Contents

3D Garage.com Bonus Videos

Located online at www/DanAblan.com/photoshop:

About the Authors

Ben Willmore

A senior engineer from NASA once said that Ben Willmore gave the best technical seminar he ever attended. That same year, a computer-phobic who had been struggling with Photoshop for years proclaimed, "He takes the bogeyman out of Photoshop!" This seems to be Ben's special gift; he has an ability to connect with users of every level and mind-set, whether it's first-timers taking their first sniff of Photoshop, or razor-sharp nerds who are on the fast track to technical illumination. The common echo that Ben leaves in his wake seems to be, "Aha! I finally *get* Photoshop!"

Known for revealing the simplicity that lies within Photoshop's complexity, Ben has personally taught over 60,000 Photoshop users on four continents. He is coauthor (with Jack H. Davis) of the best-seller *How to Wow: Photoshop for Photography*, as well as *Adobe Photoshop CS4: Up to Speed.*

Ben speaks at publishing conferences and events worldwide, including Photoshop World, the American Society of Media Photographers (ASMP), and Professional Photographers of America (PPA). He writes for numerous digital imaging and photography publications, including a monthly column for *Photoshop User* magazine. In 2004, he was inducted into the Photoshop Hall of Fame at Photoshop World. His reputation as the "expert's expert" prompted NAPP's president, Scott Kelby, to say, "When we get stuck, we call Ben!" In 2006, Ben took his Photoshop adventures on the open road in a giant touring bus. His home/office on wheels has enabled him to rekindle his great passion for photography; while many of us are hitting the snooze button, Ben is likely to be prowling around in the pre-dawn hours waiting for the perfect light. To see Ben's photos from the road, and to keep track of him while he's exploring America, visit www.WhereIsBen.com.

Dan Ablan

On Dan Ablan's LinkedIn page, a colleague from NASA Ames Research wrote, "His work has reliably exceeded all expectations, and has focused on satisfying the customer without concern for changes requested along the way. He is a professional: technically and as a businessman." Throughout a 20-year career in the digital arts, Dan's clients have proclaimed similar sentiments. Dan has the ability to explain a complex program in simple terms, whether it's 3D modeling and animation software, photography applications, or Photoshop. His knack for finding a common denominator with coworkers and students translates to the subjects he teaches.

Primarily known for his 3D books on NewTek's LightWave and Luxology's modo, such as the popular *Inside LightWave* series from New Riders Publishing, Dan's true passion is the photographic arts. With today's advancements in digital photography, it has been a natural progression for Dan to bring his years of photography and digital imaging skills to the Photoshop community.

Dan Ablan is president of AGA Digital Studios, Inc., a 3D animation and imaging company in the Chicago area. AGA Digital has produced 3D visuals for broadcast, corporate, and medical clients since 1994, and is also home to Ablan Gallery, Dan's portrait art business. Dan is the author of the international best-selling *Inside LightWave* books from New Riders Publishing (covering LightWave versions 6, 7, 8, and 9), *LightWave Power Guide* (version 5.0), *Inside LightWave 3D* (version 5.5), *LightWave 6.5 Magic*, and coauthor of *LightWave 8 Killer Tips*. He also is the author of *Digital Cinematography & Directing*, served as technical editor for *Digital Lighting & Rendering*, and was a contributor to *Adobe After Effects 5.5 Magic*. His latest books are *Inside LightWave v9*, *The Official Luxology modo 301 Guide*, and *Digital Photography for 3D Imaging and Animation*. *Adobe Photoshop CS4 Studio Techniques* marks Dan's 13th book.

Dan is the founder of 3D Garage.com, a website dedicated to high-quality video training. He has written columns and articles for *LightWave Pro* magazine, *Video Toaster User* magazine, *3D Design* magazine, *3D World* magazine, and *Computer Graphics World*, while also serving as editor in chief of *Keyframe* magazine (now *HDRI 3D* magazine) for two years. Dan has taught workshops since 1995 across the country on 3D and digital imaging, and recently started a Chicago-based, two-day one-on-one personal Photography & Photoshop workshop. Some of the companies Dan has trained include Reebok, Fox Television, ABC-TV, CBS-TV, WTTW PBS Chicago, Lockheed Martin, and many others.

An active member of the Professional Photographers of America, as well as Wedding & Portrait Photographers International (WPPI), Dan is always looking for new and exciting opportunities to capture that perfect image. Visit Dan's main site at www.DanAblan.com to see what's new, and view his photography at www.AblanGallery.com.

Thank You!

First and foremost, I have to thank Ted Waitt at Peachpit Publishing for making me a part of this book. Victor Gavenda introduced me to Ted over a year ago, probably because I wouldn't stop harassing him with ideas! I think Victor finally had enough of my incessant email messages and referred me to Ted. Not knowing any better, Ted answered my email. We started a dialogue and continued for nearly five months before the opportunity came about to revise this book. So, thanks to both of you!

What's interesting about this book is that just days after attending Ben Willmore's Photoshop seminar in Chicago, Ted emailed me about Ben's *Adobe Photoshop CS3 Studio Techniques* book. Peachpit was looking for someone to revise the series for the upcoming release of Photoshop CS4. So I have to thank Ben Willmore for the opportunity to work with your outstanding text, while still being able to add my own voice and imagery throughout the pages. Keep up the great work, Ben!

From there, my appreciation and thanks go out to Nikki McDonald and Robin Drake. These two have been the driving force behind the book, working many late nights, while tackling holidays, kids, and illness. Thanks for making this process so smooth, and making the book what it is.

Thanks also to Daniel Giordan for helping out as technical editor while he could. A bigger thanks goes to Peachpit's Lightroom Reference Guide host and all-around superhero, Rob Sylvan, for stepping in literally at the last minute to pick up the slack for our technical editing needs. Thanks, Rob! We owe you one.

There are always key people behind the scenes who really make these books come to life, such as Hilal Sala. Thank you, Hilal, for making all the "other" stuff happen so we could concentrate on content!

Thanks to all of you who have emailed, twitted, and blogged during my months of sinking my teeth into this book. Your support does not go unnoticed and is greatly appreciated.

Finally, thank you to my fantastic wife, Maria, and amazing daughter, Amelia. Your support is what keeps me going.

—Dan Ablan

I

Introduction

Introduction

Staring at a shelf full of Photoshop books at the local bookstore, it seems that there are more special-effect "cookbooks" and technical tomes than anyone would ever care to read. The problem is that none of those "cookbooks" provide enough detail to really let you feel like you understand the program (blindly following the listed steps just doesn't do it), and all of the technical books are deep into terms like *rasters*, *vectors*, and *bit-depth settings*. That's the primary reason that most people aren't truly comfortable with Photoshop. They either get the 1-2-3 steps (but no real understanding), or they get so many technical terms that Photoshop becomes impossible to grasp.

So how is this book different? Our approach is to use the same language that you use in everyday life, to explain everything from the simplest feature to the most advanced techniques. Ben Willmore acquired this approach as a result of teaching tens of thousands of people in hundreds of seminars and hands-on workshops. We still provide a fair share of step-by-step techniques, and we delve into some rather advanced features, but through it all we use metaphors and examples that make everything easy to understand and digest.

Our mission is to help you graduate from "I'm just going through the motions" to "At last, I really understand Photoshop." Once you've made that leap, you'll experience an incredible ripple effect. Your efficiency will skyrocket. Your costs will decrease. Your creative genius will come out of the closet like gangbusters, and your clients (or boss) will be thrilled. But what's most important to us is that, through learning how to master Photoshop, you'll find the passion and energy that come from knowing you're really good at something.

Will I Understand It?

Photoshop can be complex if you want it to be. But rather than boring you with technical terms and theories, this book will help you get results. It will demonstrate areas of the program that once eluded you. This book is much more than a set of recipes, and in the coming pages you'll find that mastering Photoshop CS4 is easier than you might think.

Does It Start at My Level?

If you're generally comfortable with your computer, you should be able to comprehend the information in this book, no matter how advanced the topic. We assume that you've installed Photoshop and you're using the *Photoshop User Guide* to figure out your way around the program. If you're an advanced user, don't worry. This book is very understandable, but we also get into the real meat of Photoshop and the powerful tools of version CS4.

Mac or Windows?

From a functionality standpoint, Photoshop is pretty close to identical on Mac and Windows platforms. Anything you can do on one platform, you can do on the other. But those darn keyboards are different. You can put your worries aside, because *both* Mac and Windows keyboard commands are integrated right into the text. For screen shots, we had to pick one platform and run with it, and we chose Mac OS X.

What's Missing?

This book doesn't come with a CD, and there is much more in Photoshop to discover than we could possibly fit into the allotted page count. Dan Ablan has created a number of training videos through 3D Garage.com that will help you to take your learning further. Visit www.danablan.com/photoshop to view Chapter 12, "Workflow," and a series of bonus videos on assorted useful topics.

As with Adobe Photoshop CS3, Adobe Photoshop CS4 has a hybrid version called "Extended." It has all the features of regular Photoshop, plus some features designed for more technical users (engineers, scientists, medical professionals, architects, television/film folks, 3D artists, and so on). This book is intended for photographers and graphic designers, and because the extended features are beyond the scope of that audience, we don't cover them here.

What's New in CS4?

Whether you have a previous edition of this book or you just want to jump right into the new features, it's still a good idea to start at the beginning. This entire book has been updated from *Adobe Photoshop CS3 Studio Techniques.* The text has been streamlined, and new examples and the new features of CS4 have been covered throughout the chapters where appropriate.

Ready to Get Started?

If you've read this far, you're the right person to use this book. (Most people don't read the introductory stuff—they just skip right to the good stuff.) So what are you waiting for? Turn the page and start understanding Adobe Photoshop CS4!

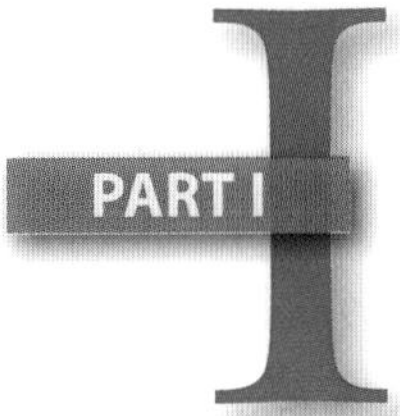

Working Foundations

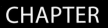

CHAPTER

1

Tools and Panels Primer

The secret of all victory lies in the organization of the non-obvious.

—Marcus Aurelius

Tools and Panels Primer

When you first open Photoshop CS4, the newly designed interface is unassuming. As you explore deeper into the tools and panels, however, you might find that the interface can quickly become cluttered, if not downright confusing. If you've worked in Photoshop previously, you might be aware that all of those panels can take up much of your screen, unless you're fortunate enough to have a second monitor to expand your workspace. This chapter will help you to become familiar with Photoshop's tools and panels so that you can manage the updated CS4 workspace effectively.

Preparing Your Workspace

With previous versions of Photoshop, you might have ended up shifting and nudging panels around the screen in order to work on a graphic or image. Along came Photoshop CS2 and CS3, packed with a huge number of panels, and adding even more tools. With CS4, the interface has been streamlined to help you work. You can easily make any panel visible—or not visible—based on your needs, organizing the clutter into an elegant arrangement in just a few seconds.

Panels and Docks

To assist you in maximizing your screen real estate, CS4 provides panel *docks*, special interface elements that allow you to collapse and expand entire groups of panels easily (**Figures 1.1a** and **1.1b**).

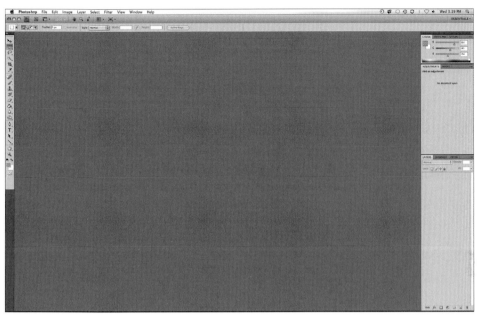

Figure 1.1a Photoshop's CS4 interface is less cluttered than previous versions, but still very customizable.

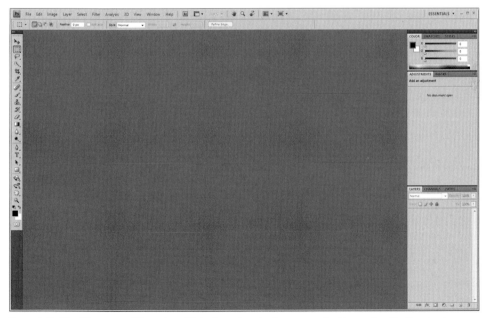

Figure 1.1b The PC version of Photoshop CS4 looks and works the same as the Mac version. You'll notice, however, that the menu bar is slightly different.

The panel well that was found in previous versions of Photoshop is no longer available. It has been completely replaced by the docking system.

By default, all panels are docked. Those gray borders around the panels are actually the docks, and they are permanently stuck to the sides of the Photoshop window. Clicking and dragging the gray boundaries doesn't move a panel dock (**Figure 1.2**), but you can expand the dock vertically or horizontally.

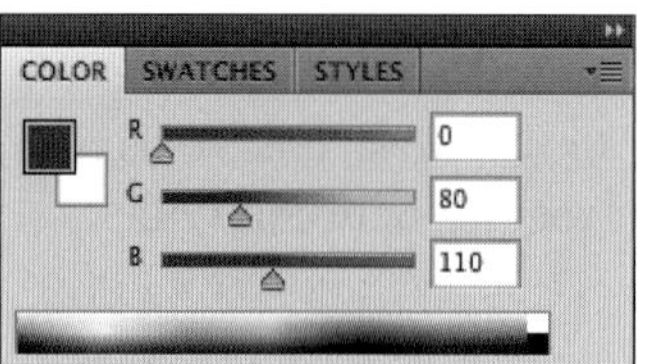

Figure 1.2 Panels are enclosed in *docks*—special constructs attached to the edge of the screen. You can't move a dock, but you can resize or collapse it.

If you want to move a panel to a different part of the screen, grab the title tab of the panel and drag it out of the dock (**Figure 1.3**).

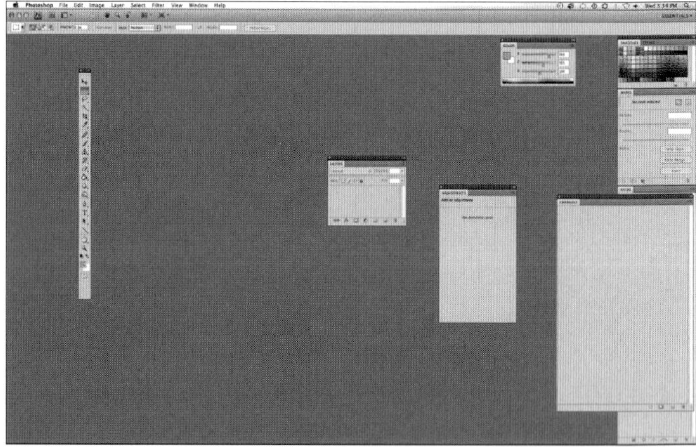

Figure 1.3 Move a panel out of the dock by clicking its title tab and dragging it. When a panel is undocked, you can place it wherever you want.

You can resize the width of any dock by clicking its edge and dragging. If you move your mouse pointer over the edge of a panel, the cursor changes to a small arrow. When you see this arrow, just click and drag to expand the panel. Within a dock, you can click the border between panels to change the size of any panel. As you enlarge one panel, its neighbors will shrink.

If you really mess things up, you can easily set all the panels back to their default locations. To do this, reselect the current Workspace by choosing Window > Workspace > Essentials.

The Tools Panel

By default, Photoshop's Tools panel, found on the left side of the interface, is now a single-column array of tools. This arrangement frees up a little bit of screen space, but if you prefer the traditional two-column Tools panel, just click the top of the Tools panel dock to toggle between the new single-column Tools panel and the old two-column version (**Figure 1.4**).

Photoshop CS4 no longer includes a launch button in the Tools panel for ImageReady (the Web graphics application that came bundled with Photoshop), because ImageReady has been discontinued. Some of its functionality has been rolled into Photoshop, and the rest is now included in Adobe Fireworks.

Another change from CS3: The Quick Mask control is now a single button (**Figure 1.5**) that toggles between Quick Mask and Standard Screen Mode, and no longer includes access to the Full Screen selector via pop-up menu. Full Screen Mode options are found under View > Screen Mode, as well as from the Application bar.

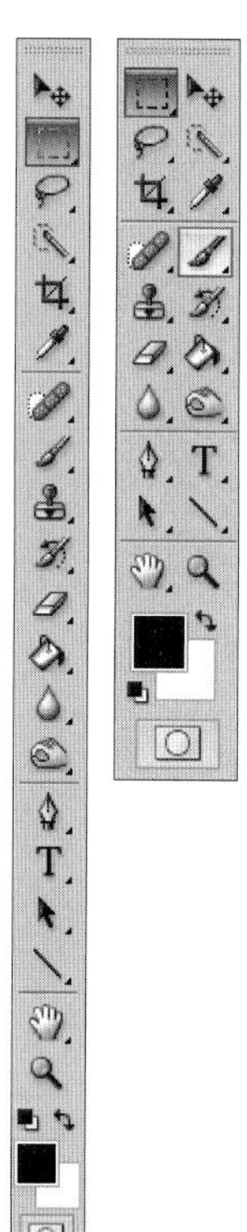

Figure 1.4 Toggle the main Tools panel between one-column and two-column layout by clicking its title bar.

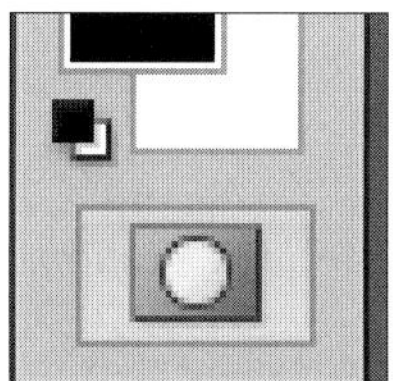

Figure 1.5 The Quick Mask toggle is now a single button at the bottom of the Tools panel.

Pressing Shift-F cycles through the screen modes.

Working with Screen Modes

While panel docks make it simple to hide and show panels, your image still doesn't use all of the available screen space. You can use the Screen Mode pop-up menu in the Application bar to solve this problem.

Standard Screen Mode

By default, Photoshop uses the Standard Screen Mode (**Figure 1.6**). You're probably used to working with this mode, with the name of your document at the top of the document window, and possibly scroll bars on the side and bottom of that window.

Figure 1.6 The Standard Screen Mode is Photoshop's default. (©2008 Dan Ablan.)

Screen Arrangements

The new CS4 *Application bar* resides just below Photoshop's menu bar. (On Windows, the Application bar is part of the menu bar; on a Mac, it's separate.) The Application bar offers a few new tools, but for now we'll concentrate on the two tools that most affect the workspace.

If you can't see the Application bar, make sure that it's enabled: Choose Window > Application Bar.

If you click and hold down the Arrange Documents icon in the Application bar, Photoshop displays a set of options. The first option is Consolidate All, which is how you can maximize an image's size onscreen. If you have multiple images open, choose one of the other options, such as Tile All in Grid, Tile All Vertically, or Tile All Horizontally (**Figure 1.7**).

Figure 1.7 You can quickly arrange your windows by choosing Tile All in Grid or one of the other options. (©2008 Dan Ablan.)

Next to the Arrange Documents pop-up menu in the Application bar is the Screen Mode pop-up menu. Here, you can choose from Standard Screen Mode (shown in Figure 1.6), Full Screen Mode with Menu Bar, and Full Screen Mode. Another option in the Arrange Documents pop-up menu is Float All in Windows. How does this option differ from using Consolidate All? Good question! If you're using the new Application Frame (found in the Window menu), loaded images are docked into neat tabs across the top of the screen (**Figure 1.8**). Choosing Float All in Windows automatically pulls these images out of their docks and floats them individually. If you'd like to return an image from floating to docked position, drag the image's title bar until it becomes transparent as you move it near the menu bar. At that point, drop the image to dock it. Conversely, you can drag an image out of its docked state to make it float. One more thing to note: If you have an image floating and not docked, you can drag and drop images into that particular image window.

Figure 1.8 With multiple images loaded, Photoshop neatly arranges the images in tabbed windows. (©2008 Dan Ablan.)

Full Screen Mode with Menu Bar

Using Full Screen Mode with Menu Bar lets the image flow all the way across the screen and slip right under the panels (**Figure 1.9**). If you choose this mode, the scroll bars disappear, so you'll have to use the Hand tool to navigate around your document. But that's okay because you can hold down the spacebar at any time to use the Hand tool temporarily. If you zoom out of a document so that it doesn't take up the entire screen, Photoshop fills the area around the image with gray.

Full Screen Mode

Full Screen Mode is a longtime favorite of serious Photoshop users. In this mode, Photoshop even turns off the menu bar! Now an image can take over the entire screen. You can still use many of the menu commands, as long as you know their keyboard shortcuts. If you zoom out while in this mode, Photoshop fills the area around the image with black. To select a new color, Control-click (Windows: right-click) somewhere in the black area.

Figure 1.9 Choosing Full Screen Mode with Menu Bar allows you to use the entire screen. (©2008 Dan Ablan.)

A great use for this mode is when you want make a presentation to clients. If you don't let them know that you're working in Photoshop, they might think that you're using a cheap little slideshow program, and won't ask you to make changes on the spot. However, you won't be able to fool anyone if all those panels are still on your screen. Just press Tab and they'll all disappear (**Figure 1.10**). Don't worry: You can get them back just as quickly by pressing Tab again.

Use the Hand tool to drag an image around as needed within the gray or black surround in the Full Screen modes.

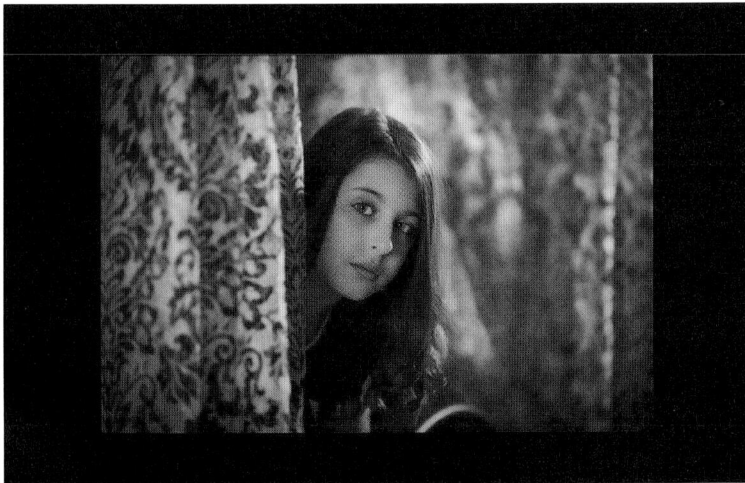

Figure 1.10 Press Tab to hide or show the panels. (©2008 Dan Ablan.)

Most of the tools have associated settings. To access these settings, take a peek at the options bar that extends across the top of the Photoshop window. Many people tend to forget about these settings when learning Photoshop.

Quick Tour of the Tools

The Tools panel in Photoshop provides dozens of tools. Describing all of them in detail would take up a huge chunk of this chapter (and you probably don't have the patience for that), so for now we'll take a look at the ones you absolutely must have. Don't worry about missing out on anything—as you work through the book, you'll get acquainted with all of the tools. In the meantime, we'll introduce you to some of the more important tool names (**Figures 1.11** and **1.12**).

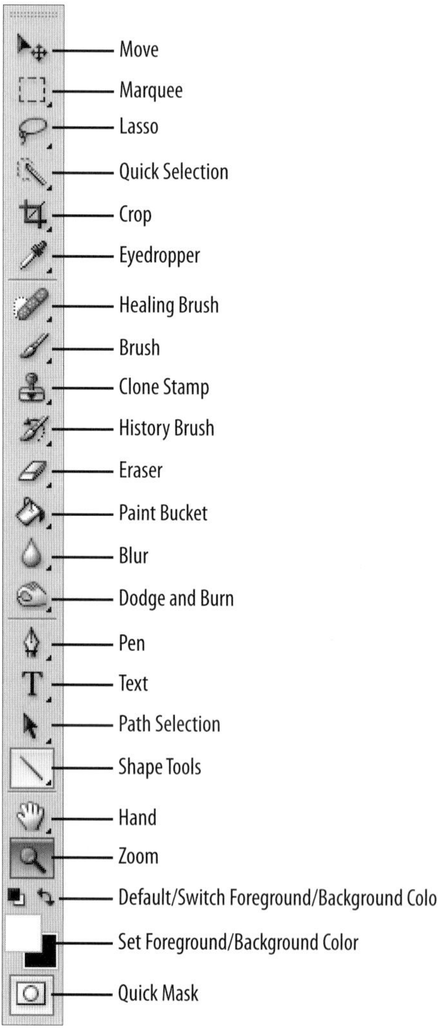

Figure 1.11 Photoshop's default Tools panel.

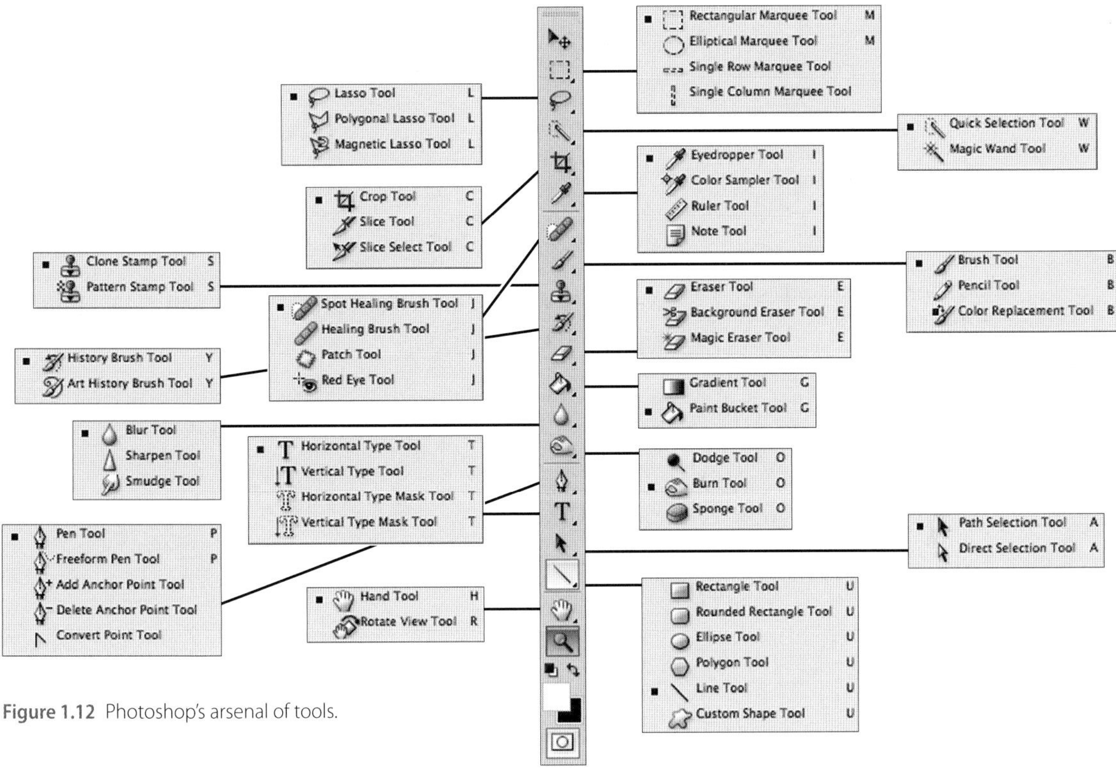

Figure 1.12 Photoshop's arsenal of tools.

Navigating Your Document

Photoshop CS4 offers great new enhancements to make panning and zooming an image smoother and more fluid than ever. A new Pixel Grid appears when you zoom into the image, providing significant flexibility over image editing while maintaining maximum clarity. When you zoom very close, the Pixel Grid automatically outlines each pixel, assisting you in editing fine details of the image.

The New Zoom Tool

The Adobe team realized that, with image sizes growing faster than computer monitors, users needed a better way to zoom and pan around the screen. You might be used to the Navigator panel, found under Window > Navigator, it has been removed from the default interface and replaced with something more efficient. The new Zoom tool is located in the options bar at the top of the interface (**Figure 1.13**). But here's what's cool about this updated Zoom tool: With an image open and the Zoom tool selected, you can just click to zoom into the image.

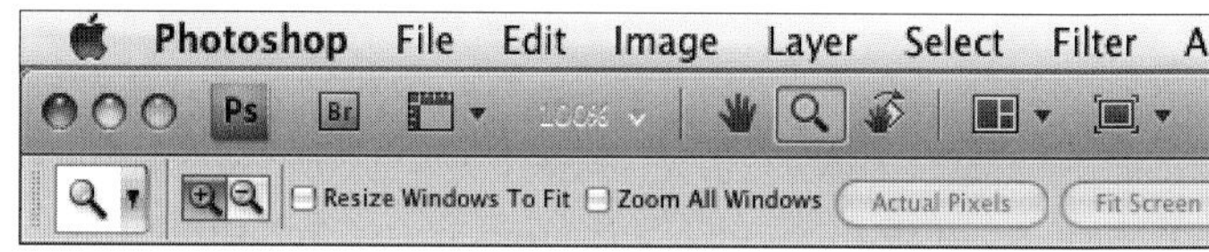

Figure 1.13 The Zoom tool on the options bar.

Photoshop CS4 takes advantage of today's graphics cards and uses OpenGL to improve moving and sizing of images. To see whether your computer's video card is up to the task, choose Preferences > Performance, and look for GPU settings. If your video card supports OpenGL, you're good to go. You can also disable OpenGL drawing with the Enable OpenGL Drawing option in the Preferences > Performance panel.

Go one step further and just hold down the mouse button. The image smoothly zooms in, taking full advantage of your system's graphics processor. Holding down Option/Alt while holding down the mouse button smoothly zooms out. But here's something even cooler. Say you've zoomed in on an image. Rather than hunting for the old Navigator panel and moving the viewing area, hold down the H key on your keyboard to activate the Hand tool, and then click. You'll suddenly jump to a bird's-eye view. Move the preview cursor to a new part of the image and release the mouse. The image will smoothly zoom in. Cool, eh?

If you still want to use the Navigator panel, open it from the Window > Navigator menu. The Navigator panel floats above the document and allows you to move around and zoom in and out of the image quickly. A little red box indicates which area of the image you're currently viewing. By dragging this box around the miniature image of the document that appears in the Navigator panel, you can change which area you're viewing in the main image window. You can also just click outside the red box, and the box will center itself on your cursor.

If you don't like the color of the little red box, or if there's so much red in the image that the box becomes difficult to see, you can change the box color by choosing Panel Options from the side menu of the panel.

When zooming in or out on an image via keyboard shortcuts in Standard Screen Mode, you can hold down Option/Alt to control whether the window that contains the image changes size with the image. On a Mac, holding down Option as you zoom causes the window containing the image to remain the same size as you zoom in or out of the image. In Windows, holding down Alt as you zoom does the opposite, causing the window to change size as you zoom. If you want to reverse the default behavior of these keyboard commands, choose Photoshop > Preferences > General and change the Zoom Resizes Windows setting.

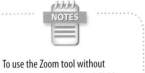

To use the Zoom tool without deselecting the active tool, hold down Command/Ctrl and the spacebar. Add the Option/Alt key to this keyboard shortcut to zoom out.

A few more notes about the Zoom tool. In addition to zooming in, you also have options for quickly zooming out. Double-click the Hand tool icon in the Tools panel (toward the bottom of the panel) to fit the entire image onscreen. You can also double-click the Zoom tool icon in the Tools panel to view the image at 100% magnification. (This technique will show you how large the image will appear when viewed in a Web browser or in any program designed for multimedia. It's not an indication of how large the image will be when printed.) Option/Alt-clicking with the Zoom tool zooms out at preset levels. Clicking the Zoom Out icon in the options bar allows you to zoom out without having to hold down a key on your keyboard. When the Zoom Out icon is chosen, holding down Option/Alt zooms in on the image.

Hand Tool

The Hand tool is definitely the most basic tool in Photoshop. By clicking and dragging with the Hand tool, now easily found in the options bar, you can scroll around the image. This tool is—excuse the pun—handy for scrolling images that are too large to fit onscreen, or for moving around without the scroll bars. Because this tool is used so often, Adobe created a special way to get to it. While working with most of Photoshop's tools, if you press the spacebar, you'll temporarily activate the Hand tool. When you release the spacebar, you'll return to the tool you were using before you switched to the Hand tool.

Full functionality of the Rotate View is dependent on your system's video card and OpenGL capabilities.

Rotate View Tool

Another new and really cool addition to CS4 is the Rotate View tool, located to the right of the Zoom tool in the Application bar. This tool allows you to rotate the canvas to just about any angle you want. Let's say that you're carefully using your tablet to brush smooth skin onto a portrait, or perhaps you're painting an illustration. It would be so much easier if you could rotate the canvas to get that perfect stroke! Select the Rotate View tool in the Application bar, and then click and drag the image. A compass-like object appears, allowing you to rotate the image freely (**Figure 1.14**). Other options: You can enter a specific angle in the options bar, choose to Rotate All Windows if you have multiple windows open, or simply click Reset View to get back to the original image position.

Figure 1.14 Photoshop's new Rotate View tool at work. (©2008 Dan Ablan.)

View Menu

If you're doing a bunch of detail work in which you need to zoom in really close on an image, you might want to create two views of the same document. Then, for instance, you can have one of the views at 16.7% magnification to give you an overall view of your image, and set the second one to 500% magnification to see all the fine details. To create a second view, use the new Arrange Documents pop-up menu in the Application bar. Click the Arrange Documents icon and choose New Window from the pop-up menu (**Figure 1.15**), or choose Window > Arrange > New Window. This action creates a second window that looks like a separate document, but it's really just another view of the same document. Choose Float All in Windows to position each image individually, and then choose Tile All Vertically from the same Arrange Documents pop-up menu. You can make your edits in either window, and both of them will show you the result of your manipulations (**Figure 1.16**).

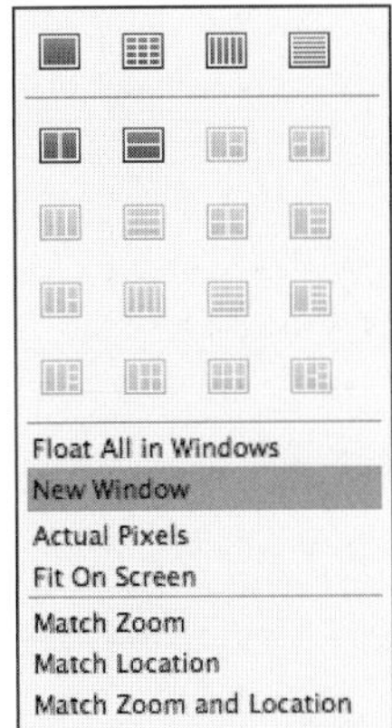

Figure 1.15 Arranging documents with the pop-up menu.

Figure 1.16 Magnification viewed at two different settings. (©2008 Dan Ablan.)

When you click the Zoom tool in the Application bar, you also can select Zoom In, Zoom Out, Resize to Fit Windows, Actual Pixels, and a few other choices from the options bar.

As you'll probably notice, each of these actions can also be accomplished by using the Zoom and Hand tools. The reason that they're listed in the options bar as well as the View menu is to enable you to use them quickly with keyboard commands.

There are indeed many ways to zoom around in Photoshop. Now all you have to do is test all the options and decide which method works best for you.

Picking Colors

Color—or is it colour? However you spell the word, the effect is the same, and it's quite important. This section will help you to work with colors in Photoshop CS4, clarifying concepts and tools that may have eluded you to this point.

Foreground and Background Colors

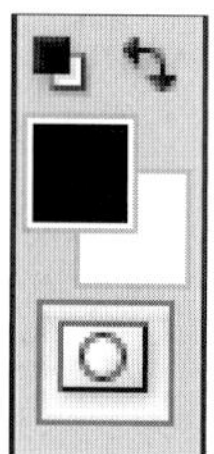

Figure 1.17 Foreground and background colors.

The two square overlapping boxes that appear toward the bottom of the Tools panel show the foreground and background colors (**Figure 1.17**). The top box is the foreground color; it determines which color will be used when you use any of the painting tools. To change the foreground color, click it to open a standard color picker. The bottom box is the background color; it's used when you're erasing the Background image or when you increase the size of your document by using Image > Canvas Size. When you use the Gradient tool with default settings, the gradient will start with the foreground color and end with the background color. You can swap the foreground and background colors by clicking the small curved arrows next to them in the Tools panel (or pressing the X key on your keyboard). You can also reset the colors to their default settings (black/white) by clicking the small squares in the lower-left corner of that same area. (Pressing D does the same thing.)

All painting tools use the current foreground color when you're painting on the image. So before you begin painting, make sure that the active foreground color is the one you want.

Color Picker

The color picker is available in many areas of Photoshop. The easiest way to get to it is to click the foreground or background color box. There are many choices in the color picker because there are many different ways to define a color. This section covers various ways in which you can choose a color. I'll start off by showing you how to preview the color you're selecting.

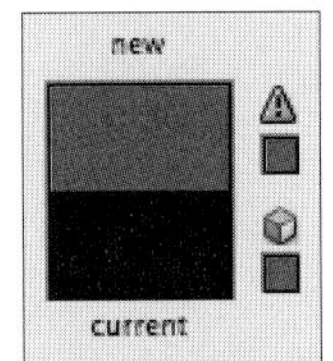

Figure 1.18 The warning triangle indicates a color that's not reproducible in CMYK mode. The cube symbol indicates that a color is not Web-safe and might appear dithered in a Web browser.

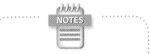

Previewing a Color

While you're choosing a color, you can glance at the two color swatches to the right of the vertical gradient to compare the color you've chosen (the top swatch) to the color you were using previously (the bottom swatch).

Be sure to watch for the out-of-gamut warning, which is indicated by a small triangle that appears next to these color swatches (**Figure 1.18**). This triangle warns you that the color you have chosen is not reproducible in CMYK mode, which means that it cannot be printed without shifting to a slightly different color. Fortunately, Photoshop provides a preview of what the color would have to shift to in order to be printable. You can find this preview in the small color swatch that appears directly below the triangle icon, and you can select this printable color by clicking the color swatch. Or, you can have Photoshop show you what all the colors would look like when printed, by choosing View > Proof Colors while the color picker is open. That option changes the look of every color that appears in the color picker, but you still have to click that little triangle symbol, because you're just seeing a preview—it doesn't actually change the colors you're choosing.

If you're working with the Basic workspace preset, the Proof Colors command isn't visible in the View menu. You'll need to click Show All Menu Items. While you're working with this chapter, keep your workspace set to Essentials.

CMYK colors are meant to be printed (which involves ink), whereas RGB colors (which involve light) are meant for multimedia. Due to impurities in CMYK inks, you can't accurately reproduce every color you see on your screen.

The Proof Colors command is accurate only when you have the proper settings specified in the Proof Setup menu (View > Proof Setup). The default setting indicates what your image will look like when converted to CMYK mode.

Choosing Web-Safe Colors

Web-safe colors are used for large areas of solid color on a Web site. By using a Web-safe color, you will prevent those areas from becoming dithered when viewed on a low-end computer (that is, simulated by using a pattern of two solid colors; for example, adding a pattern of red dots to a yellow area to create orange). If you're choosing a color that will be used in a large area on a Web page, look for the color cube symbol. Web-safe colors are within the color cube—that's why Adobe used a cube symbol for this feature. When you click the cube symbol, the color you have chosen will shift a little to become a Web-safe color.

If your method for picking white is to drag to the upper-left corner of the color field, be sure to drag beyond the edge of the square; otherwise, you might not end up with a true white. Instead, you'll get a muddy-looking white or a light shade of gray.

Selecting with the Color Field

Usually, the simplest method for choosing a color is to eyeball it. In the color picker, you can click in the vertical gradient to select the general color you want to use. Then click and drag around the large square area at the left to choose a shade of that color.

Eyedropper Tool

In addition to using the color picker and Color panel to select colors, you can use the Eyedropper tool, which is located about six icons down from the top in the Tools panel. One advantage of the Eyedropper is that you can grab colors from any open Photoshop file. After selecting the Eyedropper, click any part of an image and—bingo!—you have a new foreground color. You can also Option/Alt-click to change your background color. You don't have to click in the document you're currently editing; you can click any open image.

With Photoshop's Eyedropper tool, you can click in a document and then drag to any area of your screen to choose a color. That means that you can pick up a color from the menu bar or any other area of your screen—not just from within Photoshop, but anything you can see on your monitor. I use this feature all the time to pick colors from my Web browser.

You can also change the Sample Size setting in the options bar to choose how it looks at (samples) the area you click (**Figure 1.19**). Here are your options:

- **Point Sample:** Picks up the exact color of the pixel you click.
- **Averages:** The rest of the options average a square area of the given dimensions (3 × 3, 5 × 5, 11 × 11, 31 × 31, 51 × 51, and 101 × 101).

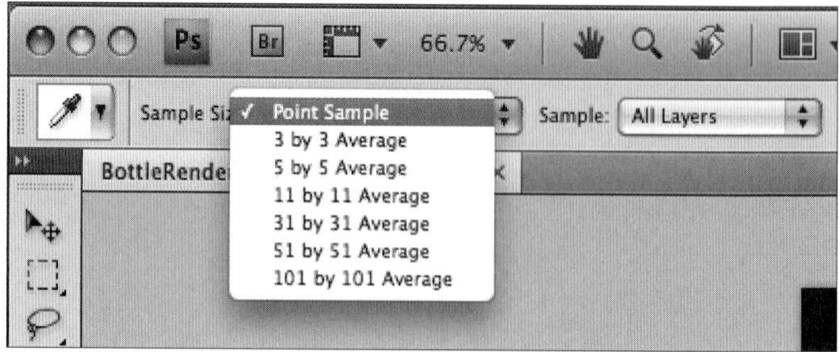

Figure 1.19 The Sample Size option determines the area the Eyedropper tool will average when you're choosing a color.

In many cases, it's helpful to use one of the Average settings. They prevent you from accidentally picking up an odd-colored speck in the area you're sampling, which ensures that the color you select correctly represents the area.

Basic Editing Tools

Just as with the majority of Photoshop's other features, there's more than meets the eye with the editing tools. For now, we'll cover their most obvious applications, but as you make your way through the rest of the book, keep in mind that these deceptively simple tools can perform some remarkable tricks. For example, the painting and gradient tools can be used for more than just painting and adding color—they can make intricate selections, composite photos, and create cool fadeouts. You can use them to create an infinite number of dazzling effects.

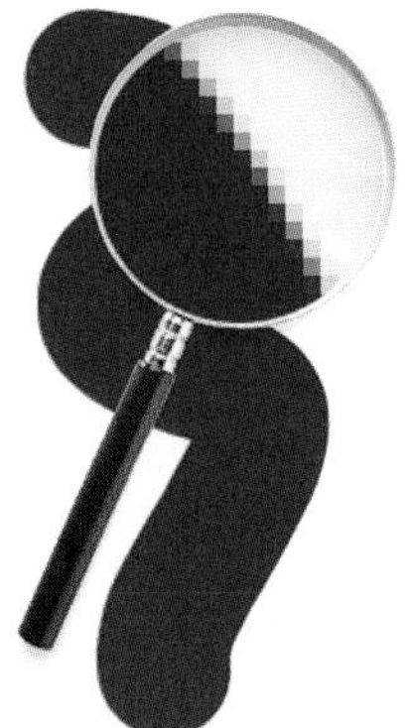

Figure 1.20 Paint stroke created with the Paintbrush tool.

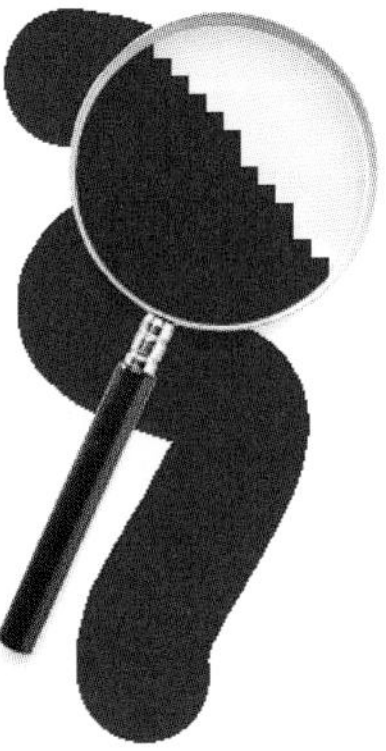

Figure 1.21 Paint stroke created with the Pencil tool.

Painting

Photoshop offers two choices for painting: the Paintbrush (Brush) tool and the Pencil tool. The only difference between the two is that the Paintbrush always delivers a soft-edged stroke—even a seemingly hard-edged brush will produce a slightly blended result—whereas the Pencil tool produces a truly crisp edge (**Figures 1.20** and **1.21**).

You can change the softness of the Paintbrush tool by choosing different brushes from the Brushes panel. When the Pencil tool is active, all brushes will have a hard edge.

Opacity

If you lower the Opacity setting of the Paintbrush tool, you can paint across the image without worrying about overlapping paint strokes (**Figure 1.22**). As long as you don't release the mouse button, the areas that you paint over multiple times won't get a second coat of paint.

To change the Opacity setting of a painting tool quickly, use the number keys on your keyboard (1 = 10%, 3 = 30%, 65 = 65%, and so on).

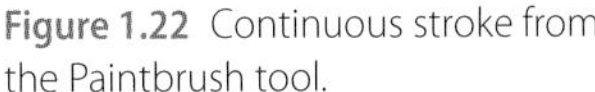

Figure 1.22 Continuous stroke from the Paintbrush tool.

If you're not familiar with the concept of opaque versus transparent, take a look at **Figures 1.23** and **1.24**.

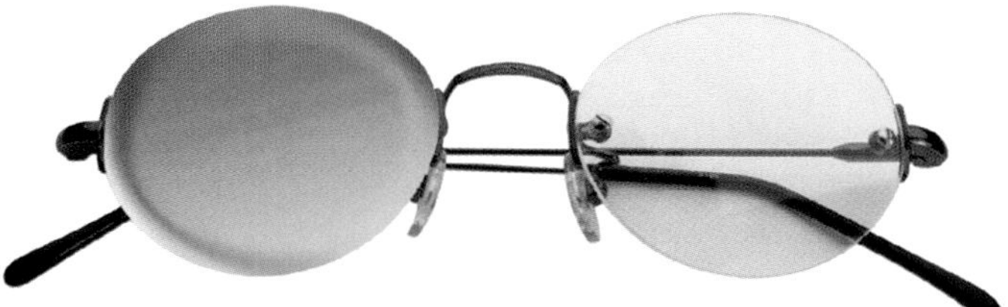

Figure 1.23 Opaque (left) versus transparent (right). (©2007 Stockbyte, www.stockbyte.com.)

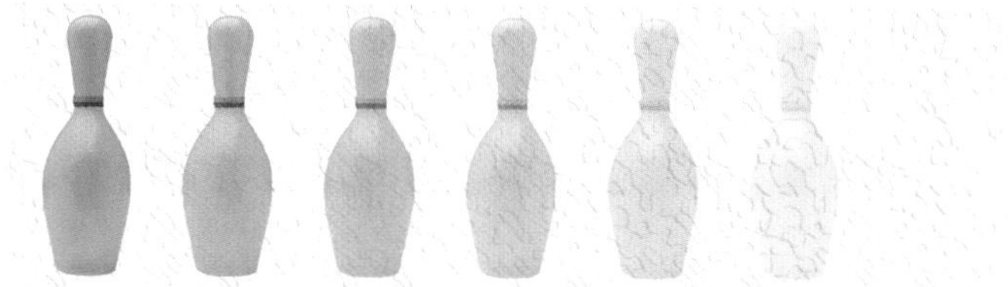

Figure 1.24 Varying opacity. (©2007 Stockbyte, www.stockbyte.com.)

Flow

Figure 1.25 Paint stroke using the Flow setting.

The Flow setting determines how much of the opacity that you've specified will show up on your first paint stroke. When Flow is set to 20%, you get 20% of the opacity you've specified in the options bar each time you paint across an area (**Figure 1.25**). Each time you pass over the same area with that setting, you build up another coat of 20% of the opacity you've chosen. No matter how many times you paint across an area, you won't be able to achieve an opacity higher than what's specified in the options bar, unless you release the mouse button. Setting Flow to 100% effectively turns off this feature, so that you get the full opacity that you've requested each time you paint. The Pencil tool doesn't use the Flow setting, and therefore delivers the desired opacity setting in a single pass.

Now let's take a look at the options available when using the painting tools.

Blending Mode

The Mode pop-up menu in the options bar is known as the *Blending Mode* menu. The options on this menu are discussed in Chapter 9, "Enhancements and Masking," so right now we'll just consider a few basic uses (**Figures 1.26** to **1.28**). If you want to change the basic color of an object, you can set the blending mode to Hue. If you're using a soft-edged brush, you can set the blending mode to Dissolve to force the edges of the brush to dissolve out.

Figure 1.26 Normal. (©2007 Stockbyte, www.stockbyte.com.)

Figure 1.27 Hue.

Figure 1.28 Dissolve.

To draw straight lines, Shift-click in multiple areas of your image; Photoshop will connect the dots (**Figure 1.29**). You can also hold down the Shift key when painting to constrain the angle to a 45-degree increment.

Figure 1.29 Shift-click to create straight lines.

Eraser Tool

If you use the Eraser tool while you're working on a Background image, it acts like one of the normal painting tools—except that it paints with the background color instead of the foreground color. It even lets you choose which type of painting tool it should mimic, by allowing you to select an option from the pop-up menu in the options bar (**Figure 1.30**).

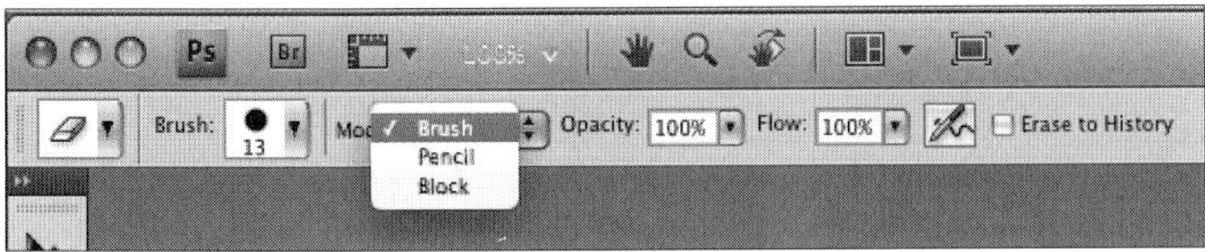

Figure 1.30 Choosing Eraser tool behavior.

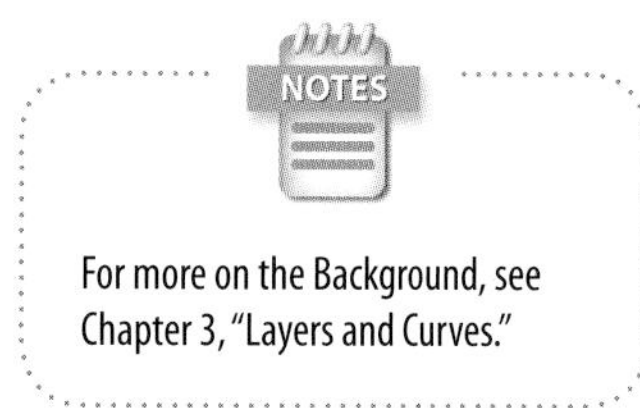

For more on the Background, see Chapter 3, "Layers and Curves."

However, when you use the Eraser tool on a non-Background layer, it really erases the area. If you lower the Opacity setting, it makes an area look partially transparent. Bear in mind that the same principle doesn't apply to the Background image. You cannot "erase" the Background.

Brush Presets Panel

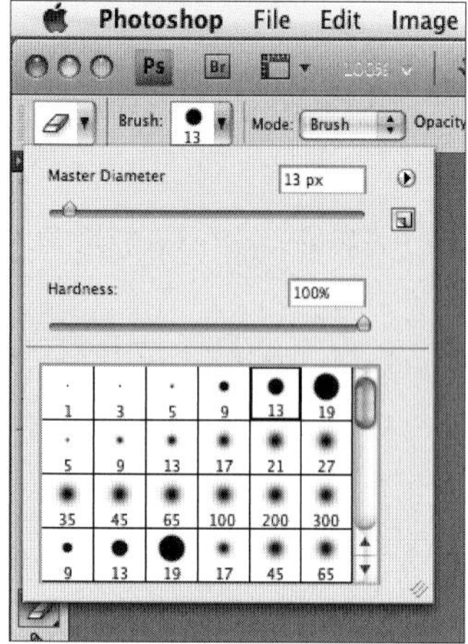

Figure 1.31 The Brush Presets panel.

Let's look at how Photoshop deals with brushes in general, and then we'll start to explore how to create custom brushes. When a painting or retouching tool is active, the currently active brush is shown in the options bar. If you click that preview, the Brush Presets drop-down panel appears (**Figure 1.31**). All of the painting and retouching tools available in the Tools panel use the Brush Presets panel to determine their brush size. Each tool remembers the last brush size you used with that tool and returns to that same size the next time you select the tool. In other words, the brush size you choose doesn't stay consistent when you switch among the tools.

You can change the active brush by clicking any brush that's available in the Brush Presets panel. (Double-clicking chooses a brush and then hides the Brush Presets panel.) The number below the brush indicates how many pixels wide the brush is.

For even more fun, keep an eye on the brush in the options bar and then press the < or > key on your keyboard (without holding down Shift). You can use these keys to cycle through all the brushes shown in the Brush Presets panel.

Brushes Panel

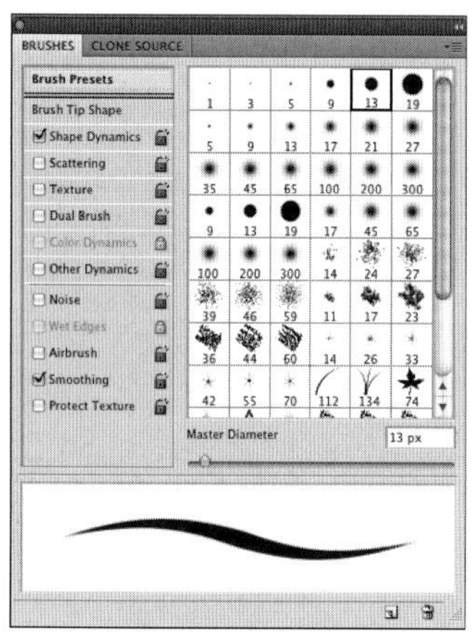

Figure 1.32 The full Brushes panel.

The Brushes panel has two versions in two different locations in Photoshop. Using the Brush Presets panel (the "diet" version), all you can do is switch between pre-made brushes. If you'd rather change the characteristics of a brush, abandon that low-calorie panel and work with the full-fat Brushes panel instead, by choosing Window > Brushes (**Figure 1.32**). In this "I want it all" version of the panel, you can still access the Brush Presets by clicking the words *Brush Presets* in the upper-left corner of the panel. But you can do a heck of a lot more by clicking the choices on the left side of the panel. When you do that, be sure to click the *words* that describe the feature you'd like to change—clicking the check boxes just lets you turn a feature on or off, and you won't see the options for that feature in the panel. Clicking the names shows you well over 30 settings that you can apply to each brush.

Looking at all these options, you might think that you'll need to go back to college to learn how to use everything. But if you look a little closer, you'll notice that the settings aren't that complicated; by combining features, you can create some pretty awesome brush effects.

You'll need to think about one thing before you start experimenting with all of Photoshop's brush settings. You can work with two types of brushes: *round* brushes and *sampled* brushes. A round brush is just what you'd expect—it's round. The second type of brush you can use is based on a picture, known as a sampled brush (**Figure 1.33**).

To work with a round brush, you must first select a round brush from the Brush Presets. To work with a sampled brush, either choose a non-round brush from the presets, or select an image area that you'd like to convert into a brush and choose Edit > Define Brush. Once you've chosen the type of brush you want, you're ready to start experimenting with all the brush settings.

Brush Tip Shape

When you click the Brush Tip Shape in the upper-left quadrant of the panel, the central portion of the panel updates to show you the settings that determine the overall look of your brush. A paint stroke is made from multiple paint daubs; that is, Photoshop fills the shape of the brush with the current foreground color, moves over a distance, and then fills that shape again (**Figure 1.34**). The Brush Tip Shape settings determine what the paint daubs will look like and how much space will be between them.

In Chapter 10, "Collage Effects," you'll learn about layer masks, which allow you to make changes as you would with the Eraser tools, but the changes aren't permanent. With a layer mask, you can bring deleted areas back even after you've saved and closed the file.

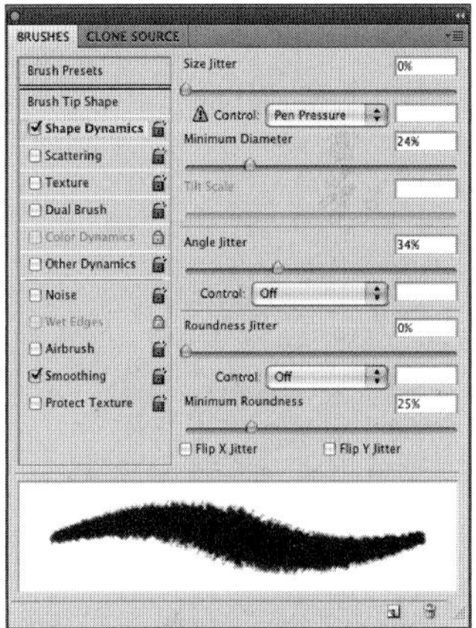

Figure 1.33 At the top of the Brushes panels are round brushes, followed by sampled brushes.

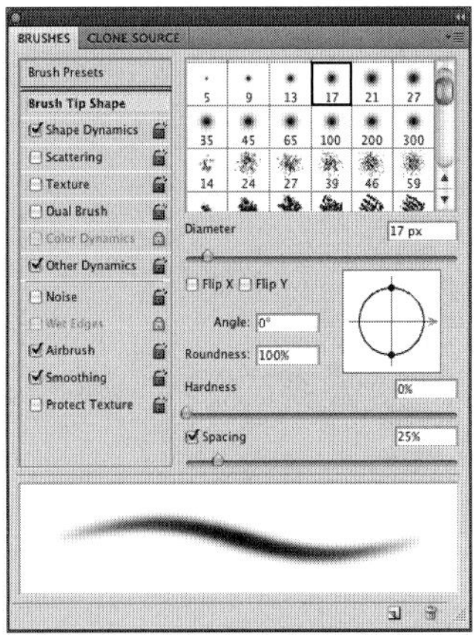

Figure 1.34 Brush Tip Shape options.

Figure 1.35 Diameter from top to bottom: 100 pixels, 50 pixels, 20 pixels.

- **Diameter:** Determines the size of the brush (**Figure 1.35**). You can use a setting between 1 and 2,500 pixels. The Use Sample Size button appears when you're using a sampled brush that has been made larger or smaller than its original size. When you click the Use Sample Size button, Photoshop resets the Diameter setting to the original size of the sampled brush, thereby delivering the highest quality. When you reduce the size of a sampled brush, it won't degrade the quality of the image much at all, but increasing the size of a sampled brush causes the brush shape to have a less crisp appearance (**Figure 1.36**).
- **Hardness:** Determines how quickly the edge fades out. Default brushes are either 100% hard or 0% hard (**Figure 1.37**). This option is only available with round brushes.
- **Roundness:** Compresses a brush in one dimension. When using round brushes, changes to the Roundness setting result in an oval-shaped brush (**Figure 1.38**). When working with a sampled brush, this setting compresses the brush vertically (**Figure 1.39**).
- **Angle:** Rotates oval and sampled brushes but has no effect on round ones (**Figure 1.40**).
- **Spacing:** Determines the distance between the paint daubs that make up a brush stroke (**Figure 1.41**). Turning Spacing off causes Photoshop to adjust the Spacing setting based on how fast you move the mouse while painting (**Figure 1.42**).

Figure 1.36 Left: Sampled brush at actual size. Right: Sampled brush scaled to be much larger than sampled size.

Figure 1.37 Hardness from top to bottom: 100, 50, 20.

Figure 1.38 Roundness from top to bottom: 100, 50, 20.

Figure 1.39 Roundness from top to bottom: 100, 50, 20.

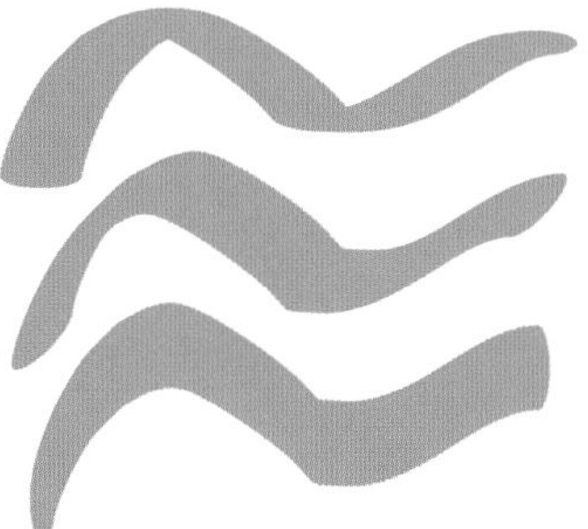

Figure 1.40 Angle from top to bottom: 0, 45, 90.

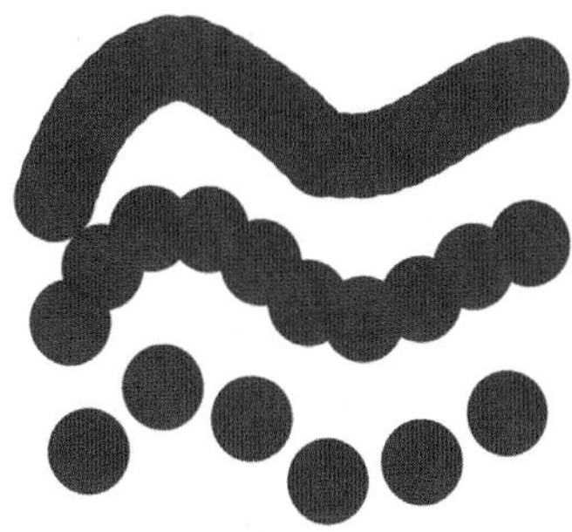

Figure 1.41 Spacing settings from top to bottom: 25%, 75%, 120%.

Figure 1.42 Turning Spacing off varies the Spacing setting based on the speed at which you paint.

The rest of the choices on the left side of the Brushes panel change how the brush tip shape is applied to an image. Three basic concepts are used over and over with the brush options:

- *Jitter* settings allow a particular option (such as size or opacity) to vary across a paint stroke (**Figure 1.43**). The higher the Jitter setting, the more the setting will vary.
- *Minimum* determines the range that the Jitter setting can use to vary a setting (**Figure 1.44**). If the Minimum option is set to 10%, the Jitter control will be able to vary a setting between the amount specified in the Brush Tip Shape panel or options bar and the amount you specified for Minimum setting. (10% means 10% of the setting that's specified in the Brush Tip Shape panel or options bar.)
- *Control* determines when Photoshop should vary a setting by using Jitter. When Control is set to Off, the Jitter command applies all the time. Fade causes the variance to fade out slowly in a particular number of brush applications. If you set Fade to 20, Photoshop starts with whatever setting is specified in the Brush Tip Shape area or options bar, and then lowers the setting over the next 20 paint daubs, where it will end up with the amount specified in the Minimum setting (**Figure 1.45**). Setting the Control pop-up menu to any of the bottom three choices (Pen Pressure, Pen Tilt, and Stylus Wheel) causes the variance to be determined by the input of a graphics tablet.

Instead of entering values for the Angle and Roundness settings, you can modify the diagram in the middle on the right side of the dialog. Drag one of the two small circles to change the Roundness setting; drag the tip of the arrow to change the Angle setting.

To prevent rough edges, lower the Spacing setting when using large, hard-edged brushes.

Use the bracket keys ([ ]) to change the diameter of your brush, or hold down Shift and use the brackets to change the hardness of the brush. If the Brush Presets panel is open, however, these keyboard shortcuts won't work.

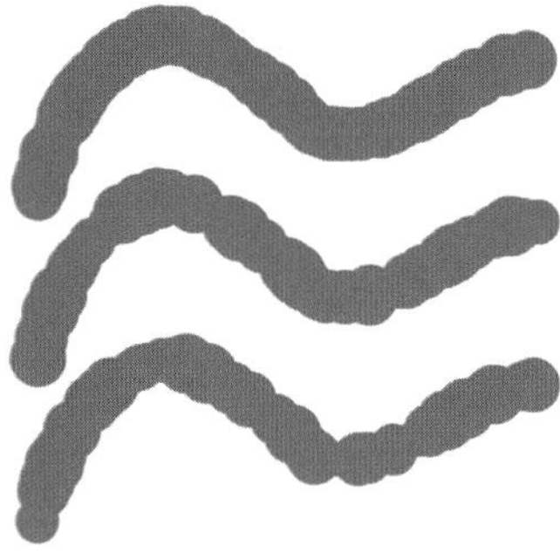

Figure 1.43 Size Jitter settings from top to bottom: 20, 50, 100.

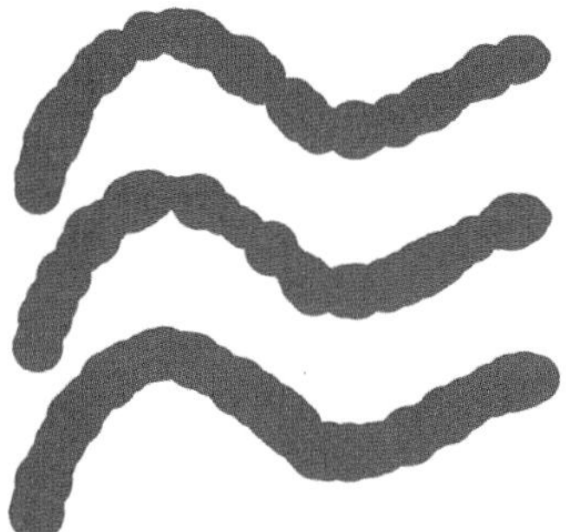

Figure 1.44 Minimum settings from top to bottom: 1, 30, 75.

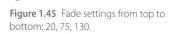

Figure 1.45 Fade settings from top to bottom: 20, 75, 130.

Shape Dynamics

The Shape Dynamics settings change the shape of the selected brush. In essence, they vary the same settings that you specified in the Brush Tip Shape section of the Brushes panel (**Figures 1.46** to **1.48**).

Scattering

The Scattering setting causes Photoshop to vary the position of the paint daubs that make up a stroke (**Figure 1.49**). The Count setting allows you to vary how many paint daubs are applied within the spacing interval that you specified in the Brush Tip Shape area of the Brushes panel (**Figure 1.50**).

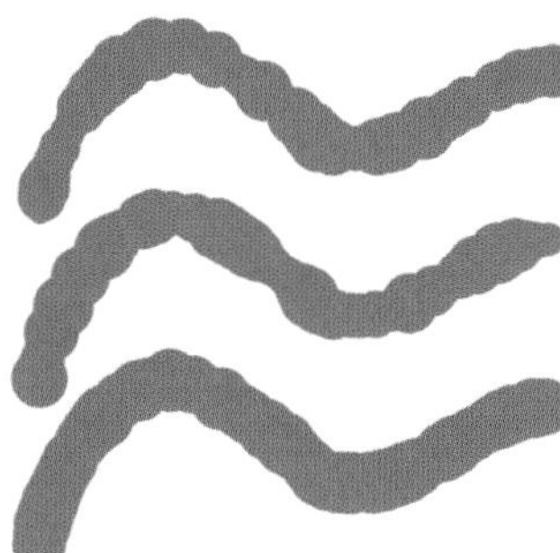

Figure 1.46 Size Jitter settings from top to bottom: 100, 50, 20. The higher the setting, the more variation in the blobs.

Figure 1.47 Angle Jitter settings from top to bottom: 100, 50, 20. The higher the setting, the more variation in the angle of the leaves.

Figure 1.48 Roundness Jitter settings from top to bottom: 100, 50, 20. This setting scales each brush tip vertically.

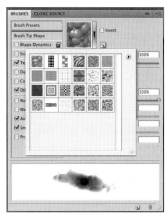

Figure 1.49 Scattering settings from top to bottom: 20, 100, 200.

Figure 1.50 Count settings from top to bottom: 1, 3, 7.

Figure 1.51 Texture settings.

Texture

The Texture settings vary the opacity of the brush based on a texture that you specify (**Figure 1.51**). The Depth Jitter setting allows Photoshop to apply the texture in varying amounts. The Texture Each Tip setting must be turned on to use the Depth Jitter setting (**Figure 1.52**). If the texture isn't changing the look of your brush, experiment with the Mode pop-up menu until you get the result you want.

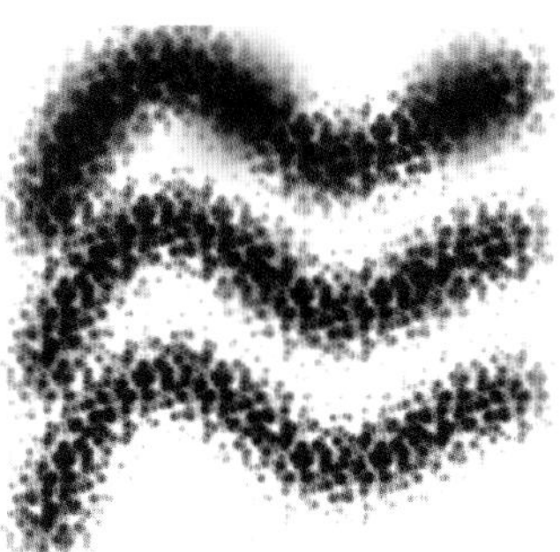

Figure 1.52 Depth Jitter settings from top to bottom: 100, 50, 20.

Dual Brush

The Dual Brush option creates a brush stroke that's made with two brushes at once. Paint shows up only where the two brush shapes would overlap (**Figure 1.53**). This is a nice way to create sponge effects. Choose a normal, round brush in the Brush Tip Shape area of the Brushes panel, and then choose a textured brush in the Dual Brush area. If the brushes aren't combining the way you'd like, experiment with the Mode pop-up menu and Spacing setting until you get the desired results.

Figure 1.53 Three examples of dual brushes.

Color Dynamics

The Color Dynamics settings vary the color of your brush across the brush stroke. The Foreground/Background setting varies the brush color between the two colors being used as foreground and background colors (**Figure 1.54**). The Hue setting changes the basic color of the brush to random colors. The higher the setting, the more it will deviate from your foreground color (**Figure 1.55**). The Saturation setting varies the vividness of the paint color (**Figure 1.56**). The Brightness setting randomly darkens the paint color (**Figure 1.57**). The Purity setting changes the saturation of the paint color. A setting of zero makes no change, negative settings lower the saturation, and positive settings increase it (**Figure 1.58**).

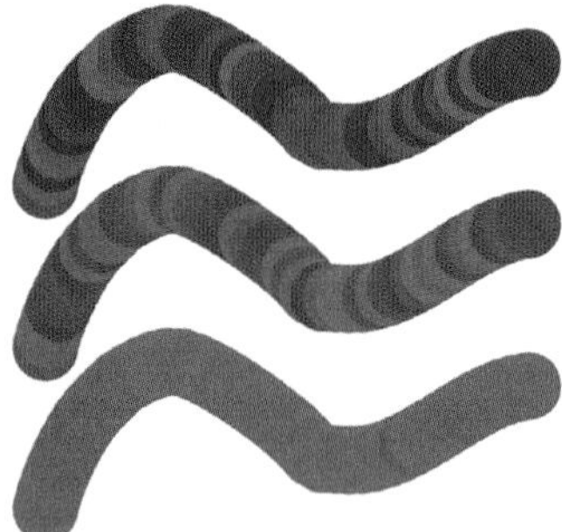

Figure 1.54 Foreground/Background using red and blue settings from top to bottom: 100, 50, 20.

Figure 1.55 Hue settings from top to bottom: 100, 50, 20.

Figure 1.56 Saturation settings from top to bottom: 100, 50, 20.

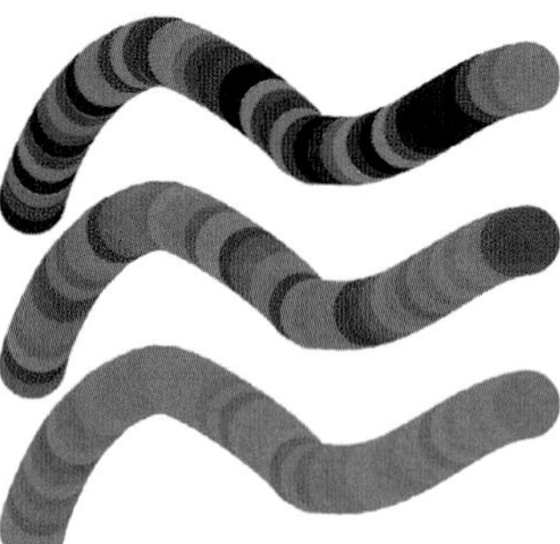

Figure 1.57 Brightness settings from top to bottom: 100, 50, 20.

Figure 1.58 Purity settings from top to bottom: +50, 0, –50.

Other Dynamics

The Opacity and Flow settings vary the settings that appear in the options bar for the current painting tool (**Figures 1.59** and **1.60**). When you use these controls, Photoshop varies the Opacity and Flow settings across a brush stroke, but will never exceed the settings specified in the options bar.

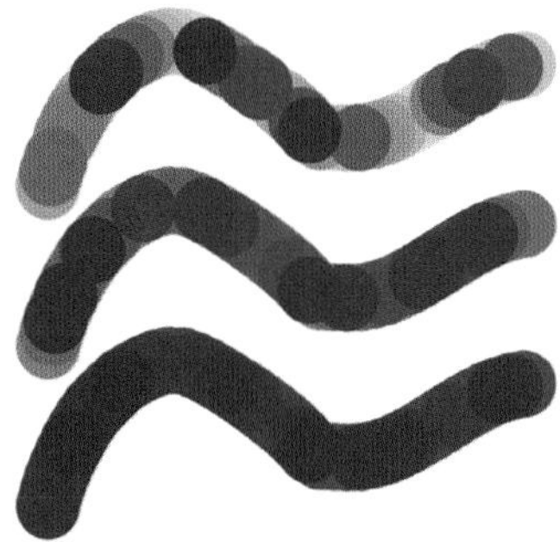

Figure 1.59 Opacity settings from top to bottom: 100, 50, 20.

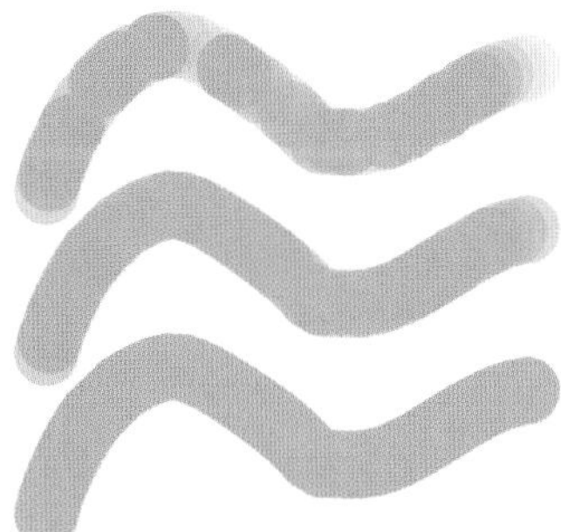

Figure 1.60 Flow settings from top to bottom: 100, 50, 20.

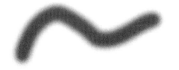

The Rest of the Brush Settings

Now let's look at the settings that are found at the bottom of the left side of the Brushes panel. The Noise setting adds a noisy look to soft-edged brushes (**Figure 1.61**). The Wet Edges setting causes the center of the brush to become 60% opaque and applies more and more paint as it gets toward the edge of the brush (**Figure 1.62**). The Airbrush setting just toggles the Airbrush icon in the options bar on or off. It works in concert with the Opacity and Flow settings found in the options bar. The Opacity setting always determines the maximum amount that you'll be able to see through your brush stroke. The Flow setting determines how quickly you will end up with the opacity that you specified. When Flow is set to 100%, you will achieve the opacity amount specified in the options bar on each paint stroke. Lower flow settings cause Photoshop to apply a lower opacity while you paint but allow you to overlap your brush strokes to build up to the Opacity setting specified in the options bar. The Airbrush setting comes into play when the Flow setting is below 100%. It causes paint to build up when you stop moving your cursor, just as it would if you held a can of spray paint in one position (**Figure 1.63**).

Figure 1.61 A brush stroke with Noise applied.

Figure 1.62 The effect of the Wet Edges setting.

Figure 1.63 The Airbrush option causes more paint to be applied wherever you pause when painting.

Saving Brushes

After you have changed the settings of a brush, you have in essence created a new brush that's no longer related to the original one that you chose in the Brushes panel. But the changed brush won't show up in the Brushes panel unless you save it by choosing New Brush from the side menu of the Brushes panel. When you have created a collection of brushes you like, you can choose Save Brushes from the side menu of the panel to save the currently loaded brushes into a file. If you ever need to get back to a saved set of brushes, choose Replace Brushes from the same menu. You can also choose Reset Brushes to set the brushes back to the default settings.

Preset brushes are located in the Brushes folder within the Presets folder in your Photoshop program folder. If you want your own brushes to show up in the Brushes drop-down panel, you'll need to store them in the same location.

Preset Brushes

Photoshop comes with a variety of preset brushes. You can load these sets by choosing either Replace Brushes or a specific name that appears at the bottom of the Brushes panel side menu (**Figures 1.64** to **1.67**).

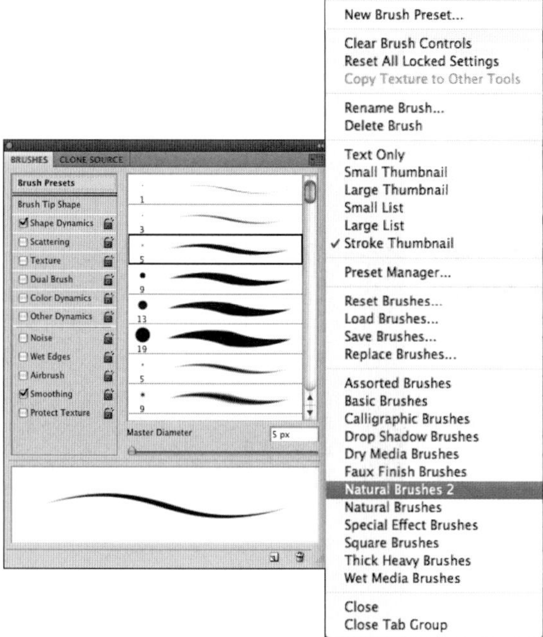

Figure 1.64 The side menu of the Brushes panel.

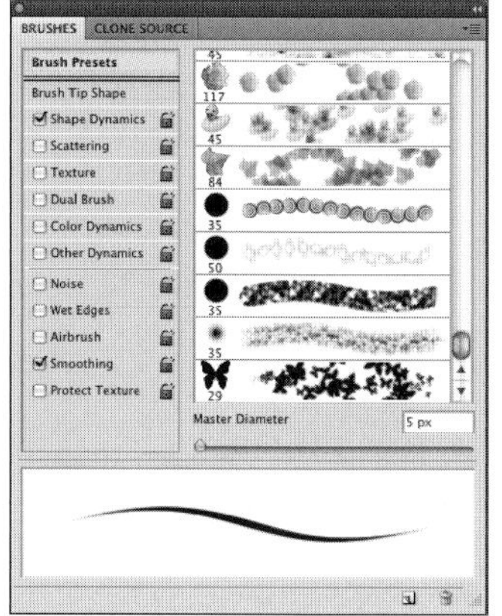

Figure 1.65 Special Effect brushes.

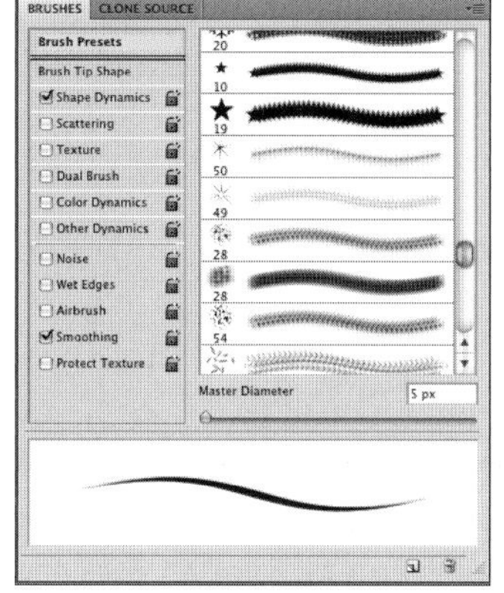

Figure 1.66 Dry Media brushes.

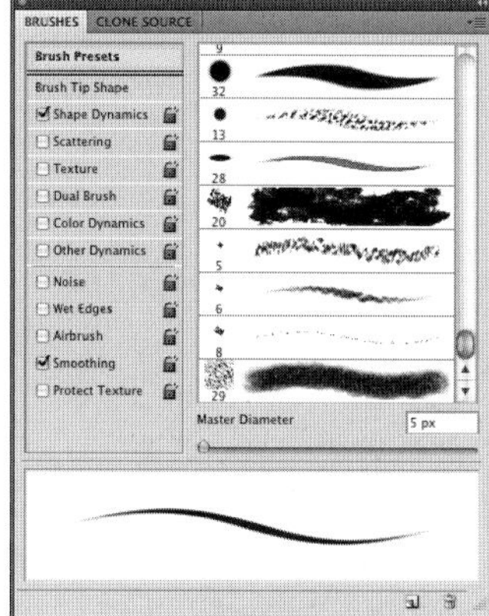

Figure 1.67 Wet Media brushes.

Paint Bucket Tool

Use the Paint Bucket tool to fill areas with the foreground color. Each time you click the image, Photoshop fills areas that contain colors similar to the one you clicked. You can specify how sensitive the tool should be by changing its Tolerance setting (**Figures 1.68** to **1.70**). Higher Tolerance settings fill a wider range of colors.

Figure 1.68 The Paint Bucket options bar.

Figure 1.69 Tolerance: 32.

Figure 1.70 Tolerance: 75.

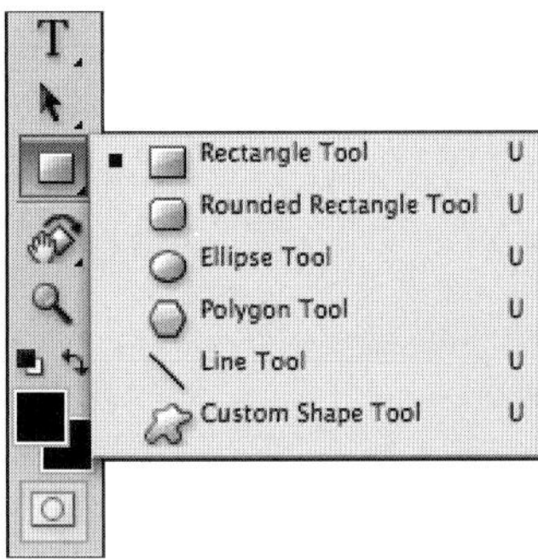

Figure 1.71 Press and hold down one of the Shape tools to see a full list of the available tools.

Figure 1.72 These three icons determine how the shape will be applied.

Shape Tools

The Shape tools are great for creating simple geometric shapes (**Figure 1.71**). These tools are much more powerful than you'd expect at first glance.

Before you dive into the Shape tools, you need to think about what kind of result you want to achieve, because you have three ways of using these tools, each of which leads you to a different outcome. The trio of choices are on the far left side of the options bar (**Figure 1.72**). The first (leftmost) choice creates a special layer. It's known as a Shape layer, and it has some very special qualities:

- It will have crisp edges when printed on a PostScript printer, even if the pixels that make up the image are large enough to cause the rest of the image to appear jagged.
- You can scale it up or down without degrading its quality. This property makes it ideal for creating button bars on Web sites where the client might decide to add more text to a button, which would require a larger button.
- You can add to or take away from it by using the other Shape tools.
- It can be filled with a solid color, gradient, pattern, or adjustment.

The second choice in the options bar delivers a path that will show up in the Paths panel. This feature can be useful when creating a vector mask, as discussed in Chapter 10. The third choice in the options bar fills an area on the active layer, using the current foreground color. I mainly use the Shape layer option (leftmost icon) because it seems to give me the most flexibility.

Once you've decided what type of result you want, you can click and drag across an image to create a shape. If you'd like a little more control over the end result, click the small triangle that appears to the right of the Shape tools in the options bar. Photoshop then presents you with options that are specific to the particular shape you're creating.

When using the Shape layer option, you can create interesting effects by choosing a style from the drop-down menu (small triangle) next to the Layer Style preview image in the options bar. A *layer style* is a collection of settings that can radically transform the look of a layer by adding dimension, shadows, and other effects to the layer. You can also apply a layer style to any layer (it doesn't have to be one that was created using a Shape tool) by opening the Styles panel and clicking one of the listed styles (**Figure 1.73**).

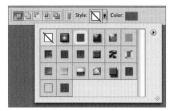

Figure 1.73 The Styles panel.

Ruler Tool

The Ruler tool allows you to measure the distance between two points or the angle of any area of the image, which can be helpful when you want to rotate or resize objects precisely. As you drag with the Ruler tool, the options bar indicates the angle (A) and length (D, for distance) of the line you're creating (**Figure 1.74**). The measurement system is the one that your rulers are using. After creating a line, you can click the line and drag it to different positions. You can also click and drag one end of the line to change the angle or distance.

Figure 1.74 The Info panel indicates the angle of the Ruler tool. (©2007 Stockbyte, www.stockbyte.com.)

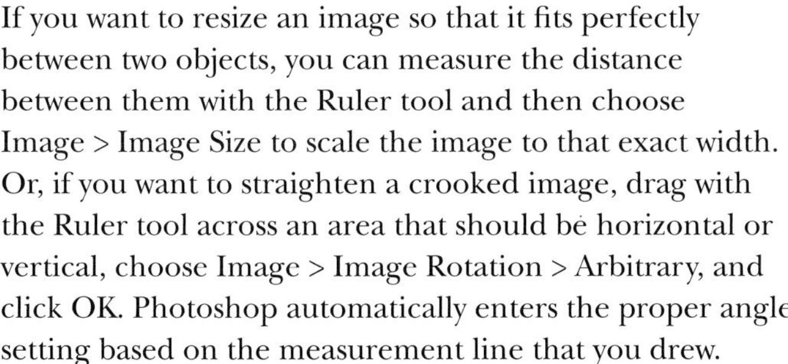

If you want to resize an image so that it fits perfectly between two objects, you can measure the distance between them with the Ruler tool and then choose Image > Image Size to scale the image to that exact width. Or, if you want to straighten a crooked image, drag with the Ruler tool across an area that should be horizontal or vertical, choose Image > Image Rotation > Arbitrary, and click OK. Photoshop automatically enters the proper angle setting based on the measurement line that you drew.

To rotate a layer to a specific angle, first use the Ruler tool to specify the angle you want; then choose Edit > Transform > Rotate. Photoshop enters the angle of the line you drew into the options bar and rotates the active layer by that amount.

You can also use the Ruler tool to determine the angle between two straight lines. If you Option/Alt-drag the end of the line, you can pull out a second line and move it to any angle you desire. The angle (A) number in both the Info panel and options bar will display the angle between those two lines.

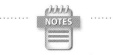

Gradient Tool

At first, you might not see any reason to get excited about using the Gradient tool. However, after we cover layers (Chapter 3), channels (see the bonus video "Channels" at www.danablan.com/photoshop), and collages (Chapter 10), you should find that the Gradient tool not only is worth getting excited about, but is downright indispensable. We want to make sure that you know how to edit and apply gradients before we get to those chapters, though, so let's give it a shot.

Unless you select an area before applying a gradient, the gradient will fill the entire image.

First, let's look at how to apply gradients to an image. To apply a gradient, simply click and drag across an image while using the Gradient tool. You'll get different results depending on which type of gradient you've chosen in the options bar (**Figure 1.75**).

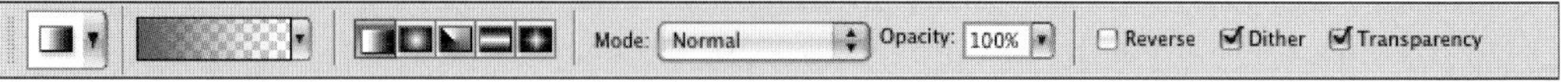

Figure 1.75 The Gradient options bar.

Here's an explanation of the gradient settings:

- **Linear:** Applies the gradient across the length of the line you make (**Figures 1.76** to **1.78**). If the line doesn't extend all the way across the image, Photoshop fills the rest of the image with solid colors (the colors with which you started and ended the gradient), or, if it's set to transparent, the gradient fades.

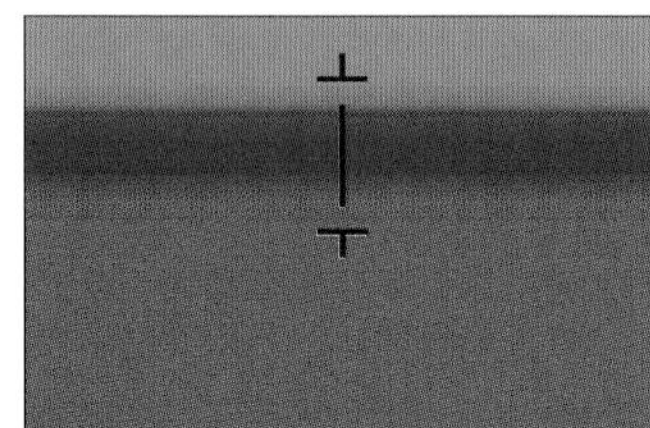

Figure 1.76 Linear gradient.

Figure 1.77 A photo from the top of the John Hancock Building in Chicago, showing the city. (©2008 Dan Ablan.)

Figure 1.78 Adding a linear gradient to the image in Figure 1.77 effectively gave a subtle shading to the skyline. (©2008 Dan Ablan.)

- **Radial:** Creates a gradient that starts in the center of a circle and radiates to the outer edge (**Figures 1.79** to **1.81**). The point where you first click determines the center of the circle; where you release the mouse button determines the outer edge of the circle. All areas outside this circle are filled with a solid color (the color with which the gradient ends).

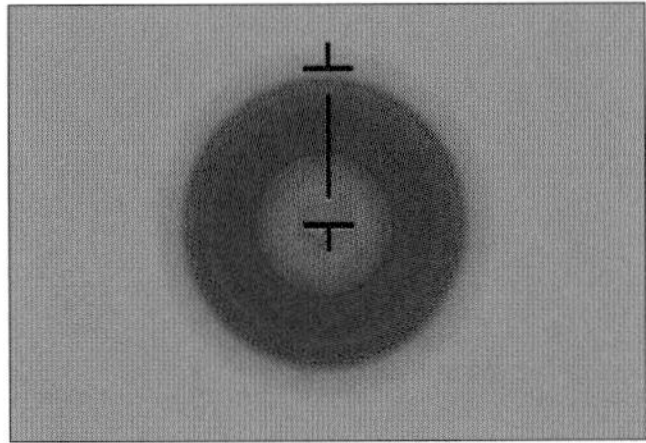

Figure 1.79 Radial gradient.

Figure 1.80 This image needs to highlight the shutter release. (©2008 Dan Ablan.)

Figure 1.81 Adding a radial gradient targets the shutter release in Figure 1.80. (©2008 Dan Ablan.)

- **Angle:** Sweeps around a circle like a radar screen (**Figures 1.82** to **1.84**). Your first click determines the center of the sweep, and then you drag to determine the starting angle.

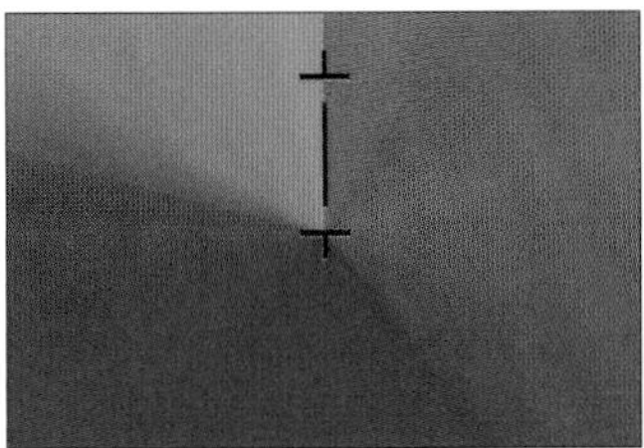

Figure 1.82 Angle gradient.

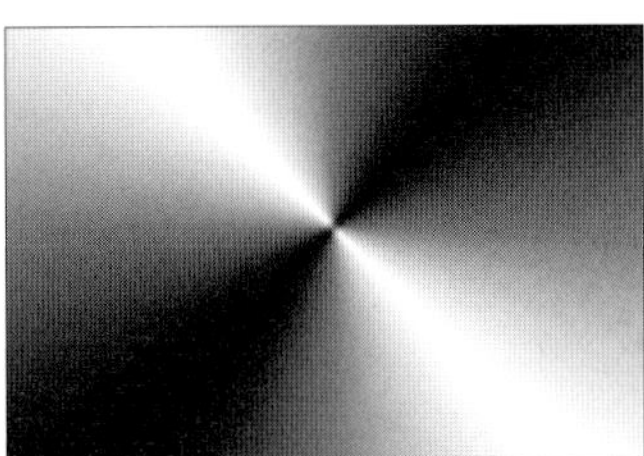

Figure 1.83 This angle gradient will be the base for an interesting trick.

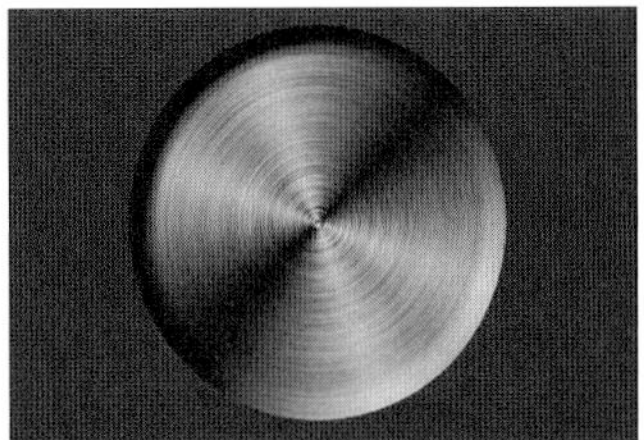

Figure 1.84 Adding texture and layer styles transformed the simple angle gradient into a drill hole in metal.

- **Reflected:** Creates an effect similar to applying a linear gradient twice, back to back (**Figures 1.85** and **1.86**).
- **Diamond:** Similar to a radial gradient except that it radiates out from the center of a square (**Figure 1.87**).

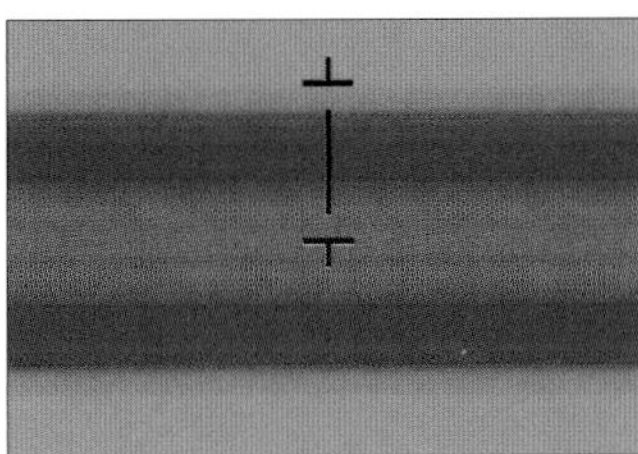

Figure 1.85 Reflected gradient.

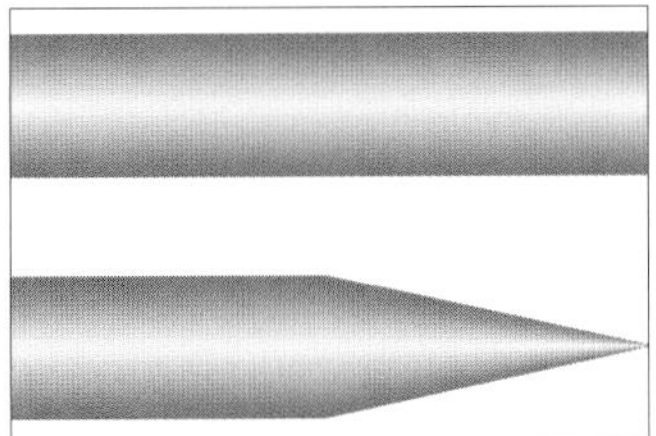

Figure 1.86 Top: A reflected gradient using metallic colors. Bottom: The end of the gradient was transformed to turn it into the tip of a pin.

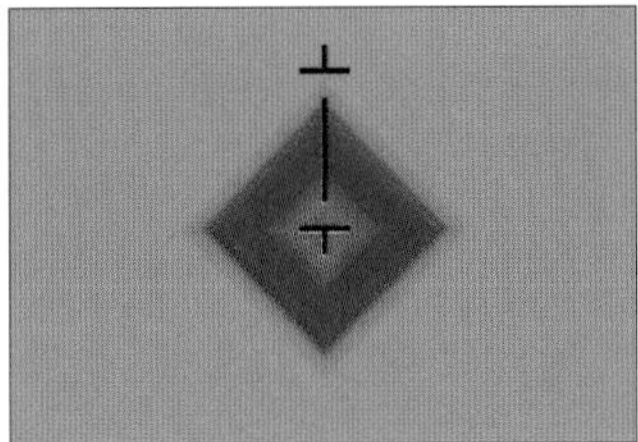

Figure 1.87 Diamond gradient.

Gradient Colors

You can choose from different preset color combinations by clicking the small triangle that appears next to the gradient preview in the options bar (**Figure 1.88**). You can also reverse the direction of the gradient by turning on the Reverse check box in the options bar. Then, if you have a gradient that usually starts with blue and ends with red, it would instead start with red and end with blue (**Figures 1.89** and **1.90**). Some of the preset gradients contain transparent areas. To disable transparency in a gradient, turn off the Transparency check box.

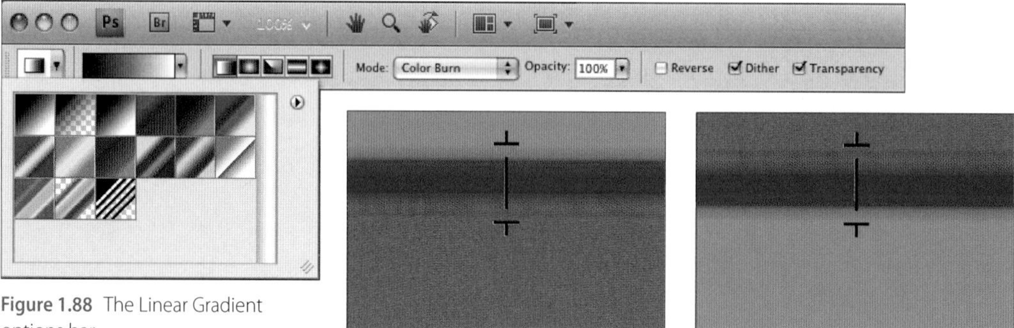

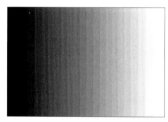

Figure 1.88 The Linear Gradient options bar.

Figure 1.89 Reverse "off."

Figure 1.90 Reverse "on."

Dithered Gradients

Figure 1.91 Dither "off."

Figure 1.92 Dither "on."

When you print an image that contains a gradient, you may notice *banding* across the gradient (also known as *stair-stepping* or *posterization*). To minimize this problem, be sure to turn on the Dither check box in the options bar. This feature adds noise to the gradient in an attempt to prevent banding. You won't be able to see the effect of the Dither check box onscreen; it just makes the gradient look better when it's printed (**Figures 1.91** and **1.92**). If you still see banding when you print the gradient, add more noise by choosing Filter > Noise > Add Noise. (Use a setting of 3 or less for most images.)

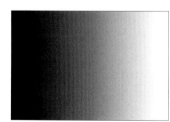

Custom Gradients

The Gradient Preset drop-down menu might not always contain the exact type of gradient you need. When that's the case, click the gradient preview in the options bar to create your own custom gradient. The Gradient Editor dialog has so many options that it can feel overwhelming, but if you take it one step at a time, you shouldn't run into any problems (**Figure 1.93**).

You can press Return/Enter to show or hide the preset gradients without accessing the options bar.

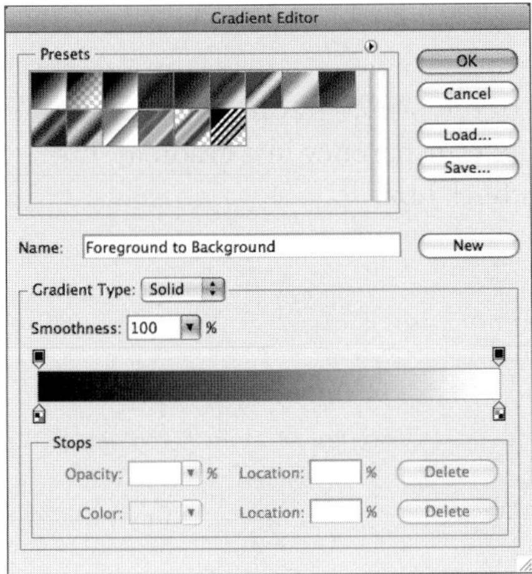

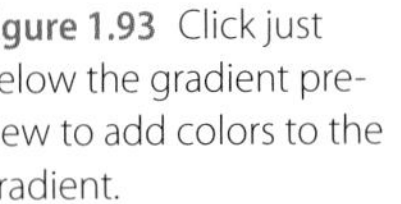

Figure 1.93 Click just below the gradient preview to add colors to the gradient.

The list at the top of the dialog shows all the gradients that usually appear in the options bar. Click any one of them, and you'll be able to preview it at the bottom of the dialog. Once you've chosen the gradient you want to edit, you can modify it by changing the gradient bar (or click New to make a copy and proceed from there). To add colors (up to a maximum of 32), click just below any part of the bar. This action adds a color swatch to the bar and changes the colors that appear in the gradient.

You have three choices of what to put into your new color swatches. These choices are on the drop-down menu to the right of the color swatch at the lower-left corner of the dialog. The Foreground and Background choices don't just grab your foreground or background colors at the time you create the gradient, as you might expect. Instead, they look at the foreground and background colors when you apply the gradient. Therefore, each time you apply the gradient, you can get a different result by changing the foreground and background colors. If you don't want the

You can remove a color swatch or a transparency swatch by simply dragging it away from the gradient bar.

gradient to contain your foreground or background colors, choose User Color from the same menu and click the color swatch to access the color picker.

After you've added a swatch of color to the gradient bar, you can reposition it by dragging it from left to right in the gradient bar or by changing the number in the Location box below. I like to click the Location number and then use the up-arrow and down-arrow keys on my keyboard to slide the color swatch around. A little diamond shape, known as the *midpoint*, appears between the color swatches; it indicates where the two colors will be mixed equally.

Transparent Gradients

You can also make areas of a gradient partially transparent by clicking just above the gradient bar. In this area, you cannot change the color of a gradient; you can only make the gradient more or less transparent. You can add and move the transparency swatches just as you would the color swatches below. Transparent areas are represented by the checkerboard pattern (**Figure 1.94**).

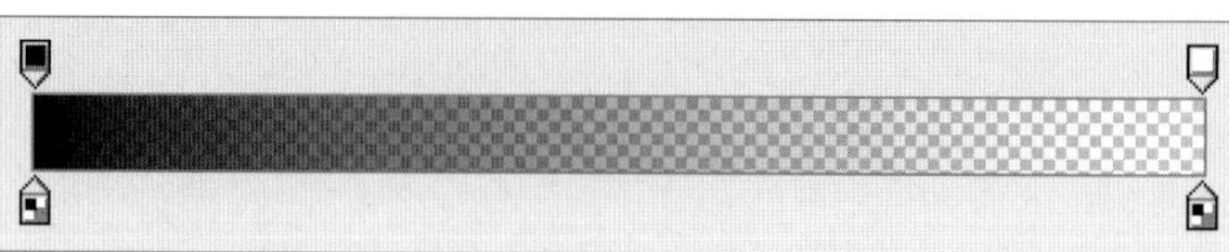

Figure 1.94 Editing the transparency of a gradient.

Tool Presets

Tool presets allow you to store and retrieve your favorite tool settings. You can access the presets in two ways: Click the Tool icon on the left side of the options bar, or choose Window > Tool Presets (**Figure 1.95**). To save a preset, click the New Preset icon at the bottom of the Tool Presets panel. (It looks like a piece of paper with the corner turned down.) The same icon appears in the upper-right area of the drop-down panel that you can access from the options bar. When you save a preset, Photoshop remembers all the settings that were specified in the options bar and the Brushes panel (if you're using a painting or

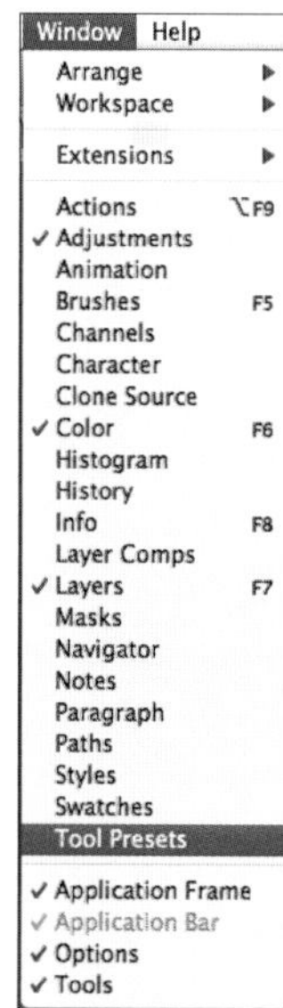

Figure 1.95 Tool Presets can be selected on the Window menu.

retouching tool). If you select the Include Color check box (when using a brush), or Include Gradient check box (when using a gradient), Photoshop will remember the active color in the options bar (**Figure 1.96**). Once you've saved a preset, you can get back to those settings at any time by clicking the name of the preset on the Tool Presets panel.

New Tool Preset	
Name: Gradient Tool 1	OK
☑ Include Gradient	Cancel

Figure 1.96 The New Tool Preset dialog.

You can work with the Tool Presets panel in two ways. The first is to use it as a replacement for Photoshop's main Tools panel. After all, when you click a preset, Photoshop switches to the referenced tool and loads the setting you saved, so you could completely replace the main Tools panel with the presets. The only problem with that strategy is that the Tool Presets panel can get rather crowded once you have four or five settings saved for each tool. It's best to select tools by using the normal Tools panel, and then streamline the selected tool in the Tool Presets panel. If you choose Show Current Tool Presets, Photoshop displays only the presets related to the active tool. You can close the panel and access it by clicking the Tool icon that appears at the left end of the options bar. That way, you can reduce screen clutter and still be able to access the presets with a quick click or two of the mouse.

The Next Step

If you've made it through this entire chapter, you've officially passed through Photoshop's welcoming committee of tools and panels. By now your screen should look neat and tidy, and you should be able to zoom in and out and scroll around an image with ease. You should also have a nodding acquaintance with a good number of the tools and panels—at least you should be familiar enough with them to know which ones you want to get more friendly with later.

Don't panic if some of this information seems like a blur. It will all begin to take shape once you spend more time with the program. After a few intense Photoshop sessions, the details you learned in this chapter will become second nature. Take some time and click around the tools, set up your own workspace, and start becoming comfortable with the tools and panels. Then, when you're ready, move on to Chapter 2 and learn about how to make selections in Photoshop.

CHAPTER

2

Selection Primer

The artist is the only one who knows that the world is a subjective creation, that there is a choice to be made, a selection of elements.

—Anaïs Nin (French-born American author of novels and short stories, 1903–1977)

Selection Primer

Whatever you do, don't skip this chapter, because the selection tools are central to your success in Photoshop. They allow you to isolate areas of your image and define precisely where a filter, painting tool, or adjustment will change the image. And, since selections can be saved and reused later, they allow you to go back and make alterations easily at any time. After you've mastered the basics, try the more advanced selections in the bonus video "Channels" at www.danablan.com/photoshop.

To launch Bridge quickly, press Option-Command-O (Mac) or Ctrl-Alt-O (Windows). That's the letter *O*, not zero. Press the same shortcut keys to return quickly to Photoshop without opening any images (for example, if you didn't find any images you liked and decided to create one from scratch). This keyboard shortcut also launches Bridge in all Adobe Creative Suite applications (Illustrator, InDesign, and so on). The shortcut Shift-Command-O (Mac) or Shift-Ctrl-O (Windows) works for Photoshop and Bridge but is not universal to other Adobe applications.

Using Adobe Bridge

Adobe Bridge is a file browsing and organizing tool bundled with Photoshop. Originally introduced with Photoshop CS2, Bridge CS4 has seen some major interface changes and now includes some important new features that will greatly streamline your workflow.

Bridge is a stand-alone application accessible from Photoshop, but you can launch it directly just like you would any other application (it installs into the same location as your Photoshop CS4 folder). Bridge lets you view thumbnail-size previews of your images, sort and rotate them, compare images side by side, add and edit metadata, add ratings and keywords, and apply a variety of automated features. Choose any of the following ways to open Bridge from within Photoshop:

- Select File > Browse in Bridge.
- Press Option-Command-O (Mac) or Ctrl-Alt-O (Windows). That's O, not zero.
- Click the Bridge icon at upper left on the options bar.

Bridge is organized into a number of tabbed panels (**Figure 2.1**). To change the view, drag the name of a tab onto another panel grouping to include that panel in the group, double-click a tab to collapse that area so it takes up minimal space, or drag the dividing bar between panels to control how much space one area uses compared to the others. Additionally, you can choose from different workspaces at the top of the interface, much like in Photoshop. Figure 2.1 shows the Essentials workspace.

Figure 2.1 Adobe Bridge CS4 interface with the Essentials workspace displayed.

Navigating Your Hard Drive

Bridge allows you to navigate your hard drive in many ways. In Bridge's default configuration, the Favorites and Folders panels appears in the upper left of the browser window. To

The fastest way to access files that reside on your desktop is to choose Desktop from the pop-up menu that appears at the top of the Bridge window.

navigate a drive in the Folders panel, click the arrows next to each folder to view its contents. Use the arrow keys on your keyboard to navigate the folder list quickly. Navigate your hard drive by using the preview area on the right side of the Bridge interface. Double-click folders within the thumbnail view to open them, or click the breadcrumb trail across the top of the interface to move one level closer to your desktop. If you've navigated to a folder that you'll want to access frequently, click the Favorites tab and drag the folder from the Content tab at the bottom of the screen to the bottom of the Favorites list (or choose File > Add Folder to Favorites). Then, when you need to access that folder, click it from within the Favorites panel or choose it from the pop-up menu that appears at the top of the Bridge window. One note of caution: This particular view is only visible in the Essentials mode.

If you're not sure in which folder an image resides, choose Edit > Find to search for the image based on its filename, date modified, keywords, or other criteria (**Figure 2.2**). One nice feature about Bridge's search capability is that it allows you to view the results even if they happen to be located in multiple folders. If you end up viewing another folder after performing a search, you can return to the search results by clicking the Back button that appears in the upper-left corner of each Bridge window.

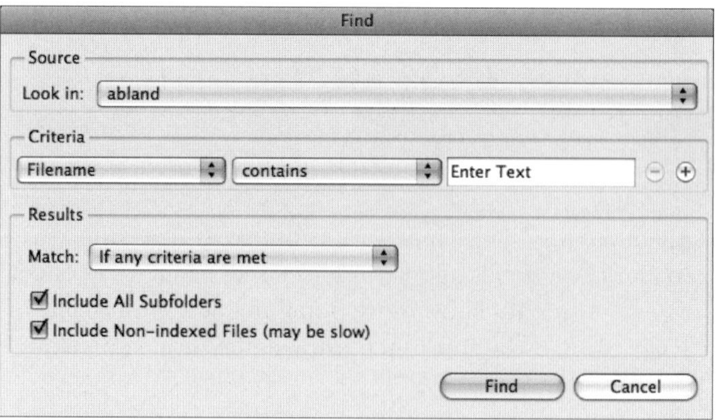

Figure 2.2 The Find dialog in Adobe Bridge.

Working with Thumbnails

The Content panel in the center of the Bridge interface presents thumbnail images of the contents of the current folder. Click any thumbnail to select that single image. Command/Ctrl-click to select additional thumbnails, or Shift-click to select a range of thumbnails. When the desired thumbnails are selected, you can do the following:

- Open the images in Photoshop by double-clicking one of the selected thumbnail images or by pressing Command/Ctrl-O (not zero).
- Delete the selected images by pressing Delete (Mac) or Backspace (Windows).
- Rotate the thumbnails by clicking one of the curved arrow icons that appear at the top of the Bridge window. (Note that although the thumbnail rotates, the image is rotated only after it has been opened in Photoshop.)
- Move an image to a different location on your hard drive by dragging it to one of the folders in the Folders or Favorites tabs. You're not limited to dragging to folders shown in Bridge; you can also drag folders and files directly to your desktop or hard drive. To move a duplicate of the image, hold down Option/Alt while dragging a thumbnail.

When you click a thumbnail, a larger version of the thumbnail appears in the Preview panel (assuming that the Preview panel is visible). If you select multiple images, all of the images will be scaled and arranged to fit in the Preview panel. This setup allows you to compare images side by side.

The largest thumbnail you can view is 512 pixels on any side, even though behind the scenes Bridge is creating thumbnail images that are 1024×768 pixels for each image.

To control the size of the thumbnails, adjust the slider that appears in the lower-right corner of the Bridge window. Smaller thumbnails allow you to see more images at once; larger thumbnails show more detail in each thumbnail image. To control how much information appears below each thumbnail, choose Preferences from the Bridge menu (Mac) or Edit menu (Windows) and change the various settings found in the Thumbnails section of the dialog.

Sorting Thumbnails

The options in the Sort menu (View > Sort) control the sorting order of the thumbnails. Sorting files by file size and resolution makes it easy to find the images that can be used at a large size easily and quickly.

Another option for choosing a sort order is to use the Sort pop-up menu located at the top of the Filter panel.

To sort images by hand, click and drag the individual images to rearrange them into whatever order you want. After you've done that, Bridge's Sort menu will indicate that your images have been sorted manually.

Controlling Thumbnail Quality

In previous versions of Bridge, images were displayed as quickly as possible when a folder was opened, with low-res thumbnails that are stored as part of most images. Then Bridge immediately began processing new thumbnails and updating the display to show those higher-quality, exposure-adjusted images. In Bridge CS4, this behavior is greatly improved. By default, Bridge now shows the stock low-res preview thumbnail and *doesn't* automatically begin generating higher-quality previews. This change makes Bridge's overall performance a lot snappier and allows for quicker navigation from folder to folder.

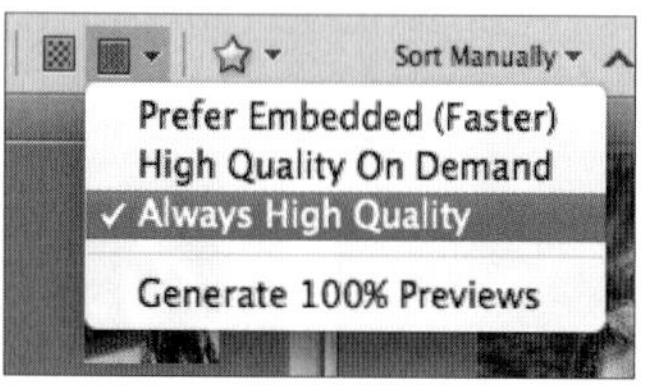

Figure 2.3 Adjusting image quality from the Thumbnail Options icon.

Like Photoshop, Bridge accesses your computer's video card for even greater image quality. If you want to see a higher-quality thumbnail (and preview image in the Preview panel), choose Always High Quality from the thumbnail options icon at the top of the interface (**Figure 2.3**). Bridge will generate a new thumbnail from your original image data.

To change the performance and file-handling options, click Adobe Bridge CS4, choose Preferences, and select the Thumbnails listing (**Figure 2.4**).

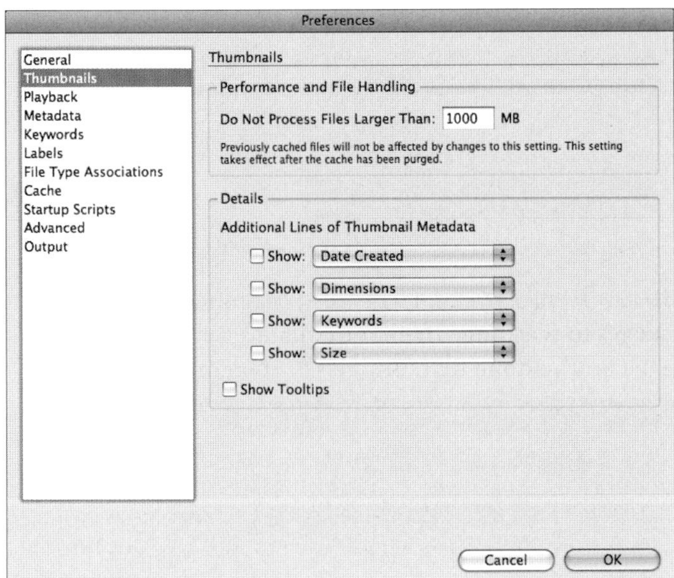

Figure 2.4 Performance and file handling options for thumbnails.

Rating and Labeling Images

You can assign a rating of 0–5 stars to any image by selecting the image(s) you want to rate and then choosing a rating from the Label menu. Alternatively, hold down the Command/Ctrl key and type a number from 0–5. To remove a rating, choose No Rating or assign a Reject rating. Note that you can also make relative changes to ratings by pressing Command/Ctrl-, (comma) to decrease the rating or Command/Ctrl-. (period) to increase the rating.

Bridge lets you assign labels to images. Just as with ratings, all you have to do is select the image(s) you want to label, and then choose the appropriate label from the Label menu.

Filtering Images

In Photoshop, the term *filters* refers to bits of plug-in code that perform image processing operations. In Bridge, *filtering* refers to the process of narrowing a selection of images to find only those that match specified criteria. For example, you might filter a folder full of images to find only those with a three-star rating, or a blue label, or both.

Filtering is very easy in Bridge CS4 thanks to the Filter panel at the lower left of the interface. Just select the items that specify the criteria for which you want to filter—JPG, Camera Raw, ISO speed, aperture values, and so on. The Filter panel is updated on the fly to include only options relevant to the images you're currently browsing. So, for example, if none of the images you're browsing have ratings, no ratings options are listed in the Filter panel.

Bridge no longer automatically adjusts the exposure of an image preview, as in the CS2 version. This functionality is not available with any of the thumbnail options.

Rating and filtering are critical parts of a post-production photography workflow. Because you'll almost always shoot more images than you need, you can use Bridge to winnow the entire shoot to just the images that are worth editing. You can assign those images a rating or label, and then quickly filter your images to find only those that match that rating.

Additionally, in the lower-right corner of the Filter panel is a Clear Filter button, which lets you clear all filtering and return to viewing all of the images in the current folder.

Changing Layouts

By default, the Bridge layout displays all of the standard panels, including a large Content panel. To resize a panel, drag its border. If you need to see more or fewer thumbnails, just resize the panel containing the thumbnails.

Bridge also provides several predefined panel layouts with different window configurations that allow for easier thumbnail viewing, larger preview viewing, or better metadata editing.

Across the top of the Bridge window are various buttons for controlling Bridge's layout and behavior. One of the more useful options is the small drop-down arrow at upper right, next to the Metadata listing. Click this arrow to choose from any of the standard workspace configurations (**Figure 2.5**), making your choice the new default. Whenever you want to return to the default workspace, just click the down-arrow button.

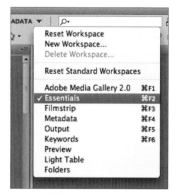

Figure 2.5 Workspace choices.

If you've reconfigured the panels in a particular way that you prefer to use, you can save that layout as a custom workspace by choosing New Workspace from the Windows menu. The New Workspace dialog (**Figure 2.6**) lets you assign a keyboard shortcut as well as elect to save the Bridge window location and current sort order as part of the workspace definition. This new workspace appears as an option directly at the top of the interface (**Figure 2.7**).

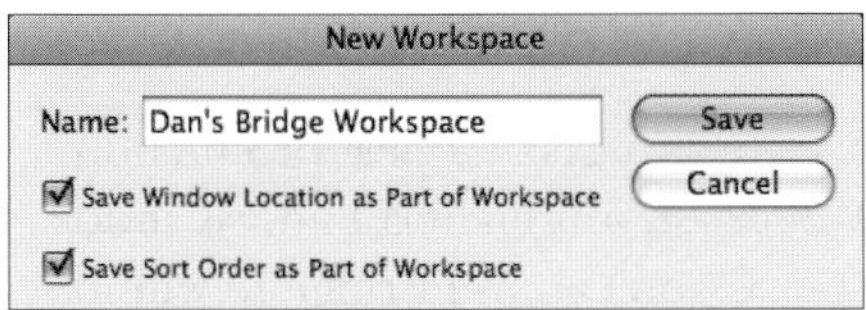

Figure 2.6 In the New Workspace dialog, specify how you want your customized workspace to be saved.

Figure 2.7 The current workspace is listed at the top of the CS4 interface.

If you'd rather present your images full screen without the distraction of thumbnail images and the rest of the Bridge interface, choose View > Slide Show. In this mode, you can press H to access an onscreen guide that lists all the keyboard shortcuts necessary to control the slide show.

Review Mode

While the slide show option is a great way to de-clutter your Bridge interface and review images, CS4 offers a new and cooler method: Choose a folder or just a select group of images and then press Command/Ctrl-B, or choose View > Review Mode. Your selected images revolve as you click the right or left arrows in the lower-left corner of the screen (**Figure 2.8**). Clicking the down arrow drops a selected image from the selection. The lower-right corner of the window offers a Loupe view icon, along with the option to create a new collection. A great way to work with Review Mode is to select an entire folder and cycle through images, clicking the down arrow to drop the unwanted images, and then create a collection when the set is complete. This is an enormous timesaver! Additionally, the Review Mode is ideal for client presentations and preview.

Review Mode is exclusive to Bridge.

Figure 2.8 The new Review Mode in CS4 makes previewing images effective and fun.

Renaming Files

To rename a file quickly, click its name in the Browser panel and then type a new name. Pressing Tab takes you to the next file in the list so you can rename that one as well, making it very easy to rename an entire folder of images. To make renaming even faster, make sure that you don't have any files highlighted in Bridge, and choose Tools > Batch Rename (**Figure 2.9**). In this dialog, you can automatically rename an entire folder's worth of images. This feature is great for when you get images off a digital camera with odd filenames like _DMA3251.NEF. Change the settings on the pop-up menus in the Batch Rename dialog to specify the naming convention you want to use. A good idea is to set the first choice to Text and enter something like "October Photoshoot." Next, click the plus sign to the right of that option to add a second choice, where you can set a Sequence Number-Three Digits, and then add a third choice, such as Current File Name-Extension. With this approach, all the images end up being named something like "October Photoshoot XXX.jpg," where XXX is a unique number for each image, beginning with 000.

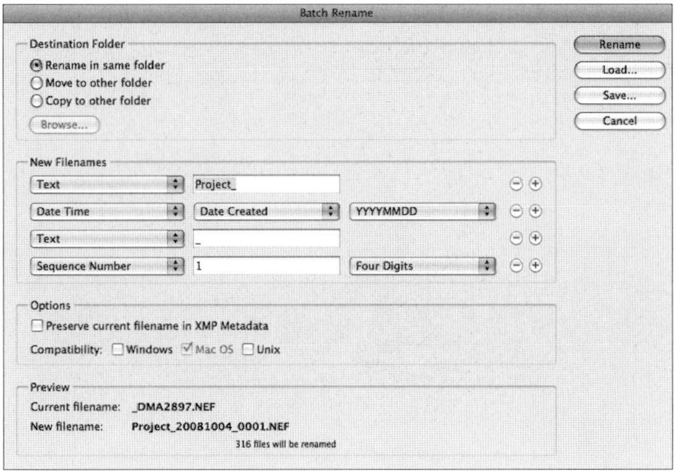

Figure 2.9 The Batch Rename dialog.

Metadata

The term *metadata* refers to all of the data that's stored in a file along with the image. Your camera packs a lot of extra data into every image you take. All of your exposure settings, white balance settings, lens choice and focal length, date and time information, and more are stored in what's called *EXIF metadata*. This data is read-only, and you can view it using Bridge's Metadata panel (**Figure 2.10**).

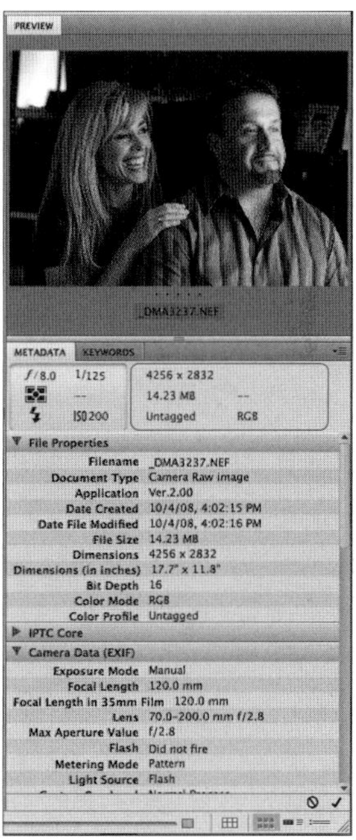

Figure 2.10 Bridge's Metadata panel makes it easy to read and edit the metadata attached to any image.

There's another type of metadata called *IPTC metadata*, which *is* editable. IPTC metadata is where you store your copyright information, name, byline, and more. You can edit all of these fields by using the Metadata panel.

In most cases, the Metadata panel contains all the metadata tags you'll need to see while browsing.

Comparing and Examining Images

One of the purposes of Bridge is to provide an easy way to compare images so that you can decide which ones you want to use in the rest of your workflow.

With early versions of Bridge, the only way to compare images was to look at their thumbnails. Although Bridge's high-quality thumbnails can be viewed at a large size, they don't always afford the most efficient use of screen space. What's more, in thumbnail view, there's no way to view just a few images unless you move them into their own folder.

In CS4, you can use the Preview panel to compare images side by side in as large a view as your monitor allows. To view images side by side, click the Filmstrip workspace at the top of the interface. Then simply Command/Ctrl-click the desired images in the Content panel. Bridge will display those selected images in the Preview panel, arranging them to maximize screen space (**Figure 2.11**). You can toggle an image on and off by Command/Ctrl-clicking it. As you select and deselect images, the Preview panel automatically changes their arrangement.

Figure 2.11 View multiple images simultaneously in the Preview panel by Command/Ctrl-clicking the images you want to view.

Loupe View

No matter what size monitor you have, if you're working with high-res images Bridge won't be able to show full resolution in the Preview panel when multiple images are selected; there simply won't be enough room.

When comparing images, you'll often want to check focus, fine detail, or even sharpness as you decide which image to use. To do so, you'll need to view the image "up close and personal." You can do this with the Loupe tool.

If you mouse over the image in the Preview panel, your cursor will change to the standard Photoshop Zoom In magnifying glass. Click the image, and Bridge's new Loupe will appear (**Figure 2.12**).

If the rating dots are visible, be careful when you're selecting an image in the Content panel. If you click the Rating portion of the thumbnail, you'll assign a rating to the image rather than select it. This is an easy way to rate images incorrectly by mistake.

Figure 2.12 The Loupe tool lets you see a 100% view of any image in the Preview panel.

Click the Loupe and drag it around for a 100% view of an image. If you want to see higher magnification, press Command/Ctrl-+ (plus sign) to zoom in. Zoom back out with Command/Ctrl-– (minus sign). These are the normal Photoshop zoom-in and zoom-out keyboard shortcuts.

To dismiss the Loupe, click the X in the lower-right corner of the Loupe.

Stacks

Figure 2.13 When you group images into a stack, a special icon shows the number of images in the stack and the thumbnail of the first image.

Very often, many of the images that you shoot are related. If you shoot a bracketed sequence of images, for example, you probably think of those frames as being part of a related group. To keep those images organized together, Bridge lets you group images into a *stack*. A stack appears in the Content panel as shown in **Figure 2.13**.

The number in the upper-left corner of the stack indicates the number of images in the stack, and the thumbnail shows a view of the first image in the stack. If you click the number, the stack opens to reveal its contents (**Figure 2.14**).

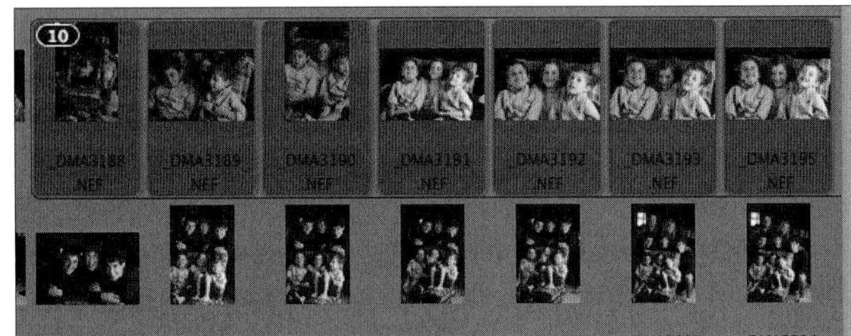

Figure 2.14 Click the stack number to reveal the stack's contents.

You cannot move a stack into another folder. If you drag a stack, only the first image will be moved.

You can preview and compare stacked images just as you would unstacked images. Stacking doesn't change the properties of any image or alter any of the operations you can perform on an image. A stack is simply a logical grouping that allows you to stay more organized and serves to free more space in the Content panel.

To create a stack, select the images you want to include in the stack and then choose Stacks > Group As Stack or press Command/Ctrl-G. To ungroup a stack, click any image in the stack. Choose Stacks > Ungroup from Stack or press Command/Ctrl-Shift-G.

To rearrange images, drag the thumbnail back and forth in the Content panel.

To add images, just drag those images into the stack. You can add images whether the stack is open or closed. To remove an image from a stack, drag it from the stack back into the Content panel.

When a stack is closed, you see only the "pick" or "hero" image from the stacked group. In a bracketed set, for example, you'll usually decide to use one image from the set. Place that image in the leftmost position in the stack, and then close the stack. Now you'll see only the selected image in the Content panel and won't have to hassle with all those additional frames. But if you ever need an alternative image, you'll be able to find it very easily.

As mentioned earlier in this section, stacks are handy for grouping bracketed sets of images, but you might also want to use them for any type of burst sequence, frames that you want to combine into a high dynamic range (HDR) image, frames that you want to stitch into a panorama, or any frames that are thematically related.

Importing Images

So far in this discussion of Bridge we've been assuming that you already have images on your computer. If you shoot with a digital camera, you can pull images into Bridge quickly. To import images from an attached camera or reader, choose File > Get Photos from Camera, or click the small camera icon in the top of the interface.

Upon first use, you'll be asked if you want Photo Downloader to launch automatically whenever a camera is connected (**Figure 2.15**). Use this option if you decide to use Bridge to manage images, iPhoto, Picasa, Windows Media, Adobe Photoshop Lightroom, ACDSee, or any other photo management program. When the Photo Downloader program opens (**Figure 2.16**), open the Get Photos From pop-up menu and choose your camera or device. If it doesn't appear, check your connections and then choose Refresh List from the menu. Configure the options in the Import Settings section and then click Get Photos.

When you're done importing, use the Eject command (File > Eject) to eject the device from which you've been importing.

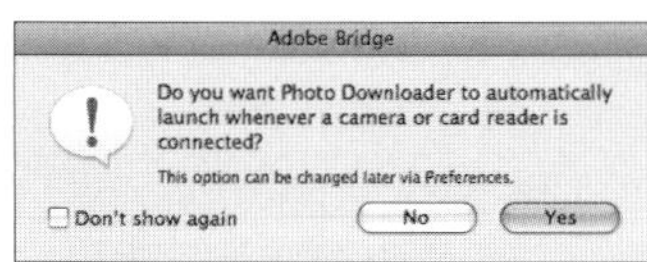

Figure 2.15 Photo Downloader imports images directly from a camera or media card.

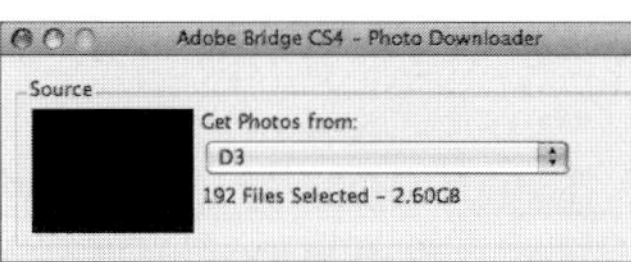

Figure 2.16 Select your camera or device in the Get Photos From pop-up menu.

Import Settings

Import settings in Photo Downloader include the following:

- **Location.** Click the Choose button next to Location to select the folder into which you want to download.
- **Create Subfolder(s).** Photo Downloader can create subfolders automatically within your chosen location. The Create Subfolder(s) pop-up menu lets you specify the metadata criteria you want to use as the basis for your subfolder structure (**Figure 2.17**).

Import Settings
Location: /.../abland/Pictures/[Shot Date] Choose...
Create Subfolder(s): Shot Date (yyyymmdd)

Figure 2.17 Use the Create Subfolder(s) pop-up menu to create a new folder to store your images.

- **Rename Files.** Your images are given initial filenames by your camera. If you want, Photo Downloader can rename the files upon import. Use the Rename Files pop-up menu to select a renaming scheme (**Figure 2.18**).

  Renaming choices that include a "custom name" option require you to enter text in the field located below the menu. An example is displayed to show you what your resulting filename structure will look like.

Figure 2.18 From the Rename Files pop-up menu, you can set a custom name for your images.

- **Open Adobe Bridge.** When you first launch Photo Downloader, it will ask whether you want to launch Photo Downloader automatically any time a camera or card reader is attached to your computer. If you choose this option, you won't always be launching Photo Downloader from within Bridge. Select the Open Adobe Bridge check box if you want to launch Bridge automatically after importing so that you can browse the imported folder immediately.
- **Convert To DNG.** If you shoot raw and use Adobe's Digital Negative (DNG) format for your images, you're already used to converting raw files to DNG. The Convert To DNG option performs this conversion for you.
- **Delete Original Files.** This option removes files from your media source after importing. It's highly

recommended that you *don't* choose this option unless you're absolutely sure that you're ready to delete your original media.

- **Save Copies To.** If you want to save a second copy of the images you import, select the Save Copies To check box and then click the Choose button to select a destination. You can choose another folder or a different volume, which allows you to import and back up your files at the same time.

Advanced Importing

If you click the Advanced Dialog button at the bottom of Photo Downloader, you'll get additional importing controls (**Figure 2.19**).

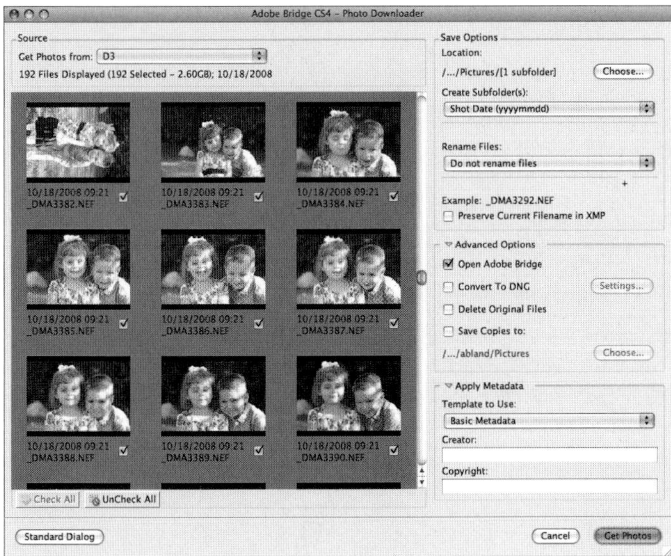

Figure 2.19 Advanced import controls include preview display and the ability to assign metadata.

In addition to all the features of Standard Dialog view, Advanced Dialog view provides a display of image thumbnails. If you deselect any images that you don't want to import, you can make your first image culling during the import step.

The Apply Metadata section allows you to tag images with metadata upon import. The default—the Basic Metadata template—lets you assign author and copyright metadata.

What Is a Selection?

When you want to edit a portion of your image, you must first select the area with which you want to work. People who paint cars for a living make "selections" very much like the ones used in Photoshop. The painters carefully place masking tape and paper over areas they don't want to paint (windows, tires, door handles, and so on). That way, they can freely spray the entire car with paint, knowing that the masked areas are protected from overspray. At the most basic level, a selection in Photoshop works in much the same way, but with a few additional advantages. In Photoshop, you can paint the car and leave the masked areas untouched, or you can paint only the masked areas and leave the rest of the car untouched. As you'll see later, you can also create areas that are only *partially* masked—as if you were using semi-opaque masking tape, which lets a fraction of the paint pass through to create a lighter shade.

When you select an area by using one of Photoshop's selection tools (Marquee, Lasso, Magic Wand, and so on), the border of the selection looks a lot like marching ants. Once you've made a selection, you can move, copy, paint, or apply numerous special effects to the selected area. **Figure 2.20** shows an unmasked photo; **Figure 2.21** shows the same image with the model selected. Notice the "marching ants" marquee around the model.

Figure 2.20 When no selection is present, you can edit the entire image. (©2008 Dan Ablan.)

Figure 2.21 When a selection is present, you change only the selected area.

There are two types of selections in Photoshop: a normal selection and a feathered selection. A normal selection

(**Figure 2.22**) has a hard edge; that is, when you paint or apply a filter to an image, you can easily see where the effect stops and starts. A feathered selection (**Figure 2.23**) slowly fades out at the edges. With a feathered selection, any painting or filters you apply will blend into an image seamlessly, without producing noticeable edges. An accurate selection makes a huge difference when you're enhancing an image in Photoshop. To see just how important it can be, compare **Figure 2.24**, in which a poor selection made for a nasty result, to **Figure 2.25**, which looks more like what the user probably had in mind.

Figure 2.22 Normal selections have hard edges.

Figure 2.23 Feathered selections have soft edges.

Figure 2.24 An amateurish selection. (©2008 Dan Ablan.)

Figure 2.25 A professional selection.

Basic Selection Tools

The Marquee, Lasso, Magic Wand, and Type Mask tools (**Figure 2.26**), as well as the new Quick Selection tool, are essential implements in your selection toolkit. You'll use these tools most often in your everyday work in Photoshop.

The Marquee tool is the most basic of all the selection tools. Don't let this tool's simplicity fool you—it can perform a surprising number of tasks. If you hold down your mouse button while your cursor is over the Marquee tool in the main Tools panel, you'll get a variety of choices in a pop-up menu.

Rectangular Marquee

The Rectangular Marquee tool is the first choice listed in the Marquee pop-up menu in the Tools panel. It can select

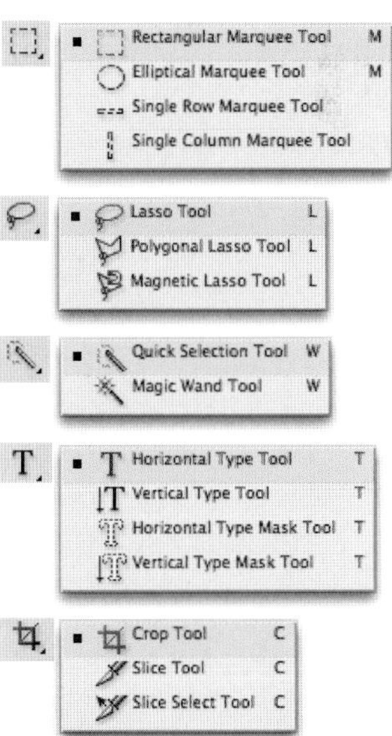

Figure 2.26 The basic selection tools.

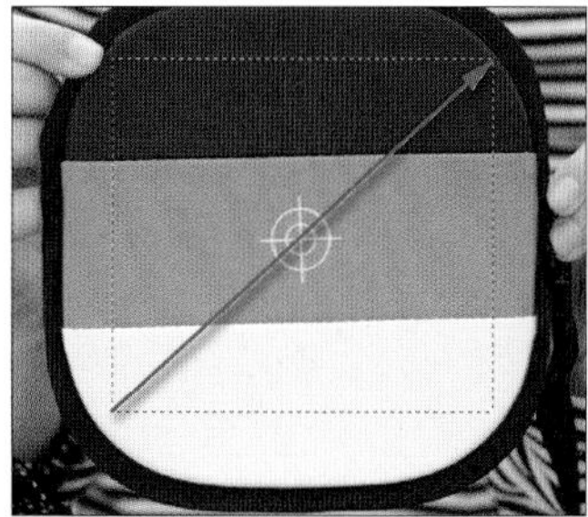

Figure 2.27 A corner-to-corner selection.

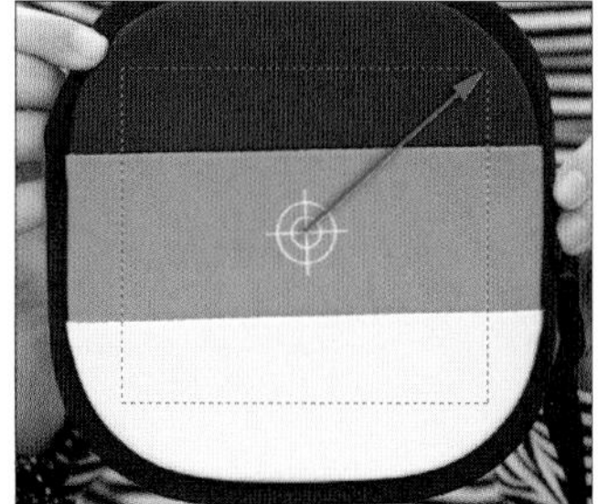

Figure 2.28 A center-to-edge selection.

only rectangular shapes. With it, you create a rectangle by clicking and dragging across your document. The first click creates one corner, and the point at which you release the mouse button denotes the opposite corner (**Figure 2.27**). To start in the center and drag to an outer edge instead of going corner to corner, hold down Option/Alt after you have started to drag (**Figure 2.28**). If you want to create a square, hold down the Shift key after you start to drag. You can even combine the Option/Alt and Shift keys to create a square selection by dragging from the center to an outer edge.

If you hold down the spacebar and drag around your screen while you're making a selection with the Marquee tool (but don't release the mouse button), you'll move the selection instead of changing its shape (**Figures 2.29** and **2.30**). This can be a real lifesaver. If you botch up the start of a selection, you can reposition it without having to start over. After you've moved the selection into the correct position, just let go of the spacebar to continue editing the selection. After you've finished making the selection, you no longer need to hold down the spacebar to move it. To move a selection after it's created, select the Marquee tool and then click and drag from within the selection outline.

If you press any combination of the Option/Alt and Shift keys before you begin a selection, they might not perform as you expect, because these keys are also used to manipulate existing selections.

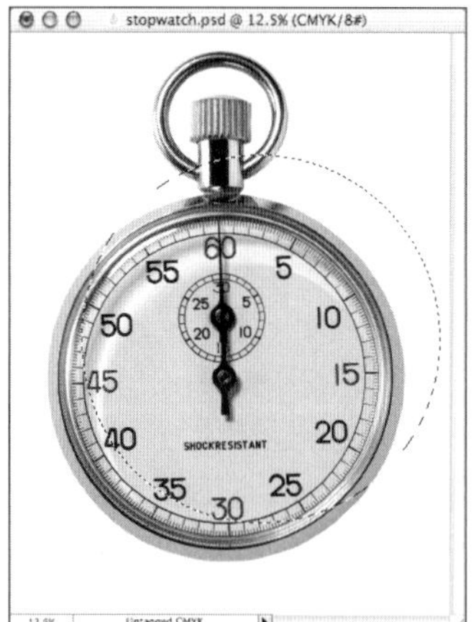

Figure 2.29 The original selection is misaligned. (©2007 Stockbyte, www.stockbyte.com.)

Figure 2.30 Use the spacebar to reposition a selection while creating it.

Elliptical Marquee

The second choice in the Marquee pop-up menu is the Elliptical Marquee tool. This tool works in the same way as the rectangular version, except that it creates an ellipse (**Figure 2.31**). It's a little bit trickier to define the elliptical marquee's size because you have to work from the "corner" of the ellipse, which doesn't really exist. (What were they thinking when they came up with this idea?) Actually, it might be easier to choose View > Show Rulers, drag out a few guides (you can get them by dragging from the rulers), and let the "corners" snap to those guides. Either that, or hold down the spacebar to reposition the selection before you release the mouse button, as just mentioned with the Rectangular Marquee tool.

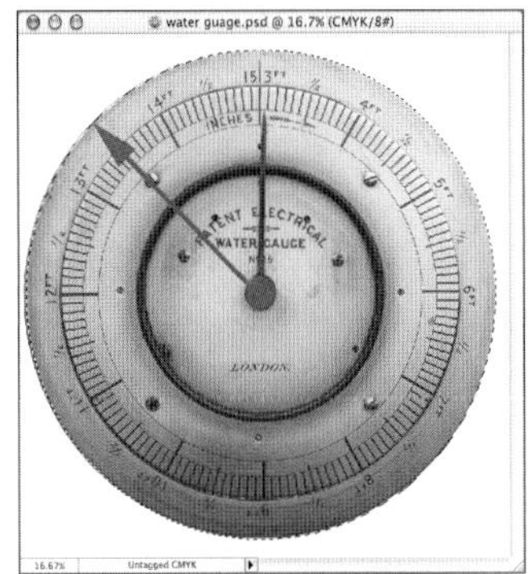

Figure 2.31 The Elliptical Marquee tool in action, selecting from center to edge. (©2007 Stockbyte, www.stockbyte.com.)

When you click any of the Marquee tools, their options will automatically be available in the options bar at the top of your screen (**Figure 2.32**):

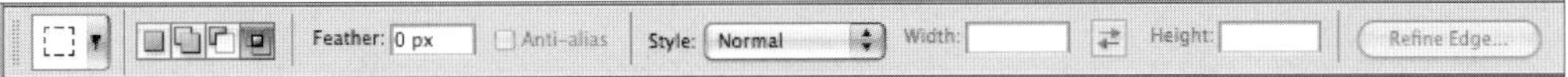

Figure 2.32 The Marquee options bar.

- **Feather:** Fades out the edge between selected and unselected areas. You'll usually want to leave this option turned off, because it's easy to forget that a Feather setting had been typed in previously, and that one little setting might mess up an otherwise great selection. Instead, use the Refine Edge command, which we'll examine later in this chapter.
- **Anti-alias:** Determines whether a one-pixel-wide border on the edge of a selection will blend with the image surrounding it. This option provides smooth transitions and helps to prevent areas from looking jagged.
- **Style menu:** Controls the shape and size of the next selection you make. When the Style pop-up menu is set to Normal, selections are not restricted in size or shape (other than having to be rectangles or ellipses). After changing this menu to the Fixed Ratio setting, you can change the Width and Height settings in order to constrain the shape of the next selection to the ratio between the Width and Height settings.

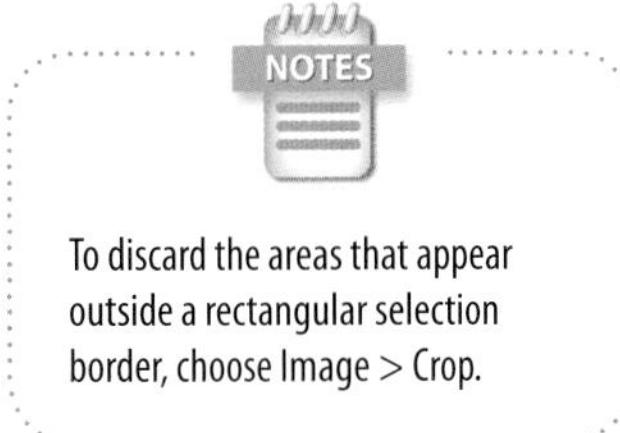

To discard the areas that appear outside a rectangular selection border, choose Image > Crop.

Single Row and Single Column Marquees

The Single Row Marquee and Single Column Marquee tools are limited in that they select only a one-pixel-tall row or one-pixel-wide column, respectively. You'll probably use them maybe once or twice a year. However, they can get you out of few tight spots, such as when you have to clean up a few stray pixels from images.

Crop

Although the Crop tool doesn't produce a selection, it allows you to isolate a certain area of an image. Using this tool, you can crop an image, resize it, and rotate it, all at the same time (**Figures 2.33** and **2.34**). Cropping requires some skill (especially if you combine cropping with rotating and/or resizing). Before you try cropping any important images, experiment with the Crop tool and its settings on the options bar until you really understand what you're doing.

Figure 2.33 The Crop tool also allows you to rotate and resize.

Figure 2.34 Result of applying a rotated and resized crop.

Lasso

The Lasso tool is the most versatile of the basic selection tools. By holding down the mouse button while you use the Lasso, you can trace around the edge of an irregularly shaped object (**Figure 2.35**). When you release the mouse button, the area will be selected. Be sure to create a closed shape by finishing the selection exactly where you started it; otherwise, Photoshop will complete the selection for you by adding a straight line between the beginning and end of the selection.

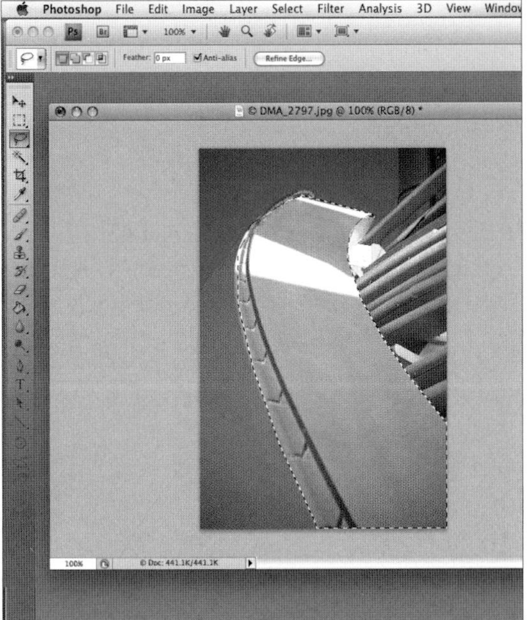

Figure 2.35 The Lasso tool in action. (©2008 Dan Ablan.)

Zoom in on your document to get a more precise view by pressing Command/Ctrl-+ (plus sign). You don't even have to let go of the mouse button—just press this key combination as you're dragging.

If you can't see the entire image, hold down the spacebar to access the Hand tool. You can do this without ever releasing the mouse button, which means that you can alternate between scrolling and selecting until you've got the whole object.

Sometimes you'll need to add a few straight segments in the middle of a freeform shape. You can do this by holding down Option/Alt and then releasing the mouse button (but not the Option/Alt key). Now, each time you click your mouse, Photoshop will connect the clicks with straight lines. To go back to creating a freeform shape, just start dragging and then release the Option/Alt key.

Polygonal Lasso

Use the Polygonal Lasso tool when you need to make a selection that consists mainly of straight lines. Using this tool, you click multiple areas of the image, and Photoshop "connects the dots" for you. If you need to create a freeform selection, hold down Option/Alt and drag (**Figure 2.36**). To finish a selection, click where the selection began; alternatively, you can double-click anywhere, which will create a straight line between where you double-clicked and where the selection started.

Figure 2.36 Hold down the Option/Alt key while dragging to create freeform selections with the Polygonal Lasso tool.

Magnetic Lasso

This tool can be a huge timesaver in that it allows you to trace around the edge of an object without having to be overly precise (**Figure 2.37**). You don't have to break a sweat making all of those tiny, painstaking movements with your mouse. Instead, you can make big sloppy selections, and the Magnetic Lasso will do the fine-tuning for you (you don't even have to hold down the mouse button). What's more, if it doesn't do a great job in certain areas, you can hold down Option/Alt to access the freeform Lasso tool temporarily. However, before using the Magnetic Lasso tool, you'll want to experiment with its settings in the options bar. If you do nothing else, pay close attention to the Edge Contrast setting.

Figure 2.37 The Magnetic Lasso tool in action, selecting the insect's wing. (©2008 Dan Ablan.)

It's possible that the Edge Contrast setting is the most important of the settings on the options bar for the Lasso tools. Edge Contrast determines how much contrast must exist between the object and the background in order for Photoshop to select the object correctly. If the object you're attempting to select has well-defined edges, use a high setting (**Figure 2.38**). You can also use a large Lasso tool width. If the edges are not well defined, use a low setting and try to be very precise when dragging.

Figure 2.38 The Magnetic Lasso tool works well when using images with strongly defined edges.

If the Magnetic Lasso tool isn't behaving itself, switch to the freeform Lasso tool temporarily by holding down Option/Alt as you drag (with the mouse button held down). You can also click periodically to add anchor points to the selection edge manually. If you want to use the Polygonal Lasso tool, hold down Option/Alt and click in multiple areas of the image (instead of dragging). If you don't like the shape of the selection, press the Delete key to remove the last anchor point. (Pressing Delete multiple times deletes multiple points.) When you have a satisfactory shape, finish the selection by pressing Return/Enter or by double-clicking. Remember, if you don't create a closed shape, Photoshop will finish it for you with a straight-line segment.

If you really practice with the Magnetic Lasso tool, you'll be able to create most of your basic selections with this tool alone. Getting used to the tool will take some time, and you'll sometimes have to supplement its use by holding down Option/Alt to access the other Lasso tools for areas where the Magnetic Lasso tool has trouble selecting. If the selection gets completely out of hand, press the Escape key to abort the selection, and then start from scratch again.

Quick Selection

The Quick Selection tool automatically makes selections for you, but it takes cues from where you point and paint to determine which pixels to select and which to leave alone.

Open an image that has something in it you'd like to select. It can be any object on any type of background. Choose the Quick Selection tool from the Tools panel by clicking it or pressing W, click the area you want to select, and begin dragging. As you drag, the selection automatically expands to add surrounding areas that are similar in color, contrast, and texture to the area over which you're dragging (**Figure 2.39**). If the Quick Selection tool selected an area that it shouldn't have, hold down the Option/Alt key and brush over the area to deselect it.

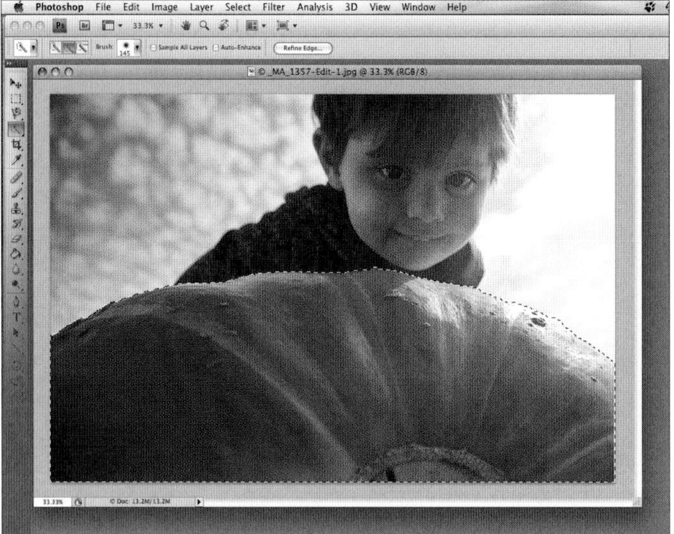

Figure 2.39 As you paint over an area with the Quick Selection tool, the selection automatically expands intelligently to select pixels with similar color, contrast, and texture. (©2008 Dan Ablan.)

The Quick Selection tool presents a number of options in the options bar (**Figure 2.40**). You can change the brush size by using the brush pop-up menu. A larger brush simply means that you don't have to work as hard to brush over the area you want to select, whereas a smaller brush lets you select a smaller area. As when using any other brush tool, you also can change the size of the brush by using the bracket keys. Pressing the right bracket (]) enlarges the brush, left bracket ([) shrinks it.

Figure 2.40 The options bar holds a few Quick Selection options.

If you select the Sample All Layers box, the Quick Selection tool analyzes all the layers in your image, rather than just the current one, to determine which pixels to select.

Auto-Enhance yields a higher-quality edge on the selection. Without Auto-Enhance, your edges will tend to be blockier. However, using Auto-Enhance exacts a slight performance penalty.

Magic Wand

The Magic Wand tool in Photoshop CS4 is located in the same menu as the Quick Selection brush. Click and hold down the Quick Selection tool and then pick the Magic Wand. (Alternatively, you can press W repeatedly until the Magic Wand tool is selected.) The Magic Wand tool is great for selecting solid (or almost solid) colored areas, because it selects areas based on color—or shades of gray in grayscale mode—as shown in **Figure 2.41**. This type of selection is helpful when you want to change the color of an area or remove a simple background.

If you hold down Shift while clicking with the Magic Wand tool, each click will add to the previous selection instead of completely replacing it.

Figure 2.41 A simple click of the Magic Wand tool can select a solid area of color with ease. (©2008 Dan Ablan.)

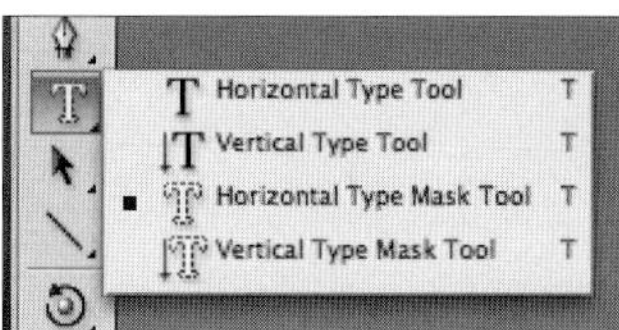

Figure 2.42 Type tools.

Figure 2.43 The selection will be previewed using a red overlay on the unselected areas.

Figure 2.44 These four choices in the options bar allow you to create, add, subtract, or intersect a selection.

Type Tool

Photoshop includes a very powerful Type tool for superimposing text on an image, but sometimes you might just want to make a selection in the *shape* of type—perhaps to fill it with a gradient or to apply a filter through it. You can do that with one of the Type Mask tools, located under the Type tool in the Tools panel (**Figure 2.42**). When you use the Type Mask, Photoshop shows a preview of the selection (with a red overlay on the image, as shown in **Figure 2.43**) while you're editing the text, and then delivers a selection when you press Return/Enter. Learn more about the options of this tool in the bonus video "Type and Background Effects" at www.danablan.com/photoshop.

Refining a Selection

Selecting complex objects in Photoshop usually requires multiple selection tools. To combine these selection tools, you'll need to use a few controls in the options bar (**Figure 2.44**) or learn a few keyboard commands that will allow you to create a new selection, add, subtract, or intersect a selection.

Adding to a Selection

To add to an existing selection, either click the second icon on the far left of the options bar (it looks like two little boxes overlapping each other) or hold down the Shift key when you start making the new selection. You must press the key *before* you start the selection; you can release it as soon as you've clicked the mouse button. If you press it too late, the original selection will be lost. Let's say, for example, that you want to select multiple round objects. One method would be to use the Elliptical Marquee tool multiple times while holding down the Shift key. But you might find it easier to use the choice available in the options bar because then you don't have to remember to hold down any keys.

Removing Part of a Selection

To remove areas from an existing selection, either click the third icon on the far left of the options bar (it looks like one little box stacked on top of another) or hold down Option/Alt when you begin making the selection. If you want to create a half circle, for example, you could start with an Elliptical Marquee tool selection, switch to the Rectangular Marquee tool, hold down Option/Alt, and drag to remove the unwanted selection while retaining the original selection (**Figures 2.45** to **2.47**).

Figure 2.45 The original selection. (©2008 Dan Ablan.)

Figure 2.46 Subtracting a second selection.

Figure 2.47 The end result.

Clicking while holding down the Option/Alt key is particularly helpful when you're using the Magic Wand tool to remove areas of a selection. With each click of the Magic Wand tool, you can use a different Tolerance setting.

Working with Intersecting Selections

To end up with only the overlapped portions of two selections, click the fourth icon on the far left of the options bar (it looks like two intersecting squares with a colored overlap area) or hold down Shift-Option/Alt while editing an existing selection. You can use the Magic Wand tool to select the background of an image and then choose Select > Inverse to get the objects of the selected image (**Figure 2.48**). However, when an image contains multiple objects, you'll often have to restrict the selection to a specific area by dragging with the Lasso tool while holding down Shift-Option/Alt.

Figure 2.48 Applying the Magic Wand tool to the background and then choosing Select > Inverse. (©2008 Dan Ablan.)

Using the Select Menu

The Select menu offers many choices that supplement the basic selection tools. Learning these features will save heaps of time in your everyday work. We'll look at these features in the order in which they appear in the menu.

Select All

Select > All selects the entire document. This can be useful when you need to trim off any part of an image that extends beyond the edge of the document (**Figure 2.49**). You can crop out those areas by choosing Select > All and then Image > Crop. Also, if you need to copy an entire image, you'll need to select everything, because without a selection, the Copy command will be grayed out.

Figure 2.49 When you crop the image, the information that used to extend beyond the document's bounds is discarded.

Deselect/Reselect

If you're done using a selection and want to work on the entire image, choose Select > Deselect. When you don't have a selection, you can work on the entire image. If there's no selection on your screen and you need to reuse the last active selection, choose Select > Reselect. This command is great when you need to use the same selection over and over again.

Inverse

As you might expect, the Inverse command selects the opposite of what you originally selected. If you have the background of an image selected, for example, after choosing Select > Inverse you'll have the subject of the image selected instead (**Figures 2.50** and **2.51**). You'll use this command constantly, especially with the Magic Wand tool. Sometimes it's just easier to select the areas that you *don't* want and then choose Select > Inverse to select what you really want to isolate. Sound backward? Think of this another way—your background might be a quick easy selection because it's made up of one solid color. Select it quickly then choose Select > Inverse.

Figure 2.50 A Magic Wand tool selection. (©2008 Dan Ablan.)

Figure 2.51 The selection after using the Select > Inverse command.

Color Range

Think of the Color Range command (Select > Color Range) as the Magic Wand tool on steroids. With Color Range, you can click multiple areas and then change the Fuzziness setting to increase or reduce the range of colors that will be selected (**Figures 2.52** and **2.53**).

Figure 2.52 The original image. (©2008 Dan Ablan.)

Figure 2.53 The image from Figure 2.52 in the Color Range dialog after clicking multiple areas within the model's blouse.

As you click and play with the Fuzziness control, notice the preview of the selection in the middle of the Color Range dialog. Areas that appear white are the areas that will be selected. The Selection and Image radio buttons let you switch between the selection preview and the main image. (You may never actually use these two controls, though, because it's often easier to switch to the image view by just holding down Command/Ctrl.) To see a preview of the selection within the main image window, change the Selection Preview pop-up menu setting to Grayscale, Black Matte, White Matte, or Quick Mask (**Figures 2.54** to **2.57**).

Figure 2.54 Choosing Grayscale displays the same preview that appears in the Color Range dialog.

Figure 2.55 Choosing Black Matte fills the unselected areas with black.

Figure 2.56 Choosing White Matte fills the unselected areas with white.

Figure 2.57 Choosing Quick Mask uses the settings in the Quick Mask dialog to create a preview of the image.

The Eyedropper tools on the right side of the dialog add and subtract colors from the selection. Using the Eyedropper with the plus symbol next to it is really helpful because it allows you to click the image multiple times. With each click, you tell Photoshop which colors you want it to find. A low Fuzziness setting with many clicks usually produces the best results.

The selections you get from the Color Range command are not ordinary selections, in that they usually contain areas that are not completely selected. For instance, if you're trying to select red areas in an image that also contains flesh tones, the fleshy areas most likely will become partially selected. If you then adjust the image, the red will be completely adjusted, and the flesh tones will shift a little bit.

If a selection is already present when you choose Select > Color Range, the command analyzes the colors only within the selected area. This feature lets you run the command multiple times to isolate smaller and smaller areas. If you want to add the Color Range command to the current selection, be sure to hold down the Shift key when choosing Select > Color Range.

You can also turn on the Localized Color Clusters option, which allows you to set a range for the area (color) sampled, rather than for all the color within the image.

Refine Edge

Beginning with CS3, Photoshop offers a much improved way of adjusting the edge of a selection. After making a selection using any of Photoshop's selection tools (or a combination of selection tools), choose Select > Refine Edge to bring up the dialog shown in **Figure 2.58**.

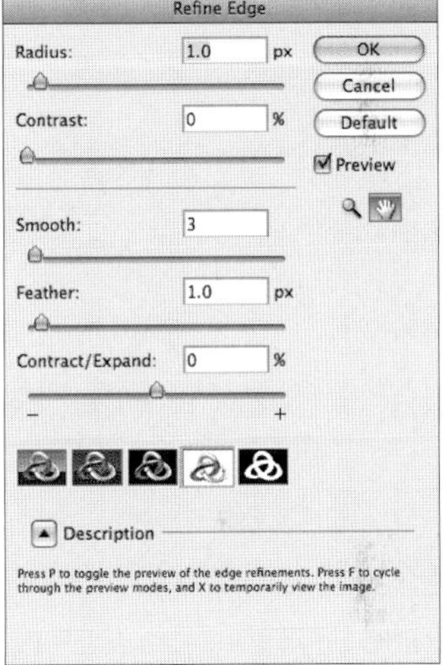

Figure 2.58 The Refine Edge dialog offers several tools for refining your selections.

The Refine Edge dialog lets you interactively preview a selection on a number of different backgrounds and provides some important controls that soften, resize, and improve the edges of the selection.

When you first open the Refine Edge dialog, your selection is shown against a white background, allowing you to see the quality of the edge. If you prefer, you can click the display buttons at the bottom of the dialog, changing the view to see your selection composited on different types of backgrounds or displayed as a regular selection of "marching ants" (**Figure 2.59**).

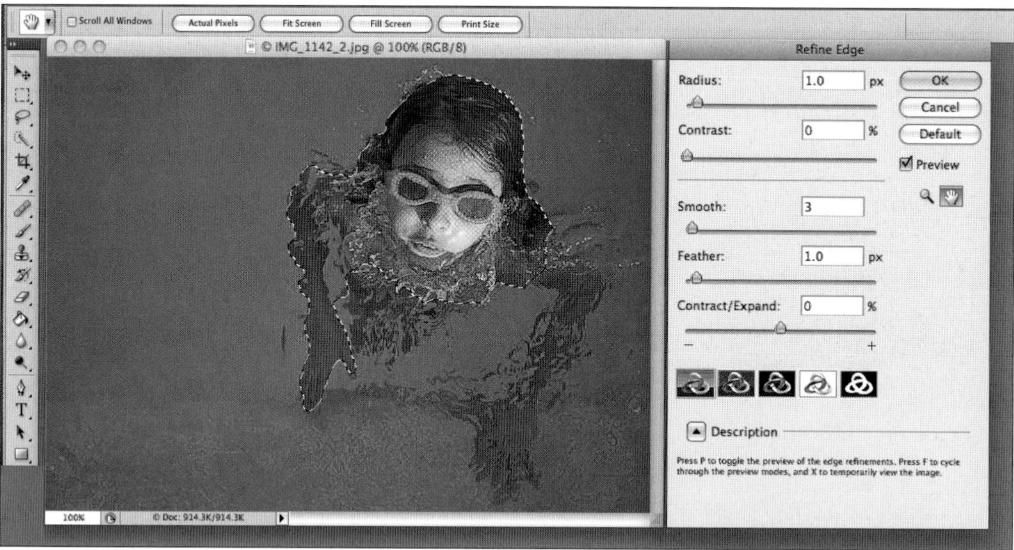

Figure 2.59 You can view your selection composited against different backgrounds. (©2008 Dan Ablan.)

Modify

The features in the Modify menu (Select > Modify) have helped artists out of many sticky situations. At first glance, it might not be obvious why you would ever use these commands, but they'll be very handy as you continue through the book. The following list describes the commands:

- **Border:** Selects a border of pixels centered on the current selection. If you use a setting of 10, the selection will be 5 pixels inside the selection and 5 pixels outside the selection. You can use this command to remove pesky halos that appear when you copy an object from a light background and paste it onto a darker background (**Figures 2.60** and **2.61**).
- **Smooth:** Attempts to round off any sharp corners in a selection (**Figure 2.62**). This trick can be especially useful when you want to create a rounded-corner rectangle.

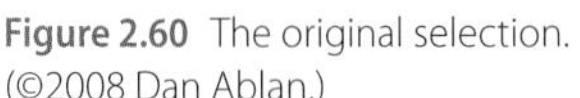

Figure 2.60 The original selection. (©2008 Dan Ablan.)

Figure 2.61 A 10-pixel border.

Figure 2.62 Smooth: 16 pixels.

- **Expand:** Enlarges the current selection while attempting to maintain its shape (**Figure 2.63**). This command works well with smooth, freeform selections, but it might not be the best choice for straight-edged selections because the selection might expand beyond the corners of the image.
- **Contract:** Reduces the size of the current selection while attempting to maintain its shape (**Figure 2.64**). The highest setting available is 16. If you need a higher setting, just use the command more than once.

Figure 2.63 Expand: 12 pixels.

Figure 2.64 Contract: 12 pixels.

- **Feather:** Unlike the Feather option in the selection tools, this command affects only the selection that's currently active; it has no effect on future selections. You can't reduce the amount of feathering with this command once it's applied. Therefore, if you apply it once with a setting of 10 and then try it again on the same selection using a setting of 5, it will simply increase the amount again. It's just like blurring an image—each time you blur the image, it becomes more and more blurry.

  You might prefer using this command instead of entering Feather settings directly into the tool's options bar (where they affect all "new" selections). If you enter values directly, days later you might not remember that you turned on that setting, and you'll spend hours trying to select an intricate object. By leaving the tools set at 0, you can press Shift-F6 to bring up the Feather dialog and enter a number to feather the selection. Because this technique affects only the current selection, it can't mess up any future selections.

  The problem with the Feather command is that there's no way to tell if a selection is feathered by just looking at the marching ants. Not only that, but most people think the marching ants indicate where the edge of a selection is, and that's simply not the case with a feathered selection. In **Figure 2.65**, the marching ants actually indicate where a feathered selection is halfway faded out. It's much better to use the Refine Edge command (Select > Refine Edge) or the Refine Edge button.

Figure 2.65 The selection area is outside the image because of a feathered selection.

Grow

The Grow command (Select > Grow) searches for colors that are similar to an area that has already been selected (**Figures 2.66** and **2.67**). In effect, it spreads the selection in every direction—but only into areas that are similar in color. It won't jump across areas that are not similar to the ones selected. The Grow command uses the Tolerance setting that's specified in the Magic Wand options bar to determine the range of colors for which it will look.

Figure 2.66 The original selection. (©2008 Dan Ablan.)

Figure 2.67 The selection after choosing Select > Grow.

Similar

The Similar command (Select > Similar) works like the Grow command except that it looks over the entire document for similar colors (**Figures 2.68** and **2.69**). Unlike the Grow command, the colors that Similar selects don't have to touch the previous selection. This feature can be very useful when you've selected one object out of a group of same-colored objects. For example, if the image shows a herd of gray elephants standing in front of a lush green jungle, you can select the first elephant and then choose Select > Similar to get the rest of the herd (provided, of course, that they're all a similar shade of gray). The same trick works for a field of flowers, and so on.

Figure 2.68 The original selection. (©2008 Dan Ablan.)

Figure 2.69 The selection after choosing Select > Similar.

Figure 2.70 The original selection. (©2008 Dan Ablan.)

Figure 2.71 After choosing Select > Transform to scale the selection.

Figure 2.72 Rotating and scaling the selection.

Control-click/right-click while transforming a selection to choose the type of distortion you want to perform.

Transform Selection

After making a selection, you can scale, rotate, or distort it by choosing Select > Transform Selection. This command places handles around the image. By dragging the handles and using a series of keyboard commands, you can distort the selection as much as you like. Look at the neat stuff you can do with Transform Selection:

- **Scale:** To scale a selection, drag any of the handles. Dragging a corner handle changes width and height at the same time. (Hold down the Shift key to retain the proportions of the original selection.) Dragging a side handle changes either the width of the selection or its height. This feature can be a great help when working with elliptical selections because it lets you drag the edges of the selection instead of its so-called corners (**Figure 2.70**).
- **Rotate:** To rotate the selection, move your cursor a little bit beyond one of the corner points; the cursor should change into an arc with arrows on each end. You can control where the pivot point of the rotation will be by moving the crosshair that appears in the center of the selection (**Figure 2.71**).
- **Distort:** To distort the shape of the selection, hold down the Command/Ctrl key and then drag one of the corner points. Using this technique, you can drag each corner independently (**Figure 2.72**).

  You can also distort a selection so that it resembles the shape of a road vanishing into the distance. Drag one of the corners while holding down Shift-Option-Command on the Mac or Ctrl-Shift-Alt in Windows (**Figures 2.73** and **2.74**).

  To move two diagonal corners at the same time, hold down Option-Command on the Mac or Ctrl-Alt in Windows while dragging one of the corner handles.

  Finalize your distortions by pressing Return/Enter (or by double-clicking inside the selection). Cancel them by pressing Esc.

Figure 2.73 The original selection. (©2008 Dan Ablan.)

Figure 2.74 Dragging the corner with Command/Ctrl.

Loading and Saving Selections

If you've spent hours perfecting a selection and think you might need to use it again in the future, apply the Save Selection command (Select > Save Selection) to store the selection as an alpha channel. Don't worry, you don't need to know anything about channels to use these commands—all you have to do is supply a name for the selection. If you want to find out more about working with channels, check out the bonus video "Channels" at www.danablan.com/photoshop.

These saved selections remain in your document until you manually remove them using the Channels panel. They won't be saved on your hard drive until you actually save the entire file. Only the Photoshop (.psd), Large Document Format (.psb), Photoshop PDF (.pdf), and TIFF (.tif) file formats support multiple saved selections.

When you want to retrieve a saved selection, choose Select > Load Selection and pick the name of the selection from the Channel pop-up menu (**Figure 2.75**). When you use this command, it's just like re-creating the selection with the original selection tool you used, only a lot faster.

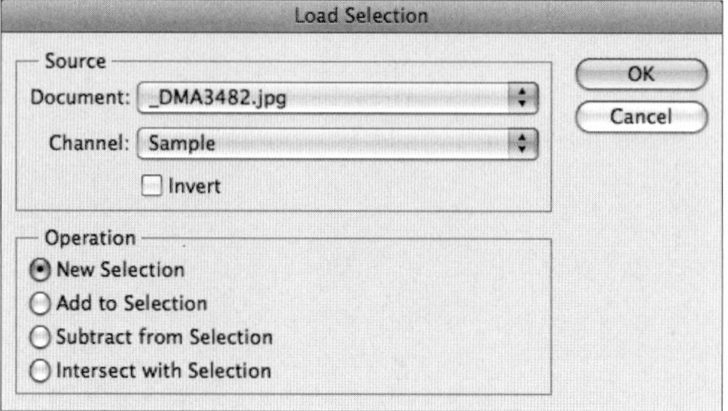

Figure 2.75 Once a selection is saved, you can load it for future work.

Quick Mask Mode

Figure 2.76 The Quick Mask icon is at the bottom of the Tools panel.

Earlier I mentioned that the marching ants marquee doesn't accurately show what a feathered selection looks like. Quick Mask mode *can* show what a feathered selection really looks like and can also help in creating basic selections. The Quick Mask icon is located directly below the foreground and background colors in the Tools panel (**Figure 2.76**).

To see how Quick Mask works, first make a selection by using the Marquee tool. Turn on Quick Mask mode by clicking the Quick Mask icon (or just press Q). In Quick Mask mode, the selected area should look normal and all the unselected areas should be covered with a translucent color (**Figures 2.77** and **2.78**).

Figure 2.77 A selection shown in Standard mode. (©2008 Dan Ablan.)

Figure 2.78 The selection from Figure 2.77, shown in Quick Mask mode.

Now that you're in Quick Mask mode, you no longer need to use selection tools to modify a selection. Instead, use standard painting tools, painting with black to take away from the selection or white to add to it. When you're done modifying the selection, switch back to Standard mode, and the marching ants will reappear (**Figures 2.79** and **2.80**).

Figure 2.79 A selection modified in Quick Mask mode.

Figure 2.80 End result after switching back to Standard mode.

Now let's see what feathered selections look like in Quick Mask mode. Make another selection using the Marquee tool. Choose Select > Modify > Feather with a setting of 10, and then switch to Quick Mask mode and take a look (**Figures 2.81** and **2.82**). Feathered selections appear with blurry edges in Quick Mask mode. This happens because partially transparent areas (that is, those that are more transparent than the rest of the mask) indicate areas that are partially selected (50% transparent means 50% selected).

Figure 2.81 Normal. (©2008 Dan Ablan.)

Figure 2.82 Feathered.

The confusing part about this process is that when you look at the marching ants that appear after you switch back to Standard mode, they only show where the selection is at least 50% selected. That isn't a very accurate picture of what it really looks like. But in Quick Mask mode, you can see exactly what's happening on the image's edge. If you want to create a feathered selection in Quick Mask mode, just paint with a soft-edged brush. Or, if you already have a shape defined, choose Filter > Blur > Gaussian Blur, which gives you the same result as feathering and shows a visual preview of the edge.

Figure 2.83 Using a selection in Quick Mask mode to restrict which areas can be edited. (©2008 Dan Ablan.)

Selections in Quick Mask Mode

You can even use a selection to isolate a particular area of the quick mask (**Figure 2.83**). Quick Mask mode can help you to create a selection that's feathered on only one side. Want to try it? Turn on Quick Mask mode, press D to reset the foreground color, and then press Option-Delete (Mac) or Alt-Backspace (Windows) to fill the quick mask. Next, choose the Marquee tool and select an area. Now use the Gradient tool set to Black, White (the third choice from the left in the Gradient Editor panel) and create a gradient within the selected area. When you're done, switch off Quick Mask mode. To see exactly how this selection will affect the image, choose Image > Adjustments > Levels and attempt to lighten that area by dragging the lower-left slider.

Quick Mask Options

Photoshop also allows you to switch where the color shows up in a Quick Mask selection. You can specify whether you want the selected or unselected areas to show up. To change this setting, double-click the Quick Mask icon and change the Color Indicates setting (**Figures 2.84** and **2.85**). Photoshop uses the term *masked areas* to describe areas that are not selected.

You can change the color that's overlaid on the image by clicking the color swatch in the Quick Mask Options dialog. The Opacity setting determines how much you'll be able to see through the Quick Mask.

Figure 2.84 Changing the Color Indicates setting changes where the color overlay appears.

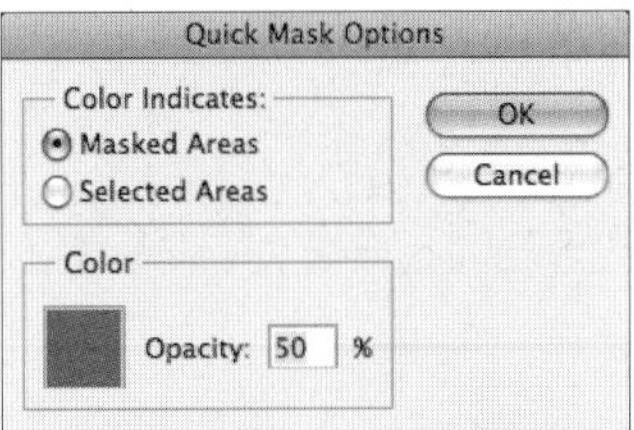

Figure 2.85 Quick Mask settings.

The Next Step

After a few practice rounds with the tools covered in this chapter, you should be selecting like a pro. We'll go over more advanced methods of creating selections in Chapter 9, "Enhancements and Masking." Meanwhile, it really is worth spending the time to build up your selection skills; you'll use them every day in Photoshop.

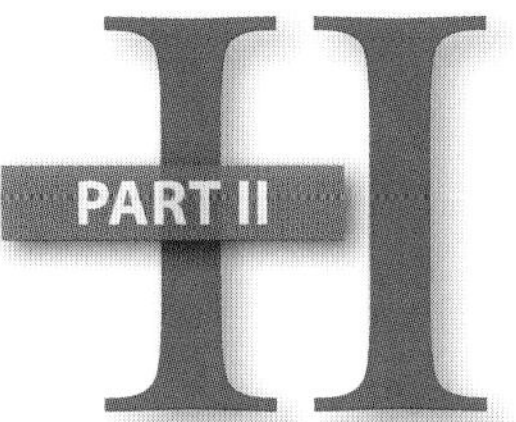

Production Essentials

CHAPTER

3

Layers and Curves

Many people who excel are self-taught.

—Herb Ritts

Layers and Curves

The Layers panel will quickly become familiar. Whether you're working on a single image or a complex graphic for a poster, the Layers panel is your home base for adjustments, masking, blending, and even just simple project organization.

How Do Layers Work?

At first glance, layers might seem complex, but the idea is really rather simple: You isolate different parts of an image onto independent layers so that you can work with them separately. Think of each layer as a piece of glass, with the individual layers stacked on top of each other as if they were separate documents (**Figure 3.1**). By putting each image on its own layer, you can change your document's look and layout freely without committing to the changes. If you paint, apply a filter, or make an adjustment, it affects only the layer on which you're working. If you get into a snarl over a particularly troublesome layer, just throw it away and start over. The rest of your document will remain untouched—safe and handy!

Layers can relate to each other in interesting ways, such as when you create a *mask* (hole) in one layer to reveal an underlying image on another layer. You'll learn some great techniques using this concept in Chapter 9, "Enhancements and Masking," and Chapter 10, "Collage Effects."

But first, you need to understand the foundations. If you've used layers for a while, you might find some of this chapter a bit too basic. On the other hand, you might find some juicy new tidbits.

Figure 3.1 Think of layers as stacks of glass that you can blend in all sorts of ways.

Meet the Layers

Before you jump in and start creating a bunch of layers, you should get familiar with their place of residence: the Layers panel (**Figure 3.2**). You're going to spend a lot of time with this panel, so take a moment now to get on friendly terms with it. It's not terribly complicated, and after you've used the Layers panel a few times you should know it like the back of your hand.

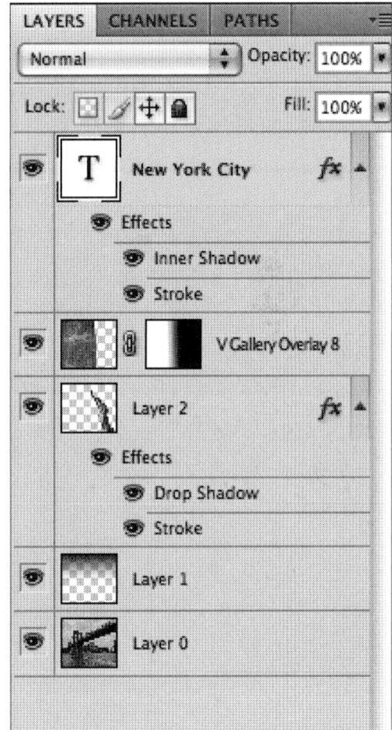

Figure 3.2 A typical Photoshop file with multiple layers, shown in the Layers panel.

As you make your way through this chapter, you'll learn more about the Layers panel and the fundamental tasks associated with it. Now, assuming that you've done your part and introduced yourself to the Layers panel, let's get on with the business of creating and manipulating layers in Photoshop.

Creating Layers

Photoshop automatically creates the majority of the layers you'll need. A new layer is added when you copy and paste an image or drag a layer between documents (we'll talk about this later in the chapter). If you're starting from scratch, however, just click the New Layer icon at the bottom of the Layers panel to create a new, empty layer.

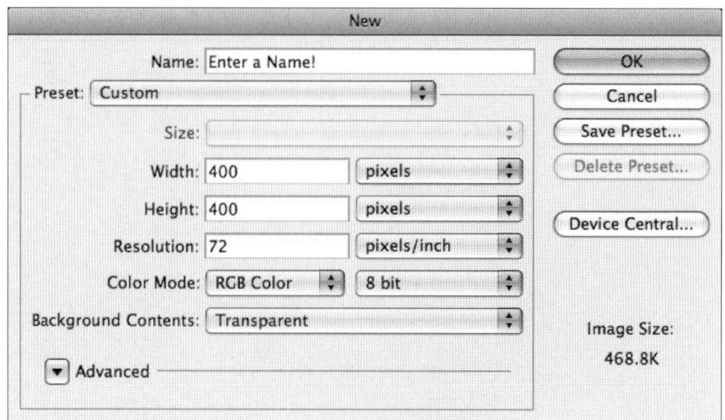

Figure 3.3 Create a new blank image with a transparent background.

If you hold down the Command/Ctrl key when clicking the New Layer icon, the new layer appears below the active layer instead of on top of it. The only time this trick won't work is when the Background is active—Photoshop can't add a new layer below the Background.

Give it a try now: Choose File > New and create an RGB document that's around 400 × 400 pixels in size, with a transparent background (**Figure 3.3**). Resolution doesn't matter at this point. Click the New Layer icon at the bottom of the Layers panel to create an empty layer. Click your foreground color and pick out a bright color. Choose the round Shape tool (Ellipse), which is grouped with the Rectangle Shape tool, below the Type tool and Path Selection tool in the Tools panel. In the options bar, click the Fill Pixels icon (**Figure 3.4**). Click and drag across your image to draw a big circle.

Figure 3.4 Click the Fill Pixels icon (on the far right) in the options bar.

When you're done with the first shape, create another layer and use the Rectangle Shape tool to draw a square, using a different color (**Figure 3.5**). Finally, create a third layer and draw a triangle with yet another color. (Create the triangle by using the Polygon Shape tool and setting Sides to 3 in the options bar.)

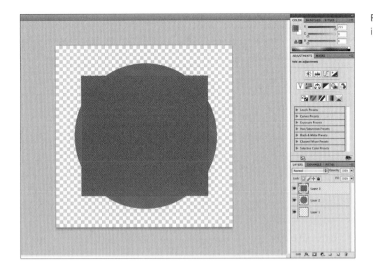

Figure 3.5 Draw a colored rectangle in a new layer.

You can use this simple document you've just created to try out the concepts in the following sections that describe the features of the Layers panel. **Figure 3.6** shows the three added layers.

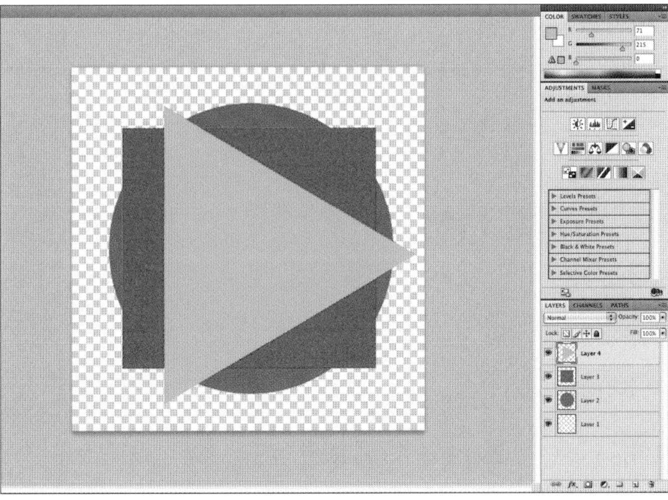

Figure 3.6 Three layers stacked above a white Background layer.

Active Layer

The current layer is highlighted in the Layers panel. To change the active layer, just click the name of another layer. Alternatively, Command/Ctrl-click the image while the

Move tool is active (press V to activate the Move tool), which causes the topmost layer containing information under your cursor to become active. As you Command/Ctrl-click different parts of an image (circle, square, triangle in this example), watch the Layers panel to see which layer becomes active. Photoshop allows you to have more than one layer active at a time, but for now we'll stick to working with one layer to keep things simple.

Try creating a new layer before using any of the painting tools or the Gradient tool. Because these tools apply changes directly to the active layer, the changes are difficult to modify once they've been applied. It's good working with a safety net, so before using these tools, you should create a new layer where you can easily edit the changes without disturbing the underlying image.

Naming Layers

Photoshop names each layer you create. However, as your projects become more complex, a stack of layers named Layer 1, Layer 2, and so on can start to get pretty confusing. To stay organized, name layers as you create them. To name a layer, click the current layer name twice and type the new name. (That is, click with a delay: click, wait, click. A double-click opens the Layer Style dialog, which we'll talk about later in this chapter.)

Layer Order

To change the order of layers, drag the name of a layer above or below the name of another layer in the Layers panel.

Layers work from the bottom up. Let's say you load a graphic or photograph. That's one layer. Then you create a new layer and draw a shape. The topmost layers will obstruct your view of the underlying images. However, changing blending modes, creating masks, and other functions make the layers work together, taking them further than just stacking them one on top of another. But for now, know that you can reorganize the layers by dragging them up or down in the Layers panel.

Background Image (Background Layer)

The Background image in Photoshop (which some people refer to as the *Background layer*) is a bit different from the other layers that make up an image. Think of the layers as individual pages in a pad of tracing paper. The Background image equates to the pad's cardboard backing. It might be the same size and it relates to the other pages in the pad, but it has some qualities that make it quite different.

The Background image has the same limitations as most of the common file formats in use today (such as JPEG and EPS): It's always 100% opaque; no part of it can extend beyond the document's bounds, and it's not actually considered a layer, since most file formats don't support layers (with a few exceptions such as .PSD and .TIFF). In fact, that's why the Background image exists. If all your document contains is the Background, you still should be able to save the image in just about any file format without losing information. That's also why most images start life as a Background image—because they originated in a file format that didn't support layers or came from a program that doesn't support layers. When you save a layered document into a file format that doesn't support layers (such as JPEG), Photoshop automatically combines all the layers that make up the image and turns the result into a Background image (known as *flattening*).

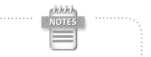

If your document doesn't have a background (because you accidentally deleted or renamed the Background image), you can convert one of the existing layers into a background by choosing Layer > New > Background from Layer. Just changing the layer's name back to "Background" won't do the job.

The Background image always displays a lock symbol to indicate that it cannot be repositioned with the Move tool, moved up or down in the layers stack, or be made transparent. For that reason, many tools will work differently when the Background image is active. For instance, the Eraser tool paints with the background color when the Background image is active, since it can't make areas of the Background image transparent.

You can change the checkerboard's appearance by choosing Edit > Preferences > Transparency & Gamut. You can even change it to solid white by changing the Grid Size setting to None.

With all that said, you don't actually have to have a Background in your document. If you want to convert the Background into a normal layer, just change its name. The Background image must be named "Background" or it becomes a normal, unlocked layer.

The Eyeballs: What They See Is What You Get

The eyeballs in the Layers panel determine which layers will be visible in your document as well as which ones will print. The eyeballs turn on and off in a toggle effect when you click them: Now you see them, now you don't.

To turn off all the visible layers in the Layers panel, Option/Alt-click any of the eyeball icons. Option/Alt-clicking a second time brings those same layers back into view. To make all the layers visible/invisible, Control-click/right-click an eyeball icon and choose Show/Hide All Other Layers.

If you turn off all the eyeballs in the Layers panel, Photoshop fills your screen with a checkerboard. This checkerboard indicates that nothing is visible in the document. (If Photoshop filled your screen with white instead, you might assume that you were looking at a visible layer filled with white.) Think of the checkerboard as the areas of the document that are empty. When you view a single layer, the checkerboard indicates the empty areas of that layer. As you turn on the other layers in the document, the checkerboard is replaced with the information contained on those layers. When multiple layers are visible, the checkerboard indicates where the underlying image will not be obstructed by the elements on the visible layers (**Figure 3.7**).

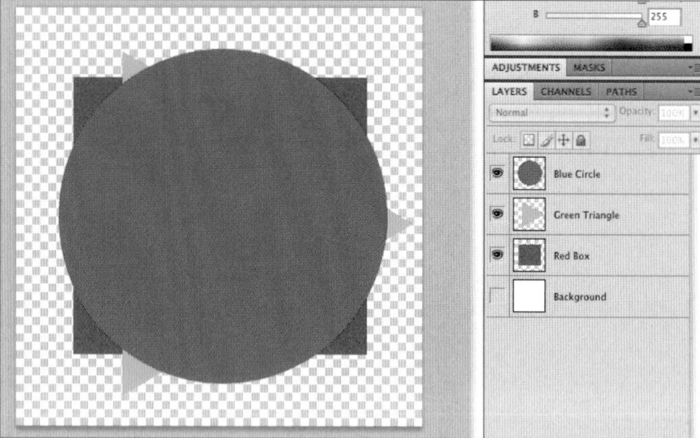

Figure 3.7 When you uncheck a visibility icon (eyeball) in the Layers panel, that particular layer no longer shows in your document.

Opacity

You can figure out the exact opacity of an area by Option/Alt-clicking a layer's eyeball icon and then opening the Info panel. Click the eyedropper in the Info panel and choose Opacity; you'll get a separate readout that indicates how opaque the area is below your cursor.

The Opacity setting at the top of the Layers panel controls the opacity of the active layer. When this setting is lowered, the entire layer becomes partially transparent (transparent is the exact opposite of opaque). To lower the opacity in a specific area rather than the entire layer, lower the opacity of the Eraser tool and then brush across the area of the layer you want to become more transparent—that is, unless the Background image is active. If you use the Eraser tool on the Background image, Photoshop simply paints with your background color instead of truly deleting areas. (Remember, the Background image is always opaque.)

Figure 3.8 Painting on a new layer, above the other layers, obstructs the layers beneath.

Figure 3.9 Lowering the opacity of a layer allows the other layers to show through.

Try this: Using the document you created earlier in this chapter, create a new layer, and press B to activate the Brush tool. Then use any painting tool to brush across the layer. Now lower the Opacity setting in the Layers panel to 70% (**Figures 3.8** and **3.9**).

Now let's compare this effect with what happens when you lower the Opacity setting of the Paintbrush tool. Create another new layer; however, this time leave the layer's Opacity setting at 100%. Click the Paintbrush tool, change the tool's Opacity setting to 70% in the options bar, and then brush across the layer (just don't overlap the paint you created earlier). The result should look like the paint that appears in the other layer (**Figure 3.10**).

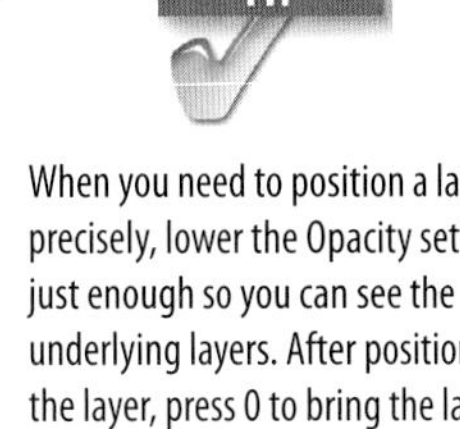

When you need to position a layer precisely, lower the Opacity setting just enough so you can see the underlying layers. After positioning the layer, press 0 to bring the layer back to 100% opacity. For really precise layer positioning, use the arrow keys on your keyboard.

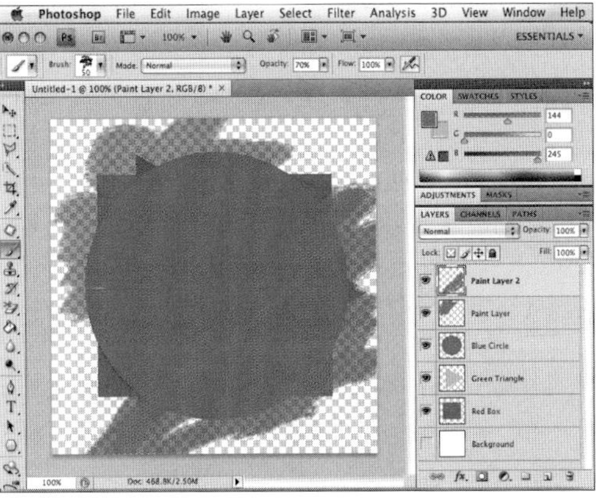

Figure 3.10 Painting on a layer with 100% opacity, but with a brush set to 70% opacity, yields the same type of result as in Figure 3.10.

Figure 3.11 Painting on a layer with 100% opacity makes a solid color covering anything below it.

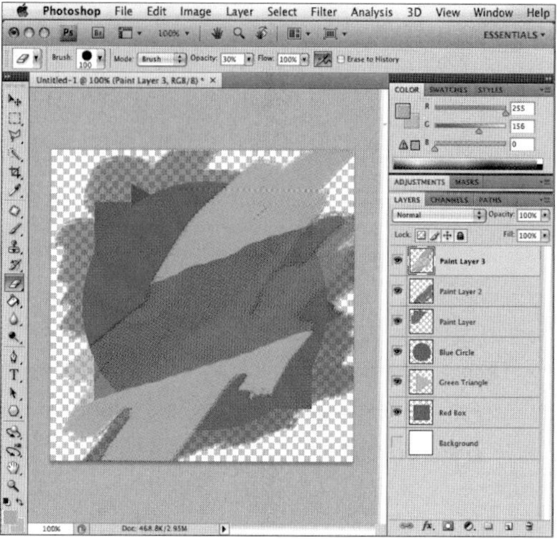

Figure 3.12 Painting a layer with the Eraser tool set at 30% opacity removes just a portion of the layer.

Finally, create one more new layer, and paint across it with the tool's Opacity setting at 100%. Now brush across an area with the Eraser tool, using an Opacity setting of 30% (**Figures 3.11** and **3.12**).

NOTES

To change the opacity of a layer quickly, switch to the Move tool (press V) and use the number keys on your keyboard (1 = 10%, 3 = 30%, 56 = 56%, and so on).

All of these options do the same thing. You just have to think a bit: Do you want to apply the Opacity setting to the entire layer? Use the Layers panel's Opacity setting. Do you want to apply the Opacity setting to only part of the layer? Use the Opacity setting in the tool's options bar. Do you want to change the opacity of an area you've already painted? Use the Eraser tool with an Opacity setting.

Moving Layers

If you want to move everything that's on a particular layer, first make that layer active by clicking its name; then use the Move tool (press V) to drag the layer around the screen. If you drag the layer onto another document window, Photoshop copies the layer into that document. If you want to move just a small area of the layer, you can make a selection and then drag from within the selected area by using the Move tool.

When the Move tool is active, you can use the arrow keys on your keyboard to nudge a layer one pixel at a time. Holding down Shift while using the arrow keys nudges the active layer 10 pixels at a time.

Selecting Multiple Layers

As you might expect, you can select more than one layer at a time. Clicking individual layers with no keys held down causes individual layers to become active. Command/Ctrl-clicking a layer adds that layer to the other layers that are selected. To select a range of layers, click the first layer you want, hold down Shift, and click the last layer you want. Photoshop selects all the layers between the first and the last layers you clicked. You can also Shift-Command-click (Mac) or Shift-Ctrl-click (Windows) within an image while the Move tool is active to add the layer that appears under your cursor to the layers that are currently selected. There is no limit to the number of layers that can be selected at one time.

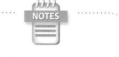

Many of Photoshop's features are unavailable when multiple layers are selected (such as filters and adjustments) because they were designed to work on only one layer at a time.

Linking Layers

When multiple layers are linked, using the Move tool or choosing Edit > Transform causes the active layer and all the layers linked to it to change (as if all the linked layers were selected). The advantage to linking layers is that the linking behavior is maintained regardless of which layer is active. So, if two layers should always relate in size and position, link them together so that that relationship remains consistent. To link layers, select the layers and then click the Link symbol at the bottom of the Layers panel (**Figure 3.13**). After linking the layers, moving or transforming the image while any one of the linked layers is selected causes all the linked layers to change. To unlink layers, select the layers you want to unlink and click the Link symbol again.

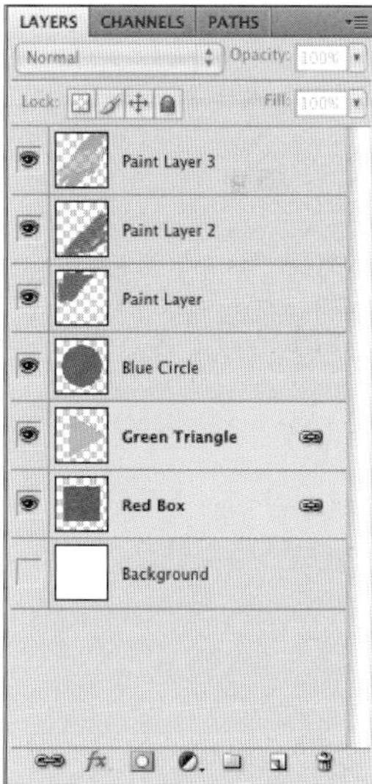

Figure 3.13 Linking layers allows certain behaviors, such as moving or rotating, to affect all the linked layers. Linked layers display the link symbol next to the layer name.

Trimming Images in Layers

If you use the Move tool to reposition a layer so that a portion of the layer extends beyond the edge of the document, that portion will no longer be visible, but Photoshop still remembers the information (**Figure 3.14**). If you move the layer away from the edge, Photoshop is able to bring back the information that wasn't visible. You can save a lot of memory by making Photoshop clip off all the information beyond the edge of the document. Here's a little trick for trimming off that fat. Just choose Select > All and then choose Image > Crop—no more wasted memory.

Figure 3.14 If an image is moved beyond the edge of a document, Photoshop remembers the part that's no longer visible—unless you crop it.

NOTES

A crop rectangle must be drawn and active for the Show/Hide commands to be visible.

WARNING

Use the "trim the fat" technique only if you're absolutely sure you won't need the information beyond the edge of the document, because you cannot get it back once you've cropped it (that is, without resorting to the History panel).

The default setting in the Crop tool is to delete the areas that extend beyond the edge of an image. You can prevent the Crop tool from deleting those areas by clicking the Hide setting in the Crop tool options bar (it will be available only in files that contain layers). That option causes Photoshop to reduce the size of the image based on the cropping rectangle you specify, but retain the information that extends beyond the edge of the image.

Extra white space around the edge of an image also wastes memory (**Figure 3.15**). Choosing Image > Trim causes Photoshop to remove any unnecessary white space (**Figure 3.16**). Just adjust the Based On setting so that Photoshop will find white information in the image (depending on which corner of the image contains white), and then specify which edge of the document you want to trim away—you can usually leave all four of the Trim Away check boxes turned on.

Figure 3.15 Extra white space around an image usually is unnecessary.

Figure 3.16 The Trim command removes unwanted space evenly.

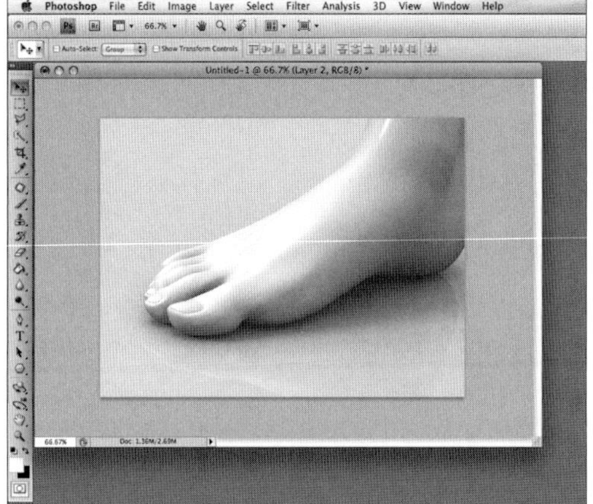

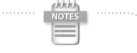

Figure 3.17 An image like this might have more to it than just what you see in the document.

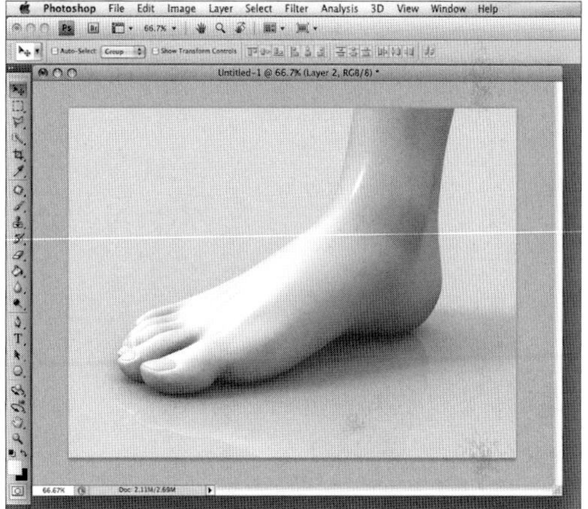

Figure 3.18 Using Reveal All allows you to see the full image.

So far we've talked about how to make images smaller to save memory and hard drive space, but now let's do the opposite with Photoshop's Reveal All command (Image > Reveal All). When you choose that command, Photoshop enlarges your document to include any information that extends beyond the bounds of the document (**Figures 3.17** and **3.18**). All the layers that you've moved beyond the edge of your document will become visible again.

When dragging between documents, Photoshop positions the copied layer(s) based on where your cursor was when you clicked the image and where you released the mouse button in the second document. Holding down Shift when dragging between documents causes the layers to end up in the center of the destination document (if no selection is active) or centered on any active selection.

Copying Layers Between Documents

When you use the Move tool, you can do more than just drag a layer around the document on which you're working. You can also drag from one image window to another. Dragging selected layers from one document into another copies the layers into the second document. The copied layers are positioned directly above the layer that was active in the second document. This is similar to copying and pasting, but takes a lot less memory because Photoshop doesn't store the image on the clipboard. You can achieve the same result by dragging the name of a layer from the Layers panel onto another document window, regardless of which tool is active.

When you drag layers between documents, occasionally an image will appear to have been scaled while it was copied. Actually, you're viewing the two images at different magnifications (**Figure 3.19**). Look at the tops of the documents; if the percentages don't match, the image size appears to change when you drag the image between the documents. It's like putting your hand under a magnifying glass: Your hand looks larger under the magnifying glass, but when you pull it out, it looks normal again.

NOTES

If the image you're dragging to another document is considerably larger than the destination document, you'll need to choose Edit > Transform > Scale to resize the image to fit the destination document. If you can't see the transformation handles, press Command/Ctrl-0 (zero) to zoom out until the handles become visible.

Figure 3.19 Image size might differ between two documents, which makes the image size appear to change when you copy the layer(s).

Duplicating Layers

If you have a picture of Elvis and you want to make Elvis twins, just drag the layer onto the New Layer icon at the bottom of the Layers panel. This icon has two purposes: It duplicates a layer that you drag onto it, or it creates a new empty layer if you just click it. You can also hold down Option/Alt when dragging a layer up or down within the layers stack, or press Command/Ctrl-J to duplicate the active layer. Just make sure that you don't have a *selection* active; otherwise, this command copies only the area that's selected, rather than the whole layer.

The Trash icon doesn't work like the Trash on a Mac or the Recycle Bin in Windows. Once you put something into it, you can't get it back without resorting to the History panel.

Deleting Layers

To delete a layer, drag its name to the Trash icon at the bottom of the Layers panel, or Option/Alt-click the Trash icon. (The Option/Alt key prevents a warning dialog from appearing.)

Transforming Layers

To rotate, scale, or distort the active layer, click one of the options in the Transform menu (Edit > Transform); then pull the handles to distort the image (**Figure 3.20**). Press Enter to commit to the change or Esc to abort.

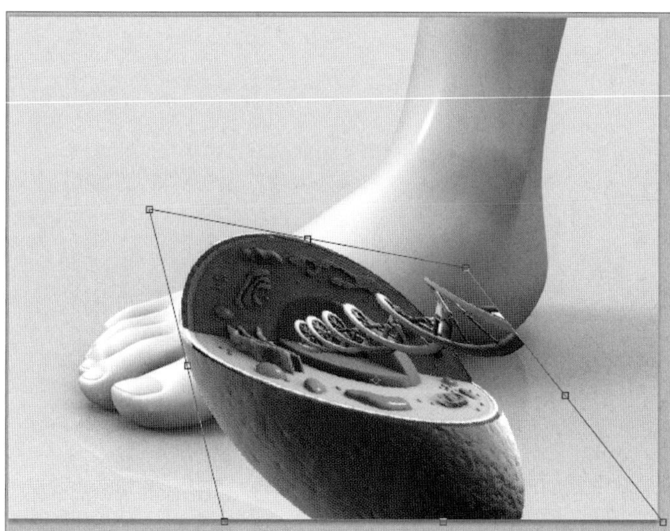

Figure 3.30 The Transform Layer tool allows you to manipulate the layer by dragging the handles.

Locking Layers

The icons at the top of the Layers panel allow you to lock the transparency, image, and position of an individual layer (**Figure 3.21**). Once a layer has been locked, changes that can be performed on that layer are limited.

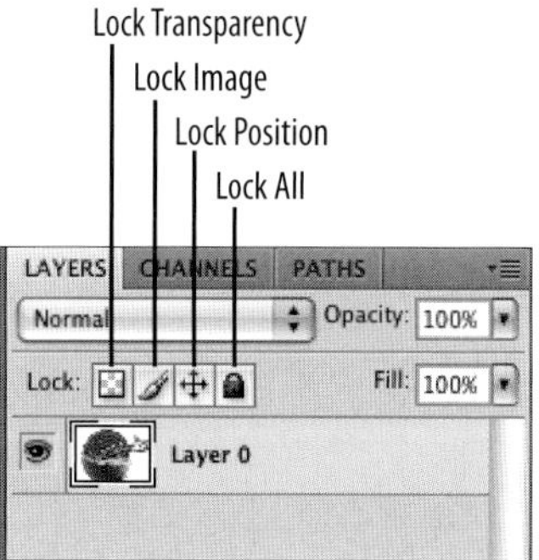

Figure 3.21 You can lock the transparency as well as the image and position of selected layers.

Lock Transparency

Lock Transparency prevents you from changing the transparency of areas. Each layer has its own Lock Transparency setting. If you turn on the Lock Transparency icon for one layer and then switch to another layer, the Layers panel displays the setting for the current layer, which might be different from setting for the previous layer.

The Eraser tool works differently when Lock Transparency is turned on. The Eraser tool usually makes areas transparent (by completely deleting them), but it starts painting with the current background color instead when Lock Transparency is turned on, filling any areas you drag over. However, if you paint across an area that's transparent, it doesn't change the image at all (because the transparent areas are being preserved). You can see how Lock Transparency can mess with your mind if you forget that you turned it on.

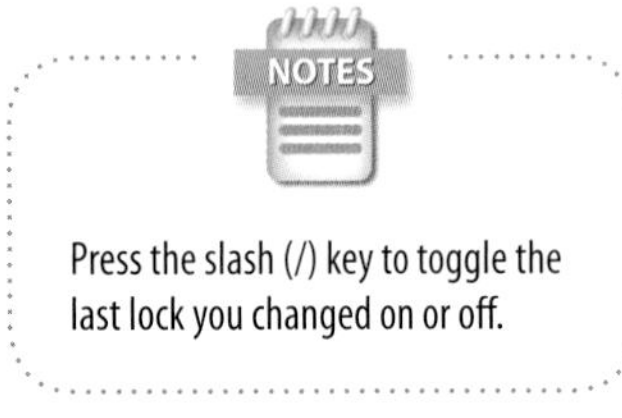

Press the slash (/) key to toggle the last lock you changed on or off.

Try this: Open a photo, and delete areas around it using the Eraser tool. To accomplish this, you'll have to change the name of the Background image first to make it a regular layer (you can poke a hole in a regular layer, but not in the Background image). Then make sure that Lock Transparency is turned off; otherwise, you can't make areas transparent. Use the Eraser tool to remove the areas that surround the subject of the photo. Choose Filter > Blur > Gaussian Blur and use a really high setting. Notice that the edge of the image fades out and blends with the transparent areas surrounding it (**Figure 3.22**). Now choose Edit > Undo and try doing the same thing with the Lock Transparency option turned on (**Figure 3.23**). Notice that the edge cannot fade out because Photoshop will not change the transparency with this option turned on.

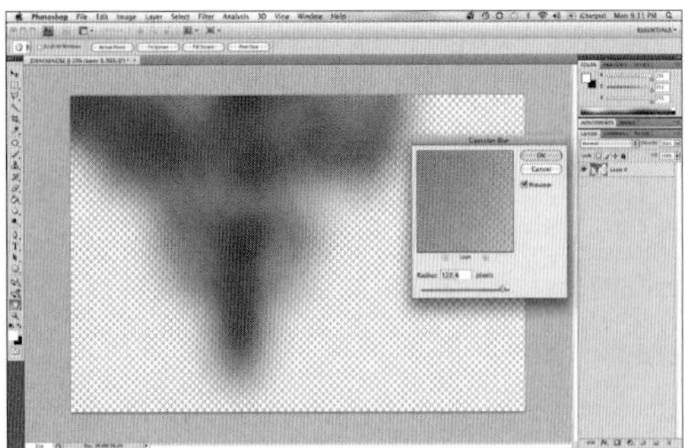

Figure 3.22 With Lock Transparency off, blurring an image takes the transparency into consideration.

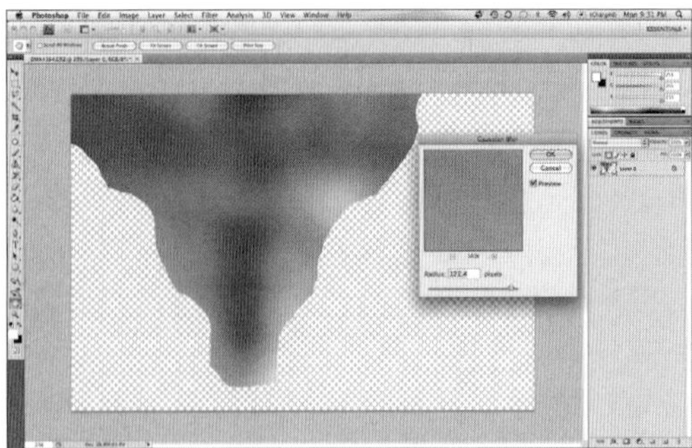

Figure 3.23 With Lock Transparency on, blurring an image ignores the transparency.

Here's another example: Create a new layer and scribble across it with any painting tool, making sure that Lock Transparency is turned off. Next, drag across the image with the Gradient tool. The gradient should fill the entire screen (**Figure 3.24**). Choose Edit > Undo, and try doing the same thing with the Lock Transparency option turned on (**Figure 3.25**). Because Photoshop can't change the transparency of the layer, it can't fill the transparent areas, and therefore is limited to changing the areas that are opaque.

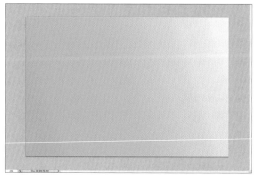

Figure 3.24 Fill the layer with a gradient.

Figure 3.25 With Lock Transparency on, a gradient will only fill the layer, not the transparency.

Lock Image

The Lock Image icon prevents you from changing the pixels that make up a layer. When the layer is locked, you can't paint, erase, apply an adjustment or filter, or do anything else that would change the look of that layer (although you can still move or transform the layer). Just as with Lock Transparency, each layer has its own Lock Image setting. Use this feature after you've finished color-correcting and retouching a layer so you don't accidentally change it later.

The Lock Image icon might prevent you from directly modifying the pixels that make up a layer, but it doesn't completely prevent changing the appearance of that layer. You can still add an adjustment layer directly above the layer in question to change its general appearance.

Lock Position

The Lock Position icon prevents you from moving the active layer. Select this feature to prevent someone else from accidentally moving an element that is positioned correctly.

Lock All

The Lock All icon locks the transparency, image, and position of the current layer.

Layer Styles

Choose Layer > Layer Style to access a bunch of really neat options. Some of the same options are available under the Layer Style pop-up menu at the bottom of the Layers panel (it's the leftmost icon). To experiment with these options, create a new, empty layer, and paint on it with any of the painting tools. Then apply one of the effects found in the Layer Style menu: Drop Shadow, Inner Shadow, Outer Glow, Inner Glow, Bevel and Emboss, and so on (**Figures 3.26** to **3.28**). You can use the default settings for now. After applying an effect, use the Eraser tool to remove some of the paint on that layer. Did you notice that the layer effect updates to reflect the changes you make to the layer? In one simple step, layer styles create results that would usually require multiple layers and a lot of memory.

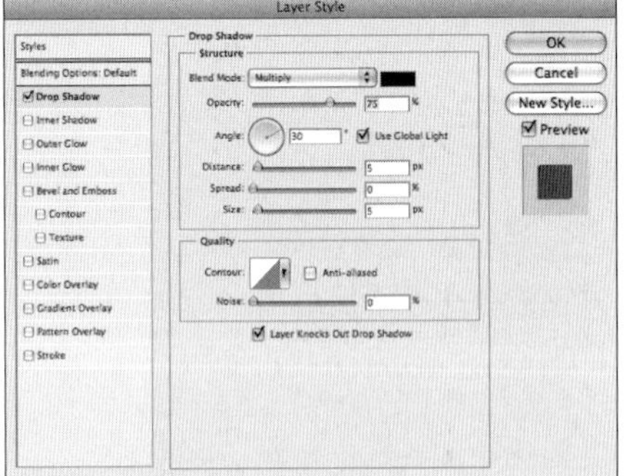

Figure 3.26 One of the most popular layer styles is the drop shadow.

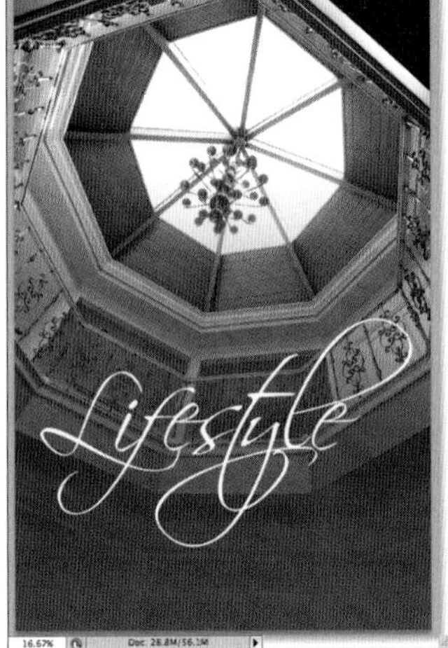

Figure 3.27 A text layer is ordinary and flat, sometimes needing a little more punch.

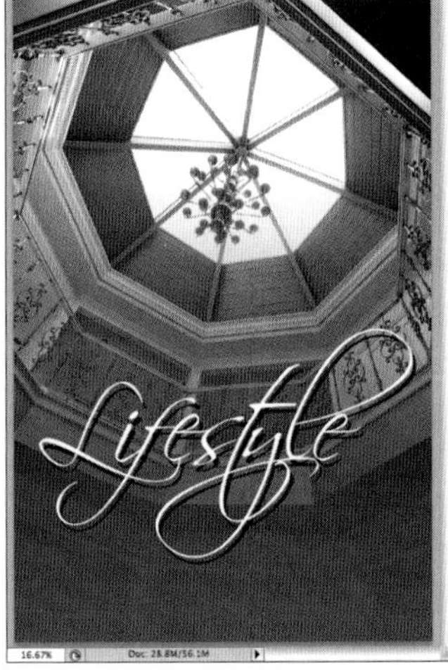

Figure 3.28 Adding a drop shadow to a text layer makes the font much clearer and adds to the overall image.

Figure 3.29 Applied layer styles appear under the *fx* symbol in the layer.

When you have at least one layer style applied to a layer, a small *fx* appears next to the layer's name in the Layers panel. That's the only indication that a layer has a layer style attached to it. Click the triangle that appears next to that symbol to see a list of the layer styles that are applied to that layer (**Figure 3.29**). If you drag one of the layer styles from that list and release the mouse button when the cursor is over another layer, that layer style moves to the selected layer. Holding down Option/Alt when dragging a style copies the style instead of moving it. Dragging the word *Effects* from the top of the list moves all of the layer styles attached to that layer. To remove a layer style, click its name in the list and drag it to the Trash icon at the bottom of the Layers panel.

You can lower the Fill setting at the top of Photoshop's Layers panel to reduce the opacity of the layer contents while keeping the layer style at full strength (**Figure 3.30**). Alternatively, hold down Shift and type a number while the Move tool is active. Choose Layer > Layer Style > Create Layer to have Photoshop create the layers that would usually be needed to create the effect. For example, you might want to choose Create Layer if you want to distort the effect separately from the layer to which it was attached. **Figures 3.31** to **3.34** show what a few of the layer styles can do to an image.

Figure 3.30 By lowering the Fill value for a layer with effects applied, you can achieve interesting results.

Figure 3.31 Use an emboss layer style to give text a softened effect.

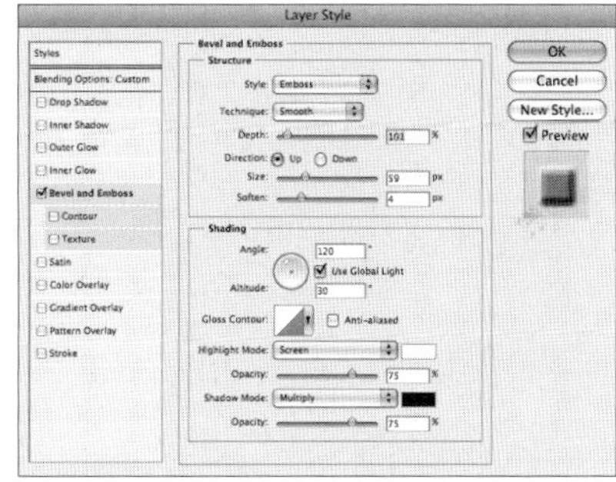

Figure 3.32 Settings for beveling and embossing.

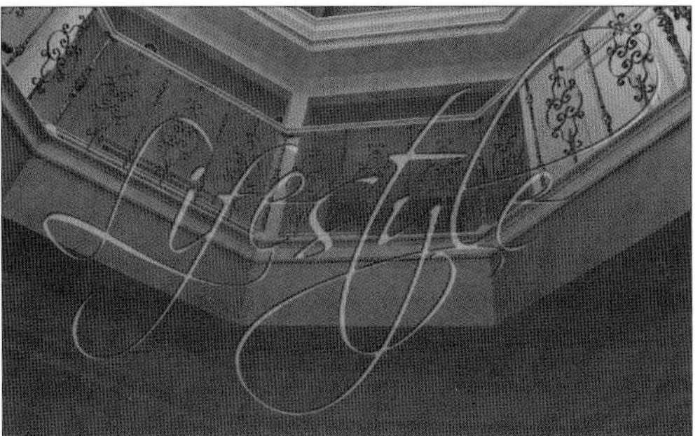

Figure 3.33 An inner shadow can create an interesting cutout effect.

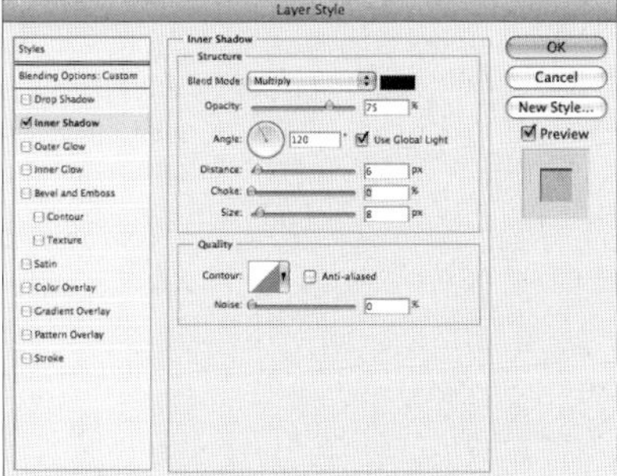

Figure 3.34 Settings for the inner shadow layer style.

Adjustment Layers

The Adjustment Layer pop-up menu at the bottom of the Layers panel (it's the half-black and half-white circle) allows you to apply adjustments that will affect multiple layers. But CS4 goes one step further with a new Adjustments panel, making the use of this key Photoshop feature even easier. This is the most versatile method for applying adjustments, and it's such a powerful feature that we've devoted an entire chapter to it (Chapter 5, "Adjustment Layers").

Fill Layers

The options in the New Fill Layer menu (Layer > New Fill Layer) add solid color, gradient, and pattern content to a layer. This feature is especially useful when combined with vector masks, as described in Chapter 10. If you don't want a fill layer to fill your entire document, make a selection before creating the fill layer, which will create a layer mask. After a fill layer has been created, you can reset your foreground and background colors to black/white by pressing D. Then you can use the Eraser tool to hide the area and the Paintbrush tool to make areas visible again.

Solid Color Layer

Choosing Layer > New Fill Layer > Solid Color brings up a dialog that asks you to name the layer you're creating. After you click OK, it opens the color picker, where you can specify the color that will be used for the solid color layer. When you've created one of these layers, you can double-click the leftmost thumbnail of the layer in the Layers panel to edit the color.

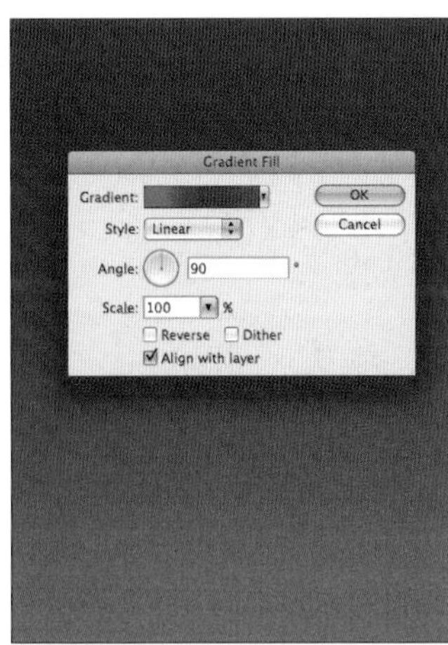

Figure 3.35 The Gradient Fill dialog is useful for creating a new layer that contains a gradient.

Gradient Layer

Choosing Layer > New Fill Layer > Gradient brings up a dialog that asks you to name the layer; this creates a new layer that contains a gradient (**Figure 3.35**). The gradient is always editable by double-clicking the leftmost thumbnail in the Layers panel. If the Align with Layer check box is turned on, the start and end points of the gradient are determined by the contents of the selected layer rather than by the document's overall size. You can change the gradient content by clicking the Gradient selection in the dialog.

Pattern Layer

Choosing Layer > New Fill Layer > Pattern allows you to create a new layer that contains a repeating pattern (**Figure 3.36**). Use this type of layer to add a brushed-aluminum look to a background. Then, if you ever decide to change the pattern, it's as simple as double-clicking the thumbnail in the Layers panel and choosing New Pattern from the drop-down menu.

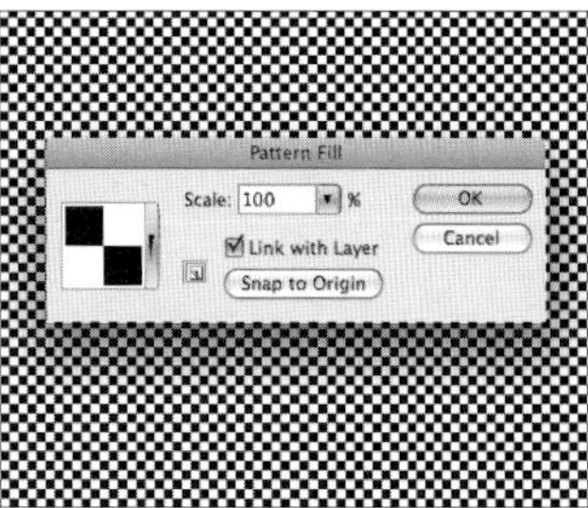

Figure 3.36 A new fill layer with a pattern makes it easy to repeat a small image throughout a larger document.

The Blending Mode Menu

The Blending Mode menu at the upper left of the Layers panel allows the information on a layer to blend with the underlying image in interesting and useful ways. Using this menu, you can quickly change the color of objects, colorize grayscale images, add reflections to metallic objects, and much more. This is an advanced feature, so you'll have to wait until you get to Chapter 9 to find out more about it.

Automatic Selections

To select everything on a particular layer, just Command/Ctrl-click the thumbnail image of the layer in the Layers panel. If the layer fills the entire screen, it will select all because this trick looks for transparent areas. You can hold down the Shift key to add to a selection that already exists or use the Option/Alt key to take away from the current selection.

Layer Via Copy

The Layers menu offers a wide variety of options for copying, merging, and manipulating layers. Let's look at one of these choices. If you select an area of an image and then choose Layer > New > Layer Via Copy, the selected area is moved from the active layer to a new layer in the same position (**Figures 3.37** to **3.39**). This feature is particularly handy when you want to move just a portion of a layer so that you can place it on top of another layer, or remove a portion of a layer and add layer styles. Very handy, but keep in mind that this won't work with vector shape or fill layers.

Figure 3.37 Making a selection is the first step to using the Layer Via Copy option.

Figure 3.38 Selecting the Layer Via Copy option moves the selection from one layer into a new layer.

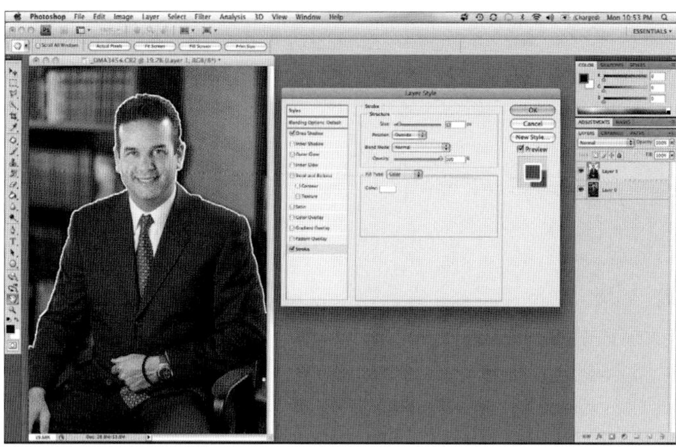

Figure 3.39 Layer Via Copy is also useful for adding various layer styles.

Use All Layers

When you're editing on a layer, some of the editing tools might not work as expected. Most of the tools act as if each layer is a separate document; they ignore all layers except the active one—unless the tool has the Use All Layers check box (labeled All Layers in the Paint Bucket tool) turned on in the options bar of the tool you're using. This check box makes the tools act as if all the layers have been combined into one layer. This possibility can work in your favor or not, depending on what you're trying to accomplish (**Figures 3.40** and **3.41**).

Figure 3.40 Using the Paint Bucket tool without the Use All Layers option checked fills the selected layer.

Figure 3.41 Using the Paint Bucket tool with the Use All Layers option checked attempts to fill all layers.

Layer Shortcuts

You'll be doing a lot of switching between layers, which can get a bit tedious. Here are some quick shortcuts:

- ▶ Command/Ctrl-click anywhere in the image window when using the Move tool to activate the layer directly below your cursor. To find out which layer is active, glance at the Layers panel.
- ▶ You won't always need the layer directly below your cursor. Control-clicking/right-clicking brings up a menu of all the layers that contain pixels below your cursor. Choose the name of the layer you want, and Photoshop switches to that layer.
- ▶ To get the Move tool temporarily at any time, hold down the Command/Ctrl key. If you press Command-Control (Mac) or hold down Ctrl and right-click (Windows), no matter what tool you're using, Photoshop presents the pop-up menu.

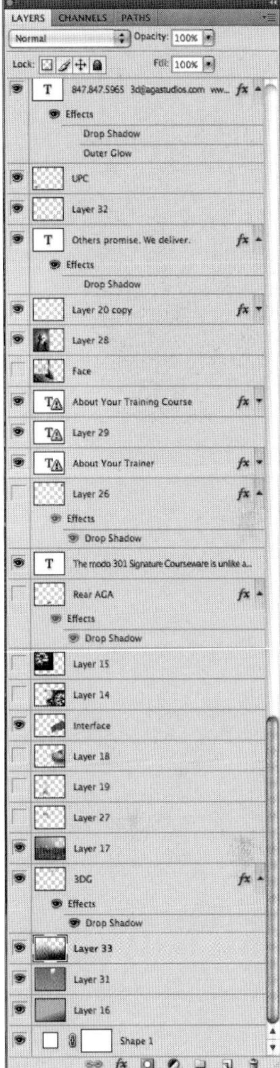

Figure 3.42 A typical project can have a full Layers panel.

Grouping Layers

Have you ever had a complicated images with dozens of layers? If so, you're probably familiar with the agony of fumbling through an endless sea of layers to find the right one. You'll be ecstatic to learn that you can group layers together. A group of layers looks like a folder in the Layers panel. You can view all the layers in the group or just the group name.

To group multiple layers, select the layers and then either Shift-click the folder icon at the bottom of the Layers panel or choose Layer > Group Layers. You can also click the folder icon (without holding down any keys) to create an empty folder. You can move any number of layers into the folder by dragging and dropping them onto the folder. The folder will have a small triangle just to its left that allows you to collapse the group down to its name or expand the group to show all the layers it contains (**Figures 3.42** and **3.43**). You can even drag one folder onto another to create a hierarchy of up to five levels of folders). This approach can greatly simplify the Layers panel, making a document of 100+ layers look as if it's made of only a few layers.

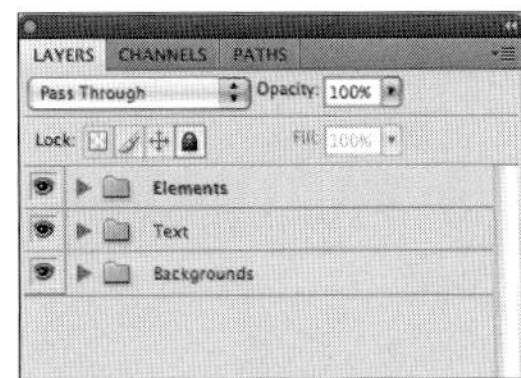

Figure 3.43 By grouping layers, you can stay organized.

Option/Alt-clicking the arrow next to a group expands or collapses all the groups and layer style lists within that group. Adding the Command/Ctrl key expands or collapses all the groups in the entire document.

To get rid of a group without throwing away the layers that are inside it, click the group to make it active, click the Trash icon at the bottom of the Layers panel, and then choose Group Only when prompted.

Groups can also be useful when you want to reorganize the layers in an image. If one of the layers within a group is active, using the Move tool affects only that layer (unless it's linked to other layers). If the group is active, using the Move tool moves all the layers within that group.

Smart Guides

When you choose View > Show > Smart Guides, Photoshop displays pink guides to indicate how the active layer aligns with the surrounding layers. These *Smart Guides* appear only when you're actively dragging a layer. Smart Guides pay attention to the top, bottom, left, right, and center of each layer, and extend the pink guides across all the layers that are aligned. The layers also snap to these alignment points, making it especially easy to get your layers in alignment. You can toggle the snapping behavior off or on by choosing View > Snap To > Layers.

Smart Guides ignore layer styles that are applied to a layer. In **Figure 3.44**, the outer ring of each object was created using the Stroke and Bevel & Emboss layer styles, so it wasn't used when determining where the edge of the layer is located. The Smart Guides also ignore any areas that have an opacity of less than 50%, which also affects any layers that have soft edges, causing the snapping behavior to treat the halfway point of the fadeout as the edge of the layer.

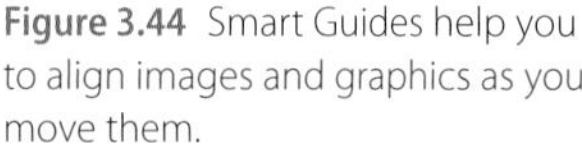

Figure 3.44 Smart Guides help you to align images and graphics as you move them.

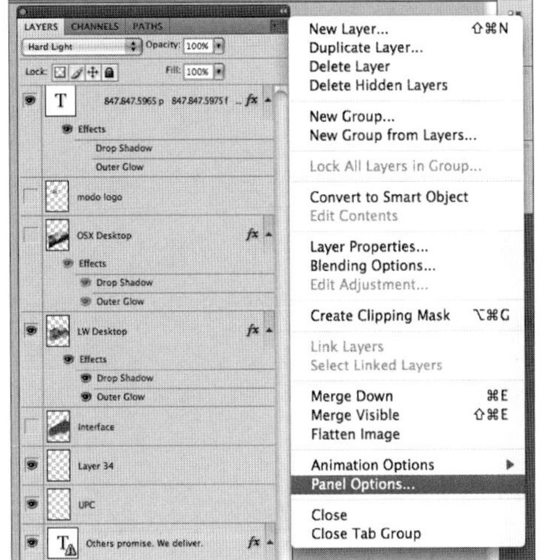

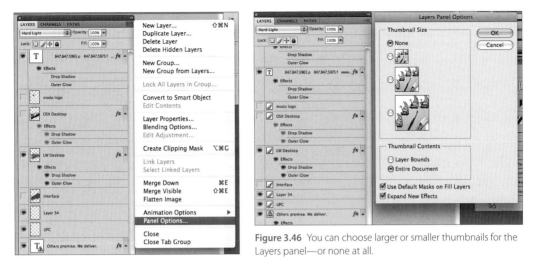

Figure 3.45 Panel options for the Layers panel are found by clicking the side menu button.

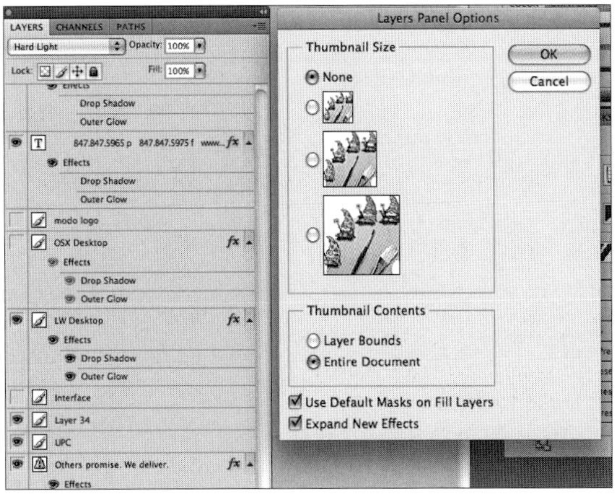

Figure 3.46 You can choose larger or smaller thumbnails for the Layers panel—or none at all.

Hiding Layer Thumbnails

If you've organized an image into layer groups, but the Layers panel is still a mess, you might want to simplify the way Photoshop displays layers. Choose Panel Options from the side menu of the Layers panel and click None in the Thumbnail Size section of the dialog to turn off the layer thumbnails. Once you've done that, the list of layers takes up a lot less space, but you still have the full functionality of all of Photoshop's features (**Figures 3.45** and **3.46**). This feature also speeds up the screen redraw of the Layers panel.

Displaying Layer Bounds

If you have many small elements on individual layers, the Layers panel might look like a sea of checkerboard. Photoshop allows you to crop the layer thumbnails so that they show the contents of a layer while ignoring any empty area surrounding the content. To get to this view, choose Panel Options from the side menu of the Layers panel and turn on the Layer Bounds setting (**Figure 3.47**).

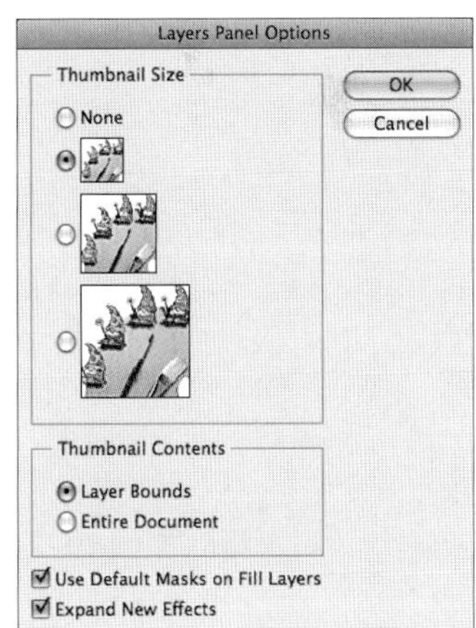

Figure 3.47 Select Layer Bounds in the Thumbnail Contents section to remove transparent areas from your thumbnails.

Color-Coding Layers

If you work within a large group of Photoshop users, it can be useful to assign colors to layers to indicate their current status. Maybe some text needs to be proofed, or the client approved a certain part of the image, or an area needs to be sent off for color correction. All you have to do is Control/right-click the name of a layer and choose Layer Properties. In the resulting dialog, you can color-code a layer or a group (**Figure 3.48**). Even easier, Control/right-click the Eyeball column to bring up color choices for that layer or group.

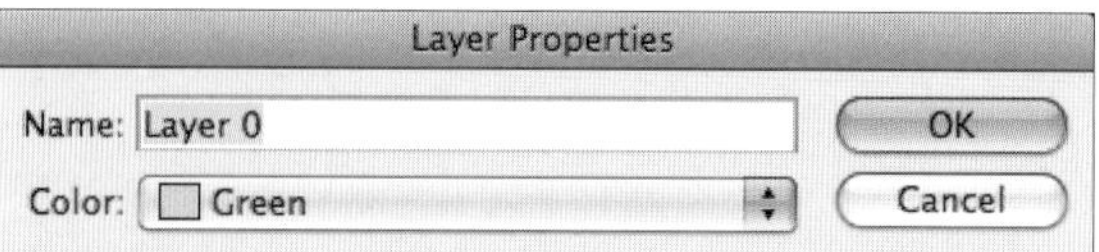

Figure 3.54 Change the color of a selected layer to help stay organized.

Merging Layers

When you create a complicated image containing dozens of layers, the project can start hogging memory, which in turn makes it difficult to manage all the layers. Every time you create a new layer and add something to it, Photoshop gobbles up more memory. Photoshop not only has to remember what's on that layer, but what's below it (even if that information is completely covered by the information on the layers above).

Whenever possible, try to simplify your images by merging layers. This action combines the layers into a single layer, which saves memory. The Layer menu and the side menu on the Layers panel provide several ways to merge layers:

- **Merge Down:** Merges the active layer into the layer directly below it.
- **Merge Visible:** Merges all the layers that are currently visible in the main image window.
- **Merge Layers:** Merges all the selected layers.
- **Merge Group:** Merges all the layers that are within the active group.

- **Flatten Image:** Merges all visible layers into the Background image, discards hidden layers, and fills empty areas with white.

If you want to know how much extra memory the layers take as you're modifying an image, choose Document Sizes from the menu that appears at the bottom center of the document (**Figure 3.49**). The number on the left should stay relatively constant (unless you scale or crop the image); it indicates how much memory the image would use if all the layers were merged. The number on the right indicates how much memory the image is using with all the layers included. This number changes as you add and modify layers. Keep an eye on it so that you can see how memory-intensive the different layers are.

Once you've merged two layers, it's awfully hard to get them apart—the only way to do so is to use the History panel. However, even with the History panel, you might lose all the changes you've made since you merged the layers.

Doc: 1.27M/1.27M

Figure 3.49 View the document's memory usage at the bottom of the document window.

The number on the right might get huge if you're using a lot of layers; however, keep in mind that by glancing at the left number you'll know exactly how large the image will be when you flatten the layers.

Layers play such a huge role in Photoshop that to deny yourself any crucial information about them is asking for trouble. With every new release, Adobe likes to pack more and more functions into the Layers panel. So, as time goes on, understanding layers will become even more essential. You should feel comfortable with them before you move on to more advanced areas of Photoshop.

The Power of Curves

Curves can be used for just about anything; in fact, it's probably the one adjustment tool you should use all the time. By mastering the Curves dialog, you'll have more control over your images than you thought possible. We're not talking about a simple bell curve here, but rather a robust adjustment system that can make ordinary images look extraordinary.

Let's consider some of the things you can do with the Curves dialog:

- Use the Sharpening filters to pull out far more detail than you can see (**Figures 3.50** to **3.52**).
- Lighten or darken areas without making selections (**Figures 3.53** and **3.54**).
- Turn ordinary text into extraordinary text (**Figures 3.55** and **3.56**).
- Enhance color and contrast in seconds (**Figures 3.57** and **3.58**).

Figure 3.50 An ordinary image can be improved with the help of Curves. (©2008 Dan Ablan.)

Figure 3.51 Making an image sharper with Curves.

Figure 3.52 Curves can make colors pop.

Figure 3.53 An ordinary image, somewhat flat. (©2008 Dan Ablan.)

Figure 3.54 With the help of Curves, the image from Figure 3.53 has areas darkened and lightened.

Figure 3.55 Original text with some layer styles applied.

Figure 3.56 The text from Figure 3.55 after a simple Curves adjustment.

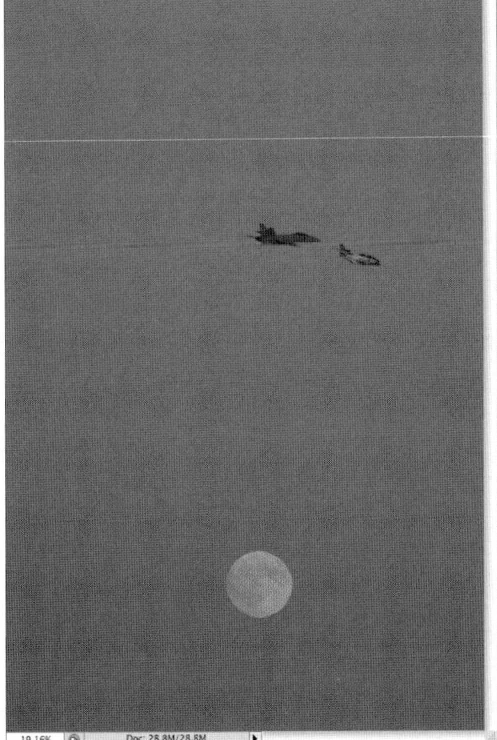

Figure 3.57 The original image. (©2008 Dan Ablan.)

Figure 3.58 The image from Figure 3.57 after simple Curves adjustments.

All the techniques mentioned in this chapter apply equally to images prepared for Web pages and those prepared for print. You might notice that we concentrate on ink settings throughout this chapter. Most users are more comfortable thinking about the effect of ink on an image, rather than the effect of light. Ink is the exact opposite of light, so Photoshop can easily translate what you're attempting to do, even if your image will be displayed using light.

None of these changes could be made by using Levels or Brightness/Contrast (that is, not without making complicated selections or losing control over the result). Now you can see why you'll want to master Curves!

Using Curves, you can perform all the adjustments available in the Levels, Brightness/Contrast, and Threshold dialogs—and much, much more. In fact, you can adjust each of the 256 shades of gray in your image independently (**Figure 3.59**).

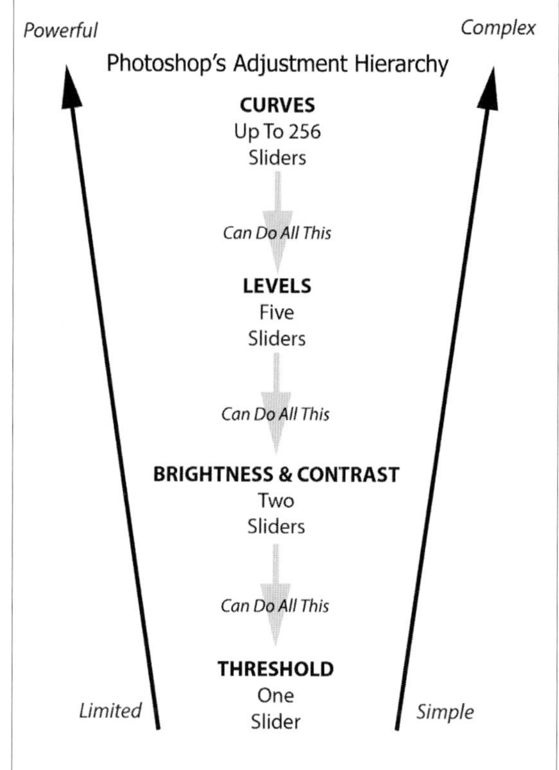

Figure 3.59 Photoshop's adjustment hierarchy.

The Concept of Curves

Before we delve deeply into Curves, let's test your present knowledge of the Curves dialog. (The lower your score, the more you should enjoy this section.)

Look at the curve shown in **Figure 3.60** and see if you can answer the following questions:

- Which shades will lose detail from this adjustment?
- Which shades will become brighter?
- What happened to 62% gray?
- What happened to the image's contrast?

If you truly understand the Curves dialog, these questions should be extremely easy to answer. However, if you hesitated before answering any of them or couldn't answer at all, this section was designed for you.

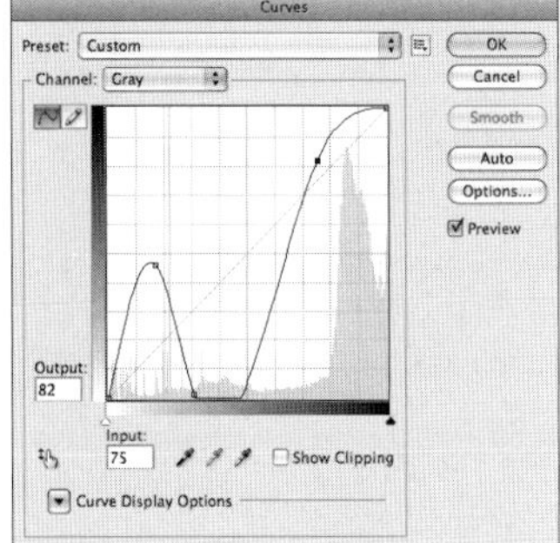

Figure 3.60 Can you figure out what this curve adjustment will do to an image?

Because the Curves dialog allows you to adjust every shade of gray in an image independently of the others (256 in all), it works quite a bit differently from the other adjustment tools. To get a clearer picture of what Curves does, let's construct our own Curves dialog from scratch, using something that's already familiar: a stylish bar graph (also called a *bar chart*).

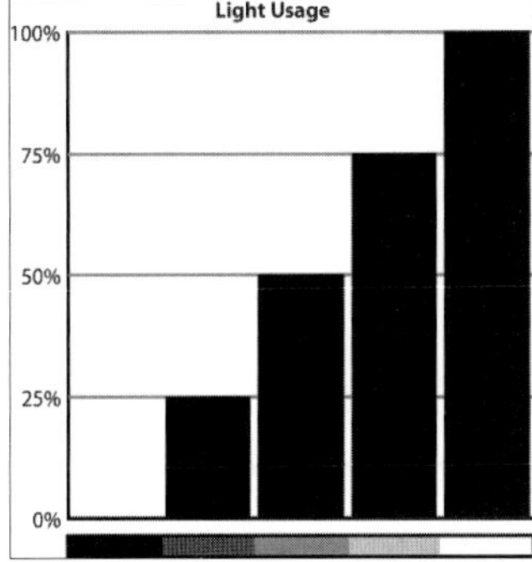

Figure 3.61 This bar graph indicates the amount of light used to display the shades of gray shown at the bottom.

Suppose you create a bar graph that indicates how much light your monitor uses to display each color in an image. This graph would be just like any other that you've seen, where taller bars mean more light and shorter bars mean less. You could show the shade of gray you're using below each bar, and then draw a line from the top of each bar over to the left so you could label how much light is being used for each shade. You'd end up with something that looks like **Figure 3.61**. Or you could just as easily change the graph to indicate how much ink your inkjet printer would use to reproduce the image. Now that we're talking about ink, short bars would mean less ink, which would produce a light shade of gray, and tall bars would mean a lot of ink and would produce a dark shade of gray. To make the change, all we'd have to do is flip all the shades at the bottom of the graph so the dark ones are below the tall bars and the bright ones are below the short bars. The result would look like **Figure 3.62**, right?

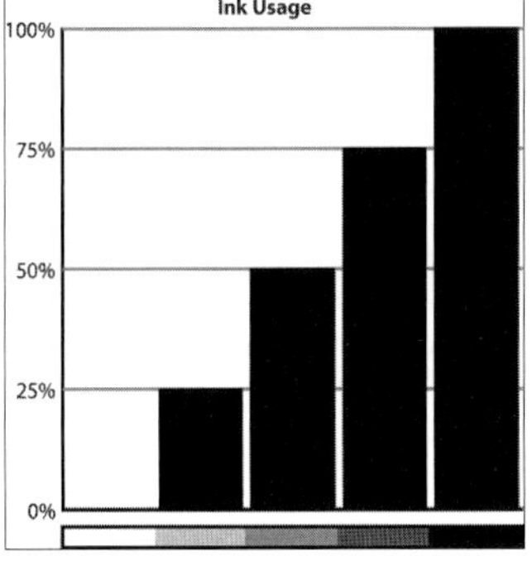

Figure 3.62 Flip the shades at the bottom, and you have a graph that represents ink usage.

Now that you've got the concept, let's expand on it to accommodate the real world. Our basic bar graph might work for a simple logo with just a few shades of gray (one bar representing each shade), but most of your images will contain many more shades. So, we just increase the number of bars (**Figure 3.63**), right? Well, sort of. The image can contain up to 256 shades of gray. But if we jam 256 bars (one for each shade) into the graph, they won't look like bars anymore; they'll just turn into a big mass (**Figure 3.64**). You can't see the individual bars because there's no space between them.

All the same, images contain up to 256 shades of gray, so we really need that many bars in our graph. Now that they're all smashed together, we don't have room to label each bar, so why don't we just overlay a grid (**Figure 3.65**) and label that instead? If that grid isn't detailed enough for you, we could add a more detailed grid, such as the one shown in **Figure 3.66**.

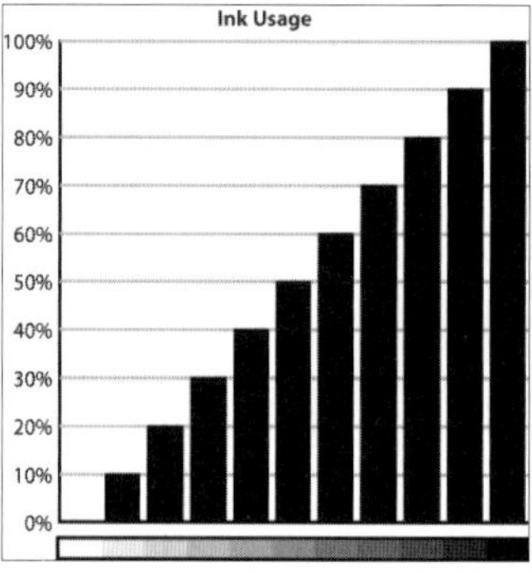

Figure 3.63 Add more bars for additional accuracy.

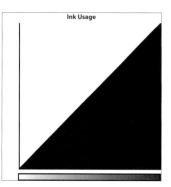

Figure 3.64 The 256 bars take up so much space that the result no longer looks like a bar graph.

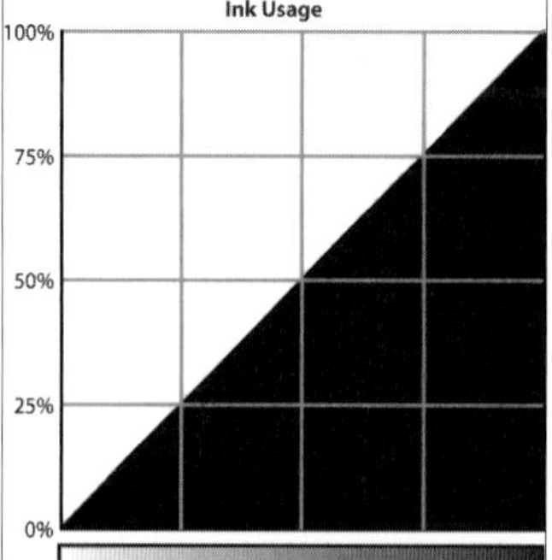

Figure 3.65 A grid can help you to figure out how much ink is used.

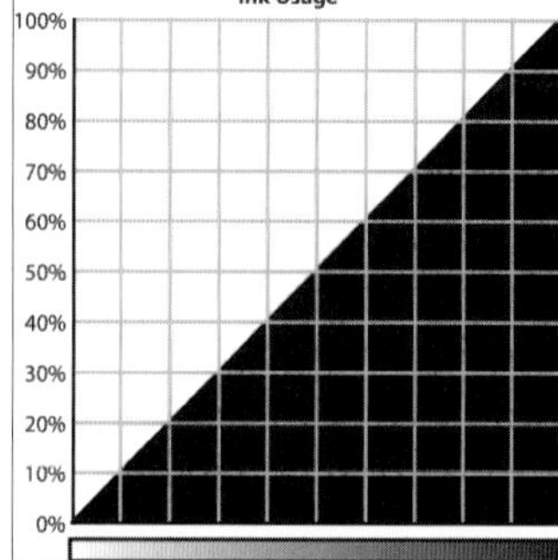

Figure 3.66 A more detailed grid allows you to be even more accurate.

The sample graph we've created isn't really all that useful—yet. It's not telling you anything you can't find in the Info or Color panels. For example, if you really want to know how much ink (or light) you'd use to reproduce a shade of gray, you could just open the Info panel by choosing Window > Info (**Figure 3.67**), and then move your pointer over the image; the Info panel would indicate how much ink would be used in that area. The Color panel (Window > Color) is set up similarly and will indicate how much ink or light makes up a shade of gray (**Figure 3.68**). The main difference between the two methods is that the Info panel gives you information about your image—specifically, what's under the pointer. The Color panel isn't image-specific but gives you generic information about how much ink or light makes up a shade of gray.

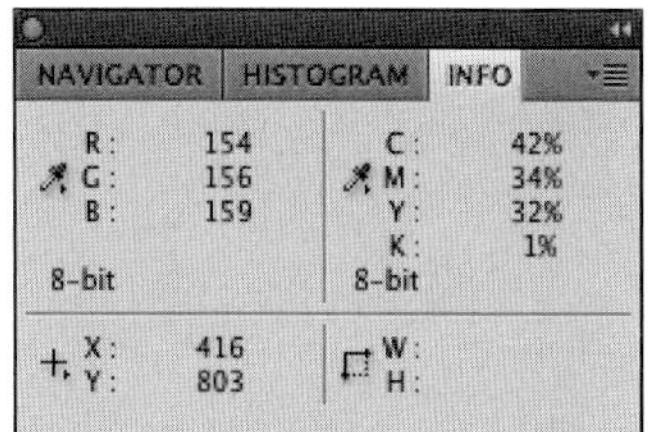

Figure 3.67 The info panel indicates how much ink or light would be used to reproduce the color under the pointer.

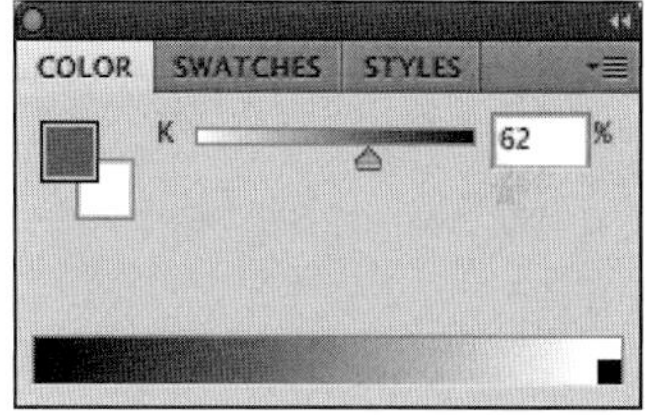

Figure 3.68 The Color panel indicates how much ink would be used to reproduce the current foreground color.

Think of the Curves dialog as just a simple bar graph—with a lot of bars that are very close together—showing how much ink or light will be used in the image. The gradient at the bottom shows all the shades of gray you could possibly have, and the graph above shows how much ink or light will be used to create each shade. But the wonderful thing about the Curves dialog is that it doesn't just sit there like a static bar graph that only gives information. Curves is interactive—you can use it to change the amount of ink (or light) used to reproduce the image (**Figure 3.69**).

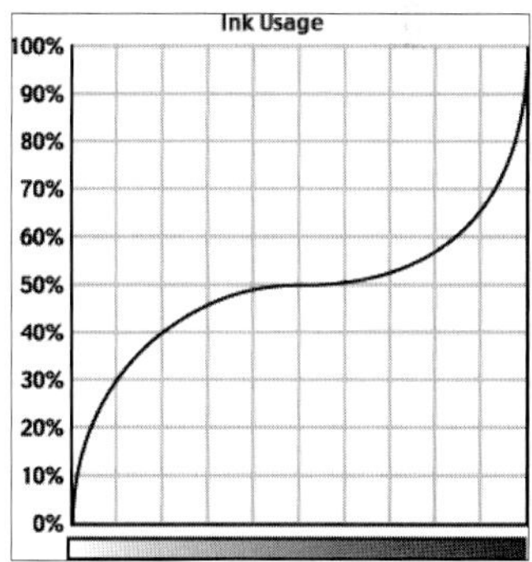

Figure 3.69 Changing the shape of the line in the Curves graph changes how much ink is used throughout the image.

Think of our ink usage bar graph: As the shades of gray get steadily darker, each shade uses slightly more ink, resulting in a straight diagonal line. But in the Curves graph, you can move points on the line. For example, you can flatten the line so that, in the modified image, many shades of gray are represented by a single shade. Or you can make a dramatic change to the line, dragging a point up or down so that a shade changes to become much darker or lighter.

Let Gradients Be Your Guide

Pick any shade of gray from the gradient, and then look above it to figure out how much ink would be used to create it (**Figure 3.70**). You can use the grid to help you calculate the exact amount of ink used (about 23% in this case). But wouldn't you rather see what 23% looks like? Suppose we replace those percentage numbers with another gradient that shows how bright each area would be (**Figure 3.71**). Just to make sure that you don't confuse the two gradients, read the next two sentences *twice*: The bottom gradient represents the shades of gray you're changing. The side gradient indicates how bright or dark a shade will become if you move the line to a certain height (**Figure 3.72**).

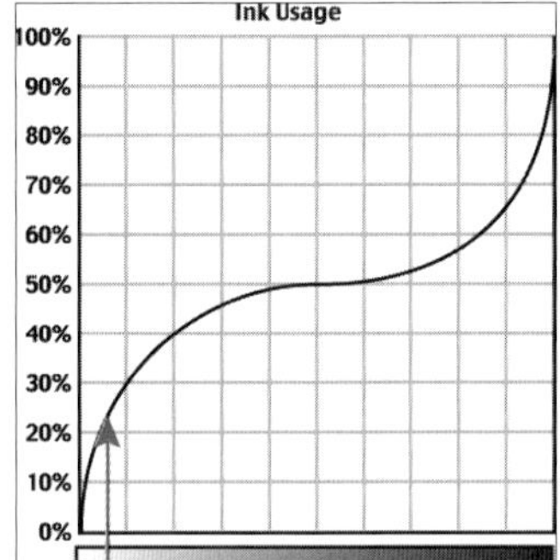

Figure 3.70 Use the grid to help determine how much ink is used in an area.

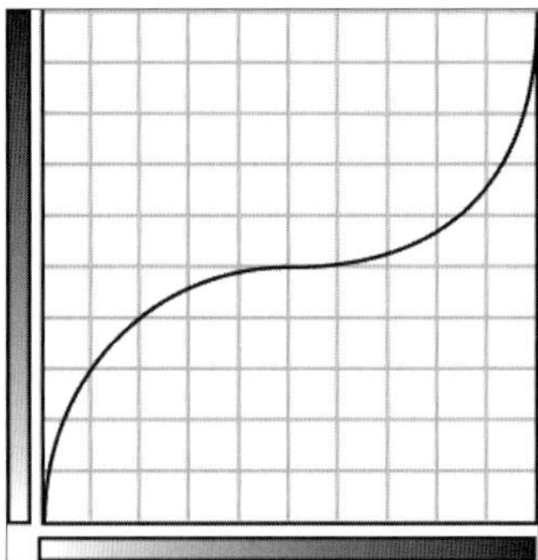

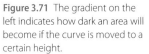

Figure 3.71 The gradient on the left indicates how dark an area will become if the curve is moved to a certain height.

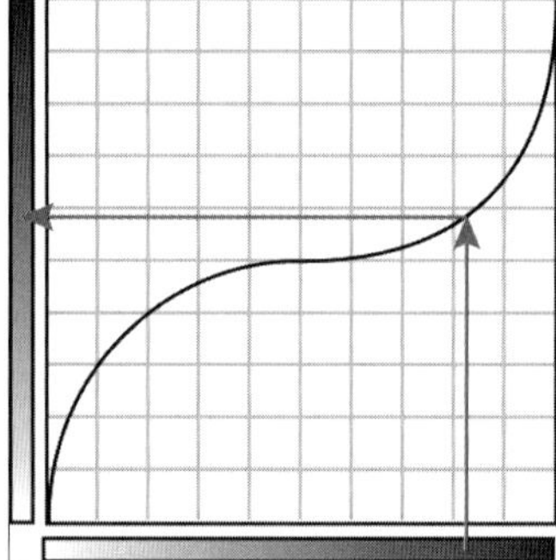

Figure 3.72 The bottom gradient scale is what you're changing. The left gradient scale shows how you changed it.

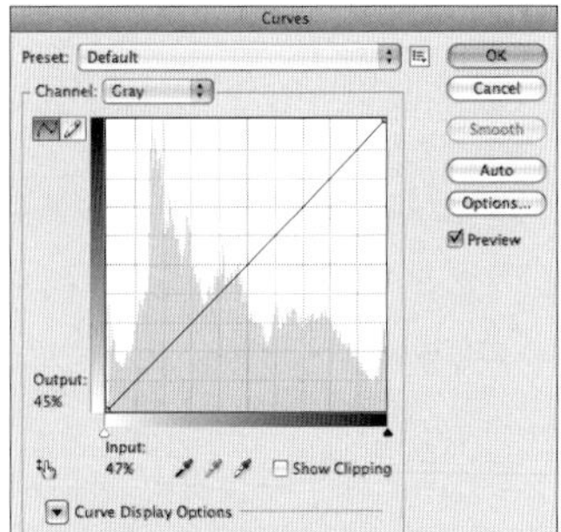

Figure 3.73 Photoshop CS4's Curves dialog.

Now you're ready to graduate from graphs and take flight with the full-fledged Curves dialog (**Figure 3.73**). Does it look familiar? It should. Along the bottom a grayscale ramp shows all of the original gray tones in the image, and running vertically along the side is a grayscale ramp showing what each point on the curve will become after you click OK.

The "curve" is the diagonal line that runs from lower left to upper right. When you first open the Curves dialog, the curve is not curvy. As you've seen, the curve indicates a correspondence between the original gray tones on the bottom and the new gray tones on the side. When the curve is a straight diagonal, all output tones are identical to the input tones.

Starting with Photoshop CS3, Adobe added a grayed-out histogram display behind the actual curve. This feature makes it easier to determine which part of the curve corresponds to specific tonal regions within the image. It also makes it easier to remember that you read the curve from black on the left to white on the right.

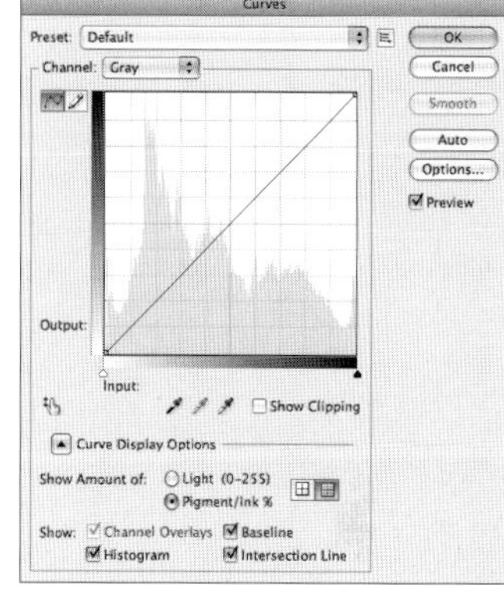

Figure 3.74 Clicking the Curve Display Options arrow displays additional controls.

Color Modes and Curves

To create the bar graph, we started by measuring how much light the monitor was using. Then we measured how much ink we'd use for printing. You can make the same change in the Curves dialog. If you click the Curve Display Options button, the Curves dialog displays additional controls (**Figure 3.74**).

The Show Amount Of setting has two radio buttons, one for light and the other for pigment/ink percentage. You can click either of these options to determine whether the curve reads from light to dark or dark to light. The grayscale ramps will reverse, just as in our bar graphs (**Figures 3.75** and **3.76**).

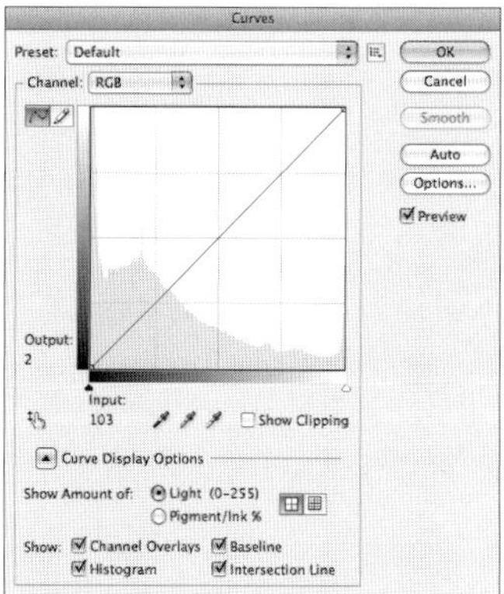

Figure 3.75 When black is at the top, you're using ink. (Remember, up means more.)

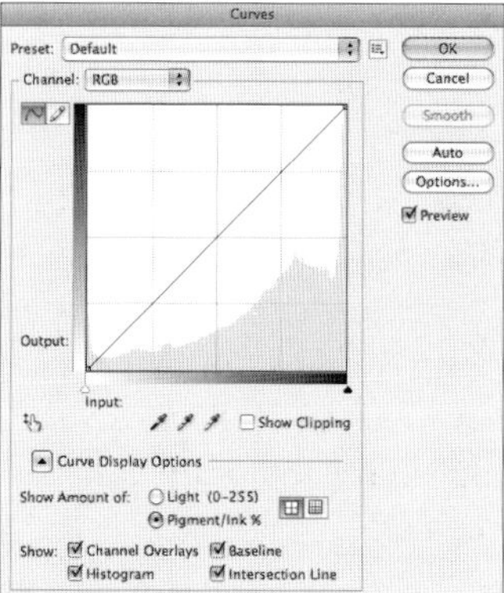

Figure 3.76 When white is at the top, you're using light. Again, up is more.

The mode of your image determines where you'll start. Photoshop assumes that images in grayscale, CMYK, or LAB mode will be printed, and defaults to using the gradient that represents ink. Because your monitor displays everything using red, green, and blue light, images in RGB mode use the gradient that represents light.

Photoshop doesn't care which system you use. It can easily translate between the two, because light is the exact opposite of ink. When you switch from one scale to the other, not only do the light and dark ends of the gradients get swapped, but the curve flips upside down. Be sure to look out for which mode is used throughout the examples in this chapter; otherwise, your result could be the opposite of what you had in mind.

Remember, the side gradient indicates what you'll get if you move a point on the curve to a certain height. You can always glance at the side to find out how much light or ink you're using. Just remember that up means more of something, and that you can use either light or ink.

Next comes the grid. Remember how we ended up with one that's more detailed than the original? You can toggle between those two grids by Option/Alt-clicking anywhere within the grid area. It doesn't affect the result you'll get in Curves; it's just a personal preference (**Figure 3.77**). You can also change grids by clicking the grid icons that appear when you open the Curve Display Options.

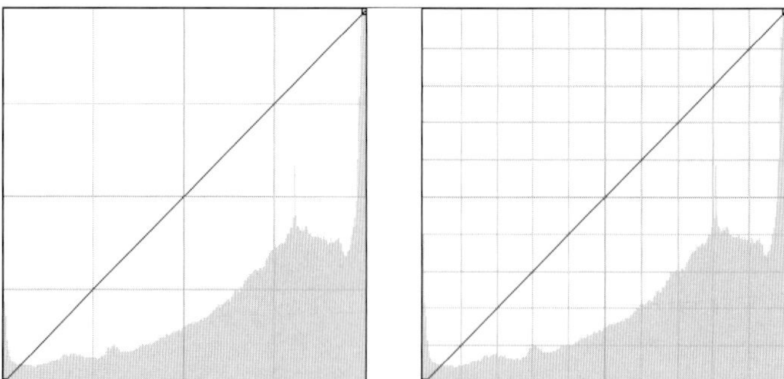

Figure 3.77 Option/Alt-click anywhere on the grid to toggle between a 25% increment grid (left) and a 10% increment grid (right)

Taking Curves for a Test Drive

Hopefully you now have a better understanding of how the Curves dialog works. So let's try it out—open an image, choose Image > Adjustments > Curves or press Command/Ctrl-M, and start messing with the curve. Click anywhere on the curve to add a point, and then drag it around to change the shape of the curve. If you want to get rid of a point, drag it off the edge of the grid. You can also click a point and then use the arrow keys on your keyboard to nudge it around the grid. You can even add the Shift key to the arrow keys to nudge in larger increments.

Hold down Option/Alt when choosing Image > Adjustments > Curves to reapply the last settings used on an image.

When you drag, Photoshop displays a set of light gray crosshairs to help you see exactly how the bottom grayscale ramp corresponds to the left ramp. If these crosshairs are distracting, turn off the Intersection Line check box in the Curve Display Options.

Photoshop also leaves a light gray *baseline* (a copy of the original flat curve), so that you can see exactly how much your new curve deviates from the original (**Figure 3.78**). As with the intersection lines, if you prefer working with a "clean" display, turn off the Baseline check box in the Curve Display Options.

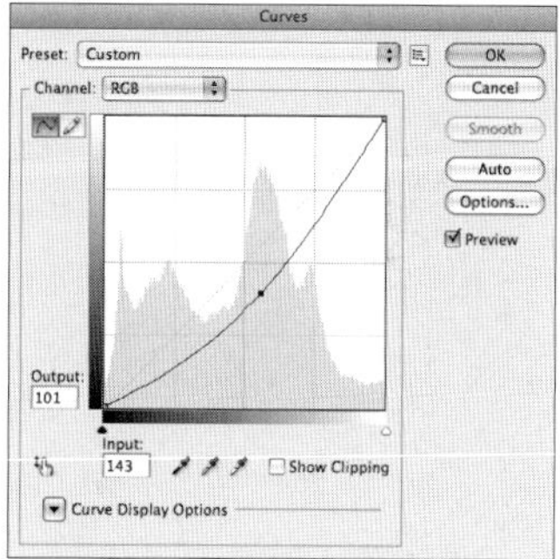

Figure 3.78 The light gray baseline represents the original line.

You should quickly find that it's pretty easy to screw up your image when you mess around with Curves. That's because we haven't yet talked about specific types of adjustments. Let's explore that final piece of the Curves puzzle.

You can compare the original and changed versions of the image by selecting or deselecting the Preview check box. As long as the check box is turned off, you'll see what the image looked like before the adjustment. When you click it on, you'll see the changes you just made.

Improving Dark Images

Try this: Open any grayscale image that you think is too dark, like the one shown in **Figure 3.79**. Next, choose Image > Adjustments > Curves and add a point by clicking the middle of the line. Pull the line straight down and see what happens to the image (**Figure 3.80**). Compare the curve with the gradient at the left of the Curves dialog. The farther you move the curve down, the less ink you use, and therefore the brighter the image becomes. If part of the curve bottoms out, the shade represented by that area becomes pure white because no ink will be used when the image is printed. (Because this is a grayscale image, the Curves dialog is using the ink percentage scale, not light, so dragging down means lighter.)

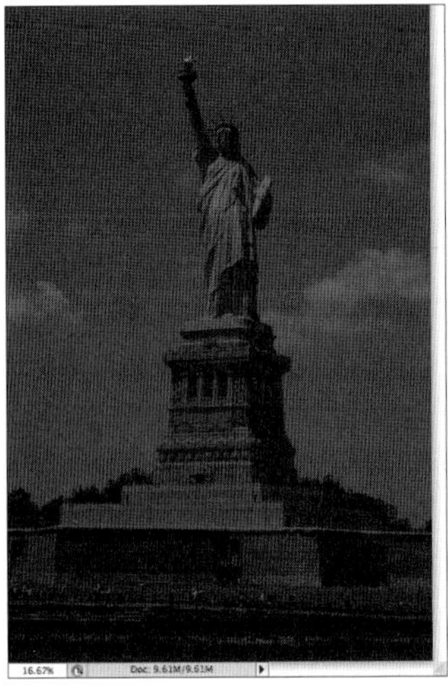

Figure 3.79 Start with a dark grayscale image. (©2008 Dan Ablan.)

Figure 3.80 Move the curve down to reduce how much ink is used.

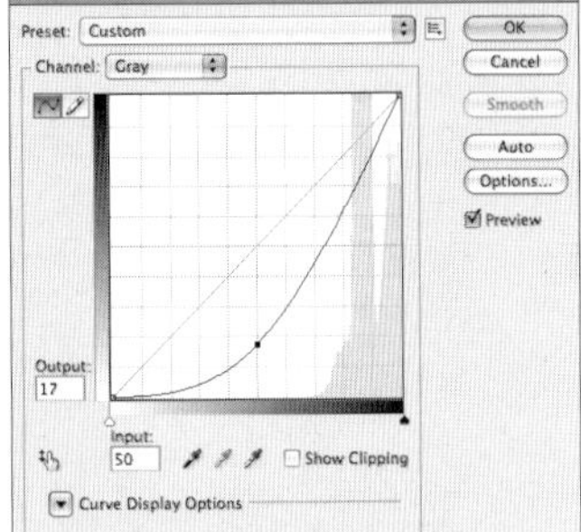

Figure 3.81 Comparing the Curve with the gradients.

Any part of a curve that's below the original line indicates an area that's using less ink, which means that it has been brightened. Look at the gradient directly below those areas to determine which shades of the image were brightened (**Figure 3.81**). The farther the line is moved down from its original position, the brighter the image will become (**Figure 3.82**).

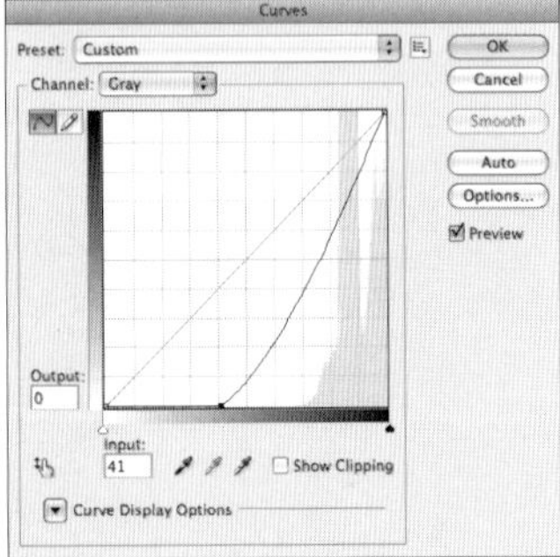

Figure 3.82 To figure out how much ink you've removed, look below where the line used to be.

Increasing Contrast and Detail

So far, you've learned that moving the curve up or down increases or decreases the amount of ink or light used to make the image. Now let's look at how changing the angle of the curve can help your images. What if you have an image where the brightest area is white and the darkest area is only 25% gray? Would it be easy to see the detail in the image? Probably not (**Figure 3.83**).

Figure 3.83 You can't see much detail in this image because the brightness is limited to 0–25%. (©2008 Dan Ablan.)

Now think about how that image would change if we applied the curve shown in **Figure 3.84**. If you look closely at this curve, you'll notice that areas that are white in the original image wouldn't change at all and areas that used to be 25% gray would end up being around 75% gray. Wouldn't that make it much easier to see the detail in the whole image? In an overexposed image like this one, you have to make the curve steeper in the lighter part of the curve. (You already learned that in an underexposed image—refer to Figure 3.79—you have to make the dark part of the curve steeper to bring out the detail.) You always have to compare the curve with the original line to determine how much of a change you've made. If you make the curve just a little steeper than the original, you'll add just a little contrast to that area. Anytime you add contrast, it becomes easier to see the detail in that area because the difference between the bright and dark parts becomes more pronounced (**Figure 3.85**). Remember to look at the gradient below the graph to figure out which shades of gray you're changing.

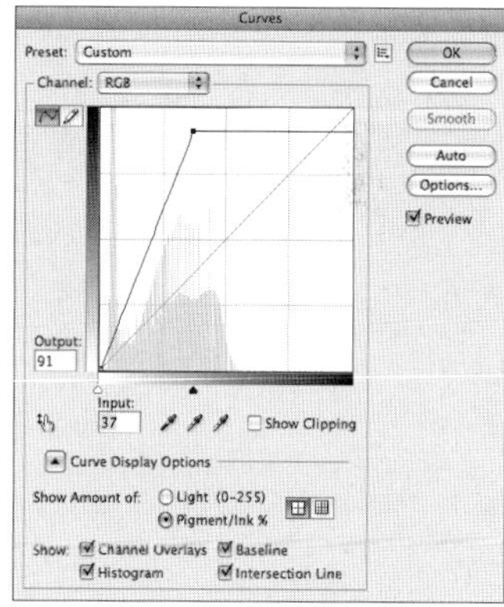

Figure 3.84 This curve adds more contrast, making it easier to see the detail in the whole image.

Figure 3.85 After making the curve steep, it's easier to see the image detail.

Figure 3.86 The original image. (©2008 Dan Ablan.)

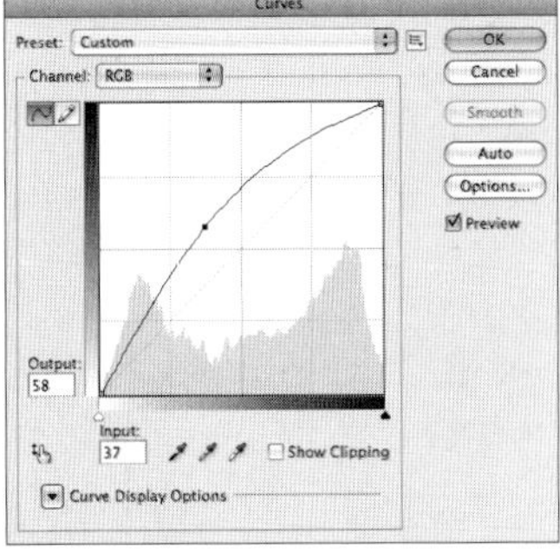

Figure 3.87 Find the range you'd like the change; then move the curve steeper. In this case, the sky is to be darkened.

Figure 3.88 The image from Figure 3.86 after making the curve steeper.

Clicking a CMYK image won't display a circle. That's because the circle's location is calculated by averaging the numbers that make up an area, and black ink throws off the calculation because it's used only in the darkest areas of an image.

Now try this. Open any image and choose Image > Adjustments > Curves. Move your pointer over the image, and then click and drag across the area where you want to exaggerate the detail. A circle appears in the Curves dialog. Photoshop is simply looking at the bottom gradient to find the shade of gray under your pointer; it then puts a circle on the curve directly above that shade. This circle indicates the area of the curve that needs to be changed to affect the area across which you're dragging. Add control points by clicking either side of this area of the curve. Next, move the top point you just added up toward the top of the graph, and move the bottom point down toward the bottom of the graph. The area you dragged across should appear to have more contrast (**Figures 3.86** to **3.88**). As contrast improves in an image, you should be able to see more details.

You might also need to fix the rest of the curve to make sure that the contrast in those areas doesn't change radically. You can do this by adding another point and moving it so that the majority of the curve looks normal—that is, diagonal (**Figure 3.89**).

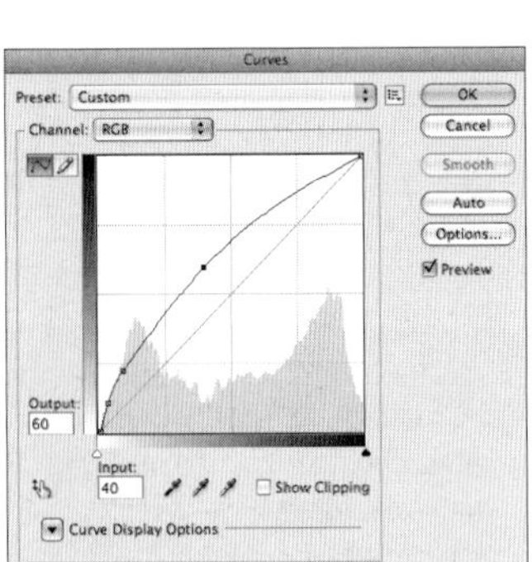

Figure 3.89 Adjust the rest of the curve so that contrast is not too exaggerated in other areas of the image.

Decreasing Contrast and Detail

Any part of the curve that's flatter (more horizontal) than the original line indicates an area where the contrast has been reduced (shades of gray become more similar). Look at the gradient directly below these areas to determine which shades of the image were changed. The flatter the line becomes, the less contrast you'll see in that area of the image. When you lower the amount of contrast in an image, it becomes harder to see detail. This can be useful if you want detail to be less visible. If the curve becomes completely horizontal in an area, you've lost all detail there (**Figures 3.90** to **3.92**). Remember, the curve is a bar graph—the same height means the same brightness.

Figure 3.90 The original image. (©2008 Dan Ablan.)

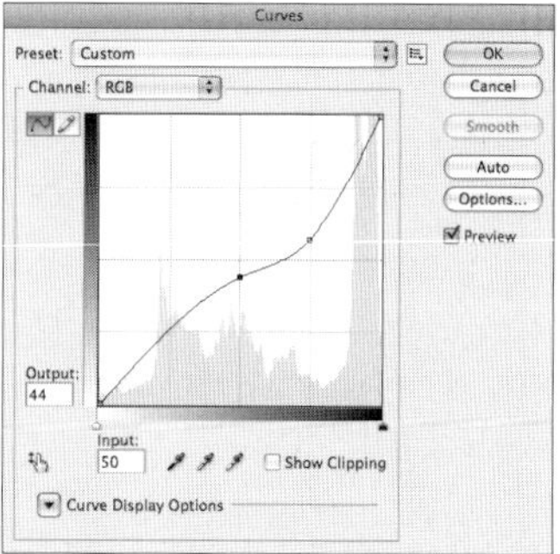

Figure 3.91 Curves used to adjust strong contrast.

Figure 3.92 The result of using Curves to reduce apparent contrast in the image from Figure 3.90.

Analyzing a Curve

Have you ever heard the tip, "Make an *S* curve"? Let's explore exactly what an *S* curve does (**Figure 3.93**).

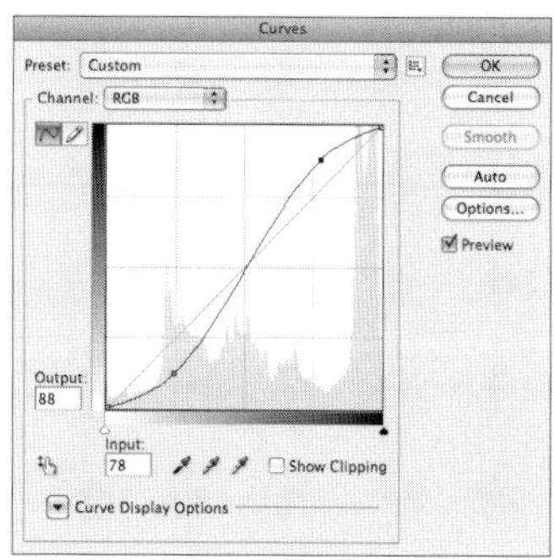

Figure 3.93 A typical *S* curve.

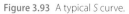

You can reset the Curves dialog to the default line by holding down Option/Alt and clicking the Reset button. The Cancel button turns into a Reset button when you hold down the proper key.

Remember, to find out what a curve is doing to your image, you should compare the curve with the original line. Look at the areas of the curve that are steeper than the original line—in this case, the middle of the curve. The shades represented by these steeper areas will appear to have more detail. Whenever you pull detail out of one part of an image, however, you'll also lose detail in another part. Therefore, look at either end of the curve, at the areas of the curve that are flatter than the original line (more horizontal). These areas appear to have less detail. Thus, an *S* curve attempts to exaggerate detail in the middle grays of the image. However, it also gives you less detail in the highlights and shadows.

Checking Ink Ranges

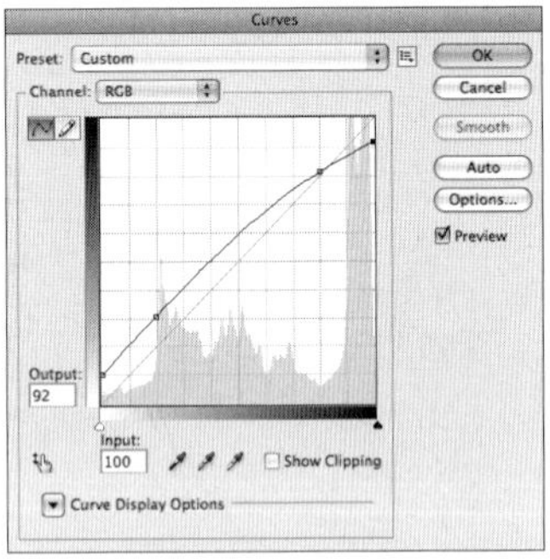

Figure 3.94 After this adjustment, this image won't contain any areas darker than 90% or brighter than 18%.

Look at **Figure 3.94**, paying particular attention to the gradient on the left side of the Curves dialog. As you know, this gradient indicates how dark an area will become if you move the curve to a particular height. Pick a shade of gray from that gradient (such as 90%); then look directly to the right of it to determine if you'll have any areas that shade of gray. Pick another shade and do the same thing. If the curve starts in the lower-left corner and ends in the upper-right corner, each one of the shades should be used somewhere in the image. However, a few shades might be used in more than one area of the curve. The adjustment shown in Figure 3.94 is analogous to using the Output sliders in the Levels dialog. What really helps set these values is the Input and Output readings within the dialog. You'll read more about this in just a few pages.

Inverting an Image

Think of Curves like a stock market graph. As long as the curve is rising, you're fine; however, if the curve starts to fall, you should expect unusual results. Look at **Figure 3.95** and try to figure out what's happening in the area that's going downhill. The dark areas of the image (around 75%) became bright, and the bright areas (around 25%)

became dark. That means you've inverted that part of the image. You'll usually want to minimize or avoid this situation unless you're going for a special effect (**Figures 3.96** and **3.97**).

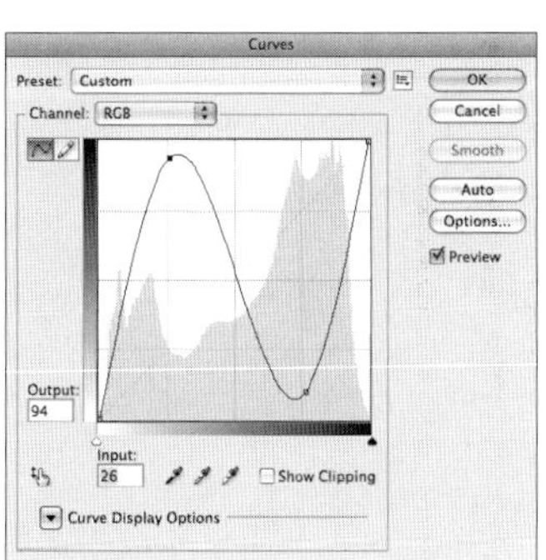

Figure 3.95 Areas between 25% and 75% have been removed.

Figure 3.96 The original image. (©2008 Dan Ablan.)

Figure 3.97 The result of applying the curve shown in Figure 3.95.

Freeform Curves

To change the curve, you're not limited to adding and moving points. Another way to define a curve is to click the Pencil icon at the top of the Curves dialog and draw a freeform shape (**Figure 3.98**). However, the shape you draw has to resemble a line moving from left to right. Go ahead, just try to draw a circle. You can't do it. That's because the Curves dialog is just like a bar graph, and you can't have two bars for a single shade. Just for giggles, draw a really wild-looking line across the grid area, and then look at your image. Drawing your own line with the Pencil tool is usually better for special effects than for simple image adjustments.

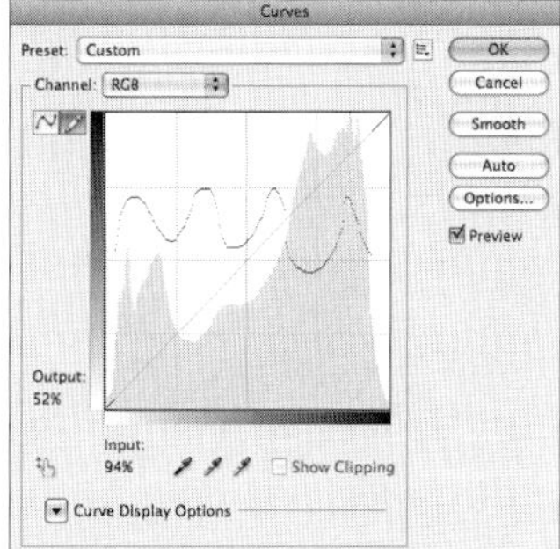

Figure 3.98 A curve created with the Pencil tool.

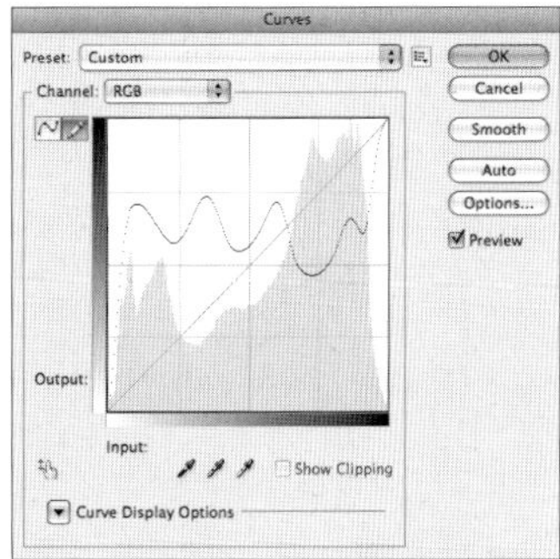

Figure 3.99 A freeform curve after smoothing is applied.

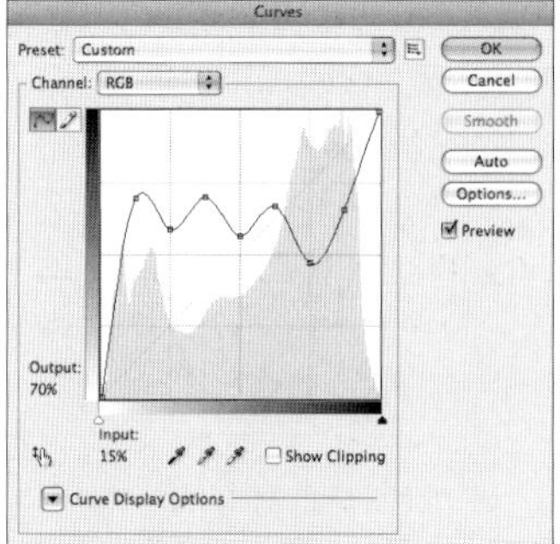

Figure 3.100 A freeform curve converted to a normal curve.

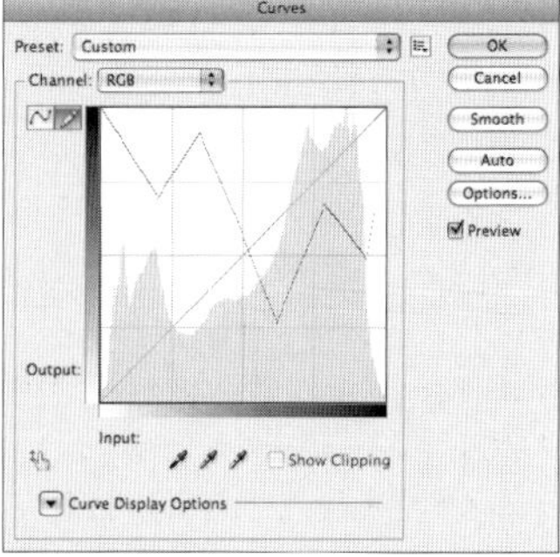

Figure 3.101 You can draw straight lines by Shift-clicking.

Let's take a quick look at some of the things you can do when working with a freeform curve:

- **Smoothing:** After creating a curve with the Pencil tool, click the Smooth button to smooth out the shape you drew (**Figure 3.99**). Keep clicking the Smooth button to further smooth the curve.
- **Converting to points:** To convert any line drawn with the Pencil tool into a normal curve, click the Curve icon (**Figure 3.100**).
- **Drawing straight lines:** You can also draw straight lines with the Pencil tool (**Figure 3.101**). Just Shift-click across the graph area, and Photoshop will connect the dots to create a straight line.
- **Posterizing:** By drawing a stair-step shape with the Pencil tool, you can accomplish the same effect as if you had used the Posterize command.

Input and Output Numbers

The Input and Output numbers at the bottom of the Curves dialog allow you to be very precise when adjusting an image. *Input* is the shade of gray being changed; *Output* is what it will become. When the points on the curve appear as hollow squares, the Input and Output numbers relate to your pointer. The Input number tells you which shade of gray is directly below your pointer. The Output number tells you what the shade of gray (height of the bar graph) would be if you moved the curve to the height of your pointer.

Try it. Click the Curve icon (not the Pencil), and then make sure that none of the points on the curve are solid. Do this by moving your pointer around until it looks like a white arrow, and then click the mouse. Now move your pointer around the grid area. Notice the Input and Output numbers changing. All they're doing is telling you which shades of gray are directly below and to the left of your pointer (**Figure 3.102**). If you trace over the shape of a curve, the Input and Output numbers will show you exactly what the curve is doing to all the shades of gray in your image.

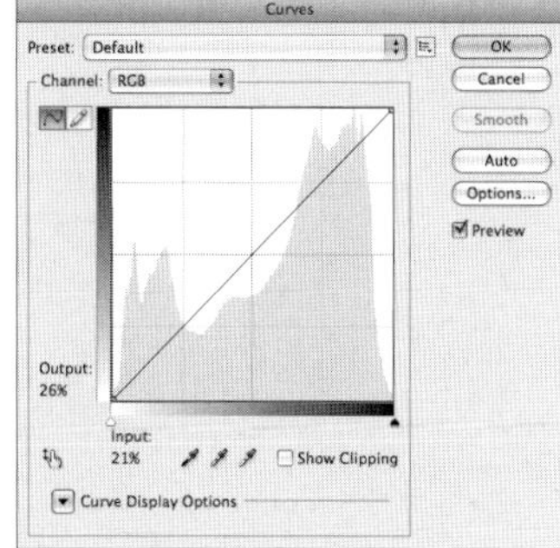

Figure 3.102 The Input and Output numbers indicate the location of your pointer relative to the two gradients in the Curves dialog.

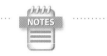

Two Numbering Systems

Two different numbering systems can be used in the Curves dialog. When you change the Show Amount Of radio button setting from Light to Pigment/Ink, Photoshop automatically changes the numbering system from the 0–255 system to percentages.

If you're working on an image that's in RGB mode, Photoshop assumes that you're going to use the image onscreen instead of printing it. Therefore, when you open Curves, it uses Input and Output numbers ranging from 0–255. These numbers represent the amount of light your monitor will use to display the image onscreen; 0 = no light (black), 255 = maximum light (white). Using this numbering system allows you to have control over each shade.

If you're working on an image that's in grayscale or CMYK mode, Photoshop assumes that you'll be printing the image. Therefore, when you open Curves, it uses numbers ranging from 0–100%. These numbers represent the amount of ink used to reproduce each level of gray in the image (0% = no ink; 100% = solid ink).

When you switch between the two numbering systems, Photoshop also reverses the gradients at the bottom and left of the graph. It does this to keep the zero point of each numbering system in the lower-left corner of the graph, which effectively changes between light and ink.

Switching the numbering system also changes the gradient on the left side of the Curves dialog. Therefore, if you're using the 0–255 numbering system, you have to move a

There are two main causes for undesirable results: making the curve flatten out (become horizontal) or making the curve go downhill (when moving from left to right). Often you can fix these problems by adding a point in the middle of the problem area (the flat or downhill part of the curve) and then moving that point so that it appears next to the point that's farthest away from the area that was causing the problem. The idea is to finesse the position of the point so that it appears next to one of the other points and is in a position that prevents the curve from becoming flat or going downhill.

When you're changing the Input and Output numbers, press the up-arrow or down-arrow key to change a number by 1, or press Shift and the arrow key to change a number by 10.

curve up to brighten the image and down to darken it—the exact opposite of what you do in the 0–100% numbering system. You should always look at the gradient on the left to remind yourself: If black is at the top of the gradient (the 0–100% system), you're using ink, and moving a curve up will darken the image. If white is at the top (the 0–255 system), you're using light, and moving a curve up will brighten the image.

Entering Numbers

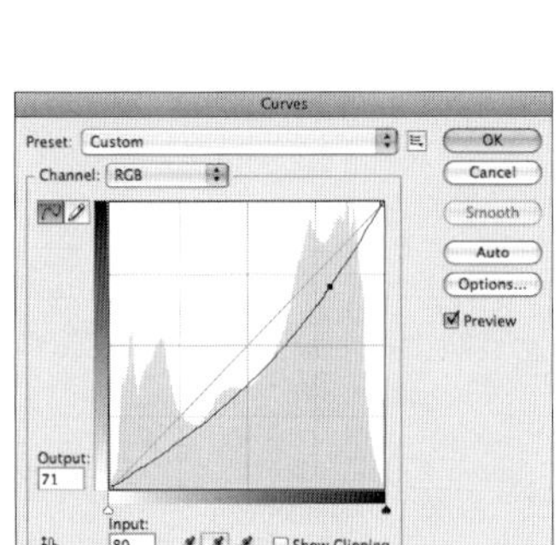

Figure 3.103 To alter the position of a point on a curve, just change one of the numbers.

After you've created a point on the curve, it appears as a solid square. This square represents the point that's currently being edited. The Input and Output numbers at the bottom of the dialog indicate the change this point will make to an image. The Input number represents the shade of gray that's being changed. The Output number indicates what's happening to that shade of gray—the value to which you're changing it. As long as the point appears as a solid square, you can type numbers into the Input and Output fields to change the location of the point (**Figure 3.103**).

Those numbers can be very useful. We'll end up depending on them once we get into color correction (Chapter 7, "Setting Up Images for Final Outpus"). For now, let's see how they can be useful when attempting to change the brightness of an image.

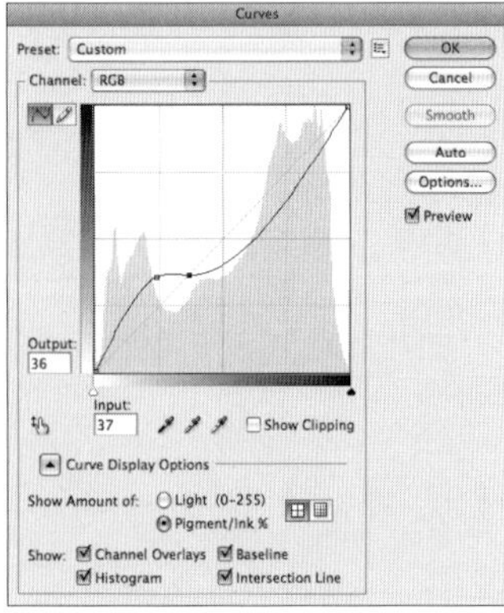

Figure 3.104 When two points are at the same height, those two areas will have the same brightness level.

Earlier, when you clicked an image, a circle appeared in the Curves dialog to indicate what part of the curve would affect the shade in that area. If you Command/Ctrl-click the image, Photoshop adds a point where that circle would show up. What if you'd like two areas of the image to have the same brightness level? Command/Ctrl-click one of them to lock in its brightness level. Then, before you release the mouse button, glance at the numbers at the bottom of the Curves dialog to see exactly how bright that area is. Command/Ctrl-click the second area, and change the Output number to match that of the first object (**Figure 3.104**). The bar graph will be the same height in both areas, which means that both areas will end up with the same brightness. But you have to be careful when using this technique, because the bar graph will flatten out between those two points. When that happens, there won't be any detail in those shades, so other parts of your image might seem to disappear (**Figures 3.105** and **3.106**).

Figure 3.105 The original image. (©2008 Dan Ablan.)

Figure 3.106 The clouds and sky now have the same brightness.

The Info Panel

The Info panel can also show you how Curves affects an image (**Figure 3.107**). When you move your pointer over the image, the Info panel indicates what's happening to that area of the image. The left number in the Info panel tells you how dark the area is before using Curves. The right number tells you how dark it will be after Curves is applied.

When using the Info panel, press the Caps Lock key to change your cursor from the default eyedropper to crosshairs.

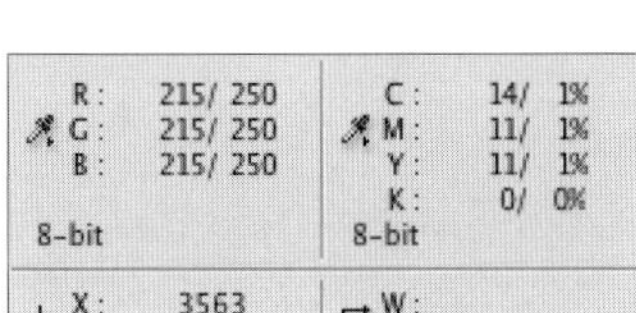

Figure 3.107 The left number is what you have before using Curves; the right number is what you get after using Curves.

Using Curves Changes Colors

The concepts and adjustments we talk about with Curves apply equally to grayscale and color images. But when you work on a color image, you have to be more careful; otherwise, you might end up shifting the colors rather than just the brightness of your image. There are two ways to apply Curves to an image, and therefore two methods for limiting its effect on the brightness of a color image.

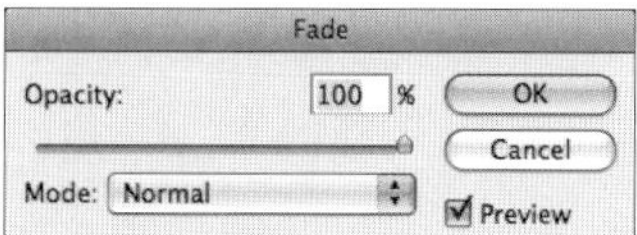

Figure 3.108 Choose Edit > Fade Curves to limit changes to the brightness of the image.

First, you can apply Curves to the active layer by choosing Image > Adjustments > Curves. Immediately after applying Curves, you can choose Edit > Fade Curves and set the Mode pop-up menu to Luminosity (**Figure 3.108**). The Fade command limits the last change you made (Curves, in this case) to changing only the brightness of the image. (*Luminosity* is just another word for *brightness.*) It won't shift the colors or change how saturated they are.

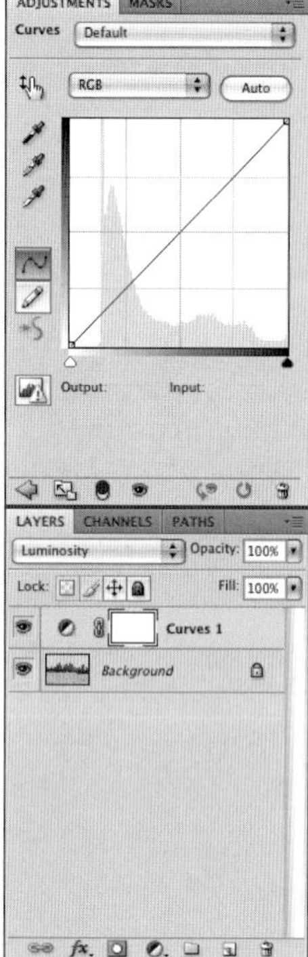

Figure 3.109 You can quickly apply a Curves adjustment as a separate layer by clicking in the Adjustments panel.

Your other choice would be to apply Curves to more than one layer by clicking the Curves icon in the Adjustments panel. Then you can change the blending mode in the Layers panel to Luminosity (**Figure 3.109**). An adjustment layer affects all the layers below it but none of the layers above it. It's also a nonpermanent change, because you can double-click the adjustment layer thumbnail in that layer to reopen the Curves dialog and make changes. Therefore, any Curves techniques you use for adjusting grayscale images will work on color images if you use the Luminosity blending mode (**Figure 3.110**).

Figure 3.110 With a Curves adjustment layer, you can make non-destructive changes to an image.

Color shifts aren't the only problems you'll encounter when adjusting color images with Curves. The mode your image is in might have an adverse effect on the adjustment. RGB color images are made from three components (red, green, and blue). A bright green color might be made out of 0 red, 255 green, and 128 blue. When you first open the

Curves dialog, the pop-up menu at the top of the dialog is set to RGB, which will cause any points to affect the same R, G, and B values. Clicking that green color in the image displays a circle at 165 on the curve, which will affect all the areas that contain 165 red, 165 blue, and 165 green.

Equal amounts of R, G, and B create gray. Simply clicking the curve of a color image usually causes the colors to shift in an unsatisfactory way, because the circle that appears when clicking the image will not accurately target the area you clicked.

While working in RGB mode, all color areas shift because their RGB mix changes as the Curves dialog shifts the RGB values in equal amounts. Ideally it would affect only the exact mix of RGB from which the color is made, but Curves doesn't work that way in RGB mode. The solution to this problem is to convert the image to LAB mode by choosing Image > Mode > Lab Color. In LAB mode, the image is made from three components: Lightness, A, and B. When you adjust the image, the Curves dialog automatically sets itself to work on the Lightness information, which prevents the adjustment from shifting the color of the image and makes the circle show up in the correct position for accurate adjustments. When you're done with the adjustment, you should convert the image back to RGB mode, because many of Photoshop's features are not available in LAB mode. You may not use LAB mode for every color image; reserve it for those images that are troublesome in RGB mode.

The word *LAB* in *LAB mode* is an acronym for what color channels it controls: Lightness, A, and B. Don't say "lab," say the letters: "L-A-B mode."

Quick Recap

To verify that you're ready to move on, make sure that you understand the general concepts of Curves:

- Flattening a curve reduces contrast and makes it more difficult to see detail.
- Making a curve steeper increases contrast and makes it easier to see detail.
- In the 0–100% system, up means darker and down means brighter.
- In the 0–255 system, up means brighter and down means darker.

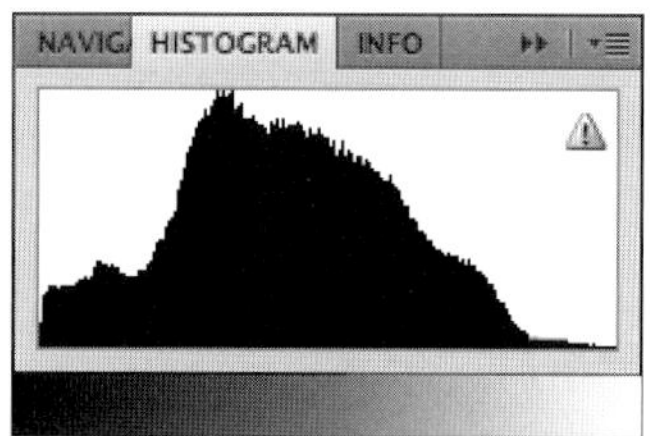

Figure 3.111 Imagine a gradient at the bottom of the Histogram panel.

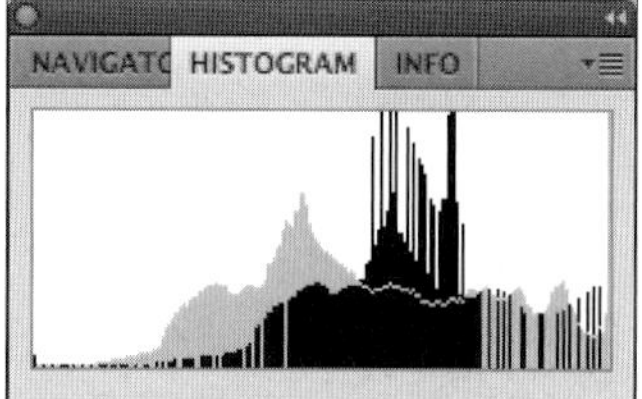

Figure 3.112 The gray histogram reflects the unadjusted image; the black version reflects the adjusted image.

Figure 3.113 An image with limited brightness. (©2008 Dan Ablan.)

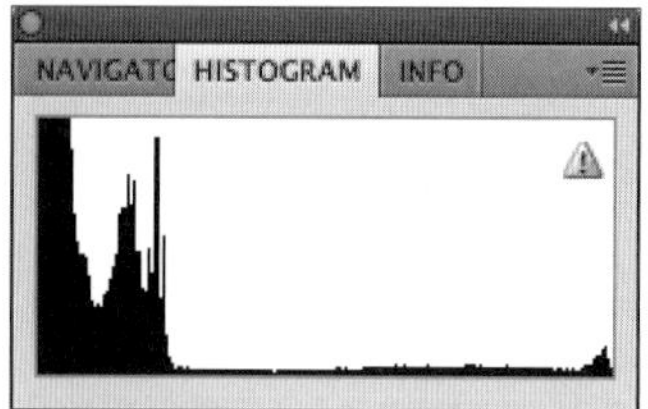

Figure 3.114 The histogram for the image in Figure 3.113.

The Histogram Panel

Used properly, the histogram that's displayed behind the curve in the Curves dialog can help you to make sure that your adjustments don't get out of control and end up harming your images instead of improving them. Photoshop's Histogram panel also can help you to ensure that you don't push your edits and adjustments too far. Now that you have an idea of how to think about Curves, let's figure out how to use these two tools to help with edits. To display the Histogram panel, choose Window > Histogram.

As you learned earlier, a histogram is a simple bar graph that shows the range of brightness levels that make up an image and the prevalence of each of these shades. When you look at the histogram, imagine that a gradient is stretched across the bottom of the bar graph, with black on the left and white on the right just as in the Curves dialog (**Figure 3.111**). If the histogram shows a bar above a particular shade of gray, that shade is used somewhere in the image. If there's no bar, that brightness level isn't used in that image. The height of the bar indicates how prevalent a particular brightness level is compared to the others that make up the image.

The Histogram panel shows the same histogram but with a bonus. When you start to adjust an image, the Histogram panel overlays a histogram that represents the current, adjusted state of the image (black) above the original histogram that shows what the image looked like before you started adjusting it (gray), as shown in **Figure 3.112**.

Achieving Optimal Contrast

If the histogram doesn't extend all the way from black to white, the image has a limited brightness range (**Figures 3.113** and **3.114**). When that's the case, you can usually move the upper-right and lower-left points on a curve toward the middle, which will widen the histogram (**Figure 3.115**). As you do, keep an eye on the histogram. Most images will look their best when the histogram extends all the way across the area available, without producing any tall spikes on either end.

Figure 3.115 The result of applying the curve to the image.

The Histogram panel can be used in two different sizes—Compact or Expanded. The Expanded version is exactly 256 pixels wide; most images contain 256 shades of gray, which makes the Expanded version of the histogram the most accurate histogram for the image. You can switch between the two different views on the side menu of the Histogram panel.

Two controls make this edit a little simpler. Notice that below the grayscale ramp beneath the curve are sliders for black point and white point, just like the one in the Levels dialog. Moving these sliders is the same as adjusting the points on the end of the curve.

Preventing Blown-Out Highlights and Plugged-Up Shadows

Because the height of the bars in the histogram indicates how prevalent each shade is within the image, tall spikes on the ends of the histogram indicate that the image contains large quantities of white or black (**Figure 3.116**). That's usually an indication of a lack of detail in the brightest or darkest areas of the image. If the image contains shiny areas that reflect light directly into the camera (shiny metal or glass, for instance), it's okay if those areas end up with no detail. But if that's not the case, part of the curve must have topped or bottomed out. You should think about moving that area of the curve away from the top or bottom so you can get back the detail that was originally in that part of the image (**Figure 3.117**).

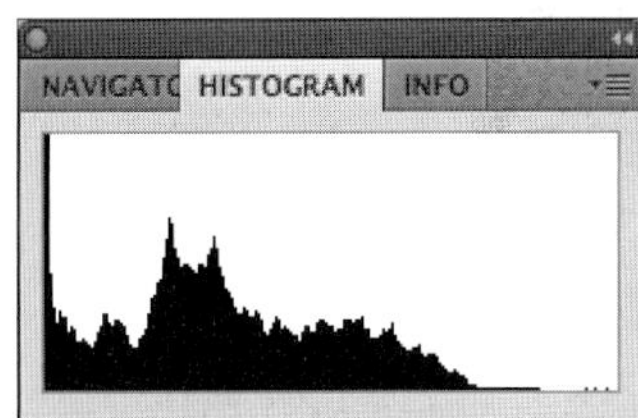

Figure 3.116 This histogram indicates a lot of black in the image because the slope is heavier on the left.

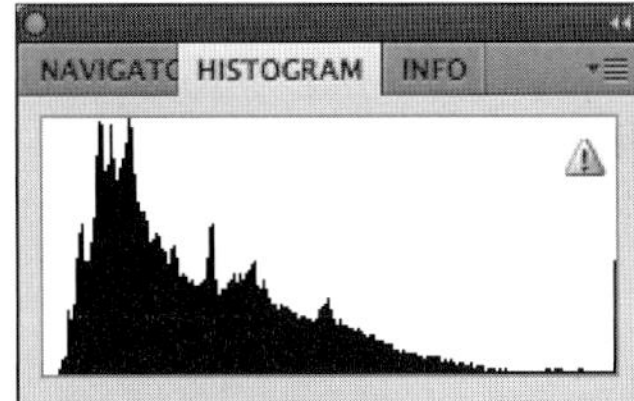

Figure 3.117 After an adjustment, the histogram shows less black and a more even shape.

Avoiding Posterization

If the histogram in the Histogram panel is showing gaps that make it look like a comb (**Figure 3.118**), keep an eye on the brightness levels directly below that area of the histogram. Gaps in a histogram indicate that certain brightness levels are not found in the image, which can indicate *posterization* (stair-stepped transitions where there would usually be a smooth transition), as in **Figure 3.119**. That usually happens when you make part of a curve rather steep. As long as the gaps are small (two to three pixels wide), it's not likely that you'll notice it in the image. If the gaps get much wider than that, you might want to inspect the image and think about making the curve less steep. The histogram in the Curves dialog doesn't show these gaps, because it only shows the original, unedited histogram.

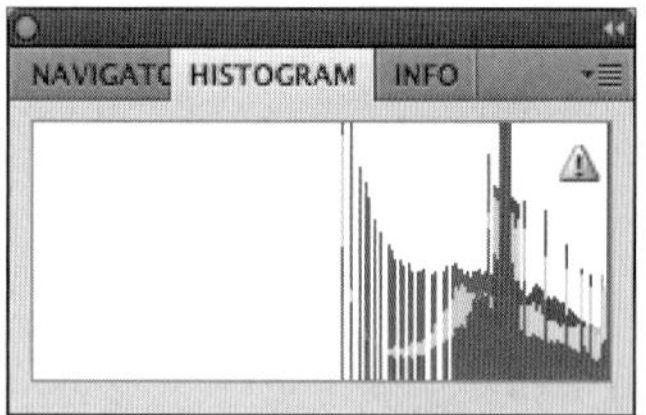

Figure 3.118 A histogram that looks like this might indicate that the image is posterized.

Figure 3.119 The posterized image based on the histogram in Figure 3.118.

To better understand posterization, try this: Create a new grayscale document, press D to reset the foreground and background colors to black and white, and then click and drag across the document with the Gradient tool. While watching the Histogram panel, choose Image > Adjustments > Posterize and experiment with different settings—the gaps don't have to be very wide before you notice posterization (**Figure 3.120**).

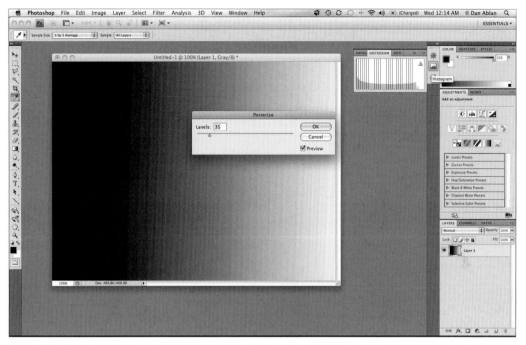

Figure 3.120 Posterize a grayscale image to get a sense of how wide the gaps can be before you see posterization in an image.

You can minimize posterization by working with 16-bit images. Unlike standard 8-bit images that are made from 256 shades of gray (or 256 shades each of red, green, and blue), 16-bit images contain up to 32,767 shades of gray. You can obtain 16-bit images from RAW format digital camera files when opening them in the Camera Raw dialog (see Chapter 4, "Using Camera Raw 5.0," for more details), or from some newer flatbed or film scanners. You can tell that you're working with a 16-bit file by looking at the title bar for the image. After the filename, you should see something like (RGB/16), which indicates that you have a 16-bit RGB-mode image.

If you notice slight posterization in the image, you might apply a little bit of noise to it (Filter > Noise > Add Noise, Amount: 3, Gaussian), which should make it less noticeable. If that doesn't do the trick, check out the manual method for eliminating posterization described in Chapter 7.

The Histogram panel usually builds its histogram by analyzing an 8-bit cached image, just to make sure that the panel display updates quickly. A cached image is a smaller version of the image with 8 bits of information. If you notice the "comb" look when adjusting a 16-bit image (**Figure 3.121**), look for the warning triangle near the upper right of the histogram. That indicates that the histogram is being created from a lower-resolution 8-bit image. Clicking the triangle causes the histogram to be redrawn directly from the high-resolution 16-bit file, which should eliminate the comb look and therefore indicate that the image isn't really posterized (**Figure 3.122**).

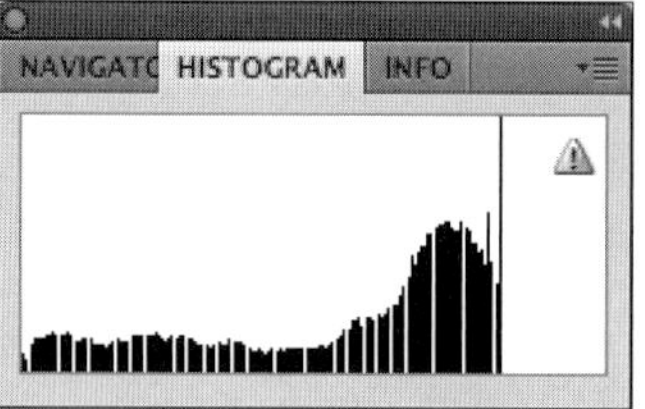

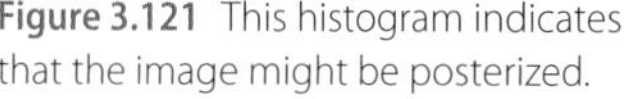

Figure 3.121 This histogram indicates that the image might be posterized.

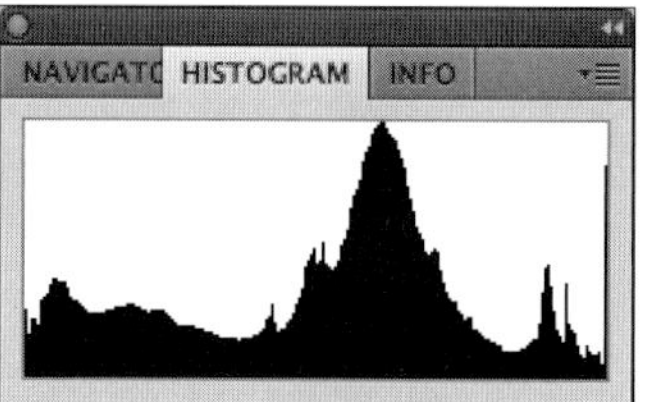

Figure 3.122 The uncached histogram is a more accurate view of the image.

Sneaky Contrast Adjustments

Flattening a curve is usually harmful to an image because the detail in the area you're adjusting will be very difficult to see. Often you can cheat, however, by analyzing the histogram to determine which areas of an image won't be harmed by flattening the curve. Because short lines in a histogram indicate shades that are not very prevalent in the image, those areas usually can be flattened in a curve without noticeable degradation to the image. Flattening one part of the curve allows you to make the rest of the curve steeper, increasing contrast in those areas and making the area appear to have more detail.

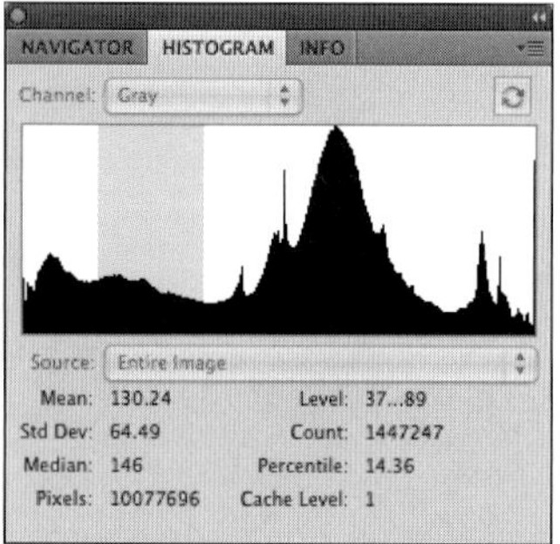

Figure 3.123 Show statistics for the histogram and drag across an area.

When you see a flat area of the histogram in the Curves dialog, place two points on the curve, one at each end of the flat section of the histogram. Here's how it works: While you're in the Curves dialog, glance over at the Histogram panel and look for short, flat areas. When you find a flat area (not all images have them), choose Show Statistics from the side menu of the Histogram panel, and then click and drag across that area in the Histogram panel, but don't release the mouse button (**Figure 3.123**). Look at the Level numbers that show up just below the histogram (if you don't see any numbers under the histogram, choose Expanded View from the side menu of the Histogram panel). Next, release the mouse button and move your cursor around the Curves dialog to see whether the numbers at the bottom are 0–100% or 0–255 numbers. If they range from 0–100%, click the Curve Display Options button and change the Show Amount Of setting to switch to the 0–255 numbering system. Now click in the middle of the curve and change the numbers that appear in the Input and Output fields at the bottom of the Curves dialog to the first number you saw in the Histogram panel (**Figure 3.124**). Add a second point and do the same for the second number you saw in the Histogram panel. Move the upper dot straight down and the lower dot straight up until the area between the two becomes almost horizontal (**Figure 3.125**). Keep an eye on the image as you do this, to see how flat you make the line without screwing up the image. That should increase the contrast across most of the image while reducing contrast in those brightness levels that are not very prevalent in the image.

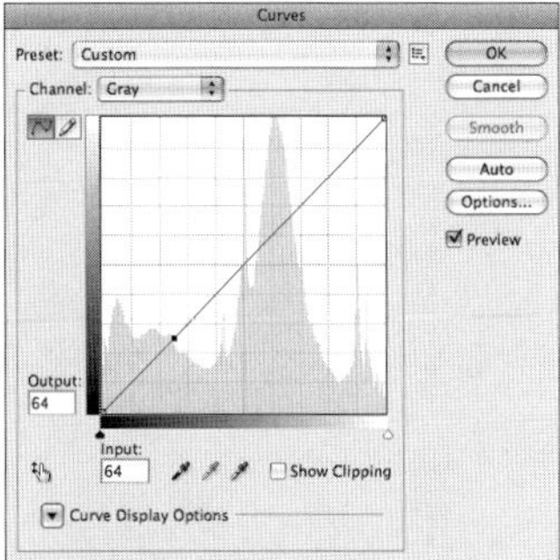

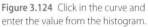

Figure 3.124 Click in the curve and enter the value from the histogram.

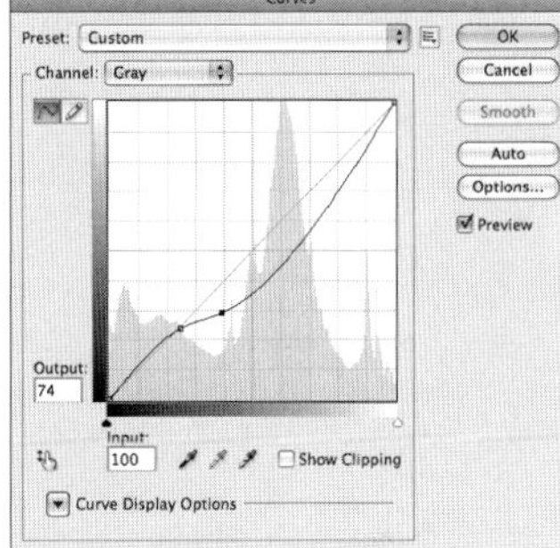

Figure 3.125 Add a second point and adjust to flatten out the curve.

Just because we've talked about the Histogram panel here in the Curves chapter, that doesn't mean that you use it only when making Curves adjustments. The Histogram panel is useful for performing any type of adjustment and for analyzing an image to determine what types of adjustments you might need to consider. Many professional cameras offer a histogram view, and the principles are the same.

In general, you shouldn't adjust images based solely on what the histogram is showing. Instead, adjust the image until you like its general appearance, and then look at the Histogram panel for signs that you might have gone too far. If you notice spikes on the ends or a huge comb taking shape, take a closer look at the image to determine if it's worth backing off from the adjustment. Who cares what the histogram looks like in the end? The visual look of your image is more important. The histogram is just like that seatbelt warning light in your car—you can ignore it, but there's a reason it's on.

Shadows/Highlights

If an image needs more pronounced shadows and/or highlight detail, the Shadows/Highlights command (Image > Adjustments > Shadows/Highlights) is a good alternative to Curves (**Figure 3.126**). In its simplest form, you just move the Shadows slider to brighten the darker areas of the image (**Figures 3.127** and **3.128**) and/or move the Highlights slider to darken the brighter areas (**Figures 3.129** and **3.130**).

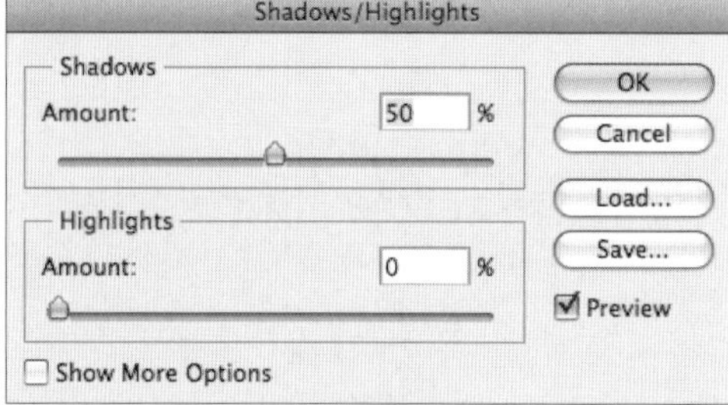

Figure 3.126 The Shadows/Highlights command is a good alternative to Curves.

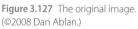

Figure 3.127 The original image. (©2008 Dan Ablan.)

Figure 3.128 The Shadows slider brightens darker areas of the image.

Figure 3.129 The original image. (©2008 Dan Ablan.)

Figure 3.130 The Highlights slider darkens brighter areas of the image.

If you need more control over the adjustment, click the Show More Options check box to see the full range of settings available (**Figure 3.131**). Start by setting Amount to 0%, Tonal Width to 50%, and Radius to 30px in both the Shadows and Highlights areas of the dialog. The Amount setting determines how radical a change you'll make to the image. Because you're starting with that setting at zero, these settings won't do a thing to the image—yet.

If you want to pull out some detail in the dark areas of an image, move the Amount slider in the Shadows area toward the right while you watch the image. Keep moving it until the dark areas of the image reach the desired brightness. Now start changing the Tonal Width setting, which

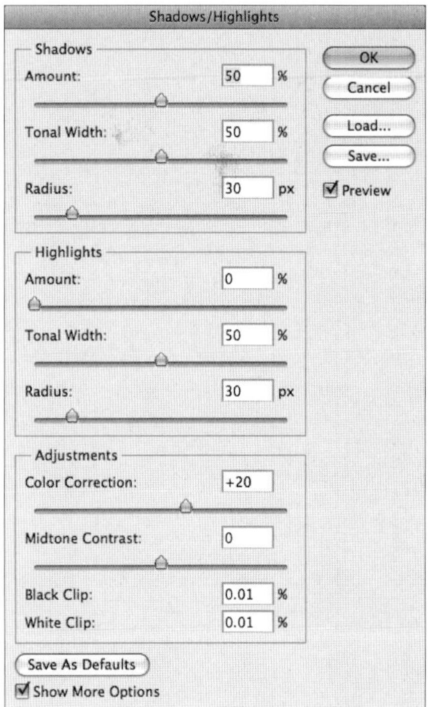

Figure 3.131 The Shadows/Highlights dialog offers more advanced controls when needed.

If you're having trouble seeing exactly what an adjustment is doing to an image, experiment with an extremely simple image until you get the hang of it. Try it on a new grayscale image to which you've applied a gradient.

controls the brightness range in the image. Extremely low settings limit the adjustment to the darkest areas of the image; higher settings allow the adjustment to creep into the brighter areas of the image (**Figures 3.132** and **3.133**). The Shadows/Highlights command adjusts areas based on the brightness level of the surrounding image. So, once you've defined the brightness range you want (via the Tonal Width slider), you'll need to experiment with the Radius slider. That setting determines how much of the surrounding image Photoshop uses when determining how to blend the changes you're making into the surrounding image. Just slide it around until the changes to the dark areas of the image look appropriate considering their surroundings. Moving the slider toward the right will cause the area you're adjusting to blend into the surrounding image more, whereas moving it to the left causes a more pronounced difference between the shadows and midtones of the image. When you've finished your first round with the settings, you'll most likely want to go back to the Amount and Tonal Width settings to fine-tune the result.

Figure 3.132 The original image. (©2008 Dan Ablan.)

Figure 3.133 The image from Figure 3.132 after shadow and tonal adjustments.

The Highlights adjustments work just like the Shadows adjustments, but attempt to darken the brightest areas of the image to exaggerate the detail in that area.

When you brighten the shadows or darken the highlights, you'll often exaggerate any color that was lurking in those areas (**Figures 3.134**). If the color is a little too distracting, try moving the Color Correction slider toward the left to make the areas you've adjusted less colorful (**Figure 3.135**). On the other hand, if you'd like to make those areas even more colorful, move the slider toward the right. The default setting is +20, which is a good starting point.

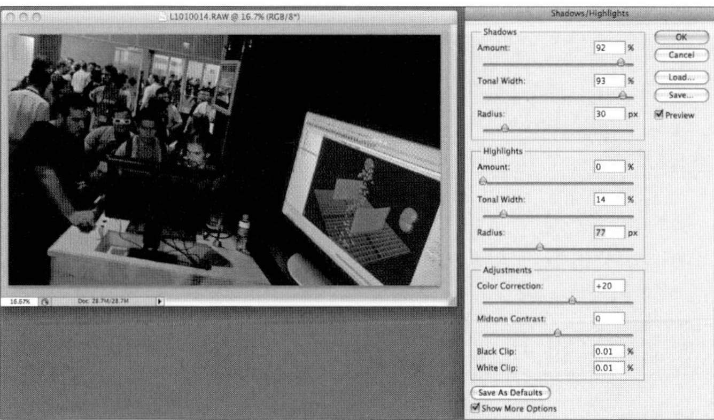

Figure 3.134 By brightening shadows, you might enhance colors. (©2008 Dan Ablan.)

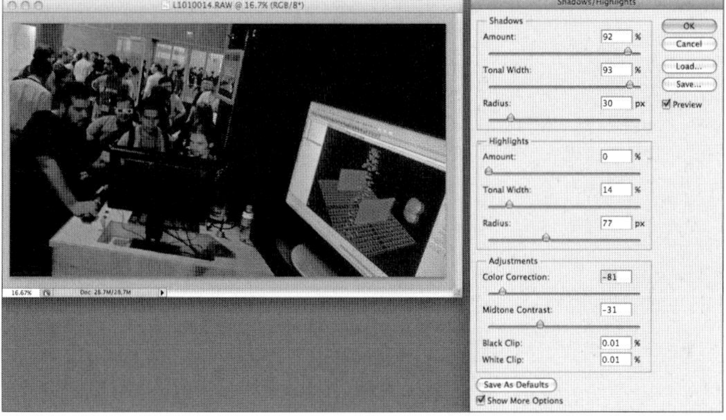

Figure 3.135 Bring the Color Correction slider to the left to pull out the color within the image.

When the brightness and color look good, you'll need to fine-tune the contrast in the areas of the image that you haven't changed. You can do that by moving the Midtone Contrast slider to the left (to lower contrast) or right (to

The Shadows/Highlights command cannot be used as an adjustment layer because it's too complex an adjustment. Adjustment layers are limited to things that can take any input (any shade of gray or color) and know what to do with it without having to know how the rest of the image looks. Because Shadows/Highlights compares the area you're adjusting to its surroundings, it's not simple enough to be implemented as an adjustment layer.

increase contrast). There aren't any set rules for using these sliders. Your image is your guide.

Darkening the highlights on some images can make them look rather dull, especially when working with something that contains shiny objects. For something to look truly shiny, the brightest areas of the image (usually direct reflections of light into the camera lens) need to be pure white. If it's not white, you get just a dull image. If you notice those bright reflections becoming darker when you adjust the Highlights setting, adjust the White Clip setting at the bottom of the Shadows/Highlights dialog. With White Clip set to zero, Photoshop is capable of darkening all the bright areas of the image. As you raise that setting, Photoshop forces a narrow range of the brightest shades in the image to pure white. The higher the setting, the wider the range of shades that Shadows/Highlights forces to white. Just watch the image and increase the White Clip setting until those shiny reflections look nice and bright.

The Black Clip setting forces the darkest areas of the image to black to make sure that they won't be lightened when you move the Amount setting in the Shadows section of the dialog. That change can be useful if you want high-contrast shadow areas or if you have text or other line art that wouldn't look right lightened.

The Next Step

I hope that you've come to the conclusion that layers and Curves really aren't such brain twisters. And if you come out of this chapter thinking of ways you might use these features in the future, even better. Layers and Curves are among a handful of things that separate the experts from everyone else. But there's no reason why you can't propel yourself into the expert category. Get in the habit of keeping an eye on the Histogram panel (don't just use it with Curves) and spend some time working with the Shadows/Highlights dialog. These tools give you that extra bit of versatility and control that can make a big difference with your next image adjustment. The initial learning curve might be somewhat daunting, but the fringe benefits are dynamite.

CHAPTER

4

Using Camera Raw 5.0

I not only use all the brains I have, but all that I can borrow.

—Woodrow Wilson

Using Camera Raw 5.0

It has been an ongoing dilemma for digital photographers in recent years: JPG or raw? Some might say that only high-end photographers with high-end gear (read: "expensive") could afford to shoot raw, in all forms of the word. But raw-format photography is now a fairly common technique used by photographers of all skill levels to ensure maximum image quality and a higher level of editing latitude. Raw files are different from JPEG or TIFF images in that they contain all the data that was captured from the camera, but with minimal processing. Many digital cameras today shoot raw—even small pocket cameras. For this reason, understanding how to process raw files is more important than ever so you can properly evaluate your workflow.

What Is Raw Format?

Your digital camera has to do quite a bit of processing to turn the raw data from your camera into a JPEG or TIFF file. It must interpolate color, adjust for white balance, correct gamma, convert to a color profile, sharpen, and perform saturation and other adjustments before finally compressing the file into a JPEG image. Think of a raw file as the pure data that comes from the camera's sensor. Many image editors can open raw images on both PC and Mac, but occasionally raw formats won't communicate. This situation leaves you frustrated and stuck with a bunch of images you won't know how to handle. However, Photoshop CS4 can open your raw files, so don't worry. Raw offers several advantages over shooting in JPEG:

- Because the files aren't compressed, you don't have to worry about the resulting images exhibiting unsightly JPEG artifacts.
- Most digital cameras capture 10–14 bits of color per pixel, but JPEG files allow for only 8 bits per pixel, meaning that your camera must discard some of its color data when it converts to a JPEG file. With a raw image, you can keep *all* of the color data, which means that you can push your edits further before you run into posterization, poor exposure, bad color depth, etc.
- With raw format, you don't have to worry about the white balance setting on your camera, because you can specify that setting when opening the image in Photoshop.
- Raw files often allow for recovery of overexposed highlights. You read that correctly: The details in highlight areas that have blown out to complete white can be restored.
- When improved raw converters are released, you can go back to your raw images and reprocess them, possibly securing a higher-quality image. A raw file is truly like a "digital negative."
- When working with raw files in Photoshop and Bridge, you have access to handy batch-processing mechanisms that can greatly speed your raw-based workflow.

When you attempt to open a raw format image in Photoshop, the Camera Raw 5.0 dialog opens. This is where you can adjust everything from the overall color of the image to the brightness and contrast, as well as control how much sharpening will be applied.

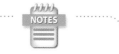

Photoshop's RAW format isn't the same as Camera Raw format. The names sound almost identical, but Camera Raw files can only originate from a digital camera, and Photoshop cannot change the file at all. Camera Raw files are locked because they're designed to contain only the information that came from the digital camera; therefore, they cannot be directly modified after the photo is taken. Think of it like the files on a CD. You can open them, but you can't save back to the CD because it's locked. That doesn't limit what you can do to the images; it just means that you have to save the changes under a different name. With Camera Raw files, changes have to be saved in a different file format (such as TIFF or JPG). Photoshop's RAW file format, on the other hand, is mainly used to export images so they can be imported into unusual software that can't handle common file formats. (I doubt that you'll ever have to use this option.)

The Camera Raw 5.0 Dialog

Let's start with a brief overview of the layout of the Camera Raw 5.0 dialog (**Figure 4.1**), and then we'll dive deeper and look at each specific setting.

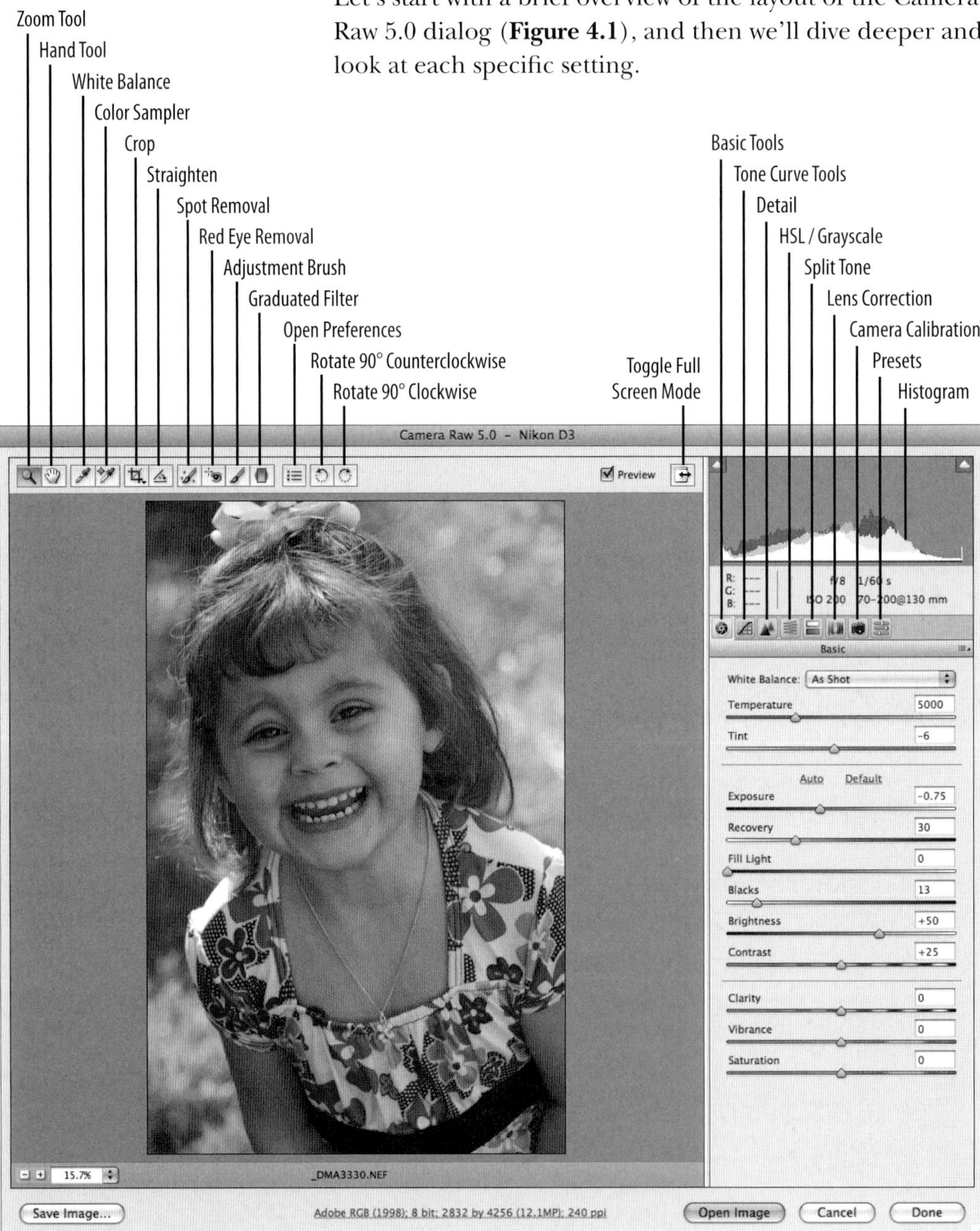

Figure 4.1 The Camera Raw 5.0 dialog opens when you load a raw image in Photoshop.

Across the top of the dialog are a set of tools and rotation icons:

- **Zoom and Hand tools.** The Zoom and Hand tools navigate around the image, like elsewhere in Photoshop, but I find the following keyboard shortcuts to be more efficient: Hold down Command/Ctrl and press the plus (+) or minus (–) key to zoom in or out on the image, and hold down the spacebar to make the Hand tool active temporarily. The current magnification is indicated just below the image.
- **Eyedropper tools.** Next to the navigation tools are two eyedropper tools. The left eyedropper (White Balance) works much like the middle eyedropper in both the Levels and Curves dialogs. The right eyedropper (Color Sampler) causes RGB readouts to appear above the image preview, much like what you'd get in the Info panel. (We talked about the Info panel and the eyedropper tools in Chapter 1, "Tools and Panels Primer.") You'll see how to use the White Balance tool shortly, when we start looking at the features that appear on the right side of the Camera Raw dialog.
- **Crop and Straighten tools.** Next to the eyedropper tools are the Crop and Straighten tools. After choosing the Crop tool, you can click and drag across an image to control how much of the image will appear when it's opened in Photoshop (**Figure 4.2**). Clicking and holding on the Crop tool presents a menu of preset width/height ratios and an option for a custom size (**Figure 4.3**). Choosing Custom allows you to enter a precise width and height, such as 8 × 10 inches (**Figure 4.4**). After you choose a preset or custom crop setting, the cropping rectangle becomes constrained when dragging over the image.

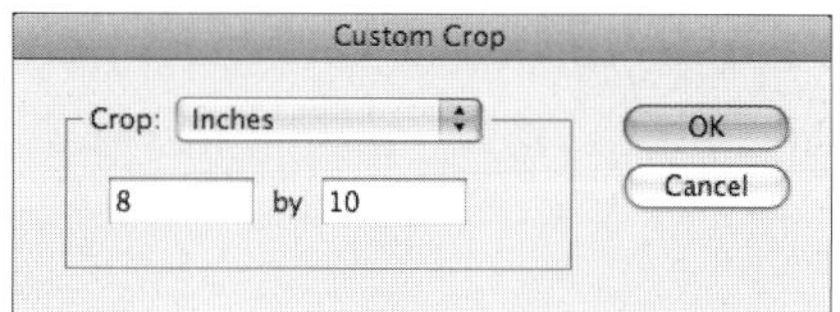

Figure 4.4 Clicking the Crop tool and choosing Custom allows you to enter a precise image size.

You can find updates to Camera Raw by visiting www.adobe.com and clicking > Support > Downloads > Photoshop. Once you've downloaded the update, double-click it to decompress the file. Place it in the following location on your hard drive: Library/Application Support/Adobe/Plug-ins/CS3/File Formats (Windows: C:/Program Files/Adobe/Plug-ins/File Formats).

Figure 4.2 The cropping rectangle indicates which portion of the image will appear when it's opened.

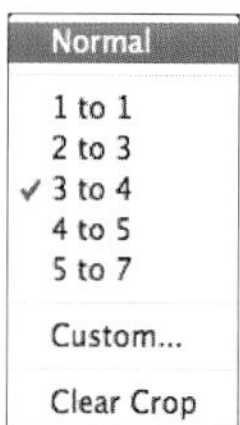

Figure 4.3 Click and hold the Crop tool to access this menu.

Figure 4.5 An image that could benefit from using the Straighten tool.

Figure 4.6 Straightening the image in the Camera Raw 5.0 dialog.

Figure 4.7 The adjusted image, opened in Photoshop. (Looks like we need to do a bit more straightening.)

If you happen to draw the first line incorrectly, click the gray area to lose the crop review, and then redraw with the Straighten tool.

If an image is crooked, click the Straighten tool and then click and drag across any straight line that should be horizontal or vertical in the image, such as the horizon line (**Figure 4.5**). Release the mouse button to display a cropping rectangle that reflects how the image will be rotated when it's opened in Photoshop (**Figure 4.6**). You can then press the Enter/Return key to confirm the cropped and rotated version, or simply click the Open Image button at the bottom of the Camera Raw 5.0 dialog to see the cropped and straightened image in Photoshop (**Figure 4.7**).

- **Spot Removal and Red Eye Removal tools.** Next to the Crop and Straighten tools are the Spot Removal and Red Eye Removal tools. The Spot Removal tool lets you perform adjustments similar to those you can do in Photoshop using the Healing Brush and Clone Stamp tools (**Figure 4.8**). The options allow you to choose from Heal or Clone. When set to Heal, the correction works similarly to the Healing Brush tool in Photoshop, except that you "stamp" your adjustments: After copying the data from the source location to the destination, Photoshop blends the copied pixels with the surrounding areas to make a cleaner patch. If you set the menu to Clone, the pixels are copied without any blending.

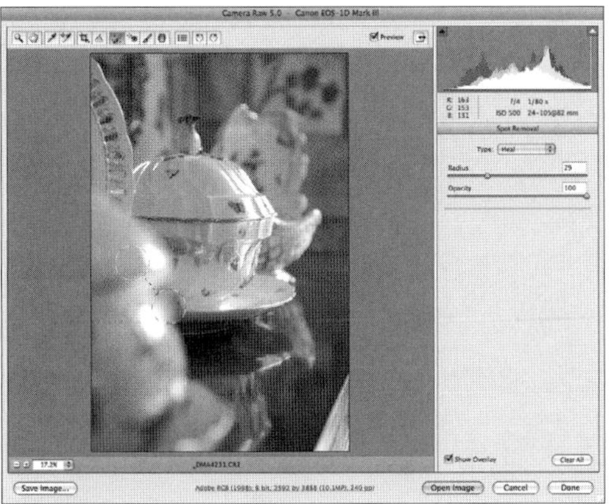

Figure 4.8 Use the Spot Removal tool to remove spots, such as sensor dust.

Figure 4.9 The Adjustment Brush increases or decreases exposure throughout an image.

The Spot Removal tool is not intended for any complex retouching or fancy effects. Rather, these tools provide a simple way to handle sensor dust and scanning artifacts that need to be removed.

We've all seen *red-eye*, the demonic look that can show up in people's eyes when the light from a camera's flash bounces off their retinas. You can correct red-eye in the Camera Raw 5.0 dialog by selecting the Red Eye Removal tool and then clicking the red part of the person's pupil. The Pupil Size and Darken sliders let you refine your correction.

- **Adjustment Brush.** New to Camera Raw 5.0, this tool allows you to paint exposure, either less or more on specific areas of an image. It's not exactly a dodge and burn function, but you can think of it in those terms when working with raw images. You can vary exposure throughout the image quickly and effectively (**Figure 4.9**). Additionally, you can paint brightness, contrast, saturation, clarity, and sharpness. Brush and feather sizes can be adjusted on the fly. Holding down the Option key lets you brush to revert the effect and allows you to tweak the Size, Feather, Flow, and Density sliders to change the brush size and behavior.

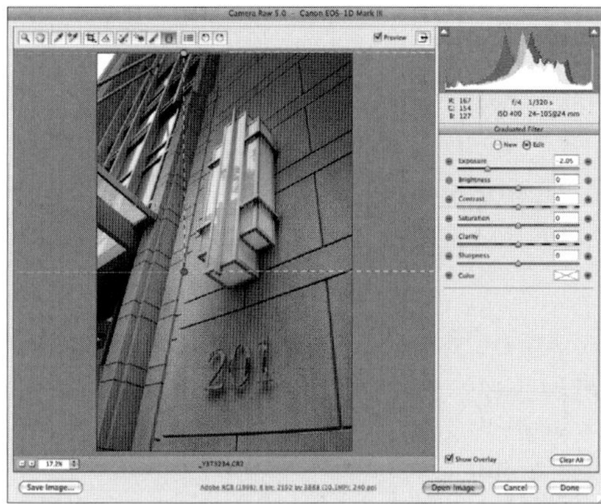

Figure 4.10 The graduated filter allows you to refocus the viewer's attention within an image.

Figure 4.11 Graduated filters are great for darkening and coloring skies.

Most raw files contain 12 bits of information, but Photoshop can deal with 8-bit or 16-bit files. That's like owning 12 cars and having to choose between an 8- or 16-car garage. The 8-car garage would cost half as much (in Photoshop, that means half the file size), but you'd have to give up something to use it. A 16-car garage might be more than you need, but since 8 or 16 are your only choices, it's the only choice that doesn't make you compromise.

- **Graduated Filter.** Also new to Camera Raw 5.0, this handy option can help to pull the viewer's eye closer to the center of an image (**Figure 4.10**). But the graduated filter is more complex than just adding a gradient to the image. **Figure 4.11** shows the filter applied to the top of an image, with the color set to a deep blue, and the contrast increased. The result is not so much a darker sky as a deeper, richer sky. Conversely, you can lighten areas of an image with the graduated filter by increasing exposure.
- **Camera Raw Preferences.** To the right of all these adjustment tools is a button for opening the Camera Raw Preferences dialog. There are a number of settings that you can customize from the Preferences dialog.
- **Rotating tools.** Finally, two tools are available for rotating the image 90° to the left or right. It might be more efficient to type L or R, respectively.
- **Management controls.** Further to the right at the top of the Camera Raw 5.0 dialog are two important window-management controls. When the Preview check box is turned on, the image is displayed with all of your corrections applied. Turn off the Preview check box to see your original, unaltered image. This feature provides a simple before-and-after switch that you can also access by simply pressing P.

The button on the far right side is the Toggle Full Screen Mode button, which expands the Camera Raw window to fill the full screen. In addition to displaying a larger image, Full Screen Mode hides other distracting interface elements and controls. As in Photoshop itself, you can toggle in and out of Full Screen Mode by pressing F.

- **Workflow options.** Beneath the image preview are the workflow settings for the image—a line of text that indicates color space, bit depth, pixel dimensions, and resolution setting (**Figure 4.12**). You might notice that these settings look like a link on a Web page; sure enough, clicking the link displays the Workflow Options dialog (**Figure 4.13**).

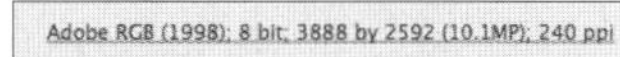

Figure 4.12 You can view your image workflow, such as resolution and color space, at the bottom of the Camera Raw dialog.

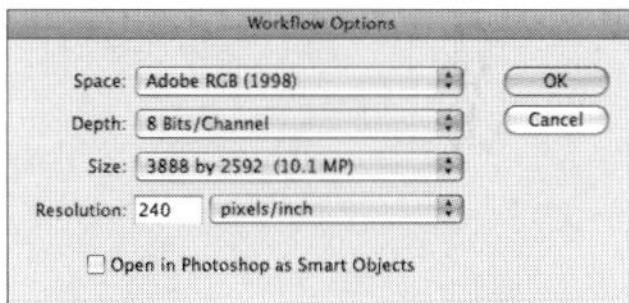

Figure 4.13 Clicking the workflow settings link at the bottom of the Camera Raw dialog displays the Workflow Options dialog.

The workflow options let you specify how much information will be delivered to Photoshop when you open the image. The Space pop-up menu controls the range of colors the image is capable of using (also known as a *color space*). It's recommended that you set it to the same RGB working space that you'll read about in Chapter 7, "Setting Up Images for Final Output." For now, you can leave it set to Adobe RGB.

The Depth pop-up menu determines how many shades Photoshop can use between black and white. Choosing 8 Bits/Channel delivers an image that contains a maximum of 256 brightness levels, which makes for 16.7 million colors. Choosing 16 Bits/Channel delivers an image that contains a maximum of 65536 brightness levels—giving you millions of colors in the image. The problem is that 16-bit files take up twice as much space as 8-bit files on your hard drive, and neither your computer screen nor your printer is capable of reproducing more than 8 bits of information.

There's a lot of hype out there about the advantages of 16-bit files, but when it comes down to the end result, the difference between 8 and 16 bits is barely detectable (except in some circumstances, which you can read about in the sidebar). Some folks out there might try to shame you into using 16-bit mode by showing

Computer monitors and desktop printers are not capable of reproducing more than 256 brightness levels (also known as *8 bits*). Are the 4096 brightness levels that come with a 12-bit image overkill, or are they worth keeping? What if you have a very dark image that only contains brightness levels from black to 90% gray, and you end up adjusting the image in Photoshop to make the brightest area white while keeping the darkest area black? Since the original image contained only 10% of the shades available, an 8-bit version would contain a maximum of 26 brightness levels and the 12-bit version would have 410! Wouldn't the 12-bit image produce a smoother result? It's only in extreme cases that the extra information is helpful, so use them only when you plan to make an extreme adjustment in Photoshop (all adjustments in the Camera Raw dialog are applied to the full 12 bits of information).

you a histogram (bar graph) that shows the difference between 8- and 16-bit results. If that ever happens to you, please ignore the bar graph and ask to see two prints side by side. If you actually see a noticeable difference between the prints, consider taking the person's advice and using 16-bit images. On the other hand, if having reasonable file sizes and a relatively fast computer are your priorities, stick with 8-bit images; your results will still look great. I suggest using 16 Bits/Channel only when you plan to make major adjustments to the images within Photoshop, or when you really don't care how large your files become or how slowly your computer runs while you're working on an image.

The Size and Resolution settings in the Workflow Options dialog determine the physical size of the image when it's opened in Photoshop. This *interpolation* is discussed in the bonus video "Resolution Solutions" at www.danablan.com/photoshop.

Finally, there's that Open in Photoshop as Smart Objects check box. We'll discuss Smart Objects in detail in Chapter 10, "Collage Effects."

Once you've configured your workflow settings, click OK to return to the Camera Raw dialog.

In the upper-right corner of the Camera Raw dialog is a histogram that shows how the sliders in the dialog affect the overall tonality of the image. You just read about histograms in Chapter 3, "Layers and Curves," and this one works the same way. The histogram and its uses will be discussed further when we get to the point where we're adjusting images.

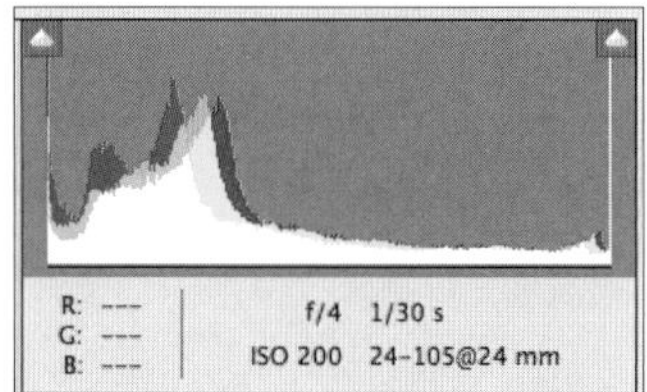

Figure 4.14 A handy histogram and the image's f-stop data are provided in the upper-right corner of the Camera Raw dialog.

Directly beneath the histogram, Adobe has conveniently placed a simple readout that shows the f-stop, shutter speed, ISO, and focal length that were used for the image (**Figure 4.14**). Next to that information is an RGB readout that shows the component color values for any pixel that you mouse over, just like the Info panel does in Photoshop.

Below these readouts are an array of sliders organized into tabs of different categories, each with its own set of controls. Let's look at these settings one at a time.

Basic Tab

The Basic tab should be your mandatory first stop in the Camera Raw dialog (**Figure 4.15**); all the other settings on the other tabs can be considered optional. The Basic tab is where you can change the overall tone and color of the image. It's often good to start with the White Balance setting. If the overall color temperature of your image is off, you'll have a difficult time evaluating the proper exposure, contrast, and other necessary values.

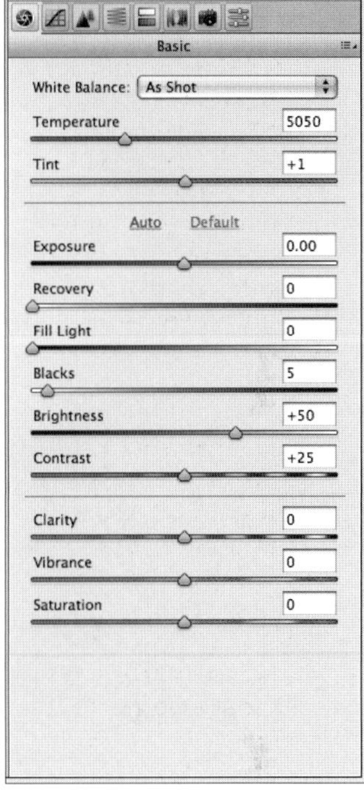

Figure 4.15 The Basic tab contains tools you'll use on all of your images.

White Balance

The White Balance setting allows you to shift the overall color of your image, making it feel warm, cool, or neutral. There are three ways to set the white balance of your image: by using the pop-up menu, the sliders, or (in most cases) the eyedropper tool.

The White Balance pop-up menu contains presets for different types of lighting conditions (Daylight, Cloudy, Tungsten, Fluorescent). If you know in which type of light an image was shot, choose that preset so Photoshop will correct for that particular light source. If you're not sure what the lighting conditions were when the image was shot, just click through the various options and watch the image change until you find the setting that makes the colors in the image look the best (**Figures 4.16** and **4.17**). If you're in a big hurry, set White Balance to Auto, and Photoshop will choose a setting that's appropriate for the lighting conditions of the image. The White Balance pop-up menu moves the Temperature and Tint sliders to preset positions. Before you start fiddling with those sliders, choose a setting on the pop-up menu to give you a good starting point, which you can then fine-tune with the sliders.

Figure 4.16 A raw image loaded into Camera Raw and set to a Fluorescent white balance preset makes the outdoors look too blue.

Figure 4.17 The image from Figure 4.16 with White Balance set to daylight.

Moving the Temperature slider to the left shifts the colors in the image toward blue; sliding it to the right shifts toward yellow. The Tint slider shifts the color in the image toward green (left) or magenta (right). The combination of these two sliders allows you to shift the image toward just about any color. For instance, if you move both the Temperature and Tint sliders to the right, you'll simultaneously shift the image toward yellow and magenta. Those two colors combined produce red, so that's the color toward which the image will shift. Moving the sliders left shifts toward both blue and green, which sends the colors toward cyan.

If you want the image to look completely neutral (not warm or cool), consider using the eyedropper tool located at upper left in the Camera Raw dialog. With the White Balance tool active, click the image, and Photoshop will figure out the proper Temperature and Tint settings to remove all the color from the area you clicked. All you have to do is find an area that shouldn't contain color and then click it (**Figures 4.18** and **4.19**). Just look for anything that appears to be a shade of gray in the image. It could be someone's gray sweatshirt, a wall that's painted white, a button on someone's shirt, or anything else that shouldn't contain a trace of color. Then, if the image looks too sterile, you can adjust the Temperature and Tint sliders to make

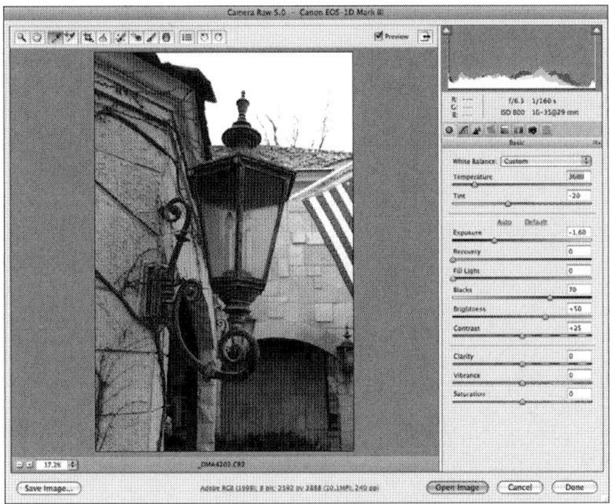

Figure 4.18 An outdoor image with the wrong white balance setting in the camera.

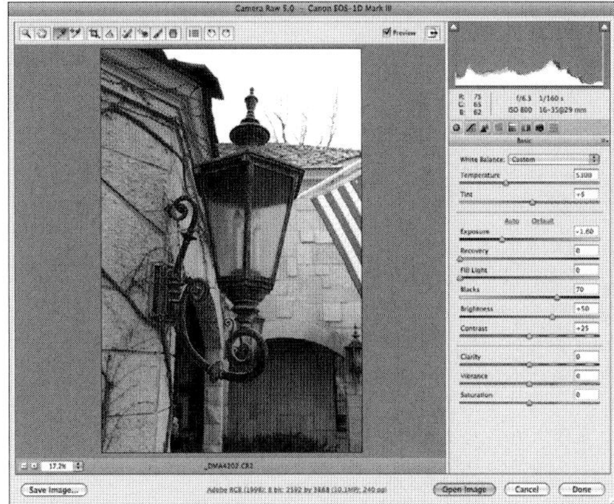

Figure 4.19 The image from Figure 4.18, quickly adjusted in Camera Raw.

the image a little warmer (move right, toward yellow and magenta) or cooler (move left, toward blue and green).

It doesn't really matter which of the three methods you use (pop-up menu, sliders, or eyedropper); all of them manipulate the Temperature and Tint sliders to produce the final result. Your personal interpretation of how you'd like the image to look will dictate the result.

Depending on how much you've zoomed in, the eyedropper will look at different numbers of pixels in the image. If you view the image at 100%, it will look at the pixel that's under the cursor when you click. Viewing the image at 50% makes the eyedropper look at an area of 2×2 pixels. When viewing at 25% or 50%, you don't have to worry about clicking an odd-colored pixel that would get averaged into the surrounding colors.

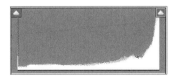

Exposure Slider

The Exposure slider controls the brightness of the brightest area of the image. As you move the Exposure slider farther to the right, more areas of the image become pure white. Be very careful; otherwise, you'll end up trashing the detail in the brightest part of the image.

There are four ways to tell if you're losing detail. The least reliable is watching the image to see whether any areas are becoming solid white or black. You often can't tell the difference between a very bright area and one that has become solid white. An alternative is to watch the histogram while adjusting the Exposure slider (**Figure 4.20**). If a spike appears on the right end of the histogram, you're starting to lose highlight detail.

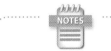

Figure 4.20 The histogram in Camera Raw can let you know if the image is clipping highlights.

As you know, an image is made out of red, green, and blue light (also known as *channels*). If the spike is in color, you're losing detail in one or two of the three colors that make up the image, but you still have detail left in the highlights. If the spike is white, on the other hand, the highlights are becoming solid white and have no detail. A spike only matters if it shows up on the absolute right end of the histogram. A spike in the middle or near the end doesn't indicate a loss of detail. (To learn more about histograms, check out Chapter 7.) The problem with this approach is that light sources and reflections of shiny objects (such as glass, water, or metal) look better when they don't contain detail, and the histogram can't distinguish between those areas and other important parts of the image.

In the upper corners of the histogram are two small buttons, one above the right side (Highlights clipping) and one above the left (Shadows clipping). Clicking the right one toggles the highlight clipping view. When it's turned on, any areas that are losing highlight detail turn red in the Camera Raw dialog (**Figure 4.21**). That makes it much easier to know when and where you're starting to lose detail. The only snag is that the red overlay doesn't differentiate between losing detail in just one or two of the three colors that make up the image (in which case you still have some detail remaining) and losing detail in all three colors, which produces solid white.

Figure 4.21 The highlights clipping warning shows red in the image where you're losing detail.

To get the most informative and useful indication of lost detail, hold down the Option/Alt key while you move the Exposure slider. That will cause Photoshop to change the way it displays the image. In this view, areas that show up as solid white have lost all detail and will end up solid white when the image is opened in Photoshop. Areas that show up in color indicate where you're losing detail in one or two of the colors that make up the image, but the areas have not become solid white yet. Finally, areas that appear solid black have detail in all three of the colors that make up the image and are therefore not at risk.

Not all clipping is bad. Sometimes you want window light completely blown out, for example; and it's okay to have some highlights lose detail, such as specular reflections.

A good approach to adjusting this slider is to move it toward the right (with Option/Alt held down) until you see the first hints of white showing up (**Figure 4.22**). Then back off a tiny amount and think of that as the farthest you'd want to move it (**Figure 4.23**)—unless the area that's becoming white is a light source or reflection of the light source, in which case forcing it to white might actually improve the look of the image. Then look at the colored areas that are showing up, and if there are areas that contain critical detail, continue to move the slider back to the left until you see only small areas of color. You shouldn't mind having large areas of color if you want the image to look really saturated, because you have to max out at least one of the colors that make up the image (red, green, and blue) in order to get a truly saturated color. Once you've found the general range that you like, release the Option/Alt key and see how this setting is affecting the brightest areas of the image, and then fine-tune if necessary. The majority of the time, you may end up leaving it at the position that was just shy of seeing solid white when you had the Option/Alt key held down.

The Exposure setting is only used to control how bright the absolute brightest areas of the image should be. Don't try to control the overall brightness of the image with this slider. There are better ways to do that, which we'll get to in a few moments. Right now, let's talk about the Recovery slider and how it can come to the rescue when the image has clipped highlights.

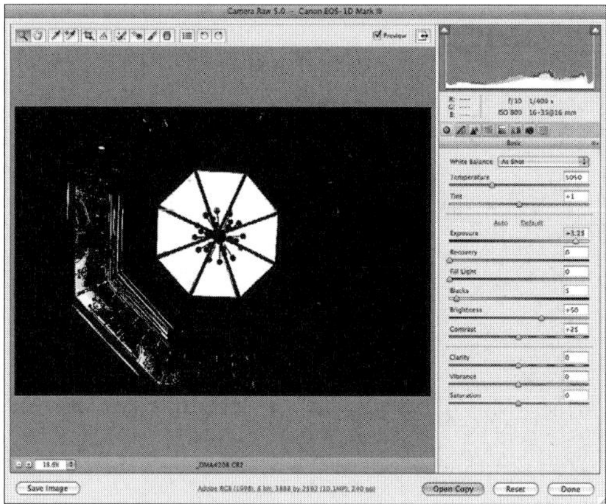

Figure 4.22 Holding down the Option/Alt key while dragging the Exposure slider helps you to determine where highlight clipping occurs.

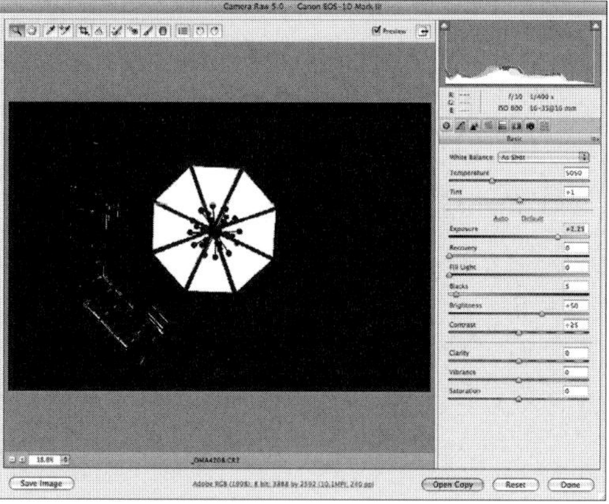

Figure 4.23 A little highlight clipping may be okay, depending on the image.

Most digital cameras also capture "headroom"—additional information above the brightest levels represented in the file. This data is necessary for some of the color and white balance calculations that must be performed to produce an image. This data is also stored in the file, and Camera Raw can reach into that data to bolster its highlight recovery efforts.

Recovery Slider

One of the most important things to take away from the previous section is the understanding that highlights don't always clip in all three channels. Very often, a highlight will clip in only one or two channels, though it might appear to be completely blown out, or to have lost detail. When a highlight is only partially clipped, there's a chance that Camera Raw can use the remaining channels to *rebuild* the clipped channels, and thus restore detail to areas that appear to be blown out. The Recovery slider attempts to do just that.

If you have clipped highlights—as evidenced by a big spike on the right side of the histogram—try sliding the Recovery slider to the right. In **Figure 4.24**, the white hat is losing detail. As you slide the Recovery slider to the right, you might very well see the spike shrink and disappear, and in the image see detail appear in the blown-out highlight sections (**Figure 4.25**).

Highlight recovery can work wonders, turning seemingly unusable images into well-exposed shots full of detail. It often works well in portraits where the model's skin gets a little too bright when the rest of the image is properly exposed. You can also perform highlight recovery by moving the Exposure slider to the left. This will perform the same recovery operation as the Recovery slider, but will also darken the midtones and shadows in the image. The

Figure 4.24 The white hat is losing detail in this image, as you can see by the spiked histogram.

Figure 4.25 A slight drag to the right of the Recovery slider restores detail in the hat, and the histogram no longer spikes.

Recovery slider constrains its effects to just the highlights in the image, which means that you won't have to do as much work later to try to restore brightness.

Fill Light Slider

Chapter 3 introduced Photoshop's Shadows/Highlights adjustment, which lets you brighten only the shadow areas of an image (or only the highlights). The Fill Light slider works just like the Shadows slider in the Shadows/Highlights dialog; slide to the right, and the shadow areas of the image brighten. It's called Fill Light here because the overall effect is very similar to what you'd see if you shined a fill light—or fired a fill flash—into the scene. Shadows under people's eyes and chins lessen, and overall contrast is reduced (**Figure 4.26**).

Figure 4.26 Using the Fill Light feature works wonders to add more light to areas that need it, such as under the brim of a hat.

The Fill Light slider lacks the refined degree of control that the Shadows/Highlights dialog provides, but having it in Camera Raw is a great convenience because it just might save you an additional processing step.

Blacks Slider

The Blacks slider controls how dark the absolute darkest areas of an image will be. It works just like the Exposure slider in that you can hold down Option/Alt to see which areas are becoming solid black (they'll look black), which areas are starting to have less detail (colored areas), and which areas haven't lost any detail (they'll look white).

The Shadows clipping button above the left side of the histogram makes areas that are losing detail appear in blue in Camera Raw. Unlike the Highlights clipping button at right above the histogram, the Shadows clipping button only indicates where an area has become solid black. It doesn't indicate areas that are losing detail in just one or two of the colors that make up the image. You may still prefer to use the Option/Alt method because you'll often want to know where you're losing detail in just one or two colors in the image. Hold down Option/Alt and move the Blacks slider until you see the first hints of pure black showing up; then back off just slightly so you don't trash the detail anywhere (**Figure 4.27**).

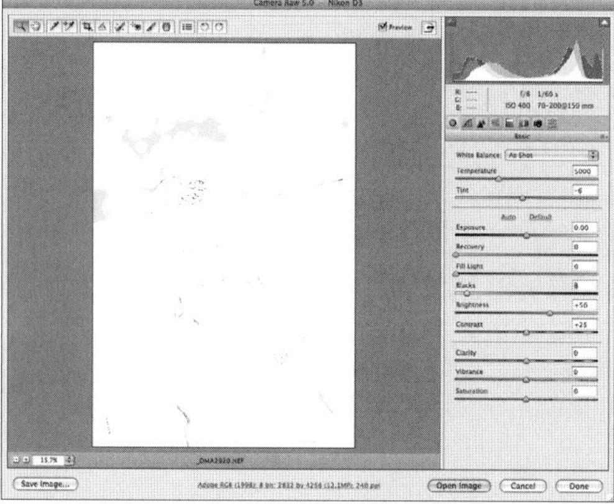

Figure 4.27 Hold down the Option/Alt key and move the Blacks slider to see where the pure black is within the image.

If you decide not to use the Shadows clipping warning feature when moving the Blacks slider, be sure to keep an eye on the histogram. If you see a spike on the left side, you're losing shadow detail. If the spike is white instead of a color, you're starting to get some solid black areas in the image. One quick way to make images really "pop" is to bring up the Blacks slider just to the point where the image is looking too dark and then bring the exposure up slightly to compensate, being careful not to overexpose the image. **Figures 4.28** and **4.29** show an image loaded and then adjusted with Blacks and Exposure. You can use the Recovery slider to pull in detail to highlight areas.

Figure 4.28 An original raw image loaded into Camera Raw. Seems okay, but lacks the punch needed for a final portrait.

Figure 4.29 The image from Figure 4.28 with the Blacks slider raised and Exposure added to compensate.

Brightness Slider

Now that we've determined how bright the brightest areas should be and how dark the darkest areas should be, it's time to adjust the brightness levels that fall between black and white.

The Brightness slider attempts to adjust the overall brightness of the image without screwing up the brightest or darkest areas. Move the slider to the left if the image needs to be darker (**Figures 4.30** and **4.31**), or move it to the right to brighten the image (**Figure 4.32**). If you're planning to make radical changes in brightness, use Curves (see Chapter 3) after you've opened the image in Photoshop. You'll have a lot more control over the process with Curves, but it won't hurt if you make a slight tweak using the Brightness slider.

Figure 4.30 An original image with the brightness set to a default of 50. (©2008 Dan Ablan.)

Figure 4.31 The image from Figure 4.30 with the Brightness slider set all the way to the left.

Figure 4.32 The image from Figure 4.30 with the Brightness slider all the way to the right.

Figure 4.33 An original image with Contrast set to 25.

Figure 4.34 The image from Figure 4.33, with Contrast set to 85.

Contrast Slider

Most of the time, you should adjust the contrast of your images using Curves, which provides much more control than you'd ever get by moving a generic Contrast slider. In a hurry, though, you might limit adjustments to what's available in the Camera Raw dialog. In those instances, it's okay to settle for the generic Contrast adjustment instead of spending the time it would take to fine-tune it with Curves (**Figures 4.33** and **4.34** show the kind of results you can get with a quick adjustment to the Contrast setting).

Clarity Slider

The Clarity slider can be used with a wide variety of photographs. It was devised to boost contrast at the micro level; even though it's a relatively subtle adjustment, it can add noticeable punch and crispness to images. Clarity is a unique adjustment in that it can't be reproduced in Curves, because it uses the image itself to make a mask on which to apply the midtone contrast adjustment. Tread lightly with this slider—a heavy hand can make the image look too contrasty (**Figures 4.35** and **4.36**).

Figure 4.35 An original image with Clarity set to 0. (©2008 Dan Ablan.)

Figure 4.36 The image from Figure 4.35 with Clarity set to 87.

Vibrance Slider

The Vibrance slider is a variation on a saturation adjustment. Rather than adjusting the saturation of the entire image, the Vibrance slider attempts to protect flesh tones. If you've ever performed a saturation boost on an image and found that skin tones ended up too red or splotchy, you'll appreciate the Vibrance slider (**Figure 4.37**).

Figure 4.37 Vibrance is a great way to boost colors in an image without oversaturing it.

Saturation Slider

You'll have much more control over your image if you adjust it in Photoshop with a Hue/Saturation adjustment. But if you're in a hurry, or you're batch-processing a large number of images using the same settings, you might decide to use the Saturation slider instead. If you have more time, test the waters with this slider and make the actual adjustments with a Hue/Saturation adjustment afterward (**Figures 4.38** through **4.40**).

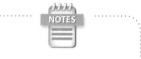

Toggling the Preview check box off and back on again will effectively show a before-and-after version of how the settings in the active tab (Basic, Detail, etc.) are affecting the image.

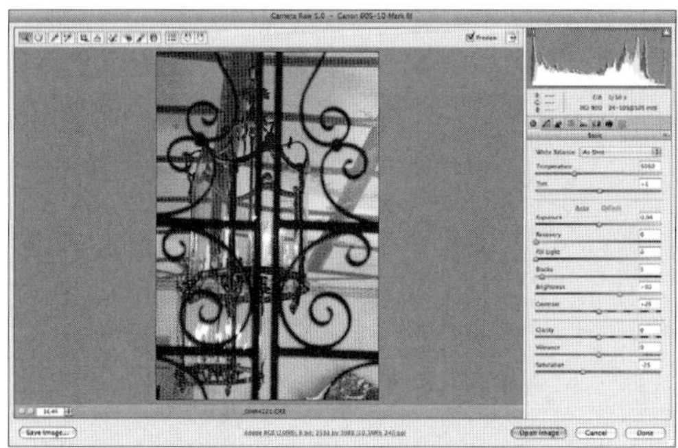

Figure 4.38 An image with a -25 saturation level.

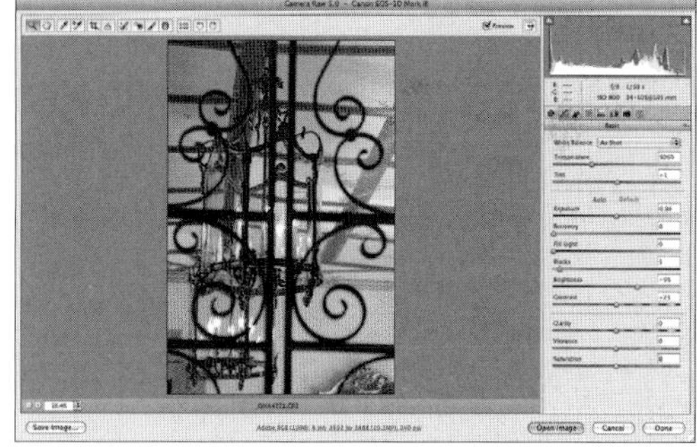

Figure 4.39 The image from Figure 4.38 with a 0 (default) saturation level.

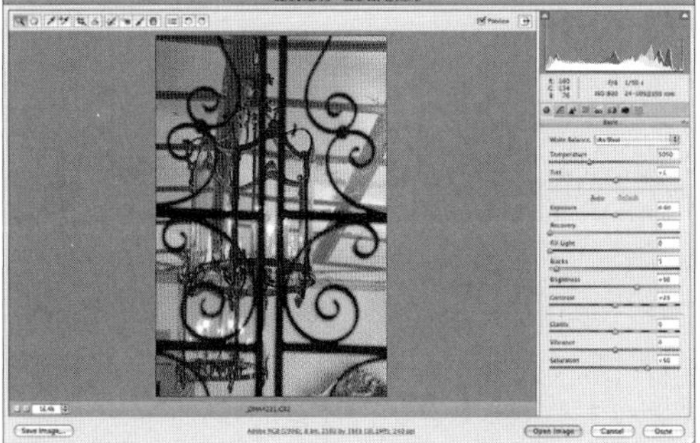

Figure 4.40 The image from Figure 4.38 set to +50 saturation.

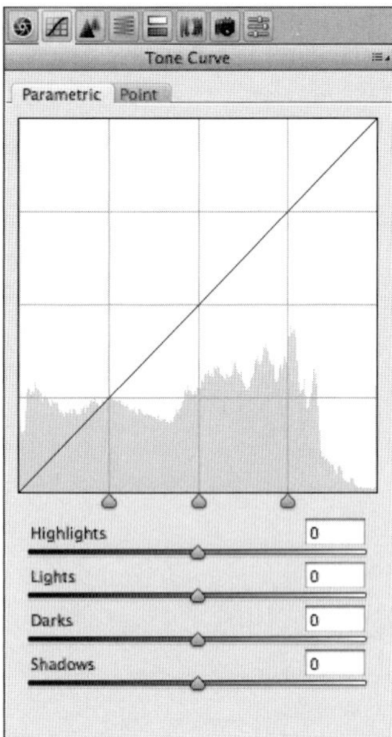

Figure 4.41 The Tone Curve tab allows you to make tonal adjustments to an image.

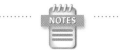

If you want a better idea of how the White Balance setting is affecting the colors of an image, you can temporarily pump up the saturation of the image with this slider. Then, once you like the overall color of the image, bring the Saturation slider back to zero.

Tone Curve Tab

The Tone Curve tab (**Figure 4.41**) works much like the Curves dialog covered in Chapter 3. The Tone Curve tab is divided into two sub-tabs: Parametric and Point, with Parametric mode as the default. Point mode is more like a normal Curves interface, so let's look at that one first.

Like the normal Curves dialog, the Tone Curve shows a histogram with an editable curve laid over it. By default, the curve includes some points that are intended to provide a medium contrast adjustment. The Tone Curve has four preset curves that you can select.

In Photoshop, you simply click the image, which causes a circle to appear on the curve. The circle indicates the area of the curve that will affect the brightness level on which you're clicking. In the Camera Raw dialog, you have to hold down the Command/Ctrl key and hover the mouse pointer over the image (without pressing the mouse button) to see the circle appear. If you click the mouse while holding down Command/Ctrl, a dot will be added where the circle appeared.

The Point and Parametric curves are not different representations of the same tone curve; they're individual curves, and you can apply both of them at the same time. Sometimes, you may find that one interface is easier for adjusting one part of the image, and the other is easier for adjusting another part of the image.

Two things to note about the Point curve: When you add a point to the curve and move it up or down, you won't see its effects until you release the mouse button; the tone curve is much more sensitive than the Photoshop Curves dialog. You'll most likely find that your curve adjustments are *very* small.

The Parametric curve provides a very different way of working, one that combines the power of Curves with the ease of a Levels adjustment. The Parametric tab has the same curve/histogram display, but beneath it are four sliders—Highlights, Lights, Darks, and Shadows. As you slide these sliders, the appropriate part of the curve will automatically bend and reshape to affect just the tonal range specified by the slider (**Figure 4.42**).

For further refinement, you can adjust the three sliders shown at the bottom of the curve display. These change the midpoint of each of the slider ranges. For example, use the bottom sliders to specify how much adjustment you want, and then use the sliders directly beneath the curve graph to fine-tune that adjustment to a very specific part of the curve (**Figure 4.43**).

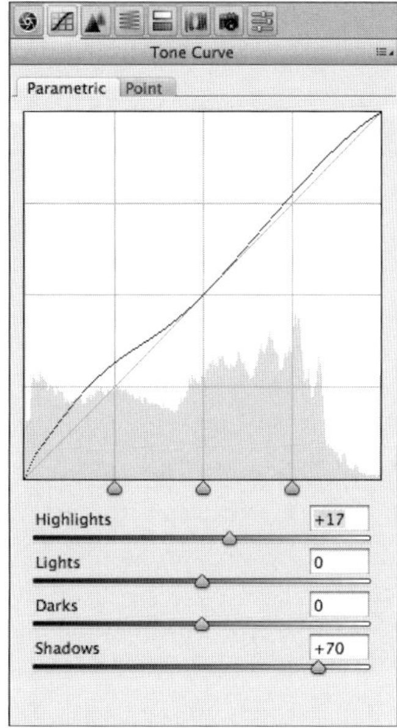

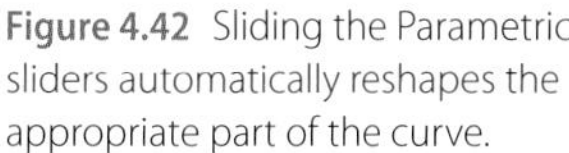
Figure 4.42 Sliding the Parametric sliders automatically reshapes the appropriate part of the curve.

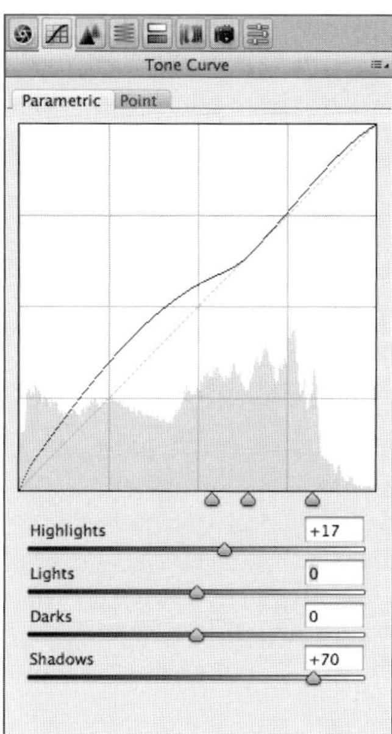

Figure 4.43 Sliding the sliders directly beneath the curve lets you adjust the midpoint of each Parametric slider.

After using the Tone Curve tab for some time, you'll probably feel that it's not as intuitive as the one built into Photoshop. You might miss the ability to use Curves combined with some of the more sophisticated features in Photoshop (adjustment layers, blending modes, layer masks, and so on), which is what really makes Curves powerful and gives you the ability to make much more precise and effective adjustments (see Chapter 3 for information on Curves, Chapter 5 for more on adjustment layers). For those reasons, you may only use the Point curve in Camera Raw when you plan on saving the image directly out of the Camera Raw dialog or when images will be used with the automated features found under the Tools menu in Adobe Bridge. For all other purposes, try to use the Curves dialog within Photoshop.

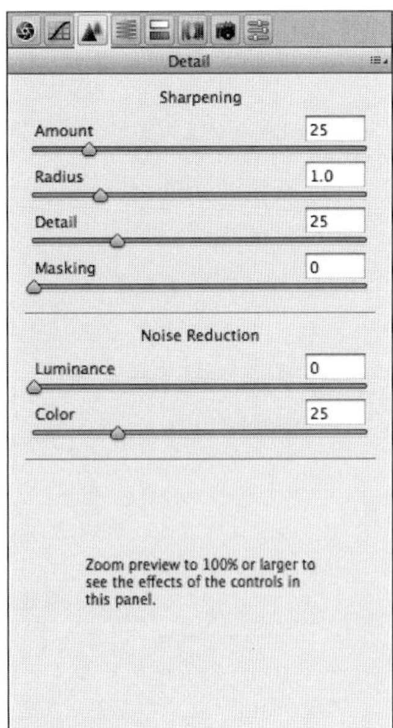

Figure 4.44 The Camera Raw Detail tab.

Detail Tab

Digital cameras often produce images that look a bit soft and can contain tiny specks of noise that are distracting. The Detail tab (**Figure 4.44**) is where you can deal with these problems and hopefully produce a sharp and noise-free image. These settings make rather subtle changes, so it's best to work with them when you're viewing the image at 100% magnification.

Sharpening

Many photographers prefer to sharpen their images as the final step before printing. Ideally, you should sharpen an image after it has been scaled down to its final size. The sharpening defaults are not set to zero, so you might want to adjust the sharpening within the Camera Raw dialog as part of your workflow.

If you're in a hurry or feeling just plain lazy, there are merits to using the Sharpening sliders. Camera Raw 5.0 has six sliders (Amount, Radius, Detail, Masking, Luminance, and Color), allowing for a great deal more control over sharpening than with previous versions. With the added controls, it might be useful to save combinations of these sliders as presets for specific image types such as portraits or landscapes. (We'll talk about the Camera Raw Presets tab later in this chapter.) In some cases, moving the sliders doesn't appear to do anything to an image. That usually happens when you're zoomed out to see the entire image. Before you start to sharpen an image, double-click the Zoom tool in the upper-left corner of the Camera Raw dialog. That will get you to 100% view, where you'll be able to see exactly what the Sharpening sliders are doing. When you're done sharpening, you can double-click the Hand tool to get back to the view that shows the entire image. I won't say much about sharpening here because Chapter 6, "Sharpening," dedicates an entire chapter to the subject.

Noise Reduction

Digital image noise comes in two flavors: *luminance* and *chrominance*, or color. The Luminance slider is designed to reduce the noise that shows up when you use high ISO settings with your digital camera. Luminance won't deal with those colorful specks you see on occasion (that's handled by Color Noise Reduction, discussed next), but it should be able to handle the dark specks that you get when you try to brighten an image that was shot in low lighting conditions. All you need to do is zoom to 100% view (double-click the Zoom tool to get there), and then experiment with the slider until the noise is minimized. Just be sure to look at the fine detail in the image to make sure that you haven't removed important detail such as freckles or skin texture.

The Color Noise Reduction slider attempts to blend in any colorful specks that appear on the image, by making them look similar to the colors that surround them. These colorful specks are often the result of shooting with high ISO settings on your digital camera. As with luminance reduction, start at 100% view and move the slider just high enough to blend the multicolored specks into your image.

Be careful with the Luminance and Color Noise Reduction sliders. Both will soften the image, which is why they're grouped in this tab with the Sharpening sliders. Be sure to toggle the Preview check box at the top of the image off and on to make sure that it's worth applying these settings. Sometimes it's better to have a noisy image that still has detail and sharpness than one with no noise that looks overly soft. Also, remember that you can always sharpen an image after you open it in Photoshop, which means that it doesn't have to remain as soft as it might appear after you apply noise reduction.

If you plan to sharpen your images in Photoshop, choose Preferences from the side menu in the upper-right corner of the Detail tab and change the Apply Sharpening pop-up menu setting to Preview Images Only. When you do that, the sharpness setting will apply only to the onscreen image preview, and no sharpening will be applied when you open the image in Photoshop.

Each HSL / Grayscale tab includes a Default link that resets the sliders for that particular tab. If you want to reset all three tabs, click each Default link individually.

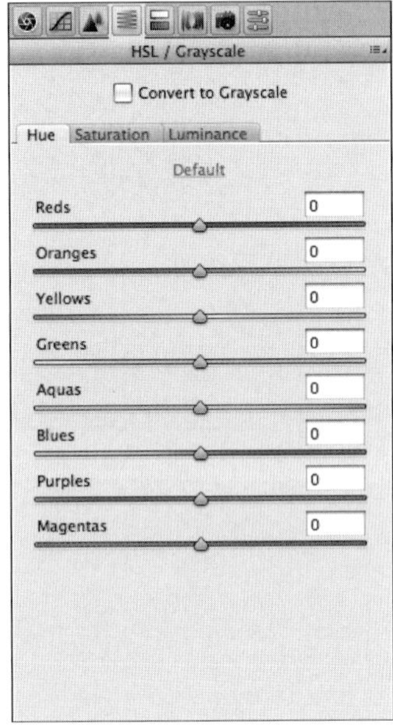

Figure 4.45 By using the sliders in the Hue tab, you can shift the hues of specific color ranges in an image.

HSL / Grayscale Tab

Sometimes you may need to make color shifts and adjustments to specific parts of the color range. For these times, Camera Raw provides the options on the HSL /Grayscale tab. Like many other additions to Camera Raw, the HSL /Grayscale control was purloined from Photoshop Lightroom.

The HSL control is divided into three tabs: Hue, Saturation, and Luminance. In each tab you'll find the same selection of color ranges: reds, oranges, yellows, greens, aquas, blues, purples, and magentas. One tab doesn't override another; you can make adjustments on each tab to create a cumulative correction. You'll probably need to switch from tab to tab to make your adjustments, however. If you increase luminance, for example, very often you'll have a different impression of the hue or saturation in your image.

Hue

In the Hue tab, you can adjust the hue of each color range simply by dragging the slider to the left or right (**Figure 4.45**). The Hue tab doesn't let you make huge swings in hue; you can't turn reds into blues, for example. For those extreme shifts, you'll need to use the hue controls in Photoshop. The Hue tab is for making slight adjustments to remove casts or slight corrections to particular color ranges. If the reds in an image are a little too orange, for example, slide the Reds slider to the left.

Saturation

The Saturation tab lets you adjust the saturation of each specific color range (**Figure 4.46**). You can adjust the saturation of just the red tones in the image, for example, by dragging the Reds slider back and forth. Slide to the left to desaturate a particular color range; slide right to increase the saturation.

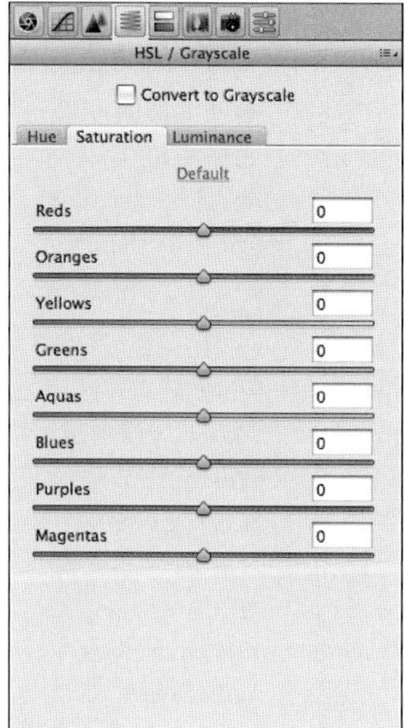

Figure 4.46 The Saturation tab's sliders let you increase or decrease the saturation of specific colors.

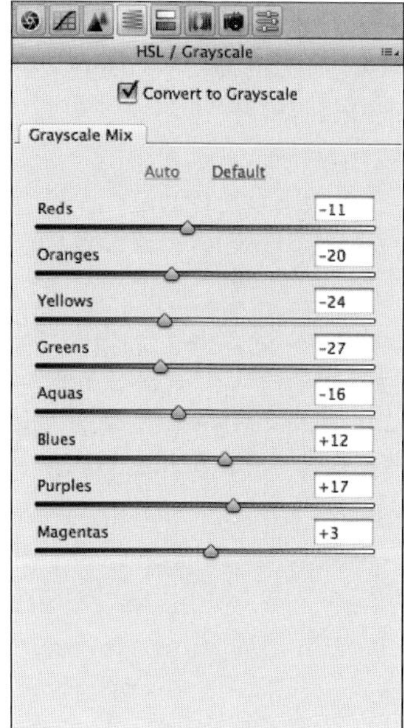

Figure 4.47 The Grayscale Mix sliders let you create custom grayscale conversions directly within Camera Raw.

Luminance

In the Luminance tab, you can adjust the luminance (brightness) of each color range. Sliding to the right brightens a color range; sliding to the left darkens colors.

Convert to Grayscale

Above the three tabs in the HSL / Grayscale tab is a Convert to Grayscale check box. If you select it, the three tabs disappear, replaced by a single Grayscale Mix tab (**Figure 4.47**). The image preview shows your new grayscale image, and the histogram changes to a single-channel histogram.

The color sliders work much like in Hue/Saturation/Luminance mode, but instead of altering hue they alter the shade of gray of those particular colors. So if you slide the Reds slider to the right, for example, any red tones in the image will get lighter.

By default, when you turn on the Convert to Grayscale check box, Camera Raw analyzes your images and calculates initial settings for the sliders. If you alter the sliders and want to go back to the initial conversion settings, click the Auto link. Clicking the Default link restores all sliders to their default positions. If you haven't changed them manually, all the default positions will be zero.

There's no image-quality advantage to be had by performing grayscale conversions in Camera Raw rather than in Photoshop (see Chapter 7). The advantage of grayscale conversion in Camera Raw is that, like all other Camera Raw adjustments, grayscale conversion is nondestructive, and you can batch-process it by using any of the normal batch-processing operations.

Remember that Camera Raw is a nondestructive editor. As you adjust settings, it constantly reprocesses your original raw camera data to present a new image onscreen. When you turn on the Convert to Grayscale check box in the HSL / Grayscale tab, the grayscale conversion is just another item added to the list of edits and adjustments that the software must make before it can show the final image onscreen. Even after you've told Camera Raw to convert the image to grayscale, you can continue to alter color and tone by using any of the program's controls (**Figure 4.48**).

Figure 4.48 After converting the image to grayscale, you can use the Grayscale Mix sliders to change the gray value of specific tones in the image. Shifting the Blues slider, for example, pulls out detail in the railings.

You're effectively changing the color of the image "underneath" the grayscale conversion. When you convert to grayscale, Camera Raw uses the original color values to determine a resulting grayscale value. So if you alter the color values by using any of Camera Raw's color-editing tools, the resulting gray values will change. This is yet another way that you can alter the gray values in your final image.

Split Toning Tab

Split toning allows you to apply separate toning to the shadows and highlights in your image. For each area, you can select different hue and saturation settings. Split toning works with either grayscale or color images, but you'll probably use it most often on grayscale pictures.

It doesn't matter whether you tone highlights or shadows first. For this example, start with the highlights. First, slide the Highlights Saturation to around 50 (**Figure 4.49**), goosing saturation because it can be difficult to see the effects of a hue choice when saturation is at zero.

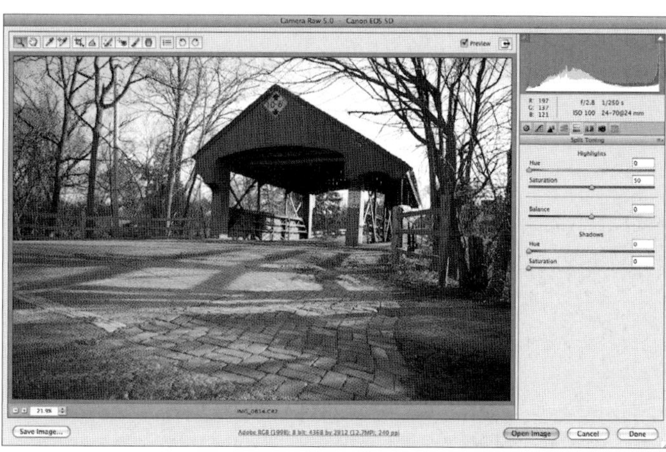

Figure 4.49 Begin your split-toning operation by increasing the Saturation setting in the Highlights section of the Split Toning tab. (©2008 Dan Ablan.)

Next, use the Hue slider to choose the hue you want for toning, and slide the Saturation slider down to something reasonable (**Figure 4.50**). Then perform the same steps using the Shadows sliders, to produce the image shown in **Figure 4.51**.

Figure 4.50 After setting the Hue slider, set the Saturation slider back to something more reasonable.

Figure 4.51 Perform the same operation on the shadow tones in your image to complete the split toning.

The Balance slider lets you shift the highlights toning more into the shadow areas, and vice versa. This option allows you to have more or less of either type of tone.

Split toning can be applied to color images or to images on which you're performing a black-and-white conversion. As explained earlier, when you're converting to black-and-white, changes to color affect the final gray tones that Camera Raw produces. So performing a split-toning operation on an image that has a grayscale conversion applied will alter the final gray tones that Camera Raw generates.

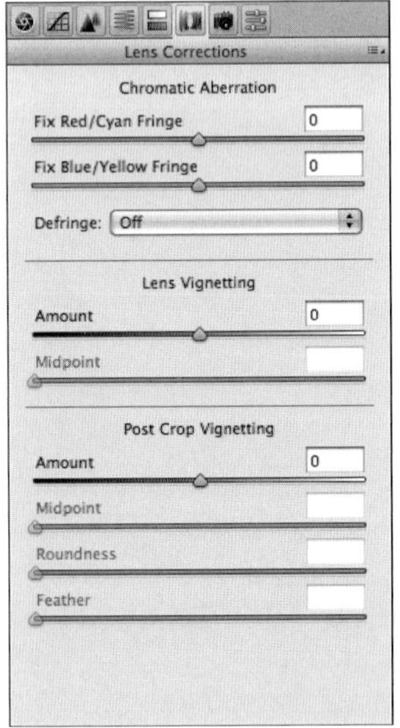

Figure 4.52 The Camera Raw Lens Corrections tab.

Lens Corrections Tab

The Lens Corrections settings are completely optional (**Figure 4.52**). You may prefer to use them only when you notice specific problems with an image. These problems are often a result of the lens that was used to shoot the images.

Some lenses—particularly wide-angle lenses—focus different wavelengths of light at different points. When that happens, you can end up with a halo of color on the edges of high-contrast lines in your image. This is called *chromatic aberration.* You might need a very fine eye to see the particular problem, but the higher the contrast between objects, the more obvious it will be. What you'll see is a shift in color around edges, or fringes within the image. This problem can happen with any lens, and chromatic aberrations are often what separate an inexpensive lens from a pricier one.

If you notice a halo of red on one side of an object and cyan on the opposite side, try moving the Fix Red/Cyan Fringe slider back and forth to see if you can reduce the halos (**Figures 4.53** and **4.54**). If you see blue and yellow halos, adjust the Fix Blue/Yellow Fringe slider instead. You might need to adjust both of the sliders, depending on what colors you're seeing on the edges of objects. Because these sliders are performing a very simple operation—scaling the colors that make up your image—they can't always get rid of this type of problem.

Figure 4.53 Looking very closely at an image, you can see bands of color pulling away from the subject. This is called *chromatic aberration*.

Figure 4.54 Camera Raw's Chromatic Aberration settings remove unwanted halos of color.

When you have images with specular highlights (such as the surface of a windy lake on a sunny day), you'll often encounter some degree of *fringing*, which is purple, red, or magenta color surrounding the hot specular highlights. The new Defringe pop-up menu in the Lens Corrections tab will help to reduce this negative effect. There are three options: Off, Highlight Edge, and All Edges. Selecting the Highlight Edge option removes most of the color additions, but there may still be a degree of fringing. Setting to All Edges removes the majority of the fringe effects, but it can negatively affect color saturation in areas where the defringing is occurring, so you'll have to decide whether this adjustment is useful on an image-by-image basis. As with sharpening and noise reduction, you really only see the effect at 100% zoom or higher.

The Vignetting sliders are designed to compensate for light falloff on the edge of an image. *Vignetting* is a photography term referring to lighter centers with darker edges. If you notice that the outer edges of an image are darker than the middle, move the Lens Vignetting Amount slider to the right until the brightness of the edge looks more like the middle of the image. Once you've done that, you'll need to adjust the Lens Vignetting Midpoint setting to control how far the brightening effect of the last slider encroaches on the center of the image. Just move it until the formerly dark edges blend into the rest of the image.

You can also use these sliders to add vignetting to your image (**Figures 4.55** and **4.56**), which will effectively darken the corners and edges of the image. Photographers often like that effect because it draws the viewer's attention toward the center of the image. You can add to the effect by lowering the Saturation and Contrast sliders under the Basic tab to simulate the look of an old, faded photo (**Figure 4.57**).

Figure 4.55 The original image is okay, but could be better.

Figure 4.56 With vignetting applied, the viewer's eye is pulled toward the center of the image.

Figure 4.57 Adjusting the saturation and contrast help give the photo a unique look.

Camera Raw 5.0 also offers the ability to set a vignette after you've cropped an image. With the Post Crop Vignetting sliders, you can set the Amount and Midpoint, as with the lens vignette, but you can also set Roundness and Feather values. You don't have to crop your image to use these tools. Sometimes they can give you a more interesting look than the standard vignetting does.

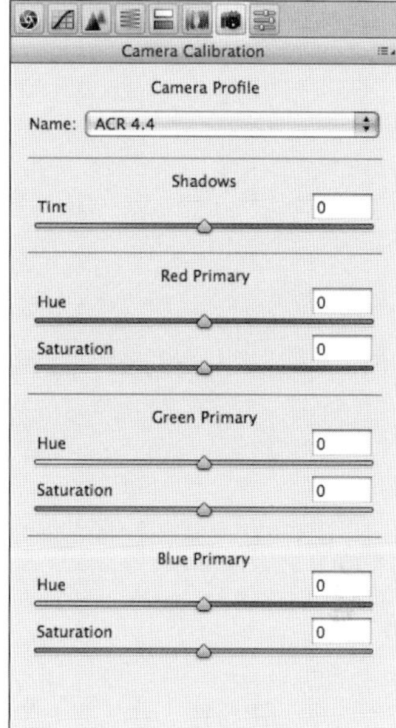

Figure 4.58 These settings allow you to change how Photoshop interprets the colors in an image.

Camera Calibration Tab

The sliders in the Camera Calibration tab (**Figure 4.58**) allow you to change the way Photoshop interprets the color information that your camera delivers. You can use these settings to simulate different film types and to compensate for problems that come with certain digital cameras.

Certain models of digital cameras produce images that have an annoying color cast in the darkest areas of an image (**Figure 4.59**). If you have one of those cameras, just about every image you open will have a cast in the shadows of the image. The Tint slider in the Shadows section allows you to shift the color of the darkest areas of the image toward green or magenta (**Figure 4.60**).

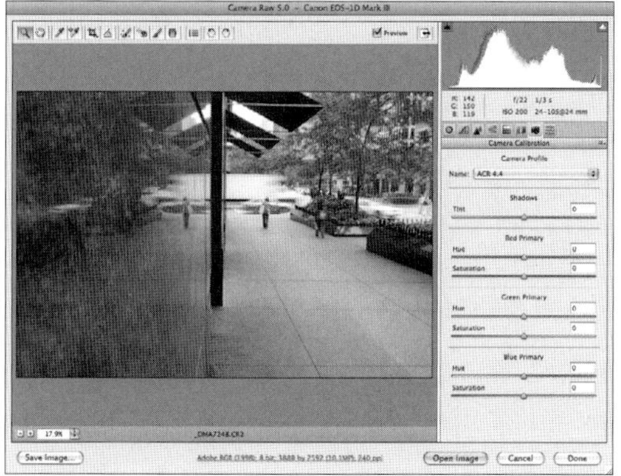

Figure 4.59 In the original image, the marble has a green tint.

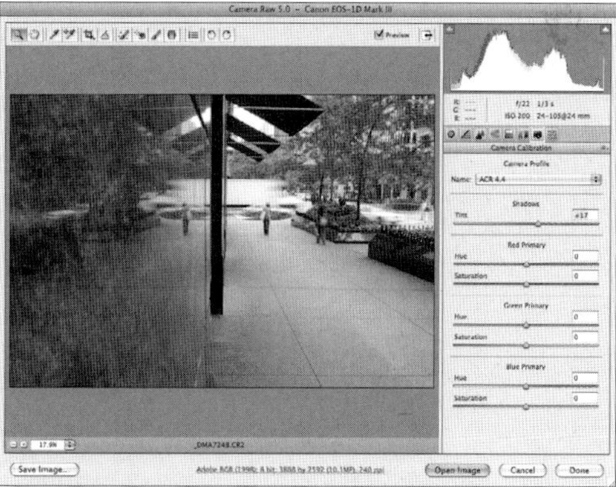

Figure 4.60 Adjusting the Shadows Tint slider helps remove unwanted color.

If you're not happy with the color in your digital camera's images, experiment with the Red Primary, Green Primary, and Blue Primary Hue and Saturation sliders. These sliders can also be used to simulate different film types (**Figures 4.61** and **4.62**).

Figure 4.61 The original image.

Figure 4.62 The image from Figure 4.61, after experimenting with the RGB settings in the Camera Calibration tab.

The sliders won't change areas that are neutral gray. The Red Primary sliders mainly affect the appearance of reds in the image, affecting yellow and magenta areas to a lesser extent. The Green Primary sliders mainly affect the appearance of greens, affecting cyan and yellow areas to a lesser extent. The Blue Primary sliders mainly affect the appearance of blues, affecting magenta and cyan areas to a lesser extent.

Presets Tab

If you regularly make the same adjustments to your images—perhaps because your camera has certain characteristics that always need to be corrected in the same way—you might want to save your adjustments as a preset, so that you can easily apply it to images in the future. A *preset* is simply a saved set of Camera Raw parameters that you can assign to any image.

Figure 4.63 Create a new preset by clicking the New Preset button at the bottom of the Presets tab.

To save a preset in Camera Raw, configure the parameters the way that you want them, switch to the Presets tab, and click the New Preset button at the bottom of the panel (**Figure 4.63**). Next, configure the New Preset dialog by selecting any items you want to save in your preset. (If you want your preset to use any of Camera Raw's auto-adjustment features, for example, turn on the Apply Auto Tone Adjustments check box.) After selecting the desired settings, enter a name for your new preset in the Name field and click OK.

To apply a preset to a raw file, open the image in Camera Raw, switch to the Presets tab, and click the preset you want to apply. The image will be adjusted according to the settings saved in the selected preset.

Adjusting Multiple Images

To adjust multiple images in the Camera Raw dialog, select more than one image in Adobe Bridge. The images will appear as thumbnails down the left side of the Camera Raw dialog (**Figure 4.64**). You can click between the thumbnails to view and adjust each image individually, or use the same keys as in Bridge to select multiple thumbnails. When multiple thumbnails are selected, a blue border appears around the thumbnail that's currently being viewed, and any changes made to the sliders in Camera Raw will affect all the selected images.

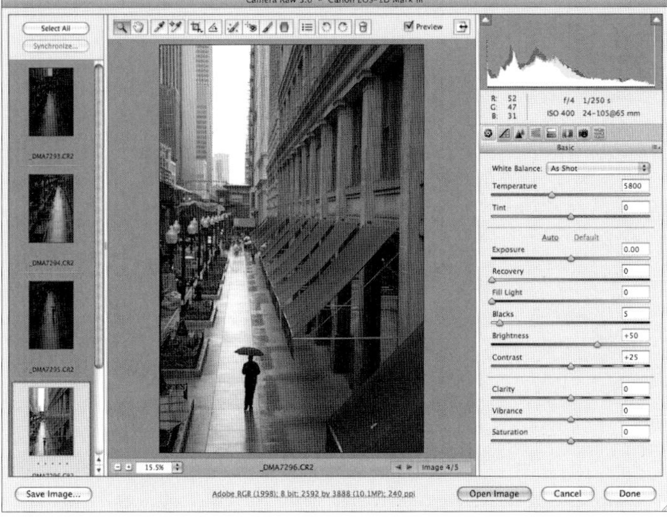

Figure 4.64 Multiple images appear as thumbnails in Camera Raw. (©2008 Dan Ablan.)

The Synchronize button above the thumbnail area presents a dialog that allows you to copy some of the settings from the image you're currently viewing and apply them to all the selected images.

Finishing Touches

Camera Raw never makes any changes to your actual raw file. In fact, it's not possible to make changes to a raw file, because it doesn't contain any finished image data. The adjustments that you make in Camera Raw are stored separately from your image data. What's great about this scheme is that you can go back at any time and change your Camera Raw settings, and then reprocess your raw file. In this way, you can derive lots of different corrections from the same file.

By default, Camera Raw stores your changes in *sidecar XMP files*. These are small text files that Camera Raw creates in the same directory as your original file. The advantage of sidecar files is that you can copy and move them along with the original raw file. The advantage of storing settings internally is that you don't have to keep track of extra data.

After you're done adjusting your settings, you need to decide what you want Camera Raw to do. At the bottom of the dialog are four buttons:

- **Done:** This button saves your settings (in either the internal database or as a sidecar XMP file, depending on your settings) and then closes the raw file.
- **Open Image:** This button does the same thing as the Done button, but also opens the image within Photoshop.
- **Cancel:** This button discards any adjustments applied to the images and closes the Camera Raw dialog.
- **Save Image:** This button saves your settings, and then saves the selected images in one of four file formats without leaving the Camera Raw dialog.

The Next Step

At first glance, the Camera Raw dialog may look like an unruly beast, but it usually takes only a few minutes to process an image once you're familiar with Camera Raw. On your next photographic adventure, even if it's just a Halloween party or a weekend get-together, shoot raw images and work through the options discussed in this chapter to create even better images.

CHAPTER

5

Adjustment Layers

"Insanity—a perfectly rational adjustment to an insane world."

—R.D. Laing

Adjustment Layers

Imagine being able to adjust the look of an original image without damaging or otherwise altering it. You can go back at any time and refine the adjustment—or remove it altogether and start over with another adjustment. Photoshop's *adjustment layers* make all of this possible. Combine adjustment layers with layer masks and blending modes, and you've got an unbeatable mixture that provides the cornerstone for working nondestructively. CS4 has made adjustment layers even easier to set up than in previous versions, thanks to the new Adjustments panel.

Adjustment layers can be used on the majority of images you'll handle. Consider this feature to be the key to working quickly, having absolute flexibility, and obtaining the highest possible quality.

Adjusting Methods

You can adjust a layer directly, or apply the adjustment through an adjustment layer. Let's look at the fundamental differences between these approaches.

Making Direct Adjustments

Figure 5.1 Choosing Image > Adjustments applies an adjustment directly to the active layer.

When you adjust a selected layer by choosing Image > Adjustments and making a selection from the submenu (**Figure 5.1**), the adjustment affects only the active layer, and the original state of the layer will be changed permanently once you save and close the document. Think of this approach as your "in a hurry and not too worried about changing it later" adjustment. Direct adjustments have two major downsides:

- If you need to isolate an area, you have to create a selection before applying the adjustment or use the History Brush after the adjustment is applied—but nothing can be done after the image has saved and closed.
- To alter the effects of a blending mode (more on this topic later in the chapter), you have to choose Edit > Fade (**Figure 5.2**) immediately after applying an adjustment—you cannot make such changes after using any other tools.

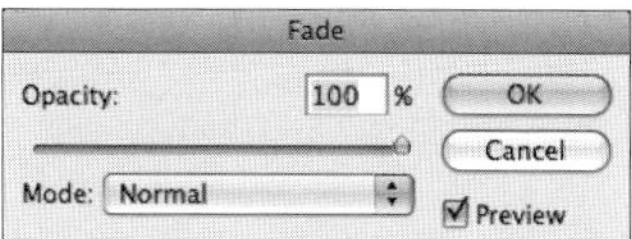

Figure 5.2 Choosing Edit > Fade immediately after adjusting a layer allows you to change the opacity and blending mode used to apply the adjustment.

There's really nothing wrong with adjusting an image directly, as long as you know what the image needs, don't want to do a lot of experimenting, and *don't make any mistakes*. If you choose to make direct adjustments, save your working image as a different file, preserving the original image. An image will not suffer in any way whatsoever by being adjusted directly. Having said that, however, we must move along on our mission to convince you that adjustment layers are by far the most efficient and nondestructive way to adjust images.

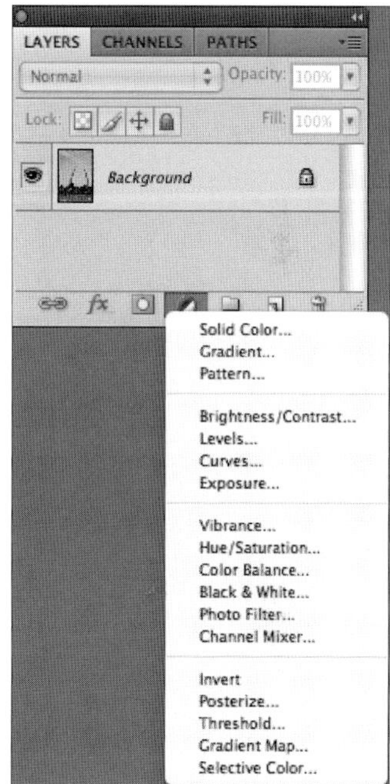

Figure 5.3 The Adjustment Layer pop-up menu at the bottom of the Layers panel.

Adding Adjustment Layers

To create an adjustment layer, you can use either of two methods:

- Choose Layer > New Adjustment Layer and then select any of the available adjustments (Levels, Curves, Hue/Saturation, and so on).
- Click the Adjustment Layer icon at the bottom of the Layers panel and choose an adjustment from the pop-up menu (**Figure 5.3**).

Once you've selected your adjustment, it will appear as a separate layer in the Layers panel (**Figure 5.4**). Think of it as if you're standing at the top of the Layers panel looking down; the adjustment layers are like filters that you attach to the lens of a camera. Anything you see through that adjustment layer (filter) will be affected by the adjustment, whereas layers that appear above the adjustment layer will not be affected (**Figures 5.5** to **5.7**).

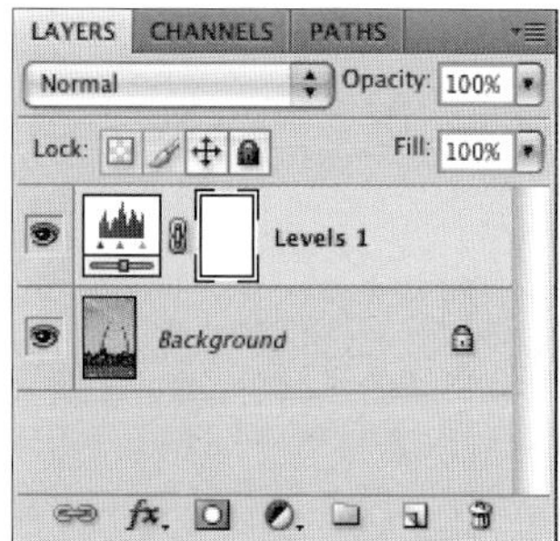

Figure 5.4 The top layer here is an adjustment layer.

Figure 5.5 The original image is made from a total of four layers.

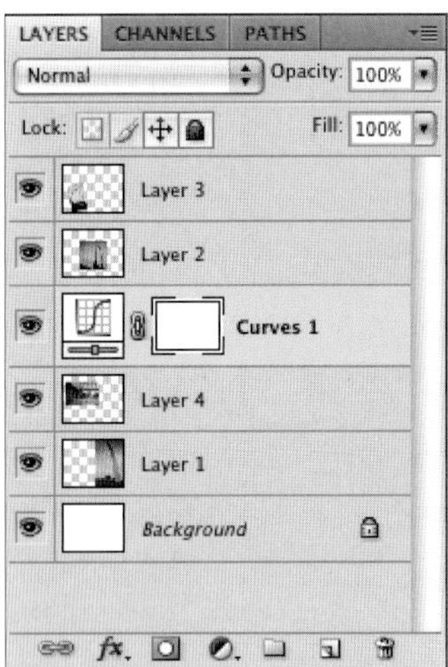

Figure 5.6 Adding an adjustment layer. (See the next section for an explanation of those icons on the adjustment layer.)

Figure 5.7 Only the layers under the adjustment layers are affected by the adjustment.

You can have only one adjustment per layer. If you want to combine adjustments, change the blending modes between them. Alternatively, you can simply open the Layer menu and choose Merge Visible for the selected adjustment layers.

If setting the Opacity to 100% doesn't produce a strong enough effect, try duplicating the adjustment layer, which will often double the effect of the adjustment (depending on the type of adjustment being applied).

The adjustment is in its own layer, isolated from the underlying image, allowing you to retain the unmodified original. At any time, you can simply turn off the eyeball icon on the adjustment layer, and the image will return to its unmodified state. In Figure 5.7, we've tinted the image by emphasizing the green color channel on the Curves adjustment layer.

To lessen the effect of the adjustment layer, lower its Opacity setting at the top of the Layers panel. Since the adjustment hasn't been applied to the image permanently, you can also double-click the adjustment layer icon at the left side of the adjustment layer to modify the adjustment settings.

Many other features can be added to the adjustment layer to limit which layers are affected by the adjustment, control which areas of the document are affected, or change how the adjustment interacts with the underlying layers. The rest of this chapter covers those topics.

Adjustment layers are much more useful than direct adjustments because the image can be saved (in formats that support layers) and then reopened in the future for more editing of the adjustment(s). Adjustments made through adjustment layers only become permanent when you merge them into the underlying image or save the image in a file format that doesn't support layers.

Adjustment Layer Features

Let's take a look at the accessories that are attached to an adjustment layer (**Figure 5.8**). After an adjustment layer is added to the Layers panel, the eyeball icon determines whether the adjustment layer is currently affecting the appearance of the image. To its right is another icon that represents the type of adjustment being applied. Simply double-click that adjustment layer icon to edit that adjustment. To the right of the adjustment layer icon is a link symbol, which really doesn't apply to adjustment layers. And to the right of that is a layer mask that allows you to limit where the adjustment will affect the underlying image. Photoshop automatically names each new adjustment layer with the selected adjustment, such as Curves. However, you can right-click the added layer, choose Layer Properties, and rename it to something more specific. Conversely, you can double-click the default layer name, which makes that name editable directly in the layer itself.

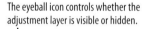

NOTES

A generic Adjustment Layer icon (which looks like a half-black and half-white circle) replaces the thumbnails in the Layers panel when the layers are too small to allow room for the full-sized versions. This can happen when the document is much wider than it is tall. You can also right-click any layer icon and choose a larger thumbnail size from the contextual menu to see the specific icon for a given layer adjustment, regardless of the document's orientation. You'll always see the generic adjustment layer icon when the No Thumbnails setting is selected.

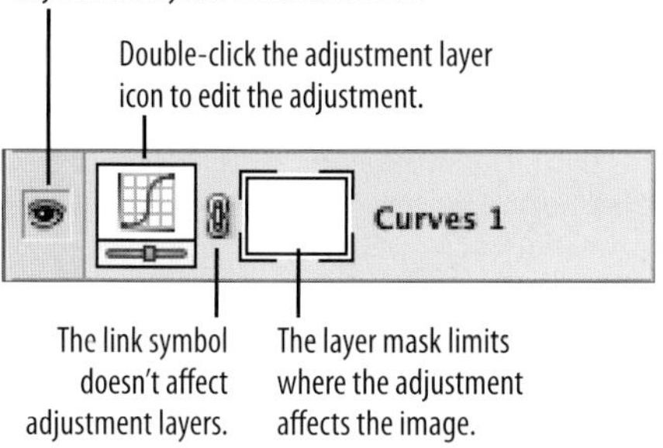
The eyeball icon controls whether the adjustment layer is visible or hidden.
Double-click the adjustment layer icon to edit the adjustment.
Curves 1
The link symbol doesn't affect adjustment layers.
The layer mask limits where the adjustment affects the image.

Figure 5.8 An adjustment layer looks like this in the Layers panel.

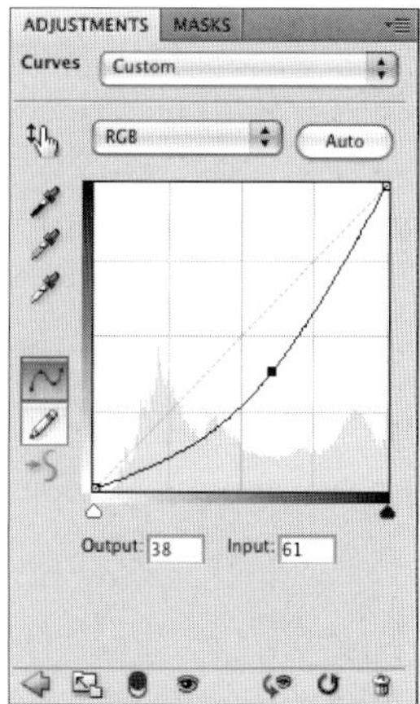
ADJUSTMENTS
MASKS
Curves
Custom
RGB
Auto
Output: 38
Input: 61

Figure 5.9 You can control an adjustment layer with the Adjustments panel.

When you add an adjustment layer in Photoshop CS4, you can control it through the new Adjustments panel (**Figure 5.9**). The Adjustments panel is a default panel in the Essentials workspace. This panel allows you to modify the adjustment settings being applied to the image; for instance, if you have selected a Curves adjustment layer, the Adjustments panel displays a smaller representation of the Curves dialog that you get by choosing Image > Adjustments.

With the Adjustments panel open (**Figure 5.10**), you can choose any one of the adjustment options. Clicking one of the icons adds that adjustment on an adjustment layer in the Layers panel (**Figure 5.11**).

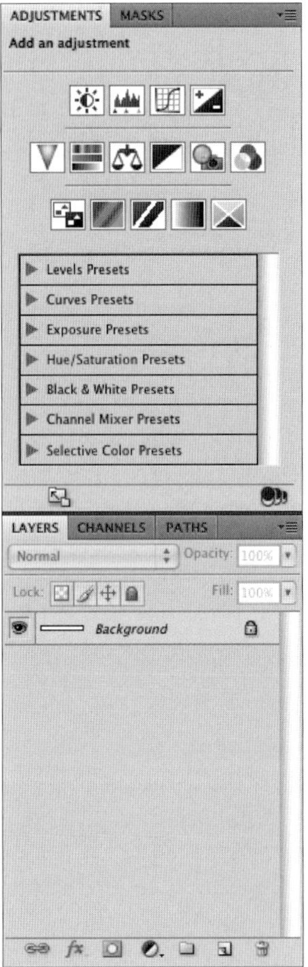

Figure 5.10 Add any of a multitude of adjustments with the Adjustments panel. (Hover your mouse pointer over the icons to see what each one does.)

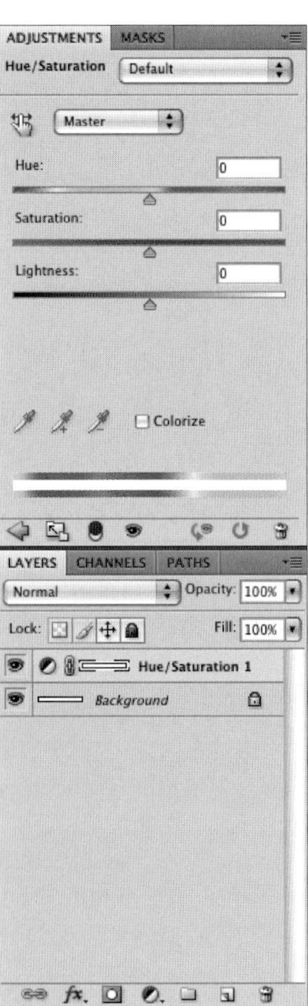

Figure 5.11 Here we've added a Hue/Saturation adjustment.

Stacking Order

When you have more than one adjustment layer on an image, the stacking order of the layers determines the order in which the adjustments are applied. Adjustment layers are applied from bottom to top, with the lowest adjustment applied first. You should always have the topmost adjustment layer active when creating a new adjustment layer, because new adjustment layers are always added directly above whichever layer is active. Try to maintain the original stacking order, always adding new adjustments to the top of the stack—adding an adjustment layer between two others, or changing the stacking order of the layers, can cause unpredictable changes to the overall look of an image.

Before-and-After Views

If your document contains multiple adjustment layers, and you want to view the original, unadjusted image, you'll have to hide all the adjustment layers by clicking their eyeball icons. To see the result of your adjustments, make the adjustment layers visible by clicking the eyeball icons again.

All that eyeball clicking makes it difficult to get a quick before-and-after view of an image. To solve this problem, hold down Option/Alt and click the eyeball icon for the Background layer (or whichever layer contains the original image). That action hides all the layers except the one you've clicked. Just repeat the process to toggle all the hidden layers back into view.

Copying Adjustment Layers to Other Documents

It's rather common for more than one photograph to needs the same type of adjustment; a set of photos might have similar subject matter and similar lighting, for example. When that's the case, you can adjust one of the documents using adjustment layers and then drag those adjustment layers on top of the second document (**Figures 5.12** and **5.13**). Select as many adjustment layers as needed and drag from either the main document window or the Layers panel. Just be aware that those layers will be deposited *above* whichever layer is active in the destination document, which can cause some unexpected results if the destination document already contains adjustment layers and the topmost layer is not active.

Figure 5.12 The image on the right has multiple adjustment layers.

Figure 5.13 Dragging the adjustment layers from the image on the right to the one on the left instantly applies those values to the new image.

Now that you have an idea of how adjustment layers operate, let's explore a simple type of adjustment so you'll have something to try as you move through the rest of this chapter.

Figure 5.14 The Photo Filter icon in the Adjustments panel.

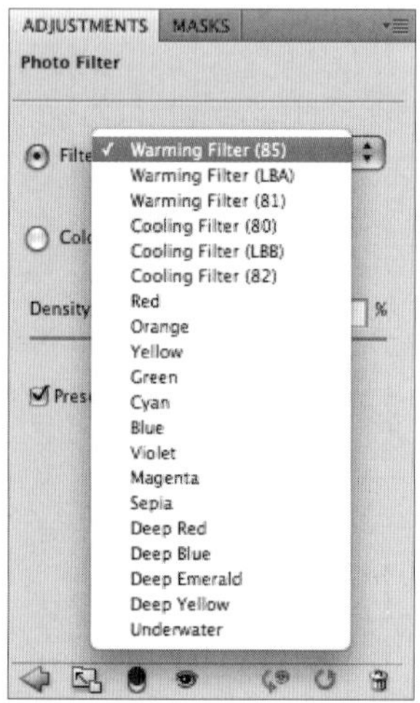

Figure 5.15 The Photo Filter adjustment has a number of presets you can use.

Sample Adjustment: Photo Filter

Let's create a special type of adjustment to give you some practice at applying adjustment layers to your own images. A photo filter adjustment layer allows you to shift the overall color in an image. The effect is much like placing a colored filter in front of a camera lens or putting on colored sunglasses. If you were on a photo shoot, say with Joe McNally, and he yelled out to you, "Grab a CTO," you'd promptly bring him a color temperature orange filter. A photo filter adjustment layer is similar to this effect (without Joe, of course).

Let's give it a try. Open an image and choose Photo Filter from the Adjustments panel (**Figure 5.14**). As soon as the new adjustment layer is selected, its control options appear. Choose a preset color from the Filter pop-up menu (**Figure 5.15**) or click the Color swatch to choose your own custom color. Then adjust the Density setting to control how radically the filter will affect the image (**Figures 5.16** to **5.18**).

Figure 5.16 The original image. (©2008 Dan Ablan.)

Figure 5.17 The photo filter adjustment with a Cooling Filter preset and 100% density.

Figure 5.18 The photo filter adjustment with a Warming Filter preset and 56% density.

If the image is getting too dark as you increase the Density setting, the Preserve Luminosity check box probably is turned off. In that case, adding a photo filter adjustment darkens the image, just as colored sunglasses allow less light to enter your eye. Turning on the Preserve Luminosity check box prevents Photoshop from changing the brightness of the image but still allows you to shift its colors. Keep Preserve Luminosity turned on for most of your images. Make a separate adjustment layer (Levels, Curves, or some other type) if you want to change the brightness of the image.

Since you probably haven't read Chapter 7, "Setting Up Images for Final Output," here's an advance peek into color adjustments in Photoshop: When you use a photo filter adjustment layer, you're pushing all the colors in the image toward one side of the color wheel. If the image has an obvious color cast, all of the colors within the image will be shifted to one side of the color wheel. When that's the case, you may be able to remove the color cast by applying a photo filter that uses the color directly across the color wheel from the color that's contaminating the image (**Figures 5.19** and **5.20**).

Figure 5.19 The original image is okay, but might be a little too warm due to white balance settings in the camera. The circled area on the color wheel represents the color case within the image. (©2008 Dan Ablan.)

Figure 5.20 A blue photo filter adjustment layer shifts the color opposite and away from the green.

Now let's start to explore the more powerful aspects of adjustment layers.

Blending Modes

The Blending Mode pop-up menu in the upper-left corner of the Layers panel determines how the active layer will interact with the underlying image. This menu can be especially useful when applying adjustment layers, since it allows you to limit how much those layers affect the image.

Three main blending modes are handy when using adjustment layers:

- **Hue blending mode** allows an adjustment to change the basic color of the underlying image while preventing the adjustment from changing the brightness or contrast of the underlying image (also known as *tonality*), or how colorful the image is (also known as *saturation*). You would primarily use this mode when you want to adjust the overall color of an image without adding color to areas that are neutral gray (**Figures 5.21** and **5.22**). It can also be useful when you notice that a color adjustment is making an image too colorful or is mellowing the color too much.

Figure 5.21 A Hue/Saturation adjustment layer overcompensates the color in the image with a Normal blending mode.

Figure 5.22 Changing the blending mode to Hue keeps the adjustment layer from affecting areas that are neutral gray.

- **Color blending mode** allows an adjustment to affect both the hue (basic color) and saturation (amount of color) of the underlying image, while preventing the adjustment from changing the tonality of the

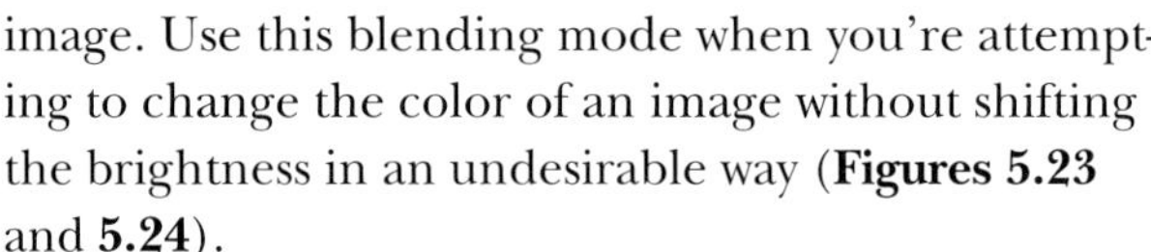
image. Use this blending mode when you're attempting to change the color of an image without shifting the brightness in an undesirable way (**Figures 5.23** and **5.24**).

- **Luminosity blending mode** limits an adjustment so that it can only affect the brightness and contrast of the underlying image, while preventing the adjustment from changing the color of the image. This mode is useful when you want to adjust the brightness of the image without shifting the color or making the image too colorful—a frequent consequence of darkening an image (**Figure 5.25**).

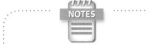

Later in this chapter, you'll see how the Normal and Pass Through settings in the Blending Mode pop-up menu can be used to affect a group of adjustment layers.

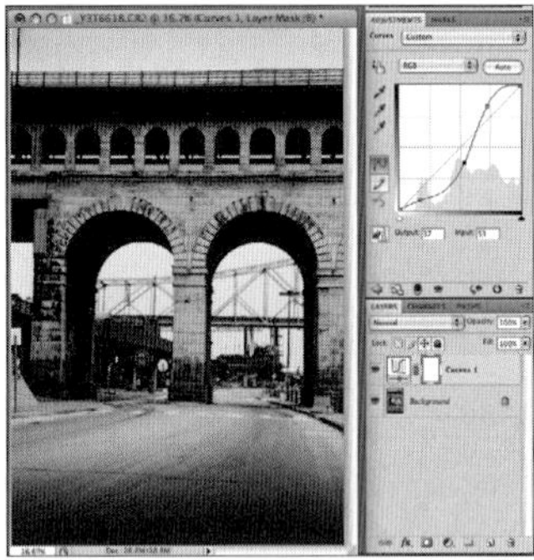

Figure 5.23 A Curves adjustment layer added to an image, with the blending mode set to Normal. (©2008 Dan Ablan.)

Figure 5.24 The image from Figure 5.23, with the adjustment layer's blending mode set to Color.

Figure 5.25 The image and curve adjustment from Figure 5.23, with blending mode set to Luminosity.

Using the pop-up Blending Mode menu at the top of the Layers panel isn't always the most ideal method for changing the blending mode of an adjustment layer, because it's only available after an adjustment has been applied. If you'd like to choose a blending mode before applying an adjustment, hold down Option/Alt when choosing an adjustment type from the Adjustment Layer pop-up menu at the bottom of the Layers panel, or from the Adjustments panel. That action opens the New Layer dialog, which includes a Mode pop-up menu where you can specify the blending mode you want for the adjustment layer you're creating (**Figure 5.26**).

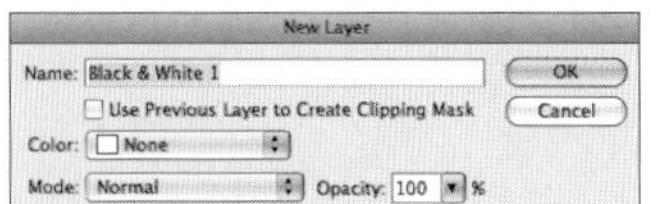

Figure 5.26 Holding down Option/Alt when adding an adjustment layer opens the New Layer dialog, which offers a blending mode choice.

Empty Adjustment Layers

Adjustment layers and blending modes can be an effective combination when applying the enhancement techniques described in Chapter 9, "Enhancements and Masking." Adjustment layers can be used anytime that you would usually duplicate a layer and change its blending mode. As an alternative, you can use a blending mode that's often referred to as an "empty adjustment layer." To do this, create a new adjustment layer, but don't change any of the settings in the Adjustments panel (so the new adjustment doesn't change the appearance of the image). This technique works because Photoshop acts as if the adjustment layer contains the result of the adjustment being applied. Since an empty adjustment doesn't change the image, it's considered to be identical to the underlying image.

Figure 5.27 You can create an adjustment layer without any actual adjustments, using it to apply a blending mode.

The advantage of using an empty adjustment layer versus duplicating a layer is that any future retouching applied to the underlying image will automatically be reflected in the empty adjustment layer (**Figures 5.27** and **5.28**)—it won't affect a duplicate layer.

Figure 5.28 The same result as in Figure 5.27, using a duplicate image layer rather than an adjustment layer.

Limiting Adjustments

Adjustment layers wouldn't be so wonderful if they always affected the entire image. To get adjustment layers to strut their stuff, combine them with layer masks, which allow you to limit which areas of the image will be affected by each adjustment layer. Let's look at all the ways in which we can work with layer masks and adjustment layers.

Layer Masks

By default, each adjustment layer comes equipped with a layer mask. This mask appears to the right of the Adjustment icon. If no selection is present when the adjustment layer was created, the layer mask will be entirely white. In a layer mask, all white causes the adjustment to affect the entire image. Black, on the other hand, prevents the adjustment from affecting areas. To control where an adjustment layer can affect an image, paint with black or

Figure 5.29 A layer mask allows you to apply an adjustment in certain areas. Here, our model is turned into a lovely orange alien, except for her eyes, which have been masked out.

white while the adjustment layer is active (**Figure 5.29**). The black and white paint will appear within the Layer Mask thumbnail image in the Layers panel.

Painting with black causes the image to revert to its unadjusted state. Keep in mind that painting with black won't always cause drastic changes to the image. If the difference between the original and the adjusted versions of the image is subtle, painting with black will cause very subtle changes to the image.

If you get sloppy and paint with black over too large an area, you can switch to painting with white, effectively undoing your painting (since the layer mask started out filled with white, and white areas allow the adjustment to apply to the image).

You're not limited to using the painting tools to modify a layer mask. Any tool that works on a grayscale image can be used to edit the layer mask. For example, you may like to use the Gradient tool to create very gradual transitions (**Figures 5.30** and **5.31**), and occasionally apply filters to a mask to generate an interesting transition or to pull back in areas that didn't need adjustment.

Figure 5.30 A Curves adjustment layer was added to enhance the trees in this photo of New York's Central Park, but in doing so, sky detail has been lost.

Figure 5.31 Using a black-to-white gradient mask, you gradually block out the effects of the Curves adjustment layer, revealing the original sky.

Working with Selections

If a selection is active at the time an adjustment layer is created, the unselected areas will be filled with black in the resulting layer mask, preventing the adjustment from affecting those areas. This approach confuses many users, because the "marching ants" that indicate the edge of a selection suddenly disappear when an adjustment layer is created. That happens because the selection has been converted into a layer mask (**Figures 5.32** and **5.33**).

TIP

Use the masking techniques described in Chapter 9 to create a selection, and then use that selection to limit which area of an image is affected by an adjustment layer.

Figure 5.32 Once you've made a selection in an image, you can apply an adjustment to just that selection.

Figure 5.33 Apply an adjustment layer to your selection, and the layer mask is created for you automatically.

Using Quick Mask Mode

If painting on a layer mask is more convenient for you than creating selections, but you'd prefer to isolate an area before applying an adjustment, try this technique: Before adjusting the image, press Q to enter Quick Mask mode (which will not change the look of the image unless you happen to have a selection active). Paint with black over the areas you don't want to be affected by the adjustment you plan to make. The areas you paint over with black will show up as a red overlay on the image (**Figure 5.34**). If you accidentally cause the red overlay to appear on an area that should be adjusted, paint with white to remove the red overlay. Once the red overlay is covering all the areas that shouldn't be adjusted, press Q again to convert the Quick Mask into a selection. With that selection active, create an adjustment layer. The areas that appeared as red in Quick Mask mode will be black in the layer mask attached to the newly created adjustment layer, which will prevent the adjustment from affecting those areas (**Figure 5.35**).

Figure 5.34 Painting in Quick Mask mode. (©2008 Dan Ablan.)

Figure 5.35 When the adjustment is applied, the Quick Mask selection is not affected.

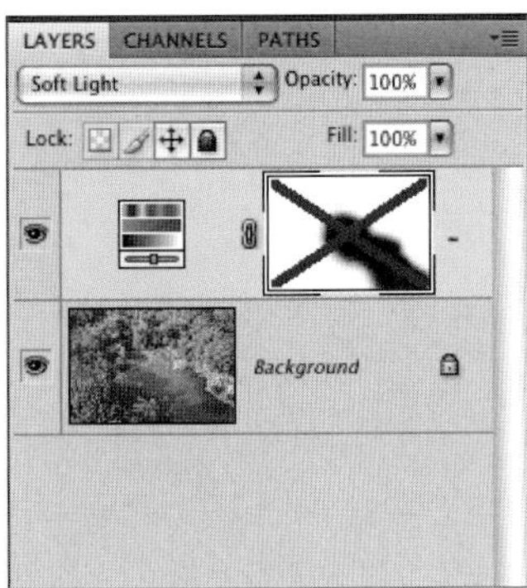

Figure 5.36 The red X over the Layer Mask thumbnail indicates that the layer mask currently isn't affecting the adjustment.

Disabling the Layer Mask

To see how an image would look if the layer mask wasn't limiting an adjustment, Shift-click the Layer Mask thumbnail to disable the mask. A red X will appear over the thumbnail to indicate that the layer mask has been disabled temporarily (**Figure 5.36**). When you're done viewing the image in that way, Shift-click the Layer Mask thumbnail a second time to turn it back on.

Viewing the Layer Mask Directly

When you paint on a layer mask, the resulting paint usually appears only in the tiny Layer Mask thumbnail image in the Layers panel, where it may be difficult to see what you're doing. To view the contents of the layer mask as a full-sized image, hold down Option/Alt and click the Layer Mask thumbnail in the Layers panel (**Figure 5.37**). You can modify the layer mask while viewing it directly, or use this view to inspect the results of painting on the Layer Mask thumbnail and to clean up unexpected problems (such as gaps between paint strokes). If you created a selection using an automated selection technique (for example, Color Range or the Background Eraser), you might notice some noise in the layer mask. In that case, try using the noise reduction techniques covered in Chapter 6, "Sharpening" to rid the mask of the noise. When you're done editing the layer mask in this view, hold down Option/Alt and click the Layer Mask thumbnail again.

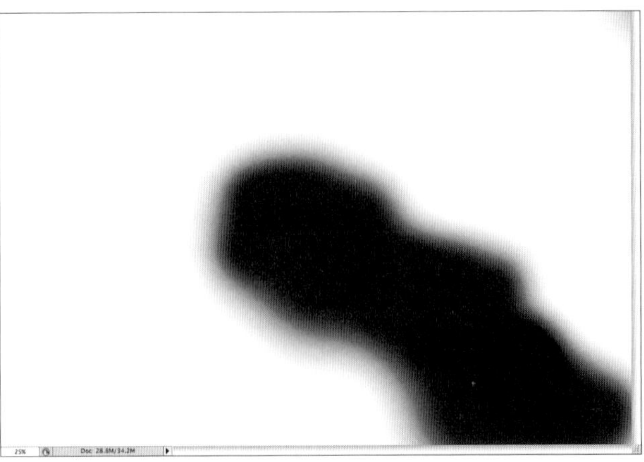

Figure 5.37 Hold down the Option/Alt key and click the Layer Mask thumbnail to see the layer mask at full size for easier masking.

Viewing the Layer Mask as a Color Overlay

You can view the contents of a layer mask as a color overlay on the image by pressing the backslash (\) key when an adjustment layer is active. (This works much like Quick Mask mode, as discussed earlier in this chapter.) Use the color overlay to see how closely your painting matches the subject of the photograph (**Figure 5.38**) and to touch up the results by painting with black or white. When you're done using this view, press the backslash (\) key a second time to turn off the color overlay. You can also modify the color being used for the overlay by double-clicking the Layer Mask thumbnail in the Layers panel (**Figure 5.39**).

Figure 5.38 Viewing the layer mask as a color overlay. (©2008 Dan Ablan.)

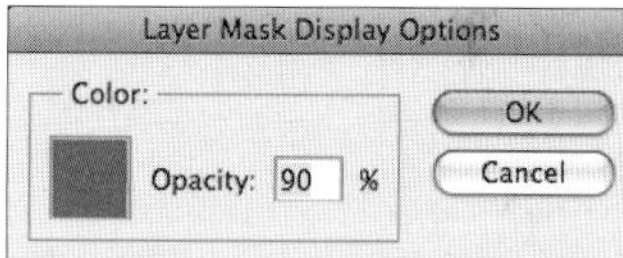

Figure 5.39 Double-clicking the Layer Mask thumbnail opens the Layer Mask Display Options dialog, in which you can specify the overlay color.

Moving or Copying the Layer Mask to Another Layer

To drag a layer mask from one layer to another, all you have to do is click in the middle of the Layer Mask thumbnail, drag the layer mask, and release the mouse button after moving the mouse onto the target layer. If you'd rather copy the layer mask instead of moving it, hold down the Option/Alt key when dragging the layer mask.

Masking Multiple Adjustment Layers

To apply multiple adjustment layers to a particular area of an image, select those adjustment layers, choose

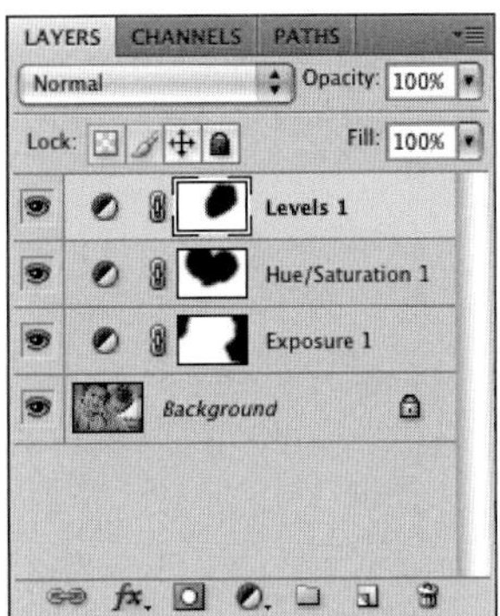

Figure 5.40 Select the layers you want to group.

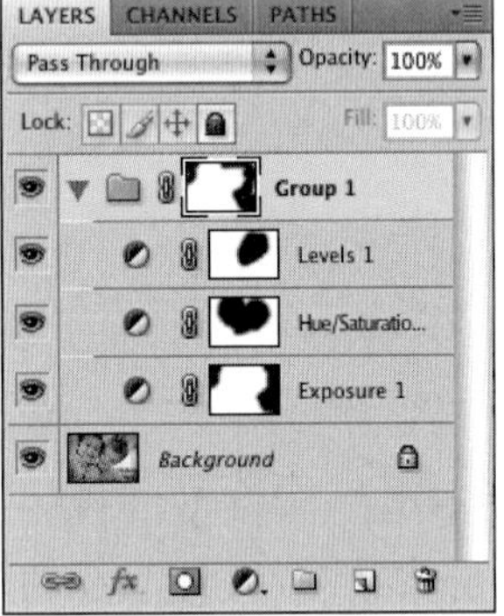

Figure 5.41 Add a layer mask to the group to mask all the layers within the group.

Layer > Group Layers, and then click the Layer Mask icon at the bottom of the Layers panel to add a layer mask to the group (**Figures 5.40** and **5.41**). Any changes made to the layer mask that's attached to the group will affect all the adjustment layers within the group. You can even paint on the layer mask attached to each adjustment layer, to further limit where it can affect the image.

Limiting the Affected Brightness Range

To limit the brightness range that an adjustment layer is able to affect, double-click to the right of the adjustment layer's name and adjust the blending sliders at the bottom of the Layer Style dialog (**Figure 5.42**).

The sliders under the This Layer heading analyze the result of the adjustment being applied and allow you to hide the dark (left slider) or bright (right slider) portions of that result so that you can see the underlying image (which is usually the original photograph). The sliders under the Underlying Layer slider cause the dark (left slider) or bright (right slider) portions of the original image to show through and therefore prevent the adjustment from affecting those areas. You can hold down Option/Alt and drag any of the sliders to split it into two halves, which will produce a gradual transition between the area that's being hidden and the rest of the image (for a more detailed explanation of the blending sliders, see Chapter 9).

Figure 5.42 To limit brightness affected by an adjustment layer, adjust the blending sliders in the Layer Style dialog.

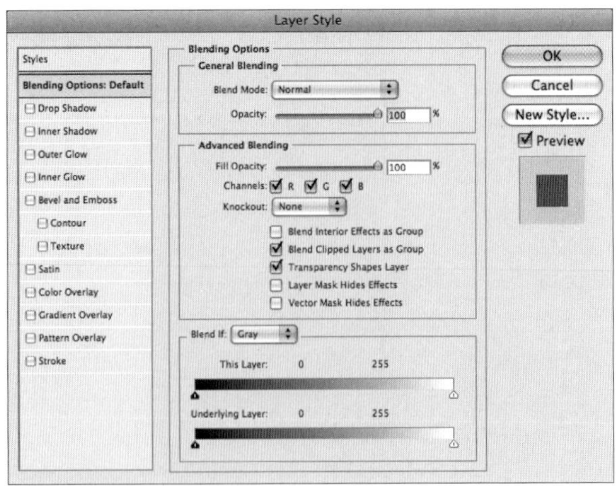

Blending sliders are particularly useful when darkening or adding contrast to part of an image using a Levels or Curves adjustment layer. Sometimes certain areas of an image change too much as you make an adjustment. By using the blending sliders to let only parts of the underlying image show through, you can prevent the adjustment from affecting the entire image.

You can also use blending sliders when colorizing an image. Create a Hue/Saturation adjustment layer (**Figure 5.43**) and turn on the Colorize check box to add some color. Then double-click just to the right of the adjustment layer's name to open the Layer Style dialog. Drag the white value of the Underlying Layer slider to the left, allowing the green of the underlying image to blend through the adjustment layer, and effectively limiting the effect of the colorized adjustment layer. (Split the sliders rather widely apart to ensure a smooth transition.) This trick is what usually separates realistic-looking images from fake-looking ones, because not much color shows up in the darkest areas of most color photographs (**Figure 5.44**).

Figure 5.43 The original image, with an adjustment layer added.

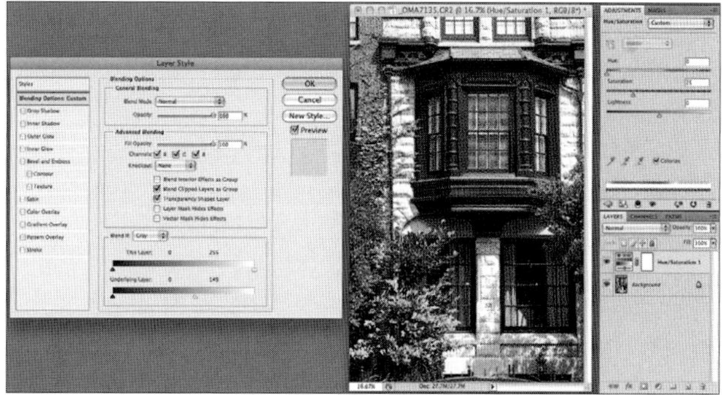

Figure 5.44 The result of using the blending sliders to limit how much color from the adjustment layer is applied.

Limiting the Layers Affected by an Adjustment Layer

The techniques we've talked about up until now work great when you're working with single image documents. When you graduate to more complex collages that contain a multitude of images and many layers, you'll have to supplement those techniques with ones that allow you to control the number of layers affected by an adjustment.

Adjusting a Single Layer

You can limit an adjustment layer to affecting a single layer by creating a clipping mask. To try this technique, create a new adjustment layer and hold down the Option/Alt key when choosing an adjustment either from the Adjustment Layer pop-up menu at the bottom of the Layers panel, or from the Adjustments panel. When the New Layer dialog appears, turn on the Use Previous Layer to Create Clipping Mask check box. A small down arrow appears in the adjustment layer, indicating that the adjustment layer applies only to the underlying layer (**Figures 5.45** and **5.46**).

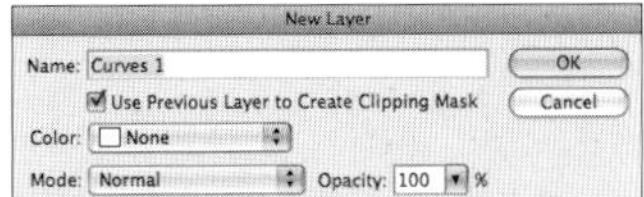

Figure 5.45 Create an adjustment layer while holding down the Option/Alt key; then choose Use Previous Layer to Create Clipping Mask.

To clip more than one adjustment layer to a single layer, hold down the Option/Alt key and click the horizontal line that separates the adjustment layers from the layer you want to adjust. When using this technique, start from the bottom adjustment layer and work your way up to the top adjustment layer that you want to apply to the image.

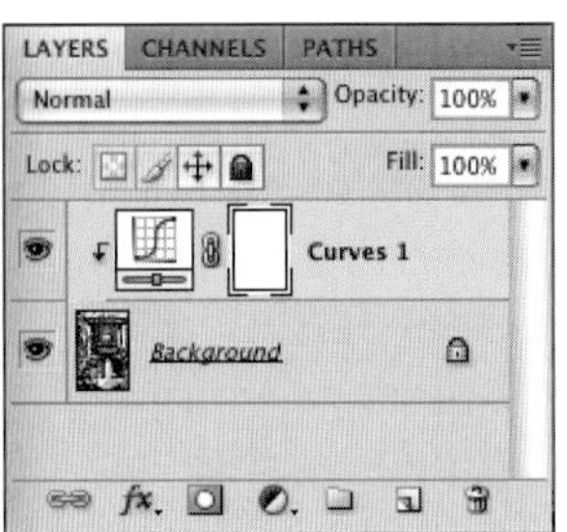

Figure 5.46 When the adjustment layer is added to the Layers panel, it's indented slightly and displays a down arrow pointing to the layer beneath.

To add a clipping mask to an existing adjustment layer, position the adjustment layer directly above the layer you want to affect, click the adjustment layer to select it, and choose Layer > Create Clipping Mask.

Adjusting a Limited Number of Layers

There are two methods for causing one or more adjustment layers to affect a limited number of layers:

- **Group the layers into a folder.** Start by selecting the adjustment layers and all the layers they should affect (**Figure 5.47**). To place those layers into a group, hold down Shift and click the Group icon (which looks like a folder) at the bottom of the Layers panel. Then click the newly created group and change the setting in the Blending Mode pop-up menu at the top of the Layers panel: Pass Through allows the adjustments to affect layers that are outside the group. Normal limits all adjustment layers and blending modes used within the group to affecting the layers within the group (**Figures 5.48** and **5.49**).

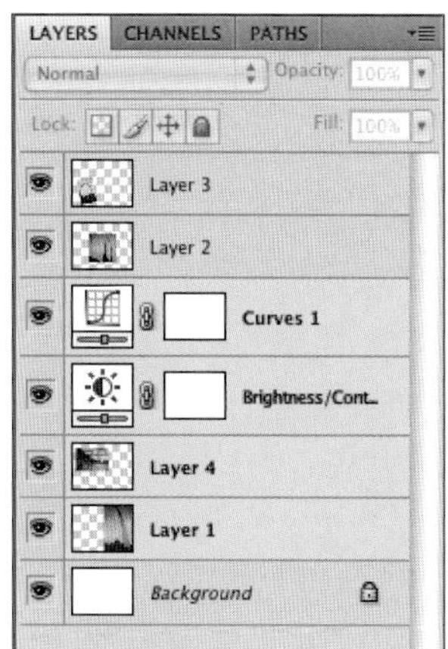

Figure 5.47 Select the image and adjustment layers you want to group.

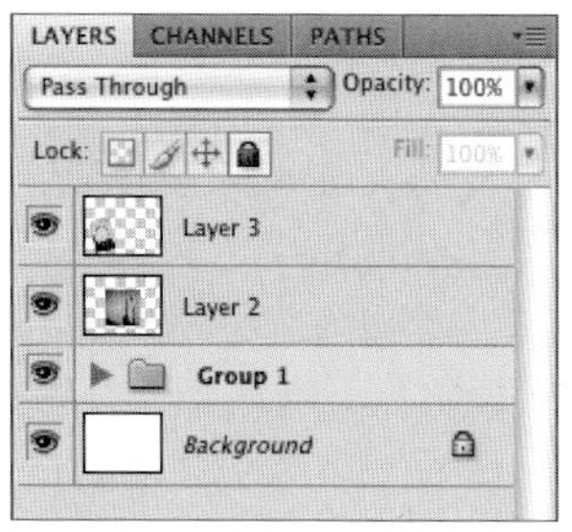

Figure 5.48 Change the blending mode to Pass Through.

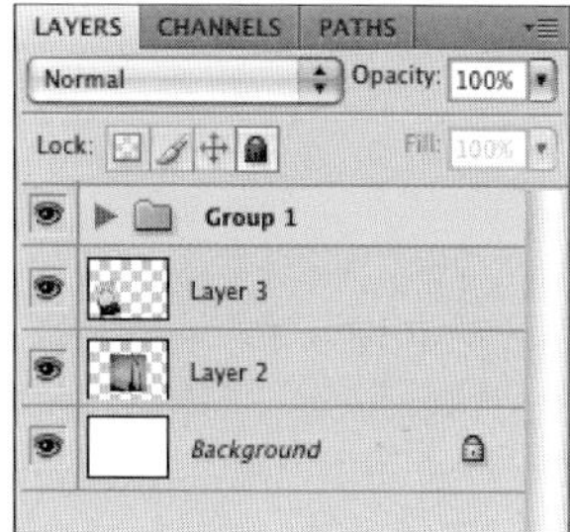

Figure 5.49 A group set to Normal blending mode. By moving the Group 1 layer to the top of the layers, you can really change the group effect.

- **Group the layers into a Smart Object.** Adjustment layers contained in a Smart Object cannot affect layers that appear outside of the Smart Object. As with the previous technique, start by selecting the adjustment layers and all the layers they should affect, but this time right-click in the Layers panel (somewhere away from the icons) and choose Convert to Smart Object, which causes all the selected layers to be encapsulated into a single Smart Object layer (**Figures 5.50** and **5.51**).

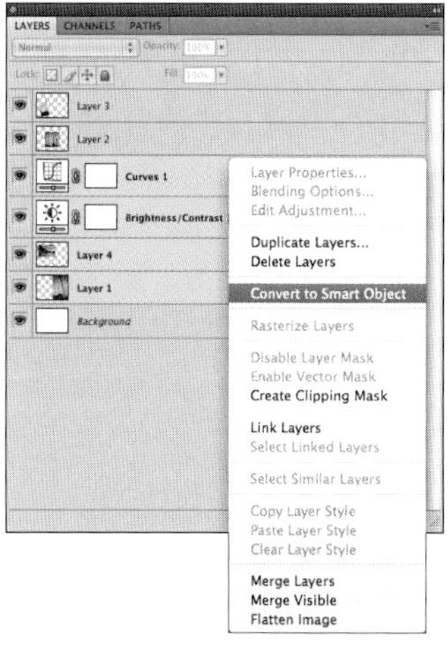

Figure 5.50 Select the image and adjustment layers; then right-click in the Layers panel and choose Convert to Smart Object.

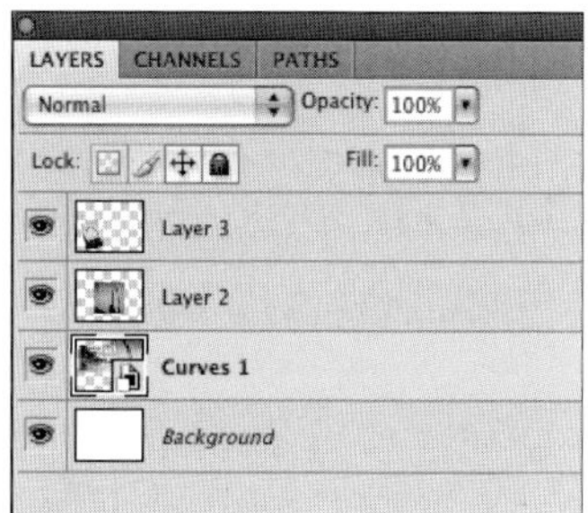

Figure 5.51 The converted Smart Object in the Layers panel.

Figure 5.52 This image contains bright and dark areas that are not part of the actual photograph. (©2008 Dan Ablan.)

To edit the contents of the Smart Object layer, double-click the Smart Object layer's thumbnail image in the Layers panel, which causes the encapsulated layer to appear as a separate layer. This is the preferred method when you plan to drag the affected layers into a more complex document, because it simplifies the Layers panel view of the image (which usually reduces confusion when working with complex documents). For more information on working with Smart Objects, check out Chapter 10, "Collage Effects."

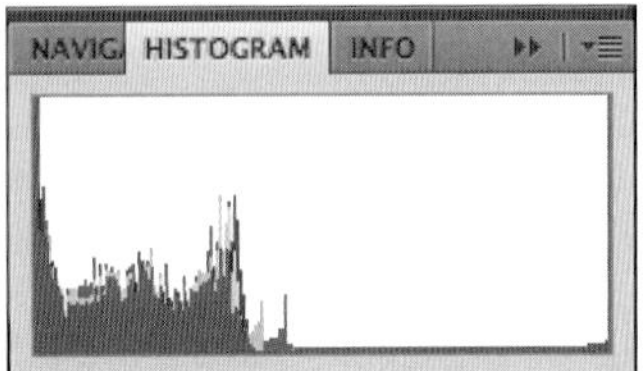

Figure 5.53 The histogram analyzes the entire image, including its border and background.

Histograms and Automatic Adjustments

When you work with images that contain large areas of white/black (like ones with fancy borders, as in **Figure 5.52**), the Histogram panel can be less than useful, because the histogram indicates that the image contains the full range of brightness levels (**Figure 5.53**)—even though the image itself (minus the border) might be rather low-contrast. To get around this problem, you'll need to take steps to limit what the histogram examines when analyzing the image. You need to optimize the contrast of the important areas of the image, without having to look at spikes at the ends of the histogram that reflect the large areas of black or white in the border area. You can also use this technique when you want to enhance the contrast of an image radically, while retaining detail only in the most important areas.

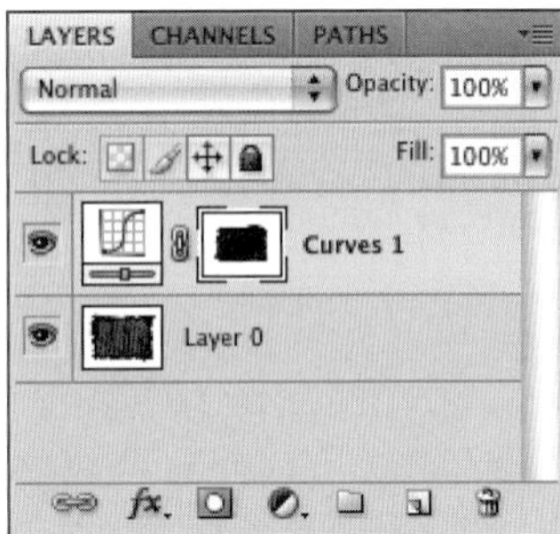

Figure 5.54 The Layers panel here includes an adjustment layer with a layer mask that's partially filled with black.

To limit the histogram, select the important areas of the image and then create a Curves adjustment layer by clicking the Curves icon in the Adjustments panel. When a selection is active, the histogram analyzes only the selected area, but the moment you create an adjustment layer, it analyzes the entire image again because the selection is converted into a layer mask. Now, look in the Layers panel (**Figure 5.54**) and Command/Ctrl-click the black-and-white Layer Mask thumbnail on the Curves adjustment layer you just created. That action brings your selection back and limits the area of the image that the histogram analyzes (**Figure 5.55**). Now you can go to the Adjustments panel and adjust away.

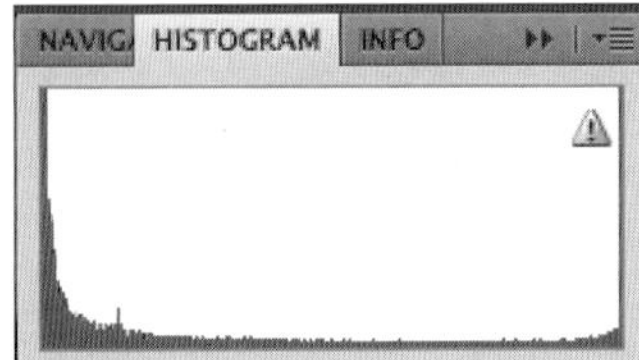

Figure 5.55 This histogram analyzes only the selected area of the image.

When you use this technique, the adjustment applies only to that same selected area (**Figure 5.56**). But don't worry—as long as you used an adjustment layer, you'll be able to force the adjustment to apply to the entire image. The layer mask that's attached to the adjustment layer should contain some black, limiting the areas of the image to which the adjustments apply. All you have to do to get the adjustment to apply to the entire image is choose Select > Deselect, press D to reset the foreground color, and then press Option-Delete (Mac) or Alt-Backspace (Windows) to fill the Layer Mask thumbnail on that layer with white. This trick adjusts the whole image (**Figure 5.57**); the histogram only looks at the selected area of the image—but in the end, the adjustment applies to the entire image. It sounds like a lot of steps, but a few times doing this procedure and it becomes second nature.

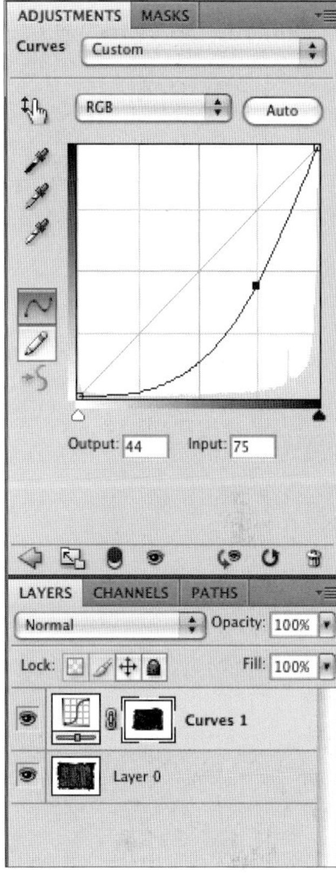

Figure 5.56 The adjustment is affecting only the selected areas.

Figure 5.57 After you fill the Layer Mask thumbnail with white, the adjustment affects the entire image.

When a layer mask is active, resetting the foreground and background colors changes the foreground color to white and the background color to black—the opposite of what you get if the layer mask isn't active.

Potential Problems

Working with adjustment layers is usually a trouble-free experience, but a few areas can cause unexpected problems:

- If you drag an image along with its adjustment layers to another document, the adjustment layers will affect the entire destination document. To prevent this problem, use the techniques mentioned earlier in this chapter (such as clipping masks) to limit which layers are affected by the adjustment layers before you drag them to the destination document.
- Be careful when changing the color mode of an image; for example, when changing RGB to CMYK. Certain adjustment layers won't make the transition, and others will produce different results. For that reason, it's best to flatten the image before changing the color mode.
- If you're working with 16-bit images in Photoshop, but you need to end up with an 8-bit version, flatten the image before making the conversion. If you retain the layers, they'll be recalculated using the 8-bit version of the image, which will cause you to lose any quality difference you would have had from working with a 16-bit image. Flattening the image will cause the adjustments to be applied to the full 16 bits of data, producing a higher-quality 8-bit result.
- Be careful when retouching an image that contains adjustment layers; otherwise, you might cause the adjustments to apply to the image twice. For more information about how to avoid this problem, check out the bonus video "Workflow" at www.danablan.com/photoshop.
- It's difficult to make radical adjustments to isolated areas without causing an obvious transition between the adjusted area and the surrounding image. This problem can often be remedied by placing an empty layer at the top of the layers stack and then retouching the transition area with the Healing Brush to blend both sides of the transition, creating a smooth blend.

Limitations of Adjustment Layers

One limitation of adjustment layers prevents certain adjustments from being available as an adjustment layer: An adjustment layer must be able to be fed a single pixel and figure out how it should be modified, without having to rely on the information contained in the surrounding image. The Match Color, Replace Color, Shadows/Highlights, Exposure, and Equalize adjustments must be able to compare the area being adjusted to the surrounding image (or a second image) to determine how to adjust the image, which prevents them from being used as adjustment layers.

Five adjustments are not found in the Adjustment Layer pop-up menu at the bottom of the Layers panel: Auto Levels, Auto Contrast, Auto Color, Desaturate, and Variables. These are really shortcuts for using adjustments in certain ways. You can use the following equivalents to get the same functionality in an adjustment layer. (Note that after the Curves or Levels adjustment layer is applied, you need to click the Adjustments panel side menu and choose Auto Options, or Option/Alt-click the Auto button, to see the Auto Levels, Auto Contrast, and Auto Color choices.)

- **Auto Levels** is the same as clicking the Options button in the Levels or Curves dialog and choosing Enhance Per Channel Contrast while leaving the other settings at their defaults.
- **Auto Contrast** is the same as clicking the Options button in the Levels or Curves dialog and choosing Enhance Monochromatic Contrast while leaving the other settings at their defaults.
- **Auto Color** is the same as clicking the Options button in the Levels or Curves dialog and choosing Find Dark & Light Colors while leaving the other settings at their defaults.
- **Desaturate** is the same as moving the Saturation slider in the Hue/Saturation dialog to -100.
- **Variations** is a visual interface for a combination of the Saturation slider in Hue/Saturation, the Brightness slider in Brightness/Contrast, and the choices available in the Color Balance dialog.

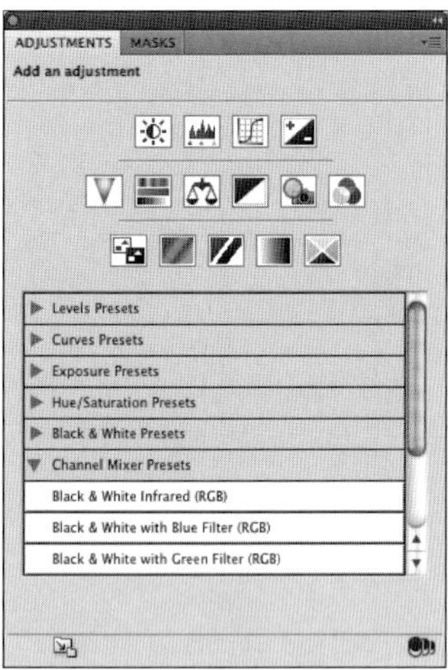

Figure 5.58 The Adjustments panel comes with a number of presets that allow you to add an adjustment layer in one click.

Final Notes on the Adjustments Panel

As you've seen, the new Adjustments panel in Photoshop CS4 makes it very easy to add an adjustment layer to an image quickly. But you can go one step further by using the various supplied presets. **Figure 5.58** shows the expanded Adjustments panel with the Channel Mixer Presets expanded. By simply clicking one of these presets, you add that preset to the Layers panel. You don't need to add an adjustment and then choose the preset—just click the preset and you're ready to go. A good way to work is to choose a preset to get you most of the way there, and then make minor modifications to suit that particular image.

At the very bottom of the Adjustments panel is a small icon (**Figure 5.59**) that allows you to toggle between two settings: New Adjustments Affect All Layers Below, and Clipping the New Layer. In most situations, as you've seen throughout this chapter, you don't need to use this option.

Figure 5.59 Use this icon in the Adjustments panel to clip a new layer.

The Next Step

I hope that this chapter not only has inspired you to use adjustment layers, but demystified them. If you commit to using adjustment layers, you'll soon wonder how you ever lived without them.

CHAPTER

6

Sharpening

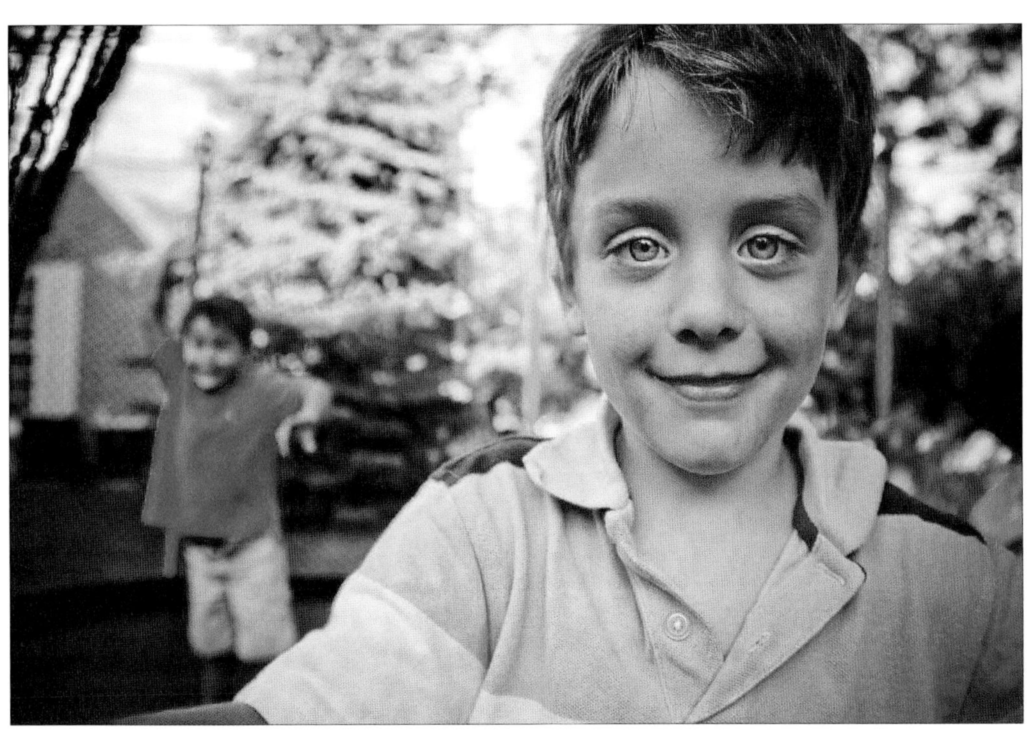

Obviously, you failed to detect the subtle diamond pattern in my tie.

—Niles Crane, on the TV show *Frasier*

Sharpening

Almost all digital images start life looking slightly soft. Too often, they're left that way when sent to the Web or to print. This chapter is about those very subtle details that can make the difference between a so-so image and one that pops off the page.

It's just a fact of life that all of our capture devices (digital cameras, scanners, and so on) can't deliver as much detail as the original image contained. (High-end drum scans are the one exception because they get sharpened during the scanning process.) Only images that are created from scratch in Photoshop or another program such as a 3D rendering application will be 100% sharp. Even those images can become soft if you attempt to make the image larger or smaller in Photoshop (known as *interpolating* the image). Finally, when you output the image to an inkjet printer, printing press, or other output device, you'll lose additional detail because most output devices simply are incapable of reproducing the amount of detail you see onscreen. By exaggerating the differences between areas (sharpening), we can attempt to compensate for all the factors that can make an image look soft.

Figure 6.1 An image out of the camera is okay, but could benefit from Photoshop's sharpening tools. (©2008 Dan Ablan.)

Figure 6.2 The image from Figure 6.1—what a difference sharpening makes!

After you learn how to sharpen images properly, they'll look much crisper when you print them, and will be an obvious improvement over unsharpened scans (**Figures 6.1** and **6.2**). But no matter how much sharpening you apply to an image, it won't compensate for an out-of-focus original, so try to stick with images that aren't overly blurry.

Removing Film Grain and Scanner/Camera Noise

Sharpening an image will exaggerate almost all the detail in the image, so any film grain will also be exaggerated (**Figures 6.3** and **6.4**). That's fine if you want an image with pronounced grain, but if you prefer a smoother look, check out the techniques in this section for removing grain from images. As we get into this topic, much of the time we'll refer to film grain as *noise*.

Figure 6.3 An old black-and-white image scanned from a 35 mm negative can have some film grain. (©2008 Dan Ablan.)

Figure 6.4 When sharpened, the noise in the image from Figure 6.3 is exaggerated.

Five main filters are used to remove noise from images: Gaussian Blur, Despeckle, Median, Dust & Scratches, and Reduce Noise. Let's look at these filters one at a time, starting with the least sophisticated and moving to the most advanced. As each filter is described, we'll show the results on two images: a simple image that contains black dots of different sizes representing noise (as in **Figure 6.5**) and a normal image (as in **Figure 6.6**) to show how much the filter trashes the real detail in the image. You'll be able to see how effective each filter is at removing noise, while at the same time learning how much image detail is lost in the process.

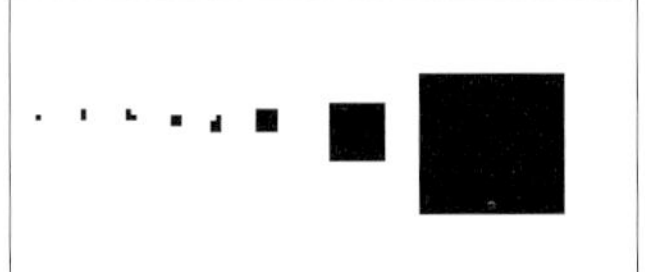

Figure 6.5 This image contains black dots that vary from one pixel to over 25 pixels wide.

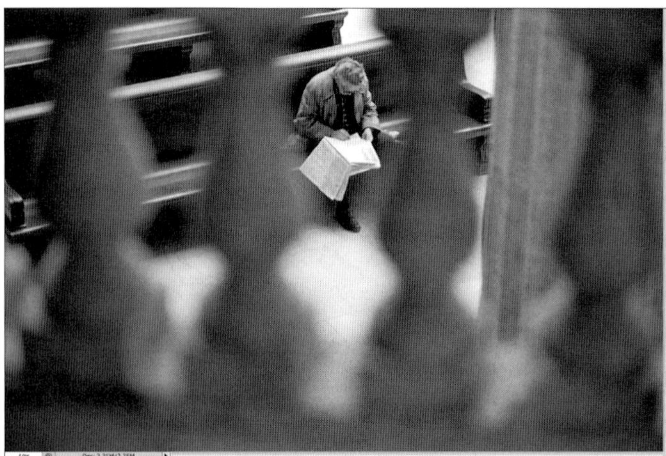

Figure 6.6 A normal image with some noise. (©2008 Dan Ablan.)

Gaussian Blur Filter

The Gaussian Blur filter (Filter > Blur > Gaussian Blur) does the opposite of what we're trying to accomplish when sharpening an image—it makes the transitions in the image less distinct, rendering the image less sharp (**Figures 6.7** and **6.8**). This is a common method used to remove noise; however, just because it's common doesn't mean that you should always use it. Much more sophisticated methods are available that won't trash the general detail in the image.

Figure 6.7 After blurring the image, it looks nowhere near as sharp as the original in Figure 6.6.

Figure 6.8 A setting of 5.0 pixels was necessary to blend the smallest dots from the example in Figure 6.5 into the surrounding image.

Despeckle Filter

The next few filters we'll explore are found in the Noise menu (Filter > Noise). The first choice in that menu is Add Noise, which is designed for adding specks to an image; the rest of the filters in the menu get rid of noise. The Despeckle filter blends the tiniest specks into the surrounding image, while leaving the major detail in the image untouched (**Figures 6.9** and **6.10**). The only problem with this filter is that it isn't always strong enough to remove noise completely from the image. If an image has minimal noise, give this filter a try; but when the noise in the image is considerable, try the other options in the Noise menu.

Figure 6.9 After applying the Despeckle filter, the single-pixel speck from the example in Figure 6.5 has changed to a light gray speck (barely visible here).

Figure 6.10 After applying the Despeckle filter to the image from Figure 6.6, the film grain has started to blend into the surrounding image. It's a subtle effect, difficult to see in print, so try it for yourself.

Median Filter

The Median filter (Filter > Noise > Median) uses an interesting approach to rid an image of unwanted noise—it rounds the corners of things, which causes tiny specks to implode. As you increase the Amount setting, the filter rounds the corners to a larger degree, which makes larger specks in the image blend into the surrounding image (**Figures 6.11** and **6.12**). What's really nice about this filter is that it doesn't make anything look blurry. You don't usually need to use settings above 2 when applying this filter.

Figure 6.11 Using the Median filter with a Radius of 1 (its lowest setting) effectively removed the small specks from the example in Figure 6.5.

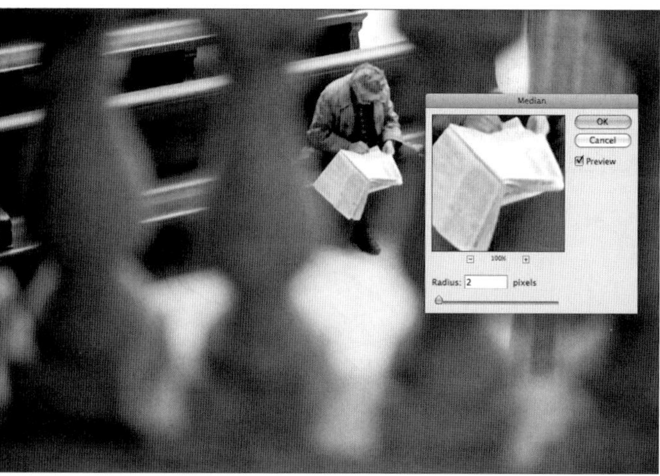

Figure 6.12 Applying the Median filter to the image from Figure 6.6 causes it to lose some detail, but it doesn't get blurry.

Dust & Scratches Filter

The Dust & Scratches filter (Filter > Noise > Dust & Scratches) uses the same technology as the Median filter, but it adds a Threshold setting to determine which shades in the image should be affected by the filter. A setting of zero allows the filter to apply to the entire image, and will therefore work exactly like the Median filter. Raising the Threshold setting limits the changes to areas that are similar in brightness. The general idea here is to start with a Threshold of zero so you work on the whole image, and then adjust the Radius setting until the noise in the image is gone. Then, to make sure that you lose the absolute minimal amount of true detail, change the Threshold setting to 255 and use the down-arrow key to change that setting slowly until you find the highest number that will rid the image of unwanted noise (**Figures 6.13** and **6.14**).

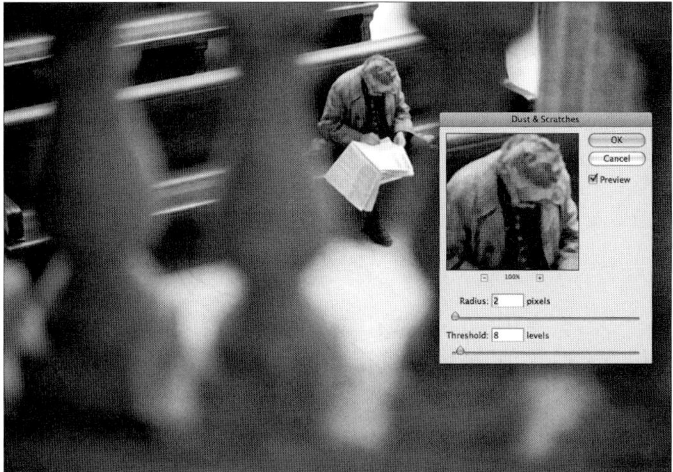

Figure 6.13 Dust & Scratches results on the image from Figure 6.6.

Figure 6.14 Using the Dust & Scratches filter with a Radius of 2 and a Threshold of 8 on the example from Figure 6.5 produced the same result on our specks as the Median filter (Figure 6.11).

Reduce Noise Filter

The Reduce Noise filter (Filter > Noise > Reduce Noise) is the most sophisticated method for reducing noise. It incorporates many of the tricks that we used to do piecemeal by using blending modes or applying filters to individual channels. It often produces a result that looks smooth while retaining much of the detail from the original image

(**Figures 6.15** and **6.16**). When applying the Reduce Noise filter, start by moving all the sliders to the far left so they have no effect on the image. Then adjust them gradually.

Figure 6.15 Using the Reduce Noise filter with a Strength of 10 and a Preserve Details setting of 1 produced minimal distortion in the largest specks from the example in Figure 6.5, while making the smaller specks fade into their surroundings.

Figure 6.16 The Reduce Noise filter produced a somewhat smoother result on the image from Figure 6.6 than the Dust & Scratches filter did in Figure 6.13, while retaining more highlight detail in the subject.

If you notice multicolored noise in the image (specks of yellow, blue, red, etc.), adjust the Reduce Color Noise slider until those colors blend into their surroundings (**Figures 6.17** and **6.18**). If the noise is primarily a single color, consider applying the features found in Advanced mode (which we'll talk about next) before continuing with the techniques mentioned here.

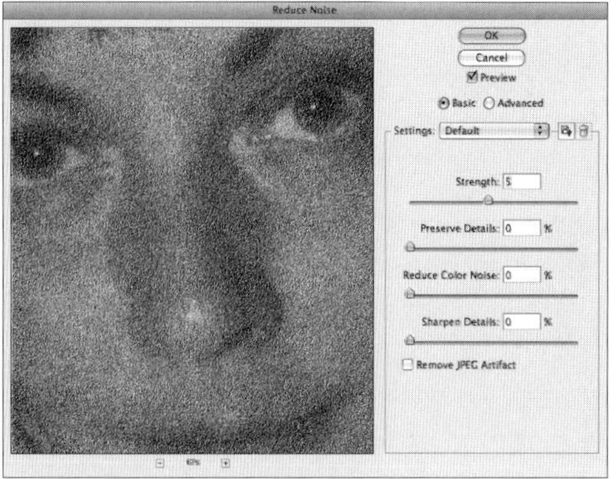

Figure 6.17 This original image contains specks of various colors. (©2008 Dan Ablan.)

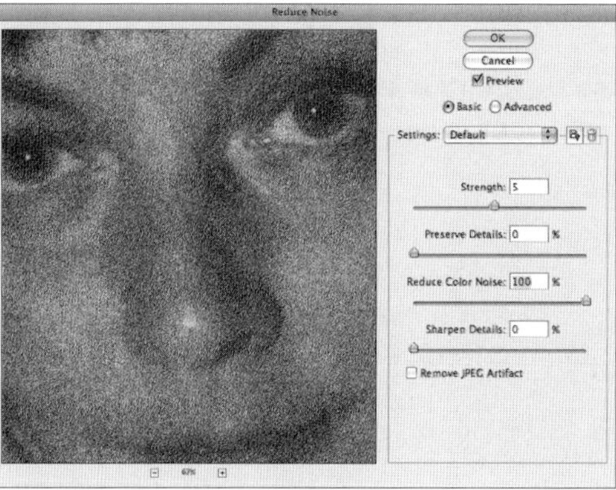

Figure 6.18 The result of adjusting the Reduce Color Noise slider for the image from Figure 6.17.

After tackling any color noise problems, it's time to rid the image of luminance noise (specks that vary in brightness instead of color). Adjust the Strength slider until you've removed as much of the remaining noise as possible. Move the Preserve Details slider all the way to the right and then lower it until you find the highest setting that gives a good balance between noise reduction and image detail (**Figure 6.19**).

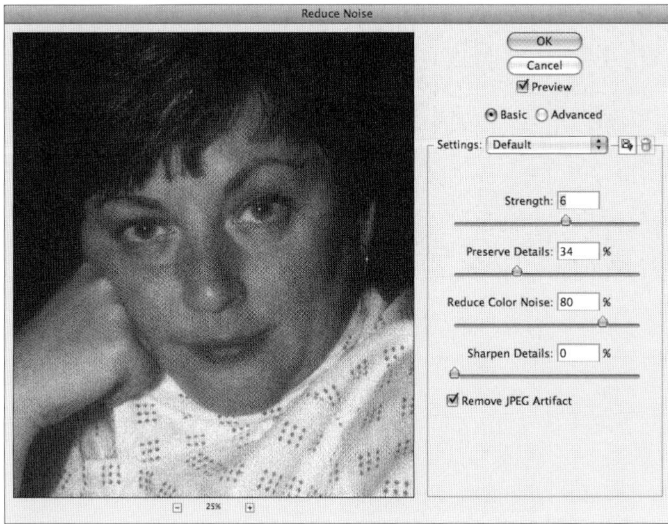

Figure 6.19 The Reduce Noise filter helps bring down noise within a scanned image.

Images saved in the JPEG file format will exhibit artifacts that make the image look as if it has been divided into squares of 8 × 8 pixels. You can attempt to blend those squares into the surrounding image by turning on the Remove JPEG Artifact check box. Just remember to inspect the image to make sure that this option doesn't destroy too much important detail in the image.

Advanced Mode

If the image has very fine detail or considerable noise, you'll need to take additional steps to ensure that you don't trash too much detail in the image when you're attempting to remove noise. Color images are made out of three (RGB) or four (CMYK) color components, which are known as color *channels*. It's rather common to find more noise in one of those channels than the others

(**Figures 6.20** to **6.22**). When that's the case, try applying the noise removal filters to the individual channels before attempting to reduce noise from the image as a whole; otherwise, you might trash the detail in most of the channels just to rid one pesky channel of noise (usually the blue or yellow channel). The next time you need to be heavy-handed with the Strength slider in the Reduce Noise dialog, try setting it to zero, switch to Advanced mode at the top of the dialog, and then click the Per Channel tab (**Figure 6.23**). After you've done that, you can cycle through the RGB or CMYK channels to see whether the noise shows up more in one channel than another, and adjust each channel accordingly. When you've done all you can to the individual channels, click the Overall tab and adjust the image further to bring back some detail (**Figure 6.24**).

Figure 6.20 The red channel. (©2008 Dan Ablan.)

Figure 6.21 The blue channel.

Figure 6.22 The green channel.

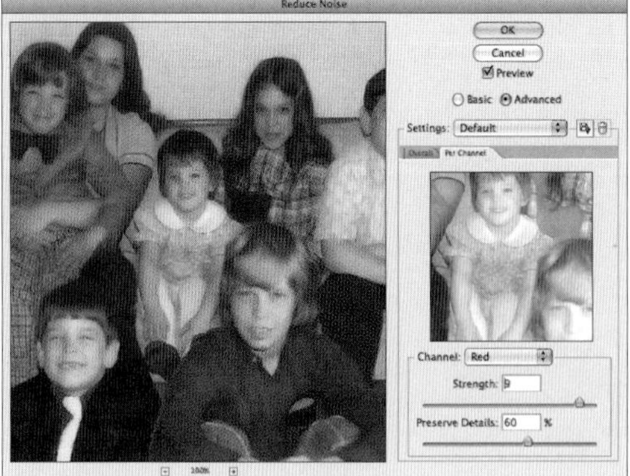

Figure 6.23 In Advanced mode, you can reduce noise in individual channels.

Figure 6.24 After reducing noise independently in channels, you can go back and adjust the overall image quality.

Reclaiming Detail with the History Brush

Applying one of the noise reduction filters may cause an image to lose important detail such as eyes or freckles. If you use the History Brush immediately after applying the noise reduction filter, you can paint back the desired detail, effectively removing the effect of the filter from the areas across which you're painting. If the History Brush presents a "no" symbol (circle with a diagonal line across it), you've either changed the dimensions of the image or changed the color mode of the image since you opened it. When that's the case, choose Window > History and click to the left of the history state that's directly above the listing for the noise reduction filter you just applied (**Figure 6.25**). After you've done that, the History Brush should work on the image. Paint across the areas that have lost important detail, and the details should come back.

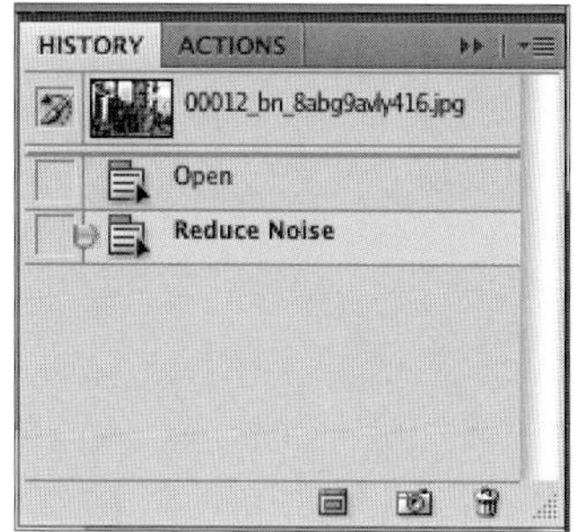

Figure 6.25 Click just to the left of the history state that's directly above the one that lists a noise reduction filter.

You can also use the History Brush with its blending mode set to Lighten or Darken to rid the image of sharpening-related halos. Use Darken mode to remove the bright halos and Lighten mode to remove the dark halos.

Now that you've seen how to rid images of unwanted noise and film grain, let's examine how sharpening can exaggerate detail, and then we'll explore the exact steps needed to sharpen any image.

How Sharpening Works

To sharpen an image, choose Filter > Sharpen. Photoshop presents a submenu of choices (**Figure 6.26**) on which the top three options might sound friendly (Sharpen, Sharpen Edges, and Sharpen More), but you might want to ignore these techniques; they're simply presets that enter different numbers into the bottom choice, Unsharp Mask. The bottom two filters in the list are the only ones that allow you to control exactly how much the image will be sharpened. We'll start by exploring the Unsharp Mask filter and then refine your knowledge by exploring Photoshop's Smart Sharpen filter.

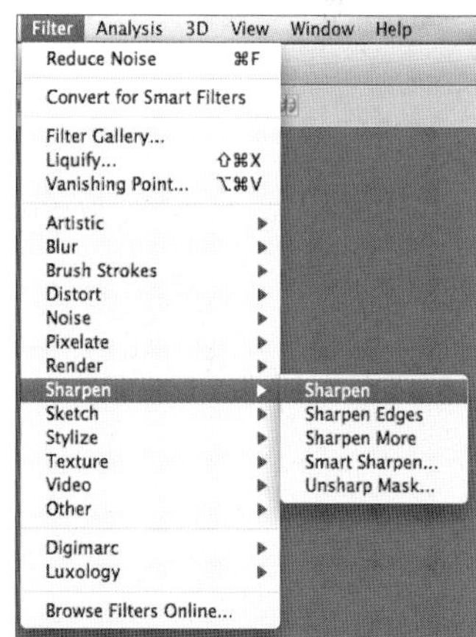

Figure 6.26 Photoshop's sharpening options.

Unsharp Mask has this confusing name because way back before people used desktop computers, they sharpened images in a photographic darkroom. They would have to go through a process that involved a blurry (unsharp) version of the image. This process would take well over an

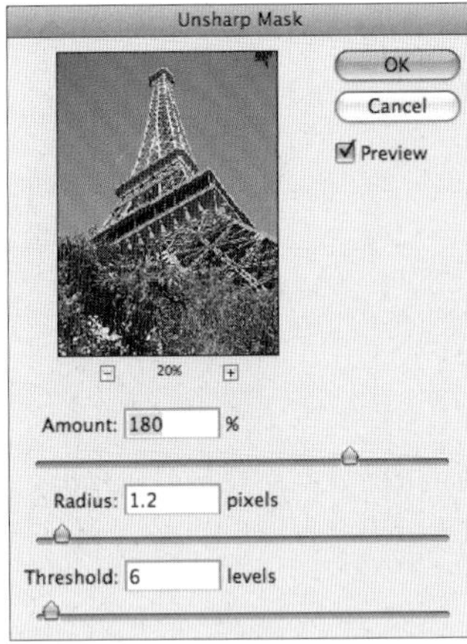

Figure 6.27 The Unsharp Mask dialog.

Figure 6.28 This simple document contains only three shades of gray.

Figure 6.29 This will be our photographic reference image. (©2008 Dan Ablan.)

hour (don't worry—in Photoshop it takes only seconds) and wouldn't be much fun. The process they'd go through in the darkroom was known as making an *unsharp mask*, so Adobe just borrowed that term.

The Unsharp Mask filter increases the contrast where two colors (or shades of gray) touch in the image, making their edges more prominent and therefore easier to see. To view the effect of the Unsharp Mask filter (**Figure 6.27**), we'll demonstrate using two documents: **Figure 6.28** contains only three shades of gray (20%, 30%, and 50%), and **Figure 6.29** is a normal photographic image.

The Unsharp Mask dialog contains three sliders:

- **Amount:** Determines how much contrast will be added to the edges of objects—and, therefore, how obvious the sharpening will be (**Figure 6.30**).
- **Radius:** Determines how much space will be used for the contrast boost that the Amount setting creates. No matter which settings you use, sharpening will produce a bright halo on one side of the edge of an object and a dark halo on the opposite side of that same edge. If you sharpen too much, you'll add a very noticeable glow around the edges of objects instead of a barely noticeable halo (**Figure 6.31**).
- **Threshold:** Determines how different two touching colors have to be for sharpening to kick in. With Threshold set at 0, everything will be sharpened. As you increase this setting, only the areas that are drastically different will be sharpened (**Figure 6.32**). If the setting is too low, unwanted artifacts like noise and film grain will be exaggerated and relatively smooth areas might start to show texture. If the setting is too high, the sharpening will apply to very few areas in the image, which will look too obvious because those areas won't fit in with their surroundings (which didn't get sharpened).

Figure 6.30 The effect of the Amount setting—left to right, settings of 100, 200, and 500. (©2008 Dan Ablan.)

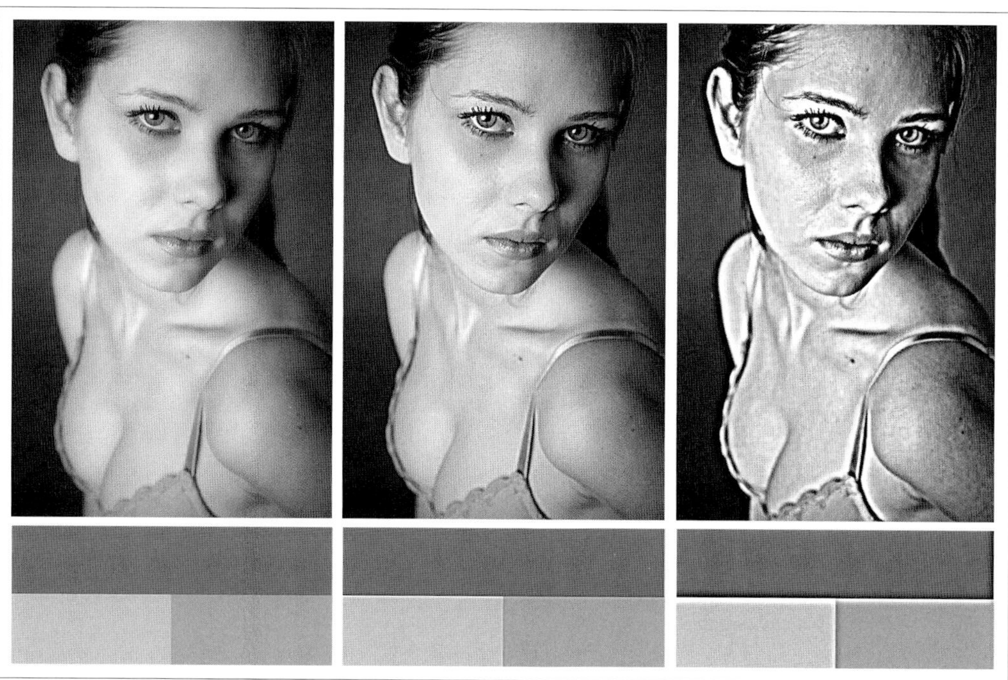

Figure 6.31 The effect of the Radius setting—left to right, settings of 1, 2, and 5.

Figure 6.32 The effect of the Threshold setting—left to right, settings of 0, 10, and 50.

Now that we've explored all the options that are available with the Unsharp Mask filter, let's get down to business and find out how to apply them to an image. But before you start applying the Unsharp Mask filter, double-click the Zoom tool in the toolbar to view the image at 100% view; otherwise, you won't be able to see the full effect of the sharpening you apply to the image.

Sharpening an Image

Load any image you might have on your drive, from a scan to a digital camera image. Then, to sharpen the image, choose Filter > Sharpen > Unsharp Mask and type the following generic settings: Amount = 500, Radius = 1, and Threshold = 0, just to make sure that you can easily see the effect of sharpening the image (**Figure 6.33**). Now adjust the Threshold setting. With Threshold set to 0, everything in the image will be sharpened. That can cause areas that used to have fine detail (such as a brick wall) or areas that used to look relatively smooth (such as a skin tone or a shadow) to have overly exaggerated detail. Those bricks

Figure 6.33 Start with the generic settings of 500, 1, and 0. (©2008 Dan Ablan.)

look noisy, and a Threshold setting of 0 will add years to anyone's face because you've exaggerated every imperfection. To avoid that problem, slowly increase the Threshold setting until those areas smooth out (**Figure 6.34**). You'll usually end up using settings in the single digits. From there, bringing the Amount value down can help to make the sharpening cleaner.

Figure 6.34 Adjust the Threshold setting until areas that should be smooth look smooth.

Next, experiment with the Radius setting, trying to find the highest setting that makes the image look like it's been sharpened—but without making it look like everything is glowing—usually in the range of .5 to 2 (**Figures 6.35** and **6.36**). Images with very fine detail look best with lower Radius settings, whereas images that contain little detail or that will be printed in large sizes and viewed from a distance look best with higher Radius settings.

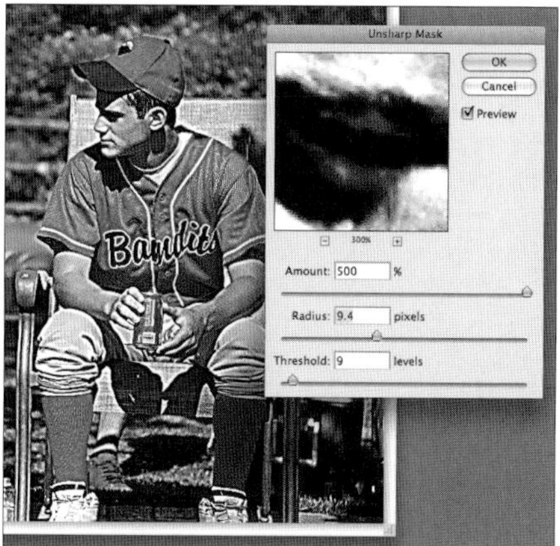

Figure 6.35 This Radius setting is too high.

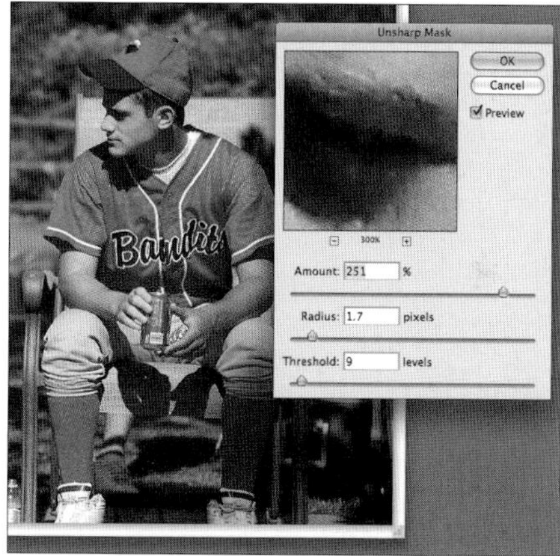

Figure 6.36 Try to find the highest Radius setting that doesn't make objects look like they're glowing.

Finally, adjust the Amount setting until the image looks naturally sharp instead of artificial, usually in the range of 15 to 250, depending on the Radius setting you used (**Figure 6.37**). Let your eyes be your guide. There are two common indicators that the Amount setting is too high:

- Obvious bright halos appear around the edge of objects. (There will always be halos; you just want to make sure that they aren't very noticeable.)
- Very fine detail (like hair, or texture in bricks) will become overly contrasty—almost pure black and pure white.

Figure 6.37 Adjust the Amount setting until the image looks realistically sharp.

The procedure we've just discussed is the usual approach to sharpening most images, but sometimes you'll need to go a different route. The Radius setting can have a radical effect on sharpening. You'll need to achieve a balance between Amount and Radius. High Amount settings (about 90–250) will require low Radius settings (.5–1.5), and low Amount settings (10–30) will require higher Radius settings (5–20). High Amount settings work for most images, and that's why we took the initial approach just mentioned.

If you have a grainy image and you want to maintain but not exaggerate the grain (**Figure 6.38**), you'll need to take a slightly different approach. A grainy image will start to look unusual when you get an Amount setting anywhere near 100–150 (**Figure 6.39**); you might even need to bring the Amount setting down to near 20 before the grain stops being exaggerated too much. At that point, you'll barely be able to tell that the image has been sharpened (**Figure 6.40**); to compensate, you'll need to get the Radius setting up until the image starts to look sharp (**Figure 6.41**). On most images, you'll be able to use much higher Amount settings without causing grain problems. In that case, you might end up with an Amount setting around 120, and then you'll need to experiment with the Radius setting to see what looks best (probably between .5 and 1.5).

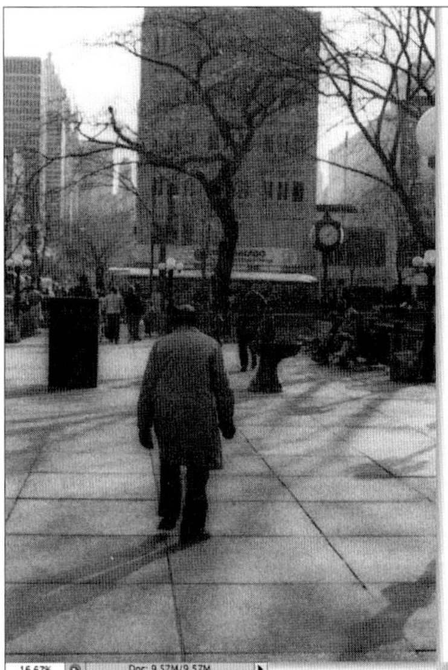

Figure 6.38 An old grainy image. (©2008 Dan Ablan.)

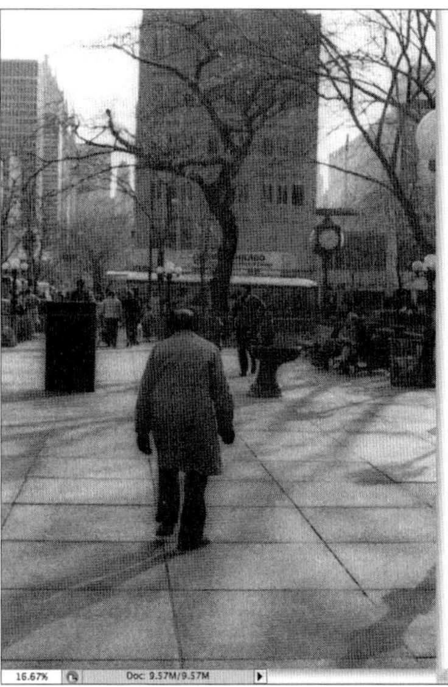

Figure 6.39 With the Amount setting at 150, the grain is becoming too obvious. (Look very closely to see the difference between this figure and Figure 6.38.)

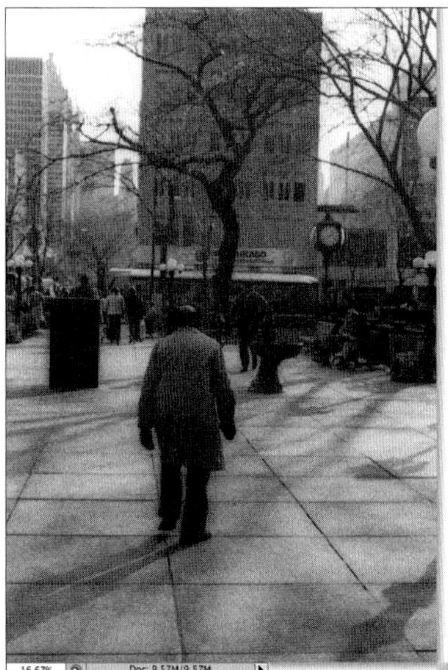

Figure 6.40 With the Amount setting at 20, the grain is less, but the image doesn't look sharp.

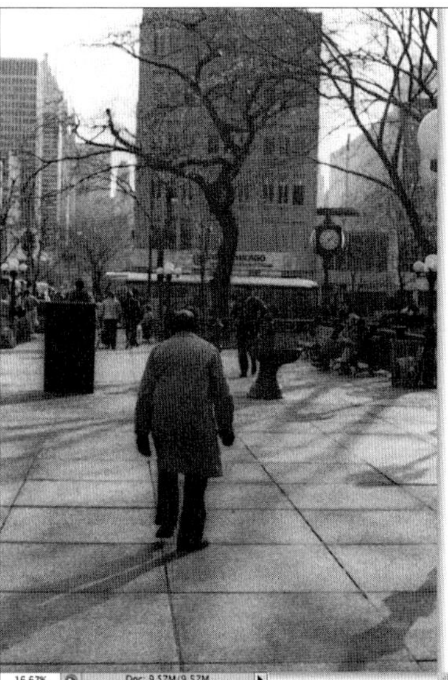

Figure 6.41 With the Amount setting at 20 or so and the Radius up to 1.5, the image becomes sharp.

Using Smart Sharpen

The Smart Sharpen filter (**Figure 6.42**) expands on the concepts of the Unsharp Mask filter to deliver a more sophisticated method for sharpening images. However, there are many instances where you might prefer the Unsharp Mask filter, for reasons explained in a moment.

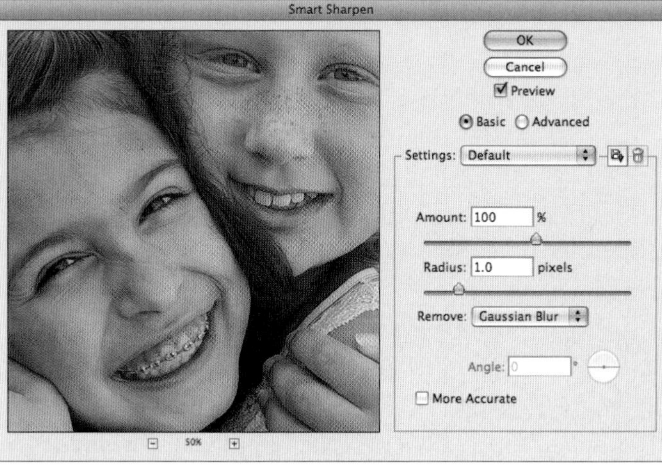

Figure 6.42 The Smart Sharpen dialog, with the Remove option set to Gaussian Blur. (©2008 Dan Ablan.)

Figure 6.43 Gaussian Blur setting.

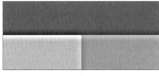

Figure 6.44 Lens Blur setting.

Figure 6.45 Lens Blur setting with More Accurate check box turned on.

The Amount and Radius settings in the Smart Sharpen filter work just like the ones in the Unsharp Mask filter. In fact, the results are identical when the Remove pop-up menu is set to Gaussian Blur (**Figure 6.43**). Setting the Remove menu to Lens Blur causes the halos that come along with sharpening to be less pronounced, which allows you to get away with higher Amount and Radius settings before the sharpening halos become overly obvious (**Figure 6.44**). You can use this setting whenever quality is more important than speed (which is often the case in normal workflow). You can also set the Remove pop-up menu to Motion Blur and then experiment with the Angle setting to reduce the blurring effect of lens shake. It's not a miracle worker, though, so it will only be effective when the camera shake was almost unnoticeable.

Turning on the More Accurate check box causes the image to be sharpened in two passes (just like applying the Unsharp Mask filter twice). This can make edges much more prominent (**Figure 6.45**), but you have to be very careful because it also has a tendency to over-exaggerate grain and noise in images.

You might find that you'll use the Unsharp Mask filter for images that contain fine texture, such as skin or brick, because the Smart Sharpen filter does not offer the Threshold setting that allows you to limit the sharpening effect to areas of more pronounced detail.

Advanced Mode

The Smart Sharpen filter also offers an Advanced mode, which allows you to control the strength of the sharpening that will be applied to the shadows and highlights of the image (**Figure 6.46**). This feature can be useful in instances when a considerable amount of noise is present in the dark portion of an image. The Fade Amount setting determines the strength of the sharpening effect; the Tonal Width setting determines the brightness range that will be affected by the sharpening, and the Radius setting determines how the sharpening effect will blend into the surrounding image. A good way to work is to start with Fade Amount at 100% and Radius at 3 so that you can see the full effect of the sharpening. Then adjust Tonal Width until the sharpening no longer affects any overly noisy areas. Finally, adjust the Fade Amount slider to see just how much sharpening you can use without exaggerating the noise in the image.

Figure 6.46 Advanced options.

More Art Than Science

The process of sharpening takes a good bit of practice before you start feeling confident. Everyone has a different idea of how sharp an image should look, and most output devices aren't capable of reproducing the amount of detail you see onscreen. Even if you sharpen the image so that it looks great onscreen, when you print the image it might still look rather soft. Following are some general thoughts on how to approach sharpening for different types of output:

- **Web/multimedia:** When the final image will be displayed onscreen, you can completely trust your screen when sharpening the image. Most of the time you'll end up with Radius settings between .5 and 1 and Amount settings below 100%. Just be aware that sharpening increases the file size of JPEG file format images (**Figures 6.47** to **6.49**). If you're planning to save the image as a JPEG file, use the absolute minimum amount of sharpening that makes the image look crisp.

Figure 6.47 The original unsharpened image. (©2008 Dan Ablan.)

Figure 6.48 The image from Figure 6.47, sharpened with settings of Amount 70, Tonal Width 5, and Radius 4.

Figure 6.49 The image from Figure 6.47, sharpened with settings of Amount 175, Tonal Width 7, and Radius 4.

- **Photographic output devices:** These devices include film recorders, LightJets, and other gadgets that use photographic film or paper to reproduce an image. They can reproduce the majority of the detail you see onscreen. With these devices you have to be very careful to make sure that the Radius setting is quite low (.25 to .7 for most images), so that the halos that come from sharpening aren't obvious on the end result.

- **Desktop printer:** This includes inkjet and laser printers. Experiment with an image that's representative of the type of image you use the most.
- **Commercial printing press:** Start by sharpening images until they look very sharp onscreen, and then analyze the printed result when you get a job back from the printing company. If the printed result doesn't look too sharp, slowly ratchet up the Amount and Radius settings on subsequent images until the printed images look very sharp, but still natural. Compare the printed result to the original digital file each time, viewing the image at 100% magnification. As you work on more and more jobs, you'll start to get a feeling for how much you need to overdo the sharpening onscreen to get a nice sharp end result. Different types of printing produce differing amounts of detail. (Newspaper images need to be sharpened much more than images that will be printed in a glossy brochure.)

If thinking about all the different settings needed for different output devices drives you crazy, consider adding a commercial plug-in filter to Photoshop. Nik Software (www.niksoftware.com) makes a set of plug-in filters known as Sharpener Pro (**Figure 6.50**), which takes a lot of the guesswork out of sharpening images. The package comes with separate filters for different types of output (including inkjet, color laser, offset printing, and Internet) and compensates for different viewing distances and image sizes, all without having to think about Amount, Radius, and Threshold settings. The results might just be a little bit too aggressive; if so, choose Edit > Fade immediately after applying the filter, and lower the Opacity setting a bit. It might be a personal preference as to what you consider to be a naturally sharp result, so the final Opacity setting will be unique to you.

Figure 6.50 Nik Sharpener Pro takes a lot of the guesswork out of sharpening.

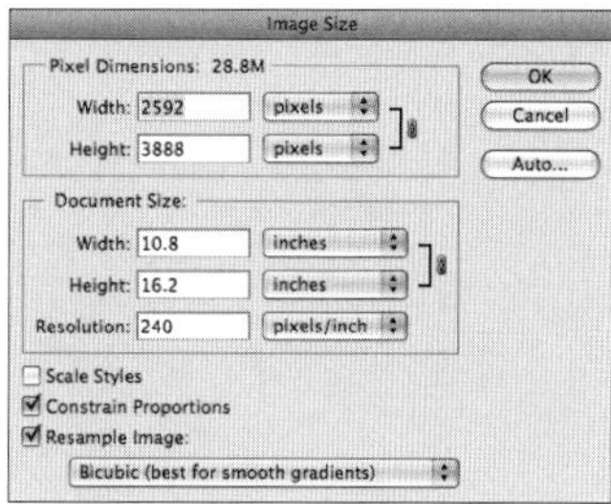

Figure 6.51 Use the Image Size dialog to specify the size and resolution of the image.

Do you plan to use an image for more than one purpose? Ideally, you should create a unique version of the image for each use. Choose Image > Duplicate to create an exact copy of an image. Then choose Image > Image Size (**Figure 6.51**) to set the proper size and resolution for the output device for which this particular image is destined. Finally, sharpen the image based on your experience with that particular device. As you repeat the process for other devices, always go back to the full-sized master image before repeating the steps.

If you simply can't deal with one image for each device, work with a single image and do the following: Set the *resolution* to what's needed for your most demanding output device (the one that needs the highest-resolution image), and *sharpen* for the device that looks closest to your screen (the one that needs the least radical sharpening). Then use that one image for all output devices. That's kind of like buying one shoe size for an entire basketball team. As long as it's large enough for the biggest person, everyone should be able to fit in it, but it won't be ideal for everyone.

Tricks of the Trade

Now that we've talked about the general process of sharpening an image, let's start to explore some more advanced ideas that will allow you to get more control over your sharpening.

Sharpen Luminosity

If you look closely at a color image after it's sharpened, you might notice bright-colored halos around objects that were not all that colorful in the original photo. (In **Figure 6.52**, notice the green fringe around the blue shirt.) To prevent that type of unwanted sharpening artifact, choose Edit > Fade Unsharp Mask immediately after sharpening an image. When the Fade dialog appears, set the Mode pop-up menu to Luminosity and then click OK (**Figure 6.53**). That will force the sharpening you just applied to affect only the brightness of the image and will prevent it from shifting or intensifying the colors in the image (**Figure 6.54**). If you read a lot of books and magazine articles about Photoshop, you might discover that many people attempt to get the same result by converting their image to LAB mode and then sharpening the image. The only problem with that approach is that any time you change the mode of an image, you lose a little quality. So try to switch modes only when you have a good reason to do so. Fading after applying the Unsharp Mask filter gives you the same benefits as converting to LAB mode, so try to leave the image in its original mode when sharpening.

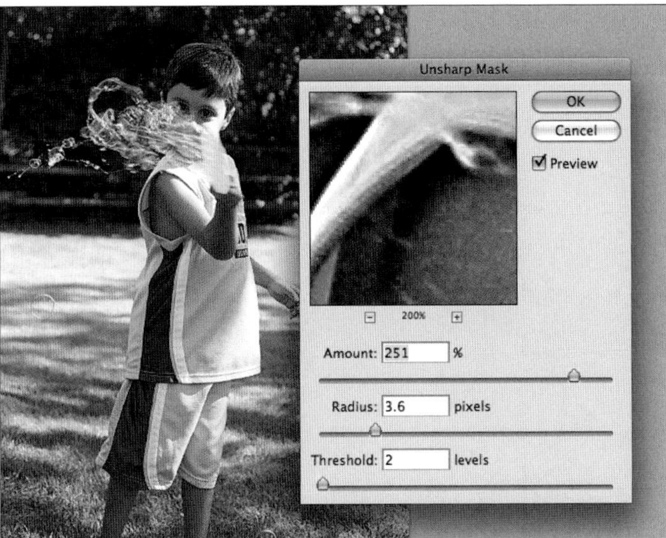

Figure 6.52 You can get colored halos around objects in an image when sharpening.

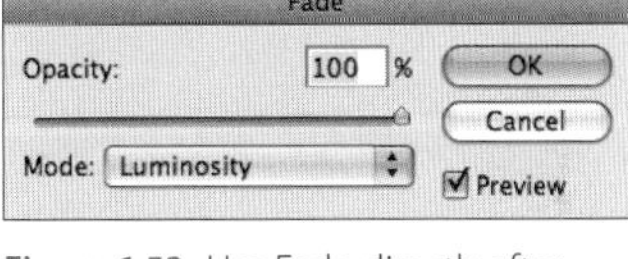

Figure 6.53 Use Fade directly after using the Unsharp Mask filter to have the sharpening affect only the brightness in the image.

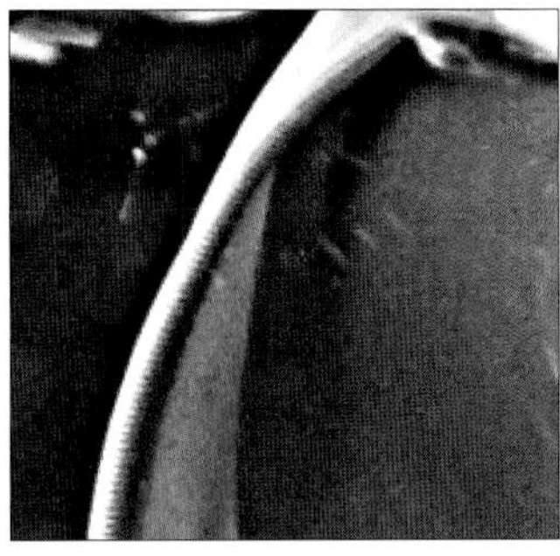

Figure 6.54 A closeup view of the sharpened image, now without fringing.

Sharpen the Black Channel

If an image is destined for CMYK mode, be sure to make an extra sharpening pass on the black channel. Just open the Channels panel (Window > Channels), click the Black channel, and sharpen away. Because black ink is mainly used in the darker areas of the image, you can get away with some rather aggressive settings. (Try these: Amount = 350, Radius = 1, Threshold = 2.) Perform this sharpening pass after you've already sharpened the full-color image (**Figures 6.55** to **6.57**).

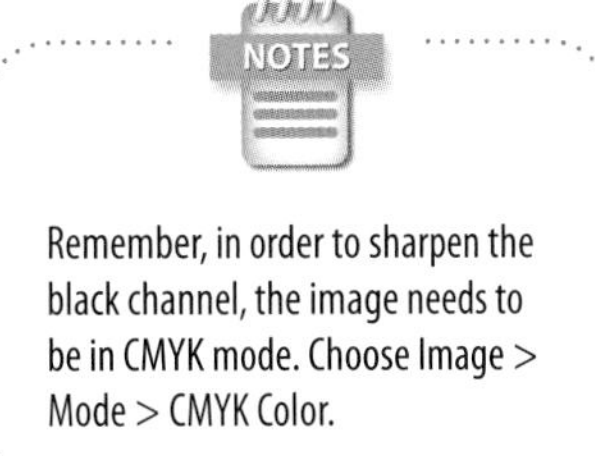

Remember, in order to sharpen the black channel, the image needs to be in CMYK mode. Choose Image > Mode > CMYK Color.

Figure 6.55 The original image, unsharpened. (©2008 Dan Ablan.)

Figure 6.56 Unsharp Mask filter applied to the RGB channels.

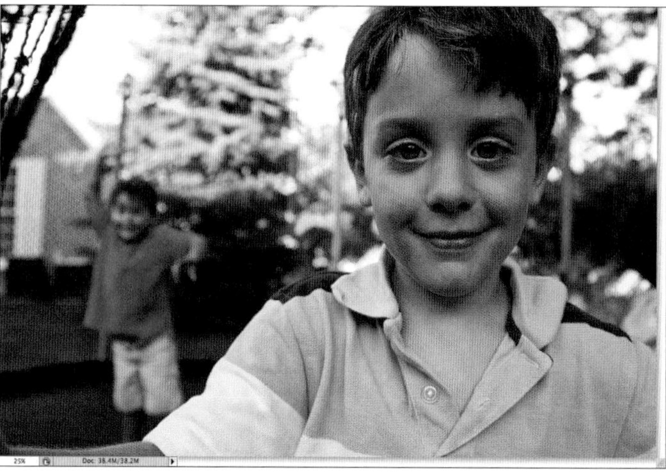

Figure 6.57 Sharpening added to just the black channel.

Sharpen Channels Separately

Certain images don't look good after being sharpened. For instance, when you sharpen a face, it sometimes seems to just fall apart, making the person look years older. Another example would be scanned images in which color noise is exaggerated. In those cases, consider clicking through the channels that appear in the Channels panel and sharpening only the channels that would help the image. For light skin, that would be the channel that's the lightest—red in RGB mode or cyan in CMYK mode (**Figures 6.58** to **6.60**). For noisy images, avoid sharpening the channel that contains the most noise—usually blue in RGB mode or yellow in CMYK mode. You shouldn't use this technique every time you want to sharpen images, but it's something to think about when sharpening a full-color image is doing more harm than good.

Figure 6.58 Red channel. (©2008 Dan Ablan.)

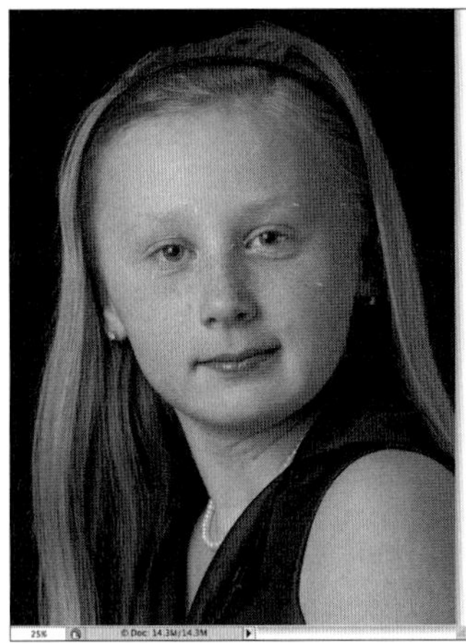

Figure 6.59 Green channel.

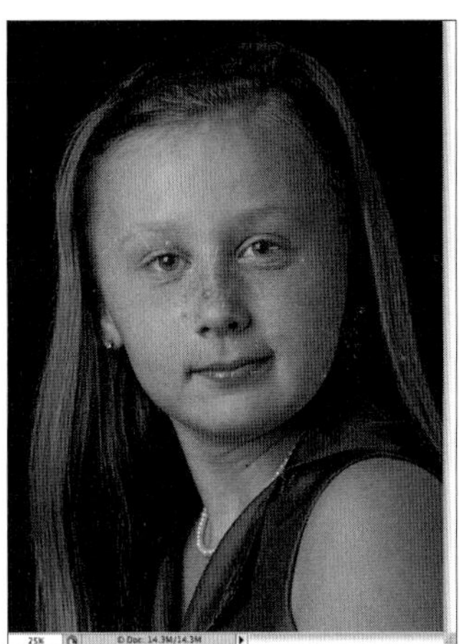

Figure 6.60 Blue channel.

Control Highlights and Shadows Separately

When you sharpen an image, Photoshop adds a dark halo on one side of an edge and a bright halo on the opposite side of the edge. When you're working with dark backgrounds, such as a deep blue sky, the bright halos can be rather easy to see (**Figure 6.61**). Try controlling the bright and dark halos separately so that you can minimize the bright halo while maintaining the dark one. You can accomplish that goal by making two duplicates of the layer you want to sharpen. Click each of the duplicate layers and set the Blending Mode pop-up menu at the top of the Layers panel to Lighten for one and Darken for the other (**Figure 6.62**). Now you can sharpen the two layers separately. The setting you apply to the layer that is set to Lighten will control the bright halos; the setting on the layer set to Darken will control the dark halo (**Figure 6.63**).

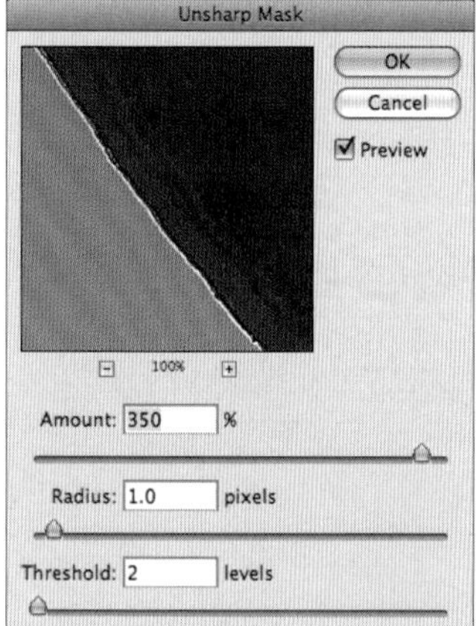

Figure 6.61 The bright halos in this image are getting obvious.

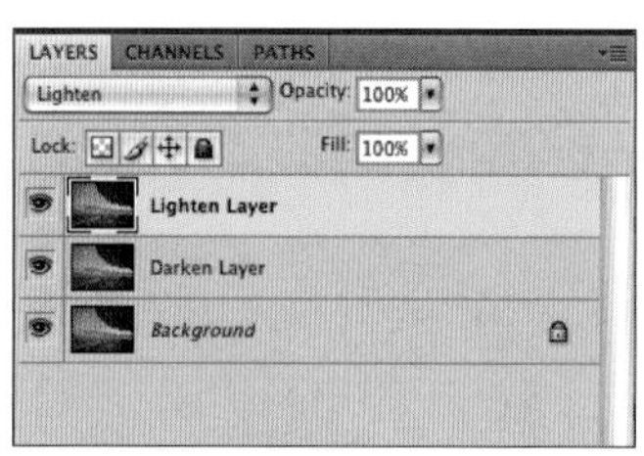

Figure 6.62 Duplicate the layer twice; set one layer to Lighten mode and the other to Darken mode.

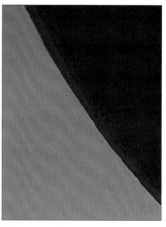

Figure 6.63 When you separate the dark and bright halos, you have more control over them.

The Next Step

If you felt like you were drowning in details in this chapter, try a few of the techniques; then come back and read it again, and things will start to gel. It may take you a while to become truly comfortable with sharpening images, but it's well worth the time because you can transform flat and lifeless images into ones that are lively and ready to pop off the page. Now, here's one more very important piece of sharpening advice before we head to the next chapter: Oversharpened images never look good, so if you're ever unsure of how much sharpening to apply, err on the side of conservatism.

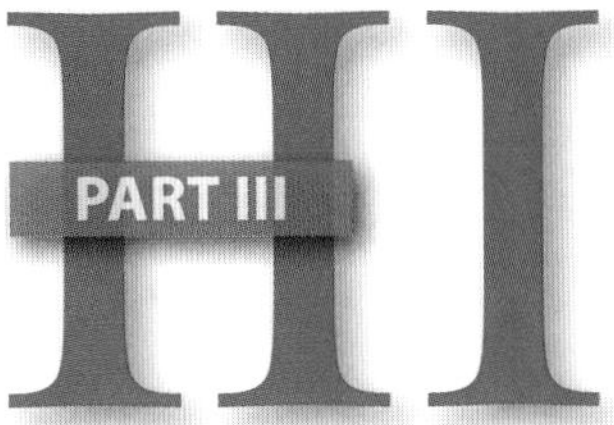

Grayscale, Color, and Print

CHAPTER

7

Setting Up Images for Final Output

Artists can color the sky red because they know it's blue. Those of us who aren't artists must color things the way they really are or people might think we're stupid.

—Jules Feiffer

Setting Up Images for Final Output

No question—your job as a photographer is to capture the image. But in today's ever-changing digital landscape, it's also your job to make sure that the image is the best it can be. And in order to do that, you need to master the color and contrast of the image.

This chapter will guide you through understanding the color and grayscale values within your imagery. You'll see the difference between Levels and Curves, while also learning that grayscale is more than just a desaturation. To begin, we'll discuss some of the more obvious variables in the image-editing process: brightness and contrast.

The techniques described in this chapter are used by the high-paid color maestros who are responsible for all of those ever-so-perfect glossy magazine ads. It will take you a while to really get the hang of these techniques, but once you do, it should take you just minutes to correct most images.

Brightness and Contrast

Years ago, Photoshop's Brightness/Contrast dialog used to adjust the entire tonal range of an image by equal amounts, which made it difficult to adjust one part of the image—say, the shadows—without destroying another part of the image, such as the highlights. However, Adobe has reengineered the Brightness/Contrast dialog with recent updates, and turned it into a very useful, very powerful tonal adjustment tool.

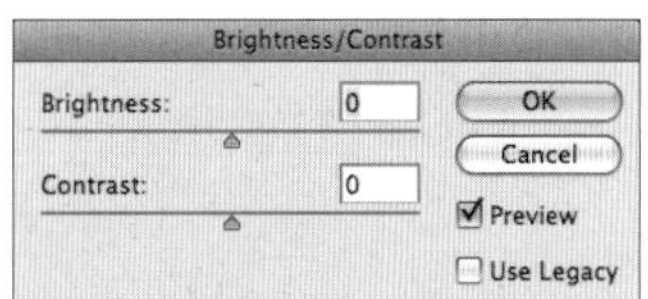

Figure 7.1 The Brightness/Contrast dialog.

To find the Brightness/Contrast adjustment, choose Image > Adjustments > Brightness/Contrast. The dialog is very straightforward (**Figure 7.1**). By sliding the Brightness slider back and forth, you can make the overall image brighter or darker. In general, the Brightness slider protects shadow areas—it won't usually let you underexpose them too far. Therefore, you need to keep a very close eye on the highlights in the image. As you adjust the slider, be careful that you don't let the highlights overexpose and blow out to complete white, losing detail (**Figure 7.2**).

Figure 7.2 As you slide the Brightness slider left or right, the image becomes darker or lighter, respectively. (©2008 Dan Ablan.)

The Contrast slider increases contrast in an image by brightening the light parts and darkening the darker areas (**Figure 7.3**). The overall effect is an image with more "pop" and better detail. Too much contrast, however, and the image can appear muddy. Moving the slider to the left lowers the contrast, resulting in a flatter image (**Figure 7.4**).

Brightness/Contrast is not the most refined tool, but it can be a great place to start if you're relatively new to Photoshop.

Figure 7.3 Use the Contrast slider to add "punch" to images.

Figure 7.4 Slide the Contrast slider left to pull contrast out of an image.

Adjusting Levels

Brightness/Contrast is especially useful if you're new to performing tonal corrections; for many images, it's all the control you'll ever need. However, Photoshop's Levels adjustment (Image > Adjustments > Levels) provides a more sophisticated tool that offers a much finer degree of control (**Figure 7.5**). Levels provides five different sliders that you can adjust, as well as a histogram (sort of like a bar graph) that indicates exactly what's happening to the image.

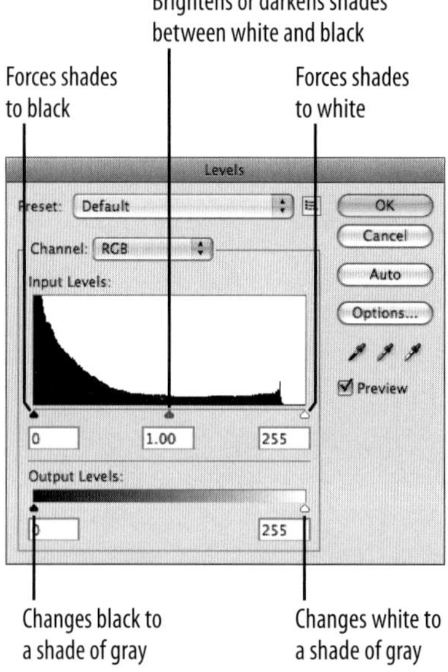

Figure 7.5 The Levels sliders.

The Histogram Is Your Guide

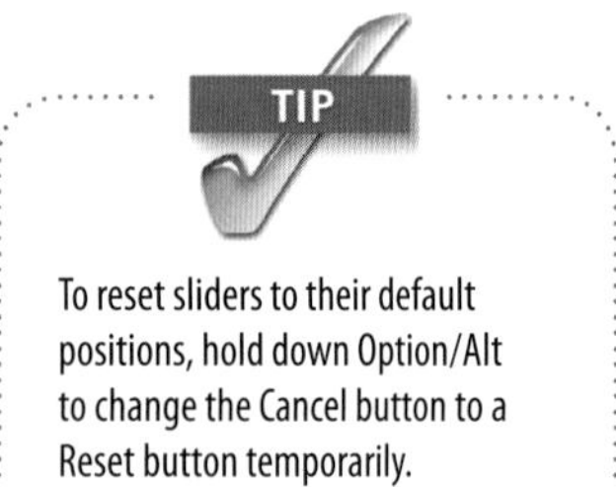

To reset sliders to their default positions, hold down Option/Alt to change the Cancel button to a Reset button temporarily.

You can use the histogram at the top of the Levels dialog to determine whether the adjustments you're making are going to harm the image or improve it. The histogram indicates which shades of gray the image uses and how prevalent those shades are within the image (**Figure 7.6**). The peaks indicate a shade of gray that takes up a lot of space in the image, and the valleys indicate a shade that isn't very prevalent in the image. A histogram that extends all the way across the space available and doesn't have tall spikes on either end indicates an image that has the full range of shades available, and is usually a sign of a good scan or a well-adjusted image. If you find a gap in the histogram, you can look at the gradient directly below it to see which shade of gray is missing from the image.

The height of the bars in a histogram suggest how much space the shades take up in an image. The height doesn't indicate an exact number of pixels; instead, it measures how much that shade is used as compared with the other shades in the image. It's as if everyone in a room stood up and you visually compared how tall each person was (without using a ruler). You wouldn't know exactly how tall anyone was, but you'd have an idea of how tall each person was as compared with the others.

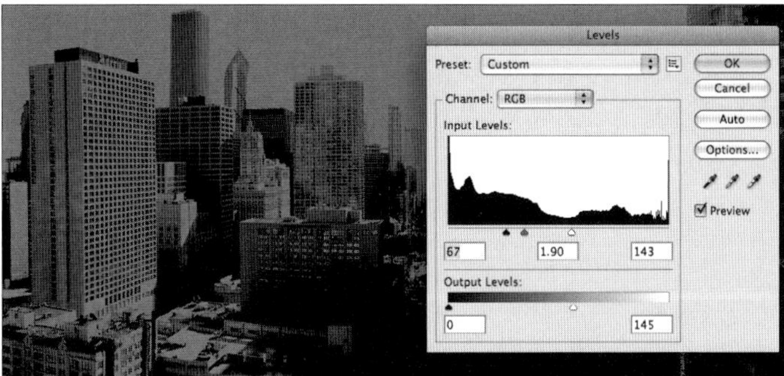

Figure 7.6 This histogram indicates that the shades between around 90% and 75% gray take up a lot of space (tall bars), and the shades between around 5% and 15% take up little space (short bars).

By looking below the left side of the histogram, you can determine the darkest shade of gray in the image. By looking below the right end of the histogram, you can determine the brightest shade of gray in the image. In **Figure 7.7**, you might notice that the image contains no pure blacks or pure whites. The darkest shade of gray is about 95%, and the brightest shade is about 6%.

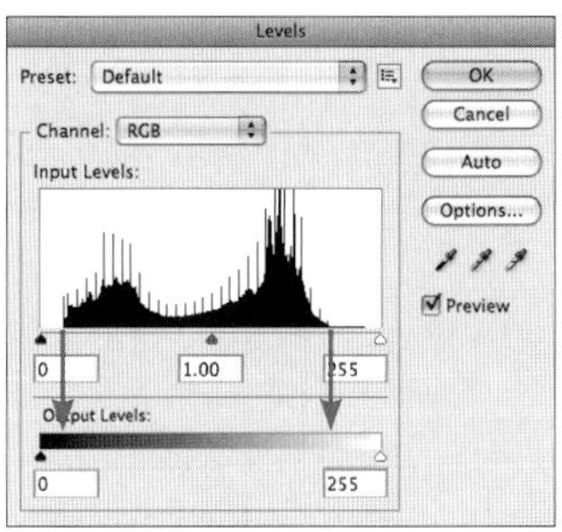

Figure 7.7 Look at the gradient bar directly below the ends of the histogram to determine the brightest and darkest shades present in the image.

There is no ideal setting for a histogram; it's simply a representation of which shades of gray are most prevalent in the image (**Figure 7.8**).

Figure 7.8 Each image has its own unique histogram. (©2008 Dan Ablan.)

NOTES

The middle slider moves when you adjust the upper-right or upper-left slider. This happens because Photoshop is attempting to keep the middle slider in the same position relative to the other two sliders. So if the middle slider is centered between the other two sliders, it will remain centered when you move one of the outer sliders.

Evaluating and Adjusting Contrast

The brightest and darkest areas of your computer monitor are nowhere near as bright or dark as the objects in the real world. The difference is even more extreme when you look at the brightest and darkest areas of a printed brochure—the paper is actually pretty dull, and the ink isn't all that dark. You'll need to use the full range of shades from black to white in order to make your photos look as close to reality as possible.

By adjusting the upper-right and upper-left sliders in the Levels dialog, you can dramatically improve the contrast of an image and make it appear more lifelike. When you move the upper-left slider in the Levels dialog, you force the shade of gray directly below it and any shade darker than it (see the gradient) to black. So moving that slider until it touches the first bar on the histogram forces the darkest shade of gray in the image to black, which should give you nice dark shadows.

When you move the upper-right slider, you force the shade that appears directly below the slider and any shade brighter than it to white. Moving the right slider until it touches the last bar on the histogram forces the brightest shade of gray to white, which should give you nice white highlights.

By adjusting both sliders, you make the image use the full range of shades available to a grayscale image (**Figure 7.9**). If you move the sliders past the beginning and end of the histogram, you'll get even more contrast, but you risk losing important detail in the process.

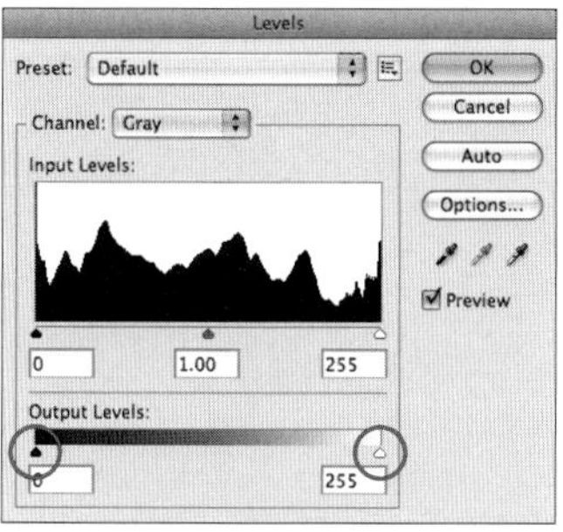

Figure 7.9 The shades that are beyond the upper-right and upper-left triangles on the Input Levels histogram become pure black and pure white, as shown on the Output Levels gradient.

Threshold Mode to the Rescue

To achieve maximum contrast without sacrificing detail, Adobe created a hidden feature in the Levels dialog. It's known as *Threshold mode*. This feature allows you to see exactly which areas are becoming black or white, and it's the key to ensuring that you don't sacrifice detail. To get to the hidden feature, hold down the Option/Alt key when you move the upper-right or upper-left slider in the Levels dialog.

When you move the upper-left slider with Threshold mode turned on, the image should turn white until the slider touches the first bar on the histogram; then small black areas should start to appear. These are the areas that will become pure black. With most images, you shouldn't force a large concentrated area to black, so move the slider only until small areas of black appear. You also want to make sure that the areas that are becoming black still contain

If you're in the market for a new scanner, be sure to compare the Dmax specifications for each scanner you're considering. Higher Dmax specs indicate a scanner that's capable of capturing more shadow detail than you'll get from a scanner with a lower Dmax spec. If you can't find the Dmax specification on the manufacturer's Web site, there's a good chance that it's too low to mention. It's often worth the extra money to get a scanner that can deliver good shadow detail.

detail. Detail will show up looking like visual "noise," so make sure that those small areas also look noisy. Repeat this process with the upper-right slider to get optimal contrast (**Figures 7.10** to **7.14**).

Figure 7.10 The original image. (©2008 Dan Ablan.)

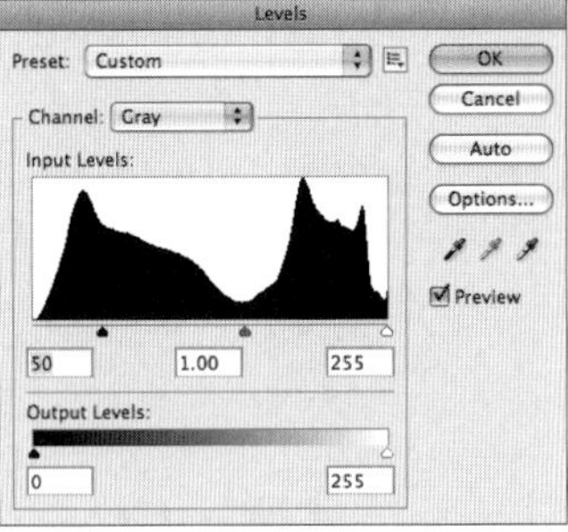

Figure 7.11 Here, the upper-left slider is adjusted much too far.

Figure 7.12 With the upper-left slider adjusted as shown in Figure 7.11, large areas of the image are losing detail and becoming pure black.

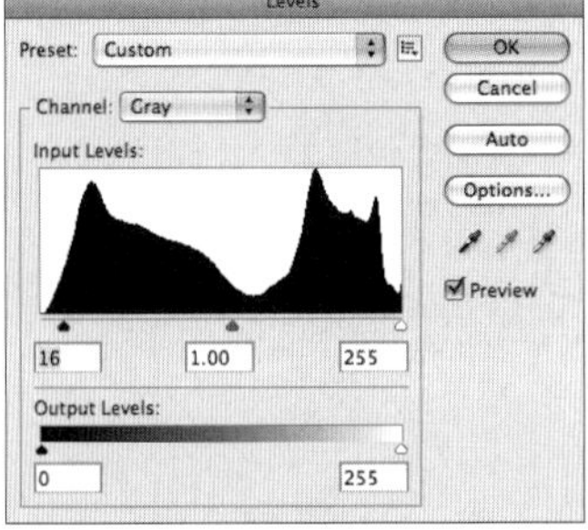

Figure 7.13 Now the upper-left slider is adjusted correctly.

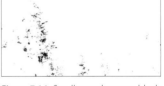

Figure 7.14 Small areas become black but still contain detail (noise).

Three things might cause an image to have large areas of black or white from the start:

- The image was scanned in, and the scanner wasn't capable of capturing good shadow detail.
- The image simply didn't have any detail in the shadows.
- The image has been adjusted without using Photoshop's Threshold mode.

The Histogram Gives You Feedback

After applying an adjustment to an image, you can see an updated histogram by choosing Image > Adjustments > Levels again. Notice that after you've adjusted the upper-right and upper-left sliders, the histogram stretches all the way across the area available. It's just like stretching out a Slinky—you remember, "It walks down stairs, alone or in pairs" (**Figure 7.15**). As you pull on the ends of a Slinky, the loops stretch out and start to create gaps. The same thing happens to a histogram—because Photoshop can't add more bars to the histogram, it can only spread out the ones that were already there. And remember, gaps in the histogram mean that certain shades of gray are missing from the image. So the more you adjust an image using Levels, the more you increase the possibility that you'll lose some of the smooth transitions between bright and dark areas (**Figure 7.16**).

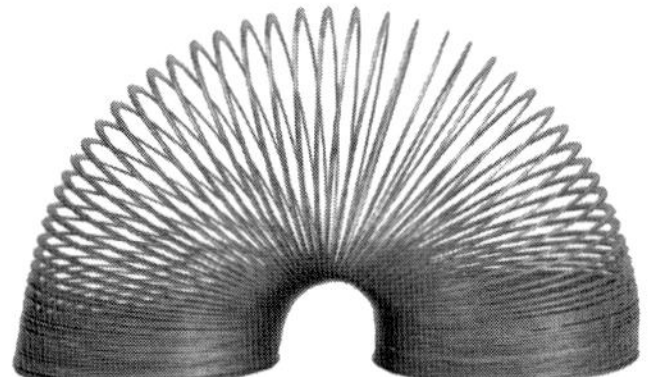

Figure 7.15 A Slinky®.

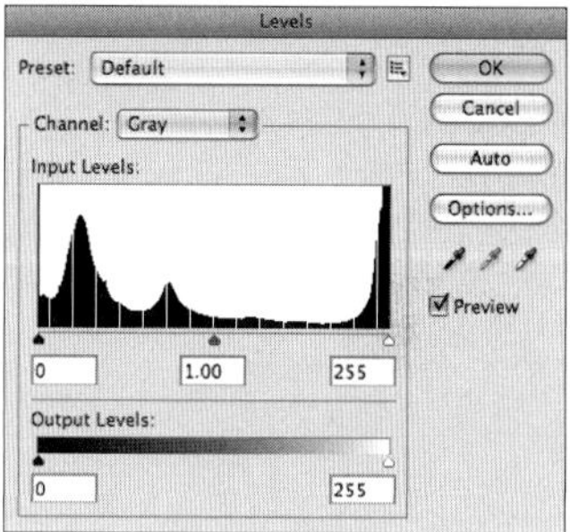

Figure 7.16 After you adjust the top two sliders, the image should use the full range of shades available.

If you see large spikes on either end of the histogram (**Figure 7.17**), it's an indication that you've lost detail. That's because you forced quite a bit of space to white or black by using Levels. But you'd know you did that, because you used the hidden feature, right? Or maybe you couldn't control yourself and used that Brightness/Contrast dialog, where you can't tell if you damaged the image! You might also get spikes on the ends of the histogram (**Figure 7.18**) if you scan an image with too high of a contrast setting, or a brightness setting that's too high or low, or if the image was scanned in and your scanner isn't capable of capturing enough shadow detail.

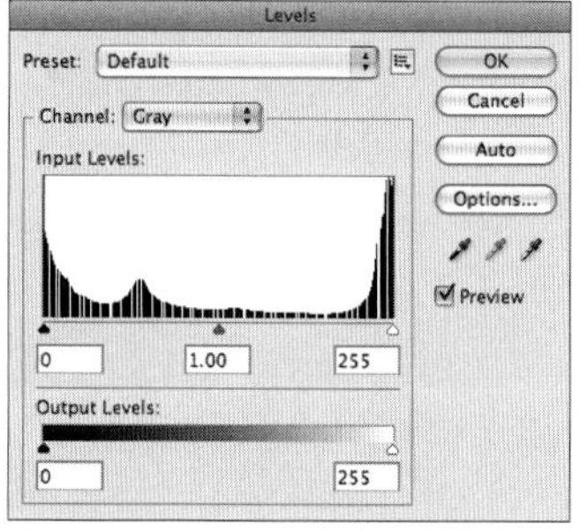

Figure 7.17 Spikes on the end of a histogram usually indicate lost detail.

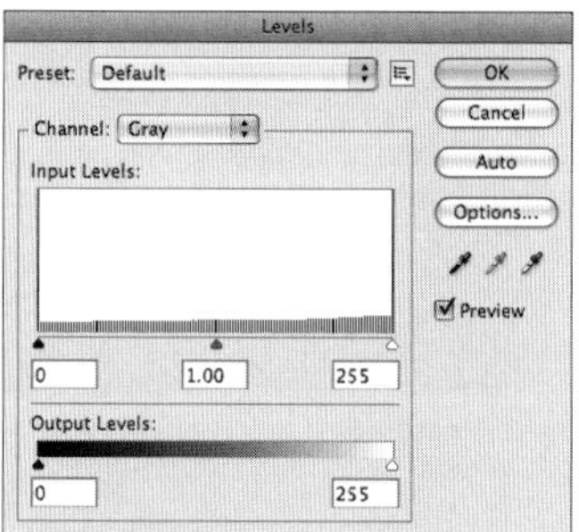

Figure 7.18 Noise.

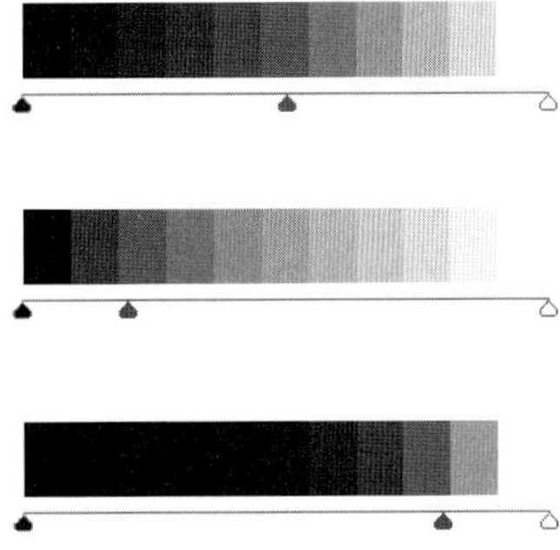

Figure 7.19 Effects of the middle slider.

To see a histogram that changes continuously to reflect any modifications you make to the image, choose Window > Histogram.

Spikes that show up after an image has been adjusted with Levels don't indicate noise. Let's say you try to squish 20 bars on the histogram into a space that's only 15 pixels wide. Five of the bars have to disappear. They're just going to pile on top of the bars next to them and make those bars about twice as tall. When this happens, you get evenly spaced spikes across part of the histogram.

Adjusting Brightness After Contrast

After you have achieved good contrast, the image might look too bright or dark. The middle slider in the Levels dialog can fix that. (Techies call this slider the *gamma setting*, but we plain folks call it the *midpoint*.) If you move the middle slider to the left, the image becomes brighter without messing up the dark areas of the image. Black areas stay nice and black. Or you can move the middle slider to the right to darken the image without messing up the bright areas. White areas stay bright white (**Figure 7.19**). This is the one setting in which you must use your own judgment, based on how bright or dark you want the image to be.

If you want to know what this adjustment is doing, just look directly below the middle slider; the shade of gray there will become 50% gray. Moving it to the left brightens the image because you're shifting what used to be a dark shade of gray to 50% gray. Moving the middle slider to the right darkens the image as you shift a bright shade to 50% gray. If you look at an updated histogram of the image, it will look like you stretched out a Slinky, and then grabbed one side and pulled it to the middle (**Figure 7.20**). Some bars get scrunched together, others spread apart.

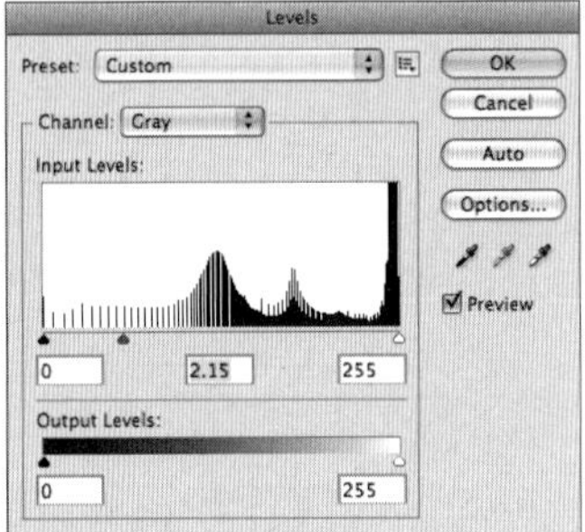

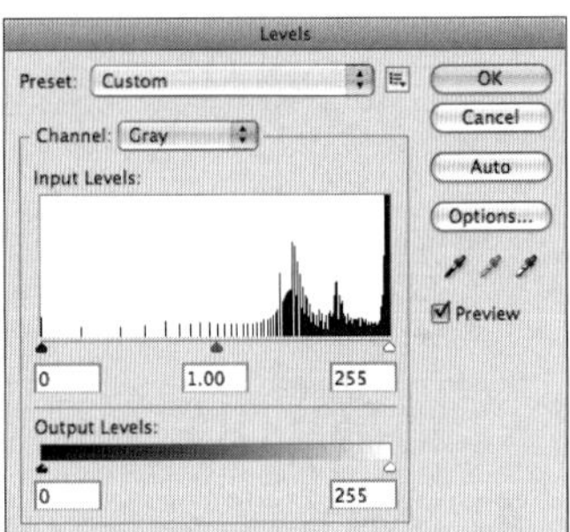

Figure 7.20 The adjustment shown on the left results in the histogram shown on the right.

Prepping for Print

If images are going to be printed on a commercial printing press, chances are that they'll end up looking a lot darker than they did when you viewed them onscreen. This is known as *dot gain*. Fortunately, Photoshop allows you to compensate for dot gain. You can tell Photoshop ahead of time how you intend to output the images, and the software will adjust the onscreen appearance of the image to look as dark as it should be when printed.

To select or enter dot gain settings, choose Edit > Color Settings. In the Working Spaces area of the Color Settings dialog, use the Gray pop-up menu (**Figure 7.21**). Ask your printing company what settings to use; otherwise, you'll just be guessing and you might not like the end result. If you don't have time to ask your printing company, you can use the settings in **Table 7.1**. After you've specified the Dot Gain setting that's appropriate for your printing conditions, choose Image > Mode > Assign Profile, and select the Working Gray setting. That will set up Photoshop to preview the image properly for the specified conditions.

Table 7.1 Dot Gain Settings

Format	Setting
Newspapers	34%
Magazines and brochures	24%
High-end brochures	22%

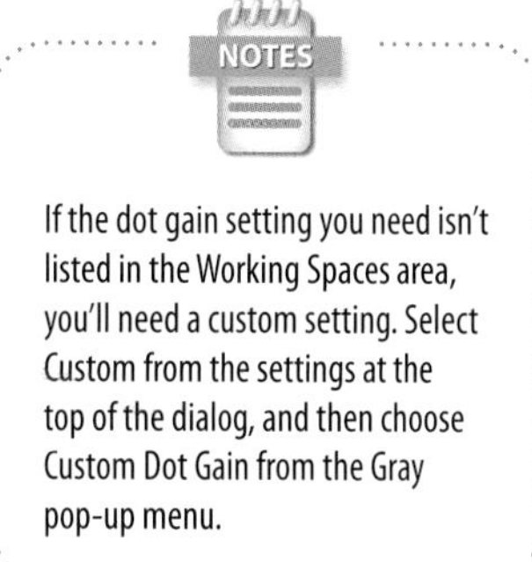

If the dot gain setting you need isn't listed in the Working Spaces area, you'll need a custom setting. Select Custom from the settings at the top of the dialog, and then choose Custom Dot Gain from the Gray pop-up menu.

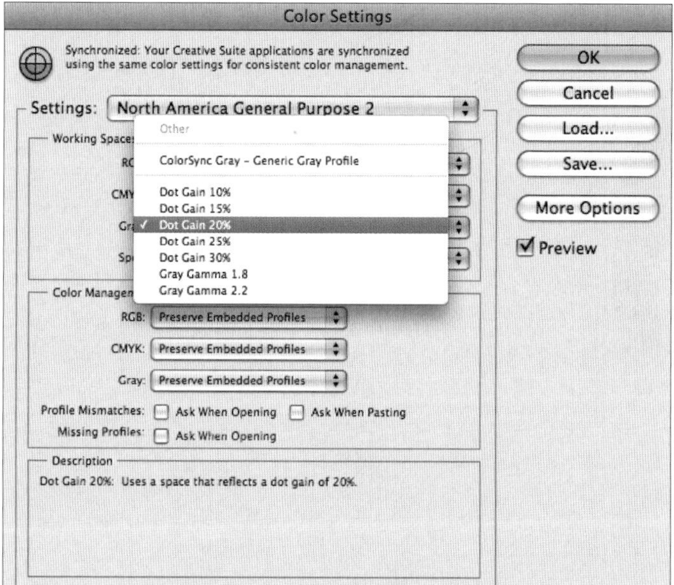

Figure 7.21 The Color Settings dialog.

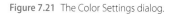

Figure 7.22 The farther the copy from the original image, the more detail lost in the brightest part of the image. (©2008 Dan Ablan.)

Preparing for a Printing Press

Take a close look at the black-and-white image in **Figure 7.22**, and imagine that you took that image to your local copy shop and made a copy of it (copy #1). Then you copied copy #1 to make copy #2. Then you took copy #2 and ran it through the copy machine in your office, making copy #3. At this point, you held copy #3 next to the original. Would you expect them to look the same? Of course not. In fact, the tiny dots that are in the brightest part of the image would have begun to disappear and become pure white—because every time you make a copy, you lose some quality.

The same thing happens when you hand over an image to a printing company; the final printed version is three levels of copying away from the original. The original is used to create a piece of metal called a *printing plate* (copy #1). The plate is put on a big roller on the printing press and flooded with water and ink. The oily ink sticks to the plate only where the images and text should be; the water makes sure that it doesn't stick to the other areas (following the principle that oil and water don't mix). Next to that roller is another one known as a *blanket*; it's just covered with rubber. The plate comes into contact with the blanket so that the ink on the plate will transfer over to the blanket—that's copy #2. Finally, the blanket transfers the ink onto a sheet of paper to create copy #3 (**Figure 7.23**).

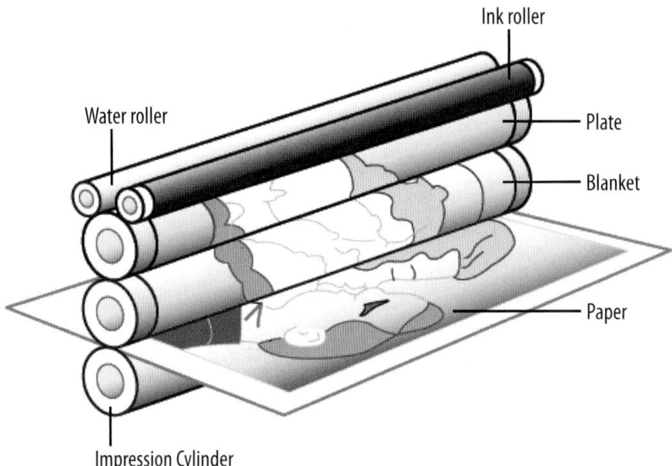

Figure 7.23 Three copies are made before the image turns into a printed page.

Each time a copy is made, you lose some of the smallest dots in the image. Until you know how to compensate for this loss, you're likely to end up with pictures of people with big white spots in the middle of their foreheads.

Before you learn how to compensate for the loss of detail in the bright areas of the image, let's take a look at what happens to the darkest areas, since you'll have to deal with them as well. When you print with ink on paper, the ink gets absorbed into the paper and spreads out—just like when you spill coffee on your morning newspaper. This spreading of ink causes the darkest areas of an image (97%, 98%, 99%) to become pure black. If you don't adjust for this potential, you'll lose detail in the shadows of the image.

If the image will be displayed only onscreen or printed on a desktop printer (such as an inkjet), change the setting in the Gray pop-up menu to the gamma choice your monitor uses. Most Macs are set to 1.8 and most Windows machines are set to 2.2.

Most printing companies create a simple test strip that prints on the edge of the job in the area that will be cropped after printing is completed. This test strip contains shades of gray from 1% to about 5%, to determine the lightest shade of gray that doesn't disappear on press and become pure white. Of course, the folks in the printing industry don't just use plain English to describe this technique; instead, they invented the term "minimum highlight dot reproducible on press." The test strip area also contains shades of gray from 99% to about 75%, so

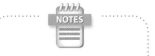

Table 7.2 Common Minimum Highlight Settings

Format	Setting
Newspapers	5%
Magazines and brochures	3%
High-end brochures	3%

Table 7.3 Common Maximum Shadow Settings

Format	Setting
Newspapers	75%
Magazines and brochures	90%
High-end brochures	95%

To measure the minimum highlight and maximum shadow settings for an output device that you own, try the highlight/shadow test at www.digitalmastery.com/test.

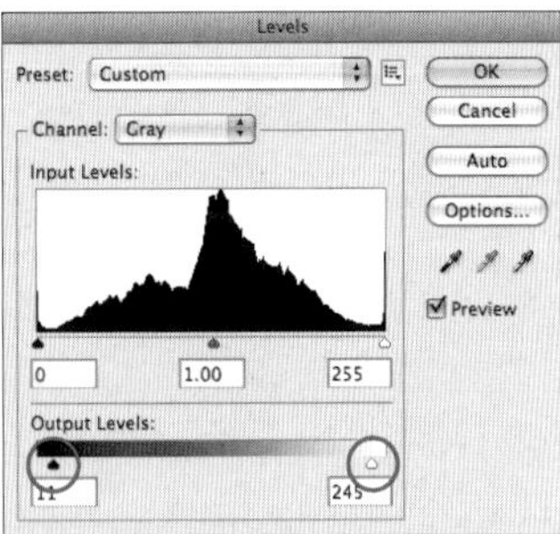

Figure 7.24 The bottom sliders reduce image contrast to compensate for the limitations of the printing press.

the printers can see the darkest shade of gray that doesn't become pure black. For that one, they came up with the term "maximum shadow dot reproducible on press." Your printing company can usually tell you exactly which settings to use. In case you don't know who will print your images, or you don't have the time to ask about settings, **Tables 7.2** and **7.3** give you some generic numbers to use.

But first, let's find out how to adjust for minimum highlight and maximum shadow dots. By moving the lower-right slider in the Levels dialog, you change white to the shade of gray to which the slider is pointing. Move this slider until it points to the *minimum highlight dot*—that is, the lightest shade of gray that won't disappear and become white on-press.

You don't want to eyeball this setting; instead of just looking at the shades of gray, use the Output Level numbers in the Levels dialog. There's one problem with these numbers, though: They range from 0 to 255 instead of 0 to 100%! This is because you can have up to 256 shades of gray in a grayscale image, and Photoshop wants you to be able to control them all. When you're using this numbering system, think about light instead of ink. If you have no light (0), that would be pitch black; if you have as much light as possible (255), you could call that white. So that you won't need a calculator, **Table 7.4** provides the conversions.

By moving the lower-left slider in the Levels dialog, you change black to the shade of gray to which the slider is pointing (**Figure 7.24**). Move this slider until it points to the darkest shade of gray that won't solidify as black (known as the *maximum shadow dot*).

At first glance, this stuff might seem complicated, but it's really quite simple. All you do is use the numbers from the tables or ask your printing company for settings. If you always print on the same kind of paper, you'll always use the same numbers.

Table 7.4 Percentage Conversion

Percentage	Output Level	Percentage	Output Level	Percentage	Output Level
100%	0	66%	87	32%	174
99%	3	65%	90	31%	177
98%	5	64%	92	30%	179
97%	8	63%	95	29%	182
96%	10	62%	97	28%	184
95%	13	61%	100	27%	187
94%	15	60%	102	26%	189
93%	18	59%	105	25%	192
92%	20	58%	108	24%	195
91%	23	57%	110	23%	197
90%	26	56%	113	22%	200
89%	28	55%	115	21%	202
88%	31	54%	118	20%	205
87%	33	53%	120	19%	207
86%	36	52%	123	18%	210
85%	38	51%	125	17%	212
84%	41	50%	128	16%	215
83%	44	49%	131	15%	218
82%	46	48%	133	14%	220
81%	49	47%	136	13%	223
80%	51	46%	138	12%	225
79%	54	45%	141	11%	228
78%	56	44%	143	10%	230
77%	59	43%	146	9%	233
76%	61	42%	148	8%	236
75%	64	41%	151	7%	238
74%	67	40%	154	6%	241
73%	69	39%	156	5%	243
72%	72	38%	159	4%	246
71%	74	37%	161	3%	248
70%	77	36%	164	2%	251
69%	79	35%	166	1%	253
68%	82	34%	169	0%	255
67%	84	33%	172		

Figure 7.25 The original image.

Figure 7.26 Result of adjusting the upper-left slider.

Figure 7.27 Result of adjusting the upper-right slider.

Figure 7.28 Result of adjusting the middle slider.

Figure 7.29 Result of adjusting the lower-left slider.

Figure 7.30 Result of adjusting the lower-right slider.

Brief Recap

Here's a quick list of the steps for adjusting each of the sliders in the Levels dialog:

To see an updated histogram after adjusting an image, you must first apply the adjustment and then reopen the Levels dialog (Image > Adjustments > Levels). You can also choose Window > Histogram to see before-and-after histograms overlaid on each other.

1. When the original image is ready (**Figure 7.25**), choose Image > Adjustments > Levels to open the Levels dialog. Move the upper-left slider in the dialog until it touches the first bar on the histogram, to force the darkest area of the image to black. Use the hidden Threshold feature—hold down Option/Alt—to go as far as possible without damaging the image (**Figure 7.26**).
2. Move the upper-right slider until it touches the last bar on the histogram, to force the brightest area of the image to white. Again, use the hidden Threshold feature—hold down Option/Alt—to go as far as possible without damaging the image (**Figure 7.27**).
3. Move the middle slider until the brightness of the image looks the way you want it (**Figure 7.28**).
4. Move the lower-left slider to make sure that the shadows won't become pure black on the printing press (**Figure 7.29**). Use the tables in the previous sections

for settings, or ask your printing company for more precise numbers.

5. Move the lower-right slider to make sure that you don't lose detail in the highlights when the smallest dots in the image disappear on the printing press (**Figure 7.30**). Use the previous tables for settings, or ask your printing company for more precise numbers.
6. When you're happy with the settings, click OK to apply them. You can usually adjust all five sliders before clicking OK.

If your scanner is 30-bit or higher and the scanning software contains a histogram and has the same adjustment controls available as in the Levels dialog, you can make adjustments within the scanning software. Most scanners can deliver a histogram without gaps because they can look back to the image and pick up extra shades of gray that would fill the gaps. These days, almost all scanners are 36-bit or higher. If your scanner is capable of delivering a 16-bit grayscale image to Photoshop, the only adjustment you need to make during scanning is to make sure that highlights and shadows still have detail. If the histogram in your scanner has spikes at the ends, lower the contrast setting and rescan until you don't get the spikes.

Post-Adjustment Analysis

When you adjust an image, you run the risk of introducing artifacts, so let's take a look at what can happen to an image after applying Levels. (Don't worry—there's usually at least one "fix" for every artifact.)

Low-Contrast Onscreen Appearance

If you've adjusted an image that will eventually be reproduced on a commercial printing press, the results most likely look rather flat onscreen (lacking contrast). This problem is temporary, since the image will gain contrast when it's printed on a press (dark areas become darker and bright areas become brighter). You may want to adjust only the top three sliders in the Levels dialog to get an acceptable image, and hold off on adjusting the bottom two sliders until you're done working on the image in Photoshop. That way, the image will have good contrast for the vast majority of the time you work on it. Just before saving the image as a final version, adjust the bottom two sliders, so that the image is ready to be reproduced on press.

Recognizing and Eliminating Posterization

Looking at an updated histogram, you might see wide gaps in the histogram between a bright area and a dark area—this *posterization* (**Figure 7.31**) happens when you should have a smooth transition between areas and instead you see a drastic jump. Some people call this *banding* or *stair-stepping*. As long as the gaps in the histogram are smaller than three pixels wide, you probably won't notice it at all in the image.

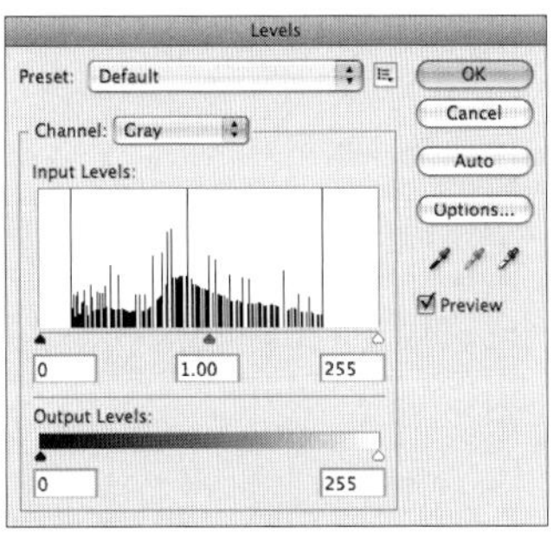

Figure 7.31 Gaps in a histogram indicate posterization.

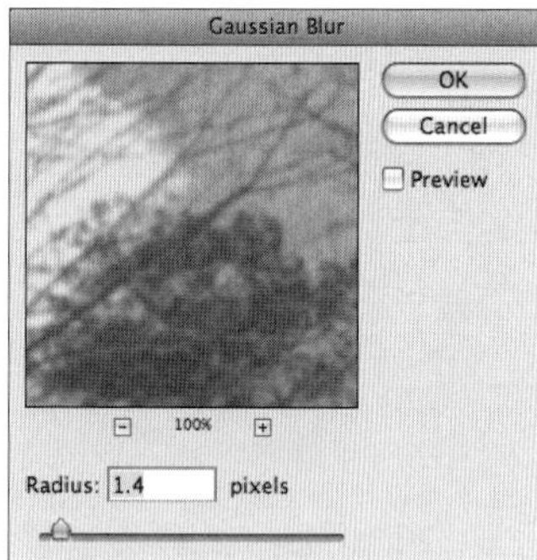

Figure 7.32 Turn off the Preview check box to see the edges of the posterized area. Then turn on the Preview check box and increase the Radius setting until the posterized area appears smooth.

Adjusting the image usually causes these gaps. As you adjust the image, the bars on the histogram spread out and gaps start to appear. The more extreme the adjustment, the wider the gaps. If you see huge gaps in the histogram, the posterization probably is noticeable enough that you'll want to fix it (it usually shows up in the dark areas of the image).

Here's a trick that can minimize the posterization. You have to apply this technique manually to each area that is posterized. Although it might take a bit of time, the results will be worthwhile. (Don't use this technique on every image—just on those that have extremely noticeable posterization.)

To begin, select the Magic Wand tool, set the Tolerance to 0, and click an area that looks posterized. Choose Select > Modify > Border, and use a setting of 2 for slight posterization or 4 for a moderate amount of posterization. Now apply Filter > Blur > Gaussian Blur until the area looks smooth (**Figure 7.32**). Repeat this process on all of the posterized areas until you're satisfied with the results.

If you don't have the time or patience to apply the technique described here to eliminate posterization, consider choosing Filter > Noise > Add Noise and using a setting of 3 or 7. This approach can help to reduce posterization, but won't be able to help in cases of extreme posterization.

If a large number of your images end up with post-scan posterization, look into getting a scanner that's capable of delivering 16-bit images to Photoshop. A typical grayscale image contains no more than 256 shades of gray, which is technically known as an *8-bit image.* That's sufficient for most images, but extreme adjustments will cause posterization. One way to avoid posterization is to use a scanner that can produce images containing thousands of shades of gray, which is technically known as a *16-bit image.* Most scanners are capable of capturing more than 256 shades of gray from a photograph, but few are capable of actually delivering all those shades to Photoshop.

Working with Color

If you surveyed hundreds of Photoshop users, you might find that the majority of them perform color correction by picking their favorite adjustment tool (Color Balance, Hue/Saturation, Curves, or the like) and then using a somewhat hit-or-miss technique. They blindly move a few sliders back and forth in the hope that the image onscreen will improve. If that approach doesn't work, they simply repeat the process with a different adjustment option. Those same people often ask for "advanced color-correction techniques" because they're frustrated and don't feel like they're really in control of the color in their images. If this describes the way you're adjusting your colors, you'll be pleasantly surprised when you learn about the science of professional color correction, where 95% of all guesswork is removed and you know exactly which tool and what settings to use to achieve great color.

If you have a color print or transparency that will be reproduced as a grayscale image, scan the original as color and then convert it to grayscale in Photoshop. Check out Chapter 8, "Color Manipulation," to learn how to produce a higher-quality grayscale conversion.

First we'll look at a general concept that will help you to color-correct an image. Then you'll walk through a step-by-step technique you can use to get good-looking color in Photoshop.

Use Gray to Fix Color?!?

For now, try to wipe out any thoughts you have of color. Seriously—this approach really works, so stick with it. The color we call "gray" is made up of equal amounts of red, green, and blue. With that in mind, open an image and find an area that you would call "gray." Then look in the Info panel to see if it really *is* gray in Photoshop (**Figure 7.33**). Don't trust your monitor *or* your eyes! If the RGB numbers in the Info panel aren't equal—no matter what it looks like on your monitor—it's not gray. If it's not gray, it must be contaminated with color. But could that color be contaminating more than the gray area? Most likely.

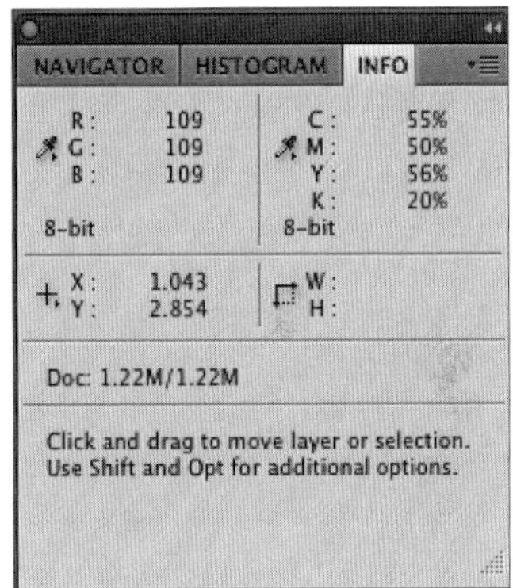

Figure 7.33 Unless the RGB numbers are equal, the selected area is not gray.

How do contaminating colors get in there? Here are a few potential culprits:

- A mixed lighting situation that confused the automatic white-balance mechanism of your camera
- Choosing the wrong manual white-balance setting
- The temperature of the chemicals used to develop the film being too hot or too cool
- Inappropriate filters used in a photographic enlarger when your prints were being made
- Aging bulbs in a scanner that might shift the colors during the scanning process

- Diffused light from surrounding elements such as trees, buildings, sky, and so on mixing together, making it nearly impossible to find complete gray

Figure 7.34 The original image. (©2008 Dan Ablan.)

We're going to use the Curves dialog to make an adjustment. But don't worry, you don't have to remember everything from Chapter 3, "Layers and Curves," to use this trick. For what we're trying to accomplish, here's what you need to know:

- Command/Ctrl-clicking the image will add a point.
- The Input number indicates what you're changing.
- The Output number determines the end result in the area you're changing.

To get started, download the image RonaldWalk.jpg (**Figure 7.34**) from www.danablan.com/photoshop (or use one of your own images). Even if you skipped the chapter on Curves, you'll still be able to color-correct images. (At this stage, we're going to adjust a curve manually. Later, you'll learn a much faster and easier method.)

Even though you'll deal with RGB settings while you learn this technique, Photoshop can translate from RGB to CMYK numbers once you start performing the steps listed in the "Professional Color Correction" section of this chapter. Look at the CMYK area of the color picker to see what you'd get in CMYK mode.

Start by putting your cursor on the gray sidewalk. Now glance over at the Info panel and write down the RGB numbers—initially, they should be approximately 114R, 111G, and 102B. (If the Info panel isn't open, press F8 or choose Window > Info.) To make that sidewalk a real gray, you'll need to make those RGB numbers equal. But you don't want to change the brightness of the sidewalk. To prevent that from happening, grab a calculator and add the three RGB numbers together to find out the total amount of light that's making up the sidewalk (114 + 111 + 102 = 327, for example). To keep from changing the brightness of the sidewalk, you'll keep the total amount of light the same, but using equal amounts of red, green, and blue. To figure out the exact numbers to use, just divide the total brightness of the sidewalk (327 in this case) by three (327 ÷ 3 = 109). Round off the result so you don't have any decimals. Now that you know your starting number (from the Info panel) and the number you want to have (from the calculator), you can adjust the image.

Choose Image > Adjustments > Curves and set the Channel pop-up menu at the top of the dialog to RGB. In the Curves chapter, you learned that if you then Command/Ctrl-click the image, you'll place a point on the curve at that tone. If you move that point up or down, you change red, green, and blue in equal amounts, which would just change the brightness of the image. But for this example, you want to work on the individual colors separately. To have Photoshop add a point to each of the red, green, and blue curves, hold down Shift-Command (Mac) or Shift-Ctrl (Windows) and click the sidewalk. To see these individual points, open the Channel pop-up menu again and select the Red, Green, or Blue channel. You should find a new point on each of those curves. The position of each one of those points is based on the numbers that showed up in the Info panel. All you need to do is switch between the red, green, and blue curves and change the output numbers for each one so that they match the number you calculated (109 in this case) in the Info panel. After you've done that, take a peek at the image to see what you've done. The sidewalk should be gray. If it's not, and you're quite sure you followed the steps correctly, your monitor may need calibration.

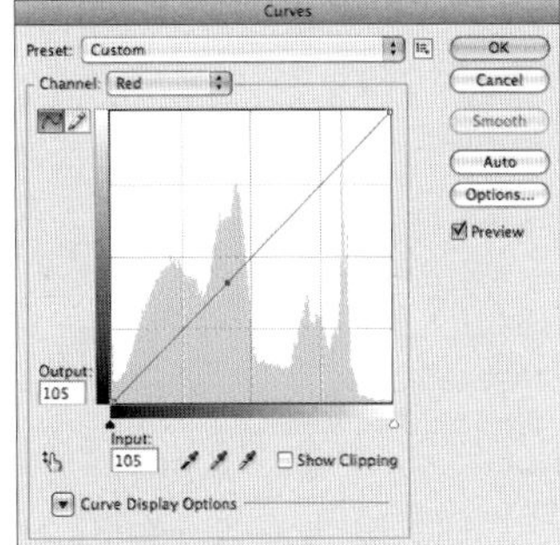

Figure 7.35 The red curve.

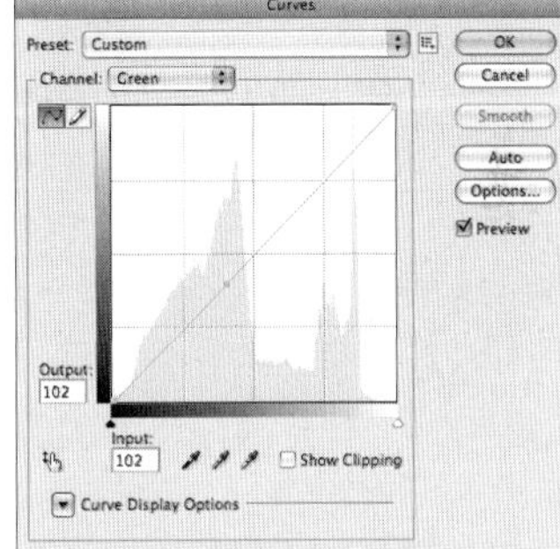

Figure 7.36 The green curve.

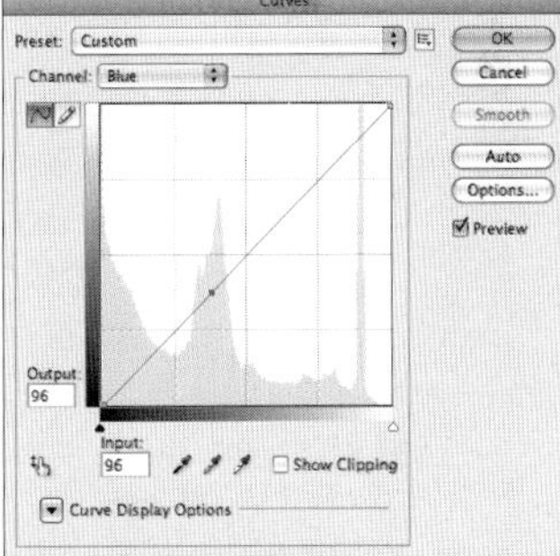

Figure 7.37 The blue curve.

Now look back at the three curves applied to this image (**Figures 7.35** to **7.37**). You measured what was wrong with the image in the gray areas, but the adjustment changed the entire image. That's logical enough, because whatever is wrong with the gray areas is also affecting the rest of the image. But when you look at those curves, does it look like you really changed the full length of the curve? Almost—but not quite. You didn't change the brightest and darkest areas. So, you really haven't accomplished the color correction, and you won't until you've taken some more steps. But from this exercise, you saw that the concept of measuring and adjusting gray works to color-correct the image. Now let's see how you can make this process faster and easier, and then you'll move on to adjusting the brightest and darkest areas.

Realizing that it might feel quite low-tech to be scribbling a bunch of numbers on a sheet of paper and using a calculator in the face of a multi-thousand-dollar computer, the folks at Adobe provided a tool that will do 99% of the work. Choose File > Revert to return the image to its original state, and then choose Image > Adjustments > Curves.

Curves is equipped to do the same basic corrections as Levels, but can also do much, much more. In general, with grayscale images you should always start out using Levels and then move on to Curves to fix any problems that Levels can't handle. Also, use Curves to work with color.

Click the middle eyedropper toward the bottom of the dialog, and then move your cursor out onto the image and click that gray sidewalk again. With a single click, it should change to gray. Photoshop is using the same concept you used when you wrote down the RGB numbers and averaged them; it's just doing it in a fraction of a second, with no paper involved. In fact, those eyedroppers will help you even more if you adjust the full range of shades from the brightest to the darkest. Let's see how it works.

Professional Color Correction

Okay, now you can start thinking in color again. Let's look at the process of professional color correction in three parts: balancing colors, adjusting skin tones, and adjusting saturation. You don't always have to perform all three parts of this process, but the more you do, the better the result.

Balancing Colors

To eliminate any color casts in the image, you'll need to look for color contamination in the gray areas of the image and then use that information to help correct the whole image. Three standard areas of an image will usually contain a shade of gray: the brightest area of the image, which is known as the *highlight*; the darkest area of the image, which is known as the *shadow* (on most photos, the highlight and shadow areas shouldn't contain color); and a gray object in the image.

Now that you know which areas need to be adjusted, go ahead and make the actual adjustment. Start by choosing Image > Adjustments > Curves. You'll be working with all three of the Curves eyedroppers. All three eyedroppers adjust the area you click, so that it ends up with a balanced combination of red, green, and blue—effectively removing any color contamination for that area. The only difference between the eyedroppers is that the one full of black makes things really, really dark; the eyedropper full of white makes things really bright; and the middle eyedropper doesn't change the brightness of an area. You'll use those eyedroppers to adjust the shadow, highlight, and gray areas, respectively. But first you have to set up things correctly.

Double-click the eyedropper on the right to bring up the color picker. This eyedropper will be used to adjust the brightest part of the image (the highlight). You don't want the highlight to become pure white, because it would look too bright. Reserve pure white for those areas that shine light directly into the camera lens (such as light bulbs and shiny reflections). The highlight should be just a bit darker than white.

When working with gray, the lightest percentage of ink you can use on a printing press is usually 3% (5% for some newspapers). Therefore, you don't want to use less than 3% of any ink in the brightest part of the image; otherwise, you might lose critical detail. But you're adjusting the image in RGB mode, and when you do that, you're using a numbering system that ranges from 0 to 255, not 0% to 100%. So let's figure out how to create a minimum of 3% ink in RGB mode.

After double-clicking the eyedropper, set the saturation setting (S) to 0 and the brightness setting (B) to 100%, and click the number next to the letter B (brightness). Use the down-arrow key to change that setting until the magenta (M) and yellow (Y) readouts indicate at least 3%. Cyan (C) will be higher, but don't worry about that. At this point, the numbers will show you exactly what RGB values are needed to produce that much ink—in **Figure 7.38**, 240R, 240G, 240B.

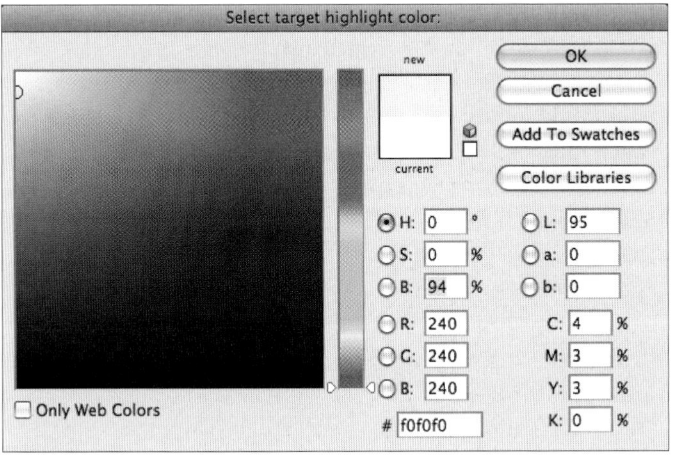

Figure 7.38 A good highlight value is 240R, 240G, 240B.

Now, on to the dark side. You're going to make the darkest area of the image pure black (0R, 0G, 0B) in order to use the full range of colors that your computer monitor is capable of displaying. Black wouldn't be a good choice if you're outputting to a printing press (you'd lose a lot of detail), but you'll set it up so that Photoshop adjusts the image automatically if you have to convert to CMYK mode. That way, no detail will be lost no matter what the output. So, double-click the left eyedropper and make sure that it's set to black. When you click OK in the Curves dialog, Photoshop asks if you would like to save the new target colors as the defaults. Go ahead and click the Yes button so that Photoshop remembers those settings and uses them every time you use the eyedroppers to color-correct images.

Now that you have everything set up properly, it's time to start adjusting images. Open any image that needs to be color-corrected, and then choose a new Curves adjustment layer from the Adjustments panel (**Figure 7.39**). Name your adjustment layer something like Color Correct. Click the black eyedropper and then click the shadow area in the image. Remember, the shadow area is the darkest area of an image—not an actual shadow. Almost all images have a shadow area, but it can sometimes be hard to locate because there may be multiple candidates.

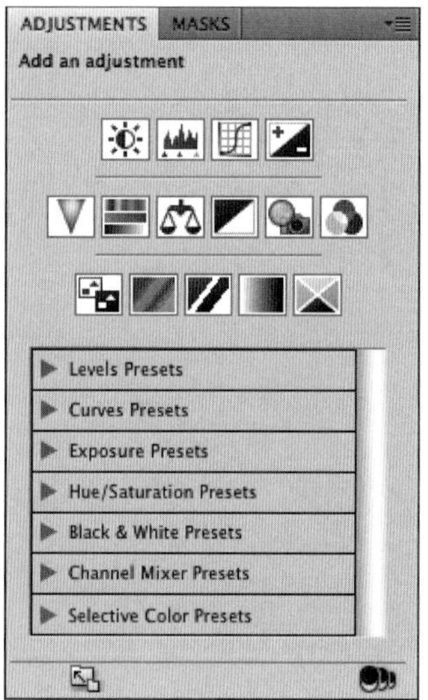

Figure 7.39 Use the new CS4 Adjustments panel to add a Curves adjustment layer.

Once you've done that, click the white eyedropper and then click the brightest part of the image. That area should still contain detail. You'll often find it in a white shirt collar or button, a Styrofoam cup, the whites of someone's eyes, or a sheet of paper. In **Figure 7.40**, for example, the brightest white is in the sky.

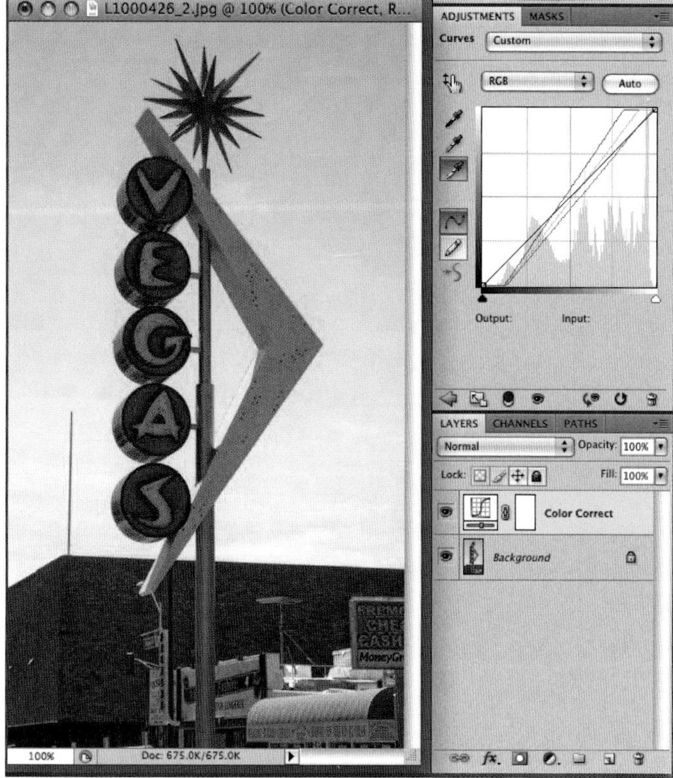

Figure 7.40 The brightest white in this image falls within the sky.

Finally, click the middle eyedropper and then click any area that should be gray in the final image—not bluish gray or pinkish gray, but pure gray (also known as *neutral* gray). You might have to really hunt for a gray; it's not always obvious. It could be a sweatshirt, a white dress shirt, or the edge of a book. On the other hand, you might run across an image that has dozens of gray areas from which you can choose. In that case, try to pick one that's not overly bright or dark, because you're already adjusting the highlight and shadow of the image. The closer you get to a middle gray, the more effective your adjustment will be. If you have any doubt at all that the area you've chosen is gray, experiment by clicking one area to see what happens; then press Command/Ctrl-Z to undo the change, and then try another area. Repeat this process until you've found an area that really causes the image to improve—but don't try too hard. Not every image contains a true gray. For example, you might not be able to find one in a photograph of a forest. If you can't find a neutral gray, then (of course) don't adjust it.

Using the Threshold Command to Locate Highlight and Shadow

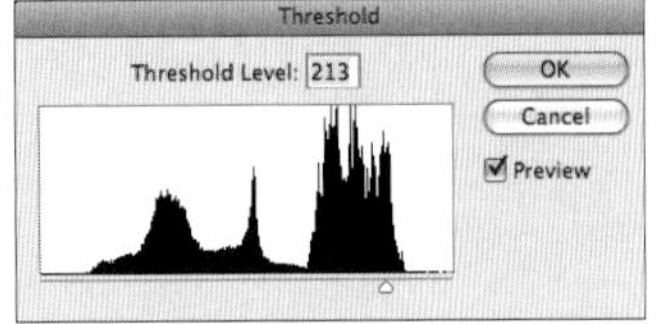

Figure 7.41 Use the Threshold command to find elusive highlights.

Here's a way to find the highlight and shadow areas without guessing. Choose Image > Adjustments > Threshold and move the slider all the way to the right; then slowly move it toward the middle (**Figure 7.41**). The brightest area of the image will be the first area that shows up as white (you can use the up- and down-arrow keys to move the slider). You don't want to find the very brightest speck (that could be a scratch or a reflection on something shiny), so be sure to look for a general area at least five or six pixels in size (something that's easy enough to click without having to be overly precise). Once you've found the correct area, Shift-click that part of the image to add a color sampler to that area. (You have to hold down Shift only if you're still in an adjustment dialog such as Threshold.) A *color sampler* is simply a visual reminder of where that area is.

Using the up- and down-arrow keys to move the Threshold slider allows you to focus on the image, instead of having to concentrate on being precise with the mouse.

Now let's use Threshold to find the darkest area of the image. This time, start with the slider all the way to the left, and then slowly move it toward the center. This shows you where the darkest area of the image is hiding. You don't want to find the darkest speck (that could be dust), so look for a general area at least five or six pixels in size. Once you've located the shadow, Shift-click that area to place a sample point on top of it, and then click Cancel to get out of the Threshold dialog. (If you click OK instead of Cancel, the image will remain completely black and white.) Now you should have two crosshairs on the image, one for the highlight and one for the shadow, as shown in **Figure 7.42**. When you use the eyedroppers in the Curves dialog, you can press Caps Lock to turn your cursor into a crosshair, which will make it easy to tell when you're lined up with those color samplers. You can get rid of the color samplers by choosing the Color Sampler tool (it's hidden under the Eyedropper tool) and clicking the Clear button in the options bar.

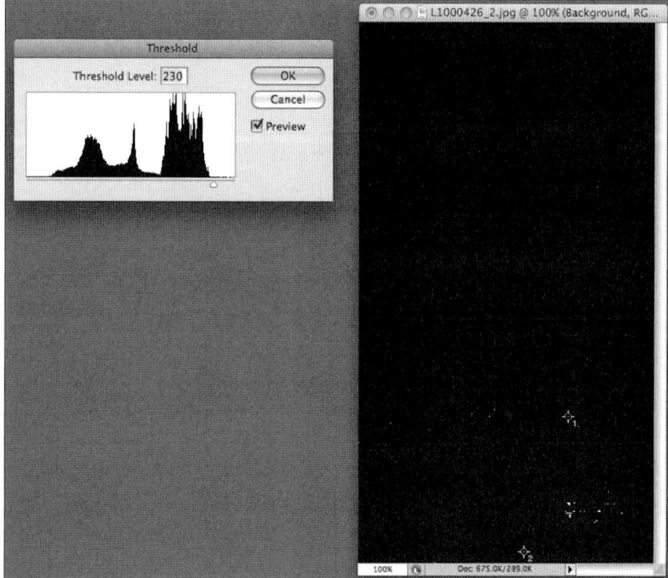

Figure 7.42 After using the Color Sampler tool, you should see crosshairs on the image.

Only use those eyedroppers that help to improve the look of the image. If one of them shifts the colors in an undesirable way, press Command/Ctrl-Z to undo that step and try another area, or don't use that eyedropper. Just because a single eyedropper harms the image, that doesn't mean that the other two eyedroppers won't help it, so always try all three, even if you think they might not help the image. You'll be surprised at how often all three can be used.

Now let's explore two alternative methods for adjusting the highlight, shadow, and gray areas of an image.

The white eyedropper doesn't help images that have desirable color casts. That's where you want the image to look warm or cool. Examples would be dinner by candlelight, a fireplace, and sunrise or sunset.

If none of the eyedroppers seems to help, check out the techniques in Chapter 8.

The grayscale correction technique is appropriate only when you want to end up with an image that looks like it was shot under a white light source. It won't improve the look of images that contain desirable color casts, such as those shot under candlelight or at sunrise or sunset.

Using Grayscale to Correct Multiple Images

Here's an interesting trick you can use when you'll be color-correcting photographed artwork or a number of images that will be shot under the same lighting conditions. Stop by a high-end camera store and ask for a *grayscale* image, also known as a *step wedge* or a *grayscale step wedge* (**Figure 7.43**). Then place it in the scene where you're about to take a large number of photos (let's say for a yearbook or a product brochure) or when shooting any kind of art. (Alternatively, you can use something like a digital calibration target from www.photovisionvideo.com.) Now, this is important—before you start shooting scenes, take a photograph of the wedge or target under the same lighting conditions you'll use for your photos, and using the same white-balance setting. As long as your settings and lighting don't change after that, you can use this first shot as a reference for correcting all of your other shots.

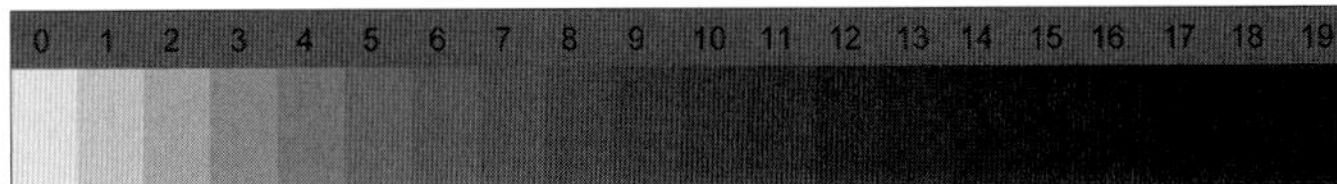

Figure 7.43 A grayscale image from a high-end camera store.

After the images are transferred to your computer (or developed, scanned, and loaded into Photoshop), create a new Curves adjustment layer on the reference image. Click the white eyedropper and then click the brightest gray rectangle on the grayscale. Next, click the black eyedropper and then click the darkest rectangle. Finally, click the middle eyedropper and then click the middle gray rectangle. These steps should remove any color cast that was present in the image.

You can apply that same adjustment to the other images by dragging the Curves adjustment layer from the grayscale image and dropping it onto another image that was photographed under the same lighting conditions. That way, you can perform color correction with no guesswork, and quickly apply the same adjustment to a large number of images.

If this technique changes the contrast of an image too much for your taste, either use the middle eyedropper (skipping the other two), or use a blending mode to control how the adjustment affects the image. If you applied your Curves adjustment directly (by choosing Image > Adjustments > Curves), choose Edit > Fade Curves immediately after applying the adjustment, and change the pop-up menu setting to Color. If you used an adjustment layer instead, change the setting in the Blending Mode menu (at the top of the Layers panel) to Color. That setting will prevent the adjustment from changing the brightness or contrast of the image, but will still allow it to shift the colors.

Auto Color

Photoshop includes a great feature that attempts to automate the process of color correction: Auto Color (**Figure 7.44**). It uses the same general concepts we've been talking about in this chapter, and it works well with a wide variety of images. You can access Auto Color by creating a new Curves adjustment layer and then clicking the Options button (hold down Alt/Option and click the Auto button). The Shadows, Midtones, and Highlights settings use the same setting that you specified when you double-clicked the eyedroppers in the Curves dialog. The only difference is that Photoshop attempts to locate the highlight, shadow, and gray areas automatically. This dialog is interactive—changes affect the image immediately.

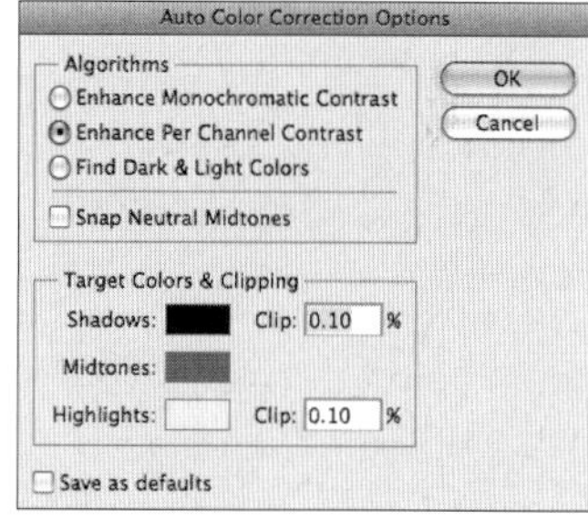

Figure 7.44 The Auto Color Correction Options dialog.

If you set the Shadows Clip value to 0.25% and the Highlights Clip value to 0.10%, and then choose the Find Dark & Light Colors option at the top of the dialog, Photoshop uses Threshold to find the bright/dark areas and applies the eyedroppers to them. Then turn on the Snap Neutral Midtones check box so Photoshop uses the middle eyedropper on areas that are close to being gray.

This automated feature works on a surprising number of images. But, as with most automated features, you might have to take over and use the old eyedroppers technique whenever Auto Color fails to deliver a satisfactory result.

If the highlights in the image become blown out (no detail), click the White Clip setting and press the down-arrow key a few times until you see the detail return. You can do the same thing with the Black Clip setting to make sure that you don't lose detail in the shadows of the image. You can generally use a .10% setting, changing it only when you notice that you're losing detail. If you're usually satisfied with the .10% values, be sure to turn on the Save as Defaults check box so Photoshop will remember those settings. With that option selected, you can quickly apply the new default settings to any image by choosing Image > Adjustments > Auto Color. If you notice the contrast of the image changing too much, choose Edit > Fade Auto Color immediately after applying that command, and set the pop-up menu option to Color. That setting will prevent any brightness or contrast shifts.

The more you get accustomed to using the techniques described in this chapter, the less you'll have to rely on stock photos for reference photos. You'll get used to knowing that the more red you pull out of an image, the more tan someone looks, and that the balance between green and blue determines how fair someone's skin looks.

Adjusting the highlight, shadow, and gray areas of an image can dramatically improve the quality of an image. But even with those adjustments, you occasionally need to fine-tune any skin tones that might be in the image.

Adjusting Skin Tones

You might be thinking that there's some kind of magic formula for creating great skin tones (kind of like what you did with grays), but if you were given just one formula, every skin tone would look identical in your images! It's much better to learn how to get a unique formula for each color of skin you might run across—dark skin, olive skin, sunburned skin, fair skin, and so on. Even better, we can do all that without trusting your monitor at all. (Of course, they'll still look good on your screen, but unless you've calibrated the screen using a hardware device, you shouldn't make critical decisions based on the screen image.)

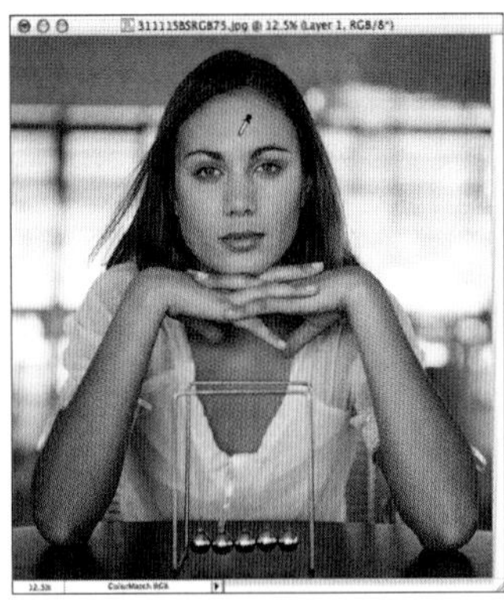

Figure 7.45 Reference photo from a stock photo catalog. (©2007 Stockbyte, www.stockbyte.com.)

Any stock photo company will have a veritable treasure trove of flesh that you can transform into your own personal stockpile of skin tones. Simply go online to any stock provider (for instance, www.istockphoto.com) and download a low-resolution comp image of the person who has the skin tone that best matches your needs. Using the Eyedropper tool, click an area of the skin that has a medium brightness (**Figure 7.45**). Then click the foreground color to see the RGB formula needed to create that exact color.

Now let's figure out how to use that information to improve the skin tones in an image. Open the image you need to correct, and use the Color Sampler tool to click the troublesome skin area. Be sure to click in an area with medium brightness, similar to the level in the other (stock photo) image. That should give you an extra readout in the Info panel (readout #1 if you just opened a fresh image, or readout #4 if you still have the three used earlier in this chapter).

Next, click the eyedropper icon that shows up next to that new readout in the Info panel. Choose HSB from the menu (**Figure 7.46**), note the brightness (B) setting, and then set that menu back to RGB. Now, click your foreground color to look at the color from the stock photo again. We want to use that basic color, but we don't want to change the brightness of the image very much. Change the brightness (B) setting to what you saw in the photo you're attempting to color-correct; then write down the RGB numbers that show up in the color picker (**Figure 7.47**). In just a moment, you're going to use those RGB numbers to tell Curves how to shift the skin color in the problem photo to match the skin color in the reference photo.

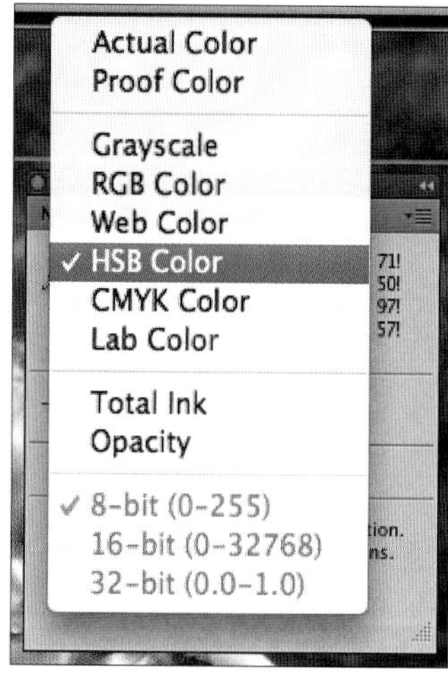

Figure 7.46 Change the sampler mode to HSB Color to determine the brightness of the area you're color-correcting.

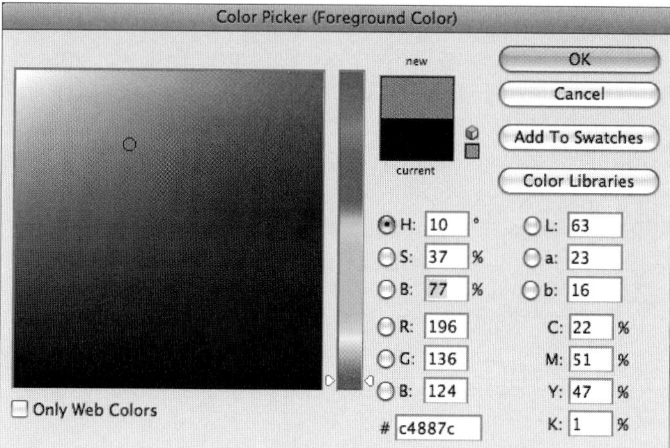

Figure 7.47 Change the brightness (B) setting to find the perfect skin tone setting.

But first, it's time to isolate the skin tones in the problem image and then make your adjustment. You can choose Select > Color Range to isolate the skin. Once you have a general selection of the skin (don't worry if it's not perfect), it's time to make the adjustment.

You can also adjust skin tones without messing with HSB numbers. Copy the RGB numbers from one image and apply them to another. Just be careful to choose areas that are not radically different in the two images; otherwise, the brightness of the area could shift dramatically.

Adjusting Saturation

If the file in progress already contains one or more adjustment layers, make sure that the top adjustment layer is active before continuing. To start the adjustment, choose Layer > New Adjustment Layer > Curves. Then, to add a point to each of the red, green, and blue curves, hold down Shift-Command (Mac) or Shift-Ctrl (Windows) and click that same medium brightness area you sampled earlier. Switch between the Red, Green, and Blue curves (use the menu at the top of the Curves dialog) and type the R, G, and B numbers you calculated and wrote down a few minutes ago (the ones you got from the color picker) in the Output of the Red, Green, and Blue curves. Once the right numbers are entered, skin tones should look much better (**Figure 7.48**).

If the skin tone adjustment was a little too much for you to handle, just start off by adjusting the highlight, shadow, and gray areas, and come back to this chapter after you're comfortable with those.

Figure 7.48 After adjusting for skin tones, the skin should look similar to the stock photo version. (Original images ©2008 Dan Ablan.)

Be sure to correct images separately before blending them together. That way, you'll be able to maintain the color integrity of each component of your "big picture." And save your edits in multiple versions, always being sure to preserve the original file.

The Next Step

Even though it has taken nearly a whole chapter to describe how to optimize grayscale and color in your photos, keep in mind that the process takes only about a minute once you're used to it.

CHAPTER

8

Color Manipulation

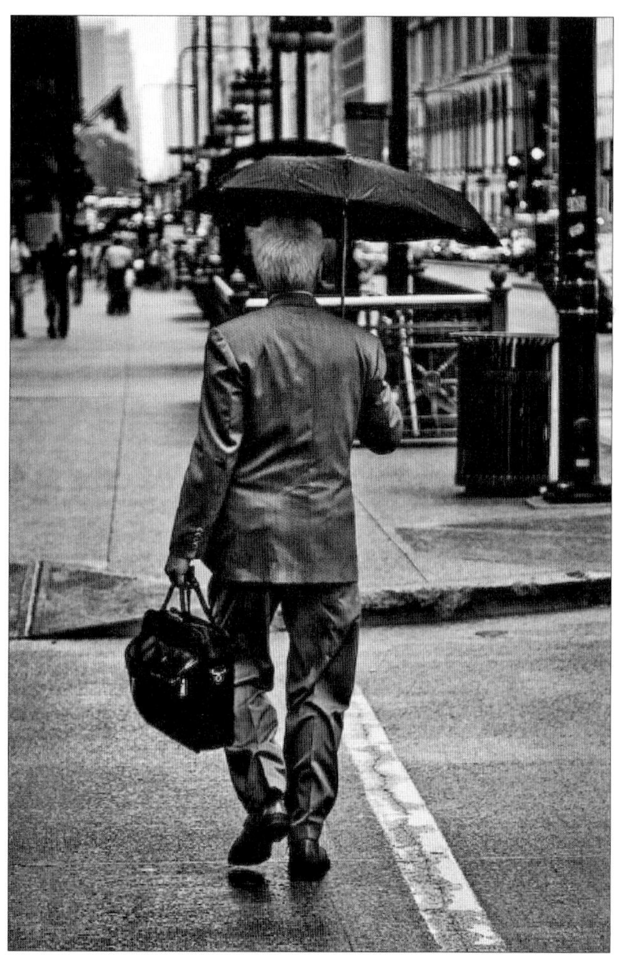

Oh, yes. Dr. Ashley felt that color has a great deal to do with the well-being of the emotionally disturbed.
—Nurse Diesel, in the film *High Anxiety* (1978)

Color Manipulation

Look at this chapter as a box chock-full of color-manipulation tools and methods. Photoshop provides an abundance of ways to shift the colors in an image. Which tools and methods you use depends on the type of original image you have and what kind of results you want. We'll start with a few popular options and progress into lesser-known techniques that might be useful from time to time.

Before we get to the fun stuff, you first need some basic knowledge about color, because that's essential to understanding what's going on behind the scenes with Photoshop's color-manipulation tools.

At the Core Is the Color Wheel

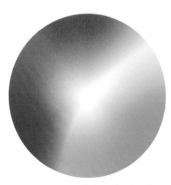

The vast majority of Photoshop's color controls are based on a classic color wheel (**Figure 8.1**). If you understand a few basic concepts about the color wheel, you'll be ahead of the game when controlling color in Photoshop.

Figure 8.1 Most of Photoshop's color-adjustment features are based on the color wheel.

Every color you've ever seen in Photoshop can be described as a combination of *hue, saturation,* and *brightness* (HSB for short). Let's look at what these terms mean.

Hue = Basic Color

In Figure 8.1, only six basic colors are shown: cyan, blue, magenta, red, yellow, and green. Every color you could imagine is based on one of those colors or the transition between them. Take red, for example. Darken it and you get maroon; make it less vivid and you have pink. But both maroon and pink are versions of red.

Photoshop describes these basic colors—*hues*—using numbers that indicate how many degrees the color is from red, going clockwise around a color wheel. If you divide the color wheel into sixths and start with red at 0, the other colors are located on the wheel as follows: yellow at 60°, green at 120°, cyan at 180°, blue at 240°, and magenta at 300° (**Figure 8.2**). You don't have to remember any of those numbers, but it will be helpful to know that hue numbers in Photoshop are based on the color wheel. When you adjust the hue (using an adjustment such as Hue/Saturation), you're effectively spinning the color wheel by moving each basic color in the image an equal amount (or angle) around the edge of the color wheel.

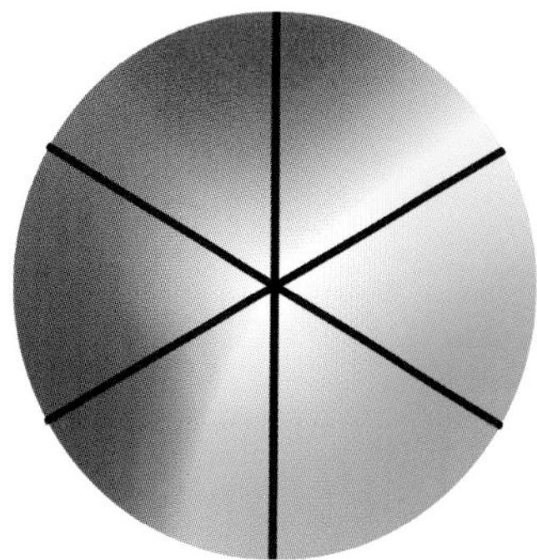

Figure 8.2 If you divide the color wheel into six equal parts, you'll find the primary colors that make up an image.

The other way to shift the basic colors in an image is to push them toward one of the six primary colors in the color wheel (using an adjustment such as Color Balance). Red, green, and blue are the exact opposites of cyan, magenta, and yellow, respectively. Cyan ink's sole job in life is to absorb red light, magenta ink absorbs green light, and yellow ink absorbs blue light. That's why you'll never find an adjustment that allows you to shift something toward cyan and red at the same time. They're opposites, so moving toward red automatically moves away from cyan. When you push an image toward one of the primary colors, all the colors within the image shift in that direction and become more similar, whereas shifting the hue by spinning the color wheel leaves colors as different as they used to be, while moving each color an equal distance around the color wheel.

Saturation = Amount of Color

If you move from the outer ring of a color wheel toward the center, the colors mellow out and become much less colorful. In fact, the shades in the absolute center of the color wheel contain no color at all (they're gray). Photoshop describes how colorful something is by using percentages, and calls this property *saturation.* If something has no saturation at all (0%), then it has no color at all (that is, no hint of any of the basic colors that show up around the outer edge of the color wheel), and therefore contains

Figure 8.3 A three-dimensional color wheel would have dark colors at the bottom and bright colors at the top.

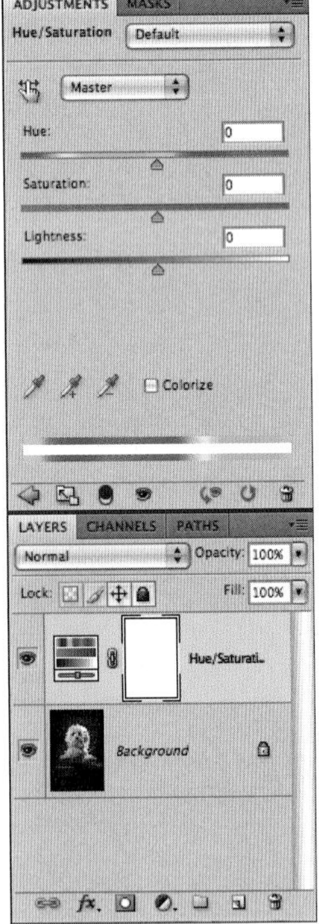

Figure 8.4 Hue/Saturation controls in the Adjustments panel.

only shades of gray. On the other hand, if something has 100% saturated colors, it will be as colorful as possible, just like the colors that appear on the outer rim of the color wheel.

The color adjustments you make shift the colors in an image based on the color wheel. Most of what you do will result in moving a color around the wheel to change its hue, or shifting it toward another color by pushing it to the opposite side of the wheel.

Brightness/Lightness/Luminosity

Missing from our color wheel are the different brightness levels for all those colors. You *could* create a 3D color wheel in the shape of a cylinder, with dark colors at its base and the brightest colors at the top (**Figure 8.3**). But because we'll probably never see anything that fancy in Photoshop, we'll just describe the brightness of a color using one of three words: *brightness, lightness,* or *luminosity*. Each of those words is just a slightly different way to describe how bright a color is. Adobe can never seem to decide which term to use, but all three terms basically mean the same thing.

Now that you have a general idea of how to think about color, jump in and see how you can mess with the colors in your images.

Hue/Saturation Changes

To get started, click the Adjustment Layer icon at the bottom of the Layers panel (the icon looks like a circle, half of which is filled with black) and choose Hue/Saturation from the pop-up menu. That action creates an adjustment layer and displays the Hue/Saturation controls in the Adjustments panel (**Figure 8.4**). You can make three types of changes with this type of adjustment—changes to hue, saturation, and lightness.

At the bottom of the Adjustments panel are two color strips, displaying all the possible hues you can use in Photoshop. Those color strips are really just a standard color wheel that's been straightened out. Notice that the color on the far left of each strip is the same as the one on the far right; if you bent the strip into a circle, it would make a color wheel. The Hue slider allows you to change the basic colors that make up the image. Go ahead and open any colorful image; then move the Hue slider around to see what happens (**Figures 8.5** to **8.7**). The bottom color strip indicates what you've done to each of the hues. Pick a color on the top strip and look straight down to the lower strip to see what Photoshop has done to it as you've adjusted the Hue slider. For now, just remember that *hue* means *basic color*, and that the Hue slider changes the basic color of everything in the image.

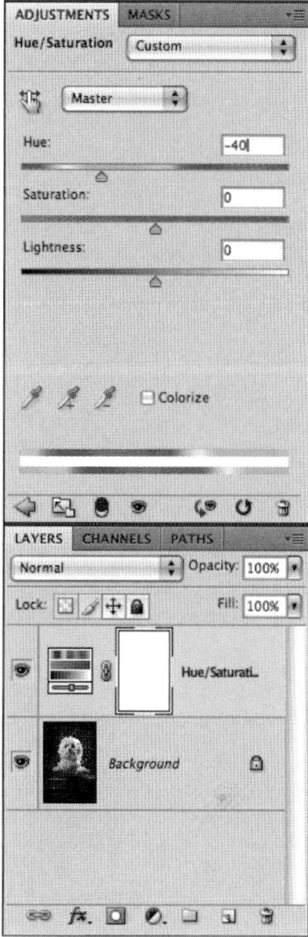

Figure 8.6 Moving the Hue slider shifts all the hues in the image.

Figure 8.5 The original image. (©2008 Dan Ablan.)

Figure 8.7 The result of applying the adjustment shown in Figure 8.6.

Later you'll learn how to get much more control over the specific colors in the image, but first let's look at the other types of changes you can make with the Hue/Saturation adjustments.

Using the same image, move the Saturation slider all the way to the left to make the image completely black-and-white. Then move the slider all the way to the right; all the colors become ridiculously vivid (**Figure 8.8**). Most images can use a modest saturation boost.

Figure 8.8 This left side of this image shows the original photo, and the right shows what can happen when you move the Saturation slider all the way to the right.

Now try the Lightness slider—slide all the way to the left and then all the way to the right to see what happens to the image. You should end up with a solid black image at one extreme and a solid white image at the other. That sort of generic adjustment can easily mess up an image (especially when applied to the entire image), so you need to be careful when adjusting Lightness. This slider becomes much more useful once you isolate a range of color to adjust. Let's consider that option next.

Isolating a Range of Colors

When the Edit pop-up menu at the top of the Hue/Saturation controls on the Adjustments panel is set to Master, any change you make will affect all the colors in the image (**Figure 8.9**). If you'd rather have your changes affect only certain colors, choose a color from that pop-up menu before adjusting the image. Watch what happens to those two color strips at the bottom of the panel as you switch between the choices that are available from the Edit pop-up menu. The tiny sliders that show up indicate the range of colors that you'll be changing. The change will apply to the hues between the two vertical bars and then fade out near the hues that appear above the triangular sliders.

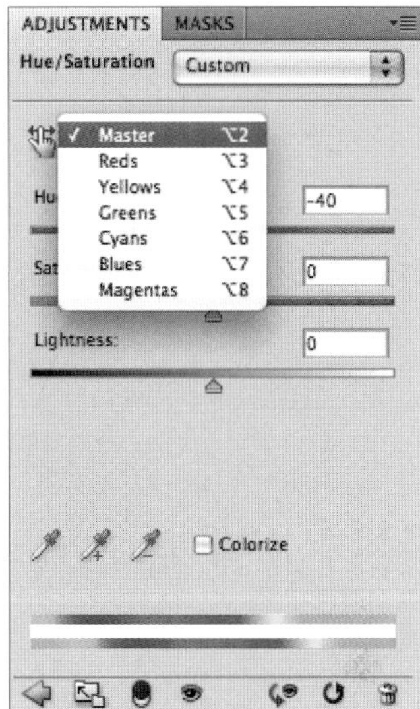

Figure 8.9 Choose Master or a color family from the Edit pop-up menu.

The Edit pop-up menu lists only six generic colors. What if the color you need to isolate is between two of those colors? To get around that six-color limitation, all you have to do is select the eyedropper, move your mouse over the image, and click the color you want to change. If you've changed the pop-up menu setting to a color other than Master, the sliders will center on the color you clicked, which puts them in the right position to work with that color. Go ahead and try it now: Create a Hue/Saturation adjustment layer (by selecting Hue/Saturation from the Adjustments panel), choose a color from the Edit pop-up menu, click the eyedropper, and then click a color in the image before moving any of the sliders.

If you really want to get precise control over the range of colors you're attempting to alter, you'll need to adjust those tiny sliders that appeared after you chose a color from the Edit pop-up menu. It might be good to start by smashing them together into one mass, which forces Photoshop to work on the narrowest range of colors possible. So go ahead and do that. To make sure that Photoshop is focusing on the right color, click the eyedropper and then click the color within the image that you want to change. (Remember that this action centers the sliders on the color you clicked.) At this point, you probably can't tell if Photoshop is going to change a wide enough range of colors, so move the Saturation slider all the way to the left just to see

Figure 8.10 Clicking in the image and lowering the Saturation setting will turn areas black-and-white. In this image, the lower-left corner is the place to select. (©2008 Dan Ablan.)

Figure 8.11 Shift-click additional colors until all the colors you want to adjust become black-and-white.

Figure 8.12 Once you've isolated the range you want to change, move all three adjustment sliders to get to the desired color.

what changes in the image. That action will make parts of the image become black-and-white (**Figure 8.10**).

If Photoshop isn't working on a wide enough range of colors, hold down the Shift key and click additional areas of the image (or click and drag across an area to get all the colors in an object). Shift-clicking spreads out the vertical sliders, causing Photoshop to work on a wider range of colors. If you accidentally click a color that you don't want to shift, hold down Option/Alt and click that area again to remove it from the range of colors that are being adjusted (narrowing the gap between the two vertical sliders). With the Saturation slider all the way to the left, all the areas you want to shift will show up as black-and-white (**Figure 8.11**). Now move the Saturation slider back to the middle and mess with all three main sliders (Hue, Saturation, and Lightness) until you get the change you want (**Figure 8.12**). Remember that the eyedropper is not selected by default when the color is changed.

The eyedropper tools also control where the sliders appear. By default, the leftmost eyedropper will be active as long as the Edit pop-up menu is set to a color, not to Master. When you click in the image with that tool selected, you center the sliders on the color you clicked. If you click the center eyedropper (the one with the plus sign) and then click in the image, Photoshop spreads out the vertical bar sliders to include the colors you clicked across, just like when you held down the Shift key. The eyedropper with the minus sign narrows the width between the vertical sliders, therefore narrowing the range of colors that are being affected—just like when Option/Alt-clicking. You can use the icons, the keyboard commands, or a combination of the two techniques.

If the area you're trying to change is in motion or out of focus, or it blends into the surrounding colors (**Figure 8.13**), you'll need to deal with the transition between that area and its surroundings. To make the adjustment fade into the surrounding colors, move one or both of the triangular sliders away from the vertical bars and watch the image until the change smoothly blends into what's around the area you were attempting to adjust (**Figure 8.14**).

Figure 8.13 You have to be careful when working with colors that blend in with their surroundings. (©2008 Dan Ablan.)

Figure 8.14 Moving the outer slider toward the color you need to blend into will fade the adjustment into those colors.

Now it's time to get to work and figure out specific uses for the Hue/Saturation options.

Saturating Colors

Many images that come from a digital camera or flatbed scanner can benefit from a boost in saturation (**Figure 8.15**). For a general boost of color, make a Hue/Saturation adjustment layer and ratchet up the Saturation slider until the colors in the image start to pop (**Figure 8.16**). When you do that, you'll probably notice that some colors become too vivid before others have reached their true potential. To avoid oversaturating, choose the objectionable color from the Edit pop-up menu, select the eyedropper tool, click the color within the image to center the color isolation sliders, and then move the Saturation slider toward the left to mellow out the oversaturated color (**Figure 8.17**).

Figure 8.15 This image could use a saturation boost. (©2008 Dan Ablan.)

Figure 8.16 After saturating the image, the yellow areas are just too colorful.

Figure 8.17 After we've isolated the yellows and lowered their saturation, none of the colors overpowers the others.

Enhancing Skies

If you've looked at a lot of photographs containing blue skies, you might have noticed that many of those skies are actually closer to a light shade of cyan than a shade of true blue (**Figure 8.18**). If you like the skies to look as genuinely blue as possible, start by creating a Hue/Saturation adjustment layer and choose Blues from the Edit pop-up menu. Select the eyedropper tool and click somewhere within the sky in the image to center the sliders. Then make the following adjustment: Move the Lightness slider toward the left to darken the sky, move the Saturation slider toward the right to make the sky more colorful, and experiment with the Hue slider until you get the best shade of blue (**Figures 8.19** and **8.20**).

Figure 8.18 This cyan-ish sky could use a tweak. (©2008 Dan Ablan.)

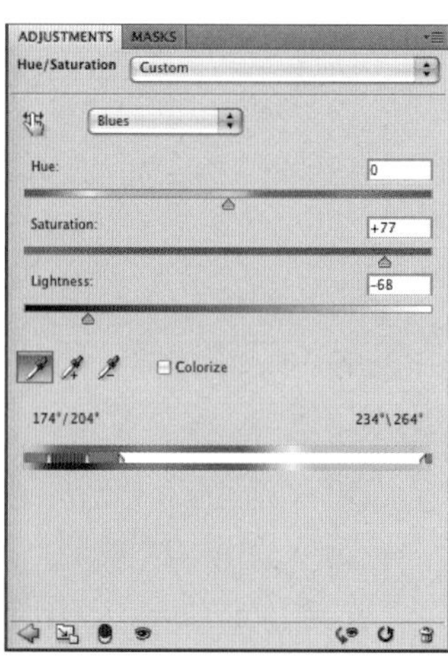

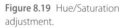

Figure 8.19 Hue/Saturation adjustment.

Figure 8.20 After adjusting the image with Hue/Saturation, the sky is true blue.

The only problem with this technique is that you might run into an image containing blue areas that are not part of the sky (**Figures 8.21** and **8.22**). If you don't want to shift those areas, you'll have to make changes after you're done creating the Hue/Saturation adjustment layer. Each adjustment layer contains a white rectangle just to the right of the adjustment layer icon for that layer. That rectangle is a *layer mask*, and it can be used to further limit the areas to which the adjustment will apply. All you have to do is grab the Paintbrush tool and paint with black at full opacity, and you'll prevent the adjustment from applying to the areas you painted. As long as the Hue/Saturation adjustment layer is active in the Layers panel, the paint you apply will affect where the adjustment applies. Painting with black hides the adjustment; painting with white brings it back. So, after enhancing a sky, you might want to grab a large, soft-edged brush and paint with black over any areas that you want to preserve (**Figure 8.23**).

Figure 8.21 The original image. (©2008 Dan Ablan.)

Figure 8.22 After adjusting the sky, areas of the foreground have shifted colors.

Figure 8.23 Painting with black on the layer mask of the adjustment layer prevents the adjustment from applying to the buildings.

Editing Hue/Saturation Adjustments

If you ever need to edit a Hue/Saturation adjustment layer that you created earlier, be extra careful. You can double-click the adjustment layer icon on the left side of the adjustment layer to change the adjustment. But before you start to make changes, you'll need to choose the same color you

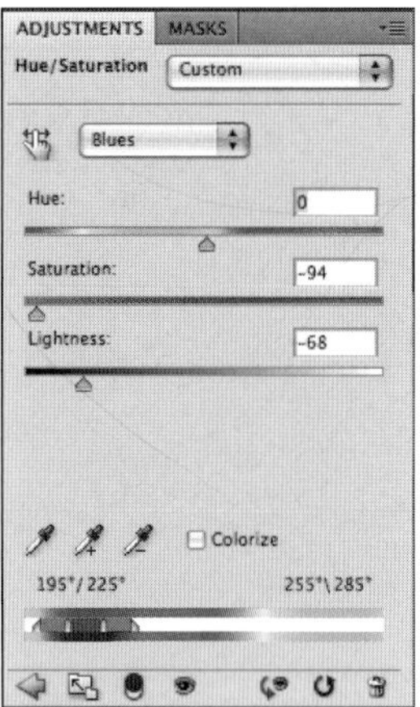

Figure 8.24 When returning to an adjustment layer, look at the color bars and try to figure out which color you adjusted previously (yellow, in this case).

Alternatively, you could set a color sample on the saturated color, set that to HSB in the Info panel, and watch those numbers while adjusting the saturation.

originally chose from the Edit pop-up menu; otherwise, any changes you make will affect the entire image because the Edit pop-up menu will be set to Master. If you can't remember which color you chose previously, glance at the color strips to see if you can figure out which areas in the bottom strip differ from the top one (**Figure 8.24**). Then look at the top strip directly above that area to figure out which color to choose from the Edit pop-up menu. Once you choose the proper color from that pop-up menu, Photoshop will get you back to adjusting the specific color you isolated when you originally created the adjustment layer.

Moving the Saturation slider too far to the right can end up distorting the relationship between the colors in an image. As one color reaches its maximum saturation, it simply can't become more saturated, but the other colors in the image will continue to become more vivid as you move the Saturation slider farther toward the right. To figure out the maximum saturation boost to give an image without distorting the relationship between the colors, pay attention to what happens in the Info panel. Choose Window > Info, click the eyedropper icon in the Info panel, and choose HSB. Then, when you're increasing the saturation of the image, move your cursor over the most saturated areas of the image, and stop increasing the saturation once you see that the "S" (Saturation) number in the HSB part of the Info panel reaches 100%. If you go any further, you'll distort the relationship between colors in the image.

Color/Grayscale Conversions

The best way to convert a color image to a grayscale image (traditionally known as a "black-and-white" image) is to use the Black and White adjustment (Image > Adjustments > Black and White). As you spend more time with Photoshop, you'll come across many methods for black-and-white conversion. But the Black and White adjustment is such a powerful tool, and so easy to use, that you can accomplish most black-and-white tasks with this tool. Best of all, the Black and White adjustment can be applied as an adjustment layer, so you get all of the advantages of adjustment layers for your grayscale conversions.

The options in the Black and White dialog let you specify exactly how you want particular color ranges in an image to be converted to grayscale (**Figure 8.25**). The sliders are very easy to use. If you move the Yellows slider to the right, for example, the yellow tones in the image will be represented by lighter shades of gray; move the slider to the left, and the yellows will darken. The other sliders work in much the same way for the other primary colors (**Figure 8.26**).

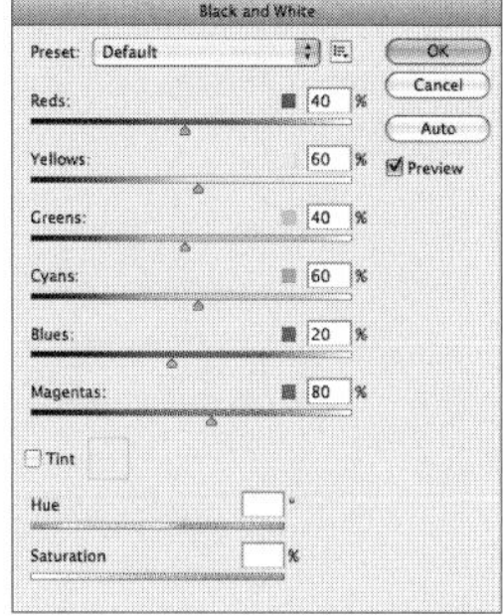

Figure 8.25 Photoshop's Black and White conversion dialog.

The Black and White dialog is actually pretty smart. If you increase the Reds setting, only those tones in the image that are truly red increase (**Figure 8.27**).

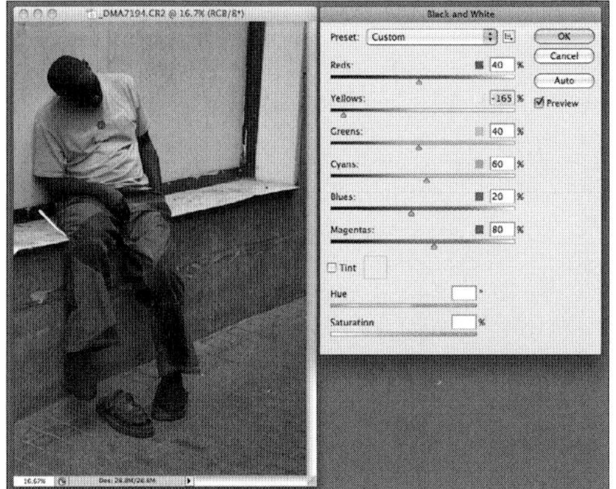

Figure 8.26 As you move the sliders in the Black and White dialog, the corresponding colors in the grayscale image become lighter or darker. (©2008 Dan Ablan.)

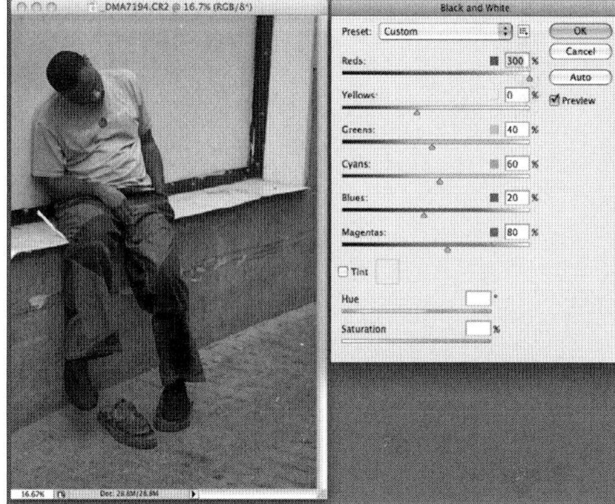

Figure 8.27 Only the reds are affected by this change in the Black and White dialog settings.

Also note that the sliders aren't interrelated. If you want to increase blue, you don't need to decrease yellow, too. The control is smart enough to know which pixels need to be affected by a particular edit.

With the Black and White adjustment, you don't have to worry about the total percentage values of the image. If the totals add up to more than 100%, you won't see a change in overall exposure in the image. However, if the total percentage value of *all* the sliders is greater than 100, the image will end up with a brighter exposure than when you started. A total value lower than 100 will result in a darker image.

The Auto button performs an automatic conversion and is well worth using to experiment. The Auto algorithm does a very good job of mapping different colors to different tones to produce a nice contrasty image.

The Black and White dialog also includes tinting controls, so you can perform black-and-white conversion and color toning in one step (**Figure 8.28**). Turn on the Tint check box to activate the tint controls; then select the hue that you want to use for tinting, and adjust the Saturation slider to specify the strength of the tint.

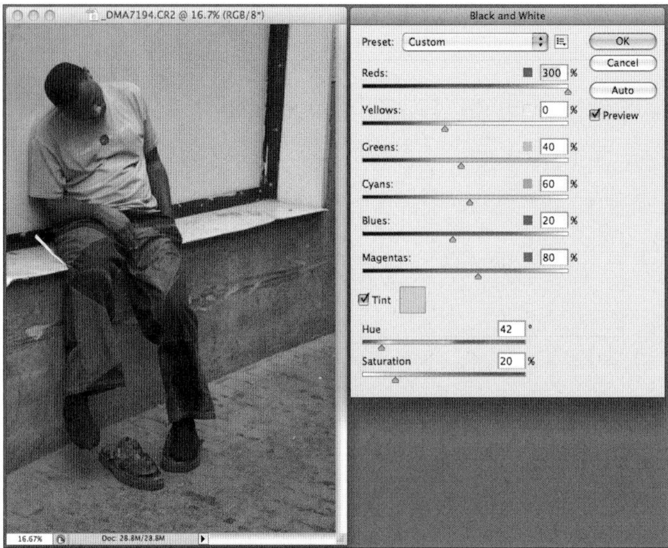

Figure 8.28 The tint controls in the Black and White adjustment let you perform grayscale conversion and tinting in one step.

The Black and White dialog is equipped with several preset configurations (**Figure 8.29**). In addition, you can save your own presets by using the Save and Load pop-up menu located to the right of the Preset menu.

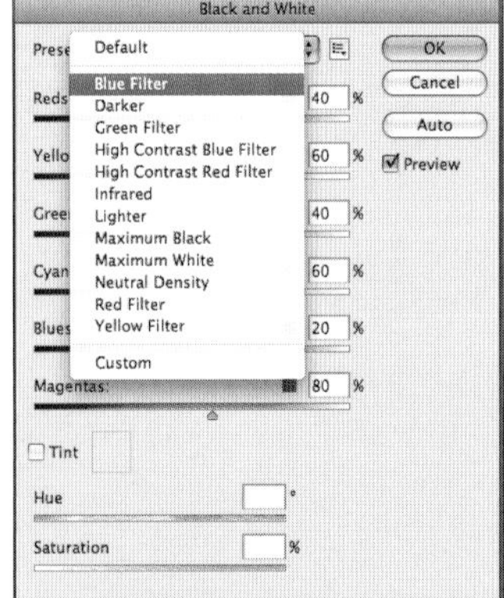

Figure 8.29 The Black and White dialog offers a variety of preset configurations.

Colorizing Grayscale Photos

If you enjoy the look of hand-tinted photographs but don't want to deal with the chemicals and mess that are usually involved, you might get excited about colorizing images with a mouse.

There are many ways to colorize a black-and-white image. For example, you can use a Hue/Saturation adjustment layer to add color to the image. Try starting out with this technique because it gives you lots of flexibility to tweak later. All you have to do is choose Image > Mode > RGB, use the color eyedropper to select one of the areas where you'd like to add color, and then create a Hue/Saturation adjustment layer. Turn on the Colorize check box, which should shift the selected area to a color similar to that of your foreground color (**Figure 8.30**). When the color has been applied, adjust the Hue setting to cycle through the full spectrum of colors. Once you've chosen the basic color, adjust the Saturation setting to control how vivid the color is, and change the Lightness setting to determine how dark the area should be (**Figure 8.31**).

Figure 8.30 When you first turn on the Colorize check box, the color you get is based on your foreground color. (©2008 Dan Ablan.)

Figure 8.31 Fine-tune the color by adjusting the Hue, Saturation, and Lightness sliders.

With this select-and-adjust approach, you use the adjustment layer to mask out areas of color (**Figure 8.32**), and then you refine the result by painting on the adjustment layer's mask with a black brush. If you remove too much of the colorization, just paint with white. Painting with white causes the adjustment to apply to a larger area of the image, whereas black limits which areas are adjusted. If the color is too intense, simply paint with a shade of gray on the adjustment layer, which causes the adjustment to apply in differing amounts. The darker the shade of gray, the less the adjustment will apply. Another option is to double-click the thumbnail icon for the adjustment layer (to the left of the layer name) to modify the settings that are being applied.

Figure 8.32 By using the Adjustments panel, you can instantly create an adjustment layer to mask out areas of color.

With this type of adjustment, usually there will be too much color in the darkest and brightest areas of the image. To limit the amount of color applied to these areas, choose Layer > Layer Style > Blending Options while the adjustment layer is active (**Figure 8.33**). Pull in the lower-left slider in the Blend If area until all the color is disappearing from the darkest areas of the image. You don't want to remove the color completely, so hold down Option/Alt and drag the left edge of the slider that you just moved until you get a smooth transition in the shadow areas of the image. Before you click OK, move the right slider a short distance and then Option/Alt-drag its right edge until the color blends into the brightest parts of the image. With a little experimentation, you'll be able to find the setting that looks best for the image (**Figures 8.34** and **8.35**).

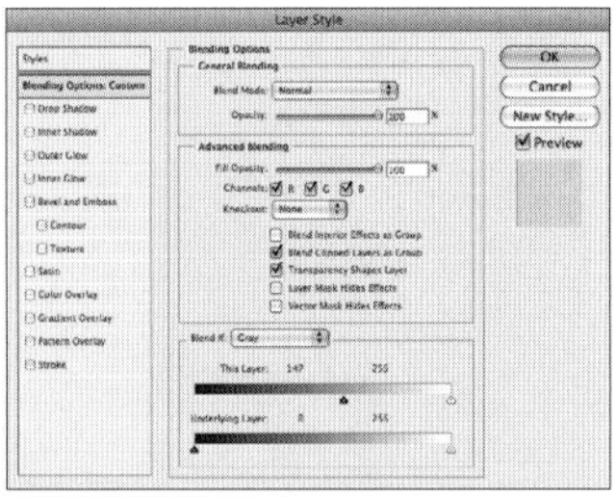

Figure 8.33 Use the Blending Options to balance areas with too much color.

Figure 8.34 The color of the backdrop could be a little less saturated.

Figure 8.35 After reducing the amount of color in the shadow areas, the image looks better.

Replacing Color

If you like the general ideas discussed so far, but didn't have complete success isolating areas based on hues, try choosing Image > Adjustments > Replace Color (**Figure 8.36**). In essence, Replace Color combines the Color Range command with the color-shifting capability found in the Hue/Saturation controls. The advantage of using Replace Color is that instead of having to figure out the exact Hue, Saturation, and Lightness settings necessary to get the desired result, you just define the desired color by clicking the color swatch at lower right in the dialog.

Figure 8.36 The Replace Color dialog is a combination of the Color Range command and the Hue/Saturation controls in the Adjustments panel. Here, the green leaves are selected, and the hue is adjusted to make them purple. (©2008 Dan Ablan.)

Unfortunately, Replace Color is not available as an adjustment layer, so you might not want to use it often. You might prefer to use the Color Range command (Select > Color Range) and then create a Hue/Saturation adjustment layer, which gives you much more flexibility if you ever need to fine-tune the initial adjustment. Another option is to duplicate a layer, apply Replace Color, and create a layer mask for added blending control.

Both Hue/Saturation and Replace Color effectively rotate the color wheel to shift the colors in an image. Now let's take a look at how we can shift the general color of an image toward one of the primary colors (red, yellow, green, cyan, blue, magenta).

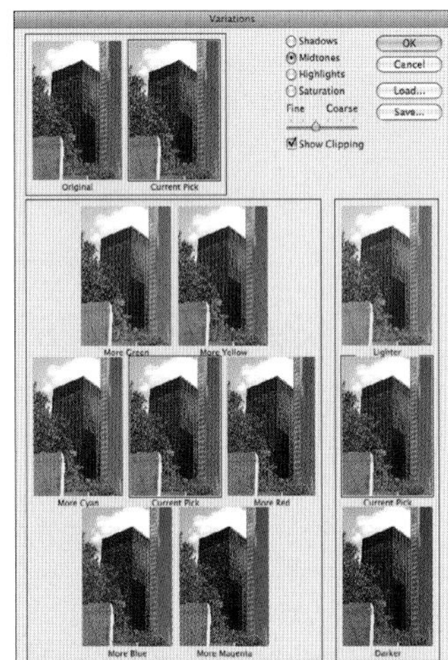

Figure 8.37 The Variations dialog presents simple previews of multiple adjustments.

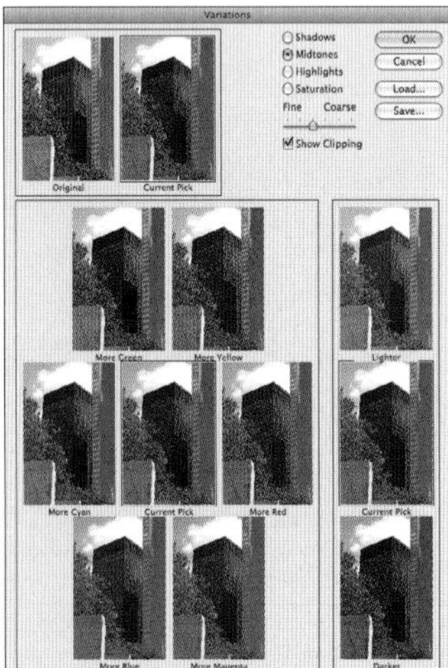

Figure 8.38 After you click one of the choices, the surrounding views repopulate with new choices.

Variations

If you like simple and easy features, you'll enjoy using the Variations command (Image > Adjustments > Variations). The Variations dialog displays your original image in the middle of a seven-image cluster (**Figure 8.37**). When you click one of the surrounding images, Variations replaces the one in the middle and repopulates the surrounding views with new alternatives (**Figure 8.38**). To control how different the alternatives are from the center image, adjust the Fine/Coarse slider at upper right in the dialog.

This type of adjustment concentrates on either the brightest areas of the image (highlights), the middle brightness levels (midtones), or the dark areas of the image (shadows). You can adjust all three areas with one adjustment, but you'll have to choose them one at a time and make an adjustment before clicking OK. After you've made a change to the image, you'll be able to compare the original to your current selection by comparing the two images that appear at upper left in the dialog.

Variations can change the brightness and saturation of the image. However, Levels and Curves are far superior for adjusting brightness, and Hue/Saturation gives you much more control over which colors become saturated. But the techniques discussed here provide a quick way to adjust color.

If you notice intense colors in areas where they don't belong (**Figure 8.39**), Photoshop most likely is warning you that you might be losing detail in that area. If you'd rather not see those unusual colors, turn off the Show Clipping option at upper right in the dialog.

Use Variations for very basic chores where you might prefer a simple visual interface; for example, when you want to tint a grayscale photo. All you have to do is change the mode of the image to RGB (Image > Mode > RGB), go to Variations (Image > Adjustments > Variations), and click away until you get the color tint you want (**Figure 8.40**).

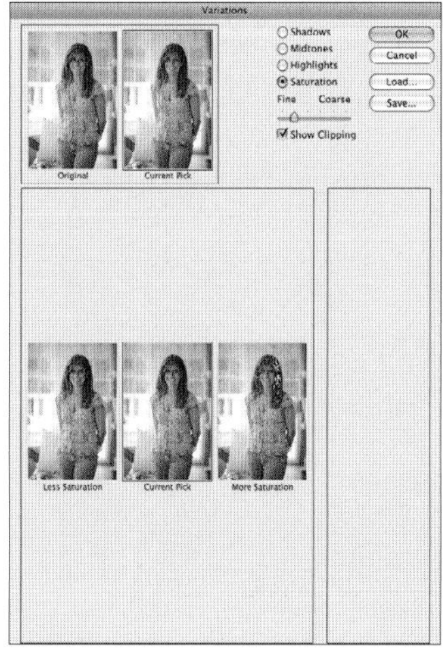

Figure 8.39 If colors look out of place, it's usually an indication that clipping has occurred, which is a sign that you might be losing detail in those areas. (©2008 Dan Ablan.)

Figure 8.40 Adding color to a grayscale image is easy with Variations. (©2008 Dan Ablan.)

Color Balance

Most of the time, you might pass over Variations in favor of the Color Balance controls in the Adjustments panel (**Figure 8.41**), which make future changes much easier. Just as in Variations, the Color Balance controls allow you to shift the color of highlights, midtones, or shadows toward one of the primary colors; the only difference is that you'll have to look at the main screen to get a preview. Moving a

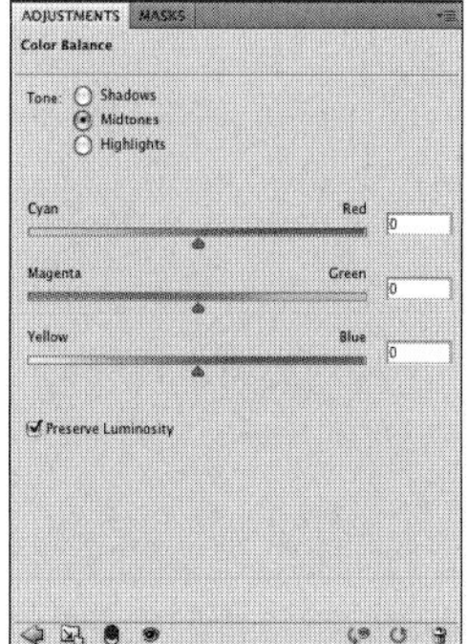

Figure 8.41 The Color Balance panel is a good alternative to the Variations dialog.

Figure 8.42 Color Balance pushes the colors in the image toward one of the primary colors.

slider to +15 or –15 is approximately the same as making one click in the Variations dialog with the default setting on the Fine/Coarse slider. But because you're not forced to make adjustments in preset increments, it's much easier to be precise with Color Balance than with Variations.

Both Variations and Color Balance effectively shift the colors of the image toward one side of the color wheel. It's almost as if you start at the center of the color wheel and then shift toward one of the primary colors (**Figure 8.42**). All the colors in the image move toward that color, whereas Hue/Saturation and Replace Color spin the color wheel, which shifts all the colors in unusual ways (not just toward one particular color).

A bunch of other commands allow you to shift toward cyan or red, magenta or green, and yellow or blue in a less obvious way. Let's take a look at a few of the adjustments that allow you to work with those primary colors.

Levels/Curves and Color

Figure 8.43 Move the curve up or down to push the colors in the image toward or away from the color you chose in the Channel pop-up menu. (©2008 Dan Ablan.)

Choosing Image > Adjustments > Curves (or selecting Curves in the Adjustments panel) allows you to pick between red, green, and blue; or cyan, magenta, and yellow (depending on which mode the image uses) in the Channel pop-up menu (**Figure 8.43**). When you work on the Red channel, you'll be able to shift the overall color of the image toward either red or cyan by moving the curve up or down; if you work on the Green channel, you'll be able to shift toward green and magenta; and the Blue channel allows you to shift toward blue and yellow.

Command/Ctrl-click the area of the image where you'd like to concentrate the adjustment. That action will add a point to the curve in the specific location needed to focus accurately on the area you clicked. Once you've done that, use the up- and down-arrow keys to shift the colors toward one of the primary colors—which one depends on the choice you made in the Channel pop-up menu (**Figure 8.44**).

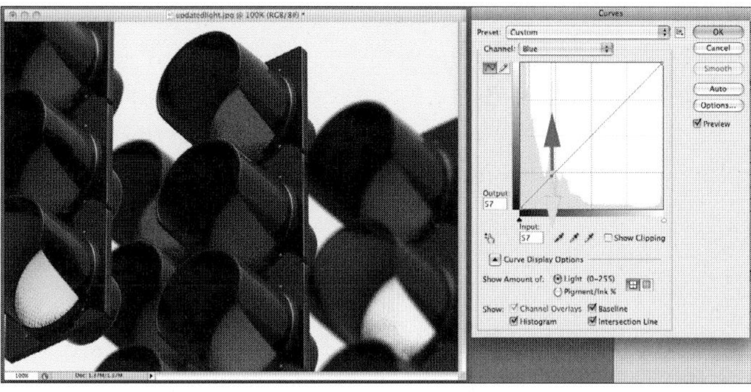

Figure 8.44 Command/Ctrl-click the image to add a point to the curve; then use the arrow keys to shift the color. (©2008 Dan Ablan.)

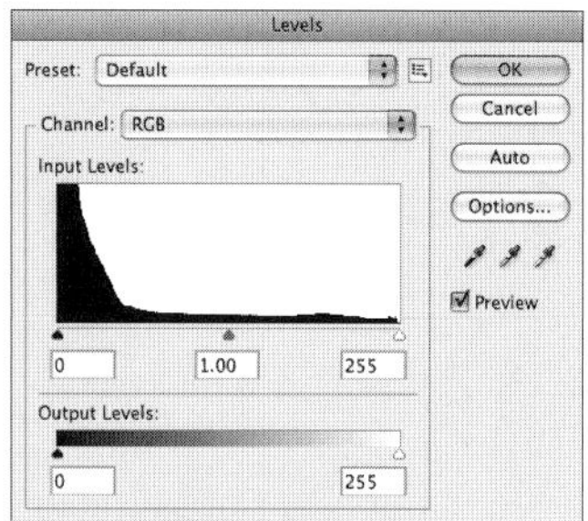

Figure 8.45 Levels can make adjustments similar to those available with Curves.

You can make similar changes by using the Levels command (Image > Adjustments > Levels). This technique also allows you to choose from the channels (RGB or CMYK) that make up the image (**Figure 8.45**). With an image in RGB mode, moving any of the upper sliders toward the left will push the color of the image toward the color you have chosen from the Channel pop-up menu. Moving the sliders toward the right will shift the colors toward the opposite color.

Auto Color Correction

Using Levels or Curves to make color adjustments might be problematic because the image can change in unexpected ways, due to the fact that you're not just controlling the highlights/midtones/shadows, as with many other adjustments. If you're having trouble getting the overall look you want, click the Options button in either Levels or Curves to open the Auto Color Correction Options dialog. Set the Algorithms setting to Enhance Monochromatic Contrast to avoid getting rid of color in the highlights or shadows of the image. Then, to shift the overall color of the image, turn on the Snap Neutral Midtones check box and click the color swatch next to Midtones. It should start with gray, but if you shift that color toward another color, the general atmosphere of the photo should change as you introduce a color cast (**Figures 8.46** and **8.47**). This technique is great for changing the overall feeling of a photo

The Options button appears in a dialog when you access it via the Image > Adjustments menu. However, you need to Alt/Option-click the Auto button when using an adjustment layer.

to make it appear more warm (toward red/orange) or cool (toward blue/cyan).

Figure 8.46 The original image. (©2008 Dan Ablan.)

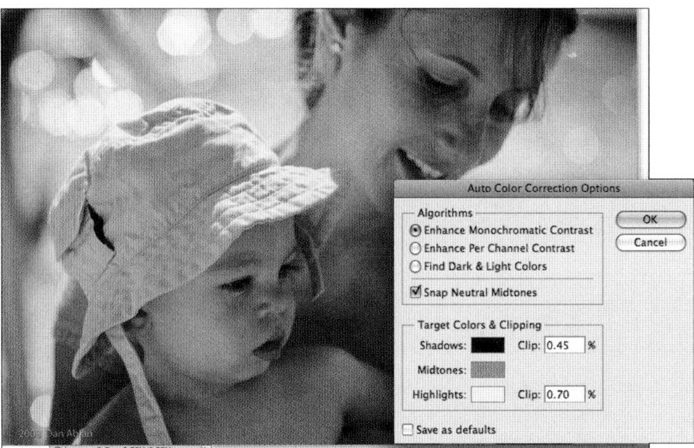

Figure 8.47 Using Auto Color to shift the image toward warm tones.

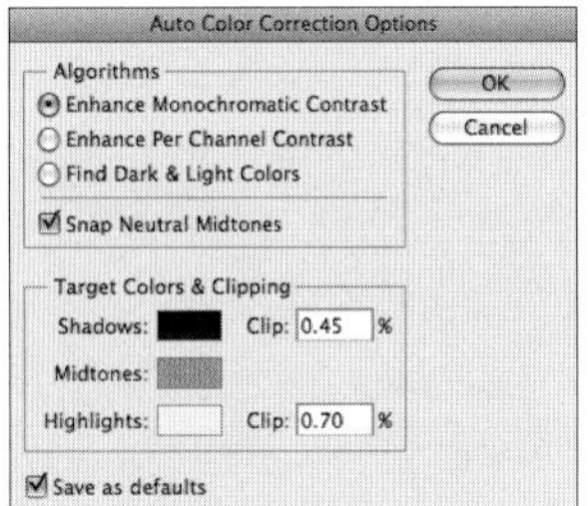

Figure 8.48 Don't check Save as Defaults unless you want to introduce a color cast to every image you adjust with Auto Color.

Check Save as Defaults in the dialog (**Figure 8.48**) only if you plan to shift the overall look of a large number of photos. Otherwise, when you use Auto Color for color correction, it will introduce color casts instead of getting rid of them.

Auto Color also is handy when you're combining two images that differ in general color (**Figures 8.49** and **8.50**). If one image has a desirable color cast and the other doesn't, the two images won't look like they belong together (**Figure 8.51**). You want Photoshop to transfer the desirable color cast to the second image by analyzing what's going on in the brightest and darkest areas of the image, because a color cast contaminates those areas that otherwise wouldn't contain any color. Here's how to do it. Place the images side by side so both documents are visible at the same time. Then, with the image that doesn't have a color cast active, choose Image > Adjustments > Curves, click the Options button, set Algorithms to Find Dark & Light Colors, and turn off the Snap Neutral Midtones check box (**Figure 8.52**).

Figure 8.49 This image has a warm color cast. (©2008 Dan Ablan.)

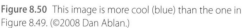

Figure 8.50 This image is more cool (blue) than the one in Figure 8.49. (©2008 Dan Ablan.)

Figure 8.51 When the two images are combined, they don't look like they belong together.

Now all you have to do is plug in the right colors in the highlights and shadows. Click the Shadows color swatch to access the color picker, move your mouse over the image containing the desirable color cast, and click the darkest area of the image (**Figure 8.53**). Next, click the Highlights color swatch to access the color picker again, and this time click the brightest area of the image that contains the desirable color cast (**Figure 8.54**)—avoiding areas that are blown out to pure white—and then click OK. That action should change the color of the active photo so that it will have a color cast similar to that of the other image (**Figure 8.55**). In this example, the devil girl now looks as if she's photographed outside with a fill flash.

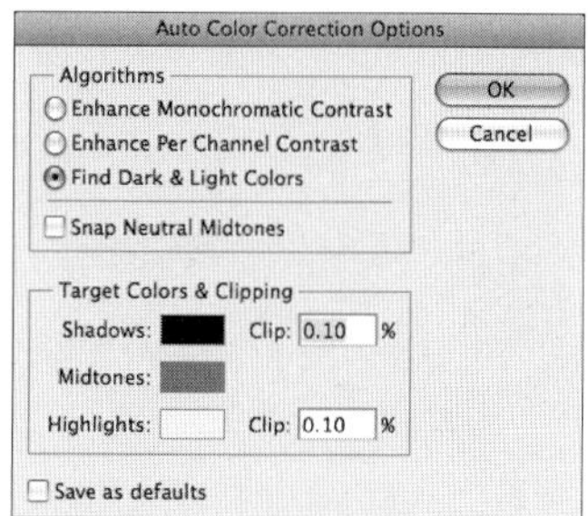

Figure 8.52 Auto settings for matching two images.

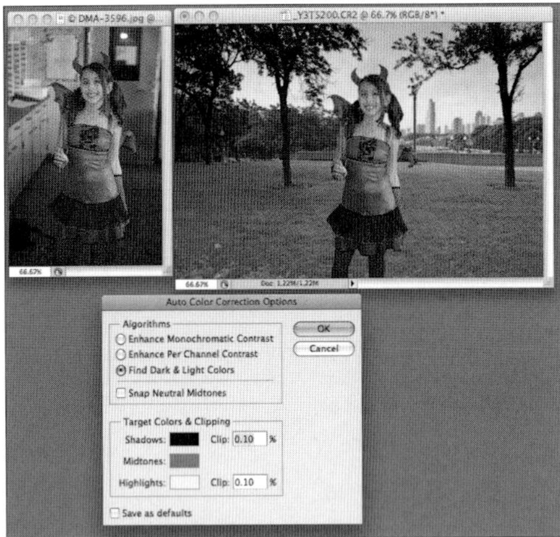

Figure 8.53 Click the Shadows swatch and then click the darkest part of the image that has the color cast.

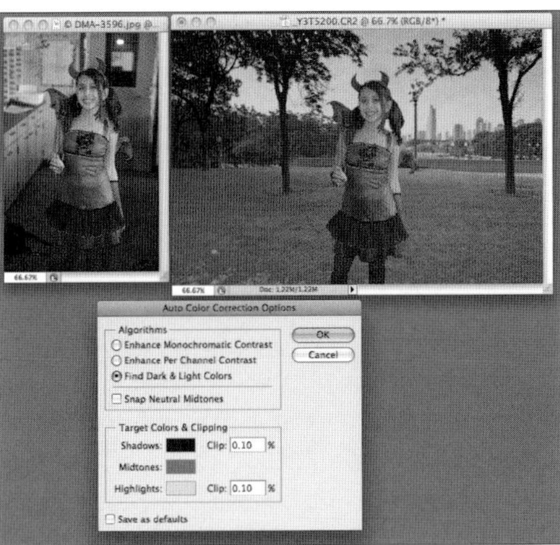

Figure 8.54 Click the Highlights swatch and then click the brightest area of the image.

Figure 8.55 After adjusting the color, the two images have similar color qualities.

Selective Color

Auto Color isn't the only way to force colors into the brightest, darkest, and neutral gray areas of an image. If you choose Image > Adjustments > Selective Color, you can select which general colors you'd like to change from the Colors pop-up menu and then shift them toward a primary color (**Figure 8.56**). Moving the sliders toward the right shifts the selected color toward the color listed to the left of the slider. Moving the slider toward the left shifts it away from the color listed and toward its exact opposite. So, even though this dialog only lists cyan, magenta, yellow, and black, you can still shift toward red, green, and blue by moving the sliders toward the left. If the Relative radio button is selected, you'll change areas relative to where they started. If you have 50% cyan and you move the Cyan slider to 10%, for instance, you'll end up with 55% cyan, because 10% of 50% is 5%. On the other hand, if you use the Absolute setting, you'll simply add the exact amount that you select. For example, if you have 50% cyan and you move the Cyan slider to 10%, you'll end up with 60% cyan, because Photoshop added the exact amount of cyan that you selected.

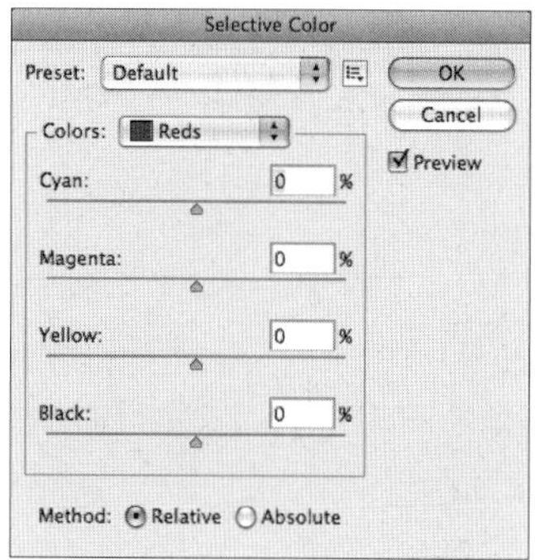

Figure 8.56 With Selective Color, you can push certain colors toward any of the primary colors.

One nice aspect of Selective Color is the capacity to shift the color of the blacks in an image. All you have to do is choose Blacks from the Colors pop-up menu, move the Black slider toward the left to lighten the area, and then move whichever color sliders you'd like to use toward the right to push color into those areas (**Figures 8.57** and **8.58**). If you're working in CMYK mode, moving the Cyan slider toward the right makes the black areas of the image richer. This adjustment is commonly used when creating large areas of black in an image that will be printed on a commercial printing press. For those areas, 40% cyan is a good setting.

Figure 8.57 The original image. (©2008 Dan Ablan.)

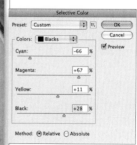

Figure 8.58 Use Selective Color to shift the color of black areas.

Selective Color also brightens highlights. Choose Whites from the Colors menu and then move the Cyan, Magenta, and Yellow sliders toward the left (**Figures 8.59** to **8.61**). This change can be useful for metallic objects, where the brightest areas need to be pure white in order to make the object appear to be highly polished and therefore shiny.

Figure 8.59 The original image. (©2008 Dan Ablan.)

Figure 8.60 After adjusting the whites, the highlights are much brighter, making the object look more polished.

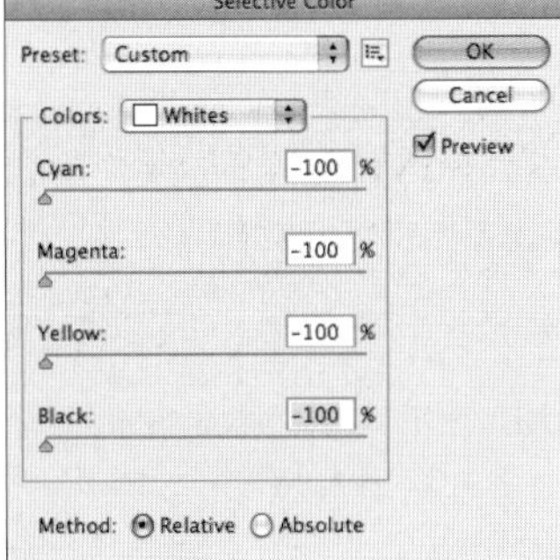

Figure 8.61 The Selective Color adjustment used to brighten the highlights.

Match Color

Match Color attempts to match the general color and contrast of two images. Let's start with simple examples and then progress into more complex and unusual solutions.

Suppose you have two images, one of which has a very cool feeling and the other of which is rather neutral, but both images have similar lighting conditions (**Figures 8.62** and **8.63**). In order to match the general feeling of the two images, open both images, click the image you'd like to change, and choose Image > Adjustments > Match Color (**Figure 8.64**). At the bottom of the Match Color dialog, change the Source pop-up menu to show the name of the image whose color you'd like to match. If the image contains adjustment layers, be sure to choose Merged from the Layer pop-up menu. That's all there is to it (**Figure 8.65**)!

Figure 8.62 This image has an overall color that we want to match. (©2008 Dan Ablan.)

Figure 8.63 This image needs adjusting. (©2008 Dan Ablan.)

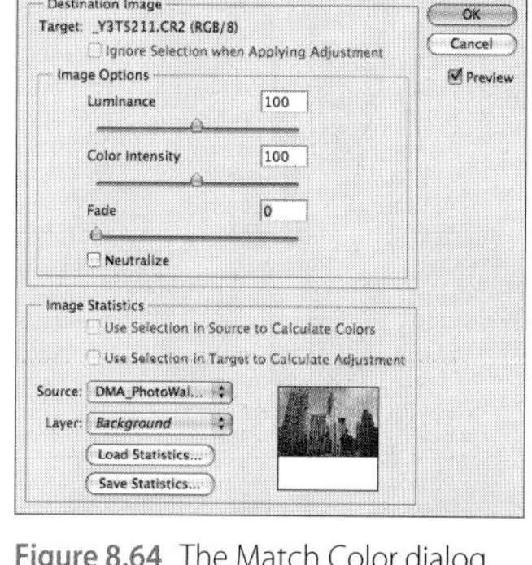

Figure 8.64 The Match Color dialog.

Figure 8.65 The result of matching the color between the two images.

After you've produced an acceptable match between the two images, adjust the Image Options settings as needed to fine-tune the end result. The Luminance slider changes the brightness of the image; the Color Intensity slider controls how saturated the colors are. If you don't want to match the reference photo precisely, but instead want to head in that general direction, try increasing the Fade setting. If you set Fade to 100, you'll see the original unchanged image (plus any Luminance and Color Intensity adjustments). Lowering the Fade setting pushes the image toward the look of the reference image. Just move the Fade slider around until you like the amount of change you're getting.

On occasion, you might need to adjust a multitude of images to match a single source image. When that's the case, set Source to the name of the image you want to match; then click the Save Statistics button and name that preset. Now, at any time in the future, you can click the Load Statistics button to use the general feeling of that photo again, and Photoshop won't need to open the file. It's easy to have a bunch of these files saved—one for warm, sunset-like images; another for cool, water-like images; yet another for high-contrast, less-colorful images; and so on. Use this technique to get a certain effect without having to remember which photo you originally matched.

The Match Color dialog is designed to match two photographs, but it's also useful on single images. Set Source to None and then play with the Image Options settings as you like. You might prefer the Color Intensity setting here versus the Saturation setting in the Hue/Saturation controls in the Adjustments panel.

If an image has an obvious color cast, such as a photo taken underwater, try turning on the Neutralize check box. That option will cause the Match Color dialog to attempt to color-correct the image. The results aren't always perfect, but it's often a good start for images that have massive color casts.

Figure 8.66 Make a selection on the reference photograph to indicate the color you'd like to match. (©2008 Dan Ablan.)

Match Color is also good for colorizing grayscale photographs. Open a full-color reference photo and select an area (such as a patch of skin that contains both bright and dark areas) so Photoshop knows what you'd like to match (**Figure 8.66**). Then switch to the grayscale photo and choose Image > Mode > RGB so that the image is in a mode that can contain color. Now make a very precise selection of the area where you'd like to add color, and choose Image > Adjustments > Match Color. To make sure that Photoshop colors only the selected areas, turn on the two check boxes at the bottom of the dialog and turn off the check box at the top. This technique produces a result that's superior to what you'd get with other tools because, instead of applying a generic color across the entire area, it will usually apply a slightly different color to the bright and dark areas of an object (**Figure 8.67**).

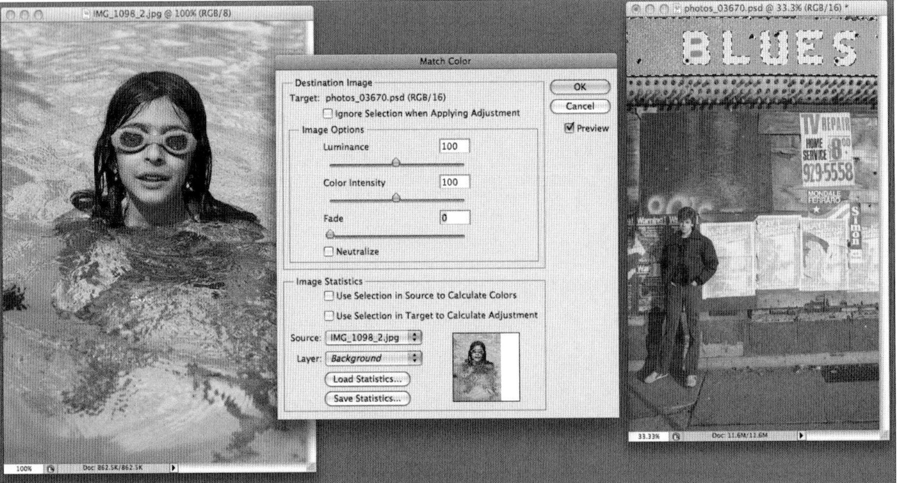

Figure 8.67 Convert the grayscale image to RGB mode, make a precise selection, and then match the color. (©2008 Dan Ablan.)

Red Eye Tool

Photoshop's Red Eye tool (which is grouped with the Healing Brush and Patch tool) is designed to quickly and easily remove red eye (**Figure 8.68**). All you have to do is click near the eye and Photoshop will search for the closest red circle, remove all the color, and then darken the area. This tool is only sensitive to red areas and therefore is not useful for the green or orange eyes that often result from animals being photographed using an on-camera flash. (In those cases, use the Color Replacement tool, which is coming up next in this chapter.)

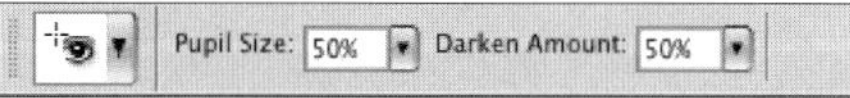

Figure 8.68 The Red Eye tool has only two settings available in the options bar.

The Darken Amount setting determines how dark the pupil will become (**Figure 8.69**). If your results look solid black, choose Edit > Undo, use a lower Darken Amount setting, and then try again.

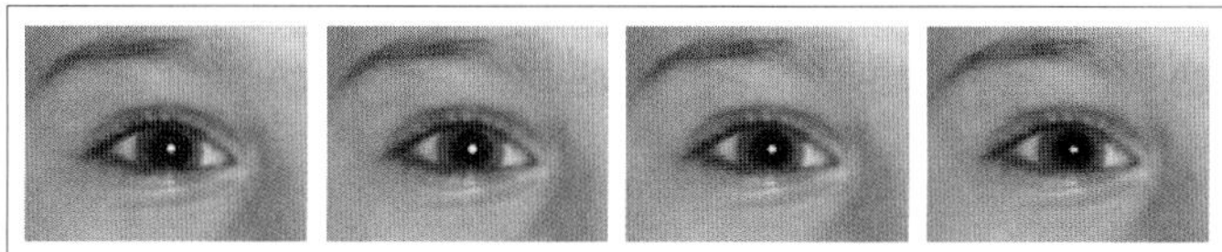

Figure 8.69 Left, the original image with red eye. Darken Amount settings from left to right: 10%, 40%, 80%. (Note: Contrast of these images has been increased to make the differences more obvious, since the onscreen difference is rather subtle and might be difficult to see in printed form.)

Low settings for Pupil Size usually produce more detail in the pupil of the eye, whereas higher settings leave little or no detail. Settings between 10% and 20% usually produce an acceptable amount of detail, and settings of 50% or above produce an almost solid black pupil.

Color Replacement Tool

The Color Replacement tool allows you to paint across an area and change its color. What's really nice about this tool is that you don't have to be overly precise with your

TIP

This tool applies your foreground color to the active layer, so remember that you can change the foreground color by holding down the Option/Alt key and clicking an area in the image that contains the desired color.

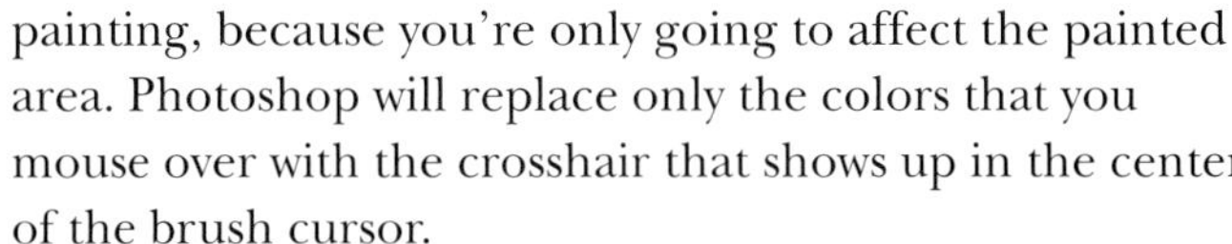

painting, because you're only going to affect the painted area. Photoshop will replace only the colors that you mouse over with the crosshair that shows up in the center of the brush cursor.

When you paint, Photoshop uses your foreground color to change what's in the active layer, based on the setting in the Mode pop-up menu in the options bar at the top of your screen (**Figure 8.70**):

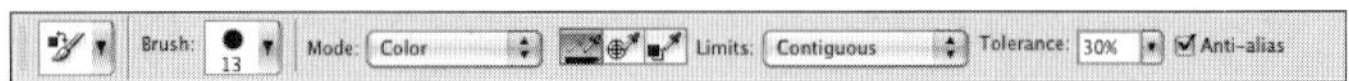

Figure 8.70 The options bar settings determine how the Color Replacement tool will interact with the image.

Figure 8.71 The dull jacket of the man crossing the street becomes a shiny purple color with a few clicks of the mouse. (©2008 Dan Ablan.)

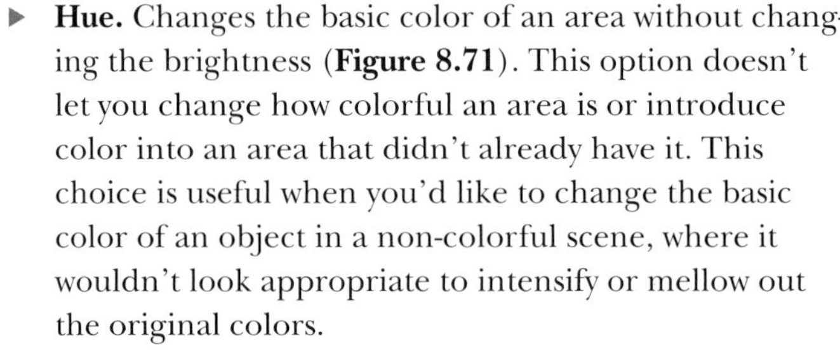

- **Hue.** Changes the basic color of an area without changing the brightness (**Figure 8.71**). This option doesn't let you change how colorful an area is or introduce color into an area that didn't already have it. This choice is useful when you'd like to change the basic color of an object in a non-colorful scene, where it wouldn't look appropriate to intensify or mellow out the original colors.

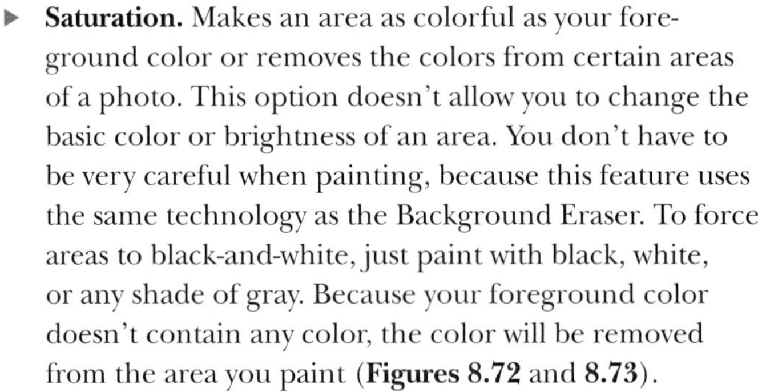

- **Saturation.** Makes an area as colorful as your foreground color or removes the colors from certain areas of a photo. This option doesn't allow you to change the basic color or brightness of an area. You don't have to be very careful when painting, because this feature uses the same technology as the Background Eraser. To force areas to black-and-white, just paint with black, white, or any shade of gray. Because your foreground color doesn't contain any color, the color will be removed from the area you paint (**Figures 8.72** and **8.73**).

Figure 8.72 The original image. (©2008 Dan Ablan.)

Figure 8.73 Color is removed from the background, using Saturation mode and painting with black.

- **Color.** Changes both the basic color and the saturation of the color, but not the brightness. In essence, this option applies the paint color to the brightness of the original image. This choice is useful when you need to push a lot of color into a particular area. Just paint with a relatively vivid version of a new color so the area becomes as colorful as the original image (**Figure 8.74**).
- **Luminosity.** Changes the brightness of an area to match the brightness of the paint color. This mode won't allow you to shift the colors at all. This option might not be used very often, but it can be helpful if you need to fix a portion of an image that's just too intense, such as a bright red baseball uniform (**Figure 8.75**).

Figure 8.74 The top half of the red bus was painted blue with the mode set to Color. (©2008 Dan Ablan.)

Figure 8.75 A few clicks on the bright red uniform reduce its intensity. (©2008 Dan Ablan.)

If you're having trouble getting good results with this tool, you need to learn more about the setting that determines which areas are changed and which are ignored. This tool uses the same technology as the Background Eraser tool, which we'll cover in detail in Chapter 9, "Enhancements and Masking." So go check out that chapter and then come back and try these ideas again.

Channel Mixer

So far, most of the adjustments in this chapter have been relatively straightforward. You tell Photoshop what you want to change (midtones, highlights, and so on) and what direction to shift the colors. But the Channel Mixer is a different beast (**Figure 8.76**). It forces you to think about how Photoshop works behind the scenes. The Channel Mixer lets you literally mix the contents of the channels that show up in the Channels panel (Window > Channels).

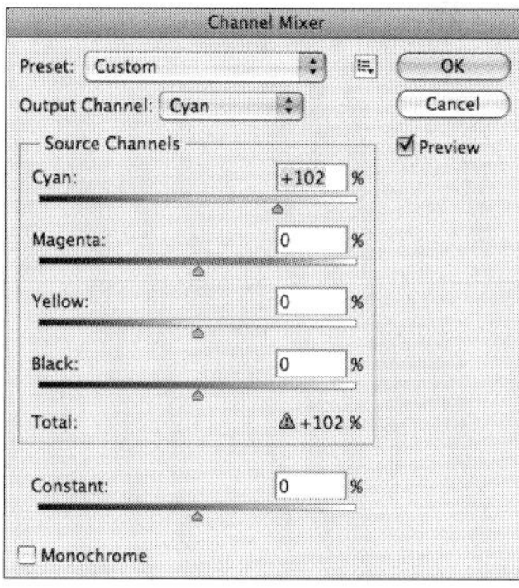

Figure 8.76 The Channel Mixer dialog.

Choose Image > Adjustments > Channel Mixer and choose the desired channel from the Output Channel pop-up menu. Then move the Source Channels sliders to brighten or darken the output channel:

- Because RGB mode creates the image out of red, green, and blue light, moving sliders toward the right adds more light and therefore brightens the output channel based on the contents of the channel whose slider you moved. Moving the slider in the opposite direction reduces the amount of light being applied to the output channel.

- CMYK mode creates the image out of four colors of ink, so moving a slider toward the right adds ink to the output channel, thereby darkening it. Moving a slider to the left in CMYK mode lessens the amount of ink in the output channel, effectively brightening it. This design might sound complicated at first, but once you see a few examples you should start to understand the simplicity behind it.

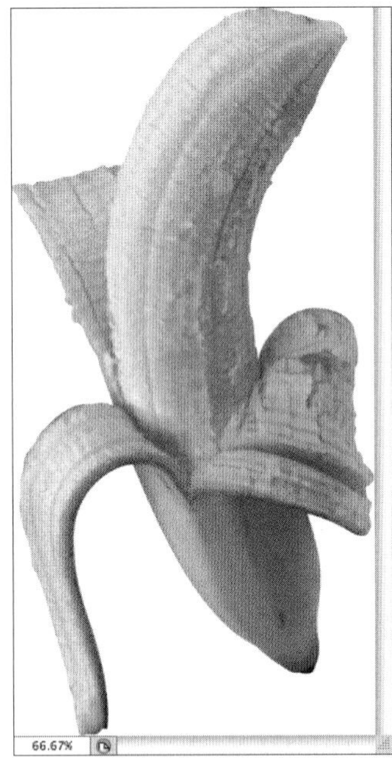

Figure 8.77 The original banana image is in CMYK mode. (©2007 Photospin.)

Let's say you have a CMYK mode image of a banana (**Figure 8.77**) and you'd like to reproduce it using only two colors of ink. That way you could save money and show your friends that you've really mastered Photoshop. You'd probably end up using yellow ink for the banana, and then use some black ink so you can get shadows that are darker than the yellow ink. Start by choosing Image > Adjustments > Channel Mixer, choose Cyan from the Output Channel pop-up menu, and move the Cyan Source Channels slider all the way to the left to indicate that you don't want to use any of what was originally in the Cyan channel (**Figure 8.78**). Then choose Magenta from the Output pop-up menu and move the Magenta slider all the way to the left to clear out the Magenta channel (**Figure 8.79**).

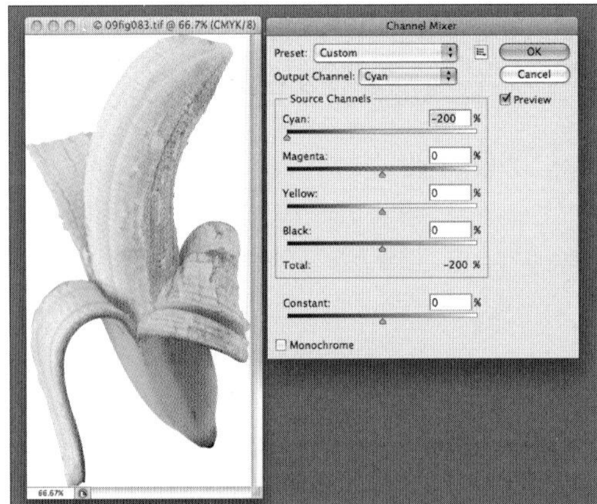

Figure 8.78 Moving the Cyan slider all the way to the left removes all cyan from the image.

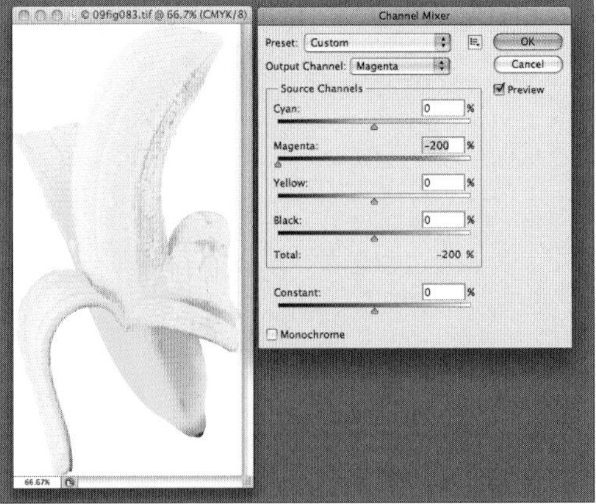

Figure 8.79 Moving the Magenta slider all the way to the left removes all magenta from the image.

Now the image should be made out of just yellow and black ink, but it most likely looks quite light because there's not enough black ink to compensate for not using any cyan or magenta ink. To fix that problem, choose Black from the Output Channel pop-up menu, and then slide the Cyan and Magenta sliders toward the right until the brightness looks as close to the original as you can get (**Figure 8.80**). Turn the Preview check box off and back on again to compare the original to the end result. Once you have the image as close as you can get to the look of the original, click OK and then drag the Cyan and Magenta channels to the trash at the bottom of the Channels panel. Finally, to get a more appropriate shade of yellow, double-click to the right of the name of the Yellow channel in the Channels panel, so you can pick a new color and experiment until the image looks the best it can (**Figure 8.81**).

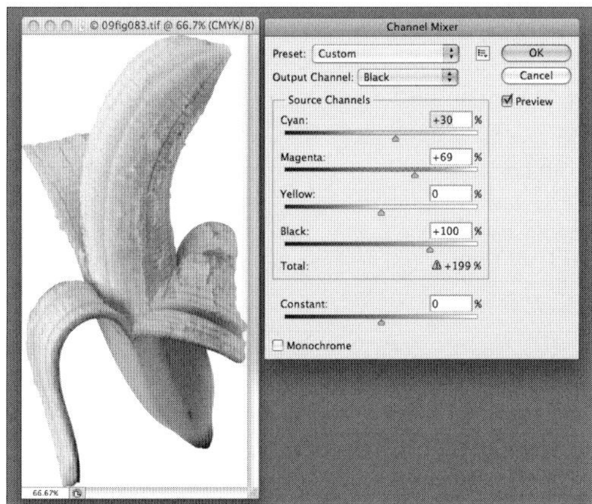

Figure 8.80 Adding what used to be in the Cyan and Magenta channels to the Black channel will compensate for using fewer inks.

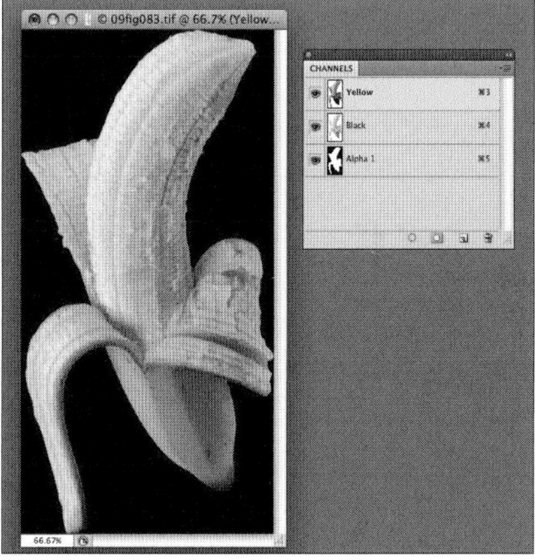

Figure 8.81 The final image is made out of only two colors of ink!

Now that you've seen one example, let's use the Channel Mixer to convert a full-color image into a grayscale version. While you might think that you could just choose Image > Mode > Grayscale and be done with it, you'll get better quality by experimenting with the Channel Mixer. But before you get started, go open the Channels panel and click through all the channels. You'll need to start with one of those channels as the base of your grayscale conversion,

With Photoshop CS4, the Black and White adjustment is the best option, but the Channel Mixer is a good alternative to other grayscale conversion methods.

so make note of which one displays the best grayscale version of the image. In **Figure 8.82**, the Red channel provides the best starting point.

Figure 8.82 The Red channel of a color RGB image. (©2008 Dan Ablan.)

Choose Image > Adjustments > Channel Mixer, and turn on the Monochrome check box at the bottom of the dialog to remove all the color from the image. To start with the channel you liked best, move the appropriate slider to the 100% position and move the other sliders to 0%. Now experiment with moving the sliders to the right and left to see how they affect the image (**Figure 8.83**). As you move a slider toward the right, the image gets brighter, necessitating that you move another slider toward the left to compensate. By using different mixes of the channels, you'll get different grayscale results. There's no obvious formula for getting the best results; you just have to experiment until you like the detail, contrast, and brightness (**Figure 8.84**). A good general rule is that getting the sliders to add up to 100% should deliver an image that's close to the same brightness as the original image. Once you like what you have, click OK and then choose Image > Mode > Grayscale.

Figure 8.83 Start with the channel that looked the best, such as the Red channel.

Figure 8.84 One of many end results you could get with a few minutes of experimentation.

Gradient Map

The Gradient Map (Image > Adjustments > Gradient Map) does a rather simple and unusual thing: It first converts an image to grayscale, and then replaces the shades of gray in the image with different colors that show up in a gradient (**Figure 8.85**). When you first open the dialog, it defaults to a black-and-white gradient, which should just make the image look grayscale. If you click the down arrow to the right of the gradient preview, you'll be able to choose a preset gradient to replace the shades of gray that were in the original image (**Figures 8.86** and **8.87**). If you prefer to bypass the preset gradients and create your own gradient, click in the middle of the gradient preview to access the Gradient Editor. To learn how to create your own gradients, read about the Gradient tool in Chapter 1, "Tools and Panels Primer."

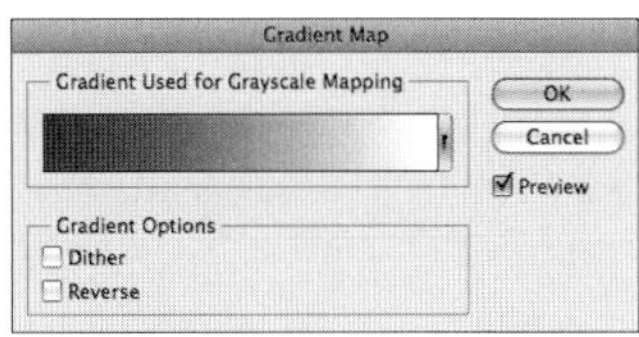

Figure 8.85 The Gradient Map dialog.

Figure 8.86 The original image. (©2008 Dan Ablan.)

Figure 8.87 Gradient Map replaces brightness levels with different colors.

You can use the Gradient Map command to transform a backlit image into one that looks like it was taken at sunset (**Figures 8.88** and **8.89**). All you have to do is create a gradient that starts with black and slowly fades to orange and then yellow (**Figure 8.90**). If you want more of a silhouetted image, just slide the black color swatch in the

Gradient Editor toward the right until you no longer see much detail in the subject of the photo (**Figure 8.91**).

Figure 8.88 The original image. (©2008 Dan Ablan.)

Figure 8.89 The result of applying a black, orange, yellow gradient map.

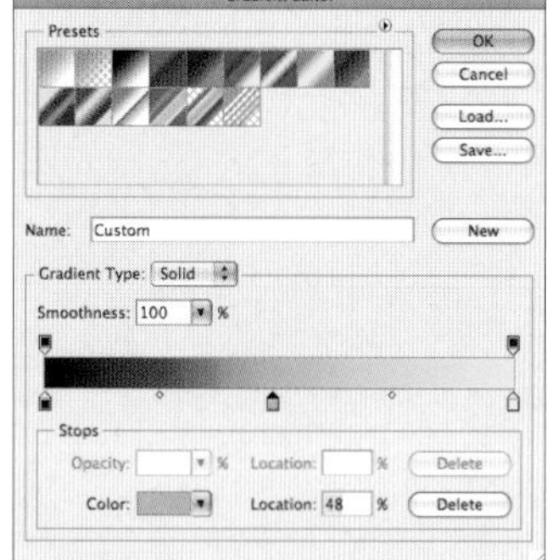

Figure 8.90 The three-color gradient used to create Figure 8.89.

Figure 8.91 The result of dragging the black slider toward the middle of the gradient.

The Next Step

As you've seen in this chapter, a mind-boggling multitude of techniques exist for manipulating the colors in your images. You don't have to know or remember how to use all of these techniques—just try the ones that seem most comfortable and stick with them for a while. Then, once you feel confident with those tricks, read this chapter again and add a few more techniques to your adjustment arsenal. Some of the best methods to use on a regular basis are Hue/Saturation, Auto Color, and the Color Replacement tool. But don't just use those three; instead, try them all and find your own favorites.

Creative Techniques

CHAPTER

9

Enhancements and Masking

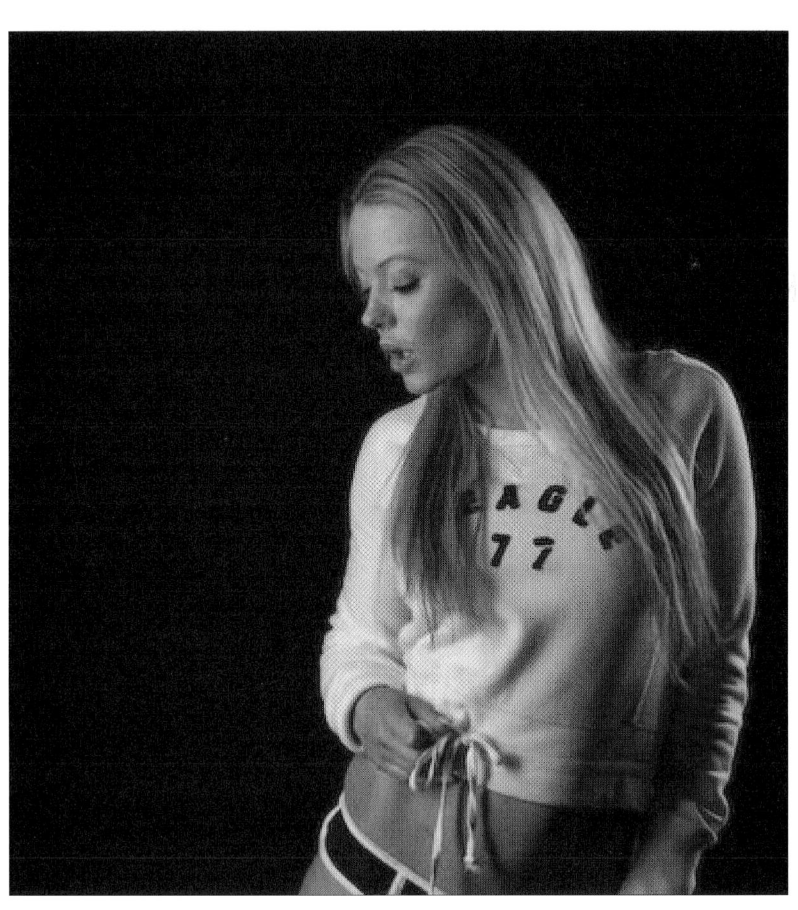

Just build a classic horseshoe of wood and plaster, and fill it with statuary and curtains, then sit back and savor the beautifully blended results.

—Michael Walsh

Enhancements and Masking

Photoshop has so many ways available to enhance an image that the possibilities are endless, limited only by your willingness to experiment.

This chapter is filled with enhancement techniques. Photoshop's blending modes kick off the chapter, followed by information on layer masks. Blending modes comprise one of the most powerful features in Photoshop—and, when mixed with layer masks, provide tremendous opportunities for image manipulation, color correction, and more.

Blending Modes

Blending modes work when you have two or more layers. The blending mode you choose determines how the active layer will interact with an underlying image. Previous chapters have looked briefly at the Blending Mode pop-up menu located at the top of the Layers panel. Chapter 5, "Adjustment Layers," pointed out that certain blending modes can be especially useful when applying adjustment layers, since the blending mode allows you to limit how much those layers affect the image.

Let's dig a little deeper into the blending modes now. Once you understand how the various modes work, you can jump in and start using them.

As with most Photoshop features, the blending modes are accessible in a variety of ways. In most situations, you'll use the Blending Mode pop-up menu at the top of the Layers panel, or the Blend Mode pop-up menu in the Layer Style dialog. For this discussion, we'll focus on the Blend Mode pop-up menu, starting at the top of the list and working our way down. The blending modes on this menu are divided into six categories, as shown in **Figure 9.1**, with Normal being the default mode.

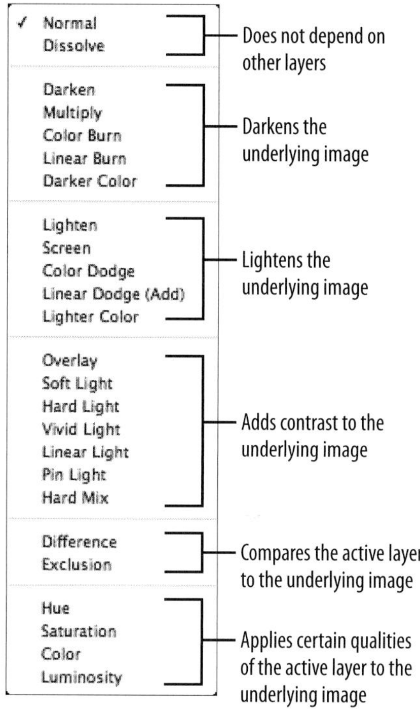

Figure 9.1 The Blend Mode pop-up menu in the Layer Style dialog is organized into six sections.

Normal Mode

Normal blending mode doesn't actually "blend" anything. Say you have a picture of a sunset in one layer, and then add another layer on top of that with a bird. With the blending mode set to Normal, you'll see each layer in its full opacity.

Dissolve Mode

The Dissolve blending mode affects only areas that are partially transparent, transforming them into a scattered spray of solid pixels. As a result, those areas end up looking noisy. For example, you might use the Dissolve blending mode for product packaging, to create a noisy-looking shadow or glow around some text. Add a Drop Shadow or an Outer Glow layer style to the layer and set its blending mode to Dissolve (**Figures 9.2** to **9.4**).

Figure 9.2 Text with drop shadow created in Photoshop's default blending mode.

Figure 9.4 The drop shadow from Figure 9.2 in Dissolve mode.

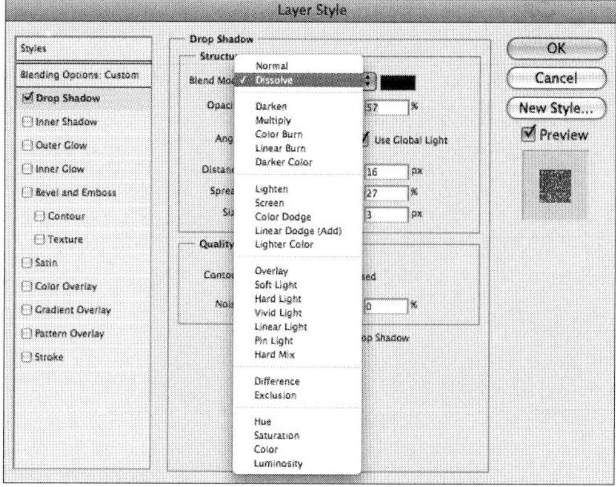

Figure 9.3 Choose Dissolve from the Blend Mode pop-up menu in the Layer Style dialog.

Behind Mode

The Behind blending mode shows up in only a few areas of Photoshop. Behind mode limits the changes you make to a layer so that they affect only the transparent areas of the active layer. If you select one of the painting tools, you'll see a blending mode selection at the top of the interface in the toolbar, where you can choose Behind mode. Using Behind mode is similar to working on a layer directly below the active layer. Painting on a layer in Behind mode gives the impression that you're painting underneath the active layer (**Figures 9.5** and **9.6**).

Figure 9.5 A layer that contains transparent areas. (©2008 Dan Ablan.)

Figure 9.6 When you're painting in Behind mode, the brush strokes appear to be underneath the active layer.

If the Behind mode isn't working as expected, glance at the top of the Layers panel to see if the Lock Transparency icon is turned on. When Lock Transparency is on, you can't change the transparent areas of the active layer; the Behind and Clear modes will be grayed out.

You can use this mode with the Fill dialog (Edit > Fill) as a quick-and-dirty way to fill the empty parts of a layer. Perhaps you might use Behind mode when you're creating a slide show and don't want to see the "checkerboard" background. Choose Edit > Fill, set the Use pop-up menu to White, and change the Mode pop-up menu to Behind to fill all transparent pixels with white.

Clear Mode

Like Behind mode, Clear mode shows up only in certain areas of Photoshop (such as in the painting tools and Edit > Fill command). Clear mode is basically the same as using the Eraser tool, or selecting an area and then pressing Delete (Mac) or Backspace (Windows).

You can generally use Clear mode to lower the opacity of a large area. Choosing Edit > Fill in Clear mode at 40% opacity, for example, reduces the opacity of the layer by 40%, leaving it 60% opaque (**Figures 9.7** and **9.8**).

Figure 9.7 The original foreground image with a white background.

Figure 9.8 The foreground image filled using Clear mode at 40% opacity.

When you use Clear mode, Photoshop completely ignores the color with which you're attempting to fill or paint. It only pays attention to the Opacity setting and uses the active paint or selection to determine which areas should be deleted.

If you'd rather not permanently lower the opacity of an area, use a layer mask instead. Clear mode is like putting gray in a layer mask. Filling with 40% opacity in Clear mode is the same as filling part of a layer mask with 40% gray.

Darken Blending Modes

The blending modes in the second section of the menu are grouped because they can only darken the underlying image. In all of these modes, white simply disappears, and in most of them, anything darker than white will darken the underlying image. Each mode has its own personality.

Darken Mode

Darken mode compares the active layer to the underlying image and allows only those areas that are darker than that image to show up. It's that simple when you're working on grayscale images, but if you try the same mode on a color image, you might be surprised by the result (**Figures 9.9** to **9.11**).

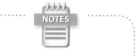

Figure 9.9 The top layer. (©2008 Dan Ablan.)

Figure 9.10 The bottom layer. (©2008 Dan Ablan.)

Figure 9.11 Result of using Darken mode on the top layer.

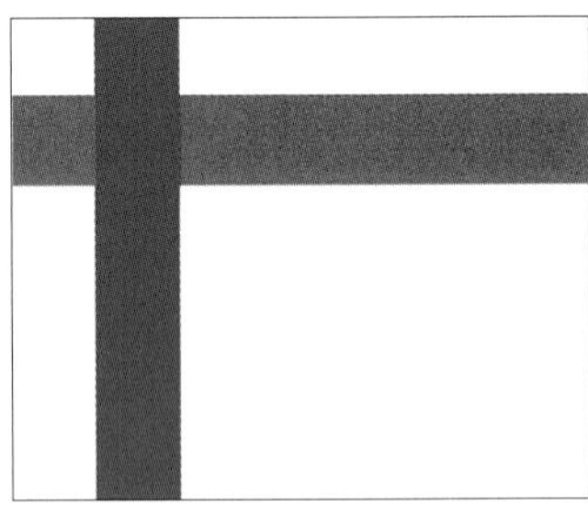

Figure 9.12 In Normal mode, the top layer obstructs your view of the underlying image.

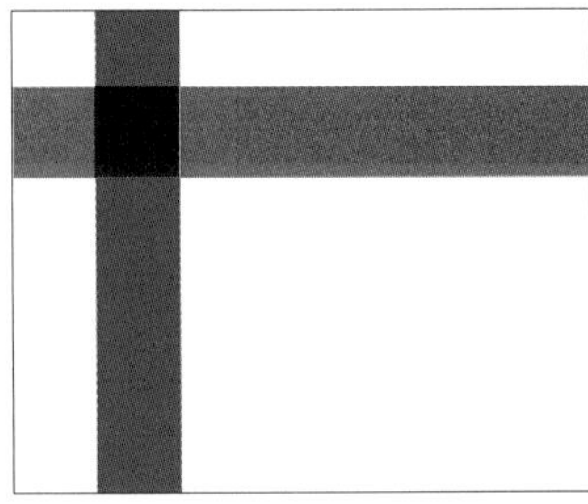

Figure 9.13 In Darken mode, Photoshop uses the darkest of the red, green, and blue components.

Darken mode compares two layers by looking at the red, green, and blue components individually. Say you have a layer with some red that's made out of 230 Red, 50 Green, and 30 Blue, and a layer above it that contains a blue made from 50 Red, 55 Green, and 200 Blue. Usually the blue in the top layer would completely cover the color below (**Figure 9.12**), but when you set the top layer to Darken mode, Photoshop compares the red, green, and blue components of each layer and uses the darkest of each. In this case, the red information on the top layer is darker—50 versus 230 (lower numbers mean less light). When comparing the green components, the bottom layer is darker, and the blue component is darkest on the bottom layer. Once Photoshop picked the darkest of each color, it would end up with 50 Red, 50 Green, and 30 Blue, which would result in a dark yellow color (**Figure 9.13**). You don't need to think about the red, green, and blue components of each layer when you're using Darken mode, but you can occasionally blame them when you don't get the intended result.

You'll mainly use Darken mode when retouching an image, but let's see how you might use it with Photoshop's filters. Suppose you've chosen Filter > Pixelate > Pointillize, but you don't like all the white areas that show up (**Figure 9.14**). Choose Edit > Fade Pointillize immediately after applying the filter, and then you can tell Photoshop how to apply that filter to the original. If you choose Darken, Photoshop compares the filtered result with the original and only allows the filter to darken the original, which should in effect get rid of the white areas, unless the original contained white (**Figure 9.15**). Try this technique after applying the Sharpen filter, when the bright halos it produces are distracting. By using Darken mode, you can limit that filter so that it creates only dark halos.

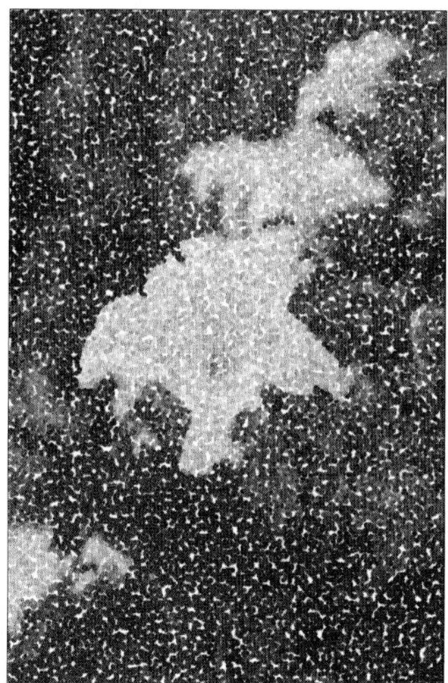

Figure 9.14 Result of applying the Pointillize filter.

Figure 9.15 Result of fading the Pointillize filter in Darken mode.

Figure 9.16 The first image. (©2008 Dan Ablan.)

Figure 9.17 Image with white background to be printed on the second pass. (©2008 Dan Ablan.)

Figure 9.18 Result of combining the two images with the top layer set to Multiply mode.

Multiply Mode

One of the most useful darkening modes is Multiply, which acts like ink. Imagine taking **Figure 9.16** and printing it on an inkjet printer. Then, imagine sending the sheet back through the printer and printing a second image on top of the first (**Figure 9.17**). All the second printing can do is darken the first, because all an inkjet printer can do is add ink to the page (**Figure 9.18**). In this mode, white simply disappears. After all, how do you print white with an inkjet printer? You don't. You just leave the paper alone. It's the same way in Multiply mode; anything darker than white will darken the underlying image.

Figure 9.19 Top text layer set to Normal mode.

Figure 9.20 Top text layer set to Multiply mode.

Figure 9.21 This tattoo will be transplanted to another image. (©Stockbyte, www.stockbyte.com.)

This is a simple way to make text or graphics "overprint" on the underlying image instead of covering it up (**Figures 9.19** and **9.20**). You can also use it anytime you have scanned text or other graphics that you'd like to print on something else.

The main problem is areas that are not completely white. Any area that is darker than white will darken the underlying image, so you'll occasionally need to choose Image > Adjustments > Levels and move the upper-right slider to make sure that the background is pure white. As an example, let's take the tattoo from **Figure 9.21** and put it on **Figure 9.22**. We place the tattoo on a layer above the second image, setting the blending mode of that layer to Multiply (**Figure 9.23**), choose Image > Adjustments > Desaturate, and then adjust the image using Levels until only the tattoo appears and the background surrounding it disappears (**Figure 9.24**).

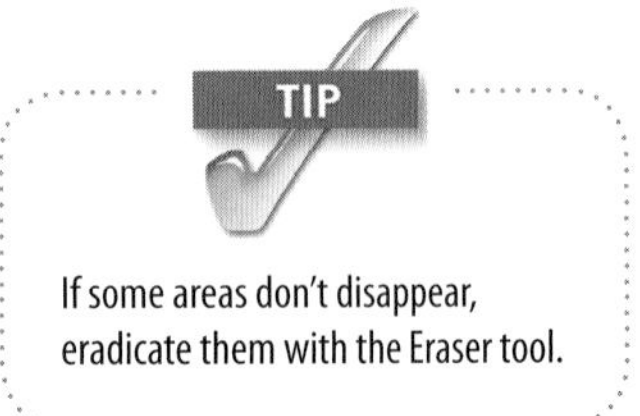

If some areas don't disappear, eradicate them with the Eraser tool.

Figure 9.22 Image to which the tattoo will be applied. (©Stockbyte, www.stockbyte.com.)

Figure 9.23 Result of setting the tattoo layer to Multiply mode.

Figure 9.24 Result of desaturating and then adjusting the image with Levels.

Earlier chapters talked about how both your screen and printer simulate a wide range of colors using only red, green, and blue light; or cyan, magenta, and yellow ink. To demonstrate this, we could create an image containing three circles, one per layer: cyan, magenta, and yellow. But they don't act like ink when they overlap (**Figure 9.25**). So we simply set the blending mode for each layer to Multiply, and then everything works the way it should (**Figure 9.26**).

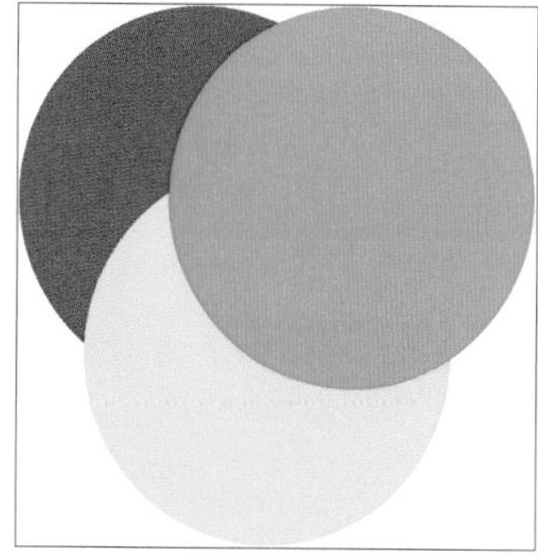

Figure 9.25 In Normal mode, the three circles don't interact with each other.

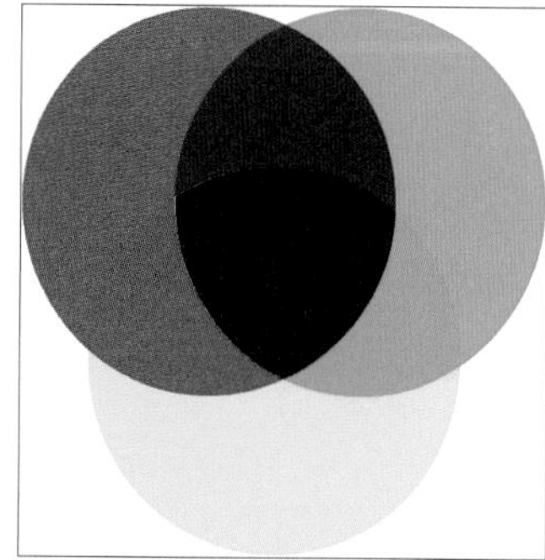

Figure 9.26 Result of setting each layer to Multiply mode.

Now let's use Multiply to create a contour drawing out of a photograph (**Figure 9.27**). Because we're going to end up with black lines and no color information, choose Image > Mode > Grayscale. To get contours, choose Filter > Stylize > Trace Contour, and move the slider around a bit (**Figure 9.28**). Trace Contour puts a black line around the edge of a particular shade of gray. But there are two problems: The contours aren't usually smooth, and there's only one contour for the entire image. To fix the first problem, smooth out the image by applying the Gaussian Blur or the Median filter. The latter requires a little more effort, and that's where we can start putting the Multiply blending mode to work.

Figure 9.27 A photograph converted to a contour drawing. (©2008 Dan Ablan.)

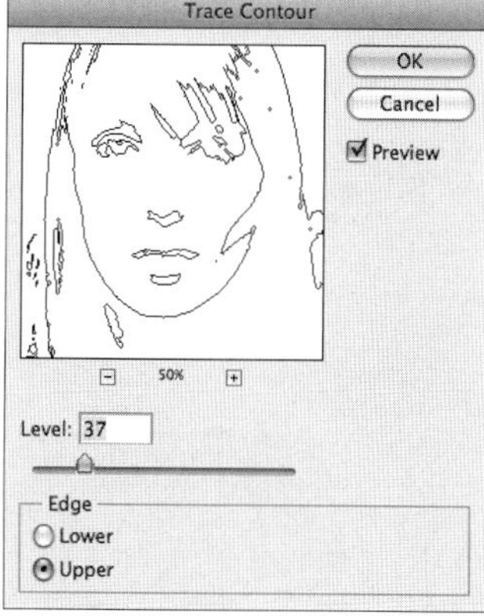

Figure 9.28 The Trace Contour dialog.

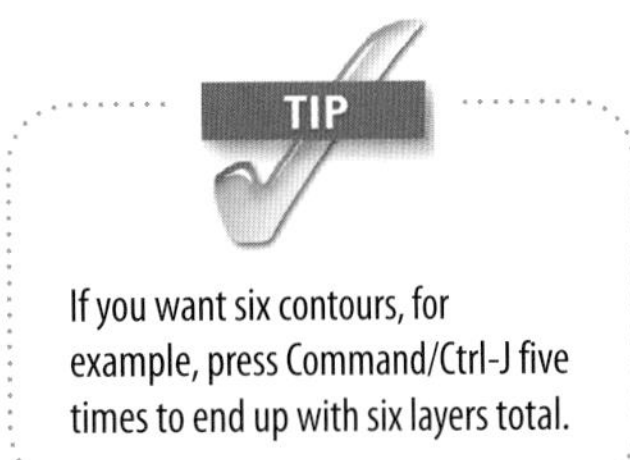

If you want six contours, for example, press Command/Ctrl-J five times to end up with six layers total.

Duplicate the layer enough times so that you have one layer for each contour that you want. Then apply the Trace Contour filter to each layer, using a different level setting each time in the Trace Contour dialog. Each layer now contains a different contour (**Figure 9.29**). To combine those images into one, set the blending mode of each layer to Multiply so they print on top of each other, which will make the white areas disappear (**Figure 9.30**).

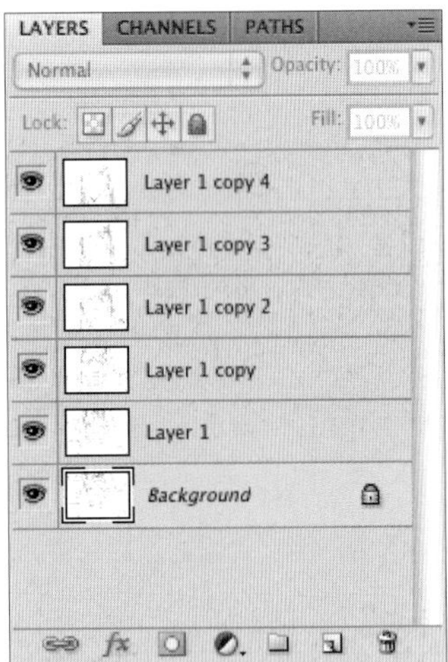

Figure 9.29 All the layers that are needed to create the drawing.

Figure 9.30 Result of combining all the layers in Multiply mode.

Here's another way of using blending modes with filters. Let's say you've opened an image and then chosen Filter > Stylize > Find Edges. Now you have a bunch of black lines representing the edges of all the objects that were in the photo (**Figure 9.31**). But what if you wanted those black lines to print on top of the original image? Immediately after applying the filter, choose Edit > Fade Find Edges and set the blending mode to Multiply. Photoshop applies the filtered image to the original as if you had printed on top of it (**Figure 9.32**).

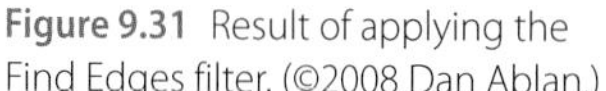

Figure 9.31 Result of applying the Find Edges filter. (©2008 Dan Ablan.)

Figure 9.32 Result of fading the edges in Multiply mode.

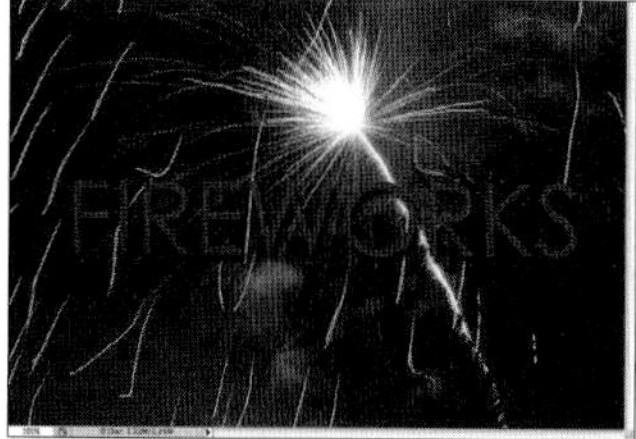

Figure 9.33 The black drop shadow doesn't contribute to the legibility of the text.

Figure 9.34 A white shadow isn't possible in Multiply mode, so the mode has been changed to Normal.

Multiply mode is used quite a bit in Photoshop's layer styles, which can be confusing when you're trying to do something unusual. Say you have some black text on a deep blue background, and you want to add a drop shadow. With the text layer active, choose Layer > Layer Style > Drop Shadow. But a black drop shadow with dark text makes the text hard to see (**Figure 9.33**), so you decide to change the shadow color to white. The shadow disappears! That's because its mode is automatically set to Multiply (in the Layer Style dialog), and white disappears in Multiply mode. To get things to work the way you wanted, change the mode to Normal (**Figure 9.34**).

Color Burn Mode

Color Burn mode isn't easy to describe or understand, but can be very useful nonetheless. As with all the darken blending modes, white doesn't do anything in Color Burn mode. Black leaves any red, green, or blue numbers that are 255 alone, forcing all others to zero. When you paint with a primary color (pure red, green, or blue), you'll end up with the amount of that primary color that was in the underlying image—and nothing else. When you paint with a color that's made out of two primaries, Photoshop strips the third primary color out of the underlying image.

Here's where the goodies come in. Paint with shades of gray to darken and intensify the colors that are in the underlying image. This can work wonders for darkening bland-looking skies, making them more colorful while at

You can use Color Burn mode to colorize grayscale images. Be sure to change the mode of the image from grayscale to RGB or CMYK. Lower the opacity of your painting tool; otherwise, you'll end up with a rather dark result.

Figure 9.35 The original image. (©2008 Dan Ablan.)

Figure 9.36 Result of painting with gray across the sky in Color Burn mode.

the same time maintaining the bright white clouds (**Figures 9.35** and **9.36**). Shadows can look good using Color Burn. If a shadow is falling on a textured background, more of the texture will come through, because it will maintain more of the highlights (**Figures 9.37** and **9.38**).

Figure 9.37 Shadow applied in Multiply mode.

Figure 9.38 Shadow applied in Color Burn mode.

Linear Burn Mode

Linear Burn mode acts much like Multiply mode but has a greater tendency to make areas pure black. It maintains more of the color from the underlying image. Use it anytime you'd think about using Multiply mode but want a higher-contrast result. If standard shadows (which usually use Multiply mode) look a little too gray, try Linear Burn; you might like the result better (**Figures 9.39** and **9.40**), although you'll need to lower the Opacity setting to avoid getting an overly dark result.

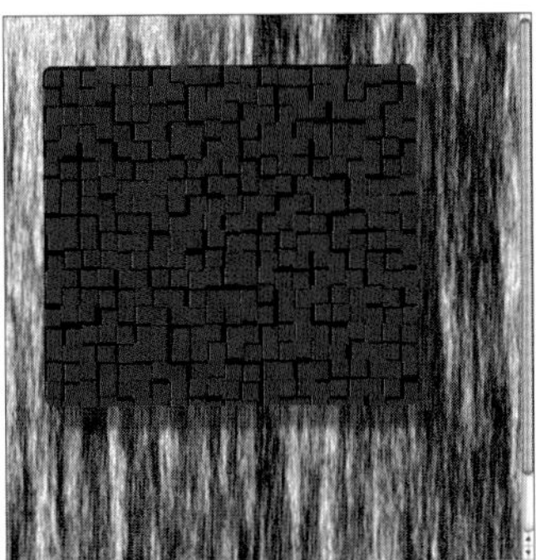

Figure 9.39 Shadow applied in Multiply mode, with Opacity reduced. (Compare the result to Figure 9.37.)

Figure 9.40 Shadow applied in Linear Burn mode.

Lighten Blending Modes

Each of the darken blending modes (Darken, Multiply, Color Burn, and Linear Burn) has an equally useful opposite mode. With all the lighten blending modes, black simply disappears, and anything brighter than black has the potential to brighten the underlying image.

Lighten Mode

Lighten mode compares the active layer to the underlying image and allows the areas of the active layer to show up that are brighter than the underlying image. But it looks at the red, green, and blue components of the image separately, which makes for some unpredictable results. Lighten mode can be a lifesaver when working with transparent surfaces, such as those of a 3D render. The only problem with combining a multiple-pass render with glass is to get both to show up at once (**Figures 9.41** and **9.42**). With both images loaded into Photoshop, one atop the other, set the blending mode of the top layer to Lighten, and—bingo, the render comes together (**Figure 9.43**).

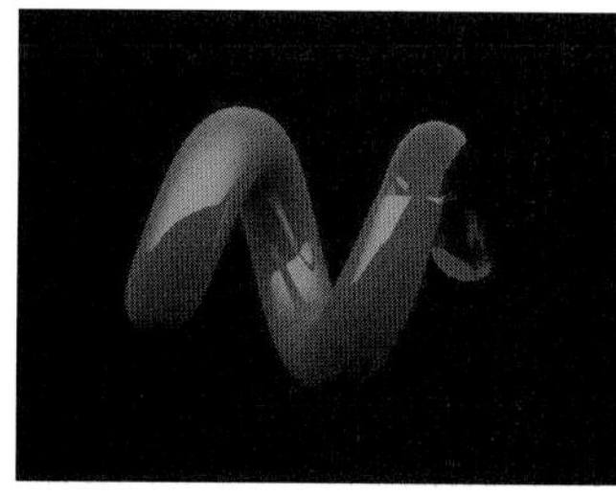

Figure 9.41 Image with bulb visible. (©2008 Luxology.com.)

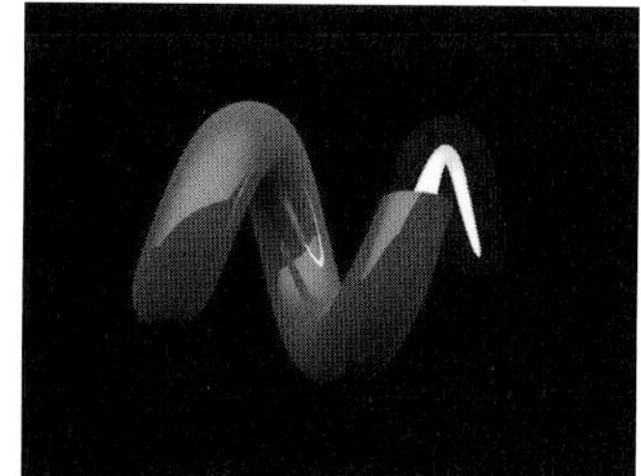

Figure 9.42 Image with filament visible.

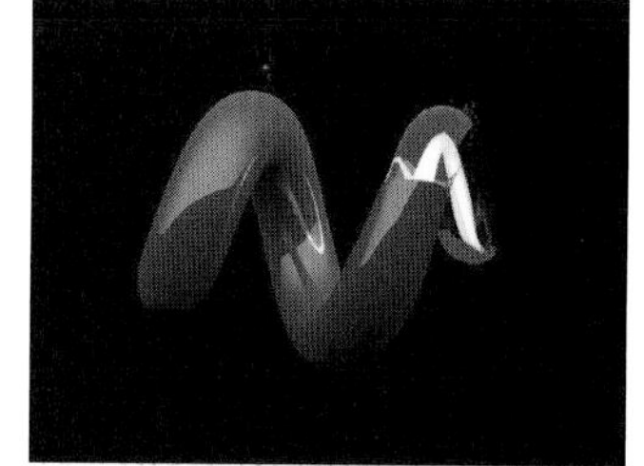

Figure 9.43 Result of combining the two images in Lighten mode.

Try Lighten mode when experimenting with filters. For instance, choosing Filter > Stylize > Glowing Edges creates bright lines where the edges of an object were in an image (**Figure 9.44**). Use this filter to add extra interest to an image by choosing Edit > Fade Glowing Edges, and then setting the blending mode to Lighten immediately after applying the filter (**Figure 9.45**). You get the bright edge effect while maintaining the overall look of the original image.

Figure 9.44 The colors shift when the Glowing Edges filter is applied. (©2008 Dan Ablan.)

Figure 9.45 More of the original image is visible after Lighten mode is used.

Lighten mode can be wonderful when sharpening an image. Duplicate the layer twice, set the top layer to Lighten and the middle layer to Darken, and then sharpen the top two layers. Then you can control the dark and bright halos separately by lowering the opacity of each of those two layers.

The same concept works great when you're using the Lighting Effects filter, which usually brightens or darkens an image. In Lighten mode, you can force that filter to brighten only (**Figures 9.46** and **9.47**). Use it after applying the Blur filter, to add a soft-focus look (**Figure 9.48**).

Figure 9.46 The original image. (©2008 Dan Ablan.)

Figure 9.47 The Lighting Effects filter brightens and darkens the image.

Figure 9.48 Result of fading the Lighting Effects filter in Lighten mode.

Screen Mode

If Multiply mode acts like ink, Screen mode is its opposite, acting like light instead. In this mode, black simply disappears, whereas anything brighter than black brightens the underlying image. Screen mode is useful when an image has a black background with anything that resembles light within it. Use it with things like sparklers and lightning; put the sparkler on a layer above another image, set the layer mode to Screen, choose Image > Adjustments > Levels, and pull the upper-left slider in until the background of the sparkler disappears (**Figures 9.49** and **9.50**).

Figure 9.49 Result of using Normal mode to combine images on two layers. (©2008 Dan Ablan.)

Figure 9.50 Result of applying Screen mode to the top layer. The black disappears.

Screen mode is used in many of Photoshop's layer styles. Say you want to add a glow around some text by choosing Layer > Layer Style > Outer Glow. That technique works fine as long as you choose a bright color like white or yellow, but doesn't look good if you use a dark color like navy blue (**Figure 9.51**). Because Photoshop uses Screen mode as the default method for applying the glow to the underlying image, shining a dark blue light at something isn't going to change it much. To remedy the situation, change the blending mode to either Normal or Multiply (**Figure 9.52**).

Figure 9.51 Dark Outer Glow on text won't be very visible in Screen Mode

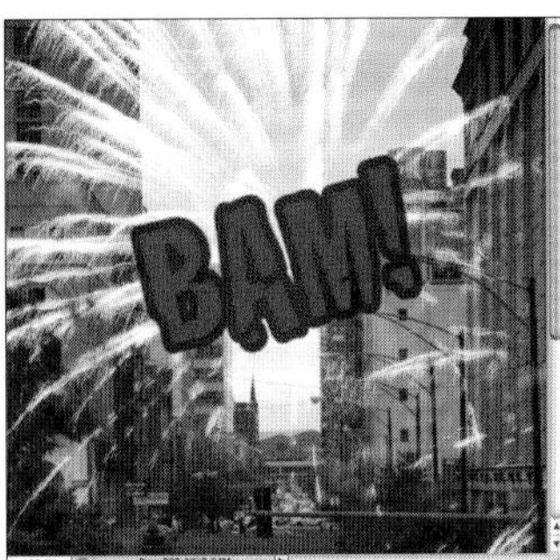

Figure 9.52 Changing the blending mode to Multiply allows the Outer Glow to be visible.

Remember the overlapping circles from Figures 9.25 and 9.26? There we were thinking ink (Multiply mode). Suppose we want circles of light instead? By setting each of the layers to Screen mode, you can get the circles in **Figure 9.53** to interact with each other as if they were circles of light (**Figure 9.54**).

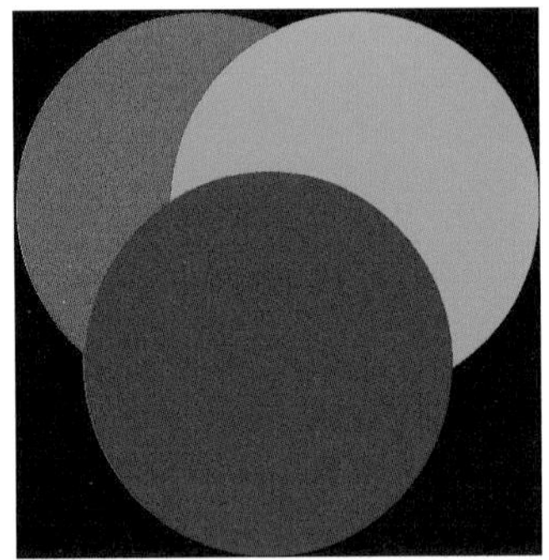

Figure 9.53 In Normal mode, the three circles don't interact with each other.

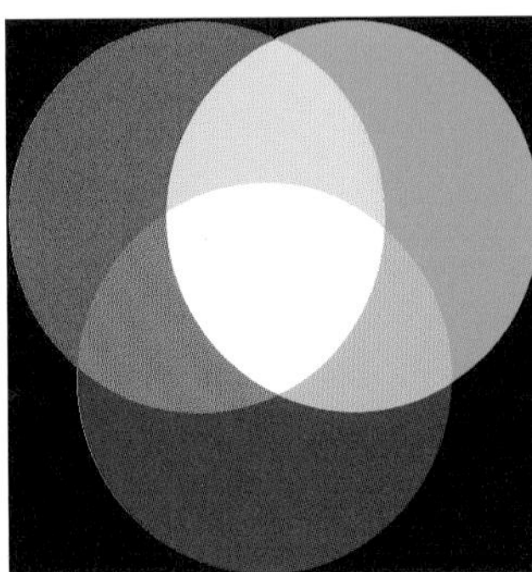

Figure 9.54 Result of switching each layer to Screen mode.

Color Dodge Mode

Color Dodge mode usually brightens the underlying image while at the same time making the colors more saturated. It's very useful because it doesn't change the darkest part of the image very much, which allows you to brighten an area while still maintaining good contrast. Use the Paintbrush tool and paint with a dark shade of gray on a layer set to Color Dodge mode (**Figures 9.55** and **9.56**). It's useful for adding more interest to otherwise dull-looking hair. (Photographers often use a separate light source to add highlights to hair.) Use Color Dodge mode as a replacement for Screen mode when you're adding an Outer Glow layer style to text (**Figures 9.57** and **9.58**).

Figure 9.55 The original image. (©2008 Dan Ablan.)

Figure 9.56 The water was brightened with gray paint in Color Dodge mode.

Figure 9.57 Yellow glow created in Screen mode. (©2008 Dan Ablan.)

Figure 9.58 The same yellow glow created in Color Dodge mode.

Figure 9.59 The same yellow glow from the earlier figures, this time created in Linear Dodge mode.

Linear Dodge Mode

Linear Dodge mode works much like Screen mode, but has a greater tendency to make areas pure white. Use it any time you're considering Screen mode but want a higher-contrast result (**Figure 9.59**).

Contrast Blending Modes

The majority of blending modes on the next section of the menu combine the ideas used as examples in the darken and lighten blending modes. In all of these modes, 50% gray simply disappears, and anything darker than 50% has the potential of darkening the underlying image, whereas areas brighter than 50% have the potential to brighten the underlying image. In essence, these modes increase the contrast of the underlying image by brightening one area while darkening another.

Overlay Mode

In Overlay mode, the information on the underlying image is used to brighten or darken the active layer. Any areas darker than 50% gray will act like ink (or Multiply mode), whereas any areas brighter than 50% gray will act like light (or Screen mode). Overlay mode is useful when you want to add color to the underlying image

Distinguishing Between the Contrast Blending Modes

Here's some general guidelines to help you know when to use which contrast blending mode:

- Overlay makes the underlying image more prominent than the active layer. Hard Light does the opposite, making the active layer more prominent. Soft Light usually makes both layers equally prominent.
- Vivid Light acts a lot like Hard Light but increases the saturation of the colors while preserving more of the highlights and shadows from the underlying image. Linear Light is also like Hard Light, but has a greater tendency to make areas pure black and pure white.
- Pin Light and Hard Mix are the loners in this group. Hard Mix increases the saturation of the colors and posterizes the image while lightening the underlying image in the highlight areas of the active layer and darkening the underlying image in the shadow areas. Pin Light compares the two layers, brightens the underlying image in the highlight areas of the active layer, and darkens the underlying image where shadows exist in the active layer (in a rather unpredictable way, though).

while maintaining its highlights and shadows (**Figures 9.60** and **9.61**), or when working with layer styles. If you use both a pattern fill and a color overlay, the color overlay always completely covers up the pattern underneath it. But if you apply the color using the Overlay blending mode, it allows the highlights and shadows from the texture to brighten and darken the color that you're applying (**Figures 9.62** and **9.63**). This allows you to create many grayscale patterns and then colorize them with the Color Overlay layer style.

Figure 9.60 The original image. (©2008 Dan Ablan.)

Figure 9.61 Result of copying the image layer and applying it as an overlay.

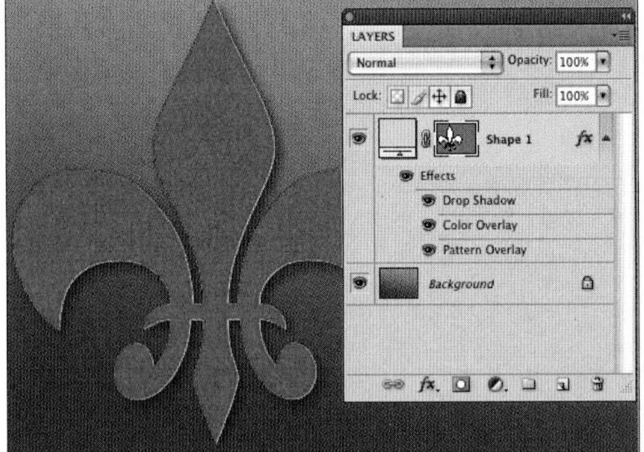

Figure 9.62 When you use color overlay and a pattern fill, the color obstructs your view of the pattern.

Figure 9.63 Applying the color overlay in Overlay mode allows it to combine with the underlying pattern.

Soft Light Mode

As with the other modes in this category, Soft Light mode makes 50% gray disappear while making brighter areas brighten and darker areas darken the underlying image. It usually does this with more subtle results than those in either Overlay or Hard Light mode. Use this mode for applying textures to photographs. Create a new, empty layer above the photograph. Press D to reset your foreground and background colors, and then choose Filter > Render Clouds. Now choose Filter > Stylize > Find Edges, and then Filter > Stylize > Emboss. Set the angle to 45°, the height to 1, and the amount as high as it can go (probably around 500). If you've done everything right, you should end up with a texture that resembles that on most "fingerprint-proof" refrigerators. To apply that texture to the underlying image, set its blending mode to Soft Light at the top of the Layers panel (**Figures 9.64** and **9.65**).

Soft Light mode is also useful when you're attempting to add a reflection. Place the image you want to reflect on a layer above the object that should be reflected, and set its blending mode to Soft Light (**Figures 9.66** and **9.67**).

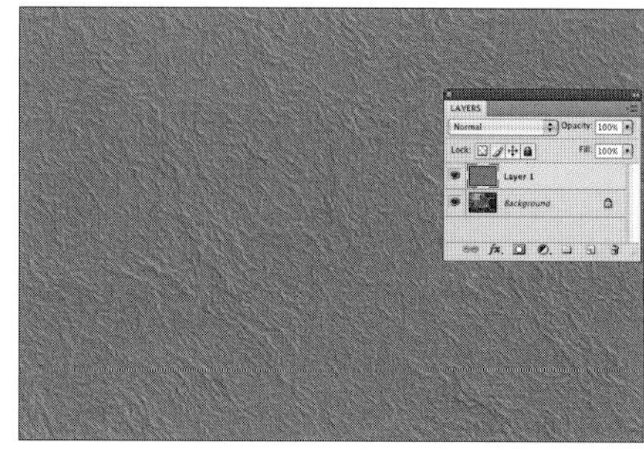

Figure 9.64 A texture applied in its own layer, above a photograph with the blending mode set to Normal. (©2008 Dan Ablan.)

Figure 9.65 The same texture now blends nicely with the photograph when the blending mode is set to Soft Light.

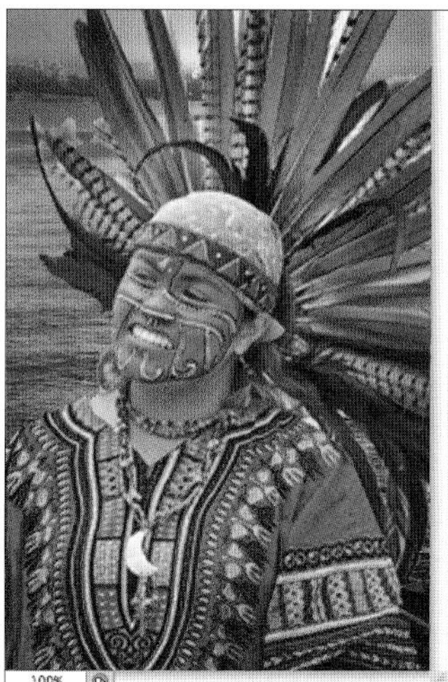

Figure 9.66 Two layers, both set to Normal mode. (©2008 Dan Ablan.)

Figure 9.67 Result of switching the top layer to Soft Light mode.

Figure 9.68 The original image. (©2008 Dan Ablan.)

Figure 9.69 The Emboss filter delivers a gray result.

Figure 9.70 Result of applying the Emboss filter in Hard Light mode.

Hard Light Mode

Hard Light mode might become one of your favorite blending modes. In essence, it's a combination of Multiply mode (which acts like ink) and Screen mode (which acts like light). In Hard Light mode, areas that are 50% gray will disappear, areas darker than 50% will darken the underlying image, and areas brighter than 50% will brighten the underlying image. Use this mode anytime you use the Emboss filter, for example. When you choose Filter > Stylize > Emboss, you end up with a gray image that has almost no hint of the colors from the original image (**Figures 9.68** and **9.69**). But the resulting gray gunk happens to be exactly 50% gray in RGB mode, which means that you can choose Edit > Fade Emboss and set the mode to Hard Light, and…bingo! The gray is gone (**Figure 9.70**). So Hard Light mode allows you to emboss an image while maintaining its color qualities.

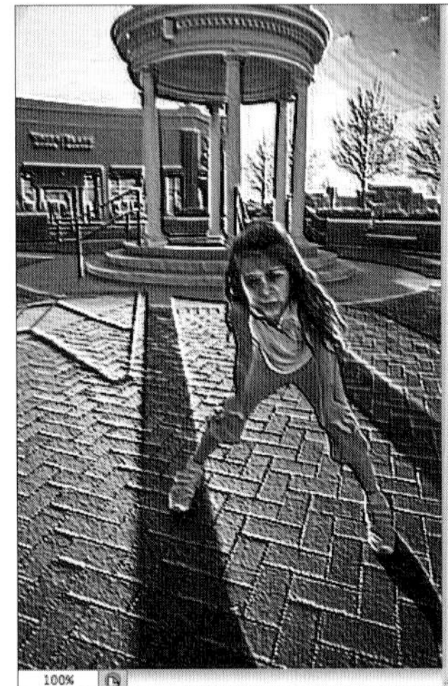

Figure 9.71 Desaturating the image prevents color residue.

You can go one better by duplicating the layer before you emboss it. Then choose Image > Adjustments > Desaturate to ensure that there won't be any color shifts (**Figure 9.71**). Set the duplicate layer to Hard Light mode, and then apply the Emboss filter. You'll get a real-time preview instead of staring at a bunch of gray stuff while you're applying the filter.

Vivid Light Mode

Vivid Light mode is a combination of Color Dodge and Color Burn. In Vivid Light mode, areas darker than 50% darken and the colors become more saturated; areas brighter than 50% brighten and the colors become more saturated. This mode is great when an image really needs some kick. Duplicate the layer and set it to Vivid Light mode. You'll most likely need to turn down the Opacity setting to get an acceptable result (**Figures 9.72** and **9.73**).

Figure 9.72 Vivid Light mode used on a duplicate layer.

Figure 9.73 Opacity is reduced slightly to prevent the image from being overly saturated.

Use Vivid Light when you want to apply a texture to an image and you're concerned that Overlay, Soft Light, or Hard Light mode will make the colors look a little too dull. For example, create a new layer above the image you want to texturize. Choose Filter > Render > Clouds, and then apply Filter > Sharpen > Unsharp Mask with settings of 500, 1.5, and 0 to create a noise pattern. Finish by applying Filter > Stylize > Emboss with settings of 145, 1, and 500. Set the texture layer to Vivid Light mode to add texture and enhance the colors in the image (**Figures 9.74** and **9.75**).

Figure 9.74 The original image could use a little texture. (©2008 Dan Ablan.)

Figure 9.75 Result of duplicating the layer and setting it to Vivid Light mode.

Linear Light Mode

Linear Light mode combines Linear Dodge and Linear Burn. Use this mode anytime you're considering using Hard Light mode but want a higher-contrast result. This is another mode that's great with textures; the highlights and shadow areas of the texture become pure white and pure black, which usually makes the texture look extra crisp. Create a new layer above the image you want to enhance, and then fill that layer with white. To make the texture, choose Filter > Artistic > Sponge, using settings of 2, 12, and 5 to pull out some contrast; then choose Image > Adjustments > Levels, and click the Auto button. Finish it off with Filter > Stylize > Emboss with settings of 135, 1, and 65. Set the blending mode to Linear Light to see the result (**Figures 9.76** and **9.77**).

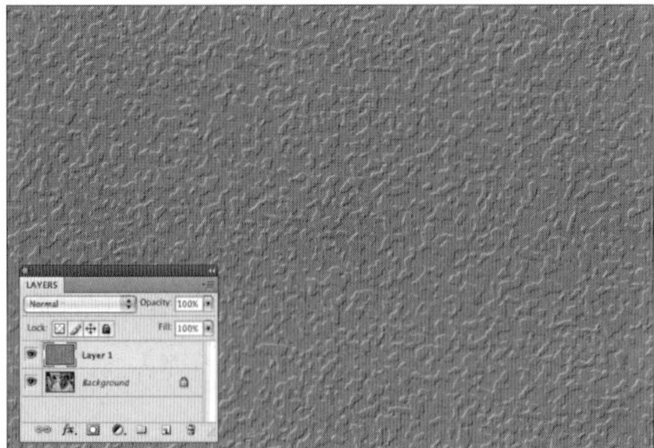

Figure 9.76 The texture that will be applied to a photo.

Figure 9.77 Applying the texture in Linear Light mode produces more saturated colors. (©2008 Dan Ablan.)

Pin Light Mode

Pin Light mode combines Lighten and Darken. Use this mode when working with filters. For example, duplicate the original layer, set the top layer to Pin Light, and leave the bottom layer set to Normal. With the top layer active, choose Filter > Sketch > Note Paper, using settings of 25, 5, and 2 to create 3D highlights. Too much of the gray background shows up (**Figure 9.78**), so choose Image > Adjustments > Levels and move the middle slider until the background disappears (**Figure 9.79**).

Figure 9.78 The Note Paper filter delivers a result containing large areas of gray.

Figure 9.79 Applying the filter in Pin Light mode and adjusting the image with Levels. (©2008 Dan Ablan.)

Hard Mix Mode

Hard Mix mode posterizes the underlying layers based on the Fill Opacity setting of the layer that uses Hard Mix. A high Fill Opacity delivers extreme posterization, whereas lower settings deliver a smoother-looking image (**Figures 9.80** and **9.81**). If the brightness of the layer is near 50% gray, the brightness of the underlying image won't change. Anything brighter than 50% gray will brighten the underlying image, whereas anything darker will darken it (**Figures 9.82** and **9.83**). A layer filled with 50% gray (RGB = 128, 128, 128) will neither brighten nor darken the underlying image, although varying the Fill Opacity will still control posterization.

Figure 9.80 Original image. (©2008 Dan Ablan.)

Figure 9.81 Using 50% gray leaves the brightness of the underlying image unchanged.

Figure 9.82 Original image. (©2008 Dan Ablan.)

Figure 9.83 Using a shade darker than 50% gray darkens the underlying image.

Use Hard Mix to create a "clipping display" like what you'd get when you Option/Alt-drag one of the sliders in Levels (Image > Adjustments > Levels) or the Camera Raw dialog.

Choose Layer > New Fill Layer > Solid Color, set the Mode pop-up menu to Hard Mix, and then work with a shade of gray. Using black shows all the areas that are being blown out to white, whereas using white shows all the areas that are plugged up to black. Simply create two layers at the top of the Layers panel and turn them on whenever you need to check to see if you've lost detail in the highlights or shadows. This technique will be useful to you only if you're knowledgeable about clipping; read Chapter 4, "Using Camera Raw 5.0," if you need a refresher.

Using Hard Mix mode with a 50% Fill Opacity often looks identical to the results you get using the Vivid Light blending mode at 100% Fill Opacity. For that reason, try Hard Mix and experiment with the Fill Opacity setting anytime you're experimenting with the Vivid Light blending mode.

Comparative Blending Modes

The Difference and Exclusion blending modes are very similar to each other. In general, they compare the active layer to the underlying image, looking for areas that are identical in both. Those areas appear as black, and all non-matching areas show up as shades of gray or color. The closer the non-matching areas are to being black in the end result, the more similar the areas are to the underlying image. In these modes, white on the active layer will invert whatever appears on the underlying image, but black on the active layer will not change the underlying image.

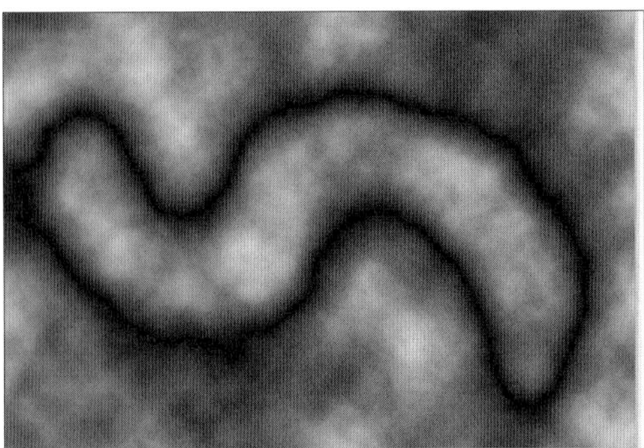

Figure 9.84 Painting on a layer below some clouds that are set to Difference mode.

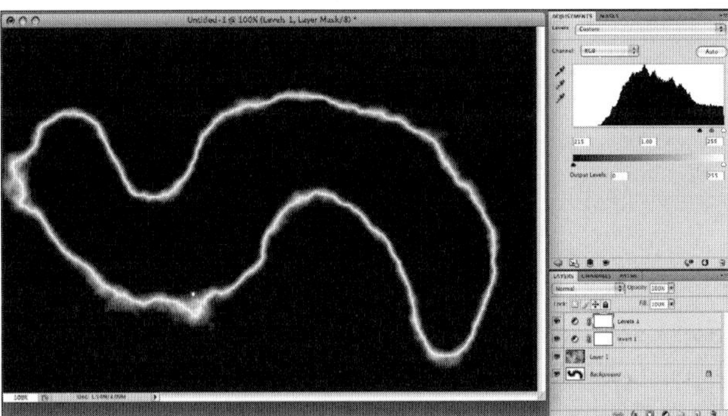

Figure 9.85 Pulling in the upper-left slider in Levels isolates the "lightning."

Difference Mode

Let's use Difference mode to create some homemade lightning. Start with a new document that contains a white background. Create a new layer, and reset your foreground and background colors by pressing D; then choose Filter > Render Clouds and set the layer containing the clouds to Difference mode. Using a large, soft-edged brush, paint with black on the bottom layer. You should end up with a cloudy-looking image that has black areas around the edges of the area where you've painted (**Figure 9.84**).

Now it's time to transform those black areas into lightning. You'll start the process by inverting the image to make black areas white. To do this, click the top layer and choose Layer > New Adjustment Layer > Invert and then Layer > New Adjustment Layer > Levels. In the Adjustments panel, move the upper-left slider to the right until all you can see is the white "lightning" (**Figure 9.85**). Now you can continue painting on the bottommost layer to create more and more lightning. When you're done, choose Layer > Merge Visible to combine the layers. To apply the lightning to another image, place your lightning on a layer above and then set the blending mode of the layer to Screen, so it acts like light.

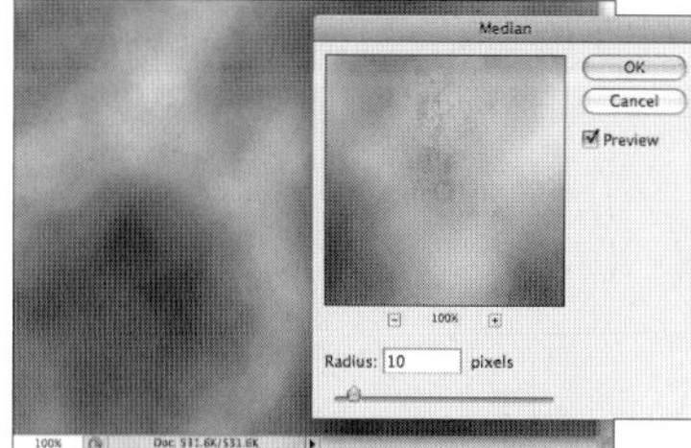

Figure 9.86 Smooth out the clouds by using the Median filter.

Exclusion Mode

Like Diffuse mode, Exclusion mode often sits around collecting dust. Let's use it to create a psychedelic, tripped-out '60s look. Create a new document. Press D to reset the foreground and background colors, choose Filter > Render Clouds, choose Filter > Noise > Median, and use a setting around 10 (**Figure 9.86**). To spice things up, select Filter > Sketch > Chrome with settings of 4 and 7. Choose Edit > Fade Chrome and try both Difference and Exclusion modes (**Figure 9.87**). Then choose Layer > New Adjustment Layer > Gradient Map and use the Color Burn blending mode. Finally, create a gradient that goes from orange to yellow, experimenting until you like what you see (**Figure 9.88**).

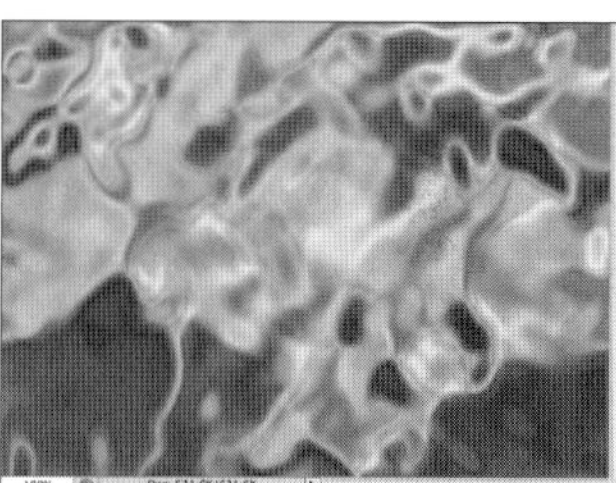
Figure 9.87 Fading the Chrome filter in Exclusion mode.

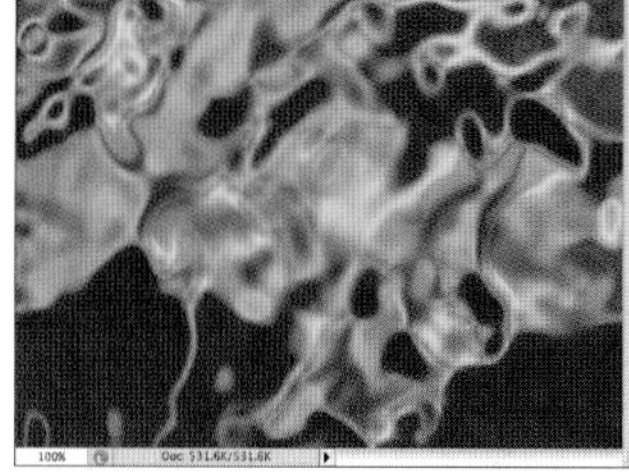
Figure 9.88 The end result after application of a gradient map.

Figure 9.89 Changing the color of an image by painting in Hue mode. (©2008 Dan Ablan.)

Figure 9.90 Adding a gradient set to Foreground to Transparent.

Figure 9.91 Final result after the Eraser tool was used to remove the color change on unwanted areas, such as the bricks.

Hue/Saturation/Brightness Blending Modes

The final set of modes divides the colors of an image into three components: hue, saturation, and brightness. Photoshop applies only one or two of these qualities to the underlying image. These are wonderfully helpful modes, with practical and obvious uses.

Hue Mode

Hue mode looks at the basic colors contained on the active layer and applies them to the brightness and saturation information on the underlying layers. Think of hue as the pure form of a color. To get to that pure form, you have to ignore how dark the color is and how vivid it is, so you can concentrate on its basic color. This mode is great for changing the colors of objects that are already in color. Create a new layer above the image, set it to Hue mode, and then paint away with the desired color (**Figure 9.89**). Use the Gradient tool to create a two-tone look (**Figure 9.90**). Set the Gradient tool to Foreground to Transparent in order to shift one area and have it slowly fade out to the original color of the image. After painting on the layer, you can really refine things by using the Eraser tool to bring areas back to normal (**Figure 9.91**).

A few things might mess you up when you're using Hue mode:

- Hue mode cannot introduce color into an area that doesn't already contain color. (To do this, it would need to change the saturation of the area.)
- It won't change the saturation of the underlying image. If an area has only a hint of color, it will still have only a hint of color after using Hue mode, because you'll only have shifted that color to a different hue.
- Hue mode can't change an area's brightness. This means that painting across a white area won't change the image, because there's no way to introduce color into a white area without darkening it. Use this mode when you need to shift the color of something that already contains color.

Saturation Mode

Saturation mode ignores how bright colors are and concentrates on how vivid they are. It changes the colors in the underlying image until they become as saturated as those on the active layer. If you paint with the most vivid green you can find, the colors in the underlying image will become just as vivid—but bear in mind that the only areas that will end up as green will be those areas that were green to start (**Figures 9.92** and **9.93**). Saturation mode can't shift any of the basic colors: Reds stay red, blues stay blue, and so on. They just become more or less vivid to match the quality of the active layer.

One common use for this mode is to force areas of an image to appear in black-and-white. Create a new layer, set its blending mode to Saturation, and then paint with any shade of gray. Because grays don't contain any color (they're pure brightness information), they'll change the underlying image to grayscale (**Figure 9.94**). If you don't want to take the image all the way to grayscale, lower the Opacity setting of your painting tool (**Figure 9.95**). You can even use the Gradient tool to make the transition fade out. Set it to Foreground to Transparent, and drag across the layer that's set to Saturation mode (**Figure 9.96**).

Figure 9.92 The original image with a layer of green. (©2008 Dan Ablan.)

Figure 9.93 Applying a vivid green color to half the image in Saturation mode.

Figure 9.94 Painting with black on a layer set to Saturation mode changes the painted areas to grayscale. Here we've removed the color from the police officer in the foreground. (©2008 Dan Ablan.)

Figure 9.95 Lowering the opacity of the painted layer brings back a hint of color.

Figure 9.96 Applying a gradient causes the color to fade gradually.

Color Mode

In essence, Color mode applies the color (both hue and saturation) of the active layer to the brightness information of the underlying image. It's like Hue mode, except that Color mode can change the saturation of an area and therefore introduce color into an area that didn't have it.

The most common (and fun) use for this mode is to colorize grayscale photographs. Change the mode of the image from grayscale to RGB or CMYK, create a new layer, set it to Color, and then paint away (**Figure 9.97**). If the color is too vivid, lower the opacity of your brush (**Figure 9.98**). If you can't get enough color into an area, try using Color Burn mode instead (**Figure 9.99**). If the highlights and shadows of the underlying image don't look right, try Overlay mode (**Figure 9.100**).

Figure 9.97 Color applied in Color mode at 100% opacity. (©2008 Dan Ablan.)

Figure 9.98 Lowering the opacity reduces the amount of color applied.

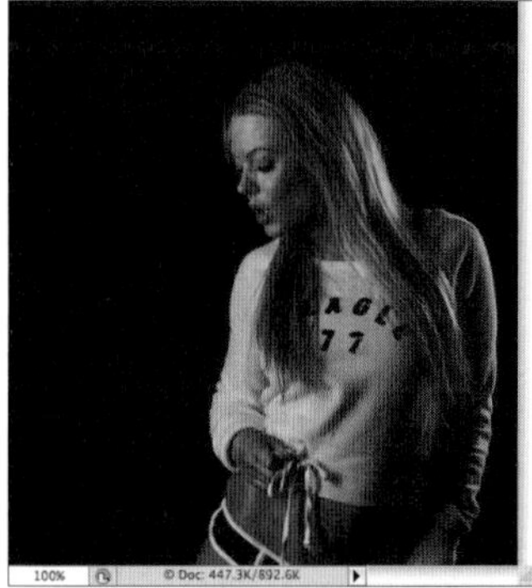

Figure 9.99 Color applied in Color Burn mode with a medium Opacity setting.

Figure 9.100 Color applied in Overlay mode.

Luminosity Mode

Luminosity mode applies the brightness information of the active layer to the color in the underlying image. It can't shift colors or change how saturated those colors are. All it can do is change their brightness. Luminosity mode can always help you, no matter what the project. Here are a few examples:

- Immediately after sharpening an image, choose Edit > Fade Unsharp Mask and set the mode to Luminosity. This prevents the sharpening from adding odd colors to the edges of objects (**Figures 9.101** and **9.102**).

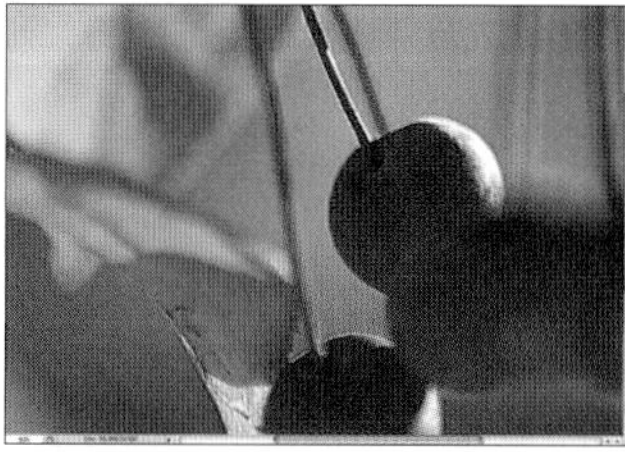

Figure 9.101 Typical sharpening halos appear after using Unsharp Mask.

Figure 9.102 Use Fade Unsharp Mask with the mode set to Luminosity to eliminate the halo effect.

- A lot of people sharpen images after converting them to LAB mode, but you can achieve the same result using the technique just mentioned. Any time you adjust the brightness or contrast of an image using Levels, Curves, or anything else, choose Edit > Fade and set the mode to Luminosity to keep the colors from becoming too vivid.
- If you're using an adjustment layer instead of applying the adjustment directly to the image, set the blending mode of the adjustment layer to Luminosity instead of using the Fade feature.
- If you apply a filter and it's shifting the color of the image, choose Edit > Fade, and then use Luminosity mode to limit the filter so that it changes only the brightness of the image.

Whew! That's the last of the blending modes. By now you should have a good understanding of which mode to use when. Let's move on and look at another crucial tool for enhancing images: masking.

Choosing the Right Masking Tool

The key to getting good at masking is to be familiar with as many masking tools as possible, with a good grasp of each tool's intended purpose, so you can choose the right tool for the job at hand. Let's take a brief look at what's available, and then we'll dig deeper and explore each feature in depth:

- **Background Eraser:** Best for crisp-edged objects that have a noticeable difference in color or brightness from the surrounding background. With this tool, you have to paint around the edges of objects to tell Photoshop which areas should be deleted, and Photoshop will try to figure out what should be kept.
- **Blending sliders:** A quick-and-dirty way to isolate objects that are radically different in brightness from their surroundings. The most obvious use is for things like fireworks, lightning, and text on a plain background.
- **Channels:** The old-fashioned way to remove the background on images. Useful when the Background Eraser would be too time-consuming. Channels are useful in a multitude of situations.
- **Pen tool:** Best with crisp-edged objects that have mainly straight lines and very smooth curves. Ideal for images that are in focus and contain manmade objects such as cars and computers.
- **Layer masks:** Mainly used to refine the results from the other masking tools. Used by themselves, layer masks are similar to manually erasing the background with the Eraser tool; however, when combined with other tools, layer masks become a powerhouse that can make the difference between mediocre and spectacular results.

Now that you have a general idea of what differentiates the various masking tools, let's jump in and explore them.

The Background Eraser

Hiding under the normal Eraser tool is a special version known as the Background Eraser. Click and hold down the Eraser tool until you see a drop-down menu—the Background Eraser is the middle tool shown in that menu (**Figure 9.103**). When you move your cursor over an image, the Background Eraser gives you a round brush with a crosshair in the middle. When you click and drag the Background Eraser on the image, Photoshop watches the color under the crosshair and deletes everything within the circle that's similar to that color (**Figure 9.104**). Trace near the edge of the object you want to keep. It's okay if the circular part of the cursor overlaps the subject. Just don't let the crosshair hit the subject; otherwise, Photoshop will start to delete that area as well (**Figure 9.105**). The settings in the options bar determine what should be kept or erased (**Figure 9.106**).

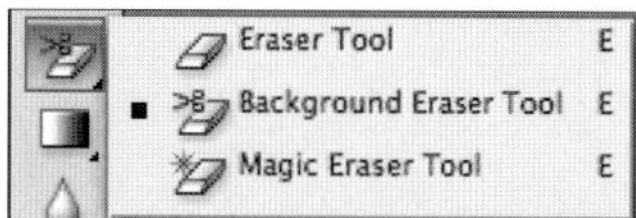

Figure 9.103 The Background Eraser tool is hidden under the Eraser tool.

The Background Eraser tool uses the Brush Presets panel that appears in the options bar. You can quickly change the size of your brush (eraser) by using the bracket keys on your keyboard ([]). To change how hard the edge of the brush is, use Shift in conjunction with the bracket keys.

Figure 9.104 Clicking deletes the color under the crosshair. Here we're erasing the light blue background.

Figure 9.105 Be careful not to let the crosshair hit the subject of the photo.

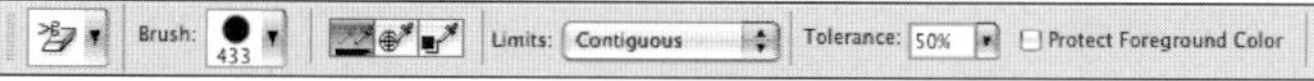

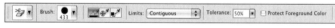

Figure 9.106 Options bar settings for the Background Eraser tool.

Tolerance Settings

Getting the right Tolerance setting on the options bar is essential to using the Background Eraser tool successfully. This setting determines how much Photoshop will be able to stray from the color under the crosshair. If the background is very similar to the subject in brightness or color, use a low Tolerance setting. If the background is quite different from the subject, try a higher Tolerance setting, so that you can quickly remove the background without having to be overly careful about dragging over the subject of the image. A good starting value is 50%.

It's easy to forget that you're protecting the foreground color, which is a problem if you start working on a different part of the image where the color you're protecting is similar to the background you're attempting to delete.

Protect Foreground Color

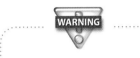

On occasion, the Tolerance setting may not be enough to isolate the subject from the background (**Figure 9.107**). In that case, use the Protect Foreground Color check box on the options bar. Photoshop deletes the color under the crosshair and keeps the foreground color (**Figure 9.108**). While the Background Eraser tool is active, you can hold down Option/Alt and click the part of the image you want to save—that will change your foreground color and therefore prevent the color you click from being deleted.

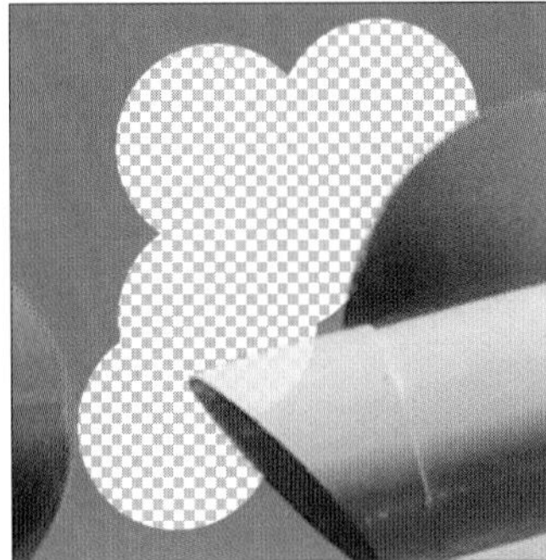

Figure 9.107 The green area here was too similar to the background for the Background Eraser to isolate it successfully.

Figure 9.108 Result of sampling a color from the brightest part of the green area and turning on the Protect Foreground Color check box.

Sampling

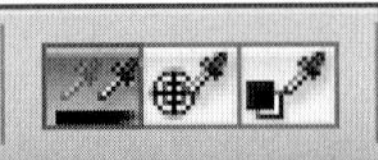

Figure 9.109 The Sampling icons from left to right: Continuous, Once, Background Swatch.

If Photoshop is forcing you to be overly precise with your mouse movements, use the Sampling icons (**Figure 9.109**). The default Continuous setting causes Photoshop to watch the color under the crosshair as you're moving your mouse (**Figures 9.110** and **9.111**). That setting works great with images that have multicolored backgrounds. If the image's background doesn't vary much in color, try the Once setting to make Photoshop pay attention to only the color under the crosshair at the exact moment that you click. It won't stray from that color, so you can click the background and then paint back and forth across the image without having to pay attention to what's under the crosshair (**Figure 9.112**). Just make sure that you don't drag across any areas of the subject that are very similar to the background color. Use this option on simple images that have a pretty big difference between the subject and background (such as a gray building and cement against an almost solid blue sky).

Figure 9.110 Original image. (©2008 Dan Ablan.)

Figure 9.111 Result of using the Continuous option.

Figure 9.112 Result of using the Once option.

The Background Swatch setting is useful on those rare occasions when you can't find an easily clickable area of background color. Use this option after you've used other tools to remove the background on an image, and you notice a slight halo around the edge of an object (**Figure 9.113**).

Figure 9.113 If halos appear after using the Background Eraser tool, use the Background Swatch option.

If the halo is too thin to target, click the background color in the color picker, choose a color that's visually similar to the halo you're trying to remove, and then experiment with the Tolerance setting until you're able to remove it.

Limits

With the default settings, the Background Eraser tool deletes only those areas that actually touch the crosshair. It can't jump across one area that shouldn't be deleted to find another area similar to the one being deleted. That limitation can cause problems when you're working with images of trees, fences, or other objects that break the background into multiple disconnected regions (**Figure 9.114**). To change that behavior, change the Limits setting from Contiguous (touching the crosshair) to Discontiguous, which allows the Background Eraser to delete the color under the crosshair from the entire circle, even if something like a tree branch isolates an area so it doesn't touch the crosshair (**Figure 9.115**).

If part of the subject is becoming semitransparent, choose Undo and try again, this time using the Find Edges setting, which tries to prevent the subject from fading out into the background.

Figure 9.114 Erasing with the Contiguous option. (©2008 Dan Ablan.)

Figure 9.115 Erasing with the Discontiguous option.

Tips and Tweaks

Now that you've seen the Background Eraser's options, let's look at ways to improve its results. The checkerboard indicating that an area has been deleted can actually hide flaws in your erasure (**Figure 9.116**). To see what you're really getting, Command/Ctrl-click the New Layer icon at the bottom of the Layers panel to create a new layer below the active layer. Change your foreground color to something that contrasts with the image (a vivid green, for instance), and then press Option-Delete (Mac) or Alt-Backspace (Windows) to fill the active layer with the foreground color. Now you should be able to see any residue that the Background Eraser left behind (**Figure 9.117**).

Remember to click the layer containing the image before you start using the Background Eraser again; you don't want to start deleting on this solid-colored layer accidentally.

Figure 9.116 The checkerboard background disguises problems. (©2008 Dan Ablan.)

Figure 9.117 Fill a layer with a solid color and place it below the image to reveal any problem areas.

Figure 9.118 Using a hard-edged brush produces abrupt transitions in soft-edged objects. (©2008 Dan Ablan.)

Stay away from hard-edged brushes when you're working with an object that has a slightly soft edge. Hard-edged brushes often produce a series of circles that can make the edge of the image resemble a pearl necklace (**Figure 9.118**). When you switch to a soft-edged brush, the edges should be nice and smooth (**Figure 9.119**).

For the ultimate in Background Eraser control, get a pressure-sensitive graphics tablet. Click the brush preview in the options bar and set the Size or Tolerance setting (or both) to Pen Pressure. Press lightly where the difference between the subject and background is slight; press harder for a more pronounced difference. This technique allows you to trace around the entire edge of an object in a single stroke, which can save quite a bit of time.

Figure 9.119 Using a soft-edged brush produces a more acceptable transition.

The Blending Sliders

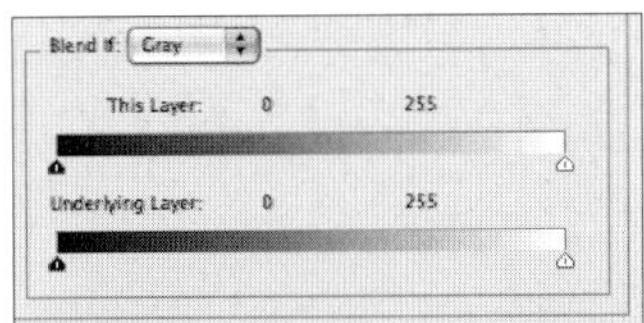

Figure 9.120 The Blending sliders.

The Blending sliders are found by choosing Layer > Layer Style > Blending Options, or by double-clicking in the empty area to the right of a layer's name in the Layers panel. Look at the top set of sliders, labeled "This Layer" (**Figure 9.120**). These sliders show or hide part of a layer based on its brightness, a very useful trick when the subject of a photograph is radically brighter (such as lightning or fireworks) or darker (such as text) than the background.

If the subject is brighter than the background (**Figure 9.121**), slide the upper-left slider toward the middle until every hint of the background disappears from view (**Figure 9.122**). Then, to control the edge quality (how soft or hard it is), hold down Option/Alt and pull on the left edge of the slider you just adjusted (**Figure 9.123**). That action causes brightness levels that are just a little darker than the subject to start to show up as partially transparent areas, which should produce a softer edge (**Figure 9.124**).

The Blending sliders are not available on the Background image. To apply them to the Background, double-click the Background image and change its name.

If the subject is darker than the background, move the upper-right slider toward the middle to hide the background. Then Option/Alt-drag the right edge of the slider to control the transition from visible areas to hidden areas.

Figure 9.121 The subject of this photo is much brighter than the background, which makes it an ideal candidate for the Blending sliders. (©2008 Dan Ablan.)

Figure 9.122 Hiding the dark areas has caused the background to disappear.

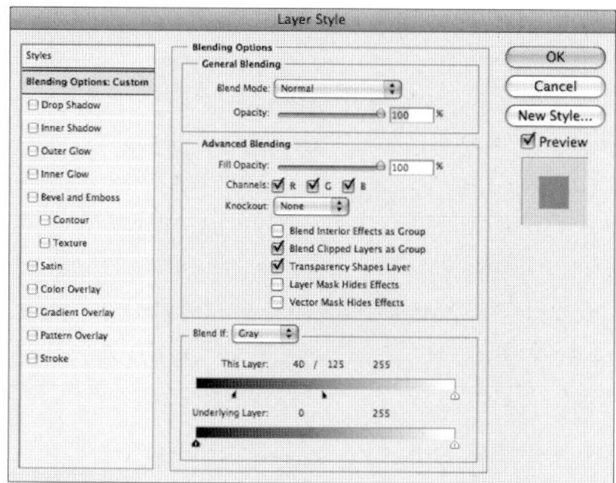

Figure 9.123 Option/Alt-drag the edge of a slider to split it into two halves and create a more gradual transition between visible and hidden areas.

Figure 9.124 The end result of splitting the sliders. Looking closely, you should notice more partially transparent areas.

If the background or subject of the image is predominantly a single color that's not found in the surrounding area (**Figure 9.125**), you might be able to use the Blend If pop-up menu to help isolate it from its surroundings. First click or open the Channels panel (Window > Channels), and then click through the channels (they show up as grayscale images) to find the one that shows the most contrast between the subject and background (**Figure 9.126**). Once you've found the right channel, take note of it, and then click the top channel to get back to your full-color image. Go to the Blending sliders, choose the name of that channel from the Blend If pop-up menu, and pull in the left or right slider (depending on whether the background in that channel is dark or bright) until the background disappears (**Figures 9.127** and **9.128**).

Figure 9.125 The Blending sliders can be very useful when the subject of a photo is a color that doesn't appear in the rest of the image. (©2008 Dan Ablan.)

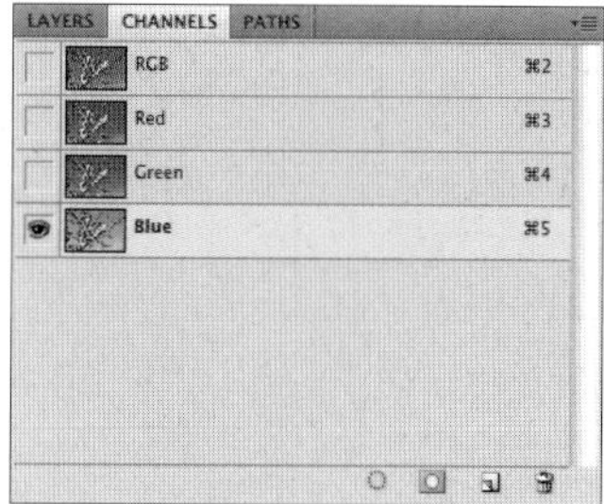

Figure 9.126 Click through the channels to determine which choice to make.

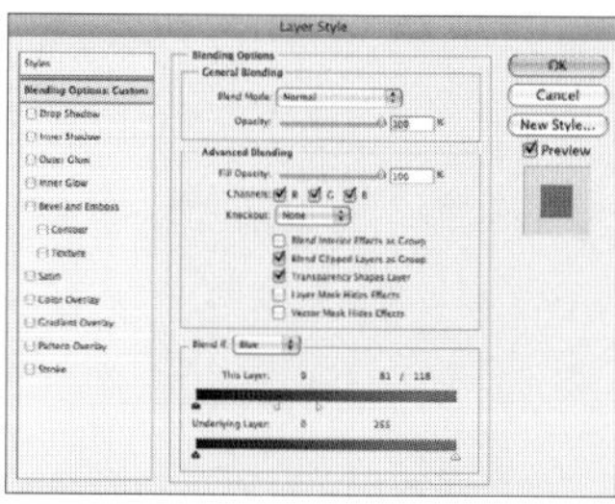

Figure 9.127 In the Blend If pop-up menu, choose the name of the channel that had the most contrast between subject and background.

Figure 9.128 The end result of applying the sliders shown in Figure 9.127.

Unlike the Background Eraser, which truly deletes the background of the image, the Blending sliders temporarily hide areas. You can move the sliders to their default locations to reveal the areas that were being hidden by the sliders. To delete the hidden areas, Command/Ctrl-click the New Layer icon at the bottom of the Layers panel to create a new layer below the one that has the sliders applied. Click the layer above the one you just created, making the slider-applied layer active. Finally, choose Layer > Merge Down, and the slider-applied layer will be combined with the empty layer. Because the underlying layer didn't have the sliders applied, Photoshop will be forced to retain the look of the slider-applied layer without actually using the sliders.

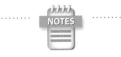

If you used the Blending sliders to hide the background, be sure to convert the result into a permanent deletion before attempting to convert it into a layer mask.

Channels

In older versions of Photoshop, you used channels to isolate complex images from their backgrounds. These days, you'll mainly use channels with simpler images, especially when working with an illustration instead of a photographic image. Often, you can convert images into spot colors so that each color in the image prints with a different color of ink (instead of printing with standard CMYK inks). Channels are the subject of one of the bonus videos on the book's website (www.danablan.com/photoshop), but for the moment let's look at how to use the Channels panel to isolate each color within an image. This might seem cumbersome at first, but read on and you'll see the value of this approach.

Let's say you have a logo or graphic that you'd like to reproduce on a commercial printing press using red, blue, and yellow ink. You should look at the original and decide which areas will use each ink and if any areas need a combination of more than one ink. In **Figure 9.129**, it's rather obvious which areas should use red and blue ink, but maybe you'd like to use a combination of yellow and red to make up the potato chips in this shot. To determine which channels you'll need, click through all the channels in the

Figure 9.129 The example image, a crunchy bag of potato chips. (©2007 PhotoSpin, www.photospin.com.)

Channels panel and look for good contrast between the color you're attempting to isolate and whatever surrounds it (**Figure 9.130**). In this example, you'll use the red channel to isolate the blue areas, the blue channel to isolate the red areas, and a combination of the red and blue channels for the potato chips.

Figure 9.130 Left to right: red channel, green channel, blue channel.

To isolate the blues, drag the red channel to the New Channel icon at the bottom of the Channels panel. (It looks like a sheet of paper with the corner folded over.) Next you need to isolate the area that should print with blue ink; if you make it black, the surrounding areas should end up white to indicate that no blue ink will be used. Choose Image > Adjustments > Levels, click the black eyedropper, and then click the darkest area that should print with blue ink. That will force the area you click to black (**Figure 9.131**). Click the white eyedropper and then click the darkest area of the image that should *not* print with blue ink, to force it to white (**Figure 9.132**). That should do most of the work needed to isolate the blues in the image. If you find any residue, just use the Eraser tool to clean it up. Set up this channel to print with blue ink by double-clicking just to the right of the channel's name in the Channels panel. In the Channel Options dialog, click Spot Color and choose the color you want to use (**Figure 9.133**).

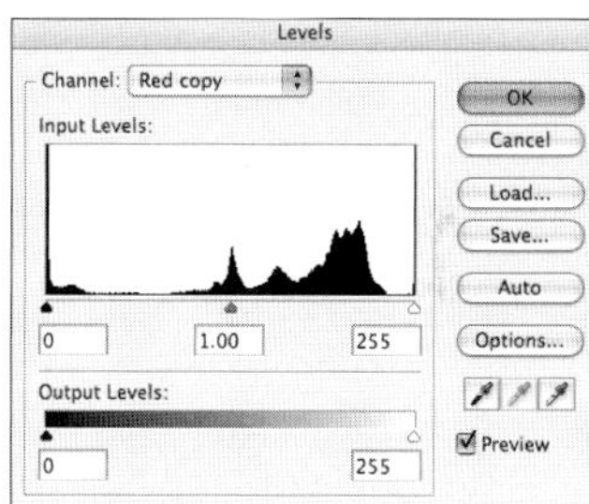

Figure 9.131 Use the eyedroppers in the Levels dialog.

Figure 9.132 Result of forcing areas to white.

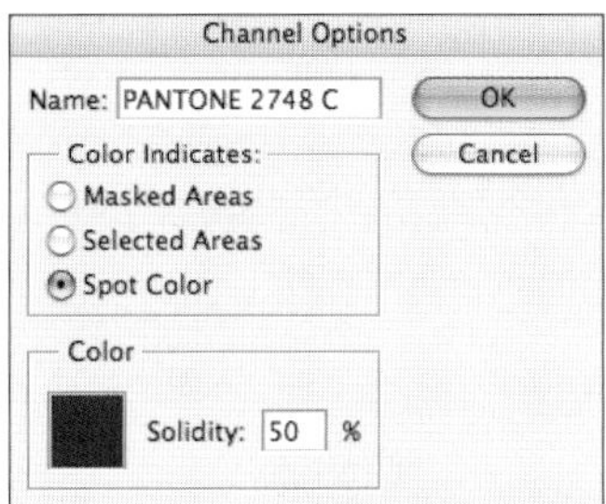

Figure 9.133 Choose Spot Color and then choose the desired color.

Figure 9.134 Result of forcing areas to white.

Figure 9.135 Result of cleaning up the remaining areas.

Duplicate the blue channel and use the Levels dialog again to isolate the reds in the image. This will force the areas that should print with red ink to black, and the areas that shouldn't be red will become white (**Figure 9.134**). You don't have to get every non-red area to become white; just get as much of those areas to be white as you can without sacrificing how dark the red areas look. In this case, you might need to select a few areas manually and fill them with white to get rid of the potato chips in the image (**Figure 9.135**). Once you have all the red areas isolated, double-click the channel and choose the spot color you want to use in that area (for this example, PMS 1805—151R, 40G, 46B).

The potato chips blend in with the surrounding image in each channel (no good isolation possible), so you'll have to select those areas manually with the Lasso tool. To get that information into a channel that prints with yellow ink, duplicate the blue channel, choose Select > Inverse, and then press Delete (Mac) or Backspace (Windows), assuming that your background color is white (**Figure 9.136**). Double-click the channel, set it to Spot Color, and choose a yellow color (for this example, PMS 141—228R, 199G, 109B.) Because you'll need to use a lot of yellow ink in the chips, you might need to choose Select > Deselect and then Image > Adjustments > Levels, and bring in the upper-left slider until a good portion of the chips becomes black (**Figure 9.137**). Now you can view your red, blue, and yellow ink image by turning on the eyeballs next to those three channels and turning off the eyeball on the top (RGB) channel.

Figure 9.136 Result of duplicating the blue channel and removing everything but the potato chips.

Figure 9.137 Result of adjusting the chips area with Levels.

To fine-tune the image, you'll need to reselect the chips (Select > Reselect), click the cyan channel, choose Edit > Copy, paste the chips into the red channel, and then adjust the result with Levels (**Figure 9.138**). That will put a hint of red in the chips, giving them a warmer feeling. You could also select the white parts of the bag and paste them into the blue ink channel to add some shading to the bag (**Figures 9.139** and **9.140**).

Figure 9.138 Result of adding the chips to the red channel.

Figure 9.139 Result of adding the white and gray areas of the bag to the blue channel.

Figure 9.140 Completed image.

Creating Paths with the Pen Tool

The Pen tool gives you a result that more closely resembles the work of a pair of scissors than anything else we've covered in this chapter. If you're sloppy with it, the result will look very crude. If you take your time, you can get a nice, crisp result, but you definitely wouldn't want to use this tool with an object that has a soft or blurry edge.

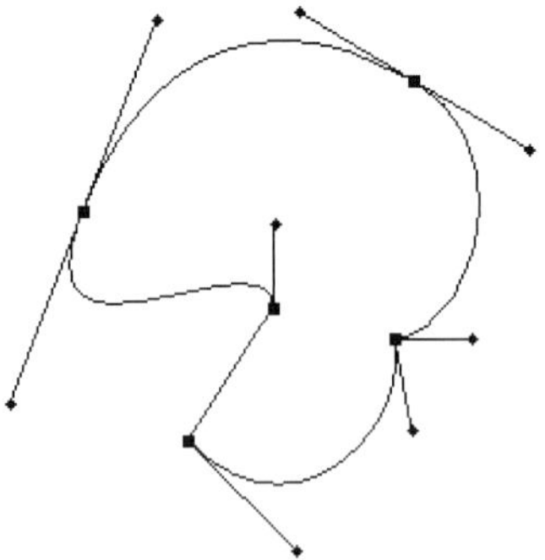

Figure 9.141 A path is made from points and directional handles.

The Pen tool can be a bit tricky to learn because it doesn't work like anything else in Photoshop. Instead of creating shapes out of a grid of pixels, the Pen tool creates shapes from a collection of points and directional handles (**Figure 9.141**). Before we get started creating paths, look in the options bar (**Figure 9.142**) and make sure that the Paths icon is active so you end up making a path instead of a shape layer. The Paths icon is the second from the left of the icons that appear just to the right of the Pen tool icon.

Figure 9.142 Options for the Pen tool.

Figure 9.143 The handle changes from a tight curve to a more gradual one where a point would be needed. (©Stockbyte, www.stockbyte.com.)

Think of the shape you want to create as being made of a series of curves and straight lines that connect to one another. Visualize tracing around the shape and looking for transitions where one curve connects with another. That might be in an area where a very tight curve starts to become more gradual, like on some coffee cup handles (**Figure 9.143**). At each of these transitions, you'll click with the Pen tool to add a point.

When adding a point, click and drag if you want to create a smooth curve. If you don't drag, you'll end up with a sharp corner instead of a curve. When you click and drag, you'll add a point and pull a set of directional handles out of that point. The angle of the directional handles determines the direction of the path when it leaves that handle, so make sure that it points in the direction in which you want the curve to go (**Figure 9.144**).

The lengths of the directional handles determine the overall shape of the curve (**Figure 9.145**). Once you've added the next point and the angle of the handle that points toward the last point is positioned correctly, it's time to adjust the length of the handles. Hold down Command/Ctrl and drag the middle of the curve that appears between the two points you just created (**Figure 9.146**). It's a little troublesome at first, but by pulling on the middle of the curve, you should be able to get the curve to fit the shape you were attempting to create. If you can't get the shape you want, one of the directional handles must be pointing in the wrong direction. If you continue to hold down the Command/Ctrl key, you'll be able to reposition the directional handles as well.

Figure 9.144 Click and drag to create a smooth curve.

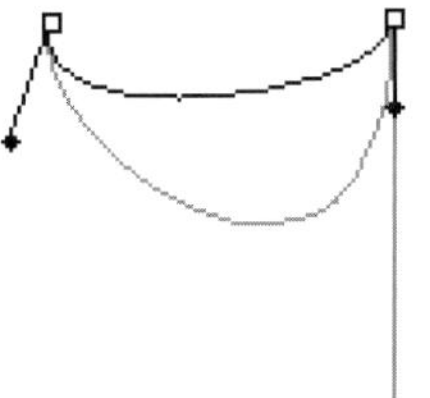

Figure 9.145 The length of the directional handles determines the overall shape of the curve.

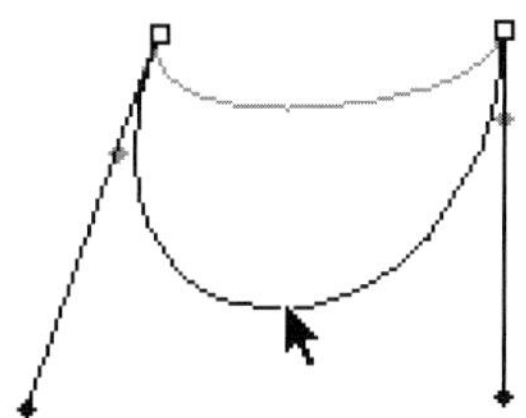

Figure 9.146 Hold down Command/Ctrl and drag the curve to adjust the length of the directional handles.

Getting the length of the handles right is difficult because the curve won't show up until the next handle is made, and its handles will also influence the shape of the curve. Keep your handles short.

On occasion, you'll need one curve to change direction abruptly instead of smoothly flowing into another curve. When that happens, remember that the directional handles determine which direction the path will go when it leaves a point. You'll need the two handles that come out of a point to be at radically different angles. You can accomplish that by holding down Option/Alt and dragging one of the handles that protrude from the point you just created (**Figure 9.147**).

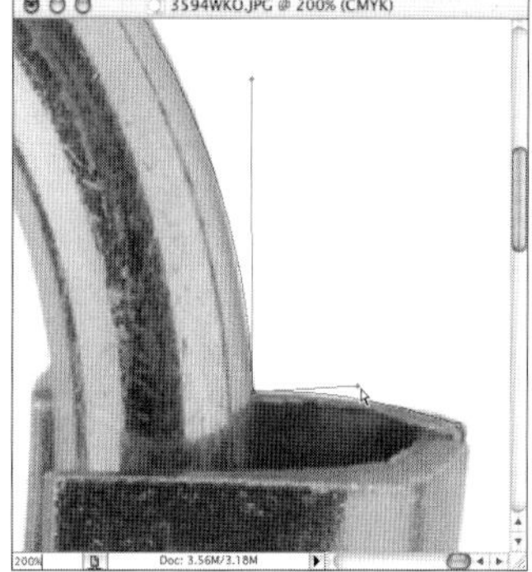

Figure 9.147 Hold down Option/Alt to change the angle of one directional handle without affecting the other handle connected to that point. (©Stockbyte, www.stockbyte.com.)

Sometimes you'll need to have a curve end at an abrupt corner, where the next portion of the shape will be a straight line. In that case, you'll need a handle on the side of the point that points toward the curve, and no handle on the side of the straight line. After adding the point and pulling out the handles, Option/Alt-click the point, and

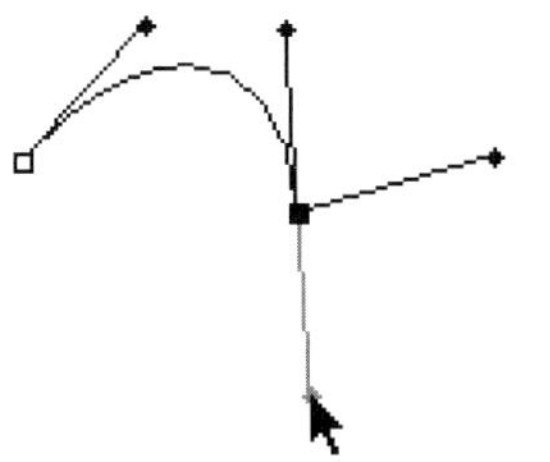

Figure 9.148 A curve ending in an abrupt corner.

Photoshop will retract the handle on the open end of the path (**Figure 9.148**).

By combining these ideas, you should be able to create just about any smooth shape. Because it's not a natural process, you might need practice to master using the Pen tool. Once you have a path, you can drag it to the selection icon (third icon from the left) at the bottom of the Paths panel (Window > Paths) to turn it into a selection.

Now that you know how to use the Pen tool, read Chapter 10 to find out how to turn a path into a vector mask.

Layer Masks

Now that you've seen how Photoshop's masking features work, let's look at how you can refine the results by using a layer mask. A layer mask hides areas of the image instead of permanently deleting them. That allows you to fix areas that don't look right, or modify the edge quality of the image.

Start with an image that you've already isolated using one of the other masking tools. In the Layers panel, Command/Ctrl-click the layer thumbnail image for the layer from which you removed the background. That action will give you a selection of the visible areas of the layer (**Figure 9.149**). To use that selection as the basis for a layer mask, click the Layer Mask icon at the bottom of the Layers panel. Now look at the active layer in the Layers panel (**Figure 9.150**). You should see two thumbnail preview images for that layer: one showing the actual layer contents and a second that's full of black wherever the layer is transparent and white where the layer contains information. That second thumbnail is the layer mask. Black hides layers in a layer mask, whereas white lets an area show up.

Figure 9.149 Command/Ctrl-click the layer to get a selection based on its contents.

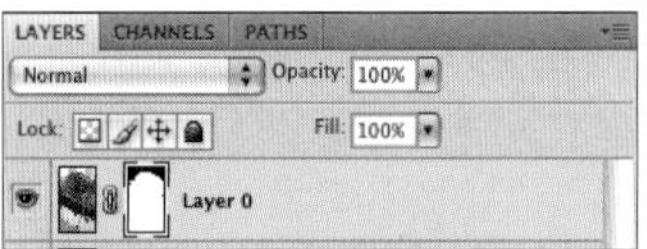

Figure 9.150 After adding a layer mask, you'll have two thumbnail preview images for that layer.

Now all you have to do is bring back the areas of the image that have been deleted, and then the layer mask will be the only thing preventing those areas from being visible. In the Layers panel, click the left thumbnail preview icon to make the image active, instead of the layer mask (brackets around the corners of the thumbnail indicate that it's active). Choose Edit > Fill. In the Fill dialog, set the Use pop-up menu to History, set Opacity to 100% and Mode to Normal, and click OK. Now, to double-check that everything worked as planned, hold down the Shift key and click in the middle of the layer mask thumbnail preview image in the Layers panel. That should cause the background of your image to become visible again, and a red X will appear over the layer mask icon (**Figure 9.151**). Shift-click it again; if the background doesn't become visible, choose Window > History, click in the empty space to the left of the step just above the one that references the masking technique you used to remove the background, and then try using Edit > Fill again.

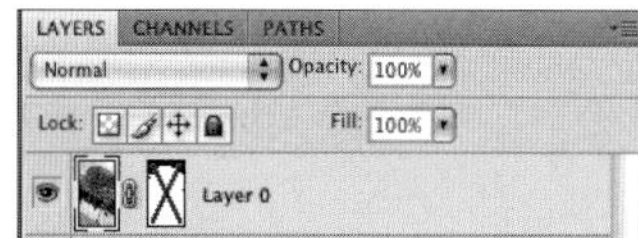

Figure 9.151 Shift-click the layer mask thumbnail to turn it off temporarily.

The "history" feature works only while you're in the same session of Photoshop. If you close your file and reopen it, the history (that is, the old background) will no longer be available.

Now that the layer mask is the only thing hiding the background, you can refine the result in a multitude of ways. Before you start, click in the middle of the layer mask thumbnail preview image in the Layers panel to make it active. (Brackets should appear on its corners.) If you want to hide additional parts of the image, click the Paintbrush tool and paint with black. To bring areas back into view, paint with white instead.

You can Option/Alt-click the layer mask preview thumbnail image in the Layers panel to view the layer mask on the main screen (**Figure 9.152**). Look for black areas that contain specks of white or gray, where the image hasn't been completely hidden. You might need to paint over those areas with black to force those parts of the image to become hidden. If you see a bunch of gray areas that shouldn't be visible, try choosing Image > Adjustments > Levels, and move the upper-left slider until those gray areas turn solid black. Or, if you see a bunch of tiny white specks, choose Filter > Noise > Despeckle. If that doesn't get rid of them, try Filter > Noise > Median, and use the lowest setting that rids the image of the specks. After cleaning up

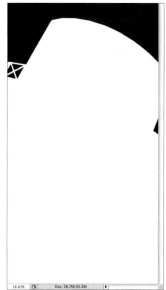

Figure 9.152 Option/Alt-click the layer mask thumbnail preview image in the Layers panel to view the mask within the document window.

the obvious problem areas, Option/Alt-click the layer mask preview thumbnail image in the Layers panel to hide the layer mask and show the image.

Next, look at areas that have soft edges and make sure that they don't look too noisy (**Figure 9.153**). You can smooth out a noisy transition or a crisp edge that looks a little jaggy by painting across the area with the Blur tool. The Blur tool will soften that edge without making the image itself blurry (**Figure 9.154**).

Figure 9.153 This soft-edged transition looks rather jagged.

Figure 9.154 After blurring the layer mask, the transition looks much smoother.

NOTES

If the Minimum and Maximum filters seem backwards, remember that they're working on the white areas of the mask instead of the black areas.

If a tiny halo of the old background shows up around the edge of an object, make a general selection that includes that area and then choose Filter > Other > Minimum. Use the Filter > Other > Maximum selection to cause more of the image to show up.

When the image looks good, make one last check by Shift-clicking the layer mask thumbnail preview image in the Layers panel to view the entire image, and then press the backslash (\) key to view the mask as a color overlay (**Figure 9.155**). Zoom in on the image and look for areas where the color overlay doesn't quite match the edge of the original image. Paint or blur the layer mask until it matches the edge of the original image. To get back to normal, press backslash (\) again to turn off the color overlay, and then Shift-click the layer mask preview again to hide the background of the image.

Figure 9.155 Double-check your work by disabling the layer mask, and then view it as an overlay by pressing the backslash (\) key.

You might occasionally copy and paste areas of a layer mask to fill in other areas that need the right texture. You can even resort to using Photoshop's funky brushes to produce the right transition on images where none of the masking tools were able to produce the correct edge—like where a white goat's hair was blown out against a backdrop of the sun. (Or just use the brush that produces something similar to grass.)

If you ever want to delete the background of an image permanently, drag the layer mask thumbnail to the Trash icon at the bottom of the Layers panel. When prompted, choose Apply, and you will permanently delete the background. To remove the empty space around the image, choose Image > Trim and use the Transparent Pixels option.

If you notice a tiny halo around the edge of objects, and you don't want to edit the layer mask, choose Layer > Matting > Defringe, and use a setting of 1, which should remove the halo.

The Next Step

If we listed all of the great enhancement techniques available in Photoshop, you'd be wading through a book 10 times the size of *War and Peace.* With this chapter, you've seen some tasty samples that should inspire you to try some more on your own. The more you work with Photoshop, the more you'll be able to add to your own personal cookbook of enhancement recipes.

A few final suggestions before you move on to Chapter 10:

- When masking the background of an image, try to make the process as easy as possible by thinking about the following concepts. Consider making a general selection of the background area and pressing Delete/ Backspace before using any of the masking tools. That way, you won't waste your time using the finer "surgical tools" to delete big obvious areas that don't require that kind of precision. Then you can let the masking tools concentrate on the difficult edge areas between the subject and background.
- Perform color correction on your image before attempting to isolate the subject from the background. Any unwanted color casts in the image will cause the subject and background to be similar in color and contrast, making it more difficult to remove the background.
- If the subject and background are rather similar, consider using a temporary adjustment layer to exaggerate the difference between subject and background before attempting to remove the background.
- Don't limit yourself to a single technique when removing a background. Instead, think about the strengths of each technique and use it wherever it's appropriate.
- If you have any control over the photography, use a simple background that contrasts with the subject of the photo so it's easy to extract.
- Finally, no tool is perfect, and sometimes you have to fall back on manual techniques like painting on layer masks or tracing objects with the Lasso tool. We all need to do that on occasion, but the more you know about Photoshop's masking tools, the less you'll have to rely on those cruder selection tools that usually produce less than elegant results.

CHAPTER

10

Collage Effects

If you think it's hard to meet new people, try picking up the wrong golf ball.

—Jack Lemmon

Collage Effects

In Photoshop, you can do more than adjust, tone, and paint images. You can create an entirely new image by blending diverse visual elements into one big picture, called *compositing* or *image blending*. This is where Photoshop really gets to strut its stuff, and where you can put your creative agility to the test. The possibilities with compositing are truly boundless. With Photoshop, all you need is your imagination and a bag full of good collage techniques.

Familiar Techniques

In this chapter, we'll explore the most useful Photoshop features for combining multiple images into one seamless composite (**Figure 10.1**). We'll get into some of the more specialized Photoshop capabilities, but you've already learned some of the most basic techniques—probably without realizing that they can be used to create collages like magic.

Figure 10.1 Photoshop allows you to combine parts of different images to create shots that are otherwise impossible to get. (©2008 Dan Ablan.)

Skeptical? If you don't believe that you've already mastered the basics, consider these simple examples:

Clipping mask: You've spent hours creating a big headline graphic for a movie poster. Now the client wants you to put flames or hot lava inside the headline, or maybe change the headline altogether. Knowing that you're a miracle worker, he gives you a deadline that's only three hours off, and hangs up. While he was still on the phone, you popped open the Layers panel and created a clipping mask to get flames inside the shape of the headline. Now you tweak the text, swap out some lava for the flames, and head off to the beach for a break before you get to show off your results.

When you create a clipping mask, the active layer shows only those places in the image where there's information on the layer directly below it. This technique is useful for simple effects like controlling where shadows fall or placing a photo inside of some text. You learned about clipping masks in Chapter 5, "Adjustment Layers."

Blending sliders: A prospective client has given you some images that you've loaded into Photoshop. One is a photograph of some billowy clouds; the other is of a pod of whales. She wants you to make the whales swim around in the clouds. In some places, she wants the whales to replace the sky behind the clouds; in other places, the whales should blend in with the clouds. Very surreal. She asks how many hours it will take to get the effect. You can nail this job in a jiffy with the Blending sliders, so while your hands are busy with the mouse, you give her a smile and reply, "I'll do it while you wait." The look on her face delivers the good news—you've got a client for life.

The Blending sliders make certain areas of a layer disappear or show up, based on how bright or dark they are. For example, it's very easy to make all the dark parts of an object disappear. You learned about the Blending sliders in Chapter 9, "Enhancements and Masking."

Layer mask: Your biggest client, a 20-year-old creative genius, wants something that looks like a skyscraper growing out of a pencil. Then he decides he wants to fuse together a hippopotamus and a ballerina. But finally he exclaims, "I know! Let's put Godzilla in an Elvis suit!" Ah, you think, a perfect day for layer masks. Without batting an eyelash, you go about the business of giving Godzilla his new outfit. Six months later, you choke on your coffee when you hear that the Elvis-Zilla ad won an award.

With layer masks, you can make any part of a layer disappear, and you can control exactly how much the edges fade out. We experimented with layer masks in Chapters 5 and 9.

See what we mean? With these techniques in your arsenal, you're well on your way to building your own collages. Now let's work on expanding your expertise.

Cool Borders and Photo Frames

A very popular Photoshop effect is the use of borders around images and artwork. Border effects with clipping masks are easy to set up, and provide a great way to present your photos, illustrations, or artwork. Begin with a background graphic—something made of a color, some brush strokes, layered images, and so on (**Figure 10.2**).

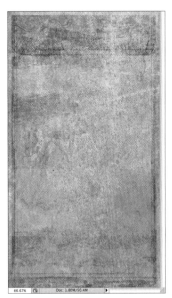

Figure 10.2 A graphic background built with various brushes.

Once you have the background graphic in place, you'll create your border in a new layer. The border can be painted with a stylized brush, or even just a plain hard- or soft-edged brush, whatever you like. Start with a box, rotate it, and then use a scattered brush to erase the edges (**Figure 10.3**). Place the photograph or illustration in a layer above the painted box (**Figure 10.4**). It will obscure the graphic frame you just painted.

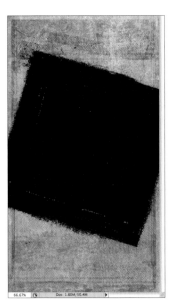

Figure 10.3 A simple black box, with edges painted away.

Figure 10.4 A photo is added in a layer above the frame. (©2008 Dan Ablan.)

This is where the clipping mask comes in. Right-click the layer with the photograph and choose Create Clipping Mask. The black frame you created acts as a window to the image above it (**Figure 10.5**). You can select either the frame layer or the picture layer and move them around for placement. When you have them lined up as you like, select both layers, right-click them, and choose Link Layers. Linking the layers locks them together so that if you choose to scale or move one, the other is also affected.

Additional techniques for creating a clipping mask:

- Option/Alt-click between two layers in the Layers panel.
- Choose Layer > Create Clipping Mask.
- Press Option-Command-G (Mac) or Alt-Ctrl-G (Windows).

Figure 10.5 The clipping mask creates a window to the image from the frame layer below.

The icon in the layer is indented to signify that it's a clipping layer. A small down-arrow indicates that this layer now relates to the layer directly below it.

Finally, to make the mask a bit cooler, paint some soft edge lines above the clipping mask and image layers. Set the layer to Overlay blending mode and perhaps another to Multiply (**Figure 10.6**). You can use this border clipping mask technique for all kinds of projects, from funky borders and edges for photographs (**Figure 10.7**), to simple, refined edges for images requiring a more subtle touch.

Spend an afternoon making a series of frames and borders to use in future projects. You can also buy frames and borders from places like GraphicAuthority.com.

Figure 10.6 Add more layers with various blending modes to finish off the look.

Figure 10.7 The clipping mask clips this photo so that it shows up only within the frame. (©2008 Dan Ablan.)

Moving Clipped Layers

Changing the stacking order of the layers may affect a clipping mask on some layers, so be careful:

- If a bunch of layers have a clipping mask applied, and you move one of them above a layer that doesn't have a clipping mask applied, you'll deactivate the clipping mask on that layer.
- If you move a layer with no clipping mask between two layers that do have clipping masks, it will suddenly have the same clipping mask applied to it.
- If you move the clipping mask layer (the one that's not indented and has all those arrows pointing to it) above or below a layer that isn't part of that clipping mask, all the layers that are affected by the clipping mask will move with it.

Place the clipping mask and related layers into a group. Simply select all the applicable layers and drag them to the small folder icon at the bottom of the Layers panel. This will create a group and place the selected contents inside.

Creating a Panoramic Image with Photomerge

The Photomerge feature automates the process of combining images into a seamless panorama. To prepare for a photomerge, you can simply take three or more photographs, usually from left to right, making sure that a portion of each image overlaps with the previous one.

To start creating your own panoramas, open the images in Photoshop and then choose File > Automate > Photomerge. The initial Photomerge dialog prompts you to specify which images you want to use to create a panorama. Because you've already opened the images you want to use, click the Add Open Files button (**Figure 10.8**). At left in the dialog are a number of layout options. For now, just choose Auto. Then check the Blend Images Together check box to create a seamless final image. With everything set, click OK to start the merging process.

If your final stitching doesn't look right, try a different layout option, or choose Reposition and position the images by hand.

With Blend Images Together turned off, Photoshop will make an old-fashioned collage of overlapping images. If you didn't shoot your panorama well enough to create a seamless image, this option can be a way to salvage the shot.

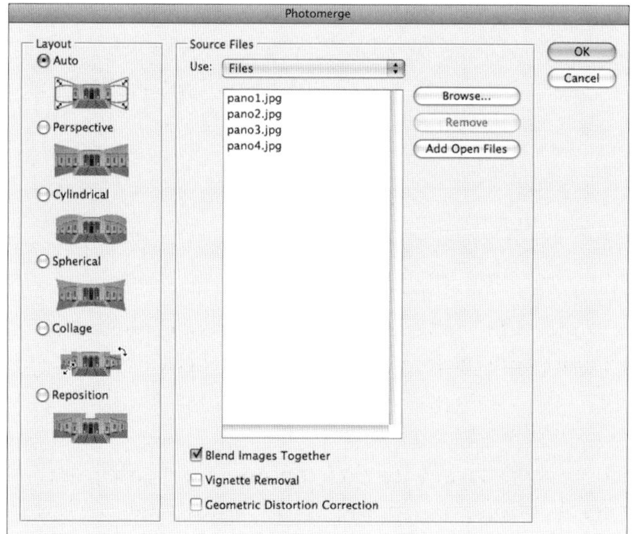

Figure 10.8 In most cases, the Photomerge dialog's Auto option works quite well.

Merging can take a while, depending on the speed of your machine, but it can be fun to watch. With the Layers and History panels open, you can get a good idea of what Photoshop is doing; basically, it's copying each image into its own layer in one document. The Auto Align and Auto Blend features perform the actual merge.

When the merge is finished, you'll have a single document with a separate layer for each image. Notice that Photoshop doesn't automatically crop the image; you'll have to do it yourself. While manual cropping may seem an extra hassle, it's actually nice to have that control, because you can choose to preserve as much image detail as you want. For example, in **Figure 10.9**, rather than cropping, you might choose to clone in some of the missing sky in order to get a larger image.

Figure 10.9 Photomerge does a fine job of seamlessly blending the images, yet doesn't crop them. (©2008 Dan Ablan.)

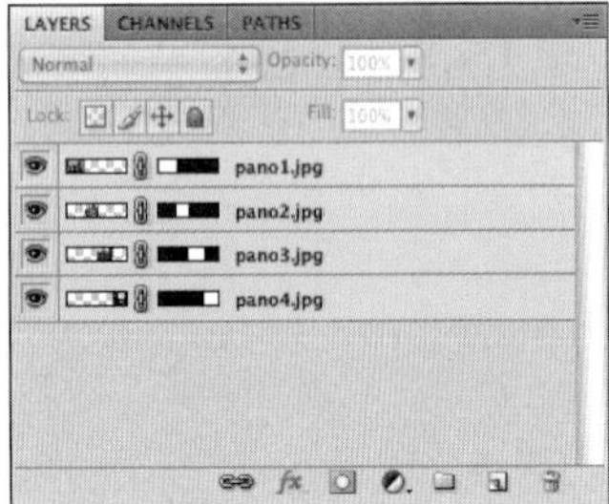

Figure 10.10 A layer mask is created for each image, giving you complete control over blending.

Notice that the Layers panel includes layer masks for each layer (**Figure 10.10**). These layer masks control which part of each layer is visible and comprise the mechanism that Photoshop uses to create the seams in the image. Since the Photomerge feature leaves the layer masks intact rather than flattening the final image, you can easily adjust a bad seam by simply painting onto that layer's layer mask.

Vector Masks

Vector masks allow you to control which area of a layer will be visible by using an easily editable, smooth-shaped, crisp-edged path; anything outside of the path will be hidden onscreen and when printed.

By the time they make it to your computer screen, all photographs are made out of pixels, and the resolution of the file determines how large the pixels will be when printed. If those pixels are large enough, the image will appear jaggy when printed. But with vector masks, you can create a low-resolution, jaggy image and still get a smooth, crisp transition between the content of a layer and the underlying image when printing to a PostScript printer.

Adding a Vector Mask

The simplest way to add a vector mask is to choose Layer > Vector Mask > Reveal All. The active layer now has two thumbnail images in the Layers panel (**Figure 10.11**). It should look like you just added a layer mask. The only difference is that with a layer mask, you paint with shades of gray to control which areas of a layer will be hidden or visible, whereas with a vector mask you use a path to define the area that will be visible.

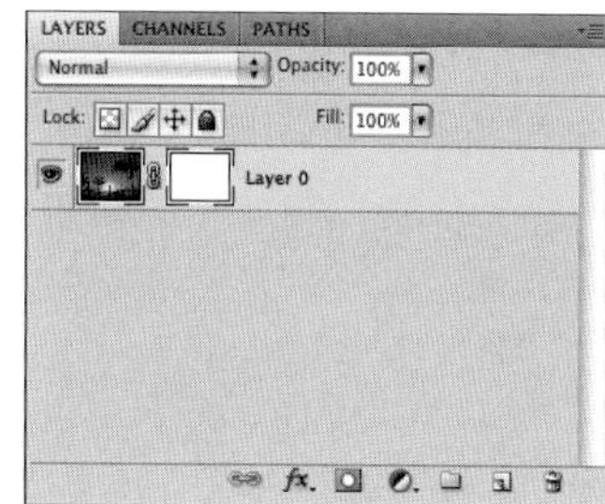

Figure 10.11 After adding a vector mask, you'll see two thumbnail images in the Layers panel.

The easiest way to define where the image should be visible is to use one of the Shape tools. Before you start creating shapes, take a peek at the settings in the options bar. Four options are available on the right side of the options bar when the active layer contains a vector mask (**Figure 10.12**). Here's what these options do, left to right:

Figure 10.12 Vector mask options on the options bar.

- Allows you to create a shape to define where the image should be visible.
- Allows you to define a shape where the image should be hidden.
- Limits the areas that are already visible, so that they show up only within the shape you draw.
- Inverts the visibility of the area inside the shape you draw, making visible areas hidden and hidden areas visible.

You can also use any of the Pen tools to create and modify a vector mask. If you're not already familiar with the Pen tools, start out with the Freeform Pen tool because it allows you to create a path by drawing a freeform shape, much like the Lasso tool allows you to create a selection. To learn how to use the Pen tool, see Chapter 9.

If you already have a path saved in the file, such as with stock photos you've purchased (it will show up in the Paths panel), you can use it as a vector mask. With the applicable layer active (you can't add a vector mask to the Background layer), click the name of the path in the Paths panel, and then choose Layer > Add Vector Mask > Current Path.

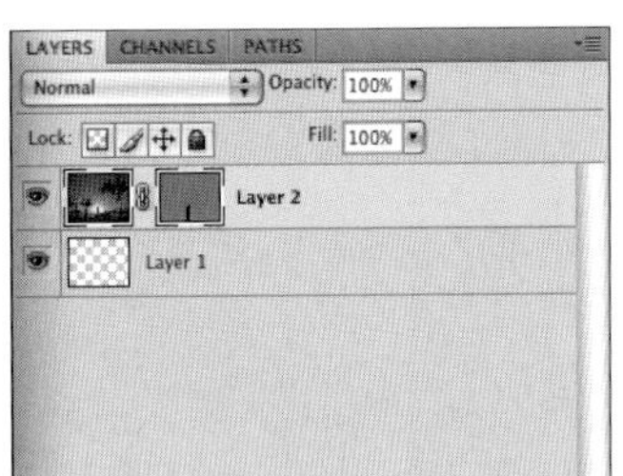

Figure 10.13 Active vector mask. When the vector mask is disabled, its thumbnail is covered by a red X.

Disabling the Vector Mask

After creating a vector mask, you can temporarily disable it by Shift-clicking its thumbnail in the Layers panel (**Figure 10.13**). With each click, you'll toggle the vector mask on and off. This feature is a great help when you want to see what a layer would look like if you didn't have a vector mask restricting where it shows up.

Using the Move Tool

When you use the Move tool to reposition a layer, the layer and the vector mask move together (**Figures 10.14** and **10.15**). If you turn off the link symbol by clicking it, you'll leave the vector mask alone and just move the image (**Figure 10.16**). To move the vector mask and leave the image stationary, use the solid arrow (Path Selection tool) that appears directly above the Pen tools (**Figure 10.17**).

Figure 10.14 Original Image with vector mask defined.

Figure 10.15 Layer and vector mask linked together.

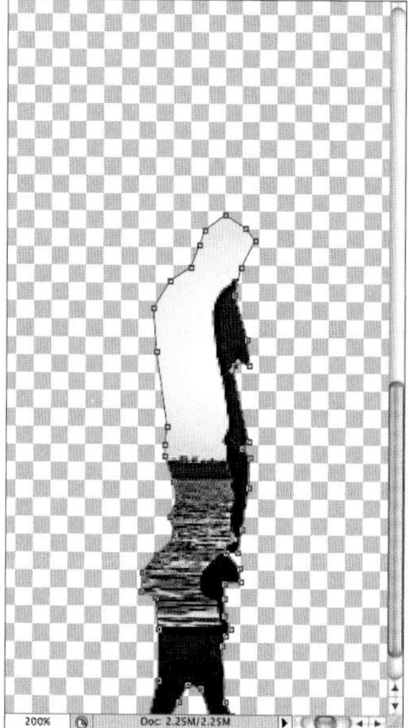

Figure 10.16 Vector mask left stationary while the layer is repositioned.

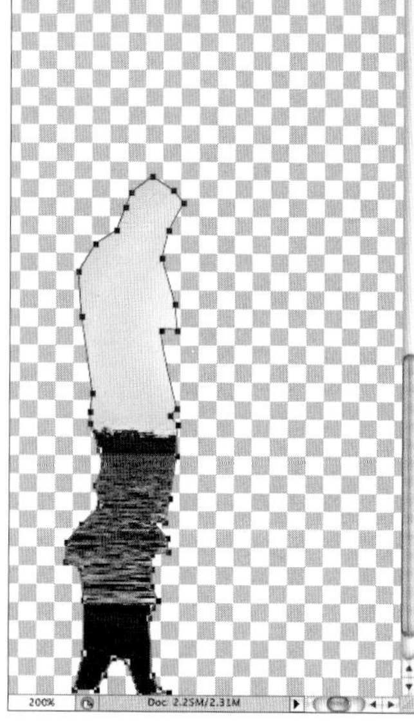

Figure 10.17 Use the Path Selection tool to reposition a vector mask.

Transforming the Vector Mask

The Edit > Transform commands are very useful when working on a vector mask. Because the path is made from a collection of points and directional handles (instead of pixels), scaling, rotating, and other transformations will not degrade the quality of the shape. Make sure that the path is visible before you choose Edit > Transform Path.

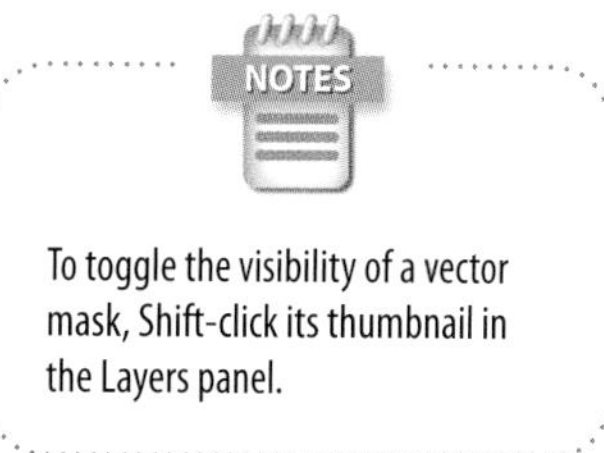

To toggle the visibility of a vector mask, Shift-click its thumbnail in the Layers panel.

Using Vector Masks with Layer Masks

You can have both a layer mask and a vector mask attached to a single layer. (Just click the Layer Mask icon twice.) When you use both, the image is visible only where both the layer mask and vector mask allow things to be visible (**Figure 10.18**). If you have multiple layers with layer masks, you can mask the cumulative effect of those layers with a vector mask. Select the layers to which you'd like to apply a vector mask. Shift-click the Create a New Group icon at the bottom of the Layers panel (**Figure 10.19**). Click the newly created group to make it active, and then add a vector mask (Layer > Vector Mask > Reveal All). Any shapes that

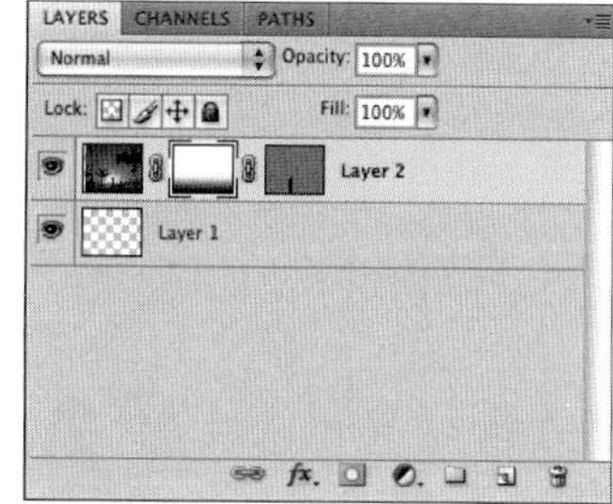

Figure 10.18 You can have a layer mask and a vector mask attached to the same layer.

you add to the vector mask will limit where all the layers that are contained in that group show up (**Figure 10.20**).

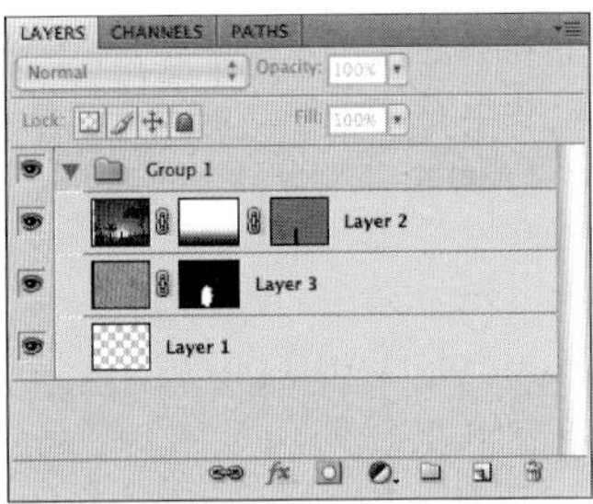

Figure 10.19 Select the layers you'd like to have in a group.

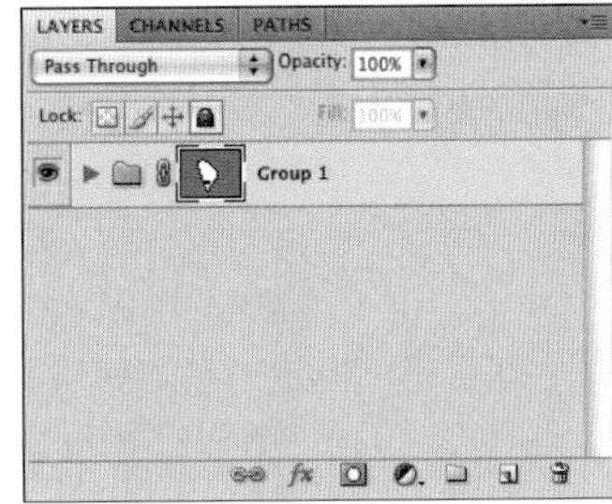

Figure 10.20 The grouped layers appear inside a folder in the Layers panel. Add a vector mask to the group to limit where all the layers within the group show up.

Removing the Vector Mask

If you want to remove the vector mask, choose Layer > Delete Vector Mask, or drag its thumbnail to the trash can icon at the bottom of the Layers panel. You can also convert a vector mask into a layer mask by choosing Layer > Rasterize > Vector Mask. But be aware that you'll lose the crisp-edged, smooth look of the path, and any transformations applied to the layer mask will cause it to appear blurry.

NOTES

Paths print with crisp edges only if you print to a PostScript output device, such as a $500+ laser printer. Most inkjet printers don't understand PostScript, so your image has the potential of appearing jaggy on those types of devices.

Saving Vector Data

If you plan to save the image and use it in a page layout program (instead of using it for a Web site), be careful about how you save it; otherwise, the crisp edge of the path may be lost. Remember that a path is different from pixels in that it's made out of points and directional handles. That's *vector* information, whereas images made from pixels are *raster* information. To maintain the crisp edges of the paths, save the image as an EPS or PDF file; those formats support vector data. When saving the file, select the Include Vector Data check box (**Figure 10.21**); this option shows up only after you click the Save button.

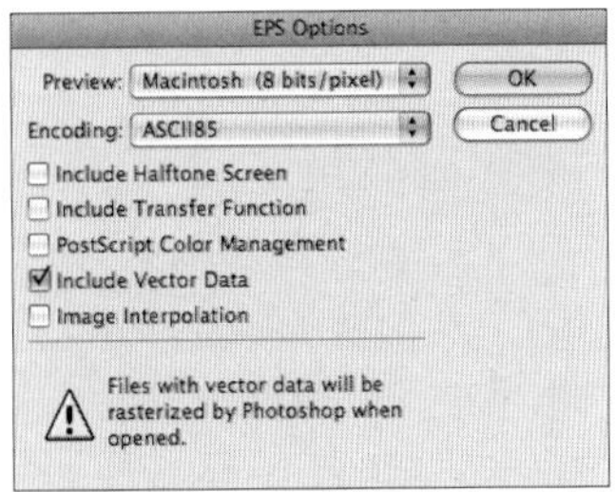

Figure 10.21 Saving an EPS file.

Clipping Paths

You can also assign a path to a document, as opposed to a single layer. A clipping path limits which areas of an image will show up and print in a page layout program (**Figures 10.22** and **10.23**). To create a clipping path, use the Pen tool or a Shape tool to create a path, and then choose Window > Paths to open the Paths panel. Next, double-click the name of the path and assign it a name. Then choose Clipping Path from the side menu of the Paths panel. When prompted, enter a Flatness setting.

Figure 10.22 Image imported without a clipping path. (©2007 www.PeterHoey.com.)

Figure 10.23 Image imported with a clipping path.

When the image is printed, it will be converted into a polygon made out of straight lines of identical length. The Flatness setting determines the length of those lines. Low settings produce short lines, which require more memory and processing time to output. If the Flatness setting is too low, the printer might run out of memory when attempting to output the image. The more complex the path (lots of points and directional handles), the higher the Flatness setting needs to be to avoid printing problems. In general, use a setting between 3 and 10, depending on the complexity of the path. After you've assigned a clipping path to an image, save it as a TIFF or EPS file so that it can be understood by a page layout program.

Working with Smart Objects

Introduced in Photoshop CS2, Smart Objects provide a completely different way of working in Photoshop. Instead of the good old one-element-per-layer tradition, images are dealt with in a way that's similar to how page layout programs link to external image files. Basically, when you place an image on a page in a page layout program, you're actually just viewing a preview of the image that's stored on your hard drive. You're free to scale, rotate, and crop the image, but you cannot edit it directly in the page layout program. Instead, you must open the linked image, make your changes, resave it, and then update the link to the image in the page layout program.

Adobe applied this idea to Photoshop in the form of *Smart Objects*. You can place an external image file or encapsulate multiple layers into a Photoshop document as a Smart Object. But instead of "linking" to external files, the images are "embedded" in the Photoshop document. The Smart Object acts much like a linked file in that you're limited to scaling, transforming, and masking its contents, but if you want to make edits, you must do so in a separate document. There are many advantages to working with Smart Objects:

- You can create a complex document without having to show all the layers that make up the image.
- You can scale a layer to a small size while retaining the ability to later enlarge the layer, using the full-sized layers that were originally used to create the Smart Object.
- You can duplicate a Smart Object multiple times and make edits to the original, and all the duplicates will automatically update to match the original.
- You can embed an Adobe Illustrator or Camera Raw file into a Photoshop file and later make changes in Illustrator or the Camera Raw dialog. You can also extract the original file at any time.
- You can apply some filters nondestructively, using the Smart Filters feature.
- You can work nondestructively with Camera Raw files, which allow you to go back and adjust your Camera Raw conversion settings at any time.

There are also limitations to what can be done to a Smart Object. The Smart Object layer cannot be edited directly, which means that you won't be able to paint or directly adjust the Smart Object without using a few special tricks, or editing the layers that make up the Smart Object.

Creating Smart Objects

There are several methods for creating a Smart Object. The easiest is to choose File > Open as Smart Object, and then select the image(s) that you want to open. (You can select more than one by Shift-clicking multiple file names.)

The image(s) open as normal and, at first glance, you won't see anything conspicuously different. However, in the title bar of each image is "<<image name>> as Smart Object" and then the usual color mode and zoom percentage stats.

The other indication that you're working with a different kind of image is in the Layers panel. There's no Background layer, as in a normal document. Instead, the image sits as a Smart Object in its own layer, with a special badge superimposed over its thumbnail (**Figure 10.24**).

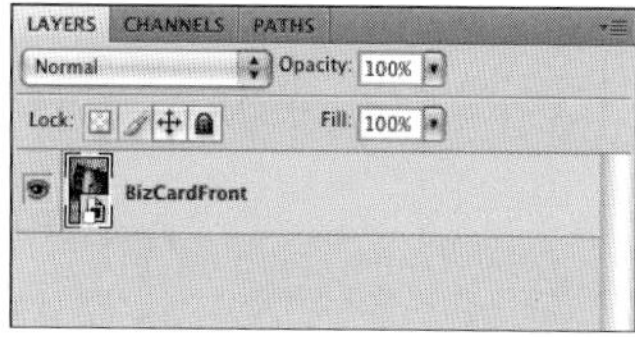

Figure 10.24 The little icon at lower right in the layer thumbnail indicates this is a Smart Object layer.

Finally, select the Brush tool and hold it over the image. A very stubborn "no" icon indicates that the tool will *not* work on this image. Remember, Smart Objects don't contain normal pixel data, and therefore can't be edited on a pixel-by-pixel basis using the normal Photoshop procedures.

To convert layers to Smart Objects, select them and choose Layer > Smart Objects > Convert to Smart Object. To use a layer or layers from an external file, choose File > Place instead. The external file can be in any file format that Photoshop can open, including Adobe Illustrator and Camera Raw files.

Grouping layers into a Smart Object prevents the individual layers within the Smart Object from interacting with layers outside of the Smart Object. The general appearance of the document might change, depending on which features were used to create it:

- The Underlying Layer sliders in the Layer Style dialog won't affect layers outside of the Smart Object.
- The layers will become adjacent to each other in the Layers panel and no longer be intermixed with other layers.
- Adjustment layers used within the Smart Object will not affect layers outside of the Smart Object.
- Blending modes used on individual layers will be limited to interacting with the other layers within the Smart Object.

Multiple Instances

Once you've created a Smart Object, you can drag it to the New Layer icon at the bottom of the Layers panel to duplicate the layer and create another instance of the same Smart Object. Each instance of the Smart Object will refer to the same set of layers that were used to create the Smart Object. Layer styles, masks, and warping can be used to modify individual instances of the Smart Object. Editing the layers that make up the Smart Object causes all the instances of that Smart Object to update to reflect the changes. In **Figure 10.25**, a single leaf was used to create a Smart Object, and then that Smart Object layer was duplicated nine times to create the other leaves, which were rotated and styled to create the composition in **Figure 10.26**. Since all ten leaves that appeared in the final image were instances of the same leaf, editing one leaf caused all ten leaves to update to reflect the change (**Figure 10.27**). In this case, a subtle change was made to a vector mask, which changed how much of the leaf was visible.

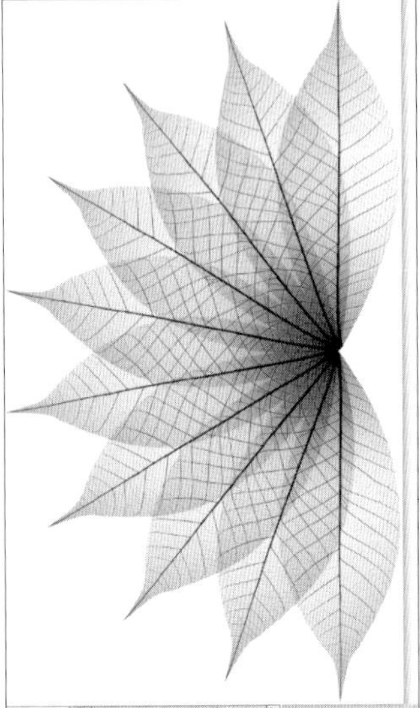

Figure 10.25 Ten instances of the same Smart Object have been rotated to create this complex image.

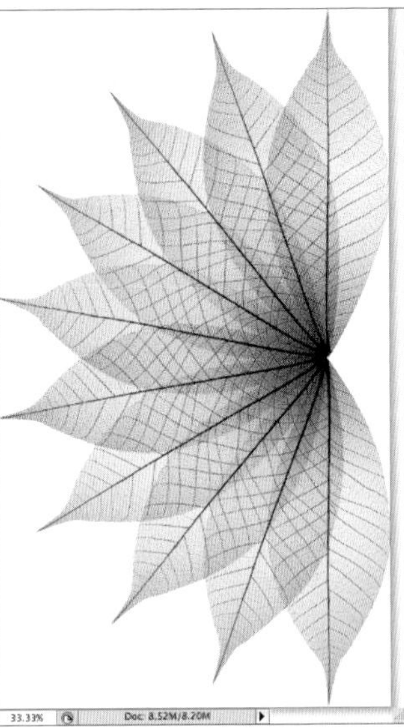

Figure 10.26 Layer styles added color to each instance of the Smart Object.

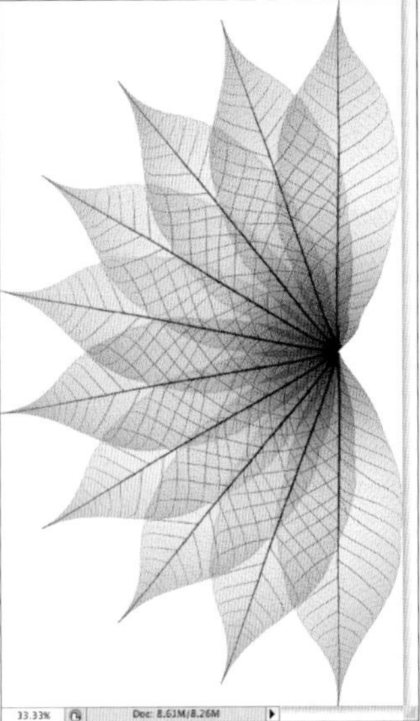

Figure 10.27 Editing the Smart Object caused all instances of the Smart Object to be updated.

Nested Smart Objects

You can nest one Smart Object within another by selecting a Smart Object and choosing Layer > Smart Objects > Group Into New Smart Object. Nested Smart Objects are useful when you want to simplify the Layers panel view of the image (**Figure 10.28**) or cause layer styles to treat multiple layers as a single object, instead of applying to each individual element that makes up the image (**Figures 10.29** and **10.30**). This will also allow you to apply warping to all the layers at once (we'll talk about warping later in this chapter).

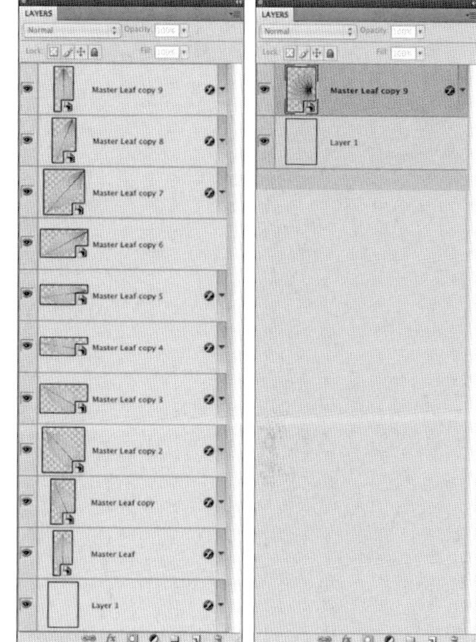

Figure 10.28 Left: Ten Smart Objects are used to create a complex document. Right: The same document viewed after nesting the ten Smart Object layers into a single Smart Object.

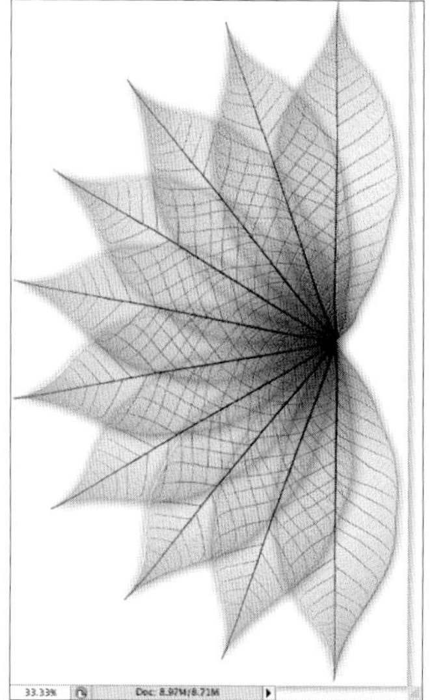

Figure 10.29 Here, a Drop Shadow layer style was applied to each of the individual leaf Smart Object layers.

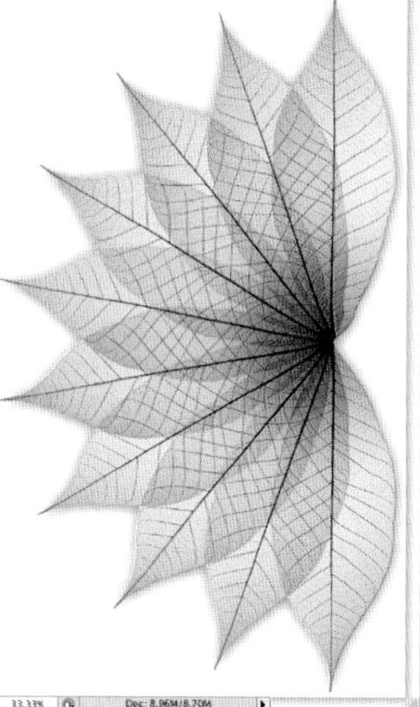

Figure 10.30 This time the Drop Shadow layer style was applied after nesting the leaf layers into a single Smart Object.

When you nest one Smart Object inside another, you cause that nested Smart Object to become independent of any other instances that are used outside of the Smart Object within which it's safely nested. Therefore, editing the nested Smart Object will only affect other instances of that Smart Object that appear within the outer Smart Object, and other Smart Objects will be unchanged. It might sound confusing just reading about it, but once you've driven this thing around the block a few times, it will make sense.

Editing Smart Objects

To edit the layers that make up a Smart Object, choose Layer > Smart Objects > Edit Contents, or double-click the Smart Object's thumbnail image in the Layers panel. The contents of the Smart Object will appear in a separate document window, where you can edit the individual layers within the Smart Object by using any of Photoshop's tools. When you're finished modifying the Smart Object, press Command/Ctrl-S to save your changes and update the parent document containing the Smart Object.

If the Smart Object contains a Camera Raw file, editing the contents will take you back to the Camera Raw dialog, where you'll be able to adjust your raw conversion parameters.

Choose Layer > Smart Objects > Replace Contents to replace the entire contents of a Smart Object with the contents of a file on your hard drive. This feature is useful when working with Camera Raw files, since it allows you to start a design with placeholder images that you can later replace with alternative images.

Smart Filters

Smart Filters allow you to apply filters to a Smart Object, just as you would to any other type of layer. Just select the filter you want from the Filter menu. The filter's dialog (if it has one) will appear as it always does, and the image will be processed. Not all filters are available as Smart Filters, but you should find all of the crucial filters—sharpening, blurring, and so on.

After the filter is added, a Smart Filters effect is added to the layer in the Layers panel (**Figure 10.31**). This is the same way that CS4 displays layer styles. As you add filters, they're added to the Smart Filter entry for that layer.

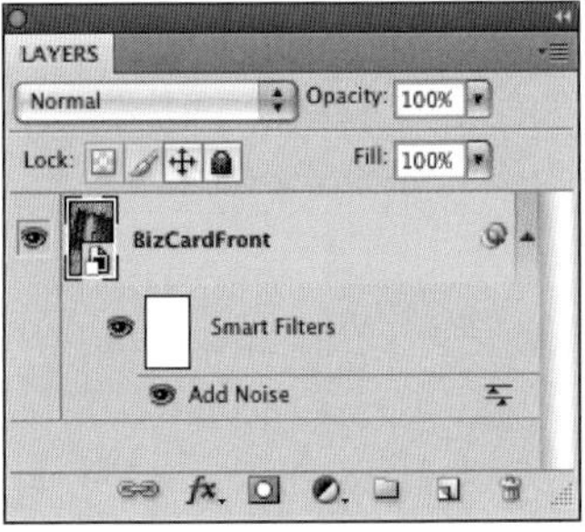

Figure 10.31 When you add a filter to a Smart Layer, it appears in a special Smart Filters effect in the Layers panel.

To change the parameters of any filter you've added, double-click its entry in the Layers panel. The filter's dialog will appear, allowing you to adjust its settings.

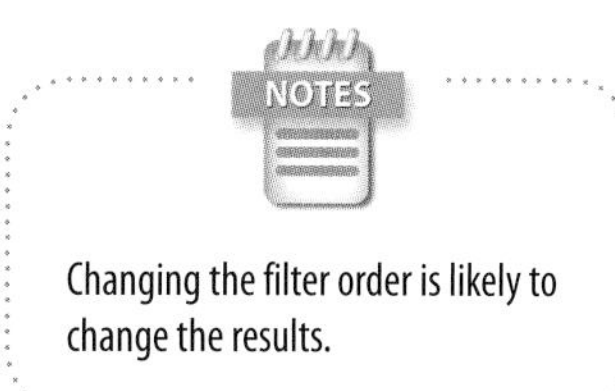

Changing the filter order is likely to change the results.

To change the order of the filters, drag them up/down the list. You can delete a filter by selecting it in the Layers panel and pressing the Delete key.

The Smart Filters collection attached to a layer has a built-in masking function that works just like a layer mask or the mask that's attached to an adjustment layer. To use the Smart Filter mask, click it in the Layers panel and then use any Photoshop painting tool to paint onto the mask (**Figure 10.32**).

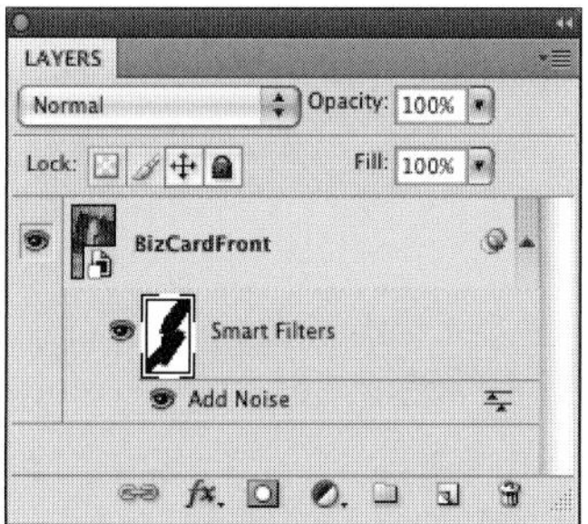

Figure 10.32 Painting onto the layer mask of a Smart Filter allows you to constrain the effects of the filter to specific areas of the image.

The layer mask applies to all filters you've added to that Smart Object. You can't create separate masks for each effect.

Smart Filters differ from adjustment layers in that they affect only the image to which they're attached. You can't use an Unsharp Mask filter to sharpen all of the layers in an image, for example. Instead, you'll need to apply separate Unsharp Mask filters to each layer in the document, configuring each of them with the same settings.

Smart Objects Tips and Tricks

Let's look at a few interesting ways to use Smart Objects. These ideas just scratch the surface of what you can do. The more you experiment, the more useful ways you'll find to use Smart Objects.

Figure 10.33 Using a single set of Camera Raw settings produced this less-than-desirable result. (©2007 Ben Willmore.)

Camera Raw

You can blend two different interpretations of the same raw format image by using Smart Objects. Embed a Camera Raw file into an existing document by choosing File > Place. In the Camera Raw dialog, you can control the tonality and color of the image—but what if you can't find a single interpretation that does justice to the entire image (**Figure 10.33**)? Choose Layer > Smart Objects > New Smart Object via Copy to create a second Smart Object that's independent of the first. Double-click the thumbnail image for the new Smart Object, causing the Camera Raw dialog to appear, and choose different settings that you want to apply to the second Smart Object. Once you have the two different interpretations of the raw file (**Figures 10.34** and **10.35**), you can add a layer mask to the top Smart Object and use it to control where each version of the raw file contributes to the final image (**Figure 10.36**).

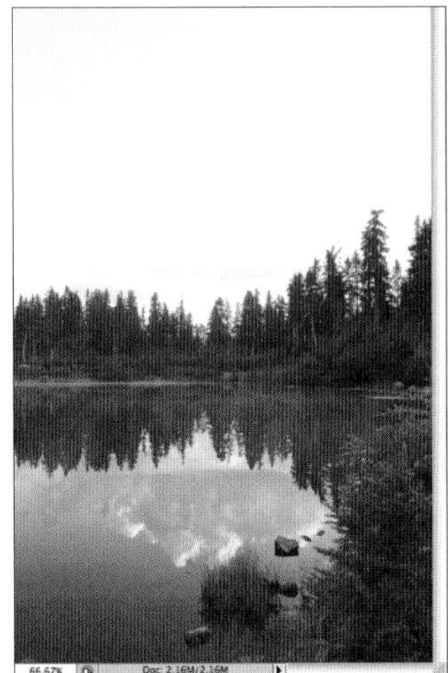

Figure 10.34 The sky was ignored and the bottom was optimized in this Camera Raw interpretation.

Figure 10.35 The bottom was ignored and the sky was optimized in this Camera Raw interpretation.

Figure 10.36 The two interpretations of the same raw file were combined by using a layer mask.

Painting and Adjustments

Many of Photoshop's tools are disabled when a Smart Object is active in the Layers panel. Here are a few tricks you can use to get around that limitation:

- To apply paint to a Smart Object, create a new layer directly above the Smart Object and choose Layer > Create Clipping Mask so that any paint applied to the layer will show up only where the Smart Object appears.
- To adjust a Smart Object without affecting the rest of the image, select the Smart Object layer, hold down Option/Alt, click the Adjustment Layer pop-up menu at the bottom of the Layers panel, and choose the adjustment you want to apply. When the New Layer dialog appears, turn on the Use Previous Layer to Create Clipping Mask check box to limit the adjustment to the Smart Object layer.
- If you want to apply a filter that's not available as a Smart Filter, first duplicate the Smart Object layer by pressing Command/Ctrl-J, and then hide the original by clicking its eyeball icon. Now apply the filter to the duplicate. Photoshop merges the layers that make up the Smart Object (also known as *rasterizing*), which turns it into a normal layer. But since you hid the original Smart Object, you still have a copy that you can later edit and then re-filter.
- Be careful when adding layers to a Smart Object. If the original Smart Object was created after opening a flat JPG file that contained no layers, adding layers will cause problems. Photoshop will act as if the Smart Object is actually a JPG file. Since JPG files can't contain layers, Photoshop will present a Save As dialog, forcing you to save the document in a file format that supports layers. That means that adding a layer will cause your edited Smart Object to be saved on your hard drive instead of being embedded in the parent document in which you used the Smart Object. To update the parent document, choose Layer > Smart Object > Replace Contents and point Photoshop to the newly saved layered file.

Warping Images

Photoshop's warping features allow you to bend and distort images in interesting ways. Choosing Edit > Transform > Warp causes various warp settings to appear in the options bar (**Figure 10.37**) and places a grid over the active layer (**Figure 10.38**). There are 15 preset warp shapes available (**Figure 10.39**). After choosing a preset from the Warp pop-up menu in the options bar, you can adjust the Bend, H (Horizontal), and V (Vertical) fields in the options bar to control the extent of the warp that's applied to the active layer. If you need to warp an image to match an element in a photograph, set the Warp pop-up menu to Custom.

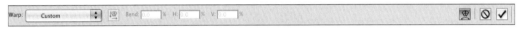

Figure 10.37 The options available when warping a layer.

Figure 10.38 Choosing Edit > Transform > Warp causes a warp grid to appear over the image. (©2008 Dan Ablan.)

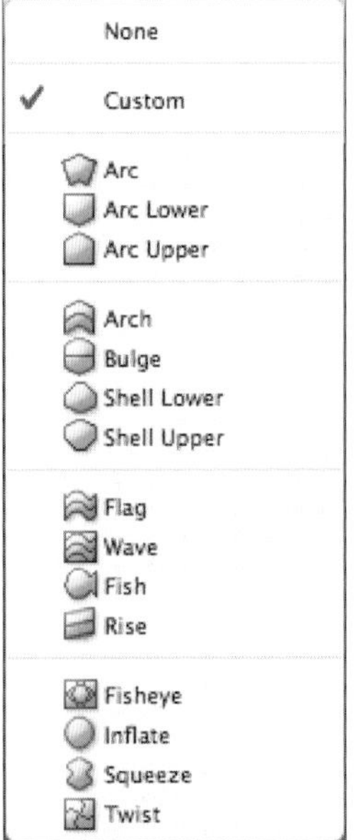

Figure 10.39 The default warp presets.

When applying a Custom warp, you can drag the corner points, handles, or grid lines to distort the image. To match the contours of an object, start by positioning the corner handles to meet the underlying image (**Figure 10.40**). Adjust the corner handles to specify the angle at which the edge of the image should match the underlying image (**Figures 10.41** and **10.42**). To fine-tune the results, drag the grid lines until the image is distorted to match the underlying object (**Figure 10.43**). If you warp a Smart Object layer, you can choose Layer > Smart Object > Replace Contents to swap out a different image while retaining the warping last applied to the layer (**Figures 10.44** and **10.45**).

Figure 10.40 Choosing Custom from the Warp pop-up menu presents a grid.

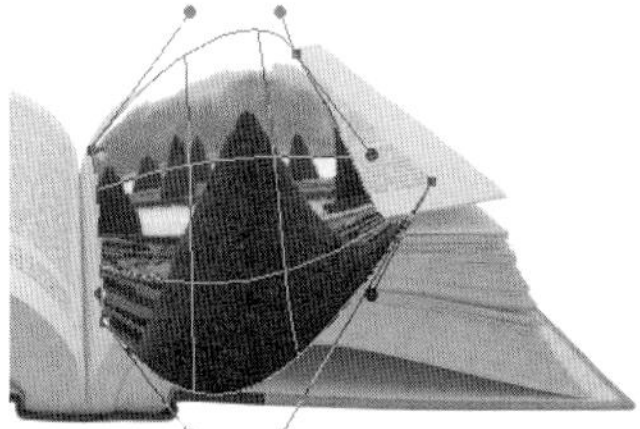

Figure 10.41 Drag the four corners of the grid so they line up with the object you're trying to match.

Figure 10.42 Adjust the corner handles.

Figure 10.43 Fine-tune the results by dragging the grid lines.

Figure 10.44 End result of warping the image to match the page. (©2007 iStockphoto.com and Ben Willmore.)

Figure 10.45 Using a Smart Object, you can swap the image while retaining the warping.

Figure 10.46 A collage on the cover of a previous edition of this book.

Creating Complex Collages

Now we're ready to put all these features together, combine them with the blending modes we explored in Chapter 9, and throw in a few other techniques to create a complex collage. If you haven't read through all of this chapter and Chapter 9, it might be difficult to follow along with this project, so make sure that you've covered that material before you dive in.

The collage in **Figure 10.46** was originally created by Regina Cleveland for the CS2 edition of this book. She challenged Ben Willmore to re-create it in Photoshop and gave him a total of four photos, which she snagged from www.istockphoto.com (**Figures 10.47** to **10.50**), along with a shot of Ben taken by his friend Andy Katz (**Figure 10.51**).

Figure 10.47 This leaf image started out as a black-and-white shot. (©2007 iStockphoto.com/BritishBeefUK.)

Figure 10.48 This pattern was used on both the head and background. (©2007 iStockphoto.com/LindaMarieB.)

Figure 10.49 The head was isolated from its background. (©2007 iStockphoto.com/puentes.)

Figure 10.50 The lens from this camera was used in the center of the image. (©2007 iStockphoto.com/avarkisp.)

Figure 10.51 This shot of Ben Willmore goofing off was used as a reflection in the lens. (©2007 Andy Katz.)

We're going to fly through this procedure, so pay close attention!

Creating the Fan of Leaves

The first element is the single leaf image, which, when later multiplied, will provide a headdress for the face. We double-click the Background image to turn it into a normal layer, and then use a vector mask to isolate the leaf from its background (**Figures 10.52** and **10.53**). Because this element is going to be scaled and rotated many times, and needs to retain as much of the original detail as possible, we convert the layer into a Smart Object.

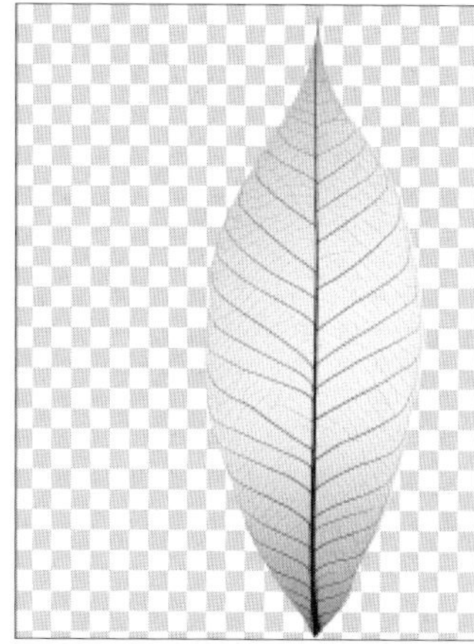

Figure 10.52 Isolate the leaf from its background by using a vector mask.

Figure 10.53 Layers panel view of the isolated leaf.

The original leaf document doesn't have enough space to create the fan of leaves, so we create a new document the exact size of the book cover plus nine points (just over 1/8 of an inch) of extra space on three sides to allow for bleed (the fourth side will merge with the spine of the book and therefore doesn't need any bleed). Once the document is open, we position three guides (using the View > New Guide command) to indicate the trimmed page size. Then, before doing any more work, we drag the leaf Smart Object to the newly created document (using the Move tool) and scale it to an appropriate size (using the Edit > Free Transform command).

The fan needs a total of ten leaves spanning a 180-degree arc. To space the leaves evenly, we divide the total degrees of rotation (180) by the number of leaves that will be used (9, since two of the leaves will end up at the same angle—straight up and down—and therefore shouldn't be counted twice). Since dividing 180 by 9 produces 20, that means that each leaf needs to be rotated by 20 degrees from the one adjacent to it.

With those calculations in hand, we duplicate the original Smart Object layer by pressing Command/Ctrl-J to create a second instance of the Smart Object. We rotate the duplicate by pressing Command/Ctrl-T to access the Free Transform command; then the pivot point (which looks like a crosshair and appears in the center of the layer that's being transformed) is dragged straight down and positioned on the bottom center transformation point (**Figure 10.54**). To get the proper amount of rotation, we enter a value of 20 in the Angle field in the options bar, which ends up rotating the image to the right—the wrong direction. Oops! Add a minus sign before the percentage to rotate it in the opposite direction. After pressing Return/Enter twice (the first time to have Photoshop accept the number and the second time to complete the rotation), we repeat the process (duplicate, move pivot point, rotate) until a total of ten leaves are in place (**Figure 10.55**).

Next, the leaves needed to interact with each other instead of obscuring each other. For each layer, the blending mode is set to Multiply, causing the layer to act as if it were being printed on top of the underlying layers using ink (**Figure 10.56**). At this point, the fan of leaves starts to look interesting, but lacks any hint of color.

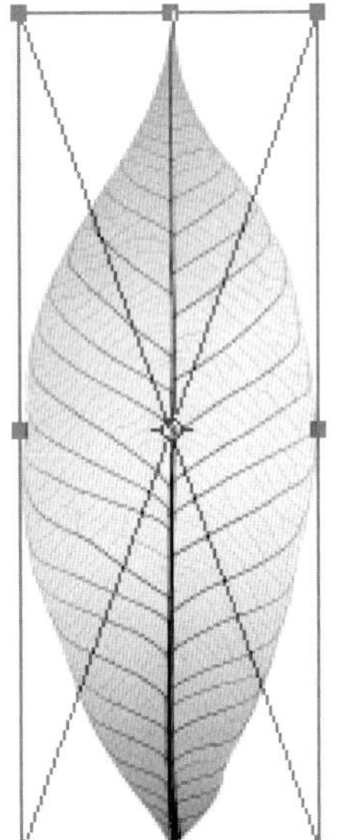

Figure 10.54 The pivot point is dragged to the tip of the leaf.

Figure 10.55 Result of duplicating and rotating the leaf Smart Object nine times.

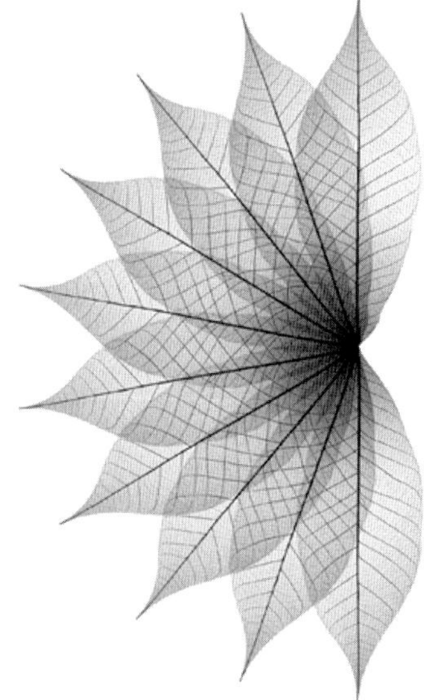

Figure 10.56 The leaves look more integrated after setting each Smart Object layer to Multiply mode.

Color is added by applying a Gradient Overlay layer style to each layer, using the Color blending mode to apply the color of the active layer to the brightness information from the underlying image. In this case, Color mode causes the Gradient Overlay to apply color to the brightness values in the leaf. We click the Gradient Overlay Preview and change the color used on one end of the gradient, and then adjust the Opacity and Angle settings until the color is affecting the leaf in just the right way (**Figure 10.57**).

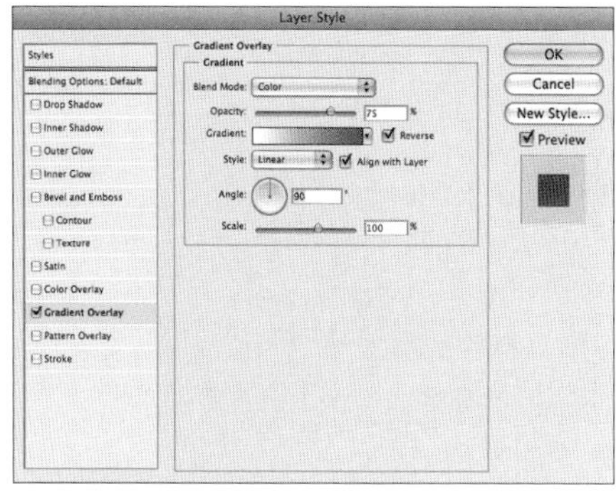

Figure 10.57 One of the Gradient Overlays that we applied to the leaves.

To apply similar settings to the other leaf Smart Objects, we Control/right-click the style-laden layer in the Layers panel, choose Copy Layer Style, select all the other Smart Object layers, Control/right-click one of the layers, and choose Paste Layer Style, which makes all the leaves take on the same color (**Figures 10.58** and **10.59**). To make each leaf a different color, double-click the Layer Style icon on each layer, change the color used in each gradient, and adjust the Angle setting to cause the color to be concentrated near the outer tip of each leaf (**Figure 10.60**).

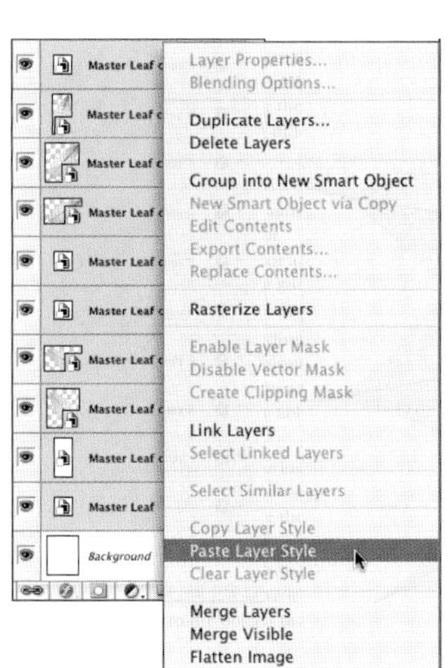

Figure 10.58 Copying and pasting the layer style applies it to each of the selected layers.

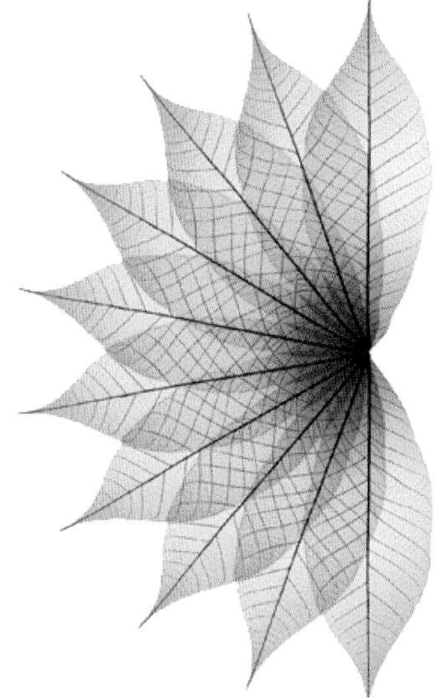

Figure 10.59 The leaves appear as a single color because we applied the same layer style to each leaf.

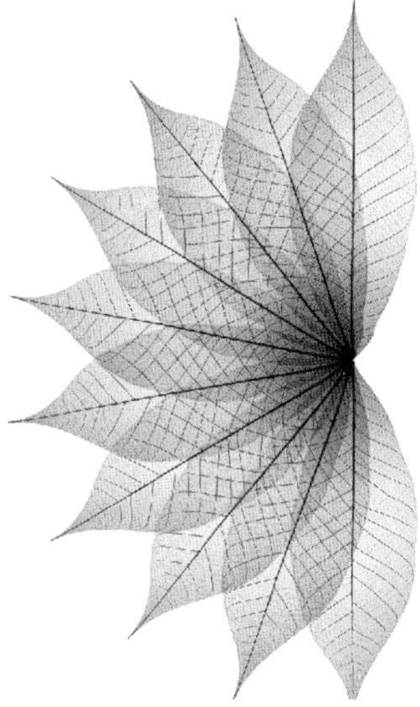

Figure 10.60 The leaves take on different colors after we modify the layer style applied to each layer.

Adding the Head

At this stage, the fan of leaves is about done, but it lacks a background. A stylistic head is the next element to tackle.

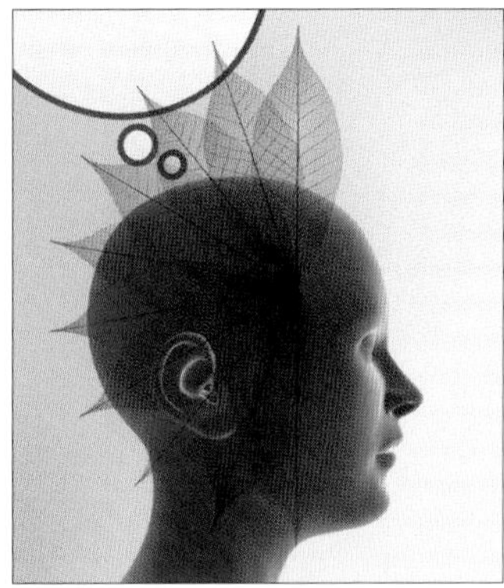

Figure 10.61 Set to Multiply mode, the leaves look like they were printed on top of the head.

Figure 10.62 The leaf layers are grouped into a Smart Object, with blending mode set to Normal.

Figure 10.63 The background is removed from the head with the Magic Wand tool and a layer mask.

We open the head image in Photoshop and drag it into the book cover document, using the Move tool. A problem develops after scaling the head layer to an appropriate size and moving it to the bottom of the Layers stack: All the leaf Smart Object layers look like they're printed on top of the head, because we set them all to use the Multiply blending mode (**Figure 10.61**).

Since we needed the Multiply mode to cause the leaves to print on top of each other instead of obscuring each other, we select all the leaf Smart Object layers and choose Layer > Smart Objects > Group into New Smart Object to nest them into a new Smart Object. This solves the problem, because the individual layers that make up a Smart Object cannot interact with layers that are outside the Smart Object. A Smart Object can only interact with the underlying image as a whole, and the blending mode for the newly created Smart Object is set to Normal, which prevents it from interacting with the rest of the image (**Figure 10.62**). Grouping the leaf layers into a Smart Object also has the added benefit of greatly simplifying the Layers panel.

The cover of this book traditionally features a white background, which means that the background of the head image needs to be removed. We start by hiding the fan of leaves Smart Object so it doesn't obstruct the view of the head layer. Removing the background on the head layer is an easy process because the background is quite different from the subject in both color and brightness. The Magic Wand tool is perfect for this job. Clicking the background probably isn't enough to select the whole area, though, so we hold down the Shift key and click unselected portions of the background. It takes less than a dozen clicks with the Magic Wand tool to get a decent selection of the background. Then, to hide the background on the head, hold down Option/Alt and click the Layer Mask icon at the bottom of the Layers panel. Holding down Option/Alt causes the selected areas to become hidden when the mask is created (**Figure 10.63**). We might have to touch up a few spots near the mouth and nose, since the original selection isn't perfect.

The head is now ready for her beauty treatment. The paisley/fractal pattern image is placed on the layer directly above the head. Then we choose Layer > Create Clipping Mask to make the pattern show up only where the head is (**Figure 10.64**). To make the pattern interact with the head, we switch to the Move tool, hold down Shift, and press the plus (+) key on the keyboard a few times to cycle through all the blending modes in the pop-up menu at the top of the Layers panel (Shift and the minus key cycles back). After going through the whole list a few times, we settle on the Overlay blending mode (**Figure 10.65**). The improved look of the head is good, but the colors aren't popping the way they did in Regina's original collage. With the pattern layer still active, we choose Gradient Overlay from the Layer Style pop-up menu at the bottom of the Layers panel, created a colorful gradient, and then experiment with the Blending Mode pop-up menu until we like the results (**Figures 10.66** and **10.67**).

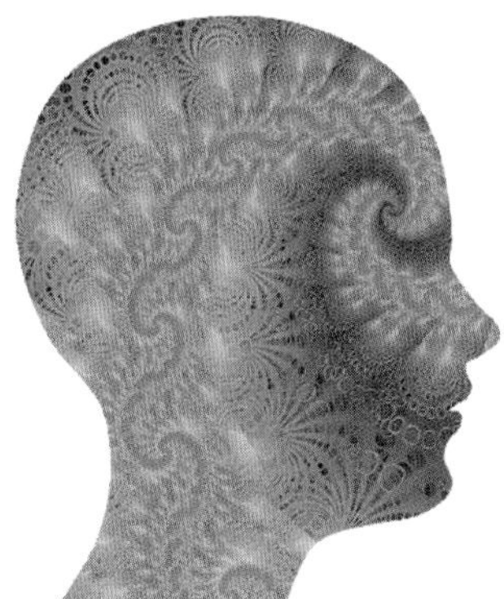

Figure 10.64 A clipping mask is used to make the pattern show up only where the head is.

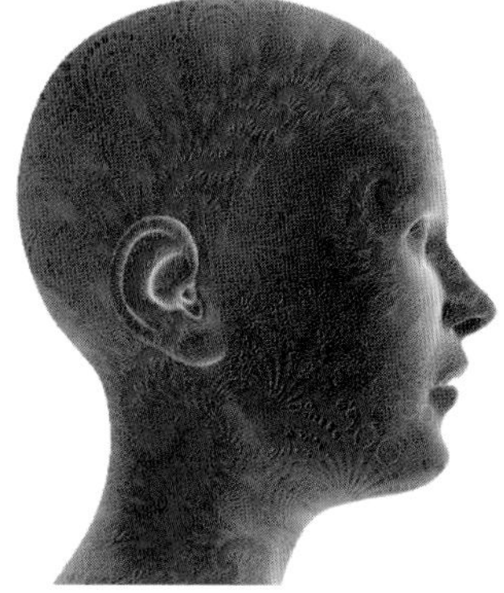

Figure 10.65 The Overlay blending mode causes the pattern to overlay onto the head.

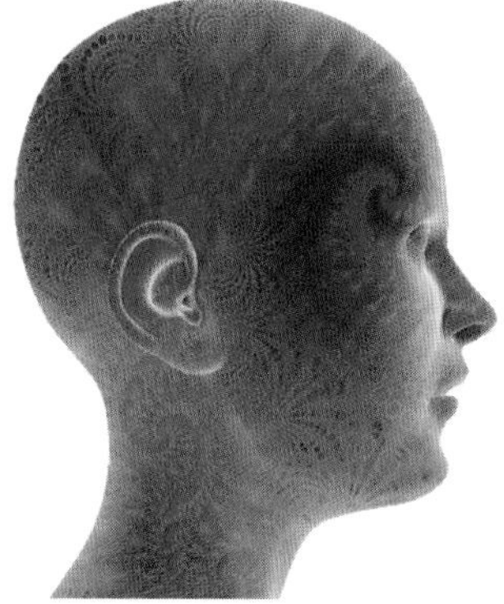

Figure 10.66 Additional color comes with a Gradient Overlay layer style on the pattern layer.

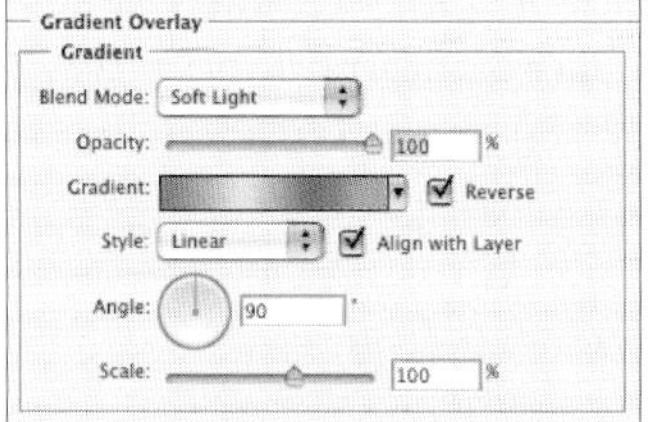

Figure 10.67 This Gradient Overlay is applied to the pattern layer.

Adding the Camera Lens

At this point, we make the fan of leaves Smart Object visible again and reposition it so that the center of the fan is close to being centered on the round part of the head (**Figure 10.68**). To add the camera lens to the middle of the fan, we open the photo of the camera, extract the camera body from the lens by using a vector mask, and then drag it into position within the collage. To add a little accent to the lens, we choose Drop Shadow from the Layer Style pop-up menu at the bottom of the Layers panel, set the blending mode to Screen, and chose a cyan color (**Figure 10.69**).

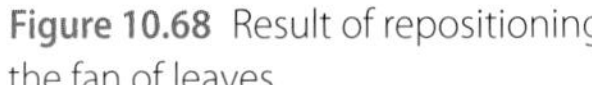

Figure 10.68 Result of repositioning the fan of leaves.

Figure 10.69 We added the camera lens and a Drop Shadow layer style.

Figure 10.70 Text and logo treatments are added to the cover.

Adding Type and Logo Treatments

It's time to add the cover text, using four Type layers. (For more about working with text, check out the bonus video "Type and Background Effects" at www.danablan.com/photoshop.) The logo that appears at lower right on the cover was supplied by the publisher as an EPS file. To add that element, we choose File > Place and point Photoshop to the logo file. That embeds the EPS file into the collage as a Smart Object layer, which allows it to be scaled to any size without losing quality. To complete the graphic elements on the cover, we add a red bar across the top of the document, using the Rectangular Shape tool (**Figure 10.70**).

Creating the Background Texture

Now we're ready to tackle the background behind the head. The pattern applied to the head was the same used for the background, so we duplicate the pattern layer, drag it to the bottom of the Layers panel, and scale and position it to fill most of the white space at the bottom of the image (**Figure 10.71**). At this stage, the head and the background contain similar colors, so we shift the color of the background: Hold down Option/Alt, choose Gradient Map from the Adjustment Layer pop-up menu at the bottom of the Layers panel, and turn on the Use Previous Layer to Create Clipping Mask check box so the adjustment affects only the background pattern. We added the gradient to force the colors in the background toward red and orange (**Figures 10.72** and **10.73**). To make the background fade into the white found at the top of the cover, we add a layer mask and apply a gradient to the mask (**Figure 10.74**).

Figure 10.71 The pattern from the head is duplicated and used as the base of the background.

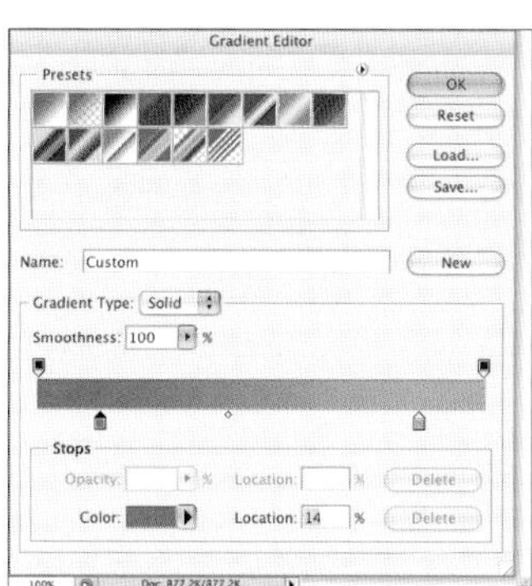

Figure 10.72 A Gradient Map adjustment layer shifts the background colors toward red and orange.

Figure 10.73 Result of shifting the colors in the background.

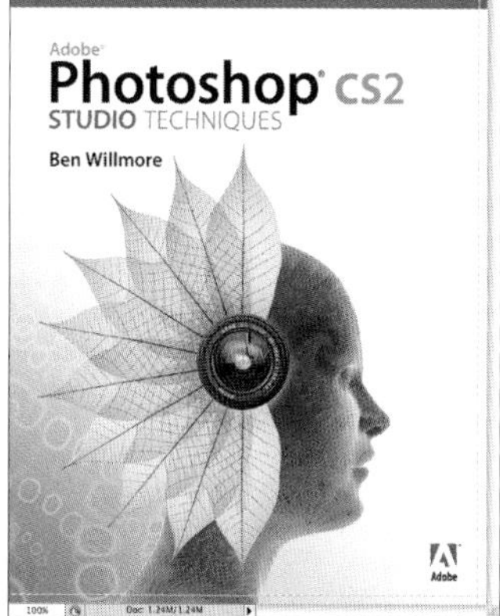

Figure 10.74 Result of masking the background with a gradient.

Final Tweaks

The cover collage now contains all of the major pieces found in the original version provided by Regina, and it just needs a few tweaks to refine the results. For the background pattern, we duplicate the fan of leaves as a Smart Object, setting its blending mode to Screen, lowering the

Figure 10.75 The finished cover, complete with lens reflection.

Opacity, and scaling it up to lighten the background, using the same shape as the leaves. To make the fan of leaves partially transparent, we add a layer mask and paint with a soft-edged brush at a low opacity, which lets the shape of the head show through. For the lens reflection effect, we add Ben's photo above the lens and use Overlay blending mode. Finally, to make a beam of light emanate from the lens, we create a new layer, make a triangular selection and fill it with white, and lower its opacity to connect the lens to the eye (**Figure 10.75**). With a big "Whew!" we consider the collage as finished, and now only need to put it into a 3-D mockup of the book's cover.

Creating a 3-D Cover Mockup

To create the 3-D cover mockup, we use a photograph of a similarly sized book, flattening the newly created collage and moving it into the book photograph image. Using the Distort command (Edit > Transform > Distort), we distort the collage to match the shape of the photographic cover (**Figure 10.76**). Finally, we use the Gradient tool in Multiply mode to add subtle shading to the cover, which adds a bit of realism to the end result (**Figure 10.77**).

Figure 10.76 The transformed cover image matches the perspective of the photograph.

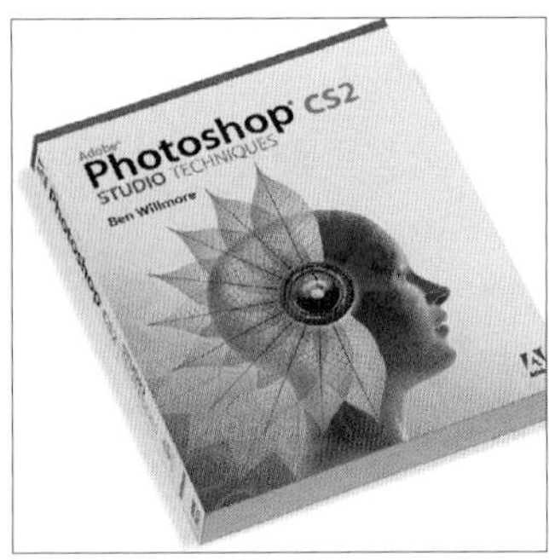

Figure 10.77 Shading with the Gradient tool helps to make the end result look more realistic.

The Next Step

Hopefully you get as much of a kick out of creating collages as we do. It's one of those things that really never gets old; you can always count on another surprise around the corner, and knowing how to create a complex image like this will help you to tackle whatever comes your way. If you want to create truly realistic-looking collages, keep the following ideas in mind:

- When combining images that were shot under different lighting conditions, be sure to color-correct the images individually before turning them into a collage; otherwise, each one will have a different color cast.
- If you're basing a collage on an image that has a desirable color cast (such as candlelight, firelight, or sunrise/sunset), use the techniques mentioned

in Chapter 8, "Color Manipulation," to infuse all the images with the same desirable color cast.

- When combining images, make sure that the direction of the light in all the images is consistent; otherwise, viewers will pick up on the fact that the image is a fake, although they might not be able to pinpoint exactly why they think that.
- The direction of the light should also dictate the direction in which shadows fall. Shadows should fall directly opposite of the light source.
- When placing objects in a scene, think about where each object appears in 3D space and make sure that it has the appropriate focus compared to its surroundings.
- The film grain that shows up in an image is usually consistent across the image, so either use the noise removal techniques covered in Chapter 6, "Sharpening," on each image, or apply the Add Noise filter (Filter > Noise > Add Noise) to make sure that all the images have the same amount of grain.

If you keep these ideas in mind, with a little practice and a lot of perspiration you should be able to create collages that fool even a trained eye. Now, move on to the last chapter, probably one of the most important subjects for photographers, "Retouching Techniques."

CHAPTER

11

Retouching Techniques

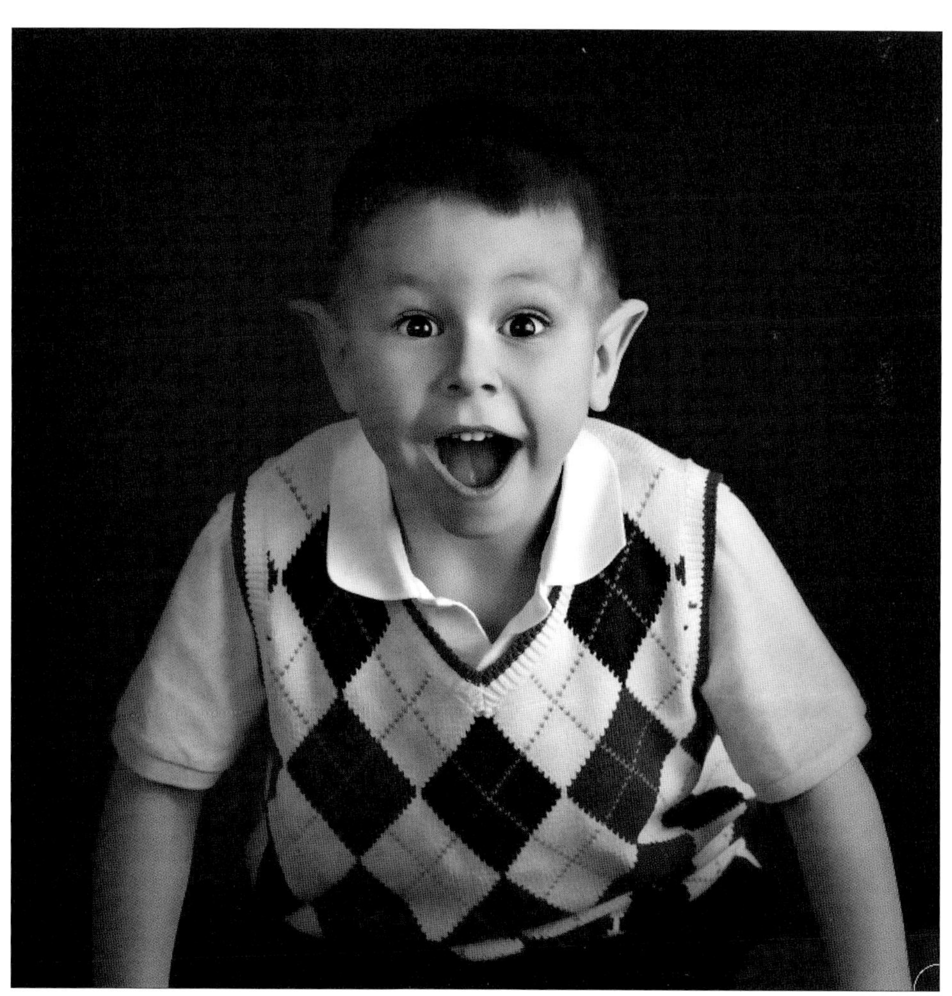

As long as the world is turning and spinning, we're gonna be dizzy and we're gonna make mistakes.

—Mel Brooks

Retouching Techniques

If you're brave enough to bring up the subject of retouching at a photographer's convention, you're likely to spark a lively debate. A purist might say that every aspect of a photograph (including the flaws) is a perfect reflection of reality and you should never tamper with it. A graphic artist, who makes a living from altering images, might say that an original photograph is just the foundation of an image, and that "tampering" is just a means of enhancing it. Either way, retouching photographs has become an everyday necessity for almost anyone who deals with graphic images. And when it comes to retouching, hands down, nothing does it better than Photoshop.

While we'll concentrate on touching up faces, don't forget that these tools can be used on any type of image. A stray light switch on a wall detracting from the shot? No problem—just use the Patch tool!

Photoshop CS4 packs an awesome arsenal of retouching tools. In this chapter, you'll learn how to do all sorts of neat things, including retouching old ripped photos, getting rid of shiny spots on foreheads, adjusting the saturation of small areas—even giving someone "instant plastic surgery."

Patch Tool

The Patch tool (hidden under the Healing Brush in the Tools panel) is innovative yet simple. You select an area of the image that needs to be touched up, such as a blemish, tattoo, or logo you don't have permission to use (**Figure 11.1**), click in the middle of the selection, and drag it to an area of the image that has similar texture but without whatever you're trying to remove. As you move the mouse, Photoshop previews the source area (from which you're copying) in the destination area you initially selected

(**Figure 11.2**). When you release the mouse button, Photoshop "patches" the destination area with the source area (**Figure 11.3**), making sure that the brightness and color is consistent with the edge of the original selection, and blending the new texture with that edge. You simply have to try it to see how cool it is.

Figure 11.1 Original image. (©2008 Dan Ablan.)

Figure 11.2 Drag the selection to an area of clean texture.

Figure 11.3 The result of using the Patch tool.

You can even sample from an area that's radically different in brightness and color (**Figure 11.4**), because the Patch tool picks up only the texture from the area that it samples (**Figure 11.5**). The main thing you should look for is a source area that has the proper texture to match the destination area you're attempting to retouch.

Figure 11.4 You can drag the selection to an area that contains radically different colors and brightness. (©2008 Dan Ablan.)

Figure 11.5 Only the texture is copied.

You still need to be careful when making selections. Try for the smallest selection that will completely encompass the defect you're trying to retouch. The larger the area being patched, the less likely it will look good (**Figures 11.6** and **11.7**).

Figure 11.6 Patching a large selection makes the model's inner arm look artificial. (©2008 Dan Ablan.)

Figure 11.7 A small selection produces a nicer blend.

This tool doesn't have many options (**Figure 11.8**). The main choice is whether to patch the source or the destination. With the Patch option set to Source (which you'll probably use 95% of the time), Photoshop replaces the area that was originally selected with a combination of the brightness and color values from its edge, along with the texture from the source area to which you drag the selection (**Figures 11.9** and **11.10**). Using the Destination setting does the opposite, letting you pick from a clean area of the original and then dragging it over the area that needs to be patched—for example, cloning a birthmark (**Figures 11.11** and **11.12**).

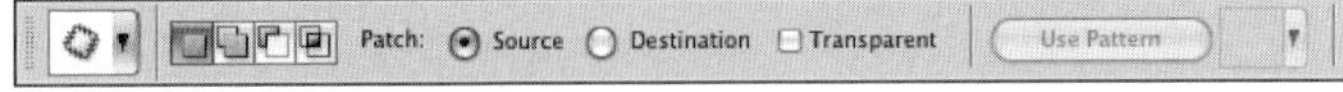

Figure 11.8 The options bar for the Patch tool.

Figure 11.9 Using the Source setting while dragging a birthmark from under the eye to an area of clean texture. (©2008 Dan Ablan.)

Figure 11.10 The clean texture is copied to the area under the eye and blended automatically.

Figure 11.11 Using the Destination setting while dragging a clean area of the skin to an area that needs retouching, or to replicate a birthmark.

If you can't find a clean area from which to steal texture, you can select a pattern by clicking the down arrow in the options bar (**Figure 11.13**) and then clicking the Use Pattern button. Patching with a pattern isn't very effective unless you've created a custom pattern for this specific purpose. Check out the bonus video "Type and Background Effects" at www.danablan.com/photoshop for details on how to create your own patterns.

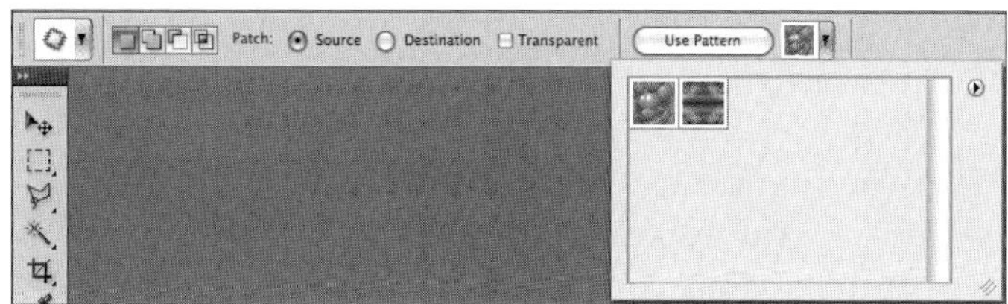

Figure 11.13 Choosing a texture.

Figure 11.12 The birthmark is blended into the surrounding image.

The Patch tool is best for situations where you're dealing with scratches, blemishes, or other defects in an area that should otherwise be relatively consistent in color (such as skin). Used on walls, floors, automobiles, and so on, it can even maintain some of the three-dimensionality of the surface with its blending capabilities (**Figures 11.14** and **11.15**). But it's not very useful for an area with multiple colors that shouldn't be blended. In that case, you should switch to the Clone Stamp tool.

Figure 11.14 The original image. (©Stockbyte, www.stockbyte.com.)

Figure 11.15 Three passes with the Patch tool covered this large area.

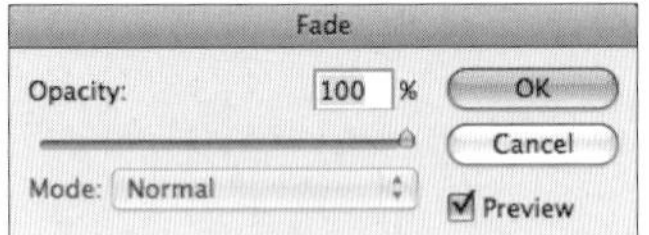

Figure 11.16 The Fade dialog.

An alternative to using the Fade command is to duplicate the original image layer before performing retouching, and then adjust the Opacity setting at the top of the Layers panel to blend the retouched layer with the underlying image.

Another alternative is to duplicate the background layer and apply the Patch tool on the duplicate. Then fade the opacity of the layer to reveal and blend the original layer to your liking.

If you use the Patch tool to remove all wrinkles and blemishes from someone's face, the person may no longer be recognizable. When you retouch facial features, choose Edit > Fade Patch Selection immediately after applying a patch (**Figure 11.16**). This feature allows you to change how the patch applies to the original image. Move the Opacity slider all the way to the left and then slowly move it toward the right until you reach the lowest Opacity setting that lessens the look of the undesirable feature without completely removing it (**Figures 11.17** to **11.19**). This technique is essential when working with shiny skin. If you use the Patch tool at full strength, you'll lose the dimensionality of the skin, but fading it back makes the area look less shiny, without completely evening out the lighting on the skin.

The Patch tool is most useful when working on large areas; it's just too cumbersome for retouching dozens of small blemishes. For that situation, switch to the Healing Brush, which can make those small retouching jobs a breeze.

Figure 11.17 The original image has shiny patches on the model's chin, chest, right shoulder, and under her right eye. (©2008 Dan Ablan.)

Figure 11.18 Using the Patch tool at full strength reduces the shine but removes some of the skin's dimensionality.

Figure 11.19 Result of fading each application of the Patch tool to about 40% opacity.

Healing Brush

The Healing Brush works using the same general concepts as the Patch tool. It attempts to patch a defect in the image by using the texture from another area and blending all the edges with the surrounding colors. The main difference between the two tools is that the Patch tool works by moving a selection, whereas the Healing Brush allows you to paint over the area that needs to be repaired.

To use the Healing Brush, Option/Alt-click the area you want to use (**Figure 11.20**), usually a part of the skin or surface that's free of blemishes, and then click and drag it onto the area that needs fixing (**Figure 11.21**). Be sure to cover the entire destination area without releasing the mouse button. Once you release the mouse button, Photoshop checks the edges of the destination area you covered to make sure that the "patch" blends with the color and brightness of the surrounding area (**Figure 11.22**).

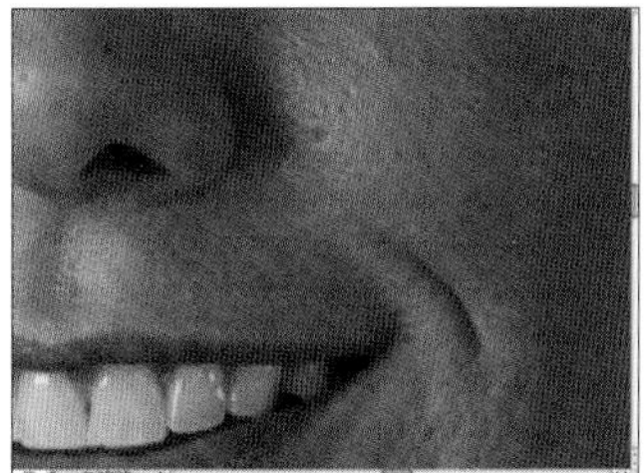

Figure 11.20 Option/Alt-click the source area to sample it. (©2008 Dan Ablan.)

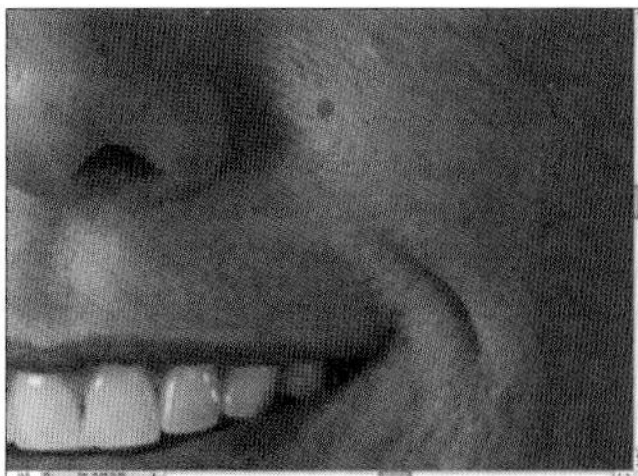

Figure 11.21 Paint across the destination area that needs to be retouched. Here we're covering some tiny dimpled areas on the model's skin to the right of her nose.

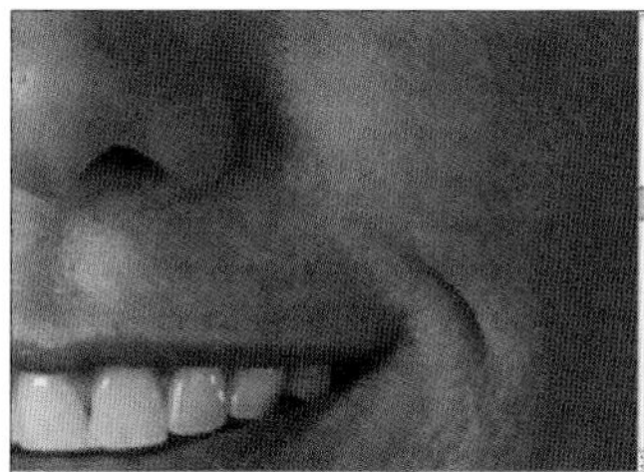

Figure 11.22 When you release the mouse button, Photoshop blends the retouched area into the surrounding image.

Choose a brush from the Brush drop-down menu in the options bar. The Healing Brush ignores the stand-alone Brushes panel because it doesn't use the advanced settings available in that panel.

If you need a really soft brush (0% hardness), use the Healing Brush with its blending mode set to Replace. That setting will make it act like the Clone Stamp tool, but it won't produce blurry results with soft-edged brushes.

You might need to use a soft-edged brush to get a good blend (**Figures 11.23** and **11.24**). A good starting point is to use a brush with a Hardness setting of 75%.

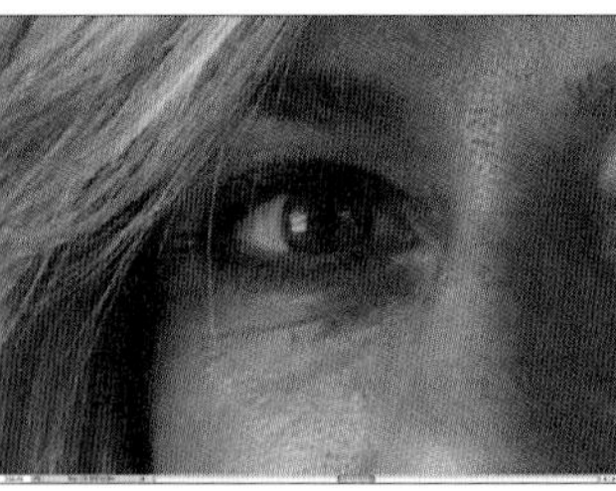

Figure 11.23 Result of using a hard-edged brush under the model's eye. (©2008 Dan Ablan.)

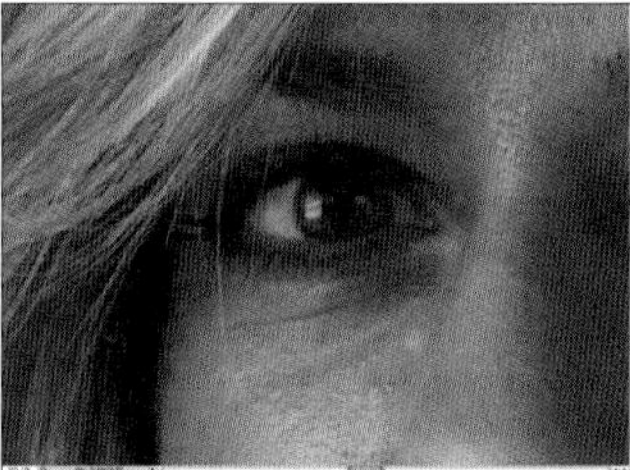

Figure 11.24 The difference is very subtle, but a soft-edged brush blends the results better with the surrounding image than the hard-edged brush does.

Layers

The Healing Brush works on one layer at a time, but you can choose to sample other layers. In the options bar for the Healing Brush, open the Sample drop-down menu and choose Current Layer, Current & Below, or All Layers (**Figure 11.25**). If you choose All Layers, Photoshop acts as if the document has no layers at all. In other words, it will be able to take from any layer below the cursor, as if all the layers were combined. However, it will apply the healing information only on the active layer.

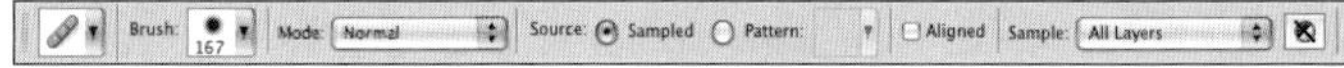

Figure 11.25 The options bar for the Healing Brush.

One handy option is to create a layer just for doing your retouching. Then you won't have to worry about making a mistake as you work, because the information you're retouching is sitting on its own layer, with the unretouched image directly below it (**Figures 11.26** to **11.28**). This technique allows you to switch over to the Eraser tool and erase small areas of that layer, or do other things such as lower the opacity of the layer.

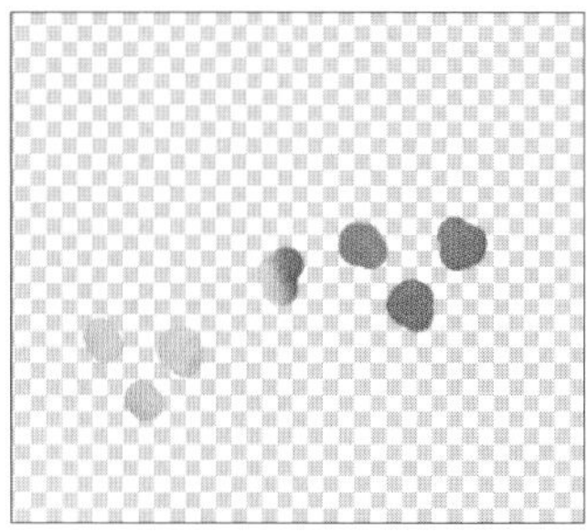

Figure 11.26 Retouch on a new layer to isolate your retouching from the underlying image.

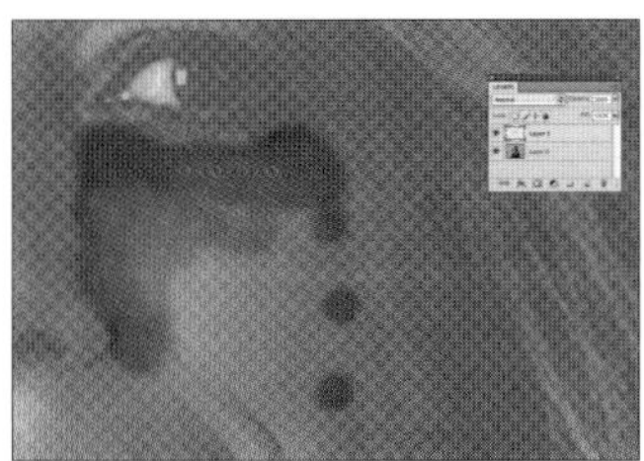

Figure 11.27 The underlying image is unaffected under the retouching layer. (©2008 Dan Ablan.)

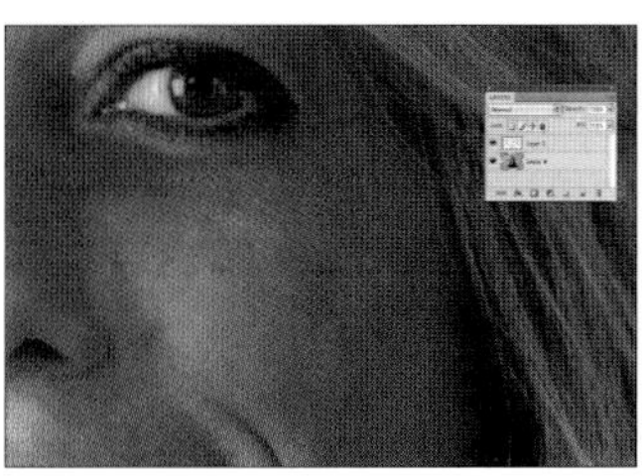

Figure 11.28 By retouching on an independent layer, you can sample from all layers, but also vary the opacity of each layer.

Blending Modes

A few blending modes, such as Multiply, are available in the options bar, but they work a little differently than usual. Most tools apply their general effect, and then, once everything is done, they apply the blending mode. But with the Healing Brush, the blending mode is applied before Photoshop does the work needed to blend the patched area with the surrounding image (**Figures 11.29** and **11.30**).

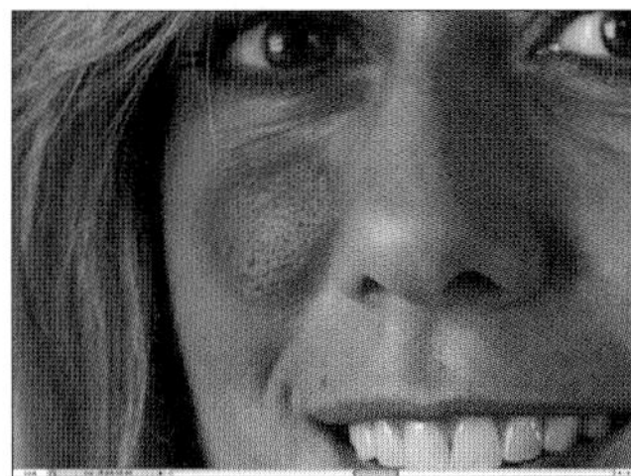

Figure 11.29 This is how Multiply mode would usually look for decreasing the hotspot on the model's cheek. (©2008 Dan Ablan.)

Figure 11.30 This is how Multiply mode looks when using the Healing Brush.

Spot Healing Brush

The Spot Healing Brush makes quick work of removing tiny defects in most images. It uses the same concepts as the Healing Brush and the Patch tool. The only difference is that it doesn't require you to choose an area of clean texture to copy. All you have to do is click and drag over a defect that needs to be removed; Photoshop analyzes the surrounding area and attempts to find appropriate texture to borrow. When you click and drag, the area that will be retouched is covered in black. When you release the mouse button, you'll see the results of the retouching (**Figures 11.31** and **11.32**). If the results don't look good, try dragging over the defect a second time, and Photoshop will pull from a different area.

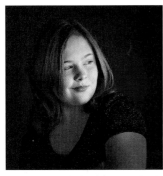

Figure 11.31 This image is scratched. (©2008 Dan Ablan.)

Figure 11.32 The scratch disappears seamlessly when painted over with the Spot Healing Brush.

If no clean areas of texture surround the defect you're attempting to retouch, try using the Create Texture setting in the options bar (**Figure 11.33**), which will cause Photoshop to create its own texture based on the surrounding image. This setting is especially useful on images that are scratched or that have a lot of detail in the surrounding area.

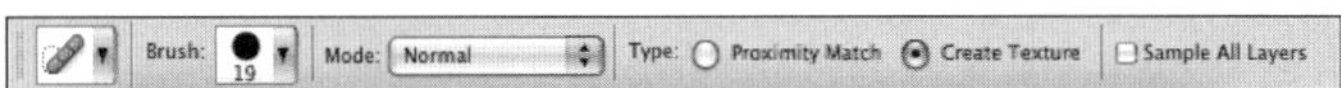

Figure 11.33 The Spot Healing Brush settings in the options bar.

Press the Home key (available on most extended keyboards) to get to the upper-left corner of the image. Then use Page Up and Page Down to move one full screen up or down (add Shift to move less than one full screen). Add Command/Ctrl to Page Up and Page Down to move one full screen to the right or left.

When you've reached the point where you think you're done working on an image, zoom in to 100% magnification (by double-clicking the Zoom tool) and look for any tiny defects in the image (such as dust, scratches, or pinholes), and fix them with the Spot Healing Brush.

The Patch tool, Healing Brush, and Spot Healing Brush are useful only when the area that needs to be retouched should match the color and brightness of the areas that surround it. When you run across an area that shouldn't blend into its surroundings, you'll have to switch over to the trusty standby—the Clone Stamp tool.

Clone Stamp

The Clone Stamp tool copies information from one area of the image and applies it somewhere else. Before using the Clone Stamp, however, there is one thing you should know: All retouching tools use the Brush Presets panel (**Figure 11.34**). The brush that you use with the Healing Brush isn't all that important because the tool will blend your retouching into the surrounding image, but the brush you choose for the Clone Stamp doesn't have those blending capabilities. You have to decide if you want what you're about to apply to fade into the image or to have a distinct edge. For most applications, it helps to have a soft edge on the brush so you can't see exactly where you've stopped retouching.

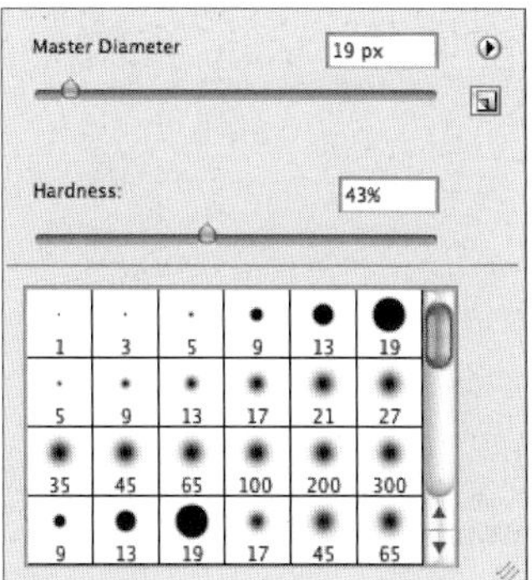

Figure 11.34 The brush determines how much your retouching work will blend into the underlying image.

The default soft-edged brushes are often too soft, which can cause the area you retouch to look blurry compared with the rest of the image. To prevent that from happening, hold down Shift and press the right bracket key (]) while keeping an eye on the brush preview in the options bar. Each time you press that key combination, you'll change the brush's hardness setting, in increments of 25%. The default brushes have a hardness of 100% for hard-edged brushes, 0% for soft ones; 25% and 50% are better for retouching with soft-edged brushes.

Cloning Around

After you've chosen a brush, hold down the Option/Alt key and click the area you want to copy. Then move to a different part of the image and click and drag the mouse (with no key held). Two cursors appear:

- The crosshair cursor shows the source of Photoshop's cloning (**Figure 11.35**).
- When you apply the Clone Stamp, a circle cursor shows exactly where it's being applied (**Figure 11.36**).

Figure 11.35 Option/Alt-click to define the spot from which you want to clone. (©iStockphoto.com/laartist.)

Figure 11.36 The Clone Stamp copies from under the crosshair and pastes into the circle.

When you move the mouse around, both of the cursors move in the same direction. As you drag, Photoshop is constantly copying from the crosshair and pasting into the circle.

Clone Aligned

The Clone Stamp operates in two different modes: Aligned and Non-aligned (it's just a simple check box in the options bar). In Aligned mode, when you apply the Clone Stamp, it doesn't matter if you let go of the mouse button and click again. Each time you let go and click again, the pieces that you're applying line up (**Figure 11.37**). It's as if you're putting together a puzzle: Once you have all of the pieces together, it looks like a complete image (**Figure 11.38**).

Unlike the Patch tool and the Healing Brush, the Clone Stamp forces you to take full control over how the retouched image matches the surrounding image. You have to think about how the brightness, color, and texture of the cloned area will affect the area you plan on retouching, as well as how the softness of the brush you choose will cause that information to blend into the surrounding image.

Figure 11.37 You can release the mouse button as many times as you want with the Aligned check box turned on, because the pieces of the cloned image line up like puzzle pieces.

Figure 11.38 Once you put all the pieces together, you'll end up with a complete image. (©iStockphoto.com/vasiliki.)

Clone Non-Aligned

If you turn off the Aligned check box, it's a different story. Apply the Clone Stamp and release the mouse button. The next time you click, the Clone Stamp resets itself, starting back at the original point from where it was cloning. For example, if you click in the middle of someone's nose, go up to the forehead, and click and drag, you'll plant a nose in the middle of the forehead. Then if you let go, move over a little bit, and click again, you'll add a second nose. But this will happen only if you have the Aligned check box turned off. For most retouching, leave Aligned turned on. That way, you don't have to be careful about letting go of the mouse button.

Opacity Settings

Sometimes you don't want to cover something—you just want to lessen its impact (**Figure 11.39**). For example, you might not want to wipe out a recognizable feature such as a birthmark, or it'll be obvious that the image was enhanced. Lowering the opacity on the Clone Stamp (**Figure 11.40**) allows you to paint over an area and partially replace it, so that the area you're applying blends with what used to be in that area.

You can press the number keys on your keyboard to change opacity. Pressing 1 gives you 10%, 2 is 20%, and so on. For 100%, just press 0 (zero).

Figure 11.39 You might want to play down some recognizable feature. (©Stockbyte, www.stockbyte.com.)

Figure 11.40 By lowering the opacity of the Clone Stamp, you can reduce the impact of undesirable features.

Straight Lines

Let's say you need to remove an image of a woman from a background containing a straight line (a wall, in **Figure 11.41**). The section of wall you use to replace the woman will have to line up perfectly with the sections of wall on either side of her head. In this kind of situation, move your cursor until it's touching the original line (edge of the wall, in this case). Option/Alt-click; then go to the area where you want the new piece of wall to appear and click where you think it would naturally line up with the other part of the wall. When you drag, the two cursors will line up just right, making the line look continuous and straight, as in **Figure 11.42**. You can even Shift-click in two spots, and Photoshop will trace a straight line with the Clone Stamp between those two areas. Other examples when this tool is useful: stairs, lampposts, or any object with straight lines that has been obstructed by another object.

Figure 11.41 On straight lines, Option/Alt-click when your cursor touches the line; then click in another area that also touches the line.

Figure 11.42 If the cursors align, the lines will remain nice and straight. (©Stockbyte, www.stockbyte.com.)

Patchwork

Sampling from one area and applying it all over the place will make it pretty obvious that you've cloned something, because shapes are repeated. To fix up the places that appear patterned, you could Option/Alt-click a random area around the place you've retouched, and then apply it on top of one of the patterned areas. But watch out—Photoshop's round brushes can be a dead giveaway, because you can easily pick out the areas that you're trying to disguise. This is a great time to use one of the odd-shaped brushes at the bottom of the Brushes panel (**Figure 11.43**). These brushes provide better cover for areas that look obviously cloned. Another trick is to apply some noise to the entire image, which will make any retouching blend right into the image. Choose Filter > Noise > Add Noise, use an amount somewhere around 3, set the Distribution to Uniform, and turn off the Monochromatic check box.

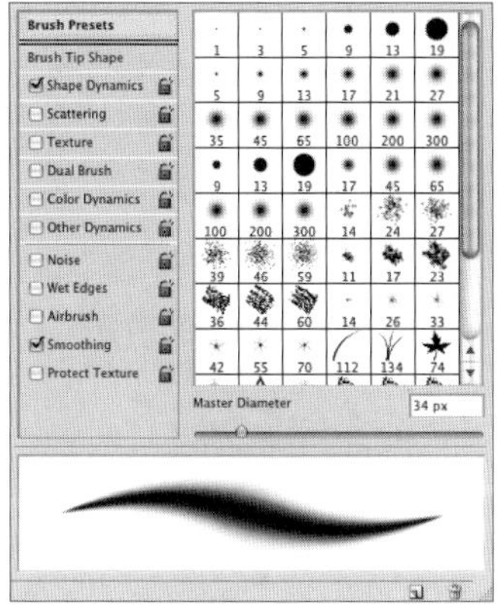

Figure 11.43 To eliminate repeated patterns, use the unusual brush shapes from the bottom of the Brushes panel.

Lighten/Darken

In most cases, the Healing Brush does an excellent job because it automatically blends into the surrounding image, but it does have one weakness: When you use it to retouch under-eye wrinkles, it sometimes tries to blend into the eyelashes, which causes the area under the eye to become too dark. When that's the case, you can use the Clone Stamp and sample the area directly below the wrinkles to clone over the wrinkles. But before you start retouching that area, experiment with the blending mode settings from the Mode selection on the options bar.

Chapter 9, "Enhancements and Masking," covers blending modes in detail. Here we're just looking at blending modes we need for the Clone Stamp.

The Lighten and Darken blending modes are both very useful when retouching. Suppose you have a light-colored scratch on an old print. You could clone from an area nearby that has the correct brightness. But before you apply the cloned material to the scratch, you might want to set the blending mode to Darken. In this mode, Photoshop can only darken the picture—never lighten it (**Figures 11.44** and **11.45**). When working with the wrinkles under eyes, try using the Lighten blending mode and lowering the Opacity setting of the Clone Stamp to around 40%.

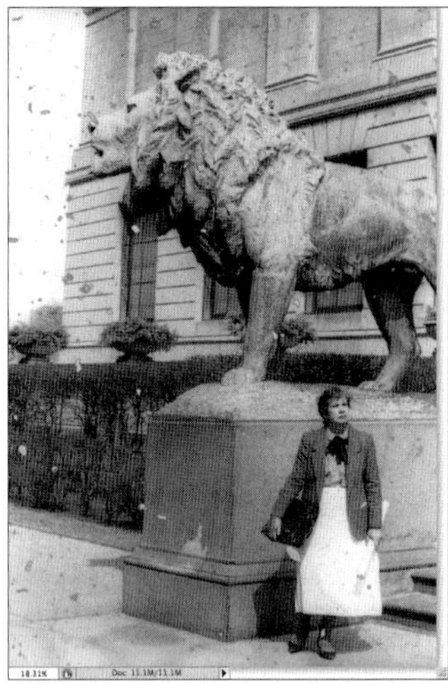

Figure 11.44 Original image with dust and scratches all over. (©2008 Dan Ablan.)

Figure 11.45 Light-colored scratches at the cement base of the lion statue are retouched by using the Clone Stamp set to Darken.

Automatic Sharpening

The automatic sharpening function in some scanners makes retouching more difficult (**Figures 11.46** and **11.47**). If possible, turn off any sharpening settings in your scanning software.

Figure 11.46 Unsharpened image.

Figure 11.47 Image sharpened during a scan.

Cloning Between Documents

With the Clone Stamp, you're not limited to cloning from the active document. You can open a second image and clone from that image as well (**Figure 11.48**). Make the second image (the cloning source) active, and then

Option/Alt-click it. Return to the first image to clone from the point you clicked in the second image.

Figure 11.48 The photo on the right was judged to be the better choice, but the girl on the right was missing. With the Clone Stamp, we can clone the girl from the photo on the left. (©2008 Dan Ablan.)

NOTES

When you're cloning between two documents, both documents must use the same color mode (RGB or CMYK).

Clone Source

A handy add-on for the Clone Stamp tool is the Clone Source panel, which sits in the panel dock (**Figure 11.49**). The Clone Source panel offers a number of useful options:

- The five buttons at the top of the panel let you store as many as five different source points, which makes it easy to switch from one source point to another during complex clone operations (such as removing a tree from in front of a building). This saves you the hassle of having to reset your clone source point repeatedly.
- Using the Source fields, you can adjust any source point numerically, making it easy to adjust a point that's off by just a pixel or two.
- The Rotate field to the immediate right of the Y field lets you rotate cloned pixels automatically. If you enter 45, for example, the resulting cloned strokes will be rotated 45 degrees.

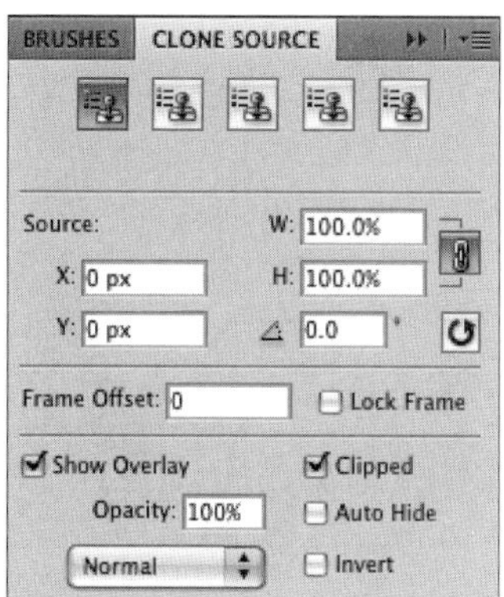

Figure 11.49 The Clone Source panel provides powerful cloning features.

- Above the Rotate field are width (W) and height (H) fields, which let you scale the source while cloning. If you unlock the lock box between those two fields, each axis will be scaled independently, allowing you to create a geometric distortion in the result.
- The Show Overlay check box provides a handy visual reference while cloning. When this box is turned on, a semi-opaque copy of the source will be superimposed over the image (how opaque it is depends on the Opacity value), giving you a preview of what your strokes will look like given the current offset (**Figure 11.50**). If you don't like the results, adjust the offset until the overlay shows the cloned results in the desired position.
- The Blending Mode pop-up menu and Invert check box provide options for improving the visibility of the overlaid source image.
- The Auto Hide option causes the overlay to disappear automatically when you start painting. When you release the mouse button, the overlay reappears.

The Opacity field controls the opacity of the overlaid image—not the opacity of your cloned strokes.

Figure 11.50 With Show Overlay turned on in the Clone Source panel, you can see exactly where the cloned image will appear. (©2008 Dan Ablan.)

Vanishing Point

All the retouching tools we've talked about until now have had one major shortcoming—they treat the world as flat! But many images contain objects that appear to change proportion as they recede from the camera. The solution is to use Photoshop's Vanishing Point filter (Filter > Vanishing Point), which creates different perspective planes in an image, thus allowing you to paint, retouch, scale, and distort in perspective.

While using Vanishing Point, you can press the X key at any time to zoom in on the image temporarily, which can help you to be more precise when defining a perspective plane or performing retouching.

The street in **Figure 11.51** has a consistent width but looks smaller in the distance due to the effects of perspective. If you were to use a standard paintbrush tool in Photoshop and paint an outline of the street, you'd end up with the shape shown in **Figure 11.52**. But with the Vanishing Point filter, you can establish the street's perspective and then paint on the image, getting quite a different result (**Figure 11.53**). Selections made in Vanishing Point will also conform to the perspective planes that make up the image (**Figures 11.54** and **11.55**).

Figure 11.51 Original image. (©2008 Dan Ablan.)

Figure 11.52 Standard perspective.

Figure 11.53 Vanishing Point perspective.

Figure 11.54 Standard Photoshop selection. (©2008 Dan Ablan.)

Figure 11.55 Selection made with the Vanishing Point filter.

Defining Planes

Before you can get all this magic to work properly, you have to educate Vanishing Point about the image by defining perspective planes. When you first open the filter (Filter > Vanishing Point), you'll be presented with a large dialog and a small tool panel. Choose the Create Plane tool (which looks like a tiny grid) and click the four corners of a flat surface in the image so Vanishing Point is aware of how the perspective affects that surface. If Vanishing Point is having trouble with the plane you're attempting to define, the lines will change color. If the grid turns red, Vanishing Point can't figure out how that shape could possibly be a flat surface as it relates to the perspective you're defining (**Figure 11.56**). If it turns yellow (**Figure 11.57**), you have a grid that could be used, but the results will be less than ideal. When the grid becomes blue (**Figure 11.58**), Vanishing Point is saying "all systems go," and you're ready to start painting or retouching the image. If you define a plane by clicking the four corners of a small object, you may need to extend the side handles so the grid covers the entire surface (or at least the area you plan to modify). If you plan to work with more than one surface in the image, you'll have to define each plane so Vanishing Point knows how those surfaces relate to each other (**Figure 11.59**).

Figure 11.56 A red outline is a sign of problems.

Figure 11.57 A yellow grid is usable, but not ideal.

Figure 11.58 A blue grid indicates that everything is okay.

Figure 11.59 Define planes for each surface you intend to modify. (©2008 Dan Ablan.)

Duplicating Areas

Once the planes are defined, you can use the other tools from Vanishing Point's tool panel. If you use the Marquee tool to make selections, you can hold down Option/Alt and drag within the selected area to move a duplicate of the selected area. As you move the selected area, Vanishing Point scales the image based on the perspective plane on which you drag (**Figures 11.60** and **11.61**). But since this chapter is all about retouching, let's check out what can be done with the main retouching tool in Vanishing Point—the Clone Stamp tool.

Figure 11.60 Sometimes moving areas produces unrealistic results.

Figure 11.61 Moving areas with the Vanishing Point filter looks more realistic.

Cloning in Perspective

Before Vanishing Point came along, Photoshop's Clone Stamp tool couldn't recognize distortions caused by perspective. Consequently, it created unacceptable results when used on an image that contained noticeable perspective distortions. The main problem is that the Clone Stamp tool is not capable of scaling the cloned area to make it match the perspective of the surface you're attempting to retouch.

Figure 11.62 This wall is distorted due to perspective. (©2007 iStockphoto.com/belterz.)

In **Figure 11.62**, the area being covered by the sign is primarily a row of larger bricks. In **Figure 11.63**, the row of large bricks ends up being patched with bricks that are much too small to look appropriate. The Clone Stamp tool in Vanishing Point can do a much better job. To start, use the Create Plane tool to click the two corners that make up the left edge of a brick; then click the two corners that make up the right edge of another brick in the same row, so Photoshop learns how the bricks are distorted by perspective (**Figure 11.64**). Then drag the size handles of the resulting grid to define the overall area that needs to be retouched (**Figure 11.65**). Once the plane has been defined, you can use the Clone Stamp tool to retouch areas, and its results will be scaled to conform to the perspective of the image (**Figure 11.66**).

Figure 11.63 Cloned areas are not scaled to the proper size and therefore don't match the surrounding image.

Figure 11.64 The initial plane lines up with a row of bricks.

Figure 11.65 Expanding the plane to cover the area that needs to be edited.

Figure 11.66 The results are scaled to be the appropriate size.

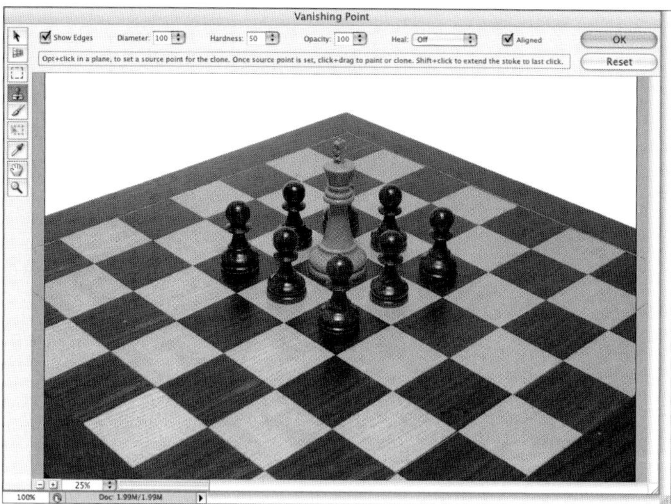

Figure 11.67 The Vanishing Point dialog with the Clone Stamp options visible. (©2007 iStockphoto.com/urbancow.)

The Vanishing Point Clone Stamp tool incorporates many of the options that are available in Photoshop's Healing Brush, along with a few that are unique to Vanishing Point (**Figure 11.67**). For retouching, the settings on the Heal pop-up menu have particular importance:

- **Off.** The Hardness setting of the brush is the only thing that causes retouching to blend into the surrounding image (**Figure 11.68**). Use this setting when the area being retouched is not similar to its surroundings.
- **Luminance.** Causes the Clone Stamp to copy both color and texture from the area that's being cloned; the brightness of the retouched area is based on the surrounding image (**Figure 11.69**). Use this setting when the surface being retouched is unevenly lit, since the Clone Stamp will match the brightness of the surrounding area.
- **On.** Causes the Clone Stamp to work like the Healing Brush, copying only texture from the cloned area and picking up the brightness and color from the area that surrounds the retouching (**Figure 11.70**). Use this setting when you want the area being retouched to have the same texture and color as the surrounding image.

Figure 11.68 Heal set to Off.

Figure 11.69 Heal set to Luminance.

Figure 11.70 Heal set to On.

The Spacing setting of your brush affects how much the image is changed when using the Dodge and Burn tools. Higher Spacing settings affect the image less.

Dodge and Burn Tools

The words *dodge* and *burn* are taken from a traditional photographic darkroom. In a darkroom, an enlarger projects an image onto a sheet of photographic paper. While the image is being projected, you could put something in the way of the light source, which would obstruct the light in such a way that it would hit certain areas less than others—a technique known as *dodging*. Or you could add light by cupping your hands together, creating just a small hole between them, and allowing the light to concentrate on a certain area more than others—a technique known as *burning*. Using a combination of these two methods, you can brighten or darken an image. Photoshop reproduces these techniques with two tools: Dodge (its icon looks like a lollipop, for dodging the light) and Burn (its icon looks like a hand with fingers cupped, for burning).

Dodge Tool

Because it can lighten the image, the Dodge tool is handy when working on photos of people with dark shadows under their eyes. An important setting for the Dodge tool is the Range menu in the options bar (**Figure 11.71**). The pop-up menu has three choices: Shadows, Midtones, and Highlights. This menu tells Photoshop which shades of gray to concentrate on when you paint across the image:

- **Shadows.** Changes the dark parts of the image. As you paint across the image, the brush brightens the areas it touches. As you get into the midtones, it applies less paint, and it doesn't change the light parts of the image much (if at all).
- **Midtones.** Affects the middle shades of gray—areas that are about 25% to 75% gray. It shouldn't change the shadows or highlights very much. They may change a little, but only so they can blend into the midtones.
- **Highlights.** Affects the lightest parts of the image, slowly blending into the midtones.

Figure 11.71 Dodge tool options bar.

With the wrong Range setting for the Dodge tool, you might cause yourself some grief. Let's say you're trying to fix dark areas around the model's eyes in **Figure 11.72**, but the Dodge tool doesn't seem to be doing the job. After dozens of tries, you finally realize that the Range pop-up menu is set to Highlights instead of Midtones (look at the eyes in **Figures 11.73** and **11.74**).

The Exposure setting on the options bar controls how much brighter the image will become. You can use the number keys on your keyboard to change this setting.

Figure 11.72 Original image. (©2008 Dan Ablan.)

Color Images

The Dodge tool works exceptionally well on grayscale images. All you have to do is choose the Range—Shadows, Midtones, or Highlights—and paint across an area. Unfortunately, the Dodge tool isn't as slick with color images. It tends to wash out some of the colors, and in some cases even change them (**Figures 11.75** and **11.76**).

Figure 11.73 Dodge tool set to Highlights is not working around the eye area.

One good solution is to duplicate the layer you're working on and set the blending mode of the duplicate to Luminosity before using the Dodge tool. That approach should maintain the original colors and limit your changes to the brightness of the image.

Figure 11.74 Dodge tool set to Midtones.

Figure 11.75 Original image. (©2008 Dan Ablan.)

Figure 11.76 Area lightened by using the Dodge tool.

Figure 11.77 Painting with a light shade of gray by using the Color Dodge mode.

Figure 11.78 Area lightened by painting with a medium shade of gray, using the Color Dodge blending mode.

Another option is to forgo the Dodge tool and just use the Paintbrush tool. You can set the Paintbrush tool's blending mode to Color Dodge and paint with a bright shade of gray. But just painting across an image is rather ridiculous, because all you're doing is blowing out the detail (**Figure 11.77**). To get the Color Dodge technique to work correctly, paint with a medium to light shade of gray (**Figure 11.78**), which allows you to create highlights or to brighten areas. Sometimes this technique works a little better than using the Dodge tool.

Figure 11.79 The original image. (©2008 Dan Ablan.)

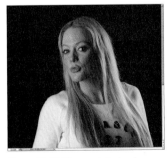

Figure 11.80 The model's cheeks, chin, and forehead are darkened with the Burn tool.

Burn Tool

The Burn tool is designed for darkening areas of an image. Like the Dodge tool, it has Range and Exposure options, and works great with grayscale images. If you're dealing with a shiny spot on someone's forehead or nose that reflects the light, you can try to fix the problem with the Burn tool (compare **Figures 11.79** and **11.80**).

Color Fixes

Like the Dodge tool, the Burn tool has trouble with color images (**Figures 11.81** and **11.82**). Try painting with a shade of gray (using the Paintbrush tool) and setting the blending mode to Color Burn, which darkens the image, making the colors more vivid while leaving the highlights largely untouched (**Figure 11.83**).

Figure 11.81 Original image. (©2008 Dan Ablan.)

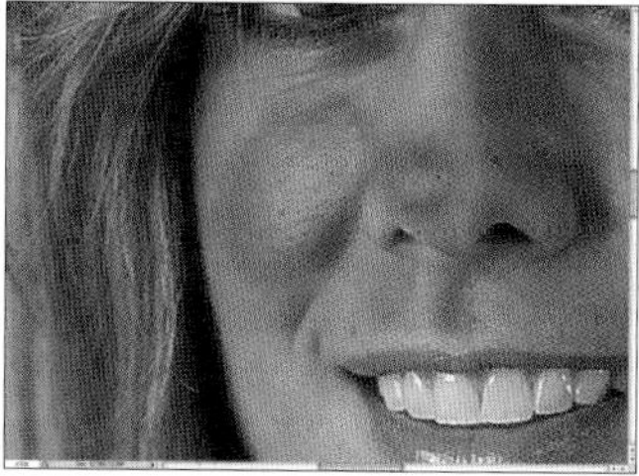

Figure 11.82 Image darkened using the Burn tool.

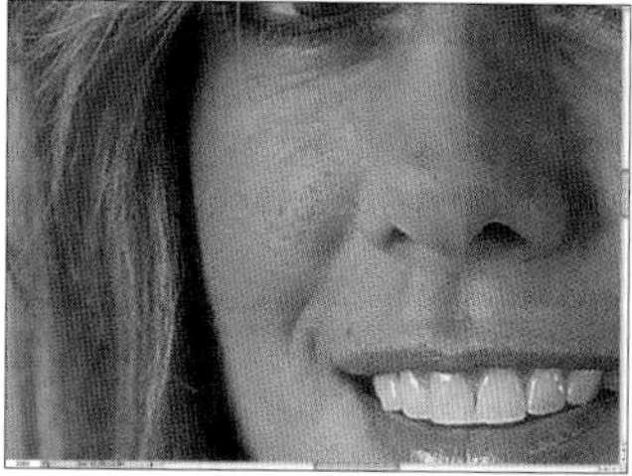

Figure 11.83 Image darkened by painting with a shade of gray in Color Burn mode.

Another technique: Option/Alt-click the New Layer icon at the bottom of the Layers panel. In the New Layer dialog, change the Mode setting from Normal to Overlay, turn on the Fill with Overlay-Neutral Color check box, and then click OK (**Figure 11.84**). With the new layer active, use the Dodge and Burn tools with the Range setting in the options bar set to Midtones (**Figures 11.85** and **11.86**). This technique allows you to dodge and burn on a separate layer, with fewer color problems.

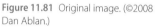

Figure 11.84 Creating a new layer in Overlay mode.

Figure 11.85 Original image. (©2008 Dan Ablan.)

Figure 11.86 Dodge and Burn used on a layer set to Overlay mode.

As you dodge and burn, especially when working on skin tones, turning on the Protect Tones check box in the options bar (new in Photoshop CS4) can help prevent haloing and washed-out colors.

Hold down Option/Alt to switch temporarily between the Dodge and Burn tools, so you don't have to go back to the Tools panel each time you want to switch from brightening to darkening the photo.

Figure 11.87 Background and foreground have been desaturated using the Sponge tool. (©2008 Dan Ablan.)

Sponge Tool

Hiding in with the Dodge and Burn tools is the Sponge tool, which works as if you have a sponge full of bleach, allowing you to paint across an image and soak up the color. Or you can do the opposite and intensify the colors—it's all determined by the Mode menu setting in the options bar.

If you choose Desaturate, the Sponge tool tones down the colors in the area you're painting. The more you paint across an area, the closer it becomes to being grayscale. This technique can be useful when you'd like to make a product stand out from an otherwise distracting background (**Figure 11.87**). With a very low Strength setting, it brightens yellowing teeth.

The Saturate setting intensifies colors as you paint over them, which is great for giving people rosy cheeks, making them stand out from a background (**Figure 11.88**), or adding a bit more color to their lips. The Sponge tool is a subtle, yet very effective tool that often is overlooked, but is exceedingly powerful for photo touchup work.

TIP

In Photoshop CS4, the Sponge tool's options bar includes a Vibrance check box that you can use to prevent oversaturation of colors that are already saturated, while boosting less-saturated colors.

Figure 11.88 The photographer was enhanced using the Sponge tool set to Saturate, and the area on the left was retouched with the Sponge tool set to Desaturate. (©2008 Dan Ablan.)

Blurring and Sharpening

When you need to blur or sharpen an area, you have two choices: Select an area and apply a filter, or use the Blur and Sharpen tools. Using filters to blur and sharpen offers a few advantages over using the tools, including getting a preview of the image before you commit to the settings, and having the ability to apply the filter effect evenly to the area you're changing. But occasionally the Blur and Sharpen tools can really help when working on small areas, so let's take a look at how they work and when to use them.

Figure 11.89 Original image. (©2008 Dan Ablan.)

Blur Tool

The Blur tool is pretty straightforward, blurring everything that the cursor passes over as you paint across the image. In the options bar, the Strength setting determines how much the Blur tool blurs the image; higher settings blur the image more. This option can be useful if itty-bitty areas of detail obstruct the image. You might prefer to use the Gaussian Blur filter instead of the Blur tool, however, because Gaussian Blur does a better job of blurring an area evenly.

Figure 11.90 Wrinkles in the forehead have been blurred using the Blur tool.

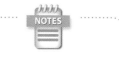

The Blur tool is good for reducing—not removing—wrinkles. If you turn the Strength setting way up and paint across a wrinkle a few times, it begins to disappear, but the result may not look very realistic (**Figures 11.89** and **11.90**). It might look as if you had smeared some Vaseline on the face. To really do a wrinkle justice, you have to take a closer look. Wrinkles are made out of two parts: a highlight and a shadow (light part and dark part). If you paint across that with the Blur tool, the darker part of the wrinkle will be lightened and the lightest part will be darkened, so that they become more similar in shade.

Don't go over the image with the Blur tool set to Lighten and then switch over to Darken and go over it again. That would be the same as leaving it set to Normal, and you would be back to Vaseline face. So use it just once, set to either Lighten or Darken. Think about what's most prominent in the wrinkle—the light area, or the dark area? That will indicate which setting you should use.

To reduce the impact of a wrinkle without completely getting rid of it (if you wanted to get rid of it, you could use the Healing Brush tool), turn the Strength setting all the way up and change the blending mode to either Darken or Lighten. If the dark area makes the wrinkle most prominent, set the blending mode to Lighten; you might also need to lower the Strength setting of the Blur tool. Then, when you paint across the area, the Blur tool will lighten that wrinkle. Remember that the Blur tool won't make the wrinkle disappear—just reduce its impact.

Consider creating a brand-new, empty layer and sampling layers with the Blur tool. With this technique, Photoshop can copy the information from the underlying layers, blur it, and then paste it onto the layer you just created, leaving the underlying layers untouched. You can easily delete areas or redo them without having to worry about permanently changing the original image.

Lens Blur Filter

To make a large area of an image blurry, try the Lens Blur filter. Unlike the standard blur filters (Blur, Blur More, and Gaussian Blur), which blur the entire image the same amount, the Lens Blur filter varies the amount of blurring, based on the contents of a grayscale image (**Figures 11.91** to **11.93**), which you can create by using the Paintbrush tool. You can specify which shade of gray represents an area that you want to keep in focus. Photoshop then makes all the other areas of the image progressively out of focus, based on how different the surrounding shades of gray are compared to the one you specified as the in-focus shade.

Figure 11.91 Original image. (©2008 Dan Ablan.)

Figure 11.92 Grayscale image used for blurring.

Figure 11.93 Result of applying the Lens Blur filter using the grayscale image shown in Figure 11.92.

The concept is easier to understand when you see this filter in action. Create a new empty layer on top of the image you want to blur. Press D to reset the foreground color to black, and then use the Paintbrush tool to paint across the areas you want to keep in focus (**Figure 11.94**). The softness of the brush determines how quickly the focus falls off, so use a really soft-edged brush if you want a smooth transition from the in-focus areas to the ones that should be blurred. To create a much softer edge, choose Filter > Blur > Gaussian Blur after you paint (**Figure 11.95**). When you're done painting, choose Edit > Fill, set the Use pop-up menu to White, set the Mode pop-up menu to Behind, and click OK (**Figure 11.96**). Photoshop fills the empty areas of the active layer with white.

Figure 11.94 Paint with black on a new layer to define the areas that should remain in focus. (©2008 Dan Ablan.)

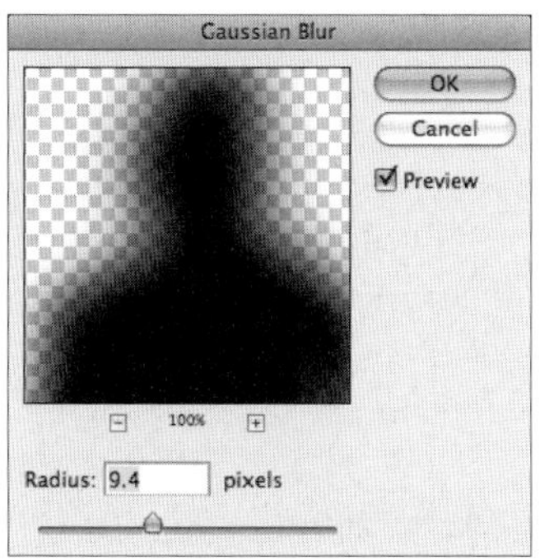

Figure 11.95 The Gaussian Blur filter

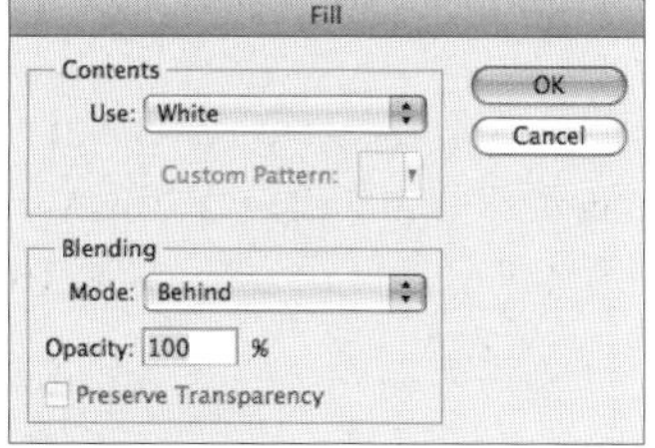

Figure 11.96 Use the Fill dialog to fill the empty parts of the layer with white.

Now we need to get the contents of the active layer to show up in an alpha channel. Open the Channels panel (Window > Channels), Command/Ctrl-click the top channel (it will be called Gray, RGB, or CMYK, depending on which mode the image uses) to get a selection, and then click the second icon from the left at the bottom of the Channels panel to generate the alpha. If necessary, click the eyeball icon to make this layer visible. To get back to working on the original image, click back to the Layers panel or choose Window > Layers, drag the layer you painted onto the trash icon, choose Select > Deselect, click the layer you want to blur, and then choose Filter > Blur > Lens Blur.

When the Lens Blur dialog appears (**Figure 11.97**), turn on the Preview check box and choose Faster for the Preview method. (The More Accurate setting is just too darn slow.) In the Source pop-up menu, choose the name of the alpha channel you created (Alpha 1, unless you renamed it). Move your mouse over the preview image and click the area you wanted to keep in focus. Clicking the image sets the Blur Focal Distance setting, specifying which shade of gray in the alpha channel will be used to represent an area that should be in focus (0 = black). If you'd rather have that area become blurry, turn on the Invert check box. To compare the blurred version of the image to the original, toggle the Preview check box off and on.

Now that you have the filter set up, it's time to figure out how you want the blurry areas of the image to look. The Radius slider determines just how blurry areas should become. When you purposefully throw an area out of focus using a camera (by using a low-aperture setting), you'll often see the shape of the aperture in the highlights of the image (**Figure 11.98**). The Shape, Blade Curvature, and Rotation settings attempt to simulate the shape of an aperture in the brightest areas of the image.

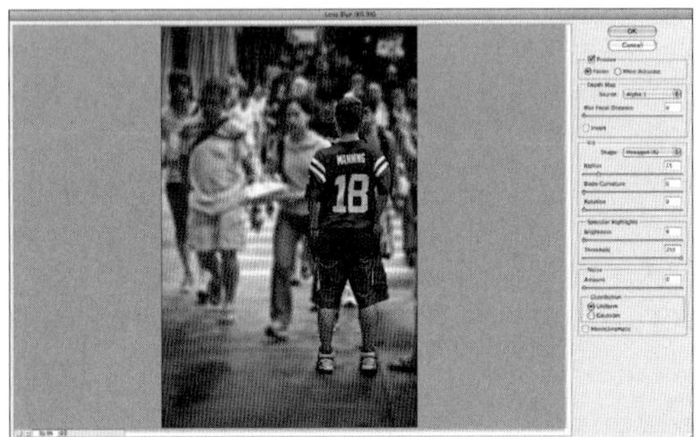

Figure 11.97 The Lens Blur dialog. (©2008 Dan Ablan.)

Figure 11.98 The shape of the camera aperture often shows up in the brightest areas of the image.

When you blur an image, the brightest areas of the image often start to look a bit dull (**Figures 11.99** and **11.100**). That happens because blurring blends those bright areas into their surroundings, which makes them become darker. To compensate, increase the Brightness setting until the highlights in the image become bright again

(**Figure 11.101**). The Threshold setting determines which shades will be brightened. Moving the slider left causes Photoshop to brighten more shades, whereas moving it right brightens only the brightest shades in the image.

Figure 11.99 Original image.

Figure 11.100 The highlights look dull after blurring the image.

Figure 11.101 Adjusting the Brightness setting brings back the brightness in the highlights.

Blurring an image usually removes any grain or noise that was in the image (**Figure 11.102**). Because the Lens Blur filter doesn't blur the entire image, you might end up with a lot of grain in the in-focus areas of the image and no grain in the blurred areas. That will make the image look very unnatural, because the original image contained consistent grain across the entire image. To add grain into the blurred areas, experiment with the Noise setting at the bottom of the Lens Blur dialog. Move the Amount slider right until the blurry areas have as much grain as the in-focus areas (**Figure 11.103**); then switch between the Uniform and Gaussian options until you determine which one delivers the best match to the grain of the original photo. Turn on the Monochromatic check box if the blurred areas look too colorful when compared to areas that haven't been blurred.

Figure 11.102 All the grain was removed when the left side of this image was blurred.

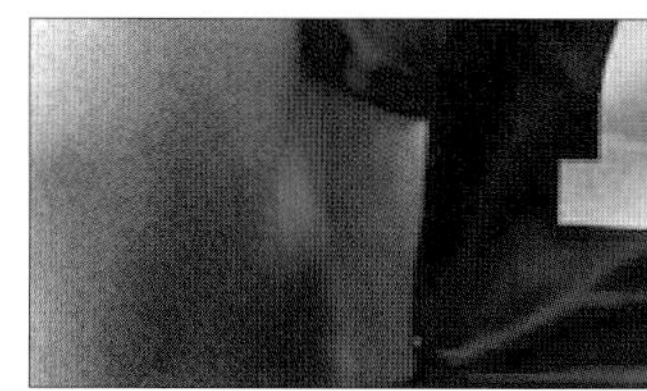

Figure 11.103 Adjusting the Noise settings added grain back into the blurred area.

Sharpen Tool

The Sharpen tool works in a fashion similar to that of its relative, the Sharpen filter. But with this tool you have to adjust the Strength setting in the options bar to determine how much to sharpen the image. Be careful, though; if you turn the Strength setting up too high or paint across an area too many times, you'll get some really weird effects (**Figures 11.104** to **11.106**).

Figure 11.104 Original image. (©2008 Dan Ablan.)

Figure 11.105 Sharpened using the Sharpen tool with a medium Strength setting.

Figure 11.106 Sharpened using the Sharpen tool with a high Strength setting.

Sharpening Reflections

When an image contains glass, metal, or other shiny objects, it usually contains extremely bright highlights (known as *specular* highlights). This usually happens when light reflects directly off one of those very shiny areas, such as the edge of a drinking glass. These extra-bright highlights often look rather flat and lifeless after being adjusted (**Figure 11.107**). This happens because whenever we adjust an image to perform color correction, or prepare it for printing or multimedia, the brightest areas of the image usually become 3% or 4% gray (instead of white). But if you sharpen those areas, you're going to brighten them and make them pure white. This will make them stand out and look more realistic. So any time you have something shiny, such as buildings, jewelry, glassware, or reflected light in people's eyes, use the Sharpen tool, bring down the Strength to about 30%, and go over those areas. That will make them almost pure white; when you print them, they'll almost jump off the page (**Figures 11.108** and **11.109**).

Figure 11.107 Metallic highlights often look a bit dull after performing color correction. (©2008 Dan Ablan.)

Figure 11.108 The areas covered in red were sharpened to make them pop.

Figure 11.109 Metallic highlights sharpened.

The Blur and Sharpen tools make subtle changes. When you want a bit more radical change, try using the Blur and Sharpen filters instead. The Lens Blur filter gives you the most control over blurring an image, but at the same time it's usually the slowest method for blurring.

Now let's get away from traditional retouching techniques and see how we can correct distorted images.

Lens Correction Filter

The Lens Correction filter (Filter > Distort) is designed to correct for distortion that's caused by the camera lens itself, or by the angle of the lens relative to the subject of the photo. Let's start off with a quick tour and then get busy fixing some images. Since this filter is often used on subjects that contain a lot of vertical and horizontal lines (such as buildings), a grid is provided to help you see when you've removed all the distortion from an image (**Figure 11.110**). You can toggle the grid on and off with the Show Grid check box, control the amount of space between grid lines with the Size setting, and reposition the grid by using the Move Grid tool (which looks like a hand on top of a grid).

You can zoom in and scroll around the image by using the Zoom and Hand tools in the Lens Correction dialog, but you might prefer to use the standard keyboard shortcuts of holding down Command/Ctrl and pressing the plus or minus keys, and using the spacebar to access the Hand tool temporarily.

Figure 11.110 The Lens Correction dialog. (©2008 Dan Ablan.)

After you've experimented with some of the Lens Correction sliders, toggle the Preview check box to see what the image looks like before and after the correction has been applied. Now that you know your way around the dialog, let's see what all those sliders can accomplish.

Remove Distortion

The Remove Distortion slider is designed to correct for barrel or pincushion distortion. That's when the image ends up bent out away from the center or bent in toward the center. You'll see this effect sometimes with very wide angle lenses and subjects shot close up, which causes vertical lines to become curved. Move the Remove Distortion slider, or drag on the image with the Remove Distortion tool (at upper left in the dialog). The grid is quite useful when adjusting this slider, since it's often hard to tell if something is perfectly straight.

Chromatic Aberration

The Chromatic Aberration sliders are designed to get rid of color fringing that often appears on the edge of high-contrast objects (**Figures 11.111** and **11.112**). This fringing is caused by light being bent as it passes through the elements that make up a camera lens, which causes the light to bend and separate much like white light turns into a rainbow of color when sent through a prism. You won't see this fringing on every image, and you'll only be able to notice it when you zoom in to 100% view.

Figure 11.111 Original image. (©2008 Dan Ablan.)

Figure 11.112 Result of correcting for chromatic aberration.

Vignette

Moving the Vignette Amount slider toward the right causes the corners of the image to become brighter, whereas moving it left darkens the corners. The Midpoint slider determines how far this brightness change intrudes toward the middle of the document. Darkened corners visually direct the viewer's attention toward the middle of the image (**Figures 11.113** and **11.114**).

You might see vignetting when shooting a Nikon digital system with lenses that are not rated for the camera at hand, such as an FX lens on a DX body.

Figure 11.113 Original image. (©2008 Dan Ablan.)

Figure 11.114 Darkening the corners with vignetting.

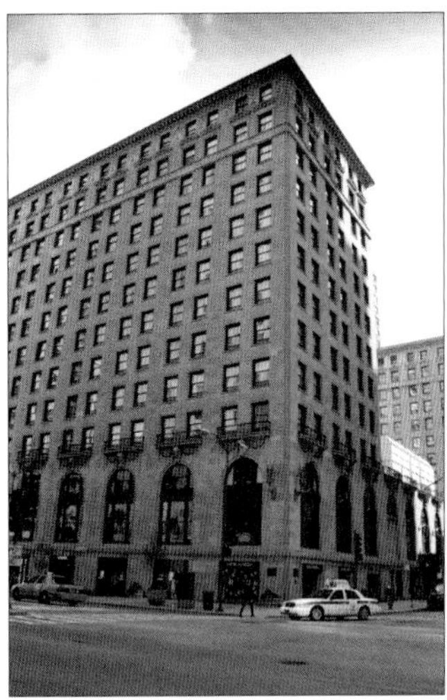

Figure 11.115 Original image. (©2008 Dan Ablan.)

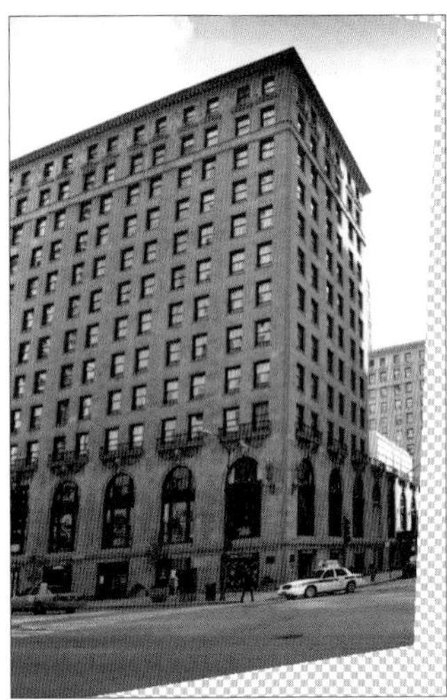

Figure 11.116 Result of adjusting vertical perspective.

Transform

The Angle setting in the Transform section of the Lens Correction dialog simply rotates the image, which can be useful if the horizon line isn't level. Click the tool and then drag across an area in the image that should be horizontal or vertical. Photoshop calculates the proper rotation setting needed to straighten the area.

The Vertical Perspective and Horizontal Perspective sliders make converging horizontal or vertical lines parallel (**Figures 11.115** and **11.116**). This is useful when you take a shot of a building by pointing your camera upward toward the top of the building, which usually causes the top of the building to appear smaller than the bottom in the resulting photograph.

The Edge setting determines what should be placed in any transparent areas of the image that are caused by the distortion correction you've applied. Leave the setting set to Transparency if you prefer to work on the transparent areas yourself.

Now that you have an idea of how to fix distorted images, let's shift gears and start applying creative distortions.

Liquify Filter

The Liquify filter allows you to pull and push on an image as if it were printed on Silly Putty. The results you get out of this filter will either be obvious (looking like a reflection in a funhouse mirror) or not noticeable to the untrained eye. It all depends on your intentions. When you choose Filter > Liquify, you'll see a dialog that dominates your screen (**Figure 11.117**). Later you can play with the more extreme uses of the Liquify tools and conjure up special effects to your heart's content, but for now let's use a more real-world approach. The incremental changes will be subtle, so pay close attention to the captions for each figure.

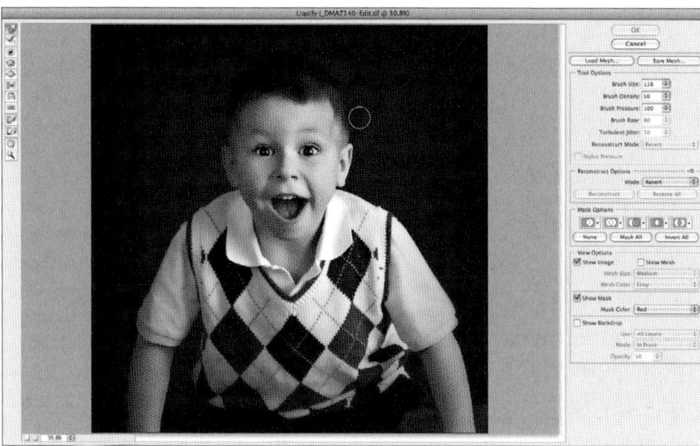

Figure 11.117 The Liquify dialog. (©2008 Dan Ablan.)

First let's consider the tools in the Liquify dialog's toolbar at upper left. The first tool is called Forward Warp. Click Forward Warp and paint on the image to push it in the direction you're dragging (**Figure 11.118**). If the results go a little too far, grab the Reconstruct tool (the next tool down) and paint across the area that you want to take back to normal (**Figure 11.119**). The more you paint across an area, the closer it becomes to the original (before you applied the Liquify command).

NOTES

The Liquify settings vary based on the image you're using and the amount of precision required to complete each task. The settings suggested here are a good starting point.

Figure 11.118 Forward Warp gives this child some cool ears. (©2008 Dan Ablan.)

Figure 11.119 Reconstruct decreases the Spock effect.

The Twirl Clockwise tool slowly rotates the area inside the cursor clockwise; hold down Option/Alt to rotate counterclockwise (**Figure 11.120**). The Pucker tool allows you to pull the image in toward the center of your brush (**Figure 11.121**), and the Bloat tool does the opposite (**Figure 11.122**).

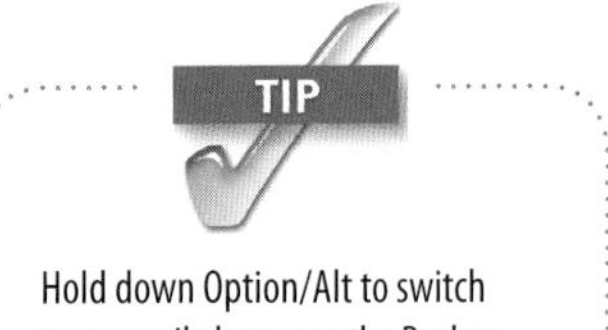

Hold down Option/Alt to switch temporarily between the Pucker and Bloat tools.

The Push Left tool acts as though the line you draw is a bulldozer, and pushes the image away from it on the left side (**Figure 11.123**). Press Option/Alt to move the image on the right side instead. The Mirror tool flips a portion of the image horizontally or vertically, depending on the direction you drag. If you drag downward, you'll reflect the area to the left of the cursor. Drag up to reflect the area to the right (**Figure 11.124**). Drag right to reflect the area below the cursor, and drag left to reflect the area above.

The Turbulence tool allows you to push and pull on the image, much like the Warp tool, but adds more of a wavy look, which can be useful when you're attempting to create water ripples and smoke (**Figure 11.125**).

Figure 11.120 Twirl tool used on the boy's hair.

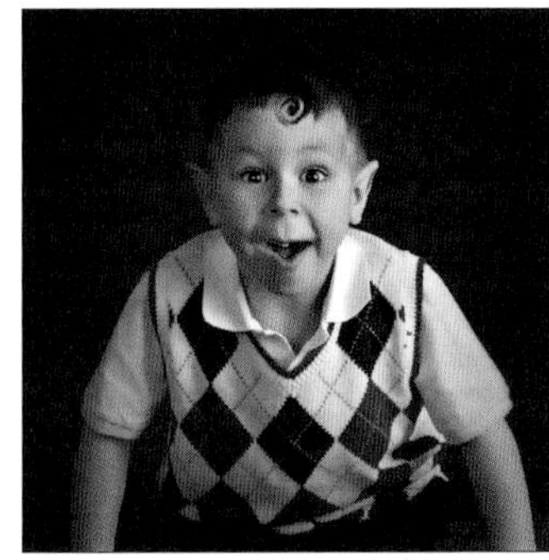

Figure 11.121 Pucker tool purses the boy's mouth.

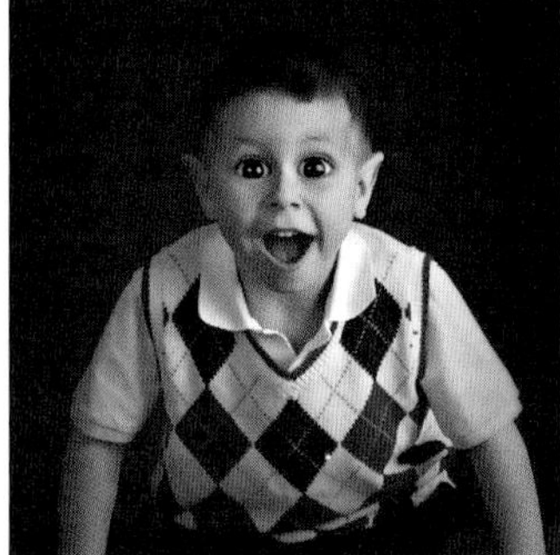

Figure 11.122 Bloat tool at work on the eyes.

Figure 11.123 Push Left tool used on the child's mouth.

Figure 11.124 Mirror tool used on his mouth.

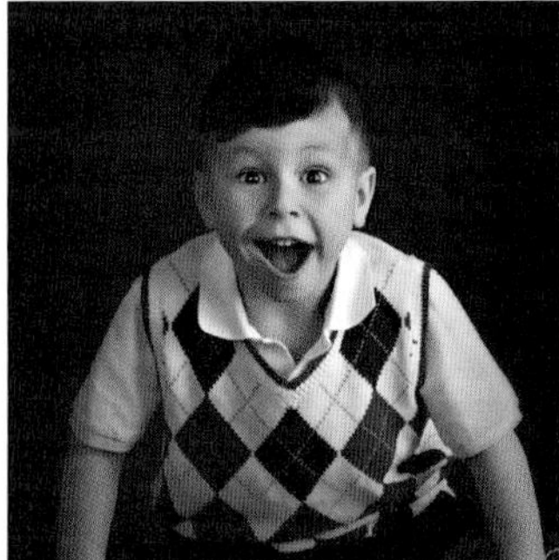

Figure 11.125 Turbulence tool used on his hair.

Now that you have an idea of what each tool does, let's explore the options at upper right in the Liquify dialog:

- **Brush Size:** There is no Brushes panel available to change the size of your brush in the Liquify dialog. The size of the brush is determined by the number entered in the Brush Size field at upper right in the dialog. You can use the bracket keys (] [) to change this setting in small increments, or press Shift with them to change the size in larger increments.
- **Brush Density:** This setting determines how thick the center of the brush is before it starts to fade out and affect the image less. Imagine that you're warping the image with your finger. You could think of this setting as how pointy your finger is when you're using it to warp the image (**Figures 11.126** to **11.128**). Low settings cause a radical change in a small area and then fade out to the edge of the brush, whereas higher settings spread the radical change into a wider area before it fades out to the edge of the brush.

Figure 11.126 Original image. (©2008 Dan Ablan.)

Figure 11.127 Image warped using a low Brush Density setting.

Figure 11.128 Image warped using a high Brush Density setting.

- **Brush Pressure:** For all of these tools, the Brush Pressure setting determines how radical a change you'll make when you paint across the image. Think of the Brush Pressure setting as determining how hard you're pushing with your finger. The harder you push, the more of the image you'll move with each paint stroke (**Figures 11.129** to **11.131**). If you have a pressure-sensitive graphics tablet, turn on the Stylus Pressure check box to make Photoshop pay attention to how much pressure you're using with the pen. With this option turned on, the Brush Pressure setting is determined by how hard you press down on the graphics tablet.

Figure 11.129 Original image. (©2008 Dan Ablan.)

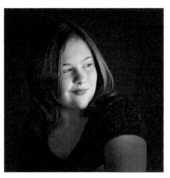

Figure 11.130 Warped using a medium Brush Pressure setting.

Figure 11.131 Warped using a high Brush Pressure setting.

- **Brush Rate:** This setting is available only with the Reconstruct, Twirl, Pucker, Bloat, and Turbulence tools. It determines how much of a change you'll make when the mouse is held stationary with the mouse button held down. The higher the setting, the more quickly the image will change when you pause the mouse on top of an area (**Figures 11.132** to **11.134**). This setting has no effect on what happens when the mouse is in motion.

Figure 11.132 Original image. (©2008 Dan Ablan.)

Figure 11.133 Bloated for three seconds using a low Brush Rate setting.

Figure 11.134 Bloated for three seconds using a high Brush Rate setting.

Figure 11.135 Turbulence tool applied to the baby's hair, with a low Turbulent Jitter setting. (©2008 Dan Ablan.)

Figure 11.136 High Turbulent Jitter setting.

Figure 11.137 When creating an image like this one, experiment with the reconstruction modes.

- **Turbulent Jitter:** This setting determines how smooth a result you'll get with the Turbulence tool (it doesn't affect the other tools). Low settings produce a smoother distortion; higher settings produce a more random distortion (**Figures 11.135** and **11.136**).
- **Reconstruct Mode:** This pop-up menu determines how the Reconstruct tool attempts to bring the image back to its original state. You'll get radically different results depending on which setting you choose. The vast majority of the time you'll use the Revert setting; in most cases, you'll only change this setting when you want a creative image (**Figure 11.137**).

You can mask an area to prevent it from changing. The Freeze Mask tool (located under the distortion tools on the left side of the dialog) applies a red overlay on the image to indicate which areas have been masked (**Figure 11.138**). The Freeze Mask tool also uses the Brush Density and Brush Pressure settings, which means that you can partially mask an area to make it change less than the unmasked areas. (For example, 50% masked areas will change half as much as unmasked areas when you paint over them.) Areas that are partially masked appear with a more transparent

Figure 11.138 The red overlay indicates an area that has been masked. (©2008 Dan Ablan.)

red overlay. If you'd rather not see the overlay, turn off the Show Mask check box. To unmask an area, use the Thaw Mask tool to remove some of the red overlay, or click None in the Mask Options area to unmask the entire image. The Freeze Mask and Thaw Mask options are great when used with the Show Backdrop setting, which allows you to see through the transparent areas of a layer to the underlying layers. This way, you can see exactly how the image lines up with the rest of the document (**Figure 11.139**).

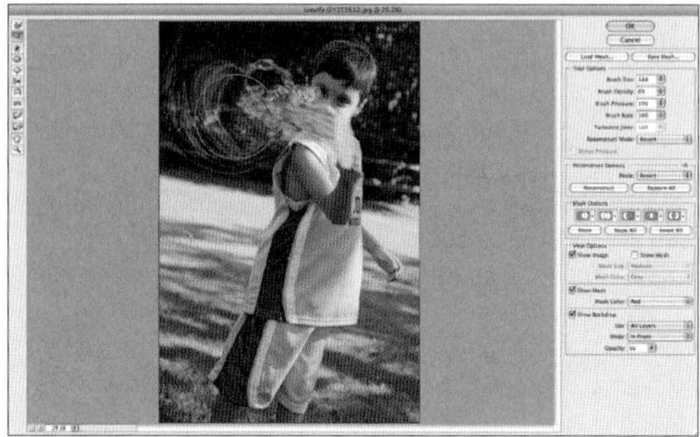

Figure 11.139 Using the Show Backdrop options, you can see the original image beneath your Liquify changes. (©2008 Dan Ablan.)

After you play around in this dialog, it may be difficult to determine the exact areas that have changed in the image. To see a different view of the changes you've made, select the Show Mesh check box (**Figure 11.140**). You might also want to turn off the Show Image check box so you can get a clear view of the mesh (**Figure 11.141**). You can control the size and color of the mesh, which can help make the changes more noticeable when viewed at the same time as the image. You can still use all the Liquify tools while the mesh is visible.

Figure 11.140 An image with the mesh visible. (©2008 Dan Ablan.)

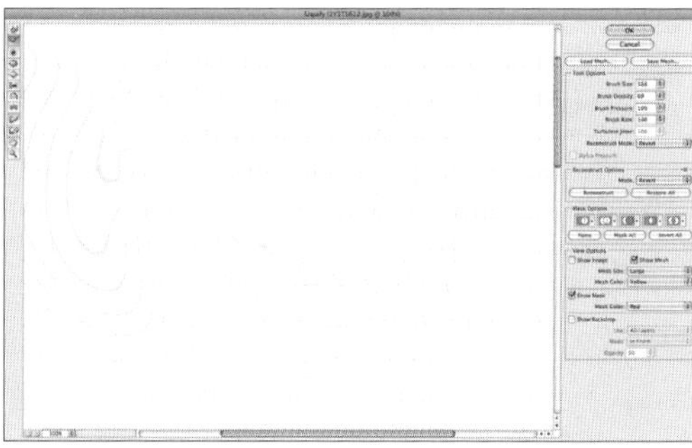

Figure 11.141 Viewing the mesh with the image hidden.

Real-World Retouching with Liquify

Let's explore how you might use the Liquify tools when retouching an image. When you're trying each of these techniques, be extra careful not to go too far with your distortions; otherwise, the changes will become obvious. The idea is to change the image so that it looks better than the original, without changing it so much that anyone would notice the tampering.

Retouching Eyes

In the world of fashion, it's not unusual to enlarge a model's eyes to draw attention to that part of his or her face. Use the Freeze Mask tool to mask off the surrounding areas of the eye that would probably look wrong if they were distorted. That usually includes the eyebrows, nose, and sometimes the sides of the head (**Figure 11.142**). Switch to the Bloat tool, move the mouse over one of the eyes, place the crosshair in the pupil, and adjust the Brush Size setting (by pressing the bracket keys) until the brush is just larger than the perimeter of the eye (**Figure 11.143**).

Figure 11.142 Mask off the areas that you don't want to distort. (©2008 Dan Ablan.)

Figure 11.143 Use a brush that's slightly wider than the eye.

Set Brush Density to 100; otherwise, you'll end up enlarging the center of the eye more than the rest of the eye. While you're at it, change Brush Rate to a low setting such as 20 so that you don't have to be overly careful about how

Figure 11.144 The final image with slightly larger eyes.

long to hold down the mouse button to get the proper change in the image. Now that you have everything set up properly, center your cursor on the pupil and then press the mouse button until the eye looks slightly larger—about a second should do it (**Figure 11.144**). Repeat the process on the other eye, holding down the mouse button for the same amount of time.

You can also use Liquify to open eyes that are partially shut (**Figure 11.145**). Liquify isn't always the best for this kind of work, however; it's better to work with multiple photos so that you can copy an open eye from one photo, paste it onto a closed eye in another image, and use the Healing Brush to blend in the edges. But for those times when you have only one shot to use, the Bloat and Warp tools can help pry open an eye (**Figure 11.146**).

Figure 11.145 Original image. (©2008 Dan Ablan.)

Figure 11.146 First try at opening an eye.

Start by choosing the Bloat tool. Set Brush Size so that the brush is about 3/4 of the width of the eye, set Brush Density to a low setting (somewhere around 20 should work) so that you mainly scale the center of the eye, and set the Brush Rate to 20. Now, click the center of the pupil four or five times so that it starts to enlarge (**Figure 11.147**). To get the rest of the eye to look natural, make a few single clicks just to the right and left of the center of the eye

(**Figure 11.148**). Finally, switch to the Warp tool, bring up the Brush Density setting to around 50, and set the Brush Pressure to around 60. Place the crosshair in the center of the brush on the eyelid and drag up or down to reshape it (**Figure 11.149**). Keep tweaking the image until each eye has the proper shape. If you mess up and create a ghoulish rendition of an eye, switch to the Reconstruct tool, bring down the Brush Pressure and Brush Rate settings to around 20, and then click or paint across the eye to see if you can smooth it out.

Figure 11.147 Click in the center of the eye a few times to pry it open.

Figure 11.148 Click the sides to even out the eye.

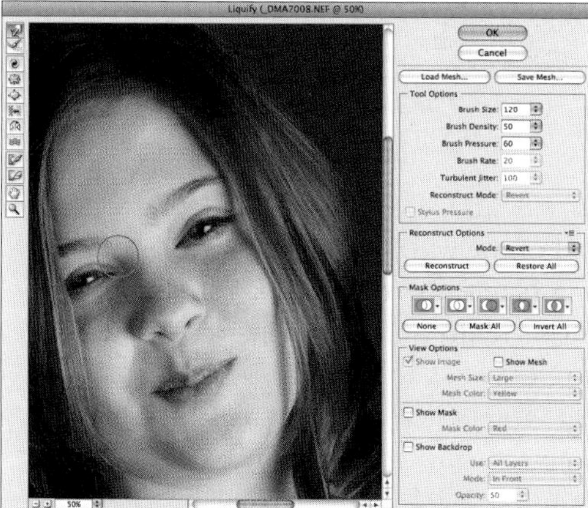

Figure 11.149 Reshape the eyelid with the Warp tool if necessary.

Retouching Mouths

Let's use the Warp tool to transform a straight mouth into a smiling one. Start by choosing the Warp tool. Change the Brush Size setting until you get a brush about half the width of the mouth, set the Brush Density to 50, and set the Brush Pressure to 50 or more. Next, move your mouse so that the crosshair is just below the right edge of the mouth, and drag upward and to the side slightly to move the corner of the mouth up and out (**Figure 11.150**). Repeat this process on the left side of the mouth. Change the Brush Size setting to get a brush slightly smaller than the one you just used, place the crosshair on the top edge of the lips (centered horizontally), and drag down a short distance (**Figure 11.151**).

When adding smiles, don't forget the cheeks. There's more to a smile than just an upward turn of the mouth.

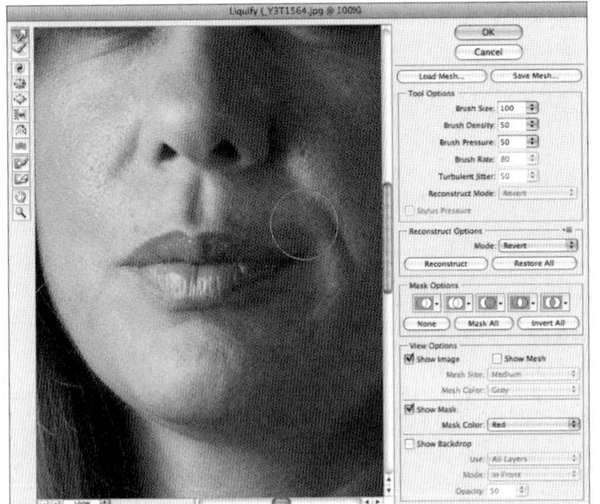

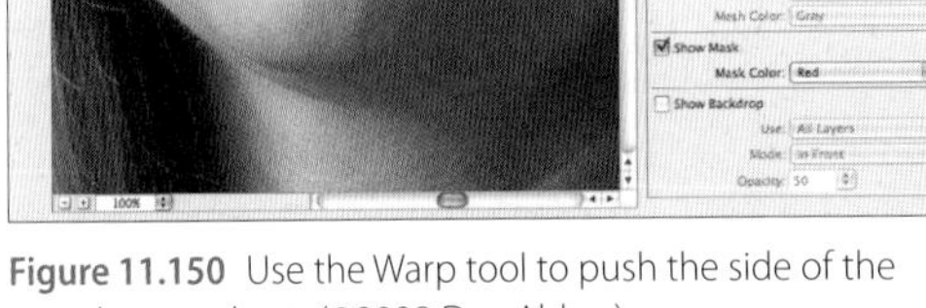

Figure 11.150 Use the Warp tool to push the side of the mouth up and out. (©2008 Dan Ablan.)

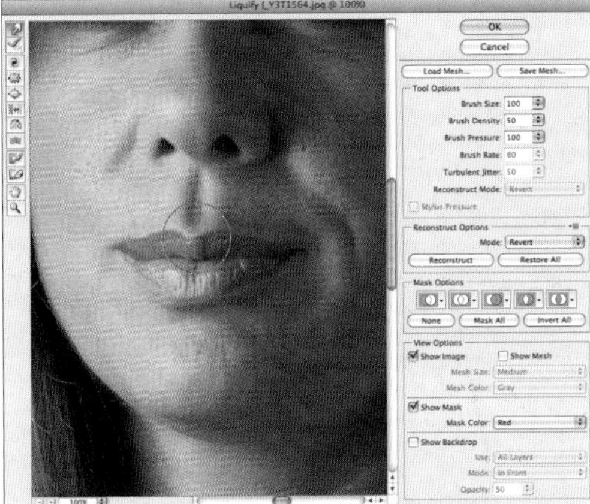

Figure 11.151 Pull the middle of the lip down slightly.

It takes some practice to get an acceptable result. If you mess up, paint across the area with the Reconstruct tool to get it closer to the original, or click the Restore All button to start over.

Digital Liposuction

If you need to nip or tuck some bulging flesh, do it by mastering the Warp, Pucker, and Push Left tools. When working on waistlines, use the Warp tool with a largish brush, a medium Brush Density setting (around 50), and a high Brush Pressure (around 80). Drag the background toward the waist (**Figures 11.152** and **11.153**).

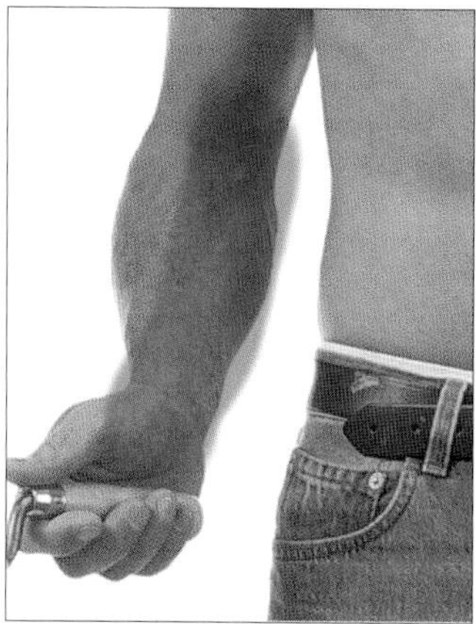
Figure 11.152 The original image with the arm masked so it won't shift. (©Stockbyte, www.stockbyte.com.)

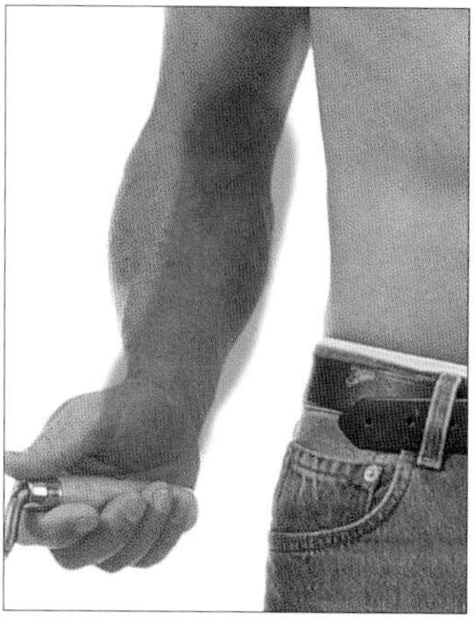
Figure 11.153 Result of warping the waist with a large brush.

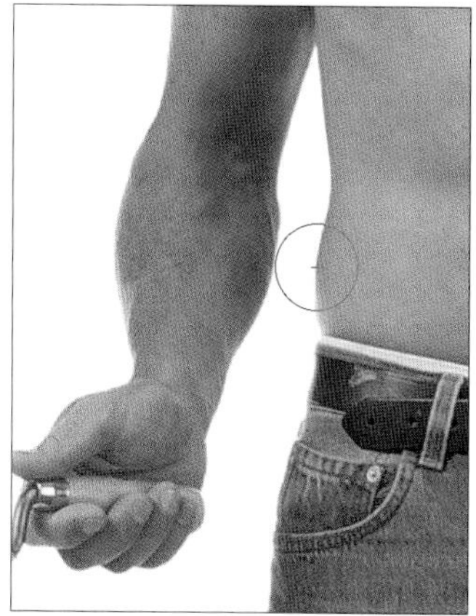
Figure 11.154 There's no need to mask when using the Push Left tool; just use a downward stroke with the crosshair on the edge that you want to push.

If you need to move a large area, consider using the Push tool. Choose a large brush, set the Brush Density to 100, and use a very low Brush Pressure (around 10). Position your cursor so that the crosshair just touches the edge you need to move, and drag to push the flesh in one direction (**Figures 11.154** and **11.155**). Drag straight down if you need to push the skin toward the right of your cursor; hold down Option/Alt if you need to move the skin in the opposite direction. If the background gets distorted too much, click OK in the Liquify dialog and use the Clone Stamp tool to replace the distorted background with something that looks more appropriate.

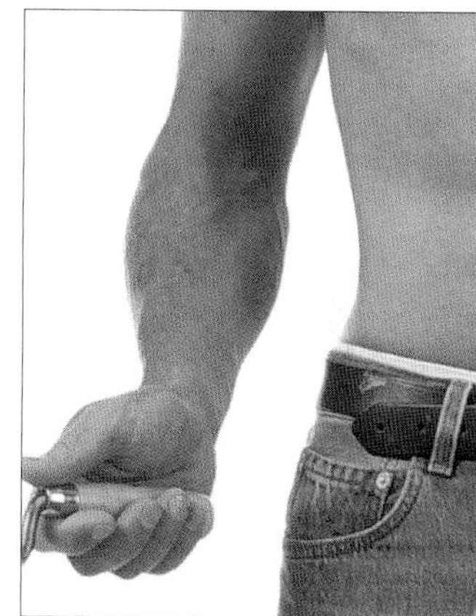
Figure 11.155 Result of pushing quite a bit of flesh, using the Push Left tool.

Content-Aware Scaling

Photoshop CS4 has introduced some new magic in the form of a scale tool. The Content-Aware Scale command allows you to take out unwanted spaces with the click and drag of a mouse. Every once in a while, you might have an image where the subjects aren't as close together as you'd like **(Figure 11.156)**. Make sure that the image is not the Background layer. (If it is, duplicate it, or double-click it to make it an editable layer.) Choose Edit > Content-Aware Scale. Handles appear around the image, like those you would see with a normal scaling operation. Click and drag.

Figure 11.156 Sometimes your subjects are too far apart. (©2008 Dan Ablan.)

Figure 11.157 The Content-Aware Scale command allows you to remove some of the unneeded green space between the three figures.

Figure 11.157 shows the result: In this example, the three figures are now closer together, with the original layer shown beneath.

Content-aware scaling is like magic, but it's not going to solve all your problems. Some images work better than others, such as a person's head against a blue sky. You'll have to experiment with the options, and see what works best for your images.

The Next Step

We've reached the end of the book, and we've covered all the tools you'll need to become a bona fide "photo doctor." Bear in mind that you don't need to limit yourself to working with photographs; the tools and techniques we've covered here can be used for non-photographic images as well.

As with everything else in Photoshop CS4, once you've gone around the block with these tools a few times, you'll probably think of a dozen other things you can do with them. From here, the learning doesn't stop. Head on over to the official book page at www.danablan.com/photoshop and view the Chapter 12 video, "Workflow," which shows image capture, color correction, global toning, and more. Thanks to 3D Garage.com, you'll also find five more bonus videos covering line art scanning, channels, shadows, type and background effects, and resolution settings.

Index

C

K

L

M

P

S

W

Z